readings
on
social
stratification

prentice-hall international, inc., London

prentice-hall of australia pty. ltd., Sydney

prentice-hall of canada ltd., Toronto

prentice-hall of india private ltd., New Delhi

prentice-hall of japan, inc., Tokyo

readings
on
social
stratification

Melvin M. Tumin
Princeton University

prentice-hall, inc./englewood cliffs, new jersey

prentice-hall readings in modern sociology series
Alex Inkeles, Editor

© 1970 by
PRENTICE-HALL, INC., Englewood Cliffs, N.J.

13–762104–3

Library of Congress Catalog Card Number: 73–76306

Printed in the United States of America

Current printing (last digit):
10 9 8 7 6 5 4 3 2 1

preface

This collection of readings in social stratification is intended to be a companion to my brief textbook, *Social Stratification* (Prentice-Hall, Inc., 1967). Almost all the articles or selections I have gathered together here are referred to at various places in the text. Since they are organized under the same headings as the chapters of the text, they form a natural extension of the text materials themselves—and that is the intention.

It will be evident to the reader that the boundaries of the field of study called "social stratification" are by no means firm or fixed. This is due mostly to the fact that various scholars differ in their conceptions of what ought properly to be included. These differing conceptions range from the minimum version, which focuses almost solely on unequal evaluation or ranking of social units, to the maximum version, which considers inequalities in power, property, and psychic gratifications to be equally important dimensions of stratification. The "minimalists" tend to see differences in power and property mainly as conditioners or shapers of evaluation and as results of it; the "maximalists" tend to see a more reciprocal network of interaction among the major kinds of inequalities that characterize all societies. The differences thus reflect differing versions of what is primary and what is derivative in the structure and function of social inequalities. My own preference is clearly for the maximalist conception.

The nagging problem in compiling a collection of readings is the matter of selection. There is a surprising and gratifying abundance of materials that are both interesting and scientifically creditable. Moreover, there is a large body of fictional literature, reportage and social-philosophical writing from which selections might have been chosen. There is little doubt that an equally valuable, informative, and sound body of alternative selections might have been gathered which would serve the intentions of this reader just as well. This possibility is testimony to the amplitude of the literature and should properly be taken as an encouraging commentary on both the salience of the concern for social inequality and the imagination and diligence with which that concern has been pursued in science and the arts. Needless to say, the brevity of the individual selections presented here and the relatively small number of selections that have been included are due to irrelevant but unavoidable considerations of publishing costs and pricing.

We are just beginning to develop systematic understanding of the ways in which inequalities emerge, take form, and function in human societies, old and new, modern and preliterate. The field is beginning to assume a recognizable shape; priorities of research and theory are becoming clearer as the quality of the materials constantly improves. I have tried in this reader and the text it accompanies to be sensitive both to some of the older "classical" literature in the field and to that newer body of materials which reflects the commendable increase in astuteness and rigor with which research and theory have lately been pursued.

MELVIN M. TUMIN

table of contents

history of
thought and theory

one

Although problems of social inequality have been matters of concern to social and political philosophers and students of society for thousands of years, it is probably true that the shape of most modern thinking on social inequality has been influenced most by Karl Marx, the 19th-century German economist, philosopher, and theoretician of revolution.

Marx was concerned with revealing the sources of inequality, and he found that these sources reside primarily in the different positions men occupy in the productive scheme. Those who own the instruments of production—whether land or capital—use their advantaged positions to accumulate disproportionate shares of the productive output and, in the process, they deprive the members of the working class, who produce the goods and services, of their fair share. Exploitation of the working class by the owning class is thus a central theme in the structure of inequality, as Marx saw it.

One might naturally expect that Marx's magnum opus *Capital* would bring this theme to an explicit focus as a logical development of the analysis of capitalist society. But Marx's manuscript breaks off just at the point where it seemed he would be turning to a dissection of capitalist class structure.

In a brilliantly imaginative piece reprinted here, Ralf Dahrendorf has attempted to imagine how that chapter on "A Theory of Class" might have read. Combining many quotations from Marx's other writings with his own versions of what Marx might have said, Dahrendorf gives us a full version of Marx's thinking about class. Class, class interests, class conflicts: these are the essence of social organization, of social inequality, and of the movement of social history. In essence, the objective differences in the positions in the productive scheme and the differing interests which arise from these positions are the determinants of social aggregation, organization, and conflict.

Max Weber is a 20th-century German sociologist to whom much of the shape of modern sociological thinking owes its origins and inspirations. A common practice among many sociologists today is to pose Weber's ideas about class and inequality against those of Marx, as though the two views were in fundamental conflict. In fact, they are not. Weber shares much of Marx's view that control over productive property gives crucial control over life in general and shapes the thinking and actions of those who exercise this control. But Weber extends Marx—

as perhaps Marx might have grudgingly extended himself under the impact of Weber's reasoning—by noting that objectively similar positions in the productive scheme are not sufficient grounds or bases in themselves to cause men either to identify with each other or to form groups with common purposes. For Weber it was important that men should perceive their common interests; only with such perception would they be likely to form common-interest groups, however "objectively" their interests might be the same. There are bases other than economic bases, then, according to Weber, that impel men to form groups or identify with each other.

"Honor" becomes a dominant concern for men in the Weberian system of thought. The desire for social honor impels men to shape their behavior and their "styles of life" in general in an effort to command this honor from other men. Honor comes from, or may be explained in terms of, or may be defined by, "status." And "status" may be defined as one's position on a ladder of evaluation of one's social worth. In this evaluation such things as money, family background, social function, and other economic and noneconomic considerations may play a large part.

As often happens, the serious, systematic, and careful thinking of great men often takes different shapes when adapted by later disciples. This is the case in the theory of W. Lloyd Warner, who tries to develop a notion of the universal requirement of stratification, conceived as unequal "social ranking," out of two Weberian notions: (1) the importance of honor, and (2) the requirement of differential power in the conduct of any social organization involving large numbers of people. However garbled Warner's version of Weber may be, it is true that Warner has been among the most influential of writers in the field of American stratification studies and his Yankee City series is surely among the most important early empirical works in the field. Warner's summary of what social class means in America is presented here, then, in view of his significant role in the field.

Unfortunately, Richard Tawney, one of the most eloquent and perceptive theorists of inequality of the 20th century, has been quite inconspicuous lately; as a result, his works are seldom read by students today. As an example of the elegance of both his style and his thought, a selection from Tawney's book on *Inequality* has been included in this volume. Tawney combines much of the best of both Marx and Weber in his dissection of the bases of social and economic inequality, revealing the ways in which the power generated by control of the basic means of production and of the basic symbols of status are skillfully and powerfully managed by those who possess them in order to entrench their own favored positions and to rationalize these positions in terms of social necessity, social welfare, and social productivity. No one has done more to lay bare the roots of inequality in English social structure than Tawney. His work is a refreshing reminder of the ease with which we tend to accept status quo situations as given, and how we can be seriously led astray in our analyses of society if we do not look for the basic sources out of which current social phenomena emerge.

Marx's Theory of Class

There have been many and violent disputes about the interpretation of the work of Marx, but no commentator has seriously doubted the central importance of the theory of class for this work. Indeed, the greatness and fatality of his work become apparent in Marx's theory of class. In this theory, the three roots of his thought are joined. Marx adopted the word from the early British political economists; its application to "capitalists" and "proletarians" stems from the French "utopian" socialists; the conception of the class struggle is based on Hegel's dialectics. The theory of class provides the problematic link between sociological analysis and philosophical speculation in the work of Marx. Both can be separated, and have to be separated, but in this process the theory of class is cut in two; for it is as essential for Marx's philosophy of history as it is for his analysis of the dynamics of capitalist society.

Marx regarded the theory of class as so important that he postponed its systematic exposition time and again in favor of refinements by empirical analysis. As a result we know it only by its application to concrete problems and by the occasional generalizations that occur throughout Marx's works. This may not be the least cause of the many controversies about the real meaning of Marx's concept and theory of class.

Reprinted from Ralf Dahrendorf, *Class and Class Conflict in Industrial Society* (Stanford, Calif.: Stanford University Press and London: Routledge & Kegan Paul Ltd., 1959), pp. 8–27, by permission of the author and Stanford University Press. © 1959 by the Board of Trustees of Leland Stanford Junior University.

Only recently the accounts of Geiger (2) and of Bendix and Lipset (1) have concluded these discussions, at least in "Western" sociology. It is not my intention, in presenting my interpretation of Marx's approach, to relight the fires of controversy. The following discussion of the concept and theory of class in the work of Marx, while not materially deviating from either Geiger or Bendix and Lipset, is designed to supplement their works and add some substance to an investigation that is indebted to Marx even in its most radical criticisms of his work.

Marx postponed the systematic presentation of his theory of class until death took the pen from his hand. The irony has often been noted that the last (52nd) chapter of the last (third) volume of *Capital*, which bears the title "The Classes," has remained unfinished. After little more than one page the text ends with the lapidary remark of its editor, Engels: "Here the manuscript breaks off." However, for the thorough reader of Marx this is no reason for despair. If he wants to, he can complete this chapter for Marx—not exactly as Marx would have written it, of course, and not entirely without interpretation either, but in any case without substantially adding to what Marx said himself. In the following section I shall try to do just this. By systematically ordering a number of quotations and connecting them to a coherent text I shall attempt to provide a basis and point of reference for critical discussion without anticipating—beyond the selection and ordering of the quotations—any interpretation.[1]

_____
[1] All quotations from Marx in the following section are in italics. Everything else is my text.

marx's theory of class   3

"THE CLASSES": THE UNWRITTEN 52ND CHAPTER OF VOL. III OF MARX'S *CAPITAL*

The Problem

It is the ultimate purpose of this work to reveal the economic laws of development of modern society (12, I, pp. 7 f). We are therefore not concerned with merely describing, much less regretting, existing conditions, but want to lay bare their revolutionary aspect. We have shown that the capitalist mode of production has become too restricted for its own forces of production. The revolution is near. But this revolution is not the product of economic forces of production or relations of production, but of the people and groups that represent these economic formations. *Of all instruments of production the greatest force of production is the revolutionary class itself* (6, p. 188).

For almost forty years we have emphasized the class struggle as the primary motive force of history, and especially the class struggle between bourgeoisie and proletariat as the great lever of modern social change (II, p. 102). *With the moment in which civilization begins, production begins to be based on the antagonism between accumulated and direct labor. Without conflict, no progress: that is the law which civilization has followed to the present day. Until now the forces of production have developed by virtue of the dominance of class conflict* (6, p. 80). And it always holds that *a change in the relation of classes is a historical change* (5, II, p. 475).

Thus we have to determine in general what constitutes a class and how class conflict emerges and expresses itself. *In a general investigation of this kind it is always assumed that real conditions correspond to their conception, or, which is the same thing, that real conditions are presented only in so far as they express their own general type* (12, III, p. 121). We are therefore not concerned with describing any one society, but with discovering the general laws which determine the trend of social development.

If we observe a given country from the point of view of political economy, we have to start with its population, its distribution into classes, town, country, sea, the different industries, export and import, annual production and consumption, commodity prices, etc. (7, p. 256). But this method presents difficulties. It leads us astray if in our abstractions we do not find the way to *the real and concrete, the real premise. Population is an abstraction if I ignore, for example, the classes of which it consists. These classes are again an empty word, if I do not know the elements on which they are based, e.g., wage labor, capital, etc.* (7, p. 256). Thus our first question concerns the elements on which classes are based; and since *modern bourgeois society is in fact our main subject* (7, p. 237), we use it for the time being as an example.

The owners of mere labor power, the owners of capital, and the landowners, whose respective sources of income are wage, profit, and rent—thus wage laborers, capitalists, and landowners—constitute the three great classes of modern society based on a capitalist mode of production.

In England, modern society has undoubtedly advanced furthest and most classically in its economic structure. Even there, however, this class structure is not displayed in a pure form. Intermediate and transitional stages obliterate the borderlines there as everywhere (although incomparably less in the country than in towns). However, this does not matter for our investigation. It has been demonstrated that it is the permanent tendency and law of development of the capitalist mode of production to separate the means of production increasingly from labor, and to concentrate the separate means of production more and more in large groups—in other words, to transform labor into wage labor, and the means of production into capital. At the same time, land ownership tends to be separated from capital and labor, and to be converted into the type of land ownership corresponding to the capitalist mode of production.

The question to be answered next is: What constitutes a class? And this results directly from the answer to the other question: What makes wage laborers, capitalists, and landowners the constituent forces of the three great social classes? (12, III, pp. 421 f.)

Two False Approaches

At first it is the identity of revenues and sources of income. They are three large social groups, whose components, i.e., the people of whom they consist, earn their living by wage, profit, and rent, i.e., by utilizing their labor power, capital, and land ownership. However, from this point of view, say, doctors and civil servants would also constitute two classes, for they belong to two different social groups whose members' incomes flow from the same source. The same would hold for the infinite fragmentation of interests and positions which the division of labor produces among workers as among capitalists and land owners (the latter, for example, into vineyard owners, field owners, forest owners, mine owners, fishing ground owners) (12, III, p. 422).

This approach does not therefore lead to a fruitful definition. The same holds for a second approach frequently adopted in explaining class differences and conflicts. The vulgar mind commutes class differences into "differences in the size of purses" and class conflict into "trade disputes." The size of the purse is a purely quantitative difference, by virtue of which two individuals of the same class can be opposed quite arbitrarily. It is well known that medieval guilds quarreled with each other "according to trade." But it is equally well known that modern class differences are by no means based on "trade." Rather, the divi-

sion of labor has created very different types of work within the same class (5, II, pp. 466 f.).

In both cases the essential point is overlooked: property, income, and source of income are themselves a result of the class structure, i.e., of the structure of economic conditions. Income and property are criteria belonging to the realm of distribution and consumption. However, the use of products is determined by the social relations of the consumers, and these social relations themselves rest on the conflict of classes (6, p. 81). And since distribution is itself a product of production, the kind of participation in production determines the particular patterns of distribution, the way in which people participate in distribution (7, p. 250).

There is no property anterior to the relations of domination and subjection which obtain in production and in the political state, and which are far more concrete relations (7, p. 258). Therefore we have to look for the elements of classes in production and in the power relations determined by it.

Property and Economic Power

The essential condition that determines the mode of production of an epoch, and that therefore provides the constituent element of classes as well as the momentum of social change, is property. The property question, relative to the different stages of development of industry, has always been the life question of any given class (5, p. 459).

However, this statement is open to misinterpretation. For the opposition of propertylessness and property as such is indifferent, and not expressed in an active relation to its inner structure, i.e., as a contradiction, so long as it is not comprehended as the opposition between labor and capital (3, p. 176).

Even in this specification property is still an abstraction, an empty concept.

*In every historical epoch property has de-
veloped differently and under different social
conditions. To define bourgeois property means
no less than to describe all the social conditions of bourgeois production. The attempt to
define property as an independent relation, a
special category, an abstract and eternal idea,
can be nothing but an illusion of metaphysics
or jurisprudence* (6, p. 169).

Only if we understand property in
the particular context of bourgeois
society, i.e., as private ownership of
the means of production, as the control
of a minority over the wealth of a whole
nation, do we in fact grasp the core of
the antagonism existing in production
and creating class conflict. *The power of
society thus becomes the private power of a
private person* (12, I, p. 138).

The essential *condition of the existence
and domination of the bourgeois class is the
accumulation of wealth in the hands of
private persons, the formation and augmenta-
tion of capital; the condition of capital is
wage labor* (14, p. 89). Thus the existence
of capital as well as wage labor, of the
bourgeoisie as well as the proletariat,
can be explained in terms of the one
condition of the particular form of property in bourgeois society, i.e., ownership of the means of production.

The authority relations within production which are given by the presence
or absence of effective property, of
control over the means of production,
are of course not the class relations
themselves. In order to determine these,
we have to look for the consequences
flowing from the relations of production
and for the social antagonisms based on
these consequences.

Relations of Production, Class Situation, and Political Power

One important consequence of the
relations of production has already been
mentioned. The division of wealth in
the sphere of distribution corresponds
to the division of property in production. Thus a person's material condition
of existence, or class situation, is based
on his position in production. *Economic
conditions have first converted the mass of the
population into workers. The rule of capital
has created for this mass a common situation*
(6, p. 187). And in a way one can state:
*In so far as millions of families live under
economic conditions which separate their way
of life, their interests, and their education
from those of other classes and oppose them
to these, they constitute a class* (8, p. 104).

However, these economic conditions
of existence are not in themselves sufficient for the formation of classes. They
are as such passive, and although they
produce the *gap between the life situations
of worker and capitalist* (12, I, p. 548),
they do not produce a real antagonism.
For in so far as there is between people
in a common material condition, or
life situation, a merely external *contact—
in so far as the identity of their interests does
not produce a community, national association, and political organization—they do not
constitute a class*. Such groups in a common situation *are therefore unable to make
their class interest heard in their own name
through a parliament or an assembly* (8, p.
104). We shall have to return to this
point.

A second and infinitely more important consequence of the distribution
of property in production is that it
determines the distribution of political
power in society. Modern relations of
production include the economic power
of the owners of private property, the
capitalists. And *the political power of the
bourgeois class arises from these modern relations of production* (5, p. 455). Indeed it
can be said that *the modern state is but an
association that administrates the common
business of the whole bourgeois class* (14, p.
83).

In this sense, authority relations in
production determine the authority relations of society in general. *The specific
economic form in which unpaid surplus labor*

is pumped out of the immediate producers determines the relation of domination and subjection as it grows directly out of and in turn determines production. On this is based the whole structure of the economic community as it comes forth from the relations of production, and thereby at the same time its political structure. It is always the immediate relation of the owners of the conditions of production to the immediate producers— a relation whose specific pattern of course always corresponds to a certain stage in the development of labor and its social force of production—in which we find the final secret, the hidden basis of the whole construction of society, including the political patterns of sovereignty and dependence, in short, of a given specific form of government (12, III, pp. 324 f.).

Finally, a third and parallel consequence of the distribution of property in production is that it also shapes the ideas that mold the character of a period. On the different forms of property and the social conditions of existence a whole superstructure of various and peculiarly formed sentiments, illusions, modes of thought, and conceptions of life is built. The whole class creates and forms these out of its material foundations and the corresponding social relations (0, p. 97).

We can say, therefore, that the ruling ideas of a period have always been nothing but the ideas of the ruling class (14, p. 93). In each epoch, the thoughts of the ruling class are the ruling thoughts; i.e., the class that is the ruling material power of society is at the same time its ruling intellectual power. The class that has the means of material production in its control, controls at the same time the means of intellectual production (13, II, p. 37).

Class Interests

We have seen that relations of property and authority constitute the basis of the formation of social classes. But we have not yet investigated the force that effects this formation. Classes do not exist in isolation, independent of other classes to which they are opposed. Individuals form a class only in so far as they are engaged in a common struggle with another class (13, II, p. 59); and the force that effects class formation is class interest. In a sense, class interests precede the formation of classes. Thus the German bourgeoisie stands in opposition to the proletariat even before it has organized itself as a class in the political sphere (5, p. 469). The proletariat has, in the beginning of its development, certain common interests, but it is nevertheless still an unorganized mass. Thus this mass is already a class in opposition to capital, but not yet a class for itself (6, p. 187).

By postulating class interests as preceding the classes themselves, we make it quite clear that class interests are not merely the random personal interests of one person or even many people. We are not concerned with what this or that proletarian or even the whole proletariat visualizes as a goal for the time being. Its goal and its historical action are obviously and irrevocably predetermined by its own life situation as by the whole organization of contemporary bourgeois society (4, p. 207). Thus the shared interest of a class exists not only in the imagination, as a generality, but above all in reality as the mutual dependence of the individuals among whom labor is divided (13, II, p. 23). As in private life we distinguish between what a man thinks and says of himself and what he really is and does, so in historical struggles we must distinguish even more carefully the catchwords and fantasies of parties from their real organism and their real interests, their conception from their reality (8, p. 38).

Class interests as "objective" interests subsuming the members of a class under a general force not only can differ from individual, personal interests, but can conflict with these interests. Although, for example, all members of the modern bourgeoisie have the same interest inasmuch as they form a class vis-à-vis another class, they have nevertheless *opposite, contradictory interests as soon as they are confronted with each other* (6, p. 140). *This conflict of interests* is not merely a possibility; it arises with a degree of necessity *from the economic conditions of their bourgeois life* (6, p. 140). For example, *the conflict between the interest of the individual capitalist and the class of capitalists makes itself felt* if the problem at hand is not the distribution of profits but that of losses, *just as before the identity of interests found its practical realization through competition* (12, III, p. 235).

The substance of class interests, in so far as they are based on the economic positions of given groups, can be expressed in various ways. To begin with, the immediate interest of the proletariat is the wage, that of the bourgeoisie the profit; and here once again we have to distinguish the *two great categories into which the interest of the bourgeoisie is divided—land ownership and capital* (8, p. 38). From these immediate concerns, confined to the sphere of production, all further interests can be derived. As a society develops to its maturity, the originally divided interests become increasingly united. More and more *it is a specific type of production, and of relations of production, which determines rank and influence of all other activities* (7, p. 264). This means that two particular interests are increasingly articulated: the conservative interest of the ruling class, and the revolutionary interest of the oppressed class. *Of all the classes with which the bourgeoisie is today confronted, only the proletariat is a truly revolutionary class* (14, p. 88). And *a class in which the revolutionary interests of society are concentrated, as soon as it has risen up, finds directly in its own situation the content and the material of its revolutionary activity: foes to be laid low; measures, dictated by the needs of the struggle, to be taken—the consequences of its own deeds*

drive it on. It makes no theoretical inquiries into its task (9, p. 42).

On the basis of these class interests, in fighting to realize them or defend them, the groups determined by the distribution of property in production, and by the distribution of political power flowing from it, organize themselves into classes.

Class Organization and Class Struggle

The organization of classes follows the progress of conflicts within the sphere of production itself. *Increasingly the collisions between the individual worker and the individual bourgeois assume the character of collisions between two classes. The workers start forming coalitions against the bourgeois; they join in order to maintain their wage* (14, p. 87). But the wage is, as we have seen, merely an undeveloped, prerevolutionary interest of the proletariat. This stage of class organization corresponds to a relatively early phase of capitalist development. *As long as the rule of the bourgeois class had not organized itself fully, and had not acquired its pure political expression, the opposition of the other classes could not come forth in its pure form either, and where it did come forth, it could not take that dangerous turn which converts every struggle against government into a struggle against capital* (8, p. 54). The development of the forces of production has to be far advanced for the formation of classes to be possible, because *the organization of the revolutionary elements as a class presupposes the complete existence of all forces of production which could possibly develop in the womb of the old society* (6, p. 188).

The formation of classes always means the organization of common interests in the sphere of politics. This point needs to be emphasized. Classes are political groups united by a common interest. *The struggle between two classes is a political struggle* (6, p. 187). We therefore speak of classes only in the realm of political conflict. Thus *every movement in which the working class as such opposes the ruling class and seeks to destroy its power by pressure from without is a political movement. The attempt, for example, to extort a limitation of working time in a single factory or trade, and from individual capitalists, by strikes, etc., is a purely economic movement; but the movement to enforce legislation stipulating an eight-hour day, etc., is a political movement. And in this manner a political movement grows everywhere out of the isolated economic movements of the workers; i.e., it is a movement of the class in order to realize its interests in a general form, in a form that possesses universal social constraining force* (10, p. 90).

Parallel with the political organization of classes there grows up a *theoretical class-consciousness* (12, I, p. 13), i.e., an awareness on the individual's part of the interests of his class generally. The positive goals of the proletariat become evident and can be formulated by its theoreticians. *As long as the proletariat has not sufficiently developed to organize itself as a class, as long as therefore the struggle of the proletariat with the bourgeoisie as yet has no political character, these theoreticians are merely utopians who invent systems in order to satisfy the needs of the oppressed classes* (6, p. 142).

Thus classes are political forces based on the relations of property and power. But although in principle every individual can be identified as a member of one of the above-named classes according to his share in property and power, it is *quite possible that a man's actions will not always be determined by the class to which he belongs; but these individual cases are as irrelevant to the class struggle as the defection of some noblemen to the Third Estate was to the French revolution* (5, p. 467).

This circulation among the classes or *exchange between them* (7, p. 266) is par-ticularly evident in two stages of the organization of interest groups into classes. We find it in the first place, for example, *in the United States of America, where although classes exist they have not yet become stabilized, but instead exchange and transfer their elements in continuous flux* (8, p. 18). That is to say, we find this exchange in an early stage of class formation when the ruling class is still concerned with consolidating its power. And *the more capable a ruling class is of absorbing the best men of the oppressed class, the more solid and dangerous is its rule* (12, III, p. 140). The second stage in which a certain exchange between the classes takes place is that immediately preceding a revolution. *In times in which the class struggle approaches its decision, the process of disintegration within the ruling class and within the whole old society assumes such a violent and glaring character that a small part of the ruling class renounces it and joins the revolutionary class, the class that carries the future in its hands. Just as earlier a part of the nobility went over to the bourgeoisie, now a part of the bourgeoisie goes over to the proletariat, in particular certain bourgeois ideologists who have achieved a theoretical understanding of the whole historical movement* (14, pp. 87 f.).

This organization of the proletarians as a class, and that means as a political party (14, p. 87), eventually furnishes the basis of the class struggle. To repeat: *Every class struggle is a political struggle* (14, p. 87). It is the deliberate and articulate conflict between two opposed interests, the interests, respectively, of preserving and of revolutionizing the existing institutions and power relations. The formation of classes as organized interest groups, the antagonism between oppressing and oppressed classes, and the resulting revolutionary changes constitute the law of development of all history up to now. *An oppressed class is the condition of existence of every society based on class conflict. Thus the liberation of the oppressed class necessarily involves the creation of a new society* (6, p. 188). *The history of all societies up to the present is the history of class struggles* (14, p. 81).

The Classless Society

Following these laws of development the proletariat has organized itself in the womb of bourgeois society, and has opened its struggle against the bourgeoisie.

Does this mean that after the downfall of the old society there will be a new class rule culminating in a new political authority? No.

The condition of the liberation of the working class is the abolition of every class, just as the condition of the liberation of the Third Estate, i.e., the establishment of the bourgeois order, was the abolition of all estates.

The working class will in the course of development replace the old bourgeois society by an association which excludes classes and their conflict, and there will no longer be any political authority proper, since it is especially the political authority that provides class conflict within bourgeois society with its official expression.

By now the conflict between proletariat and bourgeoisie is a struggle of one class against another, a struggle that means in its highest expression a total revolution. Is there any reason to be surprised that a society based on class conflict leads to brutal opposition, and in the last resort to a clash between individuals?

Nobody should say that society develops independently of politics. There is no political movement which is not at the same time a social movement.

Only in an order of things in which there are no classes and no class conflicts will social evolutions cease to be political revolutions (6, pp. 188 f.).

Sociological Elements of Marx's Theory of Class

If Marx himself had written this chapter, it would no doubt have been longer, more polemical, and more directly related to the society of his time.[2] Nevertheless the attempt to present Marx's approach to a theory of class conflict largely in his own words is more than an entertaining game. The result can serve as a fruitful basis for some more general observations which will prove useful for subsequent critical considerations. The following elements of Marx's theory of class appear particularly worth emphasizing for sociological analysis:

1. It is important to realize what Geiger called the "heuristic purpose behind the concept of class" (46, chap. ii). Wherever Marx used the concept in a sociological sense, he was not concerned with describing an existing state of society. He was concerned, rather, with the analysis of certain laws of social development and of the forces involved in this development. To use the misleading terms of modern sociology, the heuristic purpose of the concept of class was for Marx not "static" but "dynamic," not "descriptive" but "analytical." What these terms may mean and what they cannot mean will have to be discussed later in some detail.

---

[2] In this sense, Renner's attempt (3, pp. 374 ff.) to reconstruct this chapter of *Capital* is closer to Marx in style and content than the attempt here undertaken to sketch the most general elements of Marx's theory of class. Clearly, the claim that I have written the unwritten last chapter of *Capital* must not be understood literally in the sense of a philological conjecture. My main purpose has been to offer a systematic presentation of the many isolated statements about class in the work of Marx.

Here it is sufficient to emphasize that for Marx the theory of class was not a theory of a cross section of society arrested in time, in particular not a theory of social stratification, but a tool for the explanation of changes in total societies. In elaborating and applying his theory of class, Marx was not guided by the question "How does a given society in fact look at a given point of time?" but by the question "How does the structure of a society change?" or, in his own words, "What is the [economic] law of motion of modern society?"

2. This heuristic purpose explains the often criticized two-class model underlying the dynamic theory of Marx. Had Marx wanted to describe his society with photographic accuracy, this model would indeed have been most unsatisfactory. As a matter of fact, Marx does refer occasionally (without always using his concept of class in an entirely unambiguous manner) to a multitude of classes. He refers to the "two great categories into which the interest of the bourgeoisie is divided— land ownership and capital" (8, p. 43), to the petty bourgeoisie as a "transitional class" (8, p. 49), and to the class of small peasants (8, p. 118). But in principle these "intermediate and transitional stages," as Marx significantly calls them, "do not matter for our investigation" (12, III, p. 421). Not only are they unstable entities destined to be drawn sooner or later into the two great whirlpools of bourgeoisie and proletariat, but even if this were not the case, their historical role would be insignificant by comparison with that of the dominant classes of capitalist society. The concept of class is an analytical category, or, as Marx says in one of his rare but enlightening methodological remarks, "real conditions are presented only in so far as they express their own general type" (12, III, p. 121). The

general type of the real conditions of conflict that generates change, however, is the opposition of two dominant forces, two prevalent classes.

Geiger has refuted the unjustified objections to Marx's two-class model so convincingly that further discussion of them is unnecessary (2, pp. 37 ff.). But the legitimacy of assuming for analytical purposes the dominance of only two conflicting classes must not blind us to the fact that Marx has linked with his two-class model a number of additional postulates whose legitimacy appears rather more dubious. For Marx the category of class defines one side of an antagonism which entails the dominant issues of conflict in every society as well as the direction of its development. This means for Marx that (a) every conflict capable of generating structural change is a class conflict, (b) the contents of class conflict always represent the dominant issues of social conflict, and (c) the two classes stand in the relation of Hegel's "thesis" and "antithesis," in the sense that one is characterized by the affirmation (or possession) of those features of which the other is the complete negation. It is at least open to dispute whether this last approach recommends itself in social science. The other two postulates connected with Marx's two-class model, however, are empirical generalizations, the untenability of which will have to be demonstrated. Only if it is freed of these accessories can the two-class model be conceived as a feasible principle of knowledge.

3. Marx has tried to argue for the third postulate mentioned above in the most difficult part of his theory, the part concerned with the causes and origins of classes. What are the structural conditions of the formation of social classes? For simplicity's sake I shall treat this aspect of Marx's theory of class with reference to his analysis of

capitalist society, since the question remains undecided for the time being whether this theory can be applied to other types of society at all.

Marx states quite clearly that class conflicts do not originate in differences of income, or of the sources of income. His classes are not tax classes in the sense of the Roman censors. Rather, the determinant of classes is "property." Property, however, must not be understood in terms of purely passive wealth, but as an effective force of production, as "ownership of means of production" and its denial to others. In this sense, the "relations of production," i.e., the authority relations resulting from the distribution of effective property in the realm of (industrial) production, constitute the ultimate determinant of the formation of classes and the development of class conflicts. The capitalists possess factories and machines, and buy the only property of the proletarians, their labor power, in order to produce a surplus value with these means of production and augment their capital.

But our question cannot be answered all that easily. The role of property in Marx's theory of class poses a problem of interpretation, and on this interpretation the validity of Marx's theory of class stands or falls. Does Marx understand, by the relations of property or production, the relations of factual control and subordination in the enterprises of industrial production—or merely the authority relations in so far as they are based on the legal title of property? Does he conceive of property in a loose (sociological) sense—i.e., in terms of the exclusiveness of legitimate control (in which the manager also exercises property functions)—or merely as a statutory property right in connection with such control? Is property for Marx a special case of authority—or, vice versa, authority a special case of property?

These questions are of considerable significance. If one works with the narrow concept of property, class conflict is the specific characteristic of a form of production which rests on the union of ownership and control. In this case a society in which control is exercised, for example, by state functionaries, has by definition neither classes nor class conflicts. If, on the other hand, one works with the wider concept of property, class structure is determined by the authority structure of the enterprise, and the category of class becomes at least potentially applicable to all "relations of production."

Marx does not always make his answer to our questions entirely clear. But it can be shown that his analyses are essentially based on the narrow, legal concept of property. This procedure, and this procedure only, enables Marx to link his sociology with his philosophy of history—a brilliant attempt, but at the same time a fault that robs his sociological analyses of stringency and conviction, a fault made no more acceptable by the fact that orthodox Marxists have remained faithful to their master in this point to the present day.

The most striking evidence for this interpretation can be found in the preliminary attempts at an analysis of the new form of ownership characteristic of joint-stock companies which Marx presents in Volume III of *Capital*. Marx is here explicitly concerned with the phenomenon that is commonly described today as the separation of ownership and control. He discusses what he calls the "transformation of the really functioning capitalist into a mere director, an administrator of alien capital, and of the owners of capital into mere owners, mere money capitalists" (12, III, p. 477). "In joint-stock companies, function is separated from ownership of the means of production, and of surplus labor" (p. 478). Now, hard though it is for ordinary minds to see why this change in the size and legal structure of industrial enterprises should end the conflict between entrepreneurs who can command and workers who have to obey (the conflict that Marx postulates for the "pure" capitalist enterprise), Marx ascribes to the joint-stock company a peculiar place in history. Time and again he describes the joint-stock company as "private production without the control of private property" (p. 480), as "the elimination of capital as private property within the capitalist mode of production itself" (p. 477), and even as the "abolition of the capitalist mode of production within the capitalist mode of production itself" (p. 479). For him, the joint-stock company is "a necessary point on the way to reconverting capital into the property of the producers, this no longer being the private property of individual producers but their associated property, i.e., immediate social property" (p. 478). It is a "point on the way to the transformation of all functions in the process of reproduction hitherto connected with capital ownership into mere functions of the associated producers, into social functions" (p. 478). The joint-stock company, in other words, is halfway to the communist—and that means classless—society.

We cannot pursue here the manifold consequences of this strange analysis, which—correct as it may to a certain extent be empirically (if in a sense hardly intended by Marx)—would certainly have exposed Marx, had he lived longer, to many an awkward question from his most orthodox adherents. One point, however, is convincingly demonstrated by this analysis: for Marx, the relations of production as a determinant of class formation were also authority relations, but they were such only be-cause in the first place they were property relations in the narrow sense of the distribution of controlling private ownership. *Qua* property relations they are authority relations, and not vice versa, not *qua* authority relations property relations. If, therefore, the functions of the "director" and the "mere owner," the manager and the stockholder, are separated, this means a first step on the way to the complete abolition not only of effective private property itself, but also of the authority relations dependent on it, and thus a step on the way to the communist society. For Marx, classes were tied to the existence of effective private property. Their formation, existence, and struggle can occur only in a society in which some possess and others are excluded from private ownership and control of the means of production.

4 One of the critical pivots of Marx's theory of class is the undisputed identification of economic and political power and authority. Although classes are founded on the "relations of production," i.e., the distribution of effective property in the narrow sphere of commodity production, they become socially significant only in the political sphere. But both these spheres are inseparable. "The political power" of a class arises for Marx "from the relations of production" (5, p. 455). The relations of production are "the final secret, the hidden basis of the whole construction of society" (12, III, pp. 324 f.); industrial classes are *eo ipso* also social classes, and industrial class conflict is political class conflict. Nowhere has Marx explicitly discussed the basis of this empirical proposition—nor has he seen sufficiently clearly that it is an empirical proposition rather than a postulate or premise. The thesis that political conditions are determined by industrial conditions seems to stem, for

him, from the generalized assertion of an absolute and universal primacy of production over all other structures of economy and society. It is evident that a postulate of this kind requires empirical test; how it fares in this test will have to be shown.

5. Relatively thoroughly, if nowhere systematically, Marx has described the steps of the process by which groupings in the form of classes emerge from conditions of social structure. For Marx, the first stage of this process of the formation of classes is given directly by the distribution of effective private property. Possession and nonpossession of effective private property create two peculiar "common situations," "conditions of life," or class situations. These class situations have three complementary aspects: (a) that of the mere distribution of effective property, i.e., of possession or nonpossession of means of production and of authority; (b) that of the possession or nonpossession of goods and values gratifying personal needs, i.e., the "rewards" of modern sociology; and (c) that of the common situationally determined interests of those who share a class situation. By common interest in Marx's sense is not meant a conscious tendency of individual desires, but a potentially unconscious (or "falsely conscious") tendency of actual behavior shared by people in a common class situation. Common interests exist, as Marx says, "not merely in the imagination, . . . but above all in reality as the mutual dependence of the individuals among whom labor is divided" (13, II, p. 23). This is a difficult notion; for we are used to conceiving of interests above all on a psychological level. For the time being, however, we shall put off considering in what sense a concept of "objective interests" that "exist as" real conditions may be useful. At this point we merely conclude that Marx's theory of class formation starts with the postulate of a common class situation, the main components of which are a common relation to effective private property, a common socio-economic situation, and a common tendency of actual behavior determined by "objective" interests.

In accordance with the premises of class, we already find, from this point of view, a fundamental dichotomy of class situations in any given society, and of the members of a society by their class situations. Occasionally, Marx refers to the aggregates thus defined as classes. "In so far as millions of families live under economic conditions which separate their way of life, their interests, and their education from those of other classes and oppose them to these, they constitute a class" (8, p. 104). The concept of class as defined so far corresponds to Max Weber's later formulation, "'Class' shall mean any group of persons in a common class situation" (4, p. 177).[3] However, this definition has its problems. It has to be asked whether a common situation is sufficient to constitute a group in the strict sense of this term. If—as can be shown—this is not the case, it remains to be asked how an aggregate of people who are merely situated identically, without having any contact or coherence, can become an effective force in social conflict and change. Marx has asked this question, and he therefore emphasizes

---

[3] As a matter of fact, Weber is well aware of the problem under discussion. He therefore distinguishes "property classes" (as "not 'dynamic'") from "income classes" and "social classes." However, since Weber describes all three classes as consisting of all people in a common (if differently defined) class situation, his theory of class lacks the analytical strength of Marx's, which is much more precise on this point.

at many points that the mere "gap between the conditions of life," the mere "identity of interests" and class situations, is a necessary but by no means sufficient condition of the formation of classes. He continues therefore in the passage quoted above: "In so far as there is a merely local contact [among people in a common class situation]—in so far as the identity of their interests does not produce a community, national association, and political organization—they do not constitute a class. They are therefore unable to make their class interest heard. . ." (8, p. 104).

6. This may well be the most important step in Marx's theory of class formation: Classes do not constitute themselves as such until they participate in political conflicts as organized groups. Although Marx occasionally uses the concept of class in a less determinate, more comprehensive sense, a multitude of statements leave little doubt that for him class formation and class conflict were phenomena belonging to the sphere of politics. "As long as the proletariat has not sufficiently developed to organize itself as a class, . . . the struggle of the proletariat with the bourgeoisie has not yet assumed a political character" (6, p. 142). This means conversely that the carriers of class conflict have organized themselves as classes, and have become classes, only if class conflict has assumed a political character.

For Marx, this last stage of class formation has two complementary aspects. On the factual level of social structure it involves the association of people who share a class situation in a strict group, party, or political organization. Marx refers to the "organization of the proletarians as a class, and that means as a political party" (14, p. 87). On the normative and ideological level of social structure it involves the articulation of "class-consciousness," i.e., the transformation of "objective" class interests into subjectively conscious, formulated goals of organized action. The complete class is characterized not by a common though unconscious direction of behavior, but by its conscious action toward formulated goals.

7. Marx's theory of class formation is embedded in his work in a wider theory of class conflict as the moving force of social change. However, the elements of this wider theory are only partly of a sociological nature. It contains a number of theses whose validity can no longer be tested by empirical research. In summarizing those elements of Marx's theory of class conflict that are of potential use to the sociologist, we soon reach the point at which Marx the sociologist and Marx the philosopher joined forces:

a. In every society there is possession of and exclusion from effective private property. In every society there is therefore possession of and exclusion from legitimate power. The "relations of production" determine different class situations in the sense indicated above.
b. Differentiation of class situations toward the extremes of possession of and exclusion from property and power increases as a society develops.
c. As the gap between class situations grows, the conditions of class formation—i.e., of political organization and of the explicit formulation of class interests—mature. The political class struggle between "oppressors" and "oppressed" begins.
d. At its climax this conflict produces a revolutionary change, in which the hitherto ruling class loses its power position and is replaced by the hitherto oppressed class. A new society emerges, in which a new oppressed class grows up, and the process of class formation and class conflict starts anew.

It will prove necessary to subject this wider theory of Marx to severe criticism from a sociological point of view,[4] even though the most problematical aspects of Marx's theory, such as the notion of a classless society, have so far been left out of consideration. Here we are concerned merely with a résumé of the sociological elements of Marx's theory of class. It is, as we can say now, a theory of structural change by revolutions based on conflicts between antagonistic interest groups. Marx describes in detail the structural conditions and the process of formation of these interest groups. Less elaborately, but clearly enough, he also describes the process of conflict between these groups and its solution in revolutionary changes.

8. Before we leave Marx's sociology one more formal characteristic of his theory of class warrants recognition, since it is not without significance for recent sociological theory. By analyzing the change of social structures in terms of the categories mentioned, Marx introduces at least implicitly a certain image of society. Although an image of society of this kind may not be of immediate empirical relevance for sociological research, it can nevertheless become a measure of the proximity of a theoretical construction to reality, and it serves important functions as a guide to problems of research.[5]

For Marx, society is not primarily a smoothly functioning order of the form of a social organism, a social system, or a static social fabric. Its dominant characteristic is, rather, the continuous change of not only its elements, but its very structural form. This change in turn bears witness to the presence of conflicts as an essential feature of every society. Conflicts are not random; they are a systematic product of the structure of society itself. According to this image, there is no order except in the regularity of change. "Without conflict no progress: this is the law which civilization has followed to the present day" (6, p. 80).[6]

This image of society stands in clear contradiction to the images which lie at the basis of the considerations of some recent sociologists. At the same time, it appears considerably more useful for the solution of many problems of sociological analysis than all analogies, explicit or implicit, between society and organism, or society and one or another (essentially "closed") functional system. The reality of society is conflict and flux. Despite our radical criticism of Marx's theory of class, this implication may therefore be retained as a fruitful heuristic principle.

Bibliography

1. BENDIX, REINHARD, and S. M. LIPSET, eds., "Karl Marx's Theory of Social

---

[4] This holds in particular for propositions (a) and (b), which can only be empirical generalizations and are as such untenable even if Marx abandons them arbitrarily for the two societies he invented: the "original society" and the "final society" of history. Proposition (c) is also problematical; see the section on "class conflict and revolution" in Chapter IV. Generally speaking, it is my intention in this chapter—at least in so far as sociological questions are concerned—to indicate the points of departure of criticism, but to postpone the criticism itself.

[5] See Chapter III, pp. 112 ff., and Chapter V, pp. 157 ff. [of *Class and Class Conflict in Industrial Society*, by Dahrendorf] for a more elaborate discussion of "images of society."

[6] Unfortunately, the clause "to the present day" is meant to imply that one day this law will no longer hold. Here as elsewhere Marx has vitiated the value of his sociology by Hegelian philosophical additions of little plausibility. The image of society indicated in the last paragraph is for Marx an image of historical societies in the period of alienation. Communist society (as well as the early communal society of Marx's philosophical imagination) is different, and indeed in many ways not dissimilar to the constructions of modern sociological theory.

Classes," in *Class, Status and Power: A Reader in Social Stratification.* New York: The Free Press, 1953.

2. GEIGER, THEODOR, *Die Klassengesellschaft im Schmelztiegel.* Cologne and Hagen, 1949.

3. RENNER, KARL, *Die Wirtschaft als Ge-*

samtprozess und die Sozialisierung. Berlin, 1924.

4. WEBER, MAX, *The Theory of Social and Economic Organization,* trans. A. M. Henderson and Talcott Parsons. New York: Oxford University Press, Inc., 1950.

What Social Class Is in America

W. LLOYD WARNER   MARCHIA MEEKER   KENNETH EELLS

The American Dream and Social Class

In the bright glow and warm presence of the American Dream all men are born free and equal. Everyone in the American Dream has the right, and often the duty, to try to succeed and to do his best to reach the top. Its two fundamental themes and propositions, that all of us are equal and that each of us has the right to the chance of reaching the top, are mutually contradictory, for if all men are equal there can be no top level to aim for, no bottom one to get away from; there can be no superior or inferior positions, but only one common level into which all Americans are born and in which all of them will spend their lives. We all know such perfect equality of position and opportunity does not exist. All Americans are not born into families of equal position: some are born into a rich man's aristocracy on the Gold Coast; some into the solid comfort of Suburbia's middle classes; and others into a mean existence among the slum families living on the wrong side of the tracks. It is com-

Excerpted from W. Lloyd Warner, Marchia Meeker, and Kenneth Eells, *Social Class in America* (Chicago: Science Research Associates, Inc., 1949), pp. 3–10, 21, 23–26, 28–32, by permission of the authors and Harper & Row, Publishers.

mon knowledge that the sons and daughters of the Gold Coasts, the Main Lines, and Park Avenues of America are more likely to receive recognition for their efforts than the children of the slums. The distance these fortunate young people travel to achieve success is shorter, and the route up easier, than the long hard pull necessary for the ambitious children of the less fortunate middle class. Though everyone has the common right to succeed, it is not an equal "right"; though there is equality of rank for some of us, there is not equality of rank for all of us.

When some men learn that *all* the American Dream does not fit *all* that is true about the realities of our life, they denounce the Dream and deny the truth of *any* of it. Fortunately, most of us are wiser and better adjusted to social reality; we recognize that, though it is called a Dream and though some of it is false, by virtue of our firm belief in it we have made some of it true. Despite the presence of social hierarchies which place people at higher and lower levels in American communities, the principles of democracy do operate; the Christian dogma that all men are equal in the sight of God because He is our Father and we are His spiritual children, buttressed by the democratic faith in the equality of men and the insistence on their equal rights as citizens, is a powerful influence in the daily life of America.

From grade school on, we have learned to cite chapter and verse proving from the lives of many of the great men of American history that we can start at the bottom and climb to the highest peaks of achievement when we have a few brains and a will to do. Our mass magazines and newspapers print and reprint the legendary story of rags to riches and tell over and over again the Ellis-Island-to-Park-Avenue saga in the actual lives of contemporary successful immigrant men and women. From mere repetition, it might be thought the public would tire of the theme; the names are all that vary and the stories, like those of children, remain the same. But we never do tire of this theme, for it says what we need to know and what we want to hear.

Among people around us, we sometimes recognize men who have got ahead, who have been successfully upward-mobile, and who have reached levels of achievement beyond even the dreams of most men. Many Americans by their own success have learned that, for them, enough of the Dream is true to make all of it real. The examples from history, from the world around us, and from our own experience provide convincing evidence that, although full equality is absent, opportunity for advancement is present sufficiently to permit the rise of a few from the bottom and a still larger number from the middle to the higher economic and social levels. Although we know the statement that everyone is equal but that some men are higher than others is contradictory, and although some of us smile or become angry when we hear that "all of us are equal but some are more equal than others," we still accept both parts of this proposition either by understressing one part of the proposition or by letting all of it go as a paradox we feel to be true.

Our society does an excellent job in giving us an explicit knowledge of, and good argument for, the equalitarian aspects of our life. We have much scholarly knowledge about the workings of democracy, but we have little scientific knowledge about the powerful presence of social status and how it works for good and evil in the lives of all of us. Yet to live successfully and adaptively in America, every one of us must adjust his life to each of these contradictions, not just one of them, and we must make the most of each. Our knowledge of the democratic aspects of America is learned directly as part of our social heritage, but our understanding of the principle of social status tends to be implicit and to be learned obliquely and through hard and sometimes bitter experience. The lives of many are destroyed because they do not understand the workings of social class.[1]

It is the hope of the authors that this book will provide a corrective instrument which will permit men and women better to evaluate their social situations and thereby better adapt themselves to social reality and fit their dreams and aspirations to what is possible.

Our great state papers, the orations of great men, and the principles and pronouncements of politicians and statesmen tell us of the equality of all men. Each school boy learns and relearns it; but most of us are dependent upon experience and indirect statement to learn about "the wrong side of the tracks,"

---

[1] Jurgen Ruesch, Martin B. Loeb, et al., *Chronic Disease and Psychological Invalidism; a Psychosomatic Study* (New York: American Society for Research in psychosomatic Problems, 1946). A research at the University of California Hospital by Ruesch and others which demonstrates that this can be literally true; their results show how certain serious physical and mental ailments are directly attributable to social class and mobility strivings and anxieties.

"the Gold Coast and the slums," and "the top and bottom of the social heap." We are proud of those facts of American life that fit the pattern we are taught, but somehow we are often ashamed of those equally important social facts which demonstrate the presence of social class. Consequently, we tend to deny them or, worse, denounce them and by so doing deny their existence and magically make them disappear from consciousness. We use such expressions as "the Century of the Common Man" to insist on our democratic faith; but we know that, ordinarily, for Common Men to exist as a class, un-Common superior and inferior men must also exist. We know that every town or city in the country has its "Country Club set" and that this group usually lives on its Gold Coast, its Main Line, North Shore, or Nob Hill, and is the top of the community's social heap. Most of us know from novels such as those of Sinclair Lewis of the Main Streets that run through all our towns and cities, populated by Babbitts or, more explicitly stated, by "the substantial upper-middle class"; and by now, thanks to another group of novelists such as Erskine Caldwell, we know there is a low road, a Tobacco Road, that runs not only by the ramshackle houses of the poor whites of the South, but by the tarpaper shanties of the slums and river bottoms or Goat Hills of every town and city in the United States.

The "superior people" of Marquand's New England, "the North Shore crowd," divided into a top level of "old families" with a set of values and a way of life rated above those of the "new families," are matched by Philadelphia's "Main Line" families in Christopher Morley's *Kitty Foyle* and by similar groups in many other novels which report on the dominance of "the upper classes" in all regions of the United States. Reading them, together

with similar novels reporting on Suburbia and Main Street for the middle classes and those on the Tobacco Roads and the city slums for the lower levels, gives one the understanding that throughout the towns and cities of America the inhabitants are divided into status levels which are ways of life with definite characteristics and values. Talking to and observing the people of these communities demonstrate that they, too, know how real these status levels are, and they prove it by agreeing among themselves about the levels and who belongs to them in their particular city.

Although well aware of social class, social scientists have been more concerned with their theories and with quarreling among themselves about what social class is than with studying its realities in the daily lives of the people. Until recently, they have lagged behind the novelists in investigating what our classes are, how they operate in our social life, and what effect they have on our individual lives.

But recent scientific studies of social class in the several regions of the United States demonstrate that it is a major determinant of individual decisions and social actions; that every major area of American life is directly and indirectly influenced by our class order; and that the major decisions of most individuals are partly controlled by it. To act intelligently and know consciously how this basic factor in American life affects us and our society, it is essential and necessary that we have an explicit understanding of what our class order is, how it works, and what it does to the lives and personalities who live in it. Our most democratic institutions, including our schools, churches, business organizations, government, and even our family life, are molded by its all-pervading and exceedingly subtle but powerful influence.

The researches on social class in the

several regions of the United States make it possible to fill in much of the missing knowledge necessary to give Americans such explicit understanding of social class and to answer some of the important questions we raise about it when adjusting to the realities of our existence. Reduced to their simplicities these questions are: What is social class? How are social classes organized? And how do they function in the individual and the community? How do we use such knowledge to adjust ourselves more satisfactorily to the world around us? What is the effect of class on buying and selling and other problems of business enterprise, on the problems of personnel, on school and education, on the church and religion, on the acceptance and rejection of the communications of mass media such as the radio, magazine, newspaper, and motion picture? And, above all, are there effective and simple techniques of studying and applying the social-class concept so that those who are not specialized class analysts can apply such knowledge to the practical problems of their business or profession or to the research problems of the scientist?

The answer to this last important question is "yes" . . . .

The Structural Imperative— Why We Have a Class System

The recognition of social class and other status hierarchies in this country comes as no surprise to students of society. Research on the social life of the tribes and civilizations of the world clearly demonstrates that some form of rank is always present and a necessity for our kind of society.

Just as students of comparative biology have demonstrated that the physical structure of the higher animals must have certain organs to survive, so students of social anthropology have shown

that the social structures of the "higher," the more complex, societies must have rank orders to perform certain functions necessary for group survival.

When societies are complex and service large populations, they always possess some kind of status system which, by its own values, places people in higher or lower positions. Only the very simple hunting and gathering tribes, with very small populations and very simple social problems, are without systems of rank; but when a society is complex, when there are large numbers of individuals in it pursuing diverse and complex activities and functioning in a multiplicity of ways, individual positions and behaviors are evaluated and ranked. This happens primarily because, to maintain itself, the society must coordinate the efforts of all its members into common enterprises necessary for the preservation of the group, and it must solidify and integrate all these enterprises into a working whole. In other words, as the division of labor increases and the social units become more numerous and diverse, the need for coordination and integration also increases and, when satisfied, enables the larger group to survive and develop.

Those who occupy coordinating positions acquire power and prestige. They do so because their actions partly control the behavior of the individuals who look to them for direction. Within this simple control there is simple power. Those who exercise such power either acquire prestige directly from it or have gained prestige from other sources sufficiently to be raised to a coordinating position. For example, among many primitive peoples a simple fishing expedition may be organized so that the men who fish and handle each boat are under the direction of one leader. The efforts of each boat are directed by the leader and, in turn, each boat is integrated into the total enterprise by its leader's taking orders from his superior. The same situation prevails in a modern factory. Small plants with a small working force and simple problems possess a limited hierarchy, perhaps no more than an owner who bosses all the workers. But a large industrial enterprise, with complex activities and problems, like General Motors, needs an elaborate hierarchy of supervision. The position in a great industrial empire which integrates and coordinates all the positions beneath it throughout all the supervising levels down to the workers has great power and prestige. The same holds true for political, religious, educational, and other social institutions; the more complex the group and the more diverse the functions and activities, the more elaborate its status system is likely to be. . . .

The studies of other societies have demonstrated one other basic point: the more complex the technological and economic structure, the more complex the social structure, so that some argue (the Marxians and many classical economists) that technological advancement is the cause of social complexity and all class and status systems. It cannot be denied that economic and technological factors are important in the determination of class and status orders. We must not lose sight of the fact, however, that the social system, with its beliefs, values, and rules, which governs human behavior may well determine what kind of technology and what kind of economic institutions will survive or thrive in any given tribe or nation. In any case, social complexity is necessary for economic advancement. Furthermore, social complexity is a basic factor determining the presence or absence of class.

The Marxians have argued that the economic changes our society is undergoing always result in a class war in which "the proletariat" will be triumphant and out of which a "classless society" will result. The authors do not agree with them for several reasons. The principal reasons are: (1) the presence of a class order does not necessarily mean class conflict—the relations of the classes can be and often are amiable and peaceful; (2) classless societies (without differential status systems) are impossible where there is complexity for the reasons previously given. Russia's communistic system, supposedly designed to produce a pure equalitarian society, necessarily has citizens who are ranked above and below each other. Generals, there, outrank privates; commissars, the rank and file; and members of the Politburo, the ordinary comrade. Occupants of these higher ranks in Russia tend to associate together; those of the lower ranks form their own groups. Their children are trained according to the rank of their parents. This means that the younger generation learns these status differences, thereby strengthening status differences between levels and fostering the further development of social class in Communistic Russia.

All this has occurred despite the fact the Russians have removed the means of production from private hands and placed them under the control of the State ("the people"). The economic factor which by Marxian doctrine produced social classes is largely absent; yet social hierarchies and social classes are present for the reason that Russia is a complex society and needs them to survive.

These status trends in Russia will undoubtedly continue, for her population is vast, her peoples diverse, her problems immensely complex; and elaborate systems of coordination and control are necessary for such a nation to maintain itself. The Communist ideals of economic and political equality cannot produce perfect equality within the complexities of Russian life.

But let us return to the United States.

We, too, have a complex, highly diverse society. We, too, possess an elaborate division of labor and a ramified technology. And we, too, possess a variety of rank orders built on the need of maintaining unity and cohesion in making our common enterprises successful. Men occupying high and low positions possess families. Their families and their activities are identified with their social position. Families of the same position tend to associate together. They do this informally or through cliques, associations, or other institutions. This social matrix provides the structure of our class system. Children are always born to their families' position. Through life they may increase or decrease their status. The family thereby strengthens and helps maintain our class order. Social status in America is somewhat like man's alimentary canal; he may not like the way it works and he may want to forget that certain parts of it are part of him, but he knows it is necessary for his very existence. So a status system, often an object of our disapproval, is present and necessary in in our complex social world.

.   .   .

The Generalities of American Class

It is now time to ask what are the basic characteristics of social status common to the communities of all regions in the United States and, once we have answered this question, to inquire what the variations are among the several systems. Economic factors are significant and important in determining the class position of any family or person, influencing the kind of behavior we find in any class, and contributing their share to the present form of our status system. But, while significant and necessary, the economic factors are not sufficient to predict where a particular family or individual will be or to explain completely the phenomena of social class. Something more than a large income is necessary for high social position. Money must be translated into socially approved behavior and possessions, and they in turn must be translated into intimate participation with, and acceptance by, members of a superior class.

.   .   .

To belong to a particular level in the social-class system of America means that a family or individual has gained acceptance as an equal by those who belong in the class. The behavior in this class and the participation of those in it must be rated by the rest of the community as being at a particular place in the social scale.

Although our democratic heritage makes us disapprove, our class order helps control a number of important functions. It unequally divides the highly and lowly valued things of our society among the several classes according to their rank. Our marriage rules conform to the rules of class, for the majority of marriages are between people of the same class. No class system, however, is so rigid that it completely prohibits marriages above and below one's own class. Furthermore, an open class system such as ours permits a person during his lifetime to move up or down from the level into which he was born. Vertical social mobility for individuals or families is characteristic of all class systems. The principal forms of mobility in this country are through the use of money, education, occupation, talent, skill, philanthropy, sex, and marriage. Although economic mobility is still important, it seems likely now that more people move to higher positions by education than by any other route. We have indicated before this that the mere possession of money is insufficient for gaining and keeping a higher social position. This is equally true of all other forms of mobility. In every case there must be social acceptance.

Class varies from community to community. The new city is less likely than an old one to have a well-organized class order; this is also true for cities whose growth has been rapid as compared with those which have not been disturbed by huge increases in population from other regions or countries or by the rapid displacement of old industries by new ones. The mill town's status hierarchy is more likely to follow the occupational hierarchy of the mill than the levels of evaluated participation found in market towns or those with diversified industries. Suburbs of large metropolises tend to respond to selective factors which reduce the number of classes to one or a very few. They do not represent or express all the cultural factors which make up the social pattern of an ordinary city.

Yet systematic studies from coast to coast, in cities large and small and of many economic types, indicate that, despite the variations and diversity, class levels do exist and that they conform to a particular pattern of organization.

How Class Operates in Our Daily Lives

Because social class permeates all parts of our existence, it is impossible to do more than indicate how it enters consciously or unconsciously into the success and failure of business, professional, and other occupations or to show how knowledge of its effects is necessary for increasing the predictive qualities of much of the research done by psychologists and social scientists.

Class is vitally significant in marriage and training children as well as in most social activities of a community. Status plays a decisive role in the formation of personality at the various stages of development, for if young people are to learn to live adaptively as mature people in our society they must be trained by the informal controls of our society to fit into their places.

Education is now competing with economic mobility as the principal route to success. Today fewer men rise from the bottom to the top places in industry and business than did a generation ago. More and more, the sons of executives are replacing their fathers in such positions, leaving fewer positions into which the sons of those farther down can climb from the ranks. Captains of industry educate their sons to take their places or to occupy similar places in other industries. Also, more and more top jobs in industry are being filled by men coming from the technical and engineering schools or from the universities. The route up for them is no longer through a hierarchy of increasing skill to management and ownership as it was two generations ago. The prudent mobile man today must prepare himself by education if he wishes to fill an important job and provide his family with the money and prestige necessary to get "the better things of life."

Social-class research demonstrates that our educational system performs the dual task of aiding social mobility and, at the same time, working effectively to hinder it. This ceases to be a paradox when all the facts are examined. In the lower grades, our public schools are filled by children from all walks of life. Since education is free in the public schools, since everyone has a right to it and our laws try to keep children in school, and since it is common knowledge that "if you want to get ahead you must get an education," it would be assumed that children at, and below, the Common Man level would stay in school and equip themselves for mobility. Such is not the case. The social and educational systems work to eliminate the majority of them and permit only a few to get through. It has been estimated that, whereas 80 per cent of the upper- and upper-middle-class children actually go to college, only 20 per cent of the lower-middle- and 5 per cent of the lower-class children get there.[2] The evidence indicates that most, if not all, of the children of the top classes complete their preparation and go on to college, whereas those from the lower classes start dropping out in the grade schools and continue to do so in increasing numbers in high school. Only a very few of them go on to college. The educational conveyor belt drops lower-class children at the beginning and bottom of the educational route and carries those from the higher classes a longer distance, nearly all the upper-class children going to the end of the line.

If the teachers and school administrators in grade and high schools know the class positions of the children who enter their schools they can predict who will and who will not get to college. Furthermore, with such knowledge the educator can act to change a negative prediction to a positive one for the bright, ambitious lower- and lower-middle-class children, whose chances for higher education are now very slight.

The reason for the high mortality rate among the lower-class children becomes apparent when one examines the relation of the teachers and the other children to them. We now know that the intelligence of lower-class children

is not responsible for their failures in school for often their I.Q.'s are equal to those of children higher up. Although inferior intelligence has been the most frequent and plausible explanation,[3] I.Q. tests equated to social class demonstrate that differential intelligence is not the answer.

Teachers, it must be said, although one of the most democratically minded groups in America, tend to favor the children of the classes above the Common Man and to show less interest in those below that level. Studies in the Deep South, New England, and the Middle West indicate that they rate the school work of children from the higher classes in accordance with their family's social position and conversely give low ratings to the work of the lower-class children.

. . . .

The democratically minded educator asks how this can be. The answer is that most of it is done through ignorance of social class and how it operates in our lives. To be more specific, part of the general answer lies within the teacher as a product of our class system. The teacher conscientiously applies his own best values to his rating of the child. The middle-class teacher, and over three-fourths of teachers are middle-class, applies middle-class values. For him, upper- and upper-middle-class children possess traits that rank high and are positive; lower-class children

---

[2] Robert J. Havighurst and Hilda Taba, *Adolescent Character and Personality* (New York: John Wiley & Sons, Inc., 1948).

[3] The unpublished studies of Allison Davis, Robert J. Havighurst, and their collaborators on the class bias *within* the I.Q. tests themselves provide strong evidence to show that the tests are not "culture free" but reflect the middle- and upper-class cultural bias of those who fabricate them. For example, the tests, being largely products of upper-middle-class people, reflect their biases and only middle- and higher-class children are properly prepared to take them.

have characteristics that are negative and are ranked low.

Perhaps the most powerful influence of social class on the educational careers of our children, and certainly one of the most decisive and crucial situations in settling the ultimate class position of children from the Common Man and lower-class levels, is the influence of other children on the child's desire to stay in school. If the world of the child is pleasant, rewarding, and increases his self-esteem, he is likely to want to stay and do well. If it is punishing and decreases his self-respect, he is likely to do poorly and want to quit.

In a study of children's ratings of other children in a middle western community, Neugarten found that the children of the upper and upper-middle classes were rated high by all other children for such traits as good looks, liking for school, leadership, friendship, and many other favorable personal traits; lower-class children were ranked low or, more often than not, were given a negative rating and were said to be bad looking, dirty, and "people you would not want for friends."[4] When it is remembered that these children were only in the fifth and sixth grades and that each child in these grades was supposedly rated by all other children with no reference to status, we can see how quickly class values influence behavior and have their decisive effect in mold ing the personalities and influencing the life careers of Americans from their earliest years. School for the children of the populous lower classes is not the satisfactory place it is for the middle and upper classes. Given children of equal intellect, ability, and interest, it can be predicted by the use of class analysis

that a large percentage of those from the lower classes will be out of school before the sophomore year in high school and that none of the upper-class children, except those physically or mentally handicapped, will quit school.

If our society is to use more effectively the brains and native talent of this great army of young people, it must learn how to train them. To do this, it must keep them in school long enough to equip them with the skills and disciplines necessary for them to function satisfactorily in our economic and social world. Children, as well as teachers and school administrators, must have a conscious and explicit understanding of social class and a simple and easy way to use such knowledge in solving problems. Personality and I.Q. tests are important instruments to guide the teacher, but unless they are supplemented with instruments to measure and count the effects of social class they are insufficient. . . .

Studies of the relations of workers and managers in business and industry demonstrate how class continues to operate selectively when the young people leave school. Management is bringing college-trained men into the lower ranks of supervisors and promoting fewer from the ranks because it finds that the workers, while good men technically, do not have the necessary knowledge about handling men and relating themselves effectively to the higher reaches of management. Their education is often insufficient to make them good prospects for continuing advancement. The hiring of formally educated men effectively puts a ceiling over the legitimate aspirations of workers expecting to rise in the ranks. The blocking of the worker's mobility and the encouragement of college-trained men is the ultimate payoff of what began in the grade schools. Mobility for workers is becoming more difficult;

<hr>

[4] Bernice L. Neugarten, "Social Class and Friendship among School Children," *American Journal of Sociology*, LI, No. 4 (January, 1946), 305–13.

this means for the United States generally that the American Dream is becoming less real.[5]

Studies of the personalities of workers and managers now being made demonstrate that the effects of social-class and mobility drives are clearly discernible and demonstrably a part of the personality of individuals.[6]

In another area, studies of magazine subscriptions show that the class factor is of real importance in the selection of magazines. Readers from different class levels prefer various magazines on the basis of the different symbolic appeal of the stories and pictures. The Yankee City research showed that class entered not only into the purchase of magazines but into newspaper reading.[7] Later research indicates it has a decided efiect on radio listening.

A casual examination of the advertising displayed in various magazines demonstrates that advertising agencies and their clients often waste their money because they are ignorant of the operation of class values in their business. This is not surprising since so many status factors have to be considered. The class distribution of readers of the periodicals published in America varies enormously. The readers of certain magazines are confined to the narrow limits of the classes above the Common Man, others to the lower classes, still others to the Common Man level, but there are some who are not confined to any one segment, being well distributed throughout all class levels. The editors of the magazines last designated, intuitively, by trial and error, or some better means, have chosen reading matter which appeals to all levels. The others, not knowing how to extend their readership or appealing deliberately to a narrow range, have a status-limited range of readers.

The readers to whom the advertiser is appealing may or may not be the potential purchasers of his product. The product may be of such a nature that it appeals to only a narrow segment of the total society; to advertise in those media which have readers largely from other strata or to pay for advertising in journals which appeal to every level is a waste of money.

Although advertising agencies often spend their money foolishly when judged by class criteria, the fault is not always theirs, for frequently the manufacturer or retailer does not know how his product appeals to the different classes. Sometimes the product will appeal to but one level, but often a product might appeal to, and be used by, all class levels, were the producer aware of how his product is valued at different social levels. It is certain that the use and meaning of most objects sold on the American market shift from class to class.

The soap opera is a product of contemporary radio. The average upper-middle-class radio listener has little interest in soap operas; in fact, most of this group are actively hostile to these curious little dramas that fill the daytime air waves. Yet, millions and millions of American women listen daily to their favorite soap operas, and advertisers of certain commodities have found them invaluable in selling their products.

---

[5] See W. Lloyd Warner and J. O. Low, *The Social System of the Modern Factory*, Vol. IV, "Yankee City Series" (New Haven: Yale University Press, 1947), for a discussion of how many of the strikes and conflicts with management are determined by the factor of worker's blocked opportunity.

[6] The ordinary tests of personnel offices fail completely to account for social mobility and class factors, yet the predictive value of these factors for the success of managers in different kinds of jobs is very high.

[7] See Warner and Lunt, *The Social Life of a Modern Community*, Chapter XIX; and W. Lloyd Warner and William E. Henry, "Radio Daytime Serial: A Symbolic Analysis," *Genetic Psychology Monographs*, XXXVII (1948), 3–71.

Research has shown that the soap opera appeals particularly to the level of the Common Man. The problems raised in these folk dramas, their characters, plot, and values have a strong positive appeal to women of this class level, whereas they have little appeal to women above the Common Man level.[8]

Other researches demonstrate that furniture, including drapes, floor coverings, chairs and other seating facilities, is class-typed.

Another phenomenon of class, social mobility, is enormously important in the daily lives of Americans and, to a very great degree, determines how they will act on the job or at home. Recent studies of executives in large business enterprises clearly demonstrate that the success or failure of all of them is partly determined by the presence or absence of a "mobility drive." Our research shows that when a family loses its desire to achieve and advance itself, this very often is reflected in the executive's "slowing down" or being

<hr>

[8] *Ibid.*

unwilling to make the effort necessary for success as a manager. On the other hand, some men are too aggressively mobile and stir up trouble by their overly ambitious desires and their ruthless competition.

Tests combining knowledge of social class and personality demonstrate the necessity of knowing not only what the man's status level is, what it has been, and what he wants it to be, but how the class values and beliefs of his early training have become integral parts of his personality, and ever-present guides for what he thinks, what he feels, and how he acts. Those concerned with selecting executives need a personality inventory and a man's I.Q. to predict how a man will function in a given job; but they also need to find out what his experiences in our status order have done to his individuality and character structure.

Every aspect of American thought and action is powerfully influenced by social class, to think realistically and act effectively, we must know and understand our status system.

Class, Status, Party

MAX WEBER

I. Economically Determined Power and the Social Order

Law exists when there is a probability that an order will be upheld by a specific staff of men who will use physical or psychical compulsion with the intention of obtaining conformity with

Reprinted from Max Weber, *From Max Weber: Essays in Sociology*, trans. and eds. H. H. Gerth and C. Wright Mills (New York: Oxford University Press, Inc., 1946), pp. 180–95, by permission of H. H. Gerth and the publisher.

the order, or of inflicting sanctions for infringement of it.[1] The structure of every legal order directly influences the distribution of power, economic or otherwise, within its respective community. This is true of all legal orders and not only that of the state. In general, we understand by "power" the chance of a man or of a number of men to realize their own will in a communal

<hr>

[1] *Wirtschaft und Gesellschaft*, part III, chap. 4, pp. 631–40. The first sentence in paragraph one and the several definitions in this chapter which are in brackets do not appear in the original text. They have been taken from other contexts of *Wirtschaft und Gesellschaft*.

action even against the resistance of others who are participating in the action.

"Economically conditioned" power is not, of course, identical with "power" as such. On the contrary, the emergence of economic power may be the consequence of power existing on other grounds. Man does not strive for power only in order to enrich himself economically. Power, including economic power, may be valued "for its own sake." Very frequently the striving for power is also conditioned by the social "honor" it entails. Not all power, however, entails social honor: The typical American Boss, as well as the typical big speculator, deliberately relinquishes social honor. Quite generally, "mere economic" power, and especially "naked" money power, is by no means a recognized basis of social honor. Nor is power the only basis of social honor. Indeed, social honor, or prestige, may even be the basis of political or economic power, and very frequently has been. Power, as well as honor, may be guaranteed by the legal order, but, at least normally, it is not their primary source. The legal order is rather an additional factor that enhances the chance to hold power or honor; but it cannot always secure them.

The way in which social honor is distributed in a community between typical groups participating in this distribution we may call the "social order." The social order and the economic order are, of course, similarly related to the "legal order." However, the social and the economic order are not identical. The economic order is for us merely the way in which economic goods and services are distributed and used. The social order is of course conditioned by the economic order to a high degree, and in its turn reacts upon it.

Now: "classes," "status groups," and "parties" are phenomena of the distribution of power within a community.

2. Determination of Class-Situation by Market-Situation

In our terminology, "classes" are not communities; they merely represent possible, and frequent, bases for communal action. We may speak of a "class" when (1) a number of people have in common a specific causal component of their life chances, in so far as (2) this component is represented exclusively by economic interests in the possession of goods and opportunities for income, and (3) is represented under the conditions of the commodity or labor markets. [These points refer to "class situation," which we may express more briefly as the typical chance for a supply of goods, external living conditions, and personal life experiences, in so far as this chance is determined by the amount and kind of power, or lack of such, to dispose of goods or skills for the sake of income in a given economic order. The term "class" refers to any group of people that is found in the same class situation.]

It is the most elemental economic fact that the way in which the disposition over material property is distributed among a plurality of people, meeting competitively in the market for the purpose of exchange, in itself creates specific life chances. According to the law of marginal utility this mode of distribution excludes the non-owners from competing for highly valued goods; it favors the owners and, in fact, gives to them a monopoly to acquire such goods. Other things being equal, this mode of distribution monopolizes the opportunities for profitable deals for all those who, provided with goods, do not necessarily have to exchange them. It increases, at least generally, their power in price wars with those who, being propertyless, have nothing to offer but their services in native form or goods in a form constituted through their own labor, and who above all are compelled to get rid of these products in order barely to subsist. This mode of distribution gives to the propertied a monopoly on the possibility of transferring property from the sphere of use as a "fortune," to the sphere of "capital goods"; that is, it gives them the entrepreneurial function and all chances to share directly or indirectly in returns on capital. All this holds true within the area in which pure market conditions prevail. "Property" and "lack of property" are, therefore, the basic categories of all class situations. It does not matter whether these two categories become effective in price wars or in competitive struggles.

Within these categories, however, class situations are further differentiated: on the one hand, according to the kind of property that is usable for returns; and, on the other hand, according to the kind of services that can be offered in the market. Ownership of domestic buildings; productive establishments; warehouses; stores; agriculturally usable land, large and small holdings—quantitative differences with possibly qualitative consequences; ownership of mines; cattle; men (slaves); disposition over mobile instruments of production, or capital goods of all sorts, especially money or objects that can be exchanged for money easily and at any time; disposition over products of one's own labor or of others' labor differing according to their various distances from consumability; disposition over transferable monopolies of any kind— all these distinctions differentiate the class situations of the propertied just as does the "meaning" which they can and do give to the utilization of property, especially to property which has money equivalence. Accordingly, the propertied, for instance, may belong to the class of rentiers or to the class of entrepreneurs.

Those who have no property but who offer services are differentiated just as much according to their kinds of services as according to the way in which they make use of these services, in a continuous or discontinuous relation to a recipient. But always this is the generic connotation of the concept of class: that the kind of chance in the *market* is the decisive moment which presents a common condition for the individual's fate. "Class situation" is, in this sense, ultimately "market situation." The effect of naked possession *per se*, which among cattle breeders gives the non-owning slave or serf into the power of the cattle owner, is only a forerunner of real "class" formation. However, in the cattle loan and in the naked severity of the law of debts in such communities, for the first time mere "possession" as such emerges as decisive for the fate of the individual. This is very much in contrast to the agricultural communities based on labor. The creditor-debtor relation becomes the basis of "class situations" only in those cities where a "credit market," however primitive, with rates of interest increasing according to the extent of dearth and a factual monopolization of credits, is developed by a plutocracy. Therewith "class struggles" begin.

Those men whose fate is not determined by the chance of using goods or services for themselves on the market, e.g. slaves, are not, however, a "class" in the technical sense of the term. They are, rather, a "status group."

3. Communal Action Flowing from Class Interest

According to our terminology, the factor that creates "class" is unambiguously economic interest, and indeed, only those interests involved in the existence of the "market." Nevertheless, the concept of "class-interest" is an ambiguous one: even as an empirical concept it is ambiguous as soon as one understands by it something other than the factual direction of interests following with a certain probability from the class situation for a certain "average" of those people subjected to the class situation. The class situation and other circumstances remaining the same, the direction in which the individual worker, for instance, is likely to pursue his interests may vary widely, according to whether he is constitutionally qualified for the task at hand to a high, to an average, or to a low degree. In the same way, the direction of interests may vary according to whether or not a *communal* action of a larger or smaller portion of those commonly affected by the "class situation," or even an association among them, e.g., a "trade union," has grown out of the class situation from which the individual may or may not expect promising results. [Communal action refers to that action which is oriented to the feeling of the actors that they belong together. Societal action, on the other hand, is oriented to a rationally motivated adjustment of interests.] The rise of societal or even of communal action from a common class situation is by no means a universal phenomenon.

The class situation may be restricted in its effects to the generation of essentially *similar* reactions, that is to say, within our terminology, of "mass actions." However, it may not have even this result. Furthermore, often merely an amorphous communal action

emerges. For example, the "murmuring" of the workers known in ancient oriental ethics: the moral disapproval of the work-master's conduct, which in its practical significance was probably equivalent to an increasingly typical phenomenon of precisely the latest industrial development, namely, the "slow down" (the deliberate limiting of work effort) of laborers by virtue of tacit agreement. The degree in which "communal action" and possibly "societal action," emerges from the "mass actions" of the members of a class is linked to general cultural conditions, especially to those of an intellectual sort. It is also linked to the extent of the contrasts that have already evolved, and is especially linked to the *transparency* of the connnections between the causes and the consequences of the "class situation." For however different life chances may be, this fact in itself, according to all experience, by no means gives birth to "class action" (communal action by the members of a class). The fact of being conditioned and the results of the class situation must be distinctly recognizable. For only then the contrast of life chances can be felt not as an absolutely given fact to be accepted, but as a resultant from either (1) the given distribution of property, or (2) the structure of the concrete economic order. It is only then that people may react against the class structure not only through acts of an intermittent and irrational protest, but in the form of rational association. There have been "class situations" of the first category (1), of a specifically naked and transparent sort, in the urban centers of antiquity and during the Middle Ages; especially then, when great fortunes were accumulated by factually monopolized trading in industrial products of these localities or in foodstuffs. Furthermore, under certain circumstances, in the rural economy of the most diverse periods, agriculture was increasingly exploited in a profit-making manner. The most important historical example of the second category (2) is the class situation of the modern "proletariat."

4. Types of "Class Struggle"

Thus every class may be the carrier of any one of the possibly innumerable forms of "class action," but this is not necessarily so. In any case, a class does not in itself constitute a community. To treat "class" conceptually as having the same value as "community" leads to distortion. That men in the same class situation regularly react in mass actions to such tangible situations as economic ones in the direction of those interests that are most adequate to their average number is an important and after all simple fact for the understanding of historical events. Above all, this fact must not lead to that kind of pseudo-scientific operation with the concepts of "class" and "class interests" so frequently found these days, and which has found its most classic expression in the statement of a talented author, that the individual may be in error concerning his interests but that the "class" is "infallible" about its interests. Yet, if classes as such are not communities, nevertheless class situations emerge only on the basis of communalization. The communal action that brings forth class situations, however, is not basically action between members of the identical class; it is an action between members of different classes. Communal actions that directly determine the class situation of the worker and the entrepreneur are: the labor market, the commodities market, and the capitalistic enterprise. But, in its turn, the existence of a capitalistic enterprise presupposes that a very specific communal action exists and

that it is specifically structured to protect the possession of goods *per se*, and especially the power of individuals to dispose, in principle freely, over the means of production. The existence of a capitalistic enterprise is preconditioned by a specific kind of "legal order." Each kind of class situation, and above all when it rests upon the power of property, *per se* will become most clearly efficacious when all other determinants of reciprocal relations are, as far as possible, eliminated in their significance. It is in this way that the utilization of the power of property in the market obtains its most sovereign importance.

Now "status groups" hinder the strict carrying through of the sheer market principle. In the present context they are of interest to us only from this one point of view. Before we briefly consider them, note that not much of a general nature can be said about the more specific kinds of antagonism between "classes" (in our meaning of the term). The great shift, which has been going on continuously in the past, and up to our times, may be summarized, although at the cost of some precision: the struggle in which class situations are effective has progressively shifted from consumption credit toward, first, competitive struggles in the commodity market and, then, toward price wars on the labor market. The "class struggles" of antiquity—to the extent that they were genuine class struggles and not struggles between status groups—were initially carried on by indebted peasants, and perhaps also by artisans threatened by debt bondage and struggling against urban creditors. For debt bondage is the normal result of the differentiation of wealth in commercial cities, especially in seaport cities. A similar situation has existed among cattle breeders. Debt relationships as such produced class action up to the time of Cataline. Along with this, and with an increase in provision of grain for the city by transporting it from the outside, the struggle over the means of sustenance emerged. It centered in the first place around the provision of bread and the determination of the price of bread. It lasted throughout antiquity and the entire Middle Ages. The propertyless as such flocked together against those who actually and supposedly were interested in the dearth of bread. This fight spread until it involved all those commodities essential to the way of life and to handicraft production. There were only incipient discussions of wage disputes in antiquity and in the Middle Ages. But they have been slowly increasing up into modern times. In the earlier periods they were completely secondary to slave rebellions as well as to fights in the commodity market.

The propertyless of antiquity and of the Middle Ages protested against monopolies, pre-emption, forestalling, and the withholding of goods from the market in order to raise prices. Today the central issue is the determination of the price of labor.

This transition is represented by the fight for access to the market and for the determination of the price of products. Such fights went on between merchants and workers in the putting-out system of domestic handicraft during the transition to modern times. Since it is quite a general phenomenon we must mention here that the class antagonisms that are conditioned through the market situation are usually most bitter between those who actually and directly participate as opponents in price wars. It is not the rentier, the share-holder, and the banker who suffer the ill will of the worker, but almost exclusively the manufacturer and the business executives who are the direct opponents of workers in price wars. This is so in spite of the fact that it is precisely the cash boxes of the rentier, the share-holder, and the banker into which the more or less "unearned" gains flow, rather than into the pockets of the manufacturers or of the business executives. This simple state of affairs has very frequently been decisive for the role the class situation has played in the formation of political parties. For example, it has made possible the varieties of patriarchal socialism and the frequent attempts—formerly, at least—of threatened status groups to form alliances with the proletariat against the "bourgeoisie."

5. Status Honor

In contrast to classes, *status groups* are normally communities. They are, however, often of an amorphous kind. In contrast to the purely economically determined "class situation" we wish to designate as "status situation" every typical component of the life fate of men that is determined by a specific, positive or negative, social estimation of *honor*. This honor may be connected with any quality shared by a plurality, and, of course, it can be knit to a class situation: class distinctions are linked in the most varied ways with status distinctions. Property as such is not always recognized as a status qualification, but in the long run it is, and with extraordinary regularity. In the subsistence economy of the organized neighborhood, very often the richest man is simply the chieftain. However, this often means only an honorific preference. For example, in the so-called pure modern "democracy," that is, one devoid of any expressly ordered status privileges for individuals, it may be that only the families coming under approximately the same tax class dance with one another. This example is reported of certain smaller Swiss cities. But status honor need not necessarily be linked with a "class situation." On the contrary, it normally stands in sharp opposition to the pretensions of sheer property.

Both propertied and propertyless people can belong to the same status group, and frequently they do with very tangible consequences. This "equality" of social esteem may, however, in the long run become quite precarious. The "equality" of status among the American "gentlemen," for instance, is expressed by the fact that outside the subordination determined by the different functions of "business," it would be considered strictly repugnant—wherever the old tradition still prevails—if even the richest "chief," while playing billiards or cards in his club in the evening, would not treat his "clerk" as in every sense fully his equal in birthright. It would be repugnant if the American "chief" would bestow upon his "clerk" the condescending "benevolence"marking a distinction of "position," which the German chief can never dissever from his attitude. This is one of the most important reasons why in America the German "clubby-ness" has never been able to attain the attraction that the American clubs have.

6. Guarantees of Status Stratification

In content, status honor is normally expressed by the fact that above all else a specific *style of life* can be expected from all those who wish to belong to the circle. Linked with this expectation are restrictions on "social" intercourse (that is, intercourse which is not subservient to economic or any other of business's "functional" purposes). These restrictions may confine normal marriages to within the status circle and may lead to complete endogamous closure. As soon as there is not a mere individual and socially irrelevant imitation of another style of life, but an agreed-upon communal action of this closing character,

the "status" development is under way.

In its characteristic form, stratification by "status groups" on the basis of conventional styles of life evolves at the present time in the United States out of the traditional democracy. For example, only the resident of a certain street ("the street") is considered as belonging to "society," is qualified for social intercourse, and is visited and invited. Above all, this differentiation evolves in such a way as to make for strict submision to the fashion that is dominant at a given time in society. This submission to fashion also exists among men in America to a degree unknown in Germany. Such submission is considered to be an indication of the fact that a given man *pretends* to qualify as a gentleman. This submission decides, at least *prima facie*, that he will be treated as such. And this recognition becomes just as important for his employment chances in "swank" establishments, and above all, for social intercourse and marriage with "esteemed" families, as the qualification for dueling among Germans in the Kaiser's day. As for the rest: certain families resident for a long time, and, of course, correspondingly wealthy, e.g., "F. F. V., i.e., First Families of Virginia," or the actual or alleged descendants of the "Indian Princess" Pocahontas, of the Pilgrim fathers, or of the Knickerbockers, the members of almost inaccessible sects and all sorts of circles setting themselves apart by means of any other characteristics and badges ... all these elements usurp "status" honor. The development of status is essentially a question of stratification resting upon usurpation. Such usurpation is the normal origin of almost all status honor. But the road from this purely conventional situation to legal privilege, positive or negative, is easily traveled as soon as a certain stratification of the social order has in fact been "lived in" and has achieved stability by virtue of a stable distribution of economic power.

7. "Ethnic" Segregation and "Caste"

Where the consequences have been realized to their full extent, the status group evolves into a closed "caste." Status distinctions are then guaranteed not merely by conventions and laws, but also by *rituals*. This occurs in such a way that every physical contact with a member of any caste that is considered to be "lower" by the members of a "higher" caste is considered as making for a ritualistic impurity and to be a stigma which must be expiated by a religious act. Individual castes develop quite distinct cults and gods.

In general, however, the status structure reaches such extreme consequences only where there are underlying differences which are held to be "ethnic." The "caste" is, indeed, the normal form in which ethnic communities usually live side by side in a "societalized" manner. These ethnic communities believe in blood relationship and exclude exogamous marriage and social intercourse. Such a caste situation is part of the phenomenon of "pariah" peoples and is found all over the world. These people form communities, acquire specific occupational traditions of handicrafts or of other arts, and cultivate a belief in their ethnic community. They live in a "diaspora" strictly segregated from all personal intercourse, except that of an unavoidable sort, and their situation is legally precarious. Yet, by virtue of their economic indispensability, they are tolerated, indeed, frequently privileged, and they live in interspersed political communities. The Jews are the most impressive historical example.

A "status" segregation grown into a "caste" differs in its structure from a mere "ethnic" segregation: the caste structure transforms the horizontal and unconnected coexistences of ethnically segregated groups into a vertical social system of super- and subordination. Correctly formulated: a comprehensive societalization integrates the ethnically divided communities into specific political and communal action. In their consequences they differ precisely in this way: ethnic coexistences condition a mutual repulsion and disdain but allow each ethnic community to consider its own honor as the highest one; the caste structure brings about a social subordination and an acknowledgment of "more honor" in favor of the privileged caste and status groups. This is due to the fact that in the caste structure ethnic distinctions as such have become "functional" distinctions within the political societalization (warriors, priests, artisans that are politically important for war and for building, and so on). But even pariah people who are most despised are usually apt to continue cultivating in some manner that which is equally peculiar to ethnic and to status communities: the belief in their own specific "honor." This is the case with the Jews.

Only with the negatively privileged status groups does the "sense of dignity" take a specific deviation. A sense of dignity is the precipitation in individuals of social honor and of conventional demands which a positively privileged status group raises for the deportment of its members. The sense of dignity that characterizes positively privileged status groups is naturally related to their "being" which does not transcend itself, that is, it is to their "beauty and excellence" ($\kappa\alpha\lambda o$-$\kappa\alpha\gamma\dot{\alpha}\vartheta\iota\alpha$). Their kingdom is "of this world." They live for the present and by exploiting their great past. The sense of the negatively privileged strata naturally refers to a future lying beyond the present, whether it is of this life or of another. In other words, it must be nurtured by the belief in a providential "mission" and by a belief in a specific honor before God. The "chosen people's" dignity is nurtured by a belief either that in the beyond "the last will be the first," or that in this life a Messiah will appear to bring forth into the light of the world which has cast them out the hidden honor of the pariah people. This simple state of affairs, and not the "resentment" which is so strongly emphasized in Nietzsche's much admired construction in the *Genealogy of Morals*, is the source of the religiosity cultivated by pariah status groups. In passing, we may note that resentment may be accurately applied only to a limited extent; for one of Nietzsche's main examples, Buddhism, it is not at all applicable.

Incidentally, the development of status groups from ethnic segregations is by no means the normal phenomenon. On the contrary, since objective "racial differences" are by no means basic to every subjective sentiment of an ethnic community, the ultimately racial foundation of status structure is rightly and absolutely a question of the concrete individual case. Very frequently a status group is instrumental in the production of a thoroughbred anthropological type. Certainly a status group is to a high degree effective in producing extreme types, for they select personally qualified individuals (e.g., the Knighthood selects those who are fit for warfare, physically and psychically). But selection is far from being the only, or the predominant, way in which status groups are formed: Political membership or class situation has at all times been at least as frequently decisive. And today the class situation is by far the predominant factor, for of course the possibility of a style of life expected for members of a status group is usually conditioned economically.

8. Status Privileges

For all practical purposes, stratification by status goes hand in hand with a monopolization of ideal and material goods or opportunities, in a manner we have come to know as typical. Besides the specific status honor, which always rests upon distance and exclusiveness, we find all sorts of material monopolies. Such honorific preferences may consist of the privilege of wearing special costumes, of eating special dishes taboo to others, of carrying arms—which is most obvious in its consequences—the right to pursue certain non-professional dilettante artistic practices, e.g., to play certain musical instruments. Of course, material monopolies provide the most effective motives for the exclusiveness of a status group; although, in themselves, they are rarely sufficient, almost always they come into play to some extent. Within a status circle there is the question of intermarriage: the interest of the families in the monopolization of potential bridegrooms is at least of equal importance and is parallel to the interest in the monopolization of daughters. The daughters of the circle must be provided for. With an increased inclosure of the status group, the conventional preferential opportunities for special employment grow into a legal monopoly of special offices for the members. Certain goods become objects for monopolization by status groups. In the typical fashion these include "entailed estates" and frequently also the possessions of serfs or bondsmen and, finally, special trades. This monopolization occurs positively when the status group is exclusively entitled to own and to manage them; and negatively when, in order to maintain its specific way of life, the status group must *not* own and manage them.

The decisive role of a "style of life" in status "honor" means that status groups are the specific bearers of all "conventions." In whatever way it may be manifest, all "stylization" of life either originates in status groups or is at least conserved by them. Even if the principles of status conventions differ greatly, they reveal certain typical traits, especially among those strata which are most privileged. Quite generally, among privileged status groups there is a status disqualification that operates against the performance of common physical labor. This disqualification is now "setting in" in America against the old tradition of esteem for labor. Very frequently every rational economic pursuit, and especially "entrepreneurial activity," is looked upon as a disqualification of status. Artistic and literary activity is also considered as degrading work as soon as it is exploited for income, or at least when it is connected with hard physical exertion. An example is the sculptor working like a mason in his dusty smock as over against the painter in his salon-like "studio" and those forms of musical practice that are acceptable to the status group.

9. Economic Conditions and Effects of Status Stratification

The frequent disqualification of the gainfully employed as such is a direct result of the principle of status stratification peculiar to the social order, and of course, of this principle's opposition to a distribution of power which is regulated exclusively through the market. These two factors operate along with various individual ones, which will be touched upon below.

We have seen above that the market and its processes "knows no personal distinctions": "functional" interests dominate it. It knows nothing of "honor." The status order means precisely the reverse, viz.: stratification in terms of "honor" and of styles of life peculiar to status groups as such. If mere economic acquisition and naked economic power still bearing the stigma of its extra-status origin could bestow upon anyone who has won it the same honor as those who are interested in status by virtue of style of life claim for themselves, the status order would be threatened at its very root. This is the more so as, given equality of status honor, property *per se* represents an addition even if it is not overtly acknowledged to be such. Yet if such economic acquisition and power gave the agent any honor at all, his wealth would result in his attaining more honor than those who successfully claim honor by virtue of style of life. Therefore all groups having interests in the status order react with special sharpness precisely against the pretensions of purely economic acquisition. In most cases they react the more vigorously the more they feel themselves threatened. Calderon's respectful treatment of the peasant, for instance, as opposed to Shakespeare's simultaneous and ostensible disdain of the *canaille* illustrates the different way in which a firmly structured status order reacts as compared with a status order that has become economically precarious. This is an example of a state of affairs that recurs everywhere. Precisely because of the rigorous reactions against the claims of property *per se*, the "parvenu" is never accepted, personally and without reservation, by the privileged status groups, no matter how completely his style of life has been adjusted to theirs. They will only accept his descendants who have been educated in the conventions of their status group and who have never besmirched its honor by their own economic labor.

As to the general *effect* of the status order, only one consequence can be stated, but it is a very important one: the hindrance of the free development of the market occurs first for those goods which status groups directly withheld from free exchange by monopolization. This monopolization may be effected either legally or conventionally. For example, in many Hellenic cities during the epoch of status groups, and also originally in Rome, the inherited estate (as is shown by the old formula for indiction against spendthrifts) was monopolized just as were the estates of knights, peasants, priests, and especially the clientele of the craft and merchant guilds. The market is restricted, and the power of naked property *per se*, which gives its stamp to "class formation," is pushed into the background. The results of this process can be most varied. Of course, they do not necessarily weaken the contrasts in the economic situation. Frequently they strengthen these contrasts, and in any case, where stratification by status permeates a community as strongly as was the case in all political communities of antiquity and of the Middle Ages, one can never speak of a genuinely free market competition as we understand it today. There are wider effects than this direct exclusion of special goods from the market. From the contrariety between the status order and the purely economic order mentioned above, it follows that in most instances the notion of honor peculiar to status absolutely abhors that which is essential to the market: higgling. Honor abhors higgling among peers and occasionally it taboos higgling for the members of a status group in general. Therefore, everywhere some status groups, and usually the most influential, consider almost any kind of overt participation in economic acquisition as absolutely stigmatizing.

With some over-simplification, one might thus say that "classes" are stratified according to the principles of their *consumption* of goods as represented by special "styles of life."

An "occupational group" is also a status group. For normally, it successfully claims social honor only by virtue of the special style of life which may be determined by it. The differences between classes and status groups frequently overlap. It is precisely those status communities most strictly segregated in terms of honor (viz. the Indian castes) who today show, although within very rigid limits, a relatively high degree of indifference to pecuniary income. However, the Brahmins seek such income in many different ways.

As to the general economic conditions making for the predominance of stratification by "status," only very little can be said. When the bases of the acquisition and distribution of goods are relatively stable, stratification by status is favored. Every technological repercussion and economic transformation threatens stratification by status and pushes the class situation into the foreground. Epochs and countries in which the naked class situation is of predominant significance are regularly the periods of technical and economic transformations. And every slowing down of the shifting of economic stratifications leads, in due course, to the growth of status structures and makes for a resuscitation of the important role of social honor.

10. Parties

Whereas the genuine place of "classes" is within the economic order, the place of "status groups" is within the social order, that is, within the sphere of the distribution of "honor." From within these spheres, classes and status groups influence one another and they influence the legal order and are in turn influenced by it. But "parties" live in a house of "power."

Their action is oriented toward the acquisition of social "power," that is to say, toward influencing a communal action no matter what its content may be. In principle, parties may exist in a social "club" as well as in a "state." As over against the actions of classes and status groups, for which this is not necessarily the case, the communal actions of "parties" always mean a societalization. For party actions are always directed toward a goal which is striven for in planned manner. This goal may be a "cause" (the party may aim at realizing a program for ideal or material purposes), or the goal may be "personal" (sinecures, power, and from these, honor for the leader and the followers of the party). Usually the party action aims at all these simultaneously. Parties are, therefore, only possible within communities that are societalized, that is, which have some rational order and a staff of persons available who are ready to enforce it. For parties aim precisely at influencing this staff, and if possible, to recruit it from party followers.

In any individual case, parties may represent interests determined through "class situation" or "status situation," and they may recruit their following respectively from one or the other. But they need be neither purely "class" nor purely "status" parties. In most cases they are partly class parties and partly status parties, but sometimes they are neither. They may represent ephemeral or enduring structures. Their means of attaining power may be quite varied, ranging from naked violence of any sort to canvassing for votes with coarse or subtle means: money, social influence, the force of speech, suggestion, clumsy hoax, and so on to the rougher or more artful tactics of obstruction in parliamentary bodies.

The sociological structure of parties differs in a basic way according to the kind of communal action which they struggle to influence. Parties also differ according to whether or not the community is stratified by status or by classes. Above all else, they vary according to the structure of domination within the community. For their leaders normally deal with the conquest of a community. They are, in the general concept which is maintained here, not only products of specially modern forms of domination. We shall also designate as parties the ancient and medieval "parties," despite the fact that their structure differs basically from the structure of modern parties. By virtue of these structural differences of domination it is impossible to say anything about the structure of parties without discussing the structural forms of social domination *per se*. Parties, which are always structures struggling for domination, are very frequently organized in a very strict "authoritarian" fashion. . . .

Concerning "classes," "status groups," and "parties," it must be said in general that they necessarily presuppose a comprehensive societalization, and especially a political framework of communal action, within which they operate. This does not mean that parties would be confined by the frontiers of any individual political community. On the contrary, at all times it has been the order of the day that the societalization (even when it aims at the use of military force in common) reaches beyond the frontiers of politics. This has been the case in the solidarity of interests among the Oligarchs and among the democrats in Hellas, among the Guelfs and among Ghibellines in the Middle Ages, and within the Calvinist party during the period of religious struggles. It has been the case up to the solidarity of the landlords (international congress of agrarian landlords), and has continued among princes (holy alliance, Karlsbad decrees), socialist workers, conservatives (the longing of Prussian conservatives for Russian intervention in 1850). But their aim is not necessarily the establishment of new international political, i.e., *territorial*, dominion. In the main they aim to influence the existing dominion.[2]

---

[2] The posthumously published text breaks off here. We omit an incomplete sketch of types of "warrior estates."

Inequality and Social Structure

R. H. TAWNEY

So to criticize inequality and to desire equality is not, as is sometimes suggested, to cherish the romantic illusion that men are equal in character and intelligence. It is to hold that, while their natural endowments differ profoundly, it is the mark of a civilized society to aim at eliminating such inequalities as have their source, not in individual differences, but in its own organisation, and that individual differences, which are a source of social energy, are more likely to ripen and find expression if social inequalities are, as far as practicable, diminished. And the obstacle to the progress of equality is something simpler and more potent than finds expression in the familiar truism that men vary in their mental and moral, as well as in their physical, characteristics, important and valuable though that truism is as a reminder that different individuals require different types of provision. It is the habit of mind which thinks it, not regrettable, but natural and desirable, that different sections of a community should be distinguished from each other by sharp differences of economic status, of environment, of education and culture

Excerpted from R. H. Tawney, *Equality* (New York: Capricorn Books, 1961), pp. 49–60, 64–68, 69–73, 75–81, 83–90, by permission of George Allen & Unwin, Ltd. Originally published 1931.

and habit of life. It is the temper which regards with approval the social institutions and economic arrangements by which such differences are emphasized and enhanced, and feels distrust and apprehension at all attempts to diminish them.

The institutions and policies in which that temper has found expression are infinite in number. At one time it has coloured the relations between the sexes; at another, those between religions; at a third, those between members of different races. But in communities no longer divided by religion or race, and in which men and women are treated as political and economic equals, the divisions which remain are, nevertheless, not insignificant. The practical form which they most commonly assume—the most conspicuous external symptom of difference of economic status and social position—is, of course, a graduated system of social classes, and it is by softening or obliterating, not individual differences, but class gradations, that the historical movements directed towards diminishing inequality have attempted to attain their objective. It is, therefore, by considering the class system that light upon the problem of inequality is, in the first place at least, to be sought, and it is by their attitude to the relations between classes that the equalitarian temper and philosophy are distinguished from their opposite.

A society which values equality will

attach a high degree of significance to differences of character and intelligence between different individuals, and a low degree of significance to economic and social differences between different groups. It will endeavour, in shaping its policy and organization, to encourage the former and to neutralize and suppress the latter, and will regard it as vulgar and childish to emphasize them when, unfortunately, they still exist. A society which is in love with inequality will take such differences seriously, and will allow them to overflow from the regions, such as economic life, where they have their origin, and from which it is difficult wholly to expel them, till they become a kind of morbid obsession, colouring the whole world of social relations.

The Meaning of Class

The idea of "class," most candid observers will admit, is among the most powerful of social categories. Its significance is sometimes denied on the ground that, as Professor Carr-Saunders and Mr. Caradog Jones remark in their valuable book, a group described as a class may "upon many an issue be divided against itself." But this is to confuse the fact of class with the consciousness of class, which is a different phenomenon. The fact creates the consciousness, not the consciousness the fact. The former may exist without the latter, and a group may be marked by common characteristics and occupy a distinctive position *vis-à-vis* other groups, without, except at moments of exceptional tension, being aware that it does so.

While, however, class is a powerful category, it is also an ambiguous one, and it is not surprising that there should be wide differences in the interpretations placed upon it both by sociologists and by laymen. War, the institution of private property, biological characteristics, the division of labour, have all been adduced to explain the facts of class formation and class differentiation. The diversity of doctrines is natural, since the facts themselves are diverse. Clearly, there are societies in which the position and relations of the groups composing them have been determined ultimately by the effect of conquest. Clearly, the rules under which property is held and transmitted have played a large part in fixing the conditions by which different groups are distinguished from each other. Clearly, there are circumstances in which the biological characteristics of different groups are a relevant consideration. Clearly, the emergence of new social groups is a natural accompaniment of the differentiation of economic functions—of the breaking up, for example, of a relatively simple and undifferentiated society into a multitude of specialized crafts and professions, each with its different economic *métier*, its different training and outlook and habit of life, which has been the most obvious consequence of the transition of large parts of Europe from the predominantly agricultural civilization of two centuries ago to the predominantly industrial civilization of today.

These different factors have, however, varying degrees of importance in different ages, different communities, and different connections. In western Europe, for example, the imposition of one race upon another by military force was of great importance during some earlier periods of its history, but in recent centuries has played but little part in modifying its social structure. Certain groups are marked, it seems, by different biological characteristics. Such characteristics require, however, the lapse of considerable periods to produce their result, while marked alterations in social structure may take place in the course of a single lifetime. It is difficult to suppose that the broad changes in social classification which have occurred in the immediate past—the profound modification of class relations, for example, which was the result of the French Revolution, or the rise of new types of class system and the obliteration of the old, which has everywhere accompanied the development of the great industry, or the more recent growth of a *nouvelle couche sociale* of technicians, managers, scientific experts, professional administrators, and public servants—are most appropriately interpreted as a biological phenomenon.

Nor, important though economic forces have been, can the gradations of classes be explained, as is sometimes suggested, purely as a case of economic specialization. It may be true, indeed, that the most useful conception of a class is that which regards it as a social group with a strong tinge of community of economic interest. But, while classes are social groups, not all social groups, even when they have common economic interests, can be described as classes. "Classes," observed Lord Bryce, in writing of the United States of a generation ago, "are in America by no means the same thing as in the greater nations of Europe. One must not, for political purposes, divide them as upper and lower, richer and poorer, but rather according to the occupations they respectively follow." His distinction between occupational and social divisions still retains its significance. Stockbrokers, barristers and doctors, miners, railwaymen and cotton-spinners represent half a dozen professions; but they are not normally regarded as constituting half a dozen classes. Postmen, bricklayers and engineers pursue sharply contrasted occupations, and often have divergent economic interests; but they are not distinguished from each other by the differences of economic status, environment, education, and opportunity, which are associated in common opinion with differences between classes. A community which is marked by a low degree of economic differentiation may yet possess a class system of which the lines are sharply drawn and rigidly defined, as was the case, for example, in many parts of the agricultural Europe of the eighteenth century. It may be marked by a high degree of economic differentiation, and yet appear, when judged by English standards, to be comparatively classless, as is the case, for example, with some British Dominions.

The conception of class is, therefore, at once more fundamental and more elusive than that of the division between different types of occupation. It is elusive because it is comprehensive. It relates, not to this or that specific characteristic of a group, but to a totality of conditions by which several sides of life are affected. The classification will vary, no doubt, with the purpose for which it is made, and with the points which accordingly are selected for emphasis. Conventional usage, which is concerned, not with the details of the social structure, but with its broad outlines and salient features, makes a rough division of individuals according to their resources and manner of life, the amount of their income and the source from which it is derived, their ownership of property or their connection with those who own it, the security or insecurity of their economic position, the degree to which they belong by tradition, education and association to social strata which are accustomed, even on a humble scale, to exercise direction, or, on the other hand, to those whose normal lot is to be directed by others. It draws its class lines, in short, with reference partly to consumption, partly to production; partly by standards of expenditure, partly by the position which different individuals occupy in the economic system. Though its criteria change from generation to generation, and are obviously changing today with surprising rapidity, its general tendency is clear. It sets at one end of the scale those who can spend much, or who have what is called an independent income, because they are dependent for it on persons other than themselves, and at the other end those who can spend little and live by manual labour. It places at a point between the two those who can spend more than the second but less than the first, and who own a little property or stand near to those who own it.

Thus conventional usage has ignored, in its rough way, the details, and has emphasized the hinges, the nodal points, the main watersheds. And in so doing, it has come nearer, with all its crudity, to grasping certain significant sides of the reality than have those who would see in the idea of class merely the social expression of the division of labour between groups engaged in different types of economic activity. For, though differences of class and differences of occupation may often have sprung from a common source, they acquire, once established, a vitality and momentum of their own, and often flow in distinct, or even divergent, channels. The essence of the latter is difference of economic function: they are an organ of co-operation through the division of labour. The essence of the former is difference of status and power: they have normally been, in some measure at least, the expression of varying degrees of authority and subordination. Class systems, in fact, in the historical forms which they most commonly have assumed, have usually been associated—hence, indeed, the invidious suggestion which the word sometimes conveys—with differences, not merely of economic *métier*, but of social position, so that different groups have been distinguished from each other, not only, like different professions, by the nature of the service they render, but in status, in influence, and sometimes in consideration and respect. Even today, indeed, though somewhat less regularly than in the past, class tends to determine occupation rather than occupation class.

Public opinion has in all ages been struck by this feature in social organization, and has used terms of varying degrees of appropriateness to distinguish the upper strata from the lower, describing them sometimes as the beautiful and good, sometimes as the fat men, sometimes as the twiceborn, or the sons of gods and heroes, sometimes merely, in nations attached to virtue rather than beauty, as the best people. Such expressions are not terms of precision, but they indicate a phenomenon which has attracted attention, and which has certainly deserved it. The note of most societies has been, in short, not merely vertical differentiation, as between partners with varying tasks in a common enterprise, but also what, for want of a better term, may be called horizontal stratification, as between those who occupy a position of special advantage and those who do not.

The degree to which such horizontal divisions obtain varies widely in the same community at different times, and in different communities at the same time. They are more marked in most parts of Europe than in America and the British Dominions, in the east of America than in the west, in England than in France; and they were obviously more marked in the England of half a century ago than they are in that of today. Being in constant motion, they are not easily photographed, and they are hardly described before the description is out of date. But such divisions exist to some extent, it will be agreed, in most societies, and, wherever they exist to a considerable extent, they are liable, it will also be agreed, to be a focus of irritation. Accepted in the past with placid indifference, they resemble, under modern political and economic conditions, a sensitive nerve which vibrates when touched, a tooth which, once it has started aching, must be soothed or extracted before it can be forgotten, and attention paid to the serious business of life. It is possible that they possess also certain grave disadvantages. The advantages—if such there are—are most likely to be enjoyed, and the disadvantages removed, if their main features, at any rate, are, in the first place, neither denounced, nor applauded, but understood.

The Economic and Social Contours

Income, economists tell us, may be regarded from either of two points of view. It may be interpreted as a product or as a dividend, as a stream of goods in process of creation, or as a stream of goods in process of consumption. And classes, which rest upon economic foundations, have two different aspects, which correspond to these different aspects of the national income. They may be regarded, on the one hand, as composed of a series of economic groups, holding different positions in the productive system, and, as employer and employed, capitalist and wage-earner, landlord, farmer, and labourer, discharging different, if occasionally somewhat attenuated, functions within it. They may be regarded, on the other hand, as a series of social groups, distinguished from each other by different standards of expenditure and consumption, and varying in their income, their environment, their education, their social status and family connections, their leisure and their amusements.

When attention is turned upon the organization of industry and the relations of the various interests engaged in it—their disputes, their agreements, their attempts to establish more effective cooperation or their failure to achieve it—it is naturally the first aspect

of the class system which springs into prominence. Society is regarded as an economic mechanism, the main elements in whose structure correspond to different classes. In discussions of the traditions, habits and manner of life by which different classes are characterized—the social institutions which they have created, the types of schools which they attend, the varying environments in which they live—the feature which attracts attention is naturally the second. Society then presents itself, not as a productive machine, but as an organism composed of groups with varying standards of life and culture. The class system takes off its overalls or office coat, and wears the costume appropriate to hours of ease.

Before goods can be consumed goods must be produced. It is obvious that these two aspects of social organization are closely connected, as obverse and reverse, or flower and root. The material fabric of civilization is always crumbling and always being renewed; the wealth which renews it is hewn daily in the gloom of the mine and fashioned unceasingly in the glare of the forge. Both the hierarchy of the world of leisure, therefore, and the hierarchy of the world of productive effort, have their common foundation in the character and organization of the economic system. But, while they have a common foundation, the lines of the one are not a mere replica of those of the other. They correspond, but they do not coincide; in England, indeed, they coincide less closely than in younger communities, such as the United States, where the action of economic forces on the structure of society encounters fewer breakwaters built by tradition, and is therefore more simple, immediate, and direct. The social fabric is stretched upon an economic framework, and its contours follow the outlines of the skeleton which supports it. But it is not strained so taut as to be free from superfluous folds and ornamental puckers. Moulded, as it was, on the different structure of the past, it has not always adjusted itself with nicety to the angles of the present. It contains elements, therefore, which, like the rudimentary organs of the human body, or the decorative appendages of the British Constitution, have survived after their function has disappeared and their meaning been forgotten.

England is peculiar in being marked to a greater degree than most other communities, not by a single set of class relations, but by two, of which one is the product of the last century of economic development, and the other, though transformed by that development and softened by the social policy of the democratic era, contains, nevertheless, a large infusion of elements which descend from the quite different type of society that existed before the rise of the great industry. It is the combination of both—the blend of a crude plutocratic reality with the sentimental aroma of an aristocratic legend—which gives the English class system its peculiar toughness and cohesion. It is at once as businesslike as Manchester and as gentlemanly as Eton; if its hands can be as rough as those of Esau, its voice is as mellifluous as that of Jacob. It is a god with two faces and a thousand tongues, and, while each supports its fellow, they speak in different accents and appeal to different emotions. Revolutionary logic, which is nothing if not rational, addresses its shattering syllogisms to the one, only to be answered in terms of polite evasion by the other. It appeals to obvious economic grievances, and is baffled by the complexities of a society in which the tumultuous impulses of economic self-interest are blunted and muffled by the sedate admonitions of social respectability.

Regarded as an economic engine, the structure of English society is sim-pler than that of some more primitive communities. In spite of the complexity of its detailed organization, its main lines are drawn not by customary or juristic distinctions, which are often capricious, but by the economic logic of a system directed towards a single objective, the attainment of which, or the failure to attain it, can be tested by the arithmetical criterion of profit or loss. Its most obvious feature is also its most characteristic. It is the separation of the groups which organize, direct and own the material apparatus of industry from those which perform its routine work, and the consequent numerical preponderance of the wage-earning population over all other sections of the community.

Such a separation and such a preponderance, on the scale on which they exist at present, are a novel phenomenon. Till a comparatively recent period in the history of most European countries, while political power was far more highly centralized than it is today, a high degree of economic centralization was, apart from certain peculiar undertakings, the exception. The legal and social cleavage which divided different classes, the noble from the *roturier*, the lord from the peasant, was often profound. But the control of the processes of economic life tended, of course with numerous exceptions, to be dispersed in the hands of large numbers of peasant farmers and small masters, who, subject to the discharge of their personal or financial obligations towards their superiors, conducted much of the humble routine of their economic affairs at their own discretion. Labour, property and enterprise were, to some considerable degree, not separated, but intertwined. Economic initiative and direction were fragmentary and decentralized. Conducted, not by mass attacks, but by individual skirmishes, the struggle with nature was ineffective because it was uncoordinated. The organization of economic life, with its numerous tiny centres of energy, and its absence of staff-work and system, resembled that, not of an army, but of a guerrilla band. In the picture drawn in the well-known estimate of Gregory King, or in the more reliable statistics of the Prussian Census, which even in 1843 showed only seventy-six work-people to every hundred masters, pre-industrial society appears, compared with our own, like a collection of fishing-smacks beside a battle fleet.

Over the greater part of the world, such, or something like it, is still the normal type of economic structure. But the organization and class relations of industrial societies are obviously different. Their note is the magnitude of the group dependent on wages, compared with those which are interested in the ownership of property and the direction of economic enterprise. Statisticians have attempted to measure the degree of "Proletarianisation" in different countries. They have produced tables in which they are graded according to the percentage which the wage-earners and humbler salaried officials form the total occupied population, from Russia, with 12 to 14 per cent of wage workers till a decade or so ago, Greece with 21, Bulgaria with 23, and France with 48, to the United States with 70 per cent, Australia with 71, Belgium and the Netherlands each with 73, and Great Britain with 78. The materials for such investigations are defective, and accurate results are not to be expected. What is significant, however, is the broad difference of type in the economic structure of communities at the two ends of the scale. At the one extreme there are those in which the wage-earners from a minority scattered up and down the interstices of a society composed predominantly of small property-owners; at the other extreme there are those in which the wage-earners form half, two-thirds, or even three-quarters of the whole occupied population.

A famous theory has suggested that the progressive concentration of ownership in the hands of a diminishing number of owners is a tendency inherent in capitalist civilization. The generalization was prompted by the contrast between the distribution of property in England in the early days of the great industry and that obtaining in the contemporary peasant societies of the Continent, where the great industry had hardly as yet got on to its feet, and it has not been confirmed by the subsequent course of economic history. While the difference between the character and significance of property in these two types of community is not less impressive than it was, it is a difference between two phases of economic development, not, as Marx is usually understood to have suggested, between the earlier and later stages of the same phase. So far from diminishing, as he seems to have anticipated would be the case, the number of property-owners in England has tended, if anything, to increase in the course of the last half-century. Though still astonishingly small, it is probably larger today than at any time since he wrote.

But, of course, the distinction between the majority, who are mainly dependent on wages, and the minority, who are largely concerned with proprietary interests, is not the only significant line of division in the economic system. There is also the familiar division between the directed and the directors; between those who receive orders and those from whom orders proceed; between the privates and the non-commissioned officers of the industrial army and those who initiate its operations, determine its objective and methods, and are responsible for the strategy and tactics on which the economic destiny of the mass of mankind depends. Since the control of industrial enterprise belongs in law to the ordinary shareholder, and in practice to the entrepreneurs who command the use of his savings and act on his behalf, the proprietary classes, either personally or through their agents, take, as seems to them expedient, the decisions upon which the organization and conduct of industry depend, and, within the limits prescribed by law or established by voluntary agreement, are responsible for their action to no superior authority. The wage-earners act under their direction; have access to the equipment, plant, and machinery, without which they cannot support themselves, on condition of complying with the rules laid down, subject to the intervention of the State and of trade unions, by their employers; and work—and not infrequently live—under conditions which, consciously or unconsciously, the latter have determined. Hence the third characteristic of the economic structure of industrial societies is the sharpness of the division between the upper and lower grades of the economic hierarchy. In the concentration of authority which springs from the separation of the functions of initiative and control on the one hand, and of execution on the other, such societies resemble a pyramid with steeply sloping sides and an acute apex.

In the course of the last two generations that concentration of authority has passed into a new and more sensational stage. In the infancy of the great industry its significance was veiled by the multitude of small undertakings and the absence of combination between them, by the general belief that, with luck and perseverance, any able man could fight his way to the top, and by the fact that, since the employer was normally an individual, not a company, the relations between management and wage-earners, if often harsher than today, were also less remote and im-

personal. In certain branches of industry and in certain communities such conditions still survive, but the current has obviously been flowing for two generations in the opposite direction. It is sometimes suggested that the growth of joint-stock enterprise, by increasing the number of small investors, has broadened the basis of industrial government. But, if joint-stock enterprise has done something to diffuse ownership, it has centralized control. The growth in the size of the business unit necessarily accelerates the process by which ever larger bodies of wage-earners are brigaded under the direction of a comparatively small staff of entrepreneurs. The movement towards combination and amalgamation, which is advancing so rapidly today in Great Britain, does the same. The emergence, side by side with questions of wages and working conditions, of questions of status and control is one symptom of the more definite horizontal cleavage which that centralization of economic command has tended to produce.

So, when English society is considered as a series of groups engaged in production, the salient characteristic of its class structure is the division between the majority who work for wages, but who do not own or direct, and the minority who own the material apparatus of industry and determine industrial organization and policy. Society is not merely, however, an economic mechanism in which different groups combine for the purpose of production; it is also a system of social groups with varying standards of expenditure and habits of life, and different positions, not only on an economic, but on a social scale. It has, therefore, a social, as well as an economic, pattern. And, though the first is moulded upon the second, it has also a character and logic of its own, which finds expression in distinctive forms of organization and give rise to separate and peculiar problems.

Regarded from the standpoint, not of the production of wealth, but of its use and consumption, the predominant characteristic of the English social system is simple. It is its hierarchical quality, and the connection of that quality with differences of wealth. All forms of social organization are hierarchical, in the sense that they imply gradations of responsibility and power, which vary from individual to individual according to his place in the system. But these gradations may be based on differences of function and office, may relate only to those aspects of life which are relevant to such differences, and may be compatible with the easy movement of individuals, according to their capacity, from one point on the scale to another. Or they may have their source in differences of birth, or wealth, or social position, may embrace all sides of life, including the satisfaction of the elementary human needs which are common to men as men, and may correspond to distinctions, not of capacity, but of circumstance and opportunity.

It is possible to conceive a community in which the necessary diversity of economic functions existed side by side with a large measure of economic and social equality. In such a community, while the occupations and incomes of individuals varied, they would live, nevertheless, in much the same environment, would enjoy similar standards of health and education, would find different positions, according to their varying abilities, equally accessible to them, would intermarry freely with each other, would be equally immune from the more degrading forms of poverty, and equally secure against economic oppression. But the historical structure and spirit of English society are of a different character. It has inherited and preserved a tradition of differentiation, not merely by economic function, but by wealth and status, and that tradition, though obviously weakened during the last two generations, has left a deep imprint both on its practical organization and on its temper and habits of thought. Thus not only is it, like all social systems, a pyramid, but it is a pyramid the successive tiers of which tend to correspond only to a small degree with differences of character and ability, and to a high degree with differences of social class. Not only is it a hierarchy, but it is a hierarchy whose gradations embrace those aspects of life where discrimination is inappropriate, because it ignores the common element in human requirements, as well as those where, because it is related to varying levels of human capacity, it is appropriate and necessary. It is marked in short, by sharp differences, not only of economic status and economic power, but of pecuniary income, of circumstances, and of opportunity.

These contrasts of circumstances are more powerful as an instrument of social stratification even than the difference of income of which they are the consequence. Most infants, high medical authorities inform us, are born healthy, but of the children—predominantly, of course, the children of wage-earners—who enter the elementary schools at the age of five, no less than one-fifth are found to be suffering from physical defects which cripple their development and sow the seeds of illness in later years. When their formal education begins, they find in the elementary schools, with all the immense improvement that has taken place in those schools in the course of the last generation, conditions of accommodation, equipment and staffing which would not be tolerated for an instant in the schools attended by the well-to-do, and which are excluded, indeed, from grant-aided secondary schools by the regulations of the Board of Education. While the provision for the earlier stages of education is defective in quality, the provision for the later stages is defective in quantity. Educational considerations—considerations of the conditions most likely to promote the growth of human beings in physique and intelligence—dictate, as has often been pointed out, that all normal children shall pass from primary education to some form of secondary education. But the proportion of children leaving the elementary schools who enter what have hitherto been known as secondary schools is, in England and Wales as a whole, less that one-seventh, and in some areas less than one-tenth, while some three-quarters of them have higherto entered fulltime wage-earning employment at the age of fourteen.

Thus, even in childhood, different strata of the population are distinguished by sharp contrasts of environment, of health, and of physical well-being. A small minority enjoy conditions which are favourable to health, and receive prolonged and careful nurture, and are encouraged to regard themselves as belonging to a social group which will exercise responsibility and direction. The great majority are exposed to conditions in which health, if not impossible, is necessarily precarious, and end their education just at the age when their powers are beginning to develop, and are still sometimes encouraged to believe that the qualities most desirable in common men are docility, and a respect for their betters, and a habit of submission. As the rising generation steps year by year into industry, it enters a world where these social contrasts are reinforced by economic contracts—by the differences of security and economic power which distinguish those who own property and control the industrial machine from those who are dependent on their daily labour and execute the routine work of the economic system. But the social contrasts continue, and are, indeed, intensified. In spite of the poets, there are no such inveterate respecters of persons as disease and death, and the disparities find expression in the difference between the liability to disease and death of impoverished and well-to-do areas—in the fact, for example, that in the less densely populated parts of Manchester the death-rate a decade ago was 10.5 per 1,000, and in the moe densely populated parts, 16, and that in a poor district of Glasgow it was approximately twice what it was where poverty was less. More recent investigations underline the same point. It has been shown—to quote only one example—that in Stockton-on-Tees the standardized death-rate during the years 1931–34 was 11.5 per 1,000 for the better-off families, and more than twice as much—26 per 1,000—for the poorest. The poor, it seems, are beloved by the gods, if not by their fellow-mortals. They are awarded exceptional opportunities of dying young.

A stratified class system appears, therefore, to have as its second characteristic the contrast described in the familiar phrase of Disraeli, the contrast not only between different levels of pecuniary income, but between different standards of physical well-being and different opportunities for mental development and civilization. And it has, in addition, a third symptom, which is little less significant than these, and which is more conspicuous, perhaps, in England than in some other countries, for example the United States, where inequality of income in hardly less pronounced. It is the general, and, till recently, the almost unquestioning, acceptance of habits and institutions, which vest in particular classes a special degree of public influence and an exceptional measure of economic opportunity.

The association of political leadership with birth and wealth is a commonplace of English history; but it is not always realized how little that association was weakened after the advent of what is usually regarded as the age of democracy. Professor Laski, in his instructive analysis of the personnel of British Cabinets between 1801 and 1924, has shown that, for nearly two generations after the Act of 1867 had enfranchised the urban working classes, the greater part of the business of government continued, nevertheless, to be conducted by a small group of owners of great properties, who were enabled by their economic advantages and social connections to step into the exercise of political power with a facility impossible to ordinary men. Of 69 Ministers who held office between 1885 and 1905, 40 were the sons of nobility, 52 were educated at Oxford and Cambridge, and 46 were educated at public schools; while, even between 1906 and 1916, 25 out of 51 Ministers were sons of nobility. To turn from these figures to the prognostications of catastrophic social changes advanced in 1832 and 1867 is to receive a lesson in the vanity of political prophecies. Of all the institutions changed by the advent of political democracy, the traditional system of government by a small knot of rich families was for half a century that which changed the least. They heard the rumblings of the democratic tumbril, but, like the patient East,

They let the legions thunder past,
And plunged in thought again,

or, if not in thought, in whatever substitute for it they found more congenial.

The political phenomenon described by Professor Laski is today no longer so conspicuous as it was. But the forces which for long made political leadership so largely dependent upon the peculiar opportunities opened by birth and wealth have left their mark, as was to be expected, upon other departments of English life. They have tended to produce, in them also, a similar, though somewhat less noticeable, restriction of leadership to particular classes, with special opportunities and connections, which is only gradually being undermined by the wider educational provision that has been made since 1902.

"If one could not be Eton and Oxford," writes Mr. Algernon Cecil of the middle of last century, "one did well in those days to be Harrow and Cambridge." The evidence presented by Mr. Nightingale, who has made a statistical analysis of the social antecedents of the personnel of the Foreign Office and Diplomatic Service between 1851 and 1929, suggests that his statement is true of a more recent period. Sixty per cent of it, he shows, has been drawn from the eleven most exclusive public schools, while, of the remaining forty per cent, well over one-half attended the lesser public schools, received a military or naval education, or were educated privately or abroad. "The unchallengeable conclusion that emerges . . . is that the British Foreign Office and Diplomatic Service has been a preserve for the sons of the aristocratic, *rentier* and professional classes. . . . The general inference which follows from a study of the effects of the various reforms in the examination regulations is that they have been substantial but not profound." Professor Ginsberg, who has recently investigated the antecedents of 1,268 British subjects admitted to Lincoln's Inn at different periods between 1886 and 1927, reaches a somewhat similar conclusion with regard to the recruitment of one section of the legal profession. Over 75 per cent of them belonged, he finds, to the group classified by the census as "upper and middle," while in no period did the sons of wage-earners amount to 1 per cent of the total admissions, except in the years 1923–27, when they formed 1.8 per cent of them.

Equality and Culture

Since life is a swallow, and theory a snail, it is not surprising that varieties of class organization should be but inadequately represented in the terminology of political science. But the absence of a word to describe the type of society which combines the forms of political democracy with sharp economic and social divisions is, none the less, unfortunate, since it obscures the practical realities which it is essential to grasp. The conventional classification of communities by the character of their constitutional arrangements had its utility in an age when the principal objective of effort and speculation was the extension of political rights. It is economic and social forces, however, which are most influential in determining the practical operation of political institutions, and it is economic and social relations that create the most urgent of the internal problems confronting industrial communities. The most significant differences distinguishing different societies from each other are, in short, not different forms of constitution and government, but different types of economic and social structure.

Of such distinctions the most fundamental is that which divides communities where economic initiative is widely diffused, and class differences small in dimensions and trivial in their effects, from those where the conditions obtaining are the opposite—where the mass of mankind exercise little influence on the direction of economic enterprise, and where economic and cultural gradations descend precipitately from one stratum of the population to another. Both types may possess representative institutions, a wide franchise, and responsible government; and both, therefore, may properly be described as democracies. But to regard them as, on that account, resembling each other— to ignore the profound differences of spirit and quality between a democracy in which class divisions play a comparatively unimportant part in the life of society, and a democracy where the influence of such differences is all-pervasive—is to do violence to realities. It is like supposing that all mammals have the same anatomical structure, or that the scenery of England resembles that of Switzerland because both countries lie in the temperate zone. Such varieties should be treated by political scientists as separate species, and should be given distinctive names. The former contain large elements, not merely of political, but of social, democracy. The latter are political democracies, but social oligarchies.

Social oligarchies have existed under widely divergent material circumstances, and in the most sharply contrasted conditions of economic civilization. In the past they were specially associated with the feudal organization of agricultural societies, so that, in the infancy of the modern economic world, the expansion of commerce and manufacture was hailed, by some with delight, by others with apprehension, as the acid which would dissolve them. Today, since in most parts of Europe the peasant farmer has come to his own, it is highly industrialized communities that are their favourite stronghold. Though it is in countries such as England and Germany, where the great industry flowed into the moulds prepared by an aristocratic tradition, that they attain their full efflorescence, they do not only conform to an old tradition of aristocracy, they also themselves create a new tradition. They appear to be the form of social organization which, in the absence of counteracting measures, the great industry itself tends spontaneously to produce, when its first outburst of juvenile energy is over, when its individualistic, levelling and destructive phase has given place to that of system and organization.

The most instructive illustration of that tendency is given by the history of industrial America, because it is in America that its operation has been at once swiftest and least anticipated. The United States started on its dazzling career as nearly in a state of innocence as a society can. It has no medieval past to bury. It was free from the complicated iniquities of feudal land-law and the European class system. It began, at least in the north, as a society of small farmers, merchants, and master-craftsmen, without either a large wage-earning proletariat or the remnants of serfdom which lingered in Europe till a century ago. It believed that all men have an equal right to life, liberty, and the pursuit of happiness. The confident hope that it would be unsullied by the disparities of power and wealth which corrupted Europe was the inspiration of those who, like Jefferson, saw in the Revolution, not merely the birth of a new state, but the dawn of a happier society.

It is the general, if partial, realization of that hope, in certain parts, at least, of America, which has made it for a century the magnet of Europe, and which still gives to American life much of its charm. It is marked, indeed, by much economic inequality; but it is also marked by much social equality, which is the legacy from an earlier phase of its economic civilization—though how long it will survive in the conditions of today is a different question, on which Americans themselves sometimes speak with apprehension. But evidently it is not in the America of which English-men hear most, but in that of which they hear least, not in the America of Wall Street and Pittsburg and the United States Steel Corporation and Mr. Morgan and Mr. Ford, but in the America of the farmer and the country town and the Middle West, that this charm is today most likely to be found. And evidently the equality of manners and freedom from certain conventional restraints, to which, partly at least, it is due, exist, not because of the industrial expansion of America, but in spite of it.

Nearly a century ago, De Tocqueville, who wrote on the first page of his *De la Démocratie en Amérique* that the general equality of conditions in America was the fundamental fact from which all others seemed to be derived, gave to one of his later chapters the significant title, "How aristocracy may be engendered by manufactures." "If ever," he wrote, "a permanent inequality of conditions and aristocracy again penetrate into the world, it may be predicted that this is the gate by which they will enter." Americans have led the world in the frequency and fullness of their official inquiries into economic organization, and, if the results of such inquiries may be trusted, that prophecy, as far as industrial America is concerned, is today not far from fulfilment. And what is true of the great industry in the United States is not less true of other industrial communities. Their natural tendency, it seems, except in so far as it is qualified and held in check by other forces, is to produce the concentration of economic power, and the inequalities of circumstance and condition, which De Tocqueville noted as the mark of an aristocratic social order.

A right to the pursuit of happiness is not identical with the right to attain it, and to state the fact is not to pronounce a judgment upon it. To see in economic concentration and social stratification the mystery of iniquity and the mark of the beast, to regard as the result of a deliberate and sinister conspiracy qualities which are the result partly of a failure to control impersonal forces, partly, not of a subtle and unscrupulous intelligence, but of its opposite—of a crude appetite for money and power among the few, and a reverence for success in obtaining them among the many—would, no doubt, be naïve. Yes, but how irrational also to suppose, as in England it is much commoner to suppose, that such characteristics are anything but a misfortune which an intelligent community will do all in its power to remove! How absurd to regard them as inevitable and admirable, to invest them with a halo of respectful admiration, and to deplore, whenever their economic foundations are threatened, the crumbling of civilization and the Goth at the gate! A nation is not civilized because a handful of its members are successful in acquiring large sums of money and in persuading their fellows that a catastrophe will occur if they do not acquire it, any more than Dahomey was civilized because its king had a golden stool and an army of slaves, or Judea because Solomon possessed a thousand wives and imported apes and peacocks, and surrounded the worship of Moloch and Ashtaroth with an impressive ritual.

What matters to a society is less what it owns than what it is and how it uses its possessions. It is civilized insofar as its conduct is guided by a just appreciation of spiritual ends, in so far as it uses its material resources to promote the dignity and refinement of the individual human beings who compose it. Violent contrasts of wealth and power, and an indiscriminating devotion to institutions by which such contrasts are maintained and heightened, do not promote the attainment of such ends, but thwart it. They are, therefore, a mark, not of civilization, but of barbarism, like the gold rings in the noses of savage monarchs, or the diamonds on their wives and the chains on their slaves. Since it is obviously such contrasts which determine the grounds upon which social struggles take place, and marshal the combatants who engage in them, they are a malady to be cured and a problem which demands solution.

But are they a malady? Granted, it is sometimes retorted, that sharp economic distinctions, with the complacency and callousness which such distinctions produce, are in themselves nauseous, are they not, nevertheless, the safeguard for virtues that would perish without them? Is not even the attachment of Englishmen to the idea of class, vulgar and repulsive as are many of its manifestations, the lantern which shelters a spark that, but for its protection, would be extinguished or dimmed?

The characteristics of a civilized society, Mr. Bell has argued in his entertaining book, are reasonableness and a sense of values, and these qualities were made possible in the ages in which, by general consent, they found their supreme and imperishable expression, because they had as their vehicle an élite— an élite which was released for the life of the spirit by the patient labour of slaves and peasants. What was true of the Athens of Pericles, and the Italy of the Renaissance, and the France of Voltaire, is true, in a humbler measure, of every society which is sufficiently mature to understand that freedom and intellectual energy are more vital to its welfare than the mechanical satisfaction of its material requirements. If it is to possess, not merely the comforts, but the graces, of existence, it must be enamoured of excellence. It must erect a standard of perfection, and preserve it inviolate against the clamour for the commonplace which is the appetite of the natural man, and of his eager hierophant, the practical reformer. But a standard of perfection, it is urged, is the achievement of a minority, and inequality is the hedge which protects it. It is the sacred grove which guards the shrine against the hooves of the multitude. Like an oasis which few can inhabit, but the very thought of which brings refreshment and hope to the sand-weary traveller, inequality, it is argued, protects the graces of life from being submerged beneath the dust of its daily necessities. It perpetuates a tradition of culture, by ensuring the survival of a class which is its visible embodiment, and which maintains that tradition in maintaining itself.

Compared with the formidable host which understands by civilization the elaboration of the apparatus and machinery of existence, as though Athens, or Florence, or Elizabethan England were objects of respectful pity when set side by side with modern London or New York, those who press such considerations are clearly on the side of light. If the Kingdom of Heaven is not eating and drinking, but righteousness and peace, neither is civilization the multiplication of motor-cars and cinemas, or of any other of the innumerable devices by which men accumulate means of ever-increasing intricacy to the attainment of ends which are not worth attaining. It is true that the mark of civilization is respect for excellence in the things of the spirit, and a readiness to incur sacrifice for the sake of fostering it. It is true that excellence is impossible in the absence of severe and exacting standards of attainment and appreciation which check the taste for cheap success and shoddy achievement by cultivating a temper which discriminates ruthlessly between the admirable and the second-rate. It is true that such a temper has no more persistent or insidious foe than the perversion of values, which confuses the ends of life with the means, and elevates material prosperity, whether the interpretation put upon it is the accumulation of wealth or the diffusion of comfort, from the position of secondary and instrumental importance that properly belongs to it, into the grand and over-mastering object of individual effort and public approval.

In order, however, to escape from one illusion, it ought not to be necessary to embrace another. If civilization is not the product of the kitchen garden, neither is it an exotic to be grown in a hot-house. Its flowers may be delicate, but its trunk must be robust, and the height to which it grows depends on the hold of its roots on the surrounding soil. Culture may be fastidious, but fastidiousness is not culture, and, though vulgarity is an enemy to "reasonableness and a sense of values," it is less deadly an enemy than gentility and complacency. A cloistered and secluded refinement, intolerant of the heat and dust of creative effort, is the note, not of civilization, but of the epochs which have despaired of it —which have seen, in one form or another, the triumph of the barbarian, and have sought compensation for defeat in writing cultured footnotes to the masterpieces they are incapable of producing. Its achievements may be admirable, but they are those of a silver age, not of a golden. The spiritual home of its votaries is not the Athens of Sophocles; it is the Alexandria of the scholiasts and the Rome of Claudian.

Clever men, it has been remarked, are impressed by their difference from their fellows; wise men are conscious of their resemblance to them. It would be ungracious to suggest that such an attitude is a mark rather of cleverness than of wisdom, but it is not wholly free from the spirit of the sect. When those who adopt it fall below themselves, when they relapse into glorifying what Bacon calls the *idola specus*, they are liable to rhapsodize over civilization in the tone of a Muggletonian dispensing damnation to all but Muggletonians, as though its secret consisted in the fact that only select minority is capable of enjoying it, as though it were a species of private entertainment to which a coterie of the right people had received an exclusive invitation.

Humanism has many meanings, for human nature has many sides, and the attempt to appropriate it as the label of a sect is not felicitous. There is the humanism of the age which the word is most commonly used to describe, the humanism of the Renaissance, with its rediscovery of human achievement in art and letters. And there is the humanism of the eighteenth century, with its confidence in the new era to be opened to mankind by the triumphs of science, and its hatred of the leaden obscurantism which impeded its progress. There is the humanism which contrasts man with God, or at least, with the God of some theologies; and there is the humanism which contrasts man with the brutes, and affirms that he is a little lower than the angels. These different senses of the word have often been at war; history is scarred, indeed, with the contentions between them. It ought not to be difficult, nevertheless, for the apostles of the one to understand the other; for indignant though some of them would be at the suggestion, they are using different dialects of a common language. If "What a piece of work is man! how noble in reason! how infinite in faculty!" is the voice of humanism, so also is "The sabbath was made for man, not man for the sabbath," and "The Kingdom of Heaven is within you." Shelley's lines,

The loathsome mask has fall'n, the man remains
Sceptreless, free, uncircumscribed, but man,
Equal, unclass'd, tribeless, and nationless,
Exempt from awe, worship, degree, the king
Over himself! just, gentle, wise, but man,

are one expression of the humanist spirit. Dante's "Consider your origin; ye were not formed to live like brutes, but to follow virtue and knowledge" is another.

Thus humanism is not the exclusive possession either of those who reject some particular body of religious doctrine or of those who accept it. It is, or it can be, the possession of both. It is not, as the fashion of the moment is disposed to suggest, the special mark of a generation which has lost its sense of the supernatural and is groping for a substitute. For, in order to be at home in this world, it is not sufficient, unfortunately, to disbelieve in another; and, in its intellectual interests, and order of life, and economic relations, such a generation is liable, in the mere innocent exuberance of its self-satisfaction, to display some traits, at least, which are not conspicuously humane. Humanism is the antithesis, not of theism or of Christianity—for how can the humanist spirit be one of indifference to issues that have been, for two thousand years, the principal concern and inspiration of a considerable part of humanity, or to a creed whose central doctrine is that God became man?—but of materialism. Its essence is simple. It is the attitude which judges the externals of life by their effect in assisting or hindering the life of the spirit. It is the belief that the machinery of existence—property and material wealth and industrial organization, and the whole fabric and mechanism of social institutions—is to be regarded as means to an end, and that this end is the growth towards perfection of individual human beings.

The humanist spirit, like the religious spirit, is not, indeed, indifferent to these things, which, on their own plane, are obviously important; but it resists their encroachment upon spheres which do not belong to them. It insists that they are not the objects of life, but its instruments, which are to be maintained when they are serviceable, and changed when they are not. Its aim is to liberate and cultivate the powers which make for energy and refinement; and it is critical, therefore, of all forms of organization which sacrifice spontaneity to mechanism, or which seek, whether in the name of economic efficiency or of social equality, to reduce the variety of individual character and genius to a drab and monotonous uniformity. But it desires to cultivate these powers in all men, not only in a few. Resting, as it does, on the faith that the differences between men are less important and fundamental than their common humanity, it is the enemy of arbitrary and capricious divisions between different members of the human family, which are based, not upon what men, given suitable conditions, are capable of becoming, but on external distinctions between them, such as those created by birth or wealth.

Sharp contrasts of opportunity and circumstance, which deprive some classes of the means of development deemed essential for others, are sometimes defended on the ground that the result of abolishing them must be to produce, in the conventional phrase, a dead-level of mediocrity. Mediocrity, whether found in the valleys of society or, as not infrequently happens, among the peaks and eminences, is always to be deprecated, though it is hardly curable, perhaps, as sometimes seems to be supposed, by so simple a process as the application to conspicuous portions of the social system of sporadic dabs of varnish and gilt. But not all the ghosts which clothe themselves in metaphors are equally substantial, and whether a level is regrettable or not depends, after all, upon what is levelled.

Those who dread a dead-level of income or wealth, which is not at the moment a very pressing danger in England, do not dread, it seems, a dead-level of law and order, and of security for life and property. They do not complain that persons endowed by nature with unusual qualities of strength, audacity or cunning are artificially prevented from breaking into houses, or terrorizing their neighbours, or forging cheques. On the contrary, they maintain a system of police in order to ensure that powers of this kind are, as far as may be, reduced to impotence. They insist on establishing a dead-level in these matters, because they know that, by preventing the strong from using their strength to oppress the weak, and the unscrupulous from profiting by their cleverness to cheat the simple, they are not crippling the development of personality, but assisting it. They do not ignore the importance of maintaining a high standard of effort and achievement. On the contrary, they deprive certain kinds of achievement of their fruits, in order to encourage the pursuit of others more compatible with the improvement of individual character, and more conducive to the good of society.

Violence and cunning are not the only forces, however, which hamper the individual in the exercise of his powers, or which cause false standards of achievement to be substituted for true. There are also, in most societies, the special advantages conferred by wealth and property, and by the social institutions which favour them. At one time there has been the aristocratic spirit, which in England is now dead, with its emphasis on subordination and the respect which is due from the lower orders to the higher, irrespective of whether the higher deserve or not to be respected. At another time there has been the plutocratic or commercial spirit, which is very much alive, with its insistence on the right of every individual to acquire wealth, and to hold what he acquires, and by means of it to obtain consideration for himself and power over his fellows, without regard to the services—if any—by which he acquires it or the use which he makes of it.

Both have some virtues, which may have been in certain periods more important than their vices. But the tendency of both, when unchecked by other influences, is the same. It is to pervert the sense of values. It is to cause men, in the language of the Old Testament, "to go a-whoring after strange gods," which means, in the circumstances of today, staring upwards, eyes goggling and mouths agape, at the antics of a third-rate Elysium, and tormenting their unhappy souls, or what, in such conditions, is left of them, with the hope of wriggling into it. It is to hold up to public admiration sham criteria of eminence, the result of accepting which is, in the one case, snobbery, or a mean respect for shoddy and unreal distinction, and, in the other case, materialism, or a belief that the only real forms of distinction are money and the advantages which money can buy.

Progress depends, indeed, on a willingness on the part of the mass of mankind—and we all, in nine-tenths of our nature, belong to the mass—to recognize genuine superiority, and to submit themselves to its influence. But the condition of recognizing genuine superiority is a contempt for unfounded pretensions to it. Where the treasure is, there will the heart be also, and, if men are to respect each other for what they are, they must cease to respect each other for what they own. They must abolish, in short, the reverence for riches, which is the *lues Anglicana*, the hereditary disease of the English nation. And, human nature being what it is, in order to abolish the reverence for riches, they must make impossible the existence of a class which is important merely because it is rich.

It is not surprising, therefore, that the ages which were permeated most deeply with the sense of the dignity of man as a rational being were also ages which appear to have felt a somewhat slender respect for capricious distinctions of birth and fortune. It is not surprising that the temper which had as one of its manifestations humanism, or the perfecting of the individual, should have had as another manifestation an outlook on society which sympathized with the attempt to bring the means of a good life within the reach of all, and regarded the subordination of class to class, and the arrogance and servility which such subordination naturally produces, as barbarian or gothic, as the mark of peoples which were incompletely civilized. It is in that spirit that Herodotus, speaking of the Athenians, who were regarded, in comparison with the Spartans, as dreadfully ungentlemanly, remarks that "it is evident, not in one thing alone, but on all sides of life, how excellent a thing is equality among men." It is in that spirit that the French writers of the eighteenth century, whose pernicious influence was denounced by Burke in the famous essay which George III said every gentleman should read, declared that equality, as well as liberty, must be the aim of the reformer.

It is true, of course, that institutions, as always, fell short of the ideal. It is true that the economic basis of Athenian society was slavery, and that one result of the victory of the liberal idea in France was the soulless commercialism which came to its own in 1830. But, compared with the practice of the world around them, compared with Persia, or even with most parts of Greece in the fifth century, or with England and Germany in the eighteenth, the influence of Athens and France was felt to make for humanism in life and manners, as well as in literature and art, and against the harshness and brutality of traditional systems of social petrification. They not only generated light, but diffused it. Within the limits set by their history and environment, it was their glory to stand for the general development of qualities which were prized, not as the monopoly of any class or profession of men, but as the attribute of man himself.

Thus the testimony of history is not so wholly on one side as is often suggested. Whether it is practicable or not to attain a large measure of equality may fairly be disputed; but it is not necessary, it seems, to be afraid of seeking it, on the ground that it is the enemy of culture and enlightenment. It is not necessary to shrink from lowering barriers of circumstance and opportunity, for fear that the quality of civilization will suffer as the radius of its influence is extended. It is true that civilization requires that there shall be free scope for activities which, judged by the conventional standards of the practical world, are useless or even pernicious, and which are significant precisely because they are not inspired by utilitarian motives, but spring, like the labor of the artist or student, from the disinterested passion for beauty or truth, or merely from the possession of powers, the exercise of which is its own reward. Experience does not suggest, however, that in modern England the plutocracy, with its devotion to the maxim *Privatim opulentia, publice egestas*, is, in any special sense, the guardian of such activities, or that, to speak with moderation, it is noticeably more eager than the mass of the population to spend liberally on art, or education, or the things of the spirit.

Nor, if the maintenance, by the institutions of property and inheritance, of a class of whose leisure these activities are the occasional by-product is one method of sheltering them, is it necessarily either the only method, or that which is most likely to encourage in society a temper that is keenly alive to their importance and disposed to make sacrifices for the sake of providing opportunities for their further development. Culture is not an assortment of æsthetic sugar-plums for fastidious palates, but an energy of the soul. It can win no victories if it risks no defeats. When it feeds on itself, instead of drawing nourishment from the common life of mankind, it ceases to grow, and, when it ceases to grow, it ceases to live. In order that it may be, not merely an interesting museum specimen, but an active principle of intelligence and refinement, by which vulgarities are checked and crudities corrected, it is necessary, not only to preserve intact existing standards of excellence, and to diffuse their influence, but to broaden and enrich them by contact with an ever-widening range of emotional experiences and intellectual interests. The association of culture with a limited class, which is enabled by its wealth to carry the art of living to a high level of perfection, may achieve the first, but it cannot, by itself, achieve the second. It may refine, or appear to refine, some sections of a community, but it coarsens others, and smites, in the end, with a blight of sterility even refinement itself. It may preserve culture, but it cannot extend it; and, in the long run, it is only by its extension that, in the conditions of today, it is likely to be preserved.

Thus a class system which is marked by sharp horizontal divisions between different social strata is neither, as is sometimes suggested, an indispensable condition of civilization nor an edifying feature of it. It may, as some hold, be inevitable, like other misfortunes to which mankind is heir, but it is not lovable or admirable. It is the raw material out of which civilization has to be made, by bringing blind economic forces under rational control and sifting the gold of past history from its sand and sediment. The task of the spirit, whatever the name most appropriate to describe it, which seeks to permeate, not merely this fragment of society or that, but the whole community, with reason and mutual understanding, is not to flatter the natural impulses which have their origin in the fact of class, but to purify and educate them. It is to foster the growth of a classless society by speaking frankly of the perversions to which the class system gives rise and of the dangers which accompany them.

The forms which such perversions assume are, of course, innumerable, but the most fundamental of them are two. They are privilege and tyranny. The first is the insistence by certain groups on the enjoyment of special advantages which are convenient to themselves, but injurious to their neighbours. The second is the exercise of power, not for the common benefit, but in order that these special advantages may be strengthened and consolidated.

It is the nature of privilege and tyranny to be unconscious of themselves, and to protest, when challenged, that their horns and hooves are not dangerous, as in the past, but useful and handsome decorations, which no self-respecting society would dream of dispensing with. But they are the enemies, nevertheless, both of individual culture and of social amenity. They create a spirit of domination and servility, which produces callousness in those who profit by them, and resentment in those who do not, and suspicion and contention in both. A civilized community will endeavour to exorcize that spirit by removing its causes. It will insist that one condition, at least, of its deserving the name is that its members shall treat each other, not as means, but as ends, and that institutions which stunt the faculties of some among them for the advantage of others shall be generally recognized to be barbarous and odious. It will aim at making power, not arbitrary, but responsible, and, when it finds an element of privilege in social institutions, it will seek to purge it.

basic processes

two

Four basic processes mix their effects in various sequences to produce the shape of any stratification system: (1) the differentiation of formally defined statuses or positions in the major institutions such as work and family; (2) the ranking of some of these positions by some criteria that have become significant for the people involved, e.g., the hardness of work or its cleanliness, or the skill required; (3) the evaluation of the social worth or importance or preferability or popularity of the status on the basis of the rank place it is assigned on the various criteria of ranking, e.g., a doctor is more highly valued than a plumber because his work requires more skill, or a minister is highly valued than a carpenter because his task is more "sacred," or a baseball player is more valued than a flutist because more people will pay to see him play; and (4) partly on the basis of the evaluations received, defferential rewards are then assigned or claimed or expected, e.g., the doctor expects higher pay than the plumber and the minister expects more honor than the carpenter.

The rewards that can be allocated include property, power, prestige, and various forms of psychic gratification. The unequal distribution of these rewards and the inequalities in evaluation that underlie them constitute the system of stratification of a society.

Inequality in "prestige," that is, the invidious value attached to a given position, is a major dimension of social stratification. The identification of the bases or criteria according to which prestige may be assigned and of the positions from which most of the differential rewards flow thus become crucial matters for sociologists.

Bierstedt's article on social power is one of the earlier but more cogent treatments in modern sociological literature. Although he does not employ terms in the same way as we have done here, Bierstedt examines the connections between power and prestige, influence, dominance, rights, force, and authority. He then proceeds to identify the locus of each of these various forms of social relationship, and concludes with a consideration of the loci, sources, and consequences of differences in power for the shape of the society in question.

In the article reprinted here, Paul K. Hatt, treating stratification as a "system of differently valued positions," inquires about the extent to which occupation, especially in modern industrial societies, may be the key position in the distribution of differential prestige and about what criteria are used in evaluating occupations. Basing his comments on a national sample study of the prestige evaluations of various occupations, Hatt suggests that there is a need to break down occupational categories into smaller units of occupational situses and families which would include occupations that people feel they can sensible compare with each other. He analyzes some of the consequences of the study of occupational mobility that would ensue from this version of occupational grouping.

Since men can occupy different rank positions on the various ladders of possible evaluation (e.g., income, education, occupation, etc.), it becomes eminently possible that any individual will find himself higher on some scales and lower on others. This dissonance or disparity is referred to as "status incongruence." Its opposite is "status crystallization." Andrzej Malewski is concerned with examining the possible reactions to perceived incongruence by the social actors involved, and he advances a number of propositions to reduce status incongruence or to avoid some of the more demeaning implications of status incongruence. The analysis reveals the kind of complexities in responses to stratified positions that one may reasonably expect from the members of a society in which status incongruence is a salient fact.

An Analysis of Social Power

ROBERT BIERSTEDT

Few problems in sociology are more perplexing than the problem of social power. In the entire lexicon of sociological concepts none is more troublesome than the concept of power. We may say about it in general only what St. Augustine said about time, that we all know perfectly well what it is—until someone asks us. Indeed, Robert M. MacIver has recently been induced to remark that "There is no reasonably adequate study of the nature of social power."[1] The present paper cannot, of course, pretend to be a "reasonably adequate study." It aims at reasonableness rather than adequacy and attempts to articulate the problem as one of central sociological concern, to clarify the meaning of the concept, and to discover the locus and seek the sources of social power itself.

The power structure of society is not an insignificant problem. In any realistic sense it is both a sociological (i.e., a scientific) and a social (i.e., a moral) problem. It has traditionally been a problem in political philosophy. But, like so many other problems of a political character, it has roots which lie deeper than the *polis* and reach into the community itself. It has ramifications which can be discerned only in a more generalized kind of inquiry than is offered by political theory and which

Reprinted from Robert Bierstedt, "An Analysis of Social Power," *American Sociological Review*, XV, No. 6 (December, 1950), 730–738, by permission of the author and the American Sociological Association.

---

[1] *The Web of Government* (New York: The Macmillan Company, 1947), p. 458. MacIver goes on to say, "The majority of the works on the theme are devoted either to proclaiming the importance of the role of power, like those of Hobbes, Gumplowicz, Ratzenhofer, Steinmetz, Treitschke, and so forth, or to deploring that role, like Bertrand Russell in his *Power*" (*ibid.*). One might make the additional comment that most of the discussions of power place it specifically in a political rather than a sociological context and that in the latter sense the problem has attracted almost no attention.

can ultimately be approached only by sociology. Its primitive basis and ultimate locus, as MacIver has emphasized in several of his distinguished books,[2] are to be sought in community and in society, not in government or in the state. It is apparent, furthermore, that not all power is political power and that political power—like economic, financial, industrial, and military power—is only one of several and various kinds of social power. Society itself is shot through with power relations— the power a father exercises over his minor child, a master over his slave, a teacher over his pupils, the victor over the vanquished, the blackmailer over his victim, the warden over his prisoners, the attorney over his own and opposing witnesses, an employer over his employee, a general over his lieutenants, a captain over his crew, a creditor over a debtor, and so on through most of the status relationships of society.[3] Power, in short, is a universal phenomenon in human societies and in all social relationships. It is never wholly absent from social interaction, except perhaps in the primary group where "personal identification" (Hiller) is complete and in those relations of "polite acquaintance" (Simmel) which are "social" in the narrowest sense. All other social relations contain components of power. What, then, is this phenomenon?

Social power has variously been identified with prestige, with influence, with eminence, with competence or ability, with knowledge (Bacon), with dominance, with rights, with force, and with authority. Since the intension of a term varies, if at all, inversely with its extension—i.e., since the more things a term can be applied to the less precise its meaning—it would seem to be desirable to distinguish power from some at least of these other concepts. Let us first distinguish power from prestige.

The closest association between power and prestige has perhaps been made by E. A. Ross in his classic work on social control. "The immediate cause of the location of power," says Ross, "is prestige." And further, "The class that has the most prestige will have the most power."[4] Now prestige may certainly be construed as one of the sources of social power and as one of the most significant of all the factors which separate man from man and group from group. It is a factor which has as one of its consequences the complex stratification of modern societies, to say nothing of the partial stratification of non-literate societies where the chief and the priest and the medicine-man occupy prestigious positions. But prestige should not be identified with power. They are independent variables. Prestige is frequently unaccompanied by power and when the two occur together power is usually the basis and ground of prestige rather than the reverse. Prestige would seem to be a consequence of power rather than a determinant of it or a necessary component of it. In any event, it is not difficult to illustrate the fact that power and prestige are independent variables, that power can occur without prestige, and prestige without power. Albert Einstein, for example, has prestige but no power in any significant sociological sense of the word. A policeman has power, but little prestige. Similarly, on the group level, the Phi Beta Kappa Society has considerable prestige—more outside ac-

[2] See especially *The Modern State* (London: Oxford University Press, 1926), pp. 221–231, and *The Web of Government, op. cit.*, pp. 82–113, *et passim*.
[3] It will be noted that not all of these examples of power exhibit the support of the state. To some of them the state is indifferent, to one it is opposed.

[4] *Social Control* (New York: The Macmillan Company, 1916), p. 78.

ademic circles than inside, to be sure—but no power. The Communist Party in the United States has a modicum of power, if not the amount so extravagantly attributed to it by certain Senators, but no prestige. The Society of Friends again has prestige but little power.

Similar observations may be made about the relations of knowledge, skill, competence, ability, and eminence to power. They are all components of, sources of, or synonyms of prestige, but they may be quite unaccompanied by power. When power does accompany them the association is incidental rather than necessary. For these reasons it seems desirable to maintain a distinction between prestige and power.

When we turn to the relationship between influence and power we find a still more intimate connection but, for reasons which possess considerable cogency, it seems desirable also to maintain a distinction between influence and power. The most important reason, perhaps, is that influence is persuasive while power is coercive. We submit voluntarily to influence while power requires submission. The mistress of a king may influence the destiny of a nation, but only because her paramour permits himself to be swayed by her designs. In any ultimate reckoning her influence may be more important than his power, but it is inefficacious unless it is transformed into power. The power a teacher exercises over his pupils stems not from his superior knowledge (this is competence rather than power) and not from his opinions (this is influence rather than power), but from his ability to apply the sanction of failure, i.e., to withhold academic credit, to the student who does not fulfill his requirements and meet his standards. The competence may be unappreciated and the influence may be ineffective, but the power may not be gainsaid.

Furthermore, influence and power can occur in relative isolation from each other and so also are relatively independent variables. We should say, for example, that Karl Marx has exerted an incalculable influence upon the twentieth century, but this poverty-stricken exile who spent so many of his hours immured in the British Museum was hardly a man of power. Even the assertion that he was a man of influence is an ellipsis. It is the ideas which are influential, not the man. Stalin, on the other hand, is a man of influence only because he is first a man of power. Influence does not require power, and power may dispense with influence. Influence may convert a friend, but power coerces friend and foe alike. Influence attaches to an idea, a doctrine, or a creed, and has its locus in the ideological sphere. Power attaches to a person, a group, or an association, and has its locus in the sociological sphere. Plato, Aristotle, St. Thomas, Shakespeare, Galileo, Newton, and Kant were men of influence, although all of them were quite devoid of power. Napoleon Bonaparte and Abraham Lincoln were men of both power and influence. Genghis Khan and Adolf Hilter were men of power. Archimedes was a man of influence, but the soldier who slew him at the storming of Syracuse had more power. It is this distinction which gives point to Spengler's otherwise absurd contention that this nameless soldier had a greater impact upon the course of history than the great classical physicist.

When we speak, therefore, of the power of an idea or when we are tempted to say that ideas are weapons or when we assert, with the above-mentioned Bonaparte, that the pen is mightier than the sword, we are using figurative language, speaking truly as it were, but metaphorically and with synecdoche. Ideas are influential, they may alter the process of history, but for the sake of logical and sociological

(part stands for whole, eg.- 50 sail means 50 ships)

clarity it is preferable to deny to them the attribute of power. Influence in this sense, of course, presents quite as serious and as complex a problem as power, but it is not the problem whose analysis we are here pursuing.

It is relatively easy to distinguish power from dominance. Power is a sociological, dominance a psychological concept. The locus of power is in groups and it expresses itself in inter-group relations; the locus of dominance is in the individual and it expresses itself in inter-personal relations. Power appears in the statuses which people occupy in formal organization; dominance in the roles they play in informal organization. Power is a function of the organization of associations, of the arrangement and juxtaposition of groups, and of the structure of society itself. Dominance, on the other hand, is a function of personality or of temperament; it is a personal trait. Dominant individuals play roles in powerless groups; submissive individuals in powerful ones. Some groups acquire an inordinate power, especially in the political sense, because there are so many submissive individuals who are easily persuaded to join them and who meekly conform to the norms which membership imposes. As an example, one need mention only the growth of the National Socialist Party in Germany. Dominance, therefore, is a problem in social psychology; power a problem in sociology.[5]

It is a little more difficult to distinguish power from "rights" only because the latter term is itself so ambiguous. It appears indeed in two senses which are exactly contradictory —as those privileges and only those which are secured by the state and as those which the state may not invade even to secure. We do not need to pursue the distinctions between various kinds of rights, including "natural rights," which are elaborated in the history of jurisprudence and the sociology of law to recognize that a right always requires some support in the social structure, although not always in the laws, and that rights in general, like privileges, duties, obligations, responsibilities, perquisites, and prerogatives, are attached to statuses both in society itself and in the separate

---

personal frustrations of soldiers interfere with the fighting efficiency of a military unit, so the personal frustrations of individuals reduce and sometimes destroy the efficiency of any organized action. Heller has an interesting comment in this connection: "The objective social function of political power may be at marked variance with the subjective intentions of the individual agents who give concrete expression to its organization and activities. The subjective motivations which induce the inhabitant to perform military service or to pay taxes are of minor importance. For political power, no less than every other type of social power, is a cause and effect complex, revolving about the objective social effect and not, at least not exclusively, about the subjective intent and attitude." See his article "Power, Political," *Encyclopedia of the Social Sciences*, Vol. VI, p. 301. In other words, the subjective factors which motivate an individual to indulge in social action, the ends he seeks and the means he employs, have nothing to do, or at best very little to do, with the objective social consequences of the action. A man may join the army for any number of reasons—to achieve financial security and early retirement, to conform with the law, to escape a delicate domestic situation, to withdraw from an emotional commitment, to see the world, to escape the pressure of mortgage payments, to fight for a cause in which he believes, to wear a uniform, or to do as his friends are doing. None of these factors will affect very much the army which he joins. Similarly, people do not have children because they wish to increase the birth rate, to raise the classification of the municipal post office, or to contribute to the military strength of the state, although the births may objectively have all of these consequences.

---

[5] This distinction, among others, illustrates the impropriety of associating too closely the separate disciplines of psychology and sociology. Many psychologists and, unfortunately, some sociologists profess an inability to see that individual and group phenomena are fundamentally different in character and that, for example, "the tensions that cause wars" have little to do with the frustrations of individuals. Just as the

associations of society. One may have a right without the power to exercise it[6] but in most cases power of some kind supports whatever rights are claimed. Rights are more closely associated with privileges and with authority than they are with power. A "right," like a privilege, is one of the perquisites of power and not power itself.[7]

We have now distinguished power from prestige, from influence, from dominance, and from rights, and have left the two concepts of force and authority. And here we may have a solution to our problem. Power is not force and power is not authority, but it is intimately related to both and may be defined in terms of them. We want therefore to propose three definitions and then to examine their implications: (1) power is latent force; (2) force is manifest power; and (3) authority is institutionalized power. The first two of these propositions may be considered together. They look, of course, like circular definitions and, as a matter of fact, they are. If an independent meaning can be found for one of these concepts, however, the other may be defined in terms of it and the circularity will disappear.[8] We may therefore suggest an independent definition of the concept of force. Force, in any significant sociological sense of the word, means the applica-

tion of sanctions. Force, again in the sociological sense, means the reduction or limitation or closure or even total elimination of alternatives to the social action of one person or group by another person or group. "Your money or your life" symbolizes a situation of naked force, the reduction of alternatives to two. The execution of a sentence to hang represents the total elimination of alternatives. One army progressively limits the social action of another until only two alternatives remain for the unsuccessful contender—to surrender or die. Dismissal or demotion of personnel in an association similarly, if much less drastically, represents a closure of alternatives. Now all these are situations of force, or manifest power. Power itself is the predisposition or prior capacity which makes the application of force possible. Only groups which have power can threaten to use force and the threat itself is power. Power is the ability to employ force, not its actual employment, the ability to apply sanctions, not their actual application.[9] Power is the ability to introduce force into a social situation; it is the presentation of force. Unlike force, incidentally, power is always successful; when it is not successful it is not, or ceases to be, power. Power symbolizes the force which *may* be applied in any social situation and supports the authority which *is* applied. Power is thus neither force nor authority but, in a sense, their synthesis.

The implications of these proposi-

---

[6] An example will subsequently be supplied.

[7] There is, of course, a further distinction between rights and privileges. Military leave, for example, is a privilege and not a right; it may be requested but it may not be demanded. It may be granted but, on the other hand, it may not.

[8] As a matter of purely technical interest, it may be observed that all definitions are ultimately circular. Every system of inference must contain undefined or "primitive" terms in its initial propositions because, if it were necessary to define every term before using it, it would be impossible ever to begin talking or writing or reasoning. An undefined term in one system is not necessarily an indefinable term, however, particularly in another system, and furthermore

this kind of circularity is no logical deficiency if the circle, so to speak, *nicht zu klein ist*. This engaging phrase comes from Herbert Feigl, a logician who has examined this problem in a paper on Moritz Schlick, *Erkenntnis* Band, VII (1937–1938), 406. Ralph Eaton also discusses this problem in his *General Logic*, p. 298, as do Whitehead and Russell in the Introduction to *Principia Mathematica*.

[9] Sanctions, of course, may be positive or negative, require or prohibit the commission of a social act.

tions will become clearer if we now discuss the locus of power in society. We may discover it in three areas, (1) in formal organization, (2) in informal organization, and (3) in the unorganized community. The first of these presents a fairly simple problem for analysis. It is in the formal organization of associations that social power is transformed into authority. When social action and interaction proceed wholly in conformity to the norms of the formal organization, power is dissolved without residue into authority.

The right to use force is then attached to certain statuses within the association, and this right is what we ordinarily mean by authority.[10] It is thus authority in virtue of which persons in an association exercise command or control over other persons in the same association. It is authority which enables a bishop to transfer a priest from his parish, a priest with his "power of the keys" to absolve a sinner, a commanding officer to assign a post of duty to a subordinate officer, a vice-president to dictate a letter to his secretary, the manager of a baseball team to change his pitcher in the middle of an inning, a factory superintendent to demand a certain job be completed at a specified time, a policeman to arrest a citizen who has violated a law, and so on through endless examples. Power in these cases is attached to statuses, not to persons, and is wholly institutionalized as authority.[11]

In rigidly organized groups this authority is clearly specified and formally articulated by the norms (rules, statutes, laws) of the association. In less rigidly organized groups penumbral areas appear in which authority is less clearly specified and articulated. Sometimes authority clearly vested in an associational status may not be exercised because it conflicts with a moral norm to which both members and non-members of the association adhere in the surrounding community. Sometimes an official may remove a subordinate from office without formal cause and without formal authority because such action, now involving power, finds support in public opinion. Sometimes, on the contrary, he may have the authority to discharge a subordinate, but not the power, because the position of the latter is supported informally and "extra-associationally" by the opinion of the community. An extreme case of this situation is exemplified by the inability of the general manager, Ed Barrow, or even the owner, Colonel Jacob Ruppert, to "fire" Babe Ruth from the New York Yankees or even, when the Babe was at the height of his fame, to trade him.

Sometimes these power relations become quite complicated. In a university organization, for example, it may not be clear whether a dean has the authority to apply the sanction of dismissal to a professor, or, more subtly, whether he has the authority to abstain from offering an increase in salary to a professor in order indirectly to encourage him to leave, or, still more subtly, whether, when he clearly has this authority of abstention, he will be accused of maladministration if he exercises it.[12] It is similarly unclear whether a Bishop of the Episcopal Church has the authority to remove a

---

[10] Authority appears frequently in another sense as when, for example, we say that Charles Goren is an authority on bridge or Emily Post on etiquette. Here it carries the implication of superior knowledge or skill or competence and such persons are appealed to as sources of information or as arbiters. In this sense authority is related to influence but not to power.

[11] This is what Max Weber called *legitime Herrschaft*, which Parsons translates as "authority." See *The Theory of Social and Economic Organization*, Parsons, ed. (New York: Oxford University Press, 1947), p. 152, n. 83.

---

[12] As in a case at the University of Illinois.

rector from his parish when the latter apparently has the support of his parishioners.[13] In other words, it sometimes comes to be a matter of unwise policy for an official to exercise the authority which is specifically vested in his position, and it is in these cases that we can clearly see power leaking into the joints of associational structure and invading the formal organization.[14]

It may be observed that the power implied in the exercise of authority does not necessarily convey a connotation of personal superiority. Leo Durocher is not a better pitcher than the player he removes nor, in turn, is he inferior to the umpire who banishes him from the game. A professor may be a "better" scholar and teacher than the dean who dismisses him, a lawyer more learned in the law than the judge who cites him for contempt, a worker a more competent electrician than the foreman who assigns his duties, and so on through thousands of examples. As MacIver has written, "The man who commands may be no wiser, no abler, may be in no sense better than the average of his fellows; sometimes, by any intrinsic standard he is inferior to them. Here is the magic of government."[15] Here indeed is the magic of all social organization.

Social action, as is well known, does not proceed in precise or in absolute conformity to the norms of formal organization. Power spills over the vessels of status which only imperfectly contain it as authority. We arrive, therefore, at a short consideration of informal organization, in which the prestige of statuses gives way to the esteem for persons and in which the social interaction of the members proceeds not only in terms of the explicit norms of the association but also in terms of implicit extra-associational norms whose locus is in the community and which may or may not conflict, at strategic points, with the associational norms. Our previous examples have helped us to anticipate what we have to say about the incidence and practice of power in informal organization. No association is wholly formal, not even the most rigidly organized. Social organization makes possible the orderly social intercourse of people who do not know each other— the crew of a ship and their new captain, the factulty of a university department and a new chairman, the manager of a baseball team and his new recruit, the citizen and the tax collector, the housewife and the plumber, the customer and the clerk. But in any association the members do become acquainted with each other and begin to interact not only "extrinsically" and "categorically," in terms of the statuses they occupy, but also "intrinsically" and "personally," in terms of the roles they play and the personalities they exhibit.[16] Sub-groups arise and begin to exert subtle pressures upon the organization itself, upon the norms which may be breached in the observance thereof, and upon the authority which, however firmly institutionalized, is yet subject to change. These sub-groups may, as cliques and factions, remain within the association or, as sects and splinter groups, break away from it. In any

---

[13] As in the Melish case in Brooklyn, which is currently a subject for litigation in the courts.

[14] That even the most highly and rigidly organized groups are not immune from these invasions of power has been illustrated, in a previous paper, with respect to the Roman Catholic Church, the United States Navy, and the Communist Party. See Robert Bierstedt, "The Sociology of Majorities," *American Sociological Review*, XIII (December, 1948), 700–710.

[15] *The Web of Government, op. cit.*, p. 13.

[16] The terms in quotation marks are E. T. Hiller's. See his *Social Relations and Structures* (New York: Harper & Row, Publishers, 1947), Chaps. 13, 14, and 38.

event, no formal organization can remain wholly formal under the exigencies of time and circumstance. Power is seldom completely institutionalized as authority, and then no more than momentarily. If power sustains the structure, opposing power threatens it, and every association is always at the mercy of a majority of its own members. In all associations the power of people acting in concert is so great that the prohibition against "combinations" appears in the statutes of all military organizations and the right of collective petition is denied to all military personnel.

Power appears, then, in associations in two forms, institutionalized as authority in the formal organization and uninstitutionalized as power itself in the informal organization. But this does not exhaust the incidence of power with respect to the associations of society. It must be evident that power is required to inaugurate an association in the first place, to guarantee its continuance, and to enforce its norms. Power supports the fundamental order of society and the social organization within it, wherever there is order. Power stands behind every association and sustains its structure. Without power there is no organization and without power there is no order. The intrusion of the time dimension and the exigencies of circumstance require continual re-adjustments of the structure of every association, not excepting the most inelastically organized, and it is power which sustains it through these transitions.[17] If power provides the initial impetus behind the organization of every association, it also supplies the stability which it maintains throughout its

---

[17] If the power of the members, informally exercised, supports an association through changes in structure, it is the structure itself which supports it through changes in personnel.

history. Authority itself cannot exist without the immediate support of power and the ultimate sanction of force.

As important as power is, however, as a factor in both the formal and informal organization of associations, it is even more important where it reigns, uninstitutionalized, in the interstices between associations and has its locus in the community itself. Here we find the principal social issues of contemporary society—labor vs. capital, Protestant vs. Catholic, CIO vs. AFL, AMA vs. FSA, Hiss vs. Chambers (for this was not a conflict between individuals), Republican vs. Democrat, the regents of the University of California vs. the faculty, Russia vs. the United States, and countless others throughout the entire fabric of society. It is not the task of our present analysis to examine these conflicts in detail but rather to investigate the role of power wherever it appears. And here we have two logical possibilities—power in the relations of like groups and power in the relations of unlike groups. Examples of the former are commerical companies competing for the same market, fraternal organizations of the same kind competing for members, religious associations competing for adherents, newspapers competing for readers, construction companies bidding for the same contracts, political parties competing for votes, and so on through all the competitive situations of society. Examples of the latter are conflicts between organized labor and organized management, between the legislative and executive branches of government, between different sub-divisions of the same bureaucracy (e.g., Army vs. Navy), between university boards of trustees and an association of university professors, and so on through an equally large number of instances. Power thus appears both in competition and in conflict and has no incidence in groups which neither compete nor conflict, i.e., between groups which do not share a similar social matrix and have no social relations, as for example the American Council of Learned Societies and the American Federation of Labor. Power thus arises only in social opposition of some kind.

It is no accident that the noun "power" has been hypostatized from the adjective "potential." It may seem redundant to say so, but power is always potential; that is, when it is used it becomes something else, either force or authority. This is the respect which gives meaning, for example, to the concept of a "fleet in being" in naval strategy. A fleet in being represents power, even though it is never used. When it goes into action, of course, it is no longer power, but force. It is for this reason that the Allies were willing to destroy the battleship *Richelieu*, berthed at Dakar, after the fall of France, at the price of courting the disfavor of the French. Indeed, the young officer attending his introductory lectures on naval strategy, is sometimes surprised to hear what he may consider an excessive and possibly even a perverse emphasis upon the phrase, "Protect the battleships." Why should the battleship, the mightiest engine of destruction afloat, require such care in assuring its protection with sufficient cruiser, destroyer, and air support? The answer is that a battleship is even more effective as a symbol of power than it is as an instrument of force.

If power is one of the imperatives of society it may also be partly a pretense and succeed only because it is inaccurately estimated, or unchallenged. This, of course, is a familiar stratagem in war. But it occurs in the majority of power relationships in society. The threat of a strike may succeed when the strike will not. Blackmail may have consequences

more dire than the exposure of the secret. The threat of a minority to withdraw from an association may affect it more than an actual withdrawal. The threat of a boycott may achieve the result desired when the boycott itself would fail. As an example of this last, movie exhibitors sometimes discover that if they ignore a ban imposed upon a picture by a religious censor, the ban not only does not diminish the attendance figures but increases them. In poker parlance—and indeed it is precisely the same phenomenon—a "bluff" is powerful, but the power vanishes when the bluff is called.

We may, in a comparatively brief conclusion, attempt to locate the sources of power. Power would seem to stem from three sources: (1) numbers of people, (2) social organization, and (3) resources. In a previous paper we have discussed in some detail the role of majorities in both unorganized and organized social groups, and in both the formal and informal aspects of the latter, and arrived at the conclusion, among others, that majorities constitute a residual locus of social power. It is neither necessary nor desirable to review this proposition here, beyond reiterating an emphasis upon the power which resides in numbers. Given the same social organization and the same resources, the larger number can always control the smaller and secure its compliance. If majorities, particularly economic and political majorities, have frequently and for long historical periods suffered oppression, it is because they have not been organized or have lacked resources. The power which resides in numbers is clearly seen in elections of all kinds, where the majority is conceded the right to institutionalize its power as authority—a right which is conceded because it can be taken. This power appears in all associations, even the most autocratic. It is the power of a majority, even in the most formally and inflexibly organized associations, which either threatens or sustains the stability of the associational structure.[18]

As important as numbers are as the primary source of social power, they do not in themselves suffice. As suggested above, majorities may suffer oppression for long historical periods, they may, in short, be powerless or possess only the residual power of inertia. We arrive therefore at the second source of social power—social organization. A well organized and disciplined body of marines or of police can control a much larger number of unorganized individuals. An organized minority can control an unorganized majority. But even here majorities possess so much residual power that there are limits beyond which this kind of control cannot be exercised. These limits appear with the recognition that the majority may organize and thus reverse the control. And an organized majority, as suggested in the paper previously referred to, is the most potent social force on earth.

Of two groups, however, equal or nearly equal in numbers and comparable in organization, the one with access to the greater resources will have the superior power. And so resources constitute the third source of social power. Resources may be of many kinds--money, property, prestige, knowledge, competence, deceit, fraud, secrecy, and, of course, all of the things usually included under the term "natural resources." There are also supernatural resources in the case of religious associations which, as agencies of a celestial government, apply supernatural sanctions as instruments of control. In other words, most of the things we have previously differentiated from power itself may now be re-introduced as among the sources of power. It is easily apparent that, in any power con-

flict, they can tip the balance when the other sources of power are relatively equal and comparable. But they are not themselves power. Unless utilized by people who are in organized association with one another they are quite devoid of sociological significance.

As a matter of fact, no one of these sources in itself constitutes power, nor does any one of them in combination with either of the others. Power appears only in the combination of all three—numbers, organization, and resources.

It may finally be of more than incidental interest to note that there is one, and only one, kind of social situation in which the power of opposing groups is completely balanced. The numbers on each "side" are equal, their social organization is identical, and their resources are as nearly the same as possible. This situation reveals itself in games and contests in which power components are cancelled out and the victory goes to the superior skill. Whether the game be baseball or bridge there is insistence, inherent in the structure of the game itself, upon an equalization of power and this is the universal characteristic of all sports and the basis of the conception "fair play."[19] It would be foolish, of course, to assert that resources are always equal. The New York Yankees, for example, have financial resources which are not available to the St. Louis Browns and one bridge partnership may have better cards than its opponent. But such inequalities excite disapproval because they deny the nature of sport. The franchise of the Browns may be transferred from St. Louis for this reason, and tournament

---

[18] For an elaboration of this theme see "The Sociology of Majorities," *op. cit.*

[19] The game of poker is an exception. Here, unless there are betting limits, resources are not initially equalized among the contestants. In this situation, as in war, deceit is encouraged and becomes a part of the structure of the game. It is for this reason, probably, that poker sometimes carries a connotation of immorality.

bridge is duplicate bridge so that all teams will play the same hands. When resources cannot be equalized, the situation ceases to be a game and sentiment supports the "underdog." We thus have here a most familiar but nevertheless peculiar power situation, one in which power is so balanced as to be irrelevant. Sport may be a moral equivalent for war, as William James wanted to believe, but it can never be a sociological equivalent. The two situations are only superficially similar. The difference between a conflict and a contest is that the former is a power phenomenon and the latter is not.

In this paper we have taken a somewhat vague and ambiguous concept, the concept of social power, and have attempted to sharpen the edges of its meaning. Among the proposals offered, the following may serve as a summary: (1) power is a social phenomenon *par excellence*, and not merely a political or economic phenomenon; (2) it is useful to distinguish power from prestige, from influence, from dominance, from rights, from force, and from authority; (3) power is latent force, force is manifest power, and authority is institutionalized power; (4) power, which has its incidence only in social opposition of some kind, appears in different ways in formal organization, in informal organization, and in the unorganized community; and (5) the sources and necessary components of power reside in a combination of numbers (especially majorities), social organization, and resources. All of these are preliminary and even primitive propositions. All of them require additional analysis.

Occupation and Social Stratification

PAUL K. HATT

The purpose of this paper is to present a theory and to suggest a method of occupational classification usable in the study of social stratification.[1] This

Reprinted from *The American Journal of Sociology*, LV, No. 6 (May, 1950), 533–543, by permission of Mrs. Genevieve Hatt and The University of Chicago Press. Copyright 1950 by the University of Chicago. Read before the Eastern Sociological Society New York, April 23, 1949. This study was made in connection with a more complete analysis of the data being made by Cecil C. North and the writer. Gratitude is expressed to Professor North as well as to the National Opinion Research Center, the Ohio State University, the College Study in Intergroup Relations, and the Social Science Research Center.

necessarily entails the description of some currently unmet problems and an evaluation of existing classifications. To apply a classification to a totally different problem from the one for which it was intended is always a dangerous and frequently an unhappy undertaking all too often found in the use of occupational indexes in stratification studies. The central role of occupation in the determination of prestige has tempted sociologists to borrow already existing occupational classifications.

Because of the utilization of manifold types of occupational classification in sociology, any argument in this area must begin with the prior problems: What is the nature of stratification? What validity has occupation as an index of position in a stratified social system? What occupational dimension,

---

[1] An excellent analysis, for other purposes, of occupational research, both existing and needed, can be found in Carlo L. Lastrucci, "The Status of Occupational Research," *American Sociological Review*, XI, No. 1 (February, 1946), 78–84.

or dimensions, if any, are suited for use in this area?

The Nature of Stratification

For the purposes of this paper the term "stratification" is strictly limited to a system of differentially valued positions in all societies. No attempt is made, at this point, to refer to the methods of selecting personnel for these positions, and consequently no implications about the degree of freedom of movement in any society are intended. Such problems are considered as belonging to the question of vertical mobility and must be put aside for the moment as related and important but separable matters.

In the sense used here, then, the concept of stratification rests upon four postulates:

1. Differential positions occur in many different social structures, e.g., religious, governmental, economic.
2. The rewards of these positions are of various types, e.g., financial gain, advantageous working conditions, and honorific value or "psychic income."
3. Some combination of all the rewards attached to any position constitutes the invidious value of that position and hence its prestige.
4. Total societal position is a summation of prestige, modified by the esteem bestowed by others as a reward for the manner in which the expectations associated with any given status are fulfilled.[2]

----

[2] These are modifications of more extensive statements made by Davis and Moore which may be found in the following works: Kingsley Davis and Wilbert E. Moore, "Some Principles of Stratification, *American Sociological Review*, X, No. 2 (April, 1945), 242–49; Kingsley Davis, "Conceptual Analysis of Stratification," *American Sociological Review*, VII, No. 3 (June, 1942), 312.

Occupation and Relative Societal Position

Sociologists have frequently pointed out, though with differing justifications, the significance of occupation as a measure of position. For Davis and Moore,[3] Parsons,[4] and similar writers this comes as the logical consequence of a larger theoretical analysis. It is presented by others as an empirical finding in studies where stratification position was determined by criteria other than occupation.[5] In still other research the dominant role of occupation is taken as given. In these cases there is some empirical evidence of the validity of the assumption, although in no case is this made a major goal of the writer.[6]

None of these has claimed occupation to be a sufficient criterion of relative position, but all are in substantial agreement that it is a usable and valid index for most purposes. In spite of such general agreement, however, not all sociologists are willing to accept it without question.[7]

The question of whether occupation

----

[3] *Op. cit.*
[4] Talcott Parsons, "An Analytical Approach to the Theory of Sociological Stratification," *American Journal of Sociology*, XLV, No. 6 (May, 1940), 841–62.
[5] E.g., see John Useem, Pierre Tangent, and Ruth Useem, "Stratification in a Prairie Town," *American Sociological Review*, VII, No. 3 (June, 1942), 333–34.
[6] Typical of these are such works as Dewey Anderson and Percy S. Davidson, *Ballots and the Democratic Class Structure* (Palo Alto, Calif.: Stanford University Press, 1943), and Richard Centers, *The Psychology of Social Classes* (Princeton, N. J.: Princeton University Press, 1949).
[7] Gross, for example, feels that Centers' uncertain results in places could perhaps be explained by the alternative hypothesis that occupation, after all, may not be an adequate reflector of social class position (Llewellyn Gross, "The Use of Class Concepts in Sociological Research," *American Journal of Sociology*, LIV, No. 5 [March, 1949], 417–18).

may be used at all as a reflection of relative societal position must depend upon the criteria set for such an index rather than upon speculation. Returning to the demands set up by the postulates of stratification, a fully accurate index should approximate total societal position and thus reflect both prestige and esteem.[8] It should thus be some sort of summarizing measure of those prestige and esteem values attached to an individual by virtue of his status within each of the social structures in which he participates.

Occupation, by definition, cannot possibly be taken as describing esteem; moreover, when it is used as an index, position in one structure is substituted for a sum of positions in many structures. Its value as an index of position therefore must be established in spite of its inability to describe in detail the relevant areas of esteem and multistructural position. Thus, in order to appraise its value as an index, occupation should be compared with other current techniques for locating societal position.

The problem posed by the number and variety of positions held by one person has been met by Professor Chapin with the construction of the Living Room Scale. Considerable evidence as to the validity of this scale exists, and, indeed, one such study indicates specifically its superiority over occupation.[9] This is evidenced by the fact that the Chapin scale best represents a cluster of items including income, occupation, education, a measure of social participation, and the Living Room Scale itself. Because this study

was conducted with only a sample of sixty-seven Minneapolis Negro homes, generalization from it is somewhat risky. It seems inevitable, however, that such a composite index as it is should be a more accurate measure than any such single characteristic as occupation. This conclusion is consistent with the second postulate of stratification: that positions occur in a variety of social structures and that total societal position is some sort of summation of religious, educational, governmental, familial, etc., as well as occupational, status. Although some relationship between occupational position and other positions may be assumed, they are not identical, and occupation is a less precise index of position in all structures than is an instrument like the "Living Room Scale."

Taking account of the esteem dimension of social position is perhaps a more difficult problem than is that of measuring multiple statuses as done by such techniques as the Chapin scale. The adequate assessment of esteem requires knowledge of all socially significant community relationships for every individual in that community. Consequently, effective calculation of the esteem component of stratification is practicable only in the local community or neighborhood.[10]

The work of Warner and his associates is perhaps the best known among those studies which have carefully investigated total prestige patterns, including the dimension of esteem. In these studies personal reputation is summed with positional prestige and the result taken as the individual's total societal position. As suggestive as

[8] A particularly lucid discussion of *esteem* may be found in Kinglsey Davis, *Human Society* (New York: The Macmillan Company, 1949).

[9] Louis Guttman, "A Review of Chapin's Social Status Scale," *American Sociological Review*, VIII, No. 3 (June, 1943), 362–69.

[10] It should perhaps be added that great genius or virtuosity may extend esteem beyond local limits, but such instances are rare and have little significance for sociological problems relating to the total pattern of stratification.

the results of the "community-reputa-tional" technique may be, they are, however, a long way from filling many pressing needs of sociologists. While they are concrete and interesting, these findings stubbornly resist generaliza-tion, so rooted are they in local idiosyn-crasy.[11] If stratification is to be studied on a national scale, or indeed in the urban milieu, this method is inadequate for the task.

These, then, are two methods for the study of stratification, each of which reflects the total prestige pattern more accurately than can any single index. However, both show critical shortcom-ings. The weakness of the "community-reputational" approach is the extreme difficulty of extending it beyond the boundaries of the community within which a scheme is developed. The weakness of the other lies most clearly in its requirement of a home interview. These methods, while useful under certain circumstances, leave a con-siderable place which must be filled by some relatively simple method of esti-mating societal position. Many second-ary data which are not susceptible to "community-reputational" analysis or to home appraisal are already tabulated by occupation, and other types of data require a simple prestige index because of limitations of time or access to respondents. In such cases, occupation is at least relatively available and simple. These characteristics plus the evidences of its validity as an index indicate a field in which it may clearly

be useful as a research tool. In order, however, to make it a really usable index, some sensible mode of classifi-cation is required.

Occupational Dimensions and Classifications

It follows from the postulates of stratification that a sound occupational classification for stratification analysis must rest upon dimensions which accurately reflect comparative societal position. The dimensions generally used in such classifications are three: the duties, the prerequisites, and the re-wards.

1. Classifications Employing Occupational Duties

The system used by the United States Census Bureau is an instance of this first type. As a result its utility lies more in studies of horizontal mobility and industrial patterns than in studies of social stratification. The census classi-cation, together with several developed by the United States Employment Service, is a more or less frozen ex-ample of the more pliable concept of *occupational family*. Shartle describes an occupational family as containing a number of occupations grouped on the basis of their similarity with respect to any criterion which may be chosen.[12] Such criteria as physical strength, manual dexterity, and educational level are common modes of delineating these families.

While the application of specific occupational families of this type to the problems of stratification is clearly unwarranted, Edwards perceived what

---

[11] Since the writing of this paper a detailed methodological statement of this approach has appeared in Lloyd Warner, Marchia Meeker, and Kenneth Eells, *Social Class in America* (Chi-cago: Science Research Associates, 1949). This is the clearest statement to have yet appeared, but even in its new form it remains a method oriented to the local community and is not ap-plicable to cross-community, regional, or na-tional studies.

[12] Carroll Shartle, *Occupational Information* (Englewood Cliffs, N. J.: Prentice-Hall, Inc., 1946), pp. 161–71.

he believed to be a value scale within the census classifications. His "socio-economic scale" of occupations is based primarily upon "head and hands" types of work as constituting a positional scale.[13] The scale itself consists of six major categories, two of which are so subdivided as to yield ten more or less hierarchically arranged groupings. While Edwards' technique is essentially oriented toward duties, it is also validated in terms of yearly income and total educational qualifications of the job occupants. In doing this, Edwards has brought into the picture both the other dimensions commonly employed.

This classification has done yeoman service in such solid researches as those of Anderson and Davidson,[14] Centers,[15] Lind,[16] and others. Its chief weakness lies in the breadth of its categories, some of which clearly overlap, and in the absence of indications that these hierarchial positions actually reflect the invidious value accorded them by the public.

2. *Classifications Employing Occupational Prerequisites*

In vocational guidance and personnel work several occupational classifications are used in which occupations are grouped according to degree of training, education, and intelligence,[17] al-

though they frequently also employ a measure of reward such as income. Such groupings, of course, not only facilitate personnel selection and vocational guidance but also suggest the possibility of scaling occupations in terms of social position. The Minnesota scale, for example, was employed in Guttman's study of Minneapolis families cited earlier.

The use of these classifications as scales of relative position is a modification of their original orientation, however, which involves somewhat dubious assumptions. It takes for granted that the responses of others toward an occupation will be essentially rational and that prestige varies directly with the complexity of skills required by any job or occupation. Such an assumption may be warranted to a certain extent. However, it may easily be carried too far by ignoring such other bases of prestige ascription as the importance of the occupation to the society, the possibility of financial rewards, the relative pleasantness of general working conditions, and so on. Consequently, occupational classifications of this type can have only limited use in the study of social stratification.

3. *Classifications Employing Occupational Rewards*

For the purposes of this paper occupational rewards are considered as falling into three categories: financial income, honorific value or "psychic income," and working conditions. While it is true that "psychic income" also attaches to high wages and "good" working conditions, the honorific aspect of a job or occupation refers here only to the amount of respect and regard conferred upon an occupation, with honorific effect of earnings and working conditions, if any, held constant.

Classifications by Financial Reward. It will be recalled that income was shown

[13] Alba M. Edwards, *Comparative Occupational Statistics for the United States* (*XVI Census, 1940*) (Washington, D.C.: Government Printing Office, 1943).

[14] *Op. cit.*

[15] *Op. cit.*

[16] Andrew W. Lind, *An Island Community* (Chicago: The University of Chicago press, 1938), Chap. xi: "Occupational Succession."

[17] Representative of this approach are Irving Lorge and Ralph Blau, "Broad Occupational Groupings by Intelligence Levels," *Occupations*, XX, No. 6 (March, 1942), 419–23; R. O. Beckman, "A New Scale for Gauging Occupational Rank," *Personnel Journal*, XIII, No. 4 (September, 1934), 225–33; and the Minnesota Occupational Scale of Goodenough and Anderson.

by Guttman to be superior to the Minnesota Occupational Scale as a measure of societal position. This may be due partially to the fact that the Minnesota scale is of the type described here as based upon job prerequisites, or it may possibly indicate "true" superiority of income to any possible occupational classification. There are certain well-known anomalies, however, which would cast doubt upon the latter hypothesis. Teachers, for example, outrank carpenters, as do bookkeepers. The carpenter, however, enjoys an earning power superior to both—at least currently—and income alone would place one them erruldously.

Income, moreover, is regarded as peculiarly private information, and, further, steadiness of employment complicates the hourly, daily, weekly, or monthly earning picture. For these reasons, then, income alone may be judged an inadequate index of occupational position,

Classification by "Honorific Value." There is no scale known to the writer which employs this dimension alone, but it can be shown that it would not be likely to provide a valid and practicable index in any case. In the first place, "psychic income" is difficult to separate from other systems of reward, and, in the second place, if it were separable, the same sort of anomalies as those found in the use of income alone would appear. Thus, although teachers probably receive greater honorific return without regard to the other rewards than do bankers, the latter clearly occupy the higher societal position. Like financial income, "psychic income" alone seems too incomplete to serve adequately as an index of occupational position.

c Classification by Working Conditions. This type of reward is inherent in such classifications as those using the classes "professionals," "proprietors and managers," "white-collar workers" and "manual workers," since the major distinction among these necessarily includes such factors as hours, control over time, cleanliness of work, type of clothing appropriate to the employment, and other similar elements. Although good use was made of such categories by Drake and Cayton, who also used the terms "clean" and "dirty" jobs to good advantage, such a classification suffers from the same weaknesses as the Alba Edwards Scale.[18] Added to this difficulty is the further one of combining diverse values in types of working conditions such as hours, time of beginning work, clothing, cleanliness, security, etc. Anomalies also exist in this dimension: the hours of a laborer are shorter than those of a physician, the work of a store clerk is cleaner than that of a carpenter, a bookkeeper wears "better" clothes than a locomotive engineer—and yet, in all these cases, other factors reverse the social position. The use of working conditions alone, then, as an index of stratification is not feasible.

Classification by a Combination of Rewards. To return to the postualates on which the concept of stratification used in this paper is based, a sort of sum of all rewards accruing to a status constitutes the element of prestige, and it seems logical that this would similarly be true of occupation. Those studies, then, which attempt to describe *occupational prestige* actually attempt a synthesis of the total reward system.

These classifications are based on the assumption that people are able to make a total positional judgment. The theoretical aspect of this assumption is well described by Goldhamer and Shils, who point out that all deference behavior is based upon such judgments

---

[18] St. Clair Drake and Horace Cayton, *Black Metropolis* (New York: Harcourt, Brace & World, Inc., 1945).

within the observer's value hierarchy.[19]

All prestige studies of occupation rest upon essentially this assumption and further utilize the same methodology, although there are differences in techniques.[20] They assume that prestige is estimable and that it lies in the opinions of others rather than in the occupation itself or in any *specific* rewards attached to that position. Consequently, the method employed is to secure judgments from others about the prestige position of a selected series of occupations.

The theory and method of these prestige studies seems to meet the necessary requirements of an index of societal position more nearly than any other method currently available. It is in their techniques that such classifications have been inadequate for general application in stratification research. This is due in varying degrees to the incompleteness and unrepresentativeness of the occupations rated or to the inadequacy of the jury which rated them or in some cases to defects in the rating scales themselves. The method to be presented in this paper is an attempt to rectify some of the weaknesses of existing prestige scales. It accepts as valid, however, the assumptions behind the use of this occupational dimension and, indeed, behind the use of occupation itself as an index of relative social position.

The Prestige Continuum

In March, 1946, the National Opinion Research Center interviewed their regular national sample, plus a special sample of youth, on the subject of occupational prestige.[21] The total number of respondents in the survey was 2,930.

A list of eighty-eight occupations was rated by the respondents on a prestige scale giving values from one to six.[22] The list of occupations was originally compiled on the basis of three criteria: (1) that it should include no "antisocial" jobs; (2) that the occupations chosen should represent as large a proportion of the gainfully employed in the United States as possible; and (3) that the fullest practical range of prestige should be covered. Owing to a particular interest of one of the agencies who made this study possible, eight scientific occupations were added to the original selections and a few were deleted because of

---

[19] Herbert Goldhamer and Edward A. Shils, "Types of Power and Status," *American Journal of Sociology*, XLV, No. 2 (September, 1939), 178 ff.

[20] W. A. Anderson, "Occupational Attitudes and Choices of a Group of College Men, I and II," *Social Forces*, VI (1927–28), 278–83, and "The Occupational Attitudes of College Men," *Journal of Social Psychology*, V (1934), 435–65; G. W. Hartmann, "The Prestige of Occupations," *Personnel Journal*, XIII (1934), 144–52; F. Wilkinson, "Social Distance between Occupations," *Sociology and Social Research*, XIII (1929), 234–44; H. C. Lehman and Paul A. Witty, "Further Study of the Social Status of Occupations," *Journal of Educational Sociology*, V (1931), 101–12; C. W. Hall, "Social Prestige Values of Selected Groups of Occupations,"

Psychological Bulletin, XXXV (1938), 696; C. Muriger, "The Social Status of Occupations for Women," *Teachers College Record*, XXXIII (1932), 696–704; W. Coutu, "The Relative Prestige of Twenty Professions as Judged by Three Groups of Professional Students," *Social Forces*, XIV (1936), 522–29; Mapheus Smith, "Empirical Scale of Prestige Status of Occupations," *American Sociological Review*, VIII (1943), 185–92.

[21] This is NORC Survey No. 244. A summary appears in Logan Wilson and William L. Kolb, *Sociological Analysis* (New York: Harcourt, Brace & World, Inc., 1949), Chap. xiii.

[22] To secure these ratings, each respondent was handed a card which bore the instruction: "For each job mentioned, please pick out the statement that best gives *your own personal opinion* of the *general standing* that such a job has." Below this instruction appeared the following: "1. *Excellent* standing. 2. *Good* standing. 3. *Average* standing. 4. *Somewhat below average* standing. 5. *Poor* standing. X. I don't know where to place that one."

the excessive length of the list. As it now stands, the prestige ratings of between two-thirds and three-fourths of the gainfully employed can be either identified exactly or estimated accurately.

The rankings were transformed into prestige scores in such a way as to yield a minimum score of twenty and a maximum of one hundred. The actual range was from thirty-three for "shoe-shiner" to ninety-six for "Supreme Court Justice" and ninety-three for "physician," the highest rating regular occupation. Of the sixty-five possible score units within the range, forty-nine are actually present. In other words, all sections of the continuum are fairly well represented.

These scores form a prestige continuum which deals with at least some of the problems unsolved in other prestige studies.[23] It thus already constitutes a method of occupational classification which, though neither complete nor definitive, is useful for many types of research.

However, while this continuum seems usable for many purposes, the presence of similar scores for such dissimilar occupations as "airline pilot," "artist who paints pictures," "owner of a factory employing about 100 people" and "sociologist" raises the problems of whether or not the continuum holds together. In other words, the question of whether these occupations were consistently ranked *by individuals* with relation to

each other needs to be answered. That is, it is not enough to know that mean scores are consistently different for any two occupations, but it is further necessary to know whether individuals consistently rate these occupations in the same relative positions.

The method selected to make this test was the Guttman Scaling Technique.[24] If the responses to the occupations form a scale in these terms, it may be assumed that they constitute a single "response universe" and can be thought of as a unified, steplike prestige series. Three different samples of twenty-five, sixteen, and twelve occupations were analyzed by this method,[25] but none of these yielded even a "quasi-scale,"[26] nor was there reason to believe that empirical manipulation would substantially improve scalability. This result made it necessary to reconsider the nature of the prestige continuum as constructed in this study and the addition of a new hypothesis. This hypothesis is that, although the full series does not scale, there are subgroupings which do scale. That is, these are subgroupings within which individuals are consistent, not only in their gross prestige judgments, but also in maintaining constant and precise differences of prestige ratings.

Such occupational categories are an extension into the field of occupational

___

[23] An indication of reliability of these scores was secured in two ways. In about four-fifths of the occupations no statistically significant difference amongfour regions (Northeast, Midwest, South, and Far West) turned up. In addition, two occupations were entered twice with slight changes in the names. These were "garage mechanic" paired with "automobile repairman" and "public school teacher" paired with "instructor in the public schools." In both, the score difference was only one point, from 62 to 63 for the one case and from 78 to 79 in the other.

[24] Louis Guttman, "A Basis for Scaling Qualitative Data," *American Sociological Review*, IX (1944), 139–50, and "On Festinger's Evaluation of Scale Analysis," *Psychological Bulletin*, XLIV, No. 5 (September, 1947), 451–65.

[25] The responses of 100 cases were used in this operation. They were randomly selected on the basis of the case numbers. These occupational series were chosen by taking every occupation in the series arranged by decreasing prestige value.

[26] A "quasi-scale" seems to indicate the presence of scalability but one with too little precision present to allow the identification of "cutting-points."

classification of what Benoit-Smullyan has called "situs," as distinct from "status."[27] These are, therefore, types of occupations whose status system may be considered as a unit. The clearest example, perhaps, of this idea is seen in the separation of agricultural occupations from industrial pursuits. The hypothesis presented here holds that status judgments within such divisions are consistent, whereas status judgment between them are not. Consequently, a series of agricultural or industrial occupations should prove scalable separately but not in combination.

Occupational Family and Situs

To test this hypothesis, the existence of a series of occupational families was posited. These were not conceived as being families in the sense of possessing relatively equal *amounts* of prestige but as categories constituting parallel status ladders. If the hypothesis is to stand, these groupings of occupations must be so related in the public mind that their relative prestige positions would be assigned consistently by the respondents.

The first step in this procedure was the construction of groups by logical assignment employing the criterion of similar relationship between occupation and the consuming public. That is, the selling relation, the client-professional relation, etc., were taken as the criterion for the first rough classifications. The resulting groups were then subjected to scale analysis by the Cornell technique and empirically rearranged until a scalable pattern appeared. Because of these empirical adjustments of occupations from one category to another no great finality for the families or situses may be claimed. It is possible, however, to observe that these groupings seem to work out, both as to reasonable scalability and as to internal similarity of relations with the general public.

It should be pointed out that both the terms "situs" and "occupational family" are used in Tables 1, 2, and 3. Occupational families are here actually subdivisions of the situses, although there are significant differences in scalability between the two. The reproducibility figures for the situses are barely, or perhaps not quite, adequate to consider them scalable, whereas in most cases the families yield a reproducibility high enough to be so considered.[28] Even in these instances, however, the number of responses scaled is often so small as to render the conclusion tenuous. For example, in the

---

[28] Guttman, "A Basis for Scaling Qualitative Data," *op. cit.* In the following tables the key figures for the evaluation of scaladility are the number of items, the number of responses scaled, and the two reproducibility indexes. Thus, the larger the number of responses scaled, the more rigorous the test and the more satisfactory the scale.

"Reproducibility" refers to the percentage of accuracy with which the scores on the *individual* items making up a scale may be predicted knowing only the total score (ratings of selected occupations in this case) of *all* occupations in that scale. A reproducibility of 80–85 may indicate adequate scalability if satisfactory levels of rigorousness on the other criteria are met but generally would reveal a quasi-scale. An index of 85 or, perhaps better, 90 indicates satisfactory scalability. Reproducibility indexes must, however, be interpreted in the light of the minimum marginal reproducibility which represents the per cent of ratings falling at the modal value. Thus, the lower the minimum marginal figure and the higher the reproducibility, the greater is the improvement in predictability of responses to the items over that which would result from chance alone.

---

[27] These "occupational families" would be of such a nature as to coincide with what Benoit-Smullyan has called situs within the broader area of stratification (Émile Benoit-Smullyan, *American Sociological Review*, IX, No. 2 [April, 1944], 154–61).

TABLE 1   **The Scalability by the Cornell Technique of Occupational Situses and Families**

Situs and family	Number of occupations scaled	Number of responses scaled	Reproduci-bility	Mininum marginal re-producibility
1. Political	7	14	84	67
National	4	8	89	70
Local	3	6	90	59
2. Professional	8	16	77	60
Free professions	4	8	88	60
Pure sciences	6	12	86	60
Applied sciences	4	8	88	66
Community professionals	5	10	85	63
3. Business	4	11	78	55
Big business	3	6	87	61
Small business	4	8	91	70
Labor organization	2	10	85	38
White-collar employees	7	14	87	58
4. Recreation and aesthetics	6	12	80	67
High arts	3	6	86	66
Journalism and radio	3	6	86	63
Recreation	2	4	90	51
5. Agriculture	4	8	87	58
Farming	2	4	93	61
Employed on farms	2	4	92	62
6. Manual work	6	14	84	59
Skilled mechanics	4	8	87	67
Construction trades	3	9	90	55
Outdoor work	4	8	86	61
Factory work	4	8	90	68
Unskilled labor	3	6	88	73
7. Military[a]	—	—	—	—
Army	2	6	84	50
Navy	—	—	—	—
Marine Corp.	—	—	—	—
Coast Guard	—	—	—	—
8. Service	4	8	89	55
"Official community"	4	8	88	60
"Unofficial community"	3	6	98	72
Personal	3	6	86	70

[a] Only one family was represented in the original data. Thus the existence of the others is merely speculation; it may well be that they do not exist in fact.

business situs reproducibility is only seventy-eight, indicating the probable existence of a "quasi-scale," whereas for the four families shown as subdivisions of this situs the figures are much higher: eighty-seven for white-collar employees, eighty-five for labor organizers, ninety-one for small business, and eighty-seven for big business. The numbers of responses scaled, however, are small; fourteen for white-collar workers, ten for labor organizers, eight for small business, and eleven for big business. Perhaps the major value of the situses as constructed is to indicate the absolute limits to which this principle of horizontal classification may be pushed, for beyond the limits of the situses even quasi-scalability disappears.

The data of this study seem to indicate the presence of at least eight situses. These are presented in Table 1 together with the families composing them and the data required to evaluate their scalability.

At this point one may only speculate about the nature of the situses, if they exist. Some clearly represent steps in

TABLE 2   Composition of the Business Situs

Situs occupational family job or occupation	Number of occupations scaled	Number of responses scaled	Reproducibility	Minimum marginal reproducibility	Prestige score
Business	4[a]	11	78	55	—
Big business	3	6	87	61	—
Banker	—	2	88	50	88
Member of board of directors	—	2	88	62	86
Owner of factory	—	2	85	70	82
Small business	4	8	91	70	—
Building contractor	—	2	88	79	79
Owner of a printing shop	—	2	94	70	74
Owner of a lunch stand	—	2	85	76	61
Fisherman—own boat	—	2	97	55	58
Labor organization	2	10	85	38	—
International union	—	5	85	44	75
Local union	—	5	85	31	62
White-collar employees	7	14	87	58	—
Accountant	—	2	82	70	81
Manager of a store	—	2	94	85	69
Traveling salesman	—	2	94	79	68
Bookkeeper	—	2	91	82	68
Insurance agent	—	2	85	76	68
Railroad agent	—	2	83	60	67
Clerk in store	—	2	82	58	58

[a] These four occupations are those correlating highest with each of the families making up the situs.

TABLE 3   Composition of the Manual Work Situs

Situs occupational family job or occupation	Number of occupations scaled	Number of responses scaled	Reproducibility	Minimum marginal reproducibility	Prestige score
Manual work	6[a]	14	84	59	—
Skilled mechanics	4	8	87	67	—
Airline pilot	—	2	88	76	83
Locomotive engineer	—	2	91	67	77
Trained machinist	—	2	82	70	73
Garage mechanic	—	2	88	54	61
Construction trades	3	9	90	55	—
Electrician	—	3	94	50	73
Carpenter	—	3	92	58	65
Plumber	—	3	86	57	63
Outdoor work	4	8	86	61	—
Truck-driver	—	2	88	60	54
Lumberjack	—	2	88	55	53
Coal-miner	—	2	82	64	49
Dock worker	—	2	85	70	47
Factory work	4	8	90	68	—
Machine operator	—	2	86	76	60
Night watchman	—	2	91	52	47
Clothes presser in laundry	—	2	91	76	46
Janitor	—	2	91	70	44
Unskilled labor	3	6	88	73	—
Section hand	—	2	88	67	48
Garbage man	—	2	85	67	35
Street sweeper	—	2	91	85	34

[a] These six occupations are those correlating highest with each of the families. Two, however, were chosen from the skilled mechanics group.

prestige, such as the agricultural situs which includes "farm tenant," "farm owner," "farm hand" and "sharecropper." Other situses, however, appear to embrace similar functions, as in the case of those which are professional or political. From the data at hand the only known characteristic is that each situs does include only jobs and occupations which can be compared consistently by most people. It is probable that further research would reveal other properties, but any statement as to the nature of these would be pure conjecture at this time.

A more detailed presentation of two of the actual situses may help to clarify the concept. As a demonstration, Tables 2 and 3 present the composition of the business and manual-work categories by both families and individual occupations.

Although the evidence in support of the situses and families as described in this paper and illustrated in Tables 2 and 3 is far from definitive, and the nature of the groupings certainly not clearly understood, it does appear that at least the principle on which they are based has promise. Further clarification of this line of thought might lead to valuable investigation and provide insights into our social structure not currently obtainable.

Possible Application of Situs Prestige Analysis

Application of such an analysis might serve to simplify many types of problems involving stratification. Two illustrations of this, however, should be sufficient to establish the point.

1. Studies of Vertical Mobility

If prestige-situs analysis is at all realistic, it follows that there are two types of vertical mobility: that which takes place entirely within a situs and that which involves movement into another.[29] If, for example, a young man begins his occupational career in the business situs as a bookkeeper, he may rise within this situs by the acquisition of skills through experience or, perhaps, merely by virtue of seniority. If, however, he decides to enter a profession and thus also move horizontally, an additional investment (the time and money involved in education) must be made. Again, should this man have remained in business and succeeded in rising to the position of business ownership, he might then elect to enter politics. Once more an investment of time to campaign and perhaps a sizable contribution to the party war chest is required. Another type of cost involved in intersitus movement may be seen as a loss of prestige while moving into a situs more advantageously located in the terms of its upper limit. Thus, for example, a carpenter may elect to accept a prestige loss in order to take a job as a salesman —thinking perhaps that he thus enters a situs ultimately more promising than the one in which he is presently located. An alternative mode of entry for him to the business situs might be by the accumulation of sufficient funds which permit him to establish his own construction company. In either case, of course, intersitus mobility costs have arisen and been paid.

The difference between inter- and intrasitus mobility is considerable. Intersitus movement is characterized by increased risk and intrasitus movement by increased security. In addition, there probably are differences between the two with reference to the potential distance which may be moved. These differences may be of sufficient importance

---

[29] This problem has been clearly seen and stated by Elbridge Sibley in "Some Demographic Clues to Stratification," *American Sociological Review*, VII, No. 3 (June, 1942), 322–30.

as to allow the obscuring of important factors in studies of vertical mobility should they be ignored.

It should also be noted that such differences apply to intergenerational as well as to career movement, so that significance attaches to the position of the son vis-à-vis his father not only with reference to the vertical dimension but also with reference to the horizontal.

2. Analyses by Differential Stratification

As an example of this type of problem differential birth rates may be used, although a variety of others would serve as well. If conclusions of a psychological nature are to be drawn concerning vertical mobility and fertility, rough position measures may once more obscure as much as they reveal. It is entirely possible, for example, that relative position within a situs represents the true "keeping up with the Joneses" rather than position with reference to the total societal structure. Studies of relative fertility as *between* status levels but *within* situses could

conceivably add much to our knowledge of differential fertility. To put it concretely, fertility differentials between physician and architect, electrician and plumber, accountant and clerk, may contain as valuable information as those differentials between physician, architect, and accountant, on the one hand, and plumber, electrician, and clerk, on the other, which is the type of analysis currently applied.

While there is insufficient evidence to put forth the occupational families and situses as finally established exactly as set forth here, there seems ample evidence to indicate both the possibility and the utility of vertical-horizontal occupational analysis. It is hoped that further research will modify or confirm this point and, perhaps, even further, that the nature of situses will be studied more exactly, to the end that a more precise method of stratification study may be developed which not only will be systematically coherent with the postulates of stratification but will also be a practical tool for empirical research.

The Degree of Status Incongruence and Its Effects

ANDRZEJ MALEWSKI

Problems

In his last book Homans defines the status of an individual as the complex set of stimuli which it presents to others (and to himself) and which are evaluated by others as better or worse, higher or

lower.[1] The particular kinds of such stimuli are defined by him as status factors.[2] According to Homans, status congruence is realized when all the stimuli presented by a man rank better or higher than the corresponding stimuli presented by another, or when all the stimuli presented by both rank as equal.[3]

According to such a definition, the status of the same individual may be con-

Reprinted from Andrzej Malewski, "The Degree of Status Incongruence and Its Effects," *The Polish Sociological Bulletin*, VII, No. 1 (1963), 9–19, by permission of Hanna Malewska and the publisher.

---

[1] G. C. Homans, *Social Behavior* (New York: Harcourt, 1961), p. 149.
[2] *Ibid.*, p. 248.
[3] *Ibid.*

grucnt in relation to certain people and incongruent in relation to others. The incongruence of status factors is thus treated here as the characteristic of a relationship and not of an individual. Secondly, it should be agreed that in every relationship in which one of the partners is evaluated as better in certain respects and worse in others, both partners are characterized by an incongruence of status factors.

The utility of concepts depends on the aims which they are supposed to serve. The concept "incongruence of status factors" can be useful for at least two purposes. First, it may be serviceable in an analysis of society as a system, and in an enquiry concerning—for example —the problem of relationships between the congruence of status factors in particular strata on the one hand, and the sharpness of social divisions, the isolation of certain strata from others and the formation of class-consciousness on the other. Secondly, the term may be useful in the analysis of differences in the behaviour of different categories of individuals and differences in relations between people depending on the degree of congruence of the status factors.

The present article deals exclusively with the second group of problems. I shall attempt to show that the integration of the regularities which appear in this domain demands a modification of the concept of "status incongruence." Thus in the present article I shall try first of all to define the meaning of the basic terms which it will be necessary to use, and then to formulate some pertinent propositions.

The Concept of "Status" and "Status Incongruence"

I shall use here the definition of "status" and "status factors" introduced by Homans.

According to these definitions every-thing which distinguishes an individual from others may become a status factor; first of all there are various characteristics of the individual himself, such as skin colour, age, education, religion, sex, income, property, home, way of dressing, skills, achievements, personal appearance, abilities, different kinds of behavior, name, etc. Secondly, there are characteristics connected with the relationship of the given individual to other individuals, groups, organizations or communities, e.g., duration of membership, seniority at work, authority, degree of independence, social origin, marital status, circle of acquaintances, etc. And thirdly, there are the characteristics which are the result of the attitude of other people to the given individual, e.g., the approval or esteem he enjoys. All of the above mentioned characteristics and many others are status factors if they are perceived by others and if they are evaluated as higher or lower, better or worse.

The idea of status as a complex set of different factors involves the problem of relationships between those factors. As a result of experience people learn that certain status factors appear linked to others, and respond with normative expectations; they expect a man who is a university professor, for instance, to be a man of learning and a company director to have a good education and presence and to be of the proper age. If, having learned this, they meet someone who is a university professor and knows very little, or who is a company director at 20 odd years old and has only a primary education, they will experience some incongruence. Generally speaking, the greater the divergence between the complex of status factors presented by a given individual and the normative expectations which have been formed in those with whom that individual is in contact, the more incongruent is the status of that individual.

One should pay attention to the two consequences of such a definition. In order to establish the incongruence of status it is not sufficient to point out, as is commonly done, that some status factors of an individual rank much higher than others. One should also show reasons for maintaining that those differences are inconsistent with the normative expectations of the environment in which the given individual moves. This throws a new light on the dispute between W. F. Kenkel[4] and G. Lenski.[5] Kenkel in his polemic with Lenski tried to show that not every concurrence of high and low status factors will cause such consequences as the rise of social radicalism. Lenski accepted this criticism and commented to the effect that status incongruence influences the behavior and views of an individual only if it concerns the most basic components of status. This answer, however, involves further questions, namely, which status factors are most basic and what should be one's guide when evaluating the importance of status factors. The world champion in the 10,000 meters race who has not completed his primary education will present one very high status factor, namely athletic talent, but his other status factor, education, will be very low. Such a complex of status factors, however, may not have any undesirable consequences for him; not because great athletic ability or education are of no importance, but because the connection between championship medals and low educational attainments may be consistent with normative expectations.

If incongruence of status depends on normative expectations which have been formed in other men, such expectations may not be the same in all cases. It has been noted many times that in the United States the status of a Negro doctor is incongruent.[6] As a medical man he is a representative of a profession that is very highly evaluated. As a Negro he represents an ethnic group which is held in very low esteem by many whites. Consequently if such a doctor were to practice in a district inhabited by white people, he would often meet reactions due to his ethnic group and not to his profession and would frequently be humiliated. This is the traditional approach to the problem and is no doubt right. But the definition given above draws attention to facts which hitherto have been generally neglected.

The status of a Negro doctor will not be incongruent in every situation, because not even in American society is the fact of being a Negro doctor incongruent with the normative expectations in every environment. One may suppose that it is not inconsistent with the expectations of progressive white people, nor inconsistent with the expectations of the majority of the Negro community. Thus if such a doctor were to live and practice exclusively in a Negro district and to have no contacts with white patients or white doctors (especially with white doctors of conservative views) he would not show any incongruence of status factors, if congruence is to be interpreted according to the definition given above. This is not only a question of terminology. It means in fact that the propo-

[4] W. F. Kenkel, "The Relationship Between Status Consistency and Politico-Economic Attitudes," *American Sociological Review*, XXI, No. 1 (1956), 365–368.

[5] G. Lenski, "Comment on Kenkel's Communication," *American Sociological Review*, XXI, No. 2 (1956), 368–369; See also L. Broom, "Social Differentiation and Stratification," in: R. Merton, L. Broom, and L. S. Cottrell, eds., *Sociology Today* (New York: Basic Books, Inc., 1960), p. 431.

[6] E. C. Hughes, "Dilemmas and Contradictions of Status," *American Journal of Sociology*, (1945), 353–359.

sitions regarding the consequences of status incongruence may not be true as applied to him.

A Negro doctor practicing exclusively in a Negro district may enjoy high esteem as a physician. As a Negro he may not meet any humiliation because all the people he meets are also Negroes. One may treat analogously the position of a worker whose personal contacts are limited to a working class group and whose skill, education or income are higher than those of his fellow workers. It is worthwhile quoting here the results obtained by E. Goffman.[7] He showed that the preference for change in the distribution of power was most strongly related to incongruences of income, education and occupational status among the upper strata, and almost unrelated to the incongruence of those three status factors among the lower strata. This apparent irregularity could be partly explained if one assumes that a large proportion of people from the lower strata classified as belonging to the category of people with incongruent status factors, did not in fact belong to this category according to the definition given above. Some other factors are discussed hereinafter.[8]

Thus far I have introduced the definition of "status incongruence." One may of course suggest many different definitions. The criterion that enables one to reject some of them and to accept others can only be their utility for formulating general propositions. I should now like to go on to present propositions concerning the consequences of status incongruences, as understood in accordance with the definition suggested here.

Incongruent Status and Behavior

The incongruence of status implies that the individual presents some contradictory stimuli to others. This is only so, however, when the incongruent status factors are perceived by the same people.

This condition is not always fulfilled. Let us suppose that in a society (e.g., in pre-war Poland or in the United States today) the possession of a squalid little room in a poor quarter of the town is strikingly different from the expectations as to the home of a higher executive of an important organization. A high executive living in this way would, in that situation, meet our definition of the incongruence of status factors. However, if his home and work environment are isolated from each other, if his colleagues never see the room and his neighbours never see him at his place of work, neither of these two groups of persons would perceive the inconsistent stimuli. In other words, if the incongruence of status is to give inconsistent stimuli, the incongruent status factors should be perceived by the same people.

The stimuli presented by the individual to others affect their reactions towards that individual. If the individual simultaneously presents two conflicting stimuli of which the first causes respect and the second contempt, other people may react to the second type of stimuli and show their contempt for the individual, although this is not justified in the light of the higher status factors. This line of reasoning leads to the formulation of the following two propositions:

1. The greater the incongruence of simultaneously perceived status factors of the given individual, the more insecure is his status. This means that others are likely to react to that individual as if he had a lower status, than the one he really enjoys.

[7] E. W. Goffman "Status Consistency and Preference for Change in Power Distribution," *American Sociology Review*, XXII, No. 3 (1957), 275–281.

[8] Cf. proposition 3, p. 86.

2. The incongruence of status factors simultaneously perceived by other people brings punishments and the elimination of that incongruence is a source of reward.

From proposition 2 one should not conclude that people will always avoid an incongruence of status factors. Status incongruence is a source of punishments and its elimination a source of rewards, but it is not the only kind of punishment and reward. A sharpening of the incongruence of status factors may at the same time raise the general status of the individual. A very young man who becomes a professor at on e of the European universities may increase the incongruence between certain factors of his status because of the conviction, widely held in Europe, that a university professor is a man of advanced age. But at the same time he can substantially increase his status and this increase of status may greatly surpass the costs of status incongruence. Even in a case of this kind, however, the incongruence of status brings certain punishments and evokes consequent attempts to get rid of them. If this is so, it must bring forth some consequences in the form of tendencies to decrease those punishments.

3. If an individual shows several incongruent status factors, some of which are evaluated as much lower than others, and if he perceives the possibility of changing the lower factors, he will tend to raise such status factors which are evaluated as lower.

For example, the *nouveau riche* in the upper class will often obliterate signs of their parvenu background: they will marry into respected families, buy family estates, demonstrate their knowledge of a foreign language widely used among the old aristocracy, fake pedigrees, boast of their friendly relations with persons of importance and emulate the older members of the elite in conformity to the norms of their new environment. Similarly, religious converts will show greater fervour for their new faith than those who have professed it from childhood.

Systematic results backing proposition 3 are furnished by the investigation made by J. Coleman, E. Katz and H. Menzel.[9] Interviews were carried out with 85 per cent of the general practitioners, internists and pediatricians practicing in four selected American cities. In the interviews the doctors were asked, among other things, which of three widely used drugs they prescribed most often and when had they started to apply the newest of the three drugs, which appeared on the market one after the other. An examination of prescriptions from local pharmacies made out by the same doctors over fifteen months revealed what they had actually prescribed. The comparison of these two sets of data showed some striking differences. Two-thirds of the doctors who, according to the prescription record, had mostly used the oldest drug, stated that they mostly used one of the two newer ones. Sixty per cent of those who had mainly prescribed the drug introduced second, stated that they mostly used the third, i.e., the newest drug. Half the total number of physicians stated that they had begun to apply the newest drug at an earlier date and often many months earlier than actually appeared to be the case from the analysis of the prescriptions. From these results it may be concluded that keeping up with the latest discoveries in pharmacology was highly approved by the doctors interviewed, while lagging behind was disapproved.

One of the status factors of a physician is his professional competence. One

---

[9] See: H. Menzel, "Public and Private Conformity under Different Conditions of Acceptance in the Group," *Journal of Abnormal and Social Psychology*, LV, No. 3 (1957), 398–402.

would assume that the status of a doctor who is treated as little competent is incongruent. The possession of a doctor's diploma and the right to practice is incongruent with a lack of real medical skill. In order to establish how the competence of each doctor was perceived by his colleagues, the interviewers asked: "When you need information or advice about questions of therapy, [. . .] on whom are you most likely to call?" When opinions regarding a given doctor were compared with the other data already collected, it appeared that those doctors seldom or never named as potential counsellors had most often tried to appear in interviews as more up-to-date than their prescription record showed. This was rarest in the case of those doctors who were mentioned as potential advisers by three or more colleagues. In other words, doctors who showed the most striking incongruence between the two status factors— their medical title and their professional competence as perceived by their colleagues—most often tried to present themselves in a better light.

However, the tendency to eliminate status incongruence by raising those status factors which are evaluated as much lower than others does not always give the desired effects. Different status factors may have different degrees of stability. Some of them cannot be changed, e.g., skin color or sex. The change of others demands a long span of time (e.g., age) or very great efforts (e.g., education). Others may be changed quite easily (e.g., one's way of dressing). These differences are linked with the difference between ascribed status and achieved status, which has often been stressed. But as in the case of the notion of status, it also seems useful here to generalize about the differences observed. In fact we need to have not two categories of status—ascribed and achieved—but a whole continuum of

status factors from those most to those least changeable. Such a distinction enables us to formulate the next proposition.

4. If an individual has several incongruent status factors, some of which are evaluated as much lower than others, and when this individual cannot raise the lower factors, he will show a tendency to avoid those people who react to them.

Proposition 4 is backed by the results of the investigation made by G. Lenski.[10] Four status factors —income, education, prestige of occupation and ethnic prestige—were chosen for investigation. The category of a high degree of status congruence and the category of a low degree of status congruence were compared regarding frequency of and motives for contacts with other people. It turned out that respondents in a low congruence category far more frequently than respondents in a high congruency category:

a. Did not maintain any lively contacts with their neighbours or fellow-workers outside business hours and did not belong to voluntary associations for any long period of time;
b. In the case of membership in voluntary associations they did not attend meetings and were not active in the organization;
c. Indicated nonsociable motives for being members of an association, i.e., motives other than a desire for pleasurable interaction with others.

All these results seem to support proposition 4 concerning the relationship between status incongruence and the tendency to avoid other people. In the light of previous reasoning, one might expect the differences to be still

---

[10] G. Lenski, "Social Participation and Status Crystallization," *American Sociological Review*, XXI, No. 4 (1956), 458–464.

more striking if one could eliminate the factor of membership in an organization or interaction with people who did not share the common American pejorative evaluation of certain status factors. For example, where members of ethnic minorities were concerned, we did not take into consideration contacts with other members of those minorities. One might expect still more striking differences if those who presented status factors consistent with the expectations of their environment were eliminated from the category of low status congruence.[11]

Our next proposition will concern another type of defence against humiliations connected with status incongruence.

5. If an individual of incongruent status cannot raise the lower factors of his status, he will tend to reject the system of evaluation which justifies his humiliations and to join those who are opposed to that system. If these others represent a tendency towards changing the existing order, the above individual mentioned will be particularly inclined to accept their total program.

This proposition is supported by many different pieces of research. Lipset, in his study of the Co-operative Commonwealth Federation, the Socialist party of the Canadian province of Saskatchewan, discovered that the majority of businessmen and professional people who were members of that party belonged to minority groups such as Ukrainians, Poles, Russians and others, whereas only a few business-men of Anglo-Saxon origin belonged to the party.[12] Many authors have noticed that Jews from the middle and upper classes have very often been members of Socialist and Communist parties.[13] Lenski established that, in the Detroit area, individuals with high incomes, high occupational or educational status and low ethnic status, or with high occupational and low educational status more often supported Democratic or Progressive candidates and were more liberal than individuals with a higher degree of status congruence.[14] Goffman reported that incongruent respondents expressed a stronger preference for changes in the distribution of power between the State government, large scale industry, the trade unions, medium industry and the federal Government than congruent respondents.[15] Studies of voting behavior have proved that in America, where differences in speech and manners between the middle and the lower classes are small and not very obvious, people who have been promoted from the lower to the middle class more often voted for the Republican party than the stable members of the middle class. In Germany, Finland, Norway and Sweden, where the differences in behavior between the lower and middle classes seem to be much more visible, people who have been promoted to the middle class more often voted for the Social Democratic and Communist

---

[11] A more detailed analysis should also control the factor of vertical mobility. Those who constantly move upwards in the social hierarchy will tend to break all old links and will have some difficulties in establishing new ones. See E. Eilis, "Social Psychological Correlates of Upward Social Mobility among Unmarried Career Women," *American Sociological Review*, XVII, No. 2 (1952), 558–563. See also Broom, *op. cit.*, p. 432.

[12] S. M. Lipset, *Agrarian Socialism* (Berkeley, Calif.: University of California Press, 1950), pp. 190–193.

[13] See R. Michels, *Political Parties* (New York: The Free Press, 1949), pp. 260–261; see also L. E. Hubbard, *Soviet Labour and Industry* (London: Macmillan, 1942), pp. 272–279; S. M. Lipset and R. Bendix, "Social Status and Social Structure," *The British Journal of Sociology*, part II (September, 1951), 243.

[14] G. Lenski, "Status Crystallization: A Non-Vertical Dimension of Social Status," *American Sociological Review*, XIX, No. 3 (1954), 405–413.

[15] Goffman, *op. cit.*

parties, probably because of their visible status incongruence.

Such results have induced many authors to accept the proposition that status incongruence always, or at least in cases where it cannot be reduced by improving the lower status factors, results in a tendency to accept leftist programs.[16] In the light of our considerations such a tendency is a particular application of a more general law, appearing in some specific conditions. If the only group rejecting the system of values justifying the humiliations felt by people with incongruent status is the radical social Left, those people will be particularly ready to accept the program of reforms launched by the Left. If, however, there are other groups, e.g., extremely Rightist ones, whose program rouses hopes for changes bringing about the increase of lower status factors, incongruent individuals also show great readiness to accept extremely Rightist programs. This is not a purely theoretical possibility. Such a tendency has in fact been discovered, e.g., by B. Ringer and D. Sills in their study of political extremists in Iran.[17]

In the above mentioned proposition 5 the tendency to reject evaluations justifying the humiliations inflicted on people with incongruent status factors, was made dependent on the absence of any real chances of improving the lower status factors. But this proposition is only approximately true. It implicitly assumes that the real absence of opportunity for improvement is adequately perceived. It is well known, however, that perception of reality is not always adequate. In a situation in which there is an objective lack of opportunity for improving some status factor, certain people may be deluded as to the existence of such a possibility. If the situation itself is unambiguous and clear and if the given individual has no motivation for distorting reality, his perception of the situation will be adequate.[18]

These conditions, however, are not always fulfilled. People who suffer humiliations because of their origin or skin colour may see rare individuals who, although they share these features, have attained the very top of the social hierarchy. This may bolster up vain hopes of overcoming these disadvantageous status factors. This will be the easier, the more firmly the given individual has internalized the values of the privileged groups, and the stronger are his aspirations towards sharing in these values. Therefore, although skin colour is one of the least changeable status characteristics, some middle class Negroes do their best to imitate white members of the middle class in their views as well as in their behavior.

Until now I have dealt mainly with status incongruence and various defensive responses aimed at minimizing this incongruence. Now I should like to make some comments on the behavior of those whose status is undeniably high and stable. Status can be considered as stable as possible if an individual has a great many congruent status factors. In that situation particular behaviors in discordance with the high status will not be able to throw it in doubt. A university professor whose deep knowledge and creative talents are obvious, may

[16] See S. M. Lipset and J. Linz, *The Social Basis of Political Diversity*, Center for Advanced Study in the Behavioral Sciences, Palo Alto, 1956 (unpublished), Chapter VIII, p. 16; S. M. Lipset and R. Bendix, *Social Mobility in Industrial Society* (Berkeley, Calif.: University of California Press, 1959), p. 68.

[17] B. Ringer and D. Sills, "Political Extremists in Iran: A Secondary Analysis of Communications Data," *Public Opinion Quarterly*, II (1952), 668–701.

[18] See A. Malewski, *Generality Levels of Theories Concerning Human Behaviour*, paper presented at the section devoted to Models and Theory Formation, International Congress of Sociology, Washington, 1962.

openly tell his students that he does not know something, or that he has no ready answer and must stop to consider the given problem. A professor whose knowledge and abilities seem very poor to others of his circle would pay a big price for such frankness. Similarly in the United States a prosperous member of the upper class may safely drive a cheap old car or work in his garden in his old overalls, for this would in no way shake his undoubted status as a member of the upper class. The same behavior of someone who has only recently been promoted to the upper class would only emphasize his dubious status. This line of reasoning leads to the following proposition:

6. People whose status is very high and stable pay less attention to behavior as the visible symbol of their higher status.

Some findings reported by H. Menzel in the paper summarized above support proposition 6. Menzel found that the doctors whose recognized professional competence was high, more often reported less up-to-date behavior during an interview than those doctors whose professional competence was more doubtful.[19] The author could not explain this phenomenon. He discussed many hypotheses which seemed to him improbable. In the light of our discussion it seems that the result was completely in accordance with what was to be expected on the basis of proposition 6. The doctors considered by others as highly competent and who in fact followed the progress of modern medicine carefully, thought it least important to show themselves to the interviewer in the best possible light. They did not feel compelled to convince everyone they met that they were up-to-date in their medical practice. They really were up-to-date and this was well known to those whose opinion was important to them. Therefore, if they did not remember exactly when they had begun to apply the new drug for the first time, they tended to give a later rather than an earlier date. They considered it not only unnecessary but also unpleasant to present themselves in a falsely flattering light. This would have wounded their own self-esteem.

Status Incongruence of Group Memders and the System of Relations in a Group

Until now we have been discussing individuals or categories of individuals who differed from each other as to their degree of status congruence.

Now I should like to discuss what would be the effect of status incongruence among group members on the system of relationships within the group. A familiar example of the situation discussed here may be: (a) an institution or an enterprise in which the director has less competence or a lower education than at least some of his subordinates; (b) a working team in which those who work poorly and are less prepared for effort have higher salaries or a higher formal position than the others; (c) a married couple where, contrary to the normative expectations of each partner, the wife holds a much higher position and has a much higher income than her husband. In groups of this kind there will be a feeling of injustice[20] and some group members will frequently react to others in a way to cause them humiliation, and thus elicit rejection or an unfriendly response.

7. The higher the degree of status incongruence among group members the lower will be the degree of mutual friendship.

_____
[19] See Menzel, *op. cit.*, p. 402.

_____
[20] M. Patchen, "A Conceptual Framework and Some Empirical Data Regarding Comparisons of Social Rewards," *Sociometry*, I (1960).

This proposition is partly supported by the results of the study made by Stuart Adams on bomber crews.[21] He took into consideration nine different status factors of crew members, i.e., age, education, length of service, length of time spent in the air, combat time, rank, function in the crew, conviction of others as to the abilities of the given airman and popularity among others. These scores were used for constructing the status congruence score of each subject. The scores of status congruence of individual crew members enabled Stuart Adams to measure the average status congruence of each crew. The subjects answered two questionnaires: (a) on the degree of confidence which the different members of the crews felt in others, and (b) on the degree of friendship with others.

It was found that the lower the average status congruence of the crew the lower was the average degree of mutual trust and friendship. This result is in full accordance with the implications of proposition 7.

Another more indirect piece of evidence for this proposition is furnished by the results of the study carried out by J. V. Clark.[22] He investigated the workers of eight large supermarkets, and in particular two categories of employees working in direct cooperation with each other: bundlers and cashiers. The cashiers occupied posts superior in relation to those of the bundlers. The most comprehensive and most immediate data concerned two supermarkets: No. 6 and No. 38. The degree of status congruence of bundlers and cashiers in the first of these supermarkets was much lower than in the other. During the time of the study numerous workers left store No. 6. This fact indirectly confirms proposition 7. The mobility of personnel depends on the attractiveness of the group in which the individual works, at least when there are alternative job opportunities, and status incongruence helps to decrease that attractiveness.

In the two above mentioned studies attention was also paid to the problem of the interdependence of the degree of status congruence among crew or personnel, and their productivity. When considering this problem Homans put forward the assumption that "when they [people] are working together as a team, we expect that the degree to which they are congruent will make a difference to their effectiveness. If they are highly congruent at least one factor that might otherwise have disturbed their cooperation has been removed."[23] Some findings, particularly those reported by Clark, provide confirmation for this conclusion. In my opinion, however, there are no grounds for expecting any general relationship here. The degree of average status congruence among a given group is one of the factors increasing the attractiveness of that group to its members. The attractiveness of the group has an effect on the degree of conformity to the norms accepted in that group. If these norms require an increase in productivity we should expect such an increase; if, however, they require a decrease in productivity, this too is to be expected. It is not surprising therefore that Adams has stated that there was no direct relationship between the average status congruence of bomber crews and their effectiveness, as measured by the number of fulfilled combat operations. The propositions discussed above described merely a fraction of the relationships emerging in connection with the incon-

[21] S. N. Adams, "Status Congruency as a Variable in Small Group Performance," *Social Forces*, XXXII (1953–54), 16–22.

[22] J. V. Clark, *A Preliminary Investigation of Some Unconscious Assumptions Affecting Labor Efficiency in Eight Supermarkets*, Harvard Graduate School of Business Administration, 1958, unpublished. Quoted after Homans, *Social Behavior, op. cit.*, pp. 255–262.

[23] Homans, *op. cit.*, p. 255.

gruence of status factors. Reactions of individuals to status incongruence, differing from those discussed above, require further investigation. The problem of the link between the average status incongruence of a group and the functioning of that group still awaits a more comprehensive analysis. The same holds true of the problem of the relationship between the degree of status congruence within various strata and the formation of class consciousness.[24] Finally, all the propositions presented in this paper will need further modification as the result of new research. It seems to me this is a field for research which deserves particular attention.

---

[24] Problem discussed more comprehensively by Broom, *op. cit.*, pp. 433–439.

variations in systems

three

Sociologists typically look both for common patterns of social organization and for differences in the ways in which these patterns may occur in various societies. Since stratification is a universal social phenomenon, it is reasonable to expect both some basic similarities and some wide ranging differences in the ways in which inequality is structured and functions.

Many social scientists, including economists, have argued that industrial society has a compelling internal logic such that any society which seeks to industrialize and to modernize is likely to show some very basic similarities to all other industrializing societies. This generalization has been applied to the shape of the stratification system that one is likely to find in industrial societies.

Goldthorpe develops this thesis in some detail in his article, inquiring into the contention that the stratification systems of modern industrial societies tend to be fundamentally similar in (1) their degree and shape of occupational differentiation, (2) their strain toward status consistency, (3) the greater amount of mobility made possible, and (4) the movement toward greater economic and social equality. Goldthorpe casts doubt on these suppositions and, by analysis of the case of the Soviet Union, questions the more general thesis that the economic demands of the industrializing society are likely to dominate and shape the political forms. By indicating the coexistence of an authoritarian social structure with an industrialized economy in the Soviet Union, and the purposive way in which the State apparatus uses stratification for its political purposes, Goldthorpe raises serious questions regarding the thesis of the expectability of basically similar patterns of stratification in all industrializing societies.

One dimension on which societies can vary is the extent of stratification, grossly measured. There can be much or little inequality. Among the outstanding examples of approaches to maximum equality often cited in the literature is that of the kibbutz, or the agricultural cooperative community in Israel. A deliberate ideology of the equal worth of all labor and of all men is the reigning spirit in the kibbutzim. Eva Rosenfeld asks whether this presumably classless society is indeed classless, or can some significant elements of inequality be found. She argues that there are differentiated strata that cause some statuses to enjoy distinctively greater rewards of various kinds than others, albeit not material rewards, but rather rewards of power and prestige. She examines the bases on which these differences arise and the consequences of these differentiations for the "classless" kibbutzim.

Puerto Rican society is an example of still another major variation on the theme of social stratification. Although marked inequalities in income, education, occupational prestige, and power exist, Tumin argues that a fundamental spirit of equality seems to pervade this culture. The subjective perception of the quality of life by people on all rungs of the class ladders is much more uniform than one would expect given the objective differences between these levels. Men at the bottom are much more optimistic and have a significantly greater sense of their worth and of the importance of their roles in society than their objective positions indicate they "ought" to have. In part, this "dissonant" perception is due to (1) the sense of the openness of the society, (2) the possibilities of improvement through available social mechanisms, (3) the constant reiteration to the most lowly people of their importance, and (4) the frequent public ritualization of this ideology. It may be that the steady and pervasive emphasis on democratic political organization and the presence of some effective means for redistributing wealth and for conveying a sense of power and dignity even to the people at the very bottom of the class ladders constitute an effective set of techniques for producing the benign view of life found among Puerto Ricans of all classes.

Social Stratification in Industrial Society

JOHN H. GOLDTHORPE

For a decade or so now, a growing interest has been apparent, chiefly among American sociologists, in the pattern of long-term social change within relatively mature industrial societies. This interest appears to derive from two main sources.

In the first place, it can be seen as resulting from broadly based studies of the sociology of industrialization, concentrating originally on the underdeveloped or developing countries of the world. For example, work conducted as part of the Inter-University Study

of Labour Problems in Economic Development led up to the theoretical statement on the "logic" of industrialism attempted by Clark Kerr and his associates in their book, *Industrialism and Industrial Man*.[1] Secondly, this interest has undoubtedly been stimulated by the revival in comparative studies of social structure and social processes in economically advanced countries. Important here, for example, has been the work of Professor Lipset and a number of other members of the Berkeley campus of the University of California; and even more so, perhaps, studies which have chiefly involved comparisons between Western and Communist societies, such as those produced in connection with the Har-

Reprinted from John H. Goldthorpe, "Social Stratification in Industrial Society," in Paul Halmos, ed., *The Development of Industrial Society, The Sociological Review Monograph*, VIII (1964), 97–122, by permission of the author, the editor, and the publisher.

[1] Clark Kerr, J. T. Dunlop, F. H. Harbison, and C. A. Myers, *Industrialization and Industrial Man* (Cambridge, Mass.: Harvard University Press, 1960).

vard Project on the Soviet Social System by Professor Inkeles and his colleagues.[2]

However, it is notable that in spite of possibly different origins, current American interpretations of the development of industrial societies often reveal marked similarities. Basically, it may be said, they tend to be alike in stressing the standardizing effects upon social structures of the exigencies of modern technology and of an advanced economy. These factors which make for uniformity in industrial societies are seen as largely overriding other factors which may make for possible diversity, such as different national cultures or different political systems. Thus, the overall pattern of development which is suggested is one in which, once countries enter into the advanced stages of industrialization, they tend to become increasingly comparable in their major institutional arrangements and in their social systems generally. In brief, a *convergent* pattern of development is hypothesized.

Kerr and his associates have been the most explicit in this connection—and also in the matter of specifying the type of society on which the process of convergence is focussed. In their conception, "the road ahead" for all advanced societies leads in the direction of what they call "pluralistic" industrialism. By this they mean a form of industrial society in which the distribution of power is neither "atomistic" nor "monistic," nor yet radically disputed by warring classes; but rather a social order in which an "omnipresent State" regulates competition and conflict between a multiplicity of interest groups on the basis of an accepted "web of rules," and

at the same time provides the means through which a degree of democratic control can be exercised over the working of the economy and over other key social processes such as the provision of welfare and public services, education and so on.[3] Other theorists have usually been a good deal more guarded than this in their formulations; but it would nonetheless be fair to say that, in the main, they have adopted views which have been broadly consistent with the Kerr thesis. In general, the "logic" of industrialism has been regarded as powerfully encouraging, even if not compelling, the emergence of a new type of society from out of former "class" and "mass" societies alike.[4]

Clearly, then, a central theme in the interpretations in question concerns the development in advanced societies of systems of social stratification. And it is perhaps indicative of the importance of this theme that it has on several occasions been singled out for special discussion. In this paper[5] my main purpose

[2] Raymond A. Bauer, Alex Inkeles, and Clyde Kluckhohn, *How the Soviet System Works* (Cambridge, Mass.: Harvard University Press, 1956); Alex Inkeles and Raymond A. Bauer, *The Soviet Citizen* (Cambridge, Mass.: Harvard University Press, 1959).

[3] *Op. cit.*, Chaps. 1, 2 and 10 especially.

[4] The issue on which, of course, there has been greatest doubt and discussion is that of whether totalitarian régimes will *inevitably* become less "monistic" with continuing industrial advance. As emerges later in this paper, Inkeles appears somewhat uncertain on this point. Another leading American theorist of industrialism, W. E. Moore, has expressly rejected the idea that industrialization necessarily engenders increased political participation and more representative government. See his section, "Industrialisation and Social Change" in B. F. Hoselitz and W. E. Moore, eds., *Industrialization and Society* (New York: Humanities Press, Inc., 1963), pp. 357-359 especially. Nevertheless, the greater part of this section is written in terms of the social exigencies of an industrial technology and economy.

[5] I am indebted to my friend M. Alfred Willener for his criticisms of an earlier draft of this paper and also to colleagues in the Faculty of Economics and Politics of the University of Cambridge who have discussed many specific points with me.

will be to consider this particular aspect of current theories of industrialism and, further, to raise certain doubts and objections which seem to me to be of a serious kind and to have negative implications for these theories *in toto*. But at the outset I should say that I in no way intend to criticize the *kind* of sociological endeavor which is here represented. On the contrary, we are, I believe, much indebted to the authors of these theories for showing us a way to escape from the cramped quarters of trivialized empiricism without falling victim to highly speculative building with "empty boxes."

The arguments concerning the development of social stratification which form a core element in American interpretations of industrialism can be usefully stated under three main heads: differentiation, consistency and mobility.[6] To begin with, I would like to consider these three sets of arguments in turn.

Differentiation

In regard to differentiation, the major proposition that is put forward is that, in course of industrial advance, there is a decrease in the degree of differentiation in all stratification subsystems or orders. In other words, to follow Inkeles'

---

[6] The following exposition is derived chiefly from Kerr *et al.*, *op. cit.*; Inkeles, "Social Stratification in the Modernization of Russia," in Cyril E. Black, ed., *The Transformation of Russian Society* (Cambridge, Mass.: Harvard University Press, 1960); and Moore, *loc. cit.*, pp. 318–322, 353–359 especially. It is, however, important to note the very marked differences in tone and style between these contributions. Kerr and his colleagues are most dogmatic and "prophetic," but also the most diffuse in their arguments; Inkeles, on the other hand, is the most explicit yet is clearly writing, as he says, "not to settle a point but to open a discussion"; while Moore, aiming at the summing-up of a body of research data, puts forward by far the most cautious and qualified statements.

formulation: "a process of relative homogenization takes place, reducing the gap or range separating the top and bottom of the scale"—in income and wealth, in status formal and informal, and in political power.[7] As a result of this process, a marked increase occurs within each stratification order in the proportion of the total population falling into the middle ranges of the distribution. The "shape" of the stratification hierarchy thus ceases to be pyramidal and approximates, rather, to that of a pentagon or even of a diamond.

This trend is related to the "logic" of industrialism in several different ways. But, primarily, the connection is seen as being through the changing division of labor. An advancing technology and economy continually repattern the occupational structure, and in ways which progressively increase the number of higher level occupational rôles; that is to say, rôles requiring relatively high standards of education and training and at the same time commanding relatively high economic rewards and social status. Thus, the middle of the stratification hierarchy becomes considerably expanded.

So far as Western societies are concerned, a further factor in this homogenizing process is also recognized in the growing intervention of the state in economic affairs; particularly in governmental policies which lead to the redistribution and control of economic power. For example, it is observed that policies of progressive taxation and of social welfare in various ways modify for

---

[7] *Loc. cit.*, p. 341. Cf. Kerr *et al.*, pp. 286–294. Moore (p. 354), claims that during early industrialization "differences in social origin, education and power of managers and workers are likely to be widest" and the following paragraph appears to support the "relative homogenization" thesis. It is not clear, however, how far Moore is prepared to regard the trend towards reduced differentiation as one which has so far continued progressively with industrial advance.

the benefit of the less privileged the division of income and balance of social advantage which would have resulted from the free operation of market mechanisms. However, in this case great stress is placed on the close relationship that exists between this expansion in the regulatory functions of government and the direct requirements of the industrialization proescs. The state, it is argued, *must* be the key regulatory organization in any advanced society: the complexity of its technology and economy demand this. At minimum, the state must be responsible for the general rate of economic progress, and thus ultimately, for the overall allocation of resources between uses and individuals, for the quality of the national labour force, for the economic and social security of individuals and so on.[8]

In other words, even where greater social equality results directly from the purposive action of governments, the tendency is to see behind this action not a particular complex of socio-political beliefs, values or interests but rather the inherent compulsions of "industrialism" itself.[9] For example, on the subject of the development of education and its consequences, Kerr and his associates write as follows:

Education is intended to reduce the scarcity of skilled persons and this after a time reduces the wage and salary differentials they receive; it also pulls people out of the least skilled and most disagreeable occupations and raises wage levels there. *It conduces to a*

new equality which has nothing to do with ideology. . . .[10]

Furthermore, one should note, a similar viewpoint is taken in arguing that greater equality in political power —in the form of a pluralistic system— will tend to emerge in societies which now have totalitarian (or autocratic) regimes. In the first place, it is held, the production technology of an industrial society is such that any regime must become increasingly interested in the consent of the mass of the labour force; for the efficient use of this technology requires responsible initiative and freely given co-operation on the part of those who operate it. Secondly, the growing complexity of technical problems arising in the process of government itself necessitates the greater involvement in decision-making of experts and professionals, and in this way the latter come to acquire some independent authority. Thus, a monolithic structure gives way to one in which there are a number of "strategic" elites and of different foci of power. In brief, industrialism is regarded as being ultimately inimical to any form of monistic political order.[11]

Consistency

In this respect, the central argument is that as societies become increasingly

---

[8] Cf. Kerr *et al.*, pp. 31, 40–41, 273–274, 290–292; Moore, pp. 357–359.

[9] For a discussion of the strengths and weaknesses of attempts to apply this approach to the explanation of the development of social policy in 19th century England, see John H. Goldthorpe, 'Le développement de la politique sociale en Angleterre de 1800 à 1914," *Sociologie du Travail*, II (1963). (English version in *Transactions of the Vth World Congress of Sociology*, IV [1964].)

[10] *Op. cit.*, p. 286 (my italics). The theme of "the end of ideology"—in the West at least— runs strongly throughout *Industrialism and Industrial Man*. Moore, by contrast, is sufficiently detached and sophisticated to recognize "the ideology of a pluralistic society."

[11] Cf. Kerr *et al.*, pp. 274–276, 288–290; Inkeles, p. 346. As earlier noted, Moore diverges here. He notes (p. 359) the empirical probability of increased political participation as societies become industrial, but argues that so far there is no evidence of a *necessary* incompatibility between industrialism and totalitarianism.

industrial, there is a growing tendency within the stratification system towards what Inkeles terms "equilibration"; that is, a tendency for the relative position of an individual or group in any one stratification order to be the same as, or similar to, their position in other orders.[12] In traditional societies, it is observed, inconsistencies in the stratification system may have been contrary to the prevailing ideology but were nonetheless frequent because of the rigidity of the levels within the different subsystems and the relatively low degree of interaction between them. For example, a merchant might become extremely wealthy yet be debarred from "noble" status; in fact, legally, he could be of peasant status and might be treated as such in certain circumstances in spite of his wealth. In industrial societies, by contrast, there are far fewer difficulties in the way of "adjustments" which serve to bring the position of individuals and groups more or less into line from one stratification order to another. Moreover, there is also a shift away from the relative diversity of the bases of stratification which is characteristic of traditional society. With industrialism, the occupational structure takes on overwhelming primacy in this respect. The occupational rôle of the individual is in general in close correlation with most other of his attributes which are relevant to his position in the stratification hierarchy as a whole: his economic situation, his educational level, his prestige in the local community and so on.[13]

In the same way as the trend towards greater equality, the trend towards greater consistency in stratification systems is also treated as an integral part of the industrialization process and as being directly linked to technological and economic advance. In industrial society, it is argued, the distribution of both economic rewards and prestige must come into a close relationship with occupational performance since this type of society in fact presupposes an overriding emphasis upon achievement, as opposed to ascription, as the basis of social position—and specifically upon achievement in the sphere of production. At the same time, though, as a result of technological progress, occupational achievement becomes increasingly dependent upon education, and in this way closer ties are formed between economic standing on the one hand and life-styles and subculture on the other. The ignorant and vulgar tycoon and the poor scholar are seen alike as figures of declining importance. In other words, the argument is that inevitably in modern societies, the various determinants of an individual's placing in the overall stratification hierarchy come to form a tight nexus; and that in this nexus occupation can be regarded as the central element—providing as it does the main link between the "objective" and "subjective" aspects of social inequality.

Implicit, then, in this interpretation is the view that in industrial societies stratification systems tend to become relatively highly integrated, in the sense

---

[12] Inkeles' "equilibration" [following E. Benoit-Smullyan, "Status Types and Status Interrelations," *American Sociological Review*, IX (1944)] thus largely corresponds to what Lenski and Landecker have referred to as "crystallization" and Adams and Homans as "congruence." See Gerhard E. Lenski, "Status Crystallization: A Non-Vertical Dimension of Social Status," *American Sociological Review*, XIX (1954); Werner S. Landecker, "Class Crystallization and Class Consciousness," *American Sociological Review*, XXVIII (1963); Stuart Adams, "Social Climate and Productivity in Small Military Groups," *American Sociological Review*, XIX (1954); G. C. Homans, "Status Congruence" in *Sentiments and Activities* (New York: The Free Press, 1962). Moore refers simply to "consistency" or "coalescence."

[13] Cf. Kerr *et al.*, pp. 272–273, 284, 292–293; Inkeles, pp. 341–342; Moore, pp. 356–357.

that specifically class differences (i.e., those stemming from inequalities in the economic order) are generally paralleled by status differences (i.e., those based on inequalities in social evaluation); and, thus, that changes in the pattern of the former will automatically result in changes in the pattern of the latter. For example, Kerr and his associates see the growth of "middle incomes" as making for a "middle class society"; that is, a society in which middle class values are widely accepted, both among manual workers and elite groups, and in which the bulk of the population share in "middle class" status.[14]

Mobility

In regard to mobility, the central proposition that is made is one which complements the previous arguments concerning differentiation and consistency. It is that once societies have reached a certain level of industrialization, their overall rates of social mobility tend to become relatively high—higher that is, than is typical in pre-industrial or traditional societies. The increasing number of intermediate positions in the stratification hierarchy widens the opportunity for movement upward from the lower levels, while the emphasis upon occupational achievement rather than on the ascription of social positions means that intergenerationally the talented will tend to rise at the expense of those whose talent is unequal to their birth. In this respect, the educational system is seen as the crucial allocative mechanism, sieving ability and matching capacity to the demands and responsibilities of occupational rôles.[15]

In other words, then, industrial society is regarded as being essentially "open" and "meritocratic". And once more, one should note, the interpretation derives from a conception of the structural and functional imperatives of this type of social order. The high level of mobility is taken as an inevitable consequence of the technologically and economically determined division of labour and of the necessary pressure within a highly dynamic form of society for the increasingly efficient use of talent. To quote again from the authors of *Industrialism and Industrial Man*:

The industrial society is an open community encouraging occupational and geographic mobility and social mobility. In this sense industrialism *must* be flexible and competitive; it is against tradition and status based upon family, class, religion, race or caste.[16]

In this approach, thus, there is little room for consideration of institutional variations or of value differences between industrial societies which might be associated with *differing* patterns of mobility. It is taken that the overall similarities in this respect are, or at any rate are certainly becoming, the feature of major significance.

These, then, in a necessarily abbreviated form, are the main arguments concerning the development of stratification systems which figure, with varying degrees of refinement or crudity, in current American theories of industrialism. I would now like to turn to what I have to say by way of criticism of these

---

[14] *Op. cit.*, pp. 272–273, 286.

[15] Cf. Kerr *et al.*, pp. 35–37; Moore, pp. 319–321, 343–344. Inkeles does not include the factor of increased mobility as a separate element in his model of the "modernization" of stratification systems. It is, however, incorporated in his discussion of both decreasing differentiation and growing consistency, e.g., in modern societies, "Movement from one to another position on the scale . . . will not be sharply proscribed. Fluidity will characterize the [stratification] system as a whole. . . .' *Loc. cit.*, p. 341.

[16] P. 35 (my italics).

arguments and, to begin with, I would like to comment on each of the three themes on which I based the foregoing exposition. My main purpose here will be to indicate that the views which I have outlined are not always in entire accord with empirical data, and in this connection I shall refer primarily to the industrial societies of the West. Subsequently, however, I shall offer certain more basic, theoretical criticisms which are suggested by a consideration of social stratification in modern Communist society.

On the question of reduced differentiation—or greater equality—in stratification systems, my remarks at this stage will be largely confined to the economic order. This is because it is chiefly in this regard that we have data which will permit, at least in principle, some test of the arguments involved; that is, data on the distributions of income and wealth.[17]

At the outset it may be said that, although the evidence is often very patchy, a broad trend towards greater economic equality *does* seem to be discernible in the case of all those societies which have so far progressed from a traditional to an industrial form. Myths of "golden ages" of economic equality in pre-industrial times are now little heeded, and, as a rough generalization, it would, I think, be widely accepted that the poorer the society, the greater the "skew" one may expect in its distributions of income and wealth alike.[18] With this view I would

not wish to quarrel—provided that it is taken merely as a formula summing up historical experience, and as one which is subject to exceptions. But there are no grounds at all, in my view, for regarding the regularity in question as manifesting the operation of some process inherent in industrialism—of some general economic law—which will necessarily persist in the future and ensure a continuing egalitarian trend. Rather, the possibility must be left quite open that where such a trend exists, it may at some point be checked—and at a point, moreover, at which considerable economic *inequality* remains. In fact, in my assessment, the relevant data suggest that such a check may already be occurring in some of the more advanced societies of the West; or, at any rate, I would say that on present evidence *this* conclusion is indicated as much as any other.

For the distributions of income and wealth alike, it is true that figures exist to show a movement towards greater equality in most western industrial societies over the years for which adequate time-series are available; that is, from the late inter-war or early post-war period onwards.[19] However, it is now becoming increasingly clear that these figures, which are largely based on tax returns, are not always to be taken at

World Social Situation, 1952, pp. 132–134; and *Report on the World Social Situation*, 1961, pp. 58–61.

[19] See, e.g., United Nations, *Economic Survey of Europe in 1956* (1957), Chap. VII; R. M. Solow, "Income Inequality since the War" in Ralph E. Freeman, ed., *Postwar Economic Trends in the United States* (New York: Harper & Row, Publishers, 1960). Recent studies relating specifically to Great Britain are H. F. Lydall, "The Long-term Trend in the Size Distribution of Income," *Journal of the Royal Statistical Society*, Part I, CXXII (1959), and H. F. Lydall and D. C. Tipping, "The Distribution of Personal Wealth in Britain," *Oxford Institute Statistical Bulletin*, XXIII (1961).

[17] It should be acknowledged, however, that for the West, at least, there is clear evidence on one other important point; that is, on the reduction, indeed virtual elimination, of *formal* inequalities of status. This has been the concomitant of the growth of "citizenship" through which all members of national communities have been granted equal civil, political and social rights. Cf. T. H. Marshall, "Citizenship and Social Class" in *Sociology at the Crossroads* (1963).

[18] Cf. United Nations, *Preliminary Report on the*

their face value. And, in general, their defects appear to be such that they tend on balance to underestimate the income and wealth which accrue to the economically more favoured groups and in this and other ways to give a somewhat exaggerated idea of the degree of "levelling" that has taken place. In fact, for some western societies at least, there are now grounds for believing that during the last twenty years or so, overall economic inequality has in reality declined only very little, if at all. And particularly so far as wealth is concerned, it is likely that such changes as have occurred have been virtually negligible in their implications for social stratification.[20] Such conclusions have been suggested for the United Kingdom, for example, in Professor Titmuss' recent study, *Income Distribution and Social Change*. It must, of course, be admitted that the whole matter remains a highly controversial one,[21] and it is not possible here to enter into all its complexities. But what is, I think, justified by the evidence, and what is certainly most relevant to my general argument, is Titmuss' contention that "we should be much more hesitant in suggesting that any equalising forces at work in Britain since 1938 can be promoted to the status of a 'natural law' and projected into the future. . . . There are other forces, deeply rooted in the social structure and fed by many complex

institutional factors inherent in large-scale economies, operating in reverse directions."[22]

A similar point of view is maintained, with reference to the United States, in Gabriel Kolko's somewhat neglected book, *Wealth and Power in America*. This study involves not only a critique of previous findings on the distribution of income and wealth in the USA but also a positive reappraisal of the situation. This is particularly important in regard to income. Kolko supplements material from official sources with generally more reliable survey data, and on this basis suggests that over as long a period as 1910 to 1959 there has been no significant *general* trend in the USA towards greater income equality.[23]

Kolko's study prompts one to note the often overlooked point that simply because there may be some levelling of incomes going on in *certain ranges* of the total income distribution, this does not necessarily mean that *overall* equality is increasing; for in other ranges inegalitarian trends may simultaneously be operating. For example, there may be a tendency towards greater equality in that the number of middle-range incomes is growing; but at the same time the position of the lower income groups, relative to the upper and middle groups alike, may be worsening.

In fact, it seems more than possible

---

[20] Chiefly, this is because much levelling which appears to have gone on at the top of the distribution has in fact taken place simply *within* families—particularly between parents and children and generally as a means of avoiding taxation. E.g., Lydall and Tipping (*op. cit.*) note the "growing tendency for owners of large properties to distribute their assets amongst the members of their families well in advance of death" (p. 85). However, it is, of course, the family, not the individual, that must be regarded as the basic unit of stratification.

[21] See, e.g., the critical review of Titmuss' book by A. R. Prest, and Titmuss' reply, in *British Tax Review* (March–April, 1963).

[22] *Income Distribution and Social Change* (Toronto: University of Toronto Press, 1962), p. 198. In this connection it should also be remembered that certain major developments which have made for greater equality in incomes in the recent past are of a non-repeatable kind—notably, the ending of large scale unemployment and the considerable expansion in the number of working class wives in gainful employment.

[23] *Wealth and Power in America* (New York: Frederick A. Praeger, Inc., 1962), Chap. I. The data in question refer to pre-tax incomes, but Kolko is prepared to argue (Chap. 2) that "Taxation has not mitigated the fundamentally unequal distribution of income . . . ."

that a pattern of change of this kind is now going on in the United States. This is indicated by a good deal of recent investigation, apart from that of Kolko, and particularly by the growing volume of work on the extent of poverty. Gunnar Myrdal, for example, has argued in his book, *Challenge to Affluence*, that while many Americans in the intermediate social strata may well be benefiting from a levelling upwards of living standards, at the base of the stratification hierarchy there is increasing inequality, manifested in the emergence of an "underclass" of unemployed and unemployable persons and families. In other words, the middle ranks of the income distribution may be swelling, but the gap between the bottom and the higher levels is, if anything, tending to widen.[24]

Moreover, what is also significant in Myrdal's study for present purposes is the way in which he brings out the *political* aspects of the problem. Myrdal observes that structural unemployment, resulting from technological innovation in industry, is a basic, and increasingly serious, cause of poverty in America, whereas, in a country like Sweden, in which technological advance is also proceeding rapidly, full employment has been steadily maintained. Again, he notes the relative failure of the United States, compared with most western European countries, to stabilize aggregate demand in its economy on a high and rising level.[25] The explanation of these differences, Myrdal then argues, while not of course entirely political, must nonetheless be regarded as being significantly so. In particular, he stresses the inadequate achievement of government in America in long-range economic planning, in redistributional reforms, and in the provision of public services and advanced social welfare schemes. And the sources of this governmental inadequacy he traces back to certain basic American socio-political dispositions and also to a relative lack of "democratic balance" in the institutional infrastructure of the American policy. On the one hand, Myrdal claims, there is among the powerful business community and within government itself a reluctance to take the long view and to envisage more central direction and control of the economy; also "a serious and irrational bias against public investment and consumption." On the other hand, among the lower strata of American society there is an unusual degree of political apathy and passivity which is most clearly seen in the general failure of the poorer sections of the population to organize themselves effectively and to press for the fundamental social reforms that would be in their interest. In this way an imbalance in organized power is brought about within the "plural society" which makes the need for initiative on the part of government all the more pressing—at the same time as it seems to paralyse this.[26]

---

[24] *Challenge to Affluence* (New York: Pantheon Books, Inc., 1963), Chap. 3. The data assembled by the Conference on Economic Progress, *Poverty and Deprivation in the United States* (1962), suggest that there was real improvement in the income position of low-income groups during World War II but that since then the economy has not greatly enhanced the living standards of the low-income population. In regard to the distribution of wealth, Robert J. Lampmen, *The Share of Top Wealth-Holders in National Wealth* (Princeton, N.J.: National Bureau of Economic Research, Princeton University, 1962), has produced data to show that the share of personal sector wealth held by the wealthiest 1 per cent of adults in the USA has steadily increased from 1949 to 1956.

[25] *Op. cit.*, pp. 13–15, 27–30.

[26] *Ibid.*, Chaps. 4, 6, and 7. A basically similar view is presented in Michael Harrington, *The Other America* (New York: The Macmillan Company 1962). On the organizational, and thus political, weakness of the poor, see pp. 13–17; on the past failure and present responsibility of the Federal Government, pp. 163–170. Cf. also Stephen W. Rousseas and James Farganis, "American Politics and the End of Ideology," *British Journal of Sociology*, XIV, No. 4 (1963).

If, then, Myrdal's analysis has any general validity,—and it has yet, I think, to be seriously disputed—it follows that we should look somewhat doubtfully on arguments about a new equality which "has nothing to do with ideology" but which is the direct outcome of technological and economic advance. Such new equality there may be for some. But for those at the base of stratification hierarchies at least—how "equal" they are likely to become seems to have a good deal to do with ideology, or at any rate with purposive social action, or lack of this, stemming from specific social values and political creeds as well as from interests.[27] And differences between some industrial societies in these respects may well be giving rise to divergent, rather than convergent, patterns of change in their stratification systems.

On the second set of arguments— those concerning growing consistency between different stratification orders— I shall have relatively little to say for the good reason that there is little empirical data which directly bears on the crucial issue here; that is, the issue of whether there really is a *continuing* increase in the degree of integration of the stratification systems of *advanced* societies. About the long-term historical trend, one would not wish to argue; but again it is a question of whether such a trend is a reliable guide to the present and the future.

My main comment is that such evidence as does appear relevant to this issue indicates that in some industrial societies, at least, on-going economic progress is resulting in stratification systems becoming, if anything, somewhat *less* well integrated in certain respects. This evidence refers to what has become known as the "new working class." It suggests that the appreciable gains in income and in general living standards recently achieved by certain sections of the manual labour force have not for the most part been accompanied by changes in their life-styles of such a kind that their *status* position has been enhanced commensurately with their *economic* position. In other words, there is evidence of cultural and, in particular, of "social" barriers still widely existing between "working class" and "middle class" even in cases where immediate material differences have now disappeared.[28] Thus it seems that, contrary to the expectations of Kerr and his associates, "middle incomes" have not resulted, as yet at least, in the generalization of "middle class" ways of life or of "middle class" status.

Moreover, there are grounds for believing that notable discrepancies in stratification will persist in industrial societies. As Kerr himself recognizes, there will still exist in the foreseeable future in such societies a division between "managers" and "managed"— between those who are in some way as-

[27] Cf. Harrington's emphasis on the fact that "If there is to be a way out (of poverty) it will come from human action, from political change, not from automatic processes," (p. 162). Similarly, Raymond Aron has observed that the present problem of poverty in the USA is not that of the "pauperization" envisaged by Marx but that "Il n'en existe pas moins et il rappelle opportunément, à ceux qui seraient enclins à oublier, que la croissance économique ou les progrès techniques no sont pas des recettes miraculeuses de paix sociale ou de relations authentiquement humaines"; and further that ". . . ni la croissance économique livrée à elle-même, ni le progrès technique, emporté par son dynamisme, ne garantissent un ordre juste ni, moins encore, des conditions de vie conformes aux aspirations d'une humanité qui a transformé le monde plus qu'elle ne c'est transformée elle-même." *La Lutte des Classes* (1964), pp.15–16.

[28] See, e.g., for Great Britain, John H. Goldthorpe and David Lockwood, "Affluence and the British Class Structure," *Sociological Review*, XI, No. 2 (1963); for the USA, Bennet Berger, *Working Class Suburb: A Study of Auto Workers in Suburbia* (1960); for France, A. Andrieux and J. Lignon, *L'Ouvrier D'Aujourd'hui* (1960). In all these contributions a common emphasis is that on the growing *disparity* between the situation of the manual worker as *producer* and *consumer*.

sociated with the exercise of authority in productive and administrative organizations and those who are not. And this division, one would suggest, will remain associated with differences in prestige, as well as in power, while at the same time managers and managed overlap to some extent in terms of living standards. One would agree that in an economically advanced society a broad stratum of workers, performing skilled or, one would add, particularly arduous or irksome jobs, are likely to earn middle-range incomes. But there are no grounds for automatically assuming that they will thereby become socially accepted and assimilated into even the lower levels of what Renner has usefully termed the "service class."[29] After all, it must be recognized that groups which have some serious basis for claiming superior status generally take advantage of this. And further, it should be borne in mind that, increasingly, the members of this "service class" will be selected through their educational attainments rather than being recruited from the rank and file. Thus, if anything, they are likely to become more set apart from the latter in terms of culture and life-styles than they are at present.

In sum, one might suggest that the "increasing consistency" argument is flawed because it fails to take into account first, that occupational roles with similar economic rewards may in some instances be quite differently related to the exercise of authority; and secondly, that relatively high income may serve as recompense for work of otherwise high "disutility" to the operative as well as for work involving expertise and responsibility.

Lastly, then, we come to the matter of social mobility. In this case, the first question which arises is that of whether it is in fact valid to regard industrial societies as having regularly higher rates of mobility than pre-industrial societies. Several writers, one should note, have recently argued that this view should not be too readily taken and have produced evidence to suggest that certain pre-industrial societies were far less rigidly stratified than seems generally to have been supposed.[30] Nevertheless, I would not wish to argue here against the more orthodox view, except to make the point that an increased rate of *inter*generational mobility in advanced societies is likely to be associated with some limitation of *intra*generational or "career" mobility. To the extent that education becomes a key determinant of occupational achievement, the chances of "getting ahead" for those who start in a lowly position are inevitably diminished. This fact is most clearly demonstrated in recent studies of the recruitment of industrial managers. These show that as the educational standards of managers have risen, the likelihood of shop floor workers being promoted above supervisory level has been reduced.[31] Furthermore, in an advanced society, increasingly dominated by large scale organizations, the possibilities for the "little man" of starting up a successful business of his own also tend to be more limited than they were at an earlier phase in the industrialization process.

[29] Karl Renner, *Wandlungen der modernen Gesellschaft; zwei Abhandlungen uber die Probleme der Nachkriegzeit* (1953).

[30] See, e.g., for China, Robert M. Marsh, *The Mandarins: the Circulation of Elites in China, 1600–1900* (New York: The Free Press, 1961), and "Values, Demand and Social Mobility," *American Sociological Review*, XXVIII (1963), also, Ping-ti Ho, *The Ladder of Success in Imperial China: Aspects of Social Mobility, 1368–1911* (New York: Columbia University Press, 1963).

[31] For Great Britain, see Acton Society Trust, *Management Succession* (1965), and R. V. Clements, *Managers: A Study of Their Careers in Industry* (1958). For the USA, see W. Lloyd Warner and James C. Abegglen, *Occupational Mobility in American Business and Industry, 1928–1952* (Minneapolis: University of Minnesota Press, 1955).

Thus, for that large proportion of the population at least, with rank-and-file jobs and "ordinary" educational qualifications, industrial society appears to be growing significantly *less* "open" than it once was.

However, other, and perhaps more basic, issues arise from the arguments concerning mobility which I earlier outlined; in particular issues relating to the determinants of mobility patterns and rates. What are the grounds, one might ask, for believing that in advanced societies the crucial factor here is the occupational distribution, and thus that from one such society to another social mobility will tend to be much the same? Support for this view can be found in the well-known Lipset and Zetterberg study which led, in fact, to the conclusion that Western industrial societies have broadly similar rates of intergenerational mobility, and which produced no evidence to suggest that factors other than the "standardizing" one of the occupational structure were of major significance."[32] Their data, the authors claim, give no backing for the idea that differences in social ideologies, religious beliefs or other aspects of national cultures exercise a decisive influence on mobility. But it has to be noted that, as Lipset and Zetterberg themselves make quite clear, their findings in this respect refer only to "mass" mobility; that is, simply to movements across the manual-nonmanual line. And indeed they point out that the investigation of some aspects of "elite" mobility—for example, the recruitment of higher civil servants—has indicated some important national variations.[33]

Moreover, we have more recently the outstanding study of comparative social mobility made by Professor S. M. Miller.[34] This covers a still greater amount of data than Lipset and Zetterberg's work and demonstrates fairly conclusively that when *range* as well as frequency of mobility is taken into consideration, industrial societies do reveal quite sizeable differences in their mobility patterns. Such differences tend to be most evident in the case of long-range mobility. This is generally low—another reason for querying just how "open" and "meritocratic" industrial societies have so far become—but certain countries, the USA and USSR, for example, appear to have attained quite significantly higher rates of "elite" mobility than do others, such as many in western Europe. Further, though, Miller shows that countries with low long-range mobility may still have relatively high short-range mobility—as, for instance, does Great Britain; there is no correlation between rates of mobility of differing distance. Thus, industrial societies have quite various "mobility profiles"; the overall similarity indicated by the study of "mass" mobility turns out to be somewhat spurious.

On this basis, then, Miller is able to argue very strongly that patterns of social mobility in advanced societies cannot be understood *simply* in terms of occupational structure[35]—or, one would add, in terms of any "inherent" features of industrialism. Their diversity precludes this. It appears necessary, rather, to consider also the effects on mobility of other, and more variable, aspects of social structure—educational institutions, for example, and their articulation with the stratification hierarchy itself—and further, possibly, *pace* Lipset and Zetterberg, the part played by cultural

[32] See S. M. Lipset and Hans L. Zetterberg, "A Theory of Social Mobility," *Transactions of the Third World Congress of Sociology*, III, (1956), 155–177, and Chap. II, "Social Mobility in Industrial Society" in S. M. Lipset and R. Bendix, *Social Mobility in Industrial Society* (Berkeley, Calif.: University of California Press, 1959).
[33] *Ibid.*, pp. 38–42.

[34] S. M. Miller, "Comparative Social Mobility," *Current Sociology*, IX, No. 1 (1960).
[35] *Ibid.*, pp. 22–23, 57–58.

values.[36] As Miller points out, what is perhaps most surprising about his data is the _lack_ of convergence in mobility patterns that is indicated between societies at broadly comparable levels of economic development. The "logic" of industrialism, it appears, is often confused by "extraneous" factors.

These, then, are some of the objections that may be made on empirical grounds to the hypotheses concerning changes in stratification systems which I previously outlined. Accepting the arguments in question on their own terms, as it were, it is possible to indicate a number of points at which they do not appear to fit well with the findings of empirical research in western industrial societies or, at least, at which they remain unproven. However, in conclusion of this paper, I would like to make a more basic objection which relates to the theoretical position underlying these arguments. Specifically, I would like to question the idea that the stratification systems of all industrial societies are _ipso facto_ of the same generic type, and thus that they may in principle be expected to follow convergent or parallel lines of development. Against this view, I would like to suggest that social stratification in the advanced societies of the Communist world—or at any rate in the USSR and its closer satellites—is _not_ of the same generic type as in the West and that,

because of this, the hypotheses earlier discussed cannot in this case really apply.

Soviet society is, of course, stratified; and, furthermore, it is true that in spite of the absence of private property in production, it appears to be stratified on an often similar pattern to the capitalist or post-capitalist societies of the West. For example, to a large degree there is apparent similarity in the connections between occupational rôle, economic rewards and social prestige, in the part played by education in determining occupational level, in the operation of an informal status system, and so on. But, I would argue, this similarity is only of a phenotypical kind: genotypically, stratification in Soviet society is significantly different from stratification in the West.

Primarily, it may be said, this difference derives from the simple fact that in Soviet society the economy operates within a "monistic," or totalitarian, political order and is, in principle at least, totally planned, whereas in advanced Western societies political power is significantly less concentrated and the economy is planned in a far less centralized and detailed way. From this it results that in the West economic, and specifically market forces act as the crucial stratifying agency within society. They are, one could say, the major source of social inequality. And consequently, the _class_ situation of individuals and groups, understood in terms of their economic power and resources, tends to be the most important single determinant of their general life-chances. This is why we can usefully speak of Western industrial society as being "class" stratified. However, in the case of Soviet society, market forces cannot be held to play a comparable rôle in the stratification process. These forces operate, of course, and differences in economic power and resources between in-

---

[36] As an example of the kind of study which would seem particularly relevant and valuable, see Ralph H. Turner, "Modes of Social Ascent through Education: Sponsored and Contest Mobility," in A. H. Halsey, Jean Floud and C. Arnold Anderson, eds., _Education, Economy and Society_ (New York: The Free Press, 1961). This paper is concerned with the relation between differences in the American and English educational systems and differences in the prevailing norms in the two societies pertaining to upward mobility. More specifically, the aim is to investigate how the _accepted mode_ of upward mobility shapes the pattern of educational institutions.

dividuals and groups have, as in the West, far-reaching social and human consequences. But, one would argue, to a significantly greater extent than in the West, stratification in Soviet society is subjected to *political* regulation; market forces are not permitted to have the primacy or the degree of autonomy in this respect that they have even in a "managed" capitalist society. Undoubtedly, the functional requirements of the economy exert pressures upon the system of stratification, and these pressures may in some cases prove to be imperative. But the nature of the political order means that far more than with Western democracy, the pattern of social inequality can be shaped throught the purposive action of the ruling party, and still more so, of course, the "life-fates" of particular persons.[37]

For example, during the years of Stalin's rule, economic inequality in the USSR generally increased. Numerous writers have in fact commented upon the progressive abandonment over this period of the egalitarian aspects of Marxist-Leninist ideology and of post-revolutionary attempts to operate egalitarian economic and social policies.[38] From the early 1930's differential rewards in relation to skill, effort and responsibility were introduced into industry and administration, and thus from this point the range of wages and salaries tended to widen. Further, changes in the 1940's in the income tax and inheritance laws were conducive to greater inequalities in incomes and personal wealth alike. Then again, high ranking officials and other favoured persons appear to have received increasingly important nonmonetary rewards in the form of cars, apartments, villas, free holidays and so on. By the end of the war decade, these developments had led to a degree of inequality in Soviet society which, in the view of many commentators, was greater than that which was generally to be found in the industrial societies of the West.[39] However, in more recent years it has become clear that contrary to most expectations, this inegalitarian trend in the USSR has been checked and, moreover, that in certain respects at least it has even been reversed. Minimum wages in industry have been increased several times since the late 1950's and the incomes of the *kolkhozy* have for the most part risen quite considerably. This latter development has had the effect of closing somewhat the income gap between industrial and agricultural workers and has also been associated with a reduction in differentials in the earnings of the *kolkhoz* peasants themselves. At the same time, there is evidence of limitations being placed on the more excessive salaries of higher officials and of more stringent measures being taken against the abuse of privileges. Finally, tax changes in the past few years have tended to favour the poorer against the richer groups, and various kinds of welfare provision have been substantially improved. In these ways, then, economic differences between the manual and nonmanual categories overall have almost certainly been reduced to some extent, as well as differences within these categories.[40]

---

[37] Also relevant here, of course, is a further distinctive feature of a totalitarian political system—the absence of the "rule of law."

[38] Probably the best analysis in this respect is that provided by Barrington Moore, Jr., *Soviet Politics—The Dilemma of Power* (New York: Harper & Row, Publishers, 1950).

[39] See, e.g., Alex Inkeles, "Social Stratification and Mobility in the Soviet Union: 1940–1950," *American Sociological Review*, XV (1950). This paper contains an excellent factual account of the ways through which both economic and status inequality was increased during the Stalin era.

[40] For a general discussion of these changes, see Robert A. Feldmesser, "Towards the Classless Society?" in *Problems of Communism*, United States Information Agency, 9 (1960), pp. 31–

Now these changes can, of course, be rightly regarded as being in some degree economically conditioned. Clearly, for instance, the increased differentiation in wages and salaries in the Stalin era must in part be understood in terms of the exigencies and consequences of rapid industrialization. But, I would argue, there can be little question that at the same time these changes were the outcome of political decisions—of choices made between realistic alternatives—and, furthermore, that frequently they were brought about with political as well as with specifically economic ends in view. Stalin, it is true, wanted rapid industrialization; but he had the further political objective that this process should be carried through under his own absolute control. Thus, this entailed not only depriving a large section of the population of material returns from their labour in order to achieve maximum expansion of industrial capacity, but also the building-up of a group of exceptionally favoured administrators and managers who would be highly motivated to retain their enviable positions through loyalty to Stalin and through high level performance. To this latter end, in fact, appropriate status as well as economic inequalities were also developed. For example, during and after the war years, formal titles, uniforms and insignia of rank were introduced into various branches of industry and the governmental bureaucracy. Moreover, the wide social distance which was in this way created between the top and bottom of the stratification hierarchy had the manifest function of insulating the "élite" from the masses and from their needs and wishes. And thus, as Professor Feldmesser has pointed out, those in high positions were helped to learn "that

success was to be had by winning the favour not of those below them but of those above them, which was exactly what Stalin wanted them to learn."[41]

Similarly, the more recent moves towards reducing inequalities have again fairly evident political aims, even though, in some cases, they may also have been economically required.[42] On the one hand, it seems clear that the present Soviet leadership is working towards a future Communist society which will be characterized by a high level of social welfare, and indeed eventually by private affluence, while still remaining under the undisputed dominance of the Party. In other words, the creation of the "good life" for all appears destined to become one of the régime's most important sources of legitimacy. In fact, as Professor Shapiro has noted, the 1961 Programme of the CPSU makes this more or less explicit. The Programme, he writes,

enunciates squarely the concrete fact that party rule has come to stay. It calls upon the Soviet citizen to recognize and accept this fact, and to abandon the illusion that in this respect, things are going to change. In return, it promises him great material benefits and prosperity.[43]

---

[41] *Op. cit.*, p. 579. This political subordination of members of the "élite," concomitant with their economic and status elevation, is the reason for using inverted commas. As Feldmesser notes, the "élite" created by Stalin is surely distinctive by virtue of its general lack of autonomy.

[42] As, e.g., in the case of the increase in peasant incomes which was essential if genuine incentives to improve production were to be offered in agriculture. Cf. Seweryn Bialer, "But Some are More Equal than Others," *Problems of Communism*, IX, No. 2 (1960).

[43] Leonard Shapiro, "From Utopia towards Realism" in Shapiro ed., *The USSR and the Future: An Analysis of the New Program of the CPSU* (1963). See also Erik Boettcher, "Soviet Social Policy in Theory and Practice," in Paul Halmos, ed., *The Development of Industrial Society, The Sociological Review Monograph*, VIII (1964). The text

---

39. Cf. also Alec Nove, "Is the Soviet Union a Welfare State?" in Alex Inkeles and Kent Geiger, eds., *Soviet Society* (Boston: Houghton Mifflin Company, 1961).

On the other hand, the security of the régime also requires that the bureaucratic and managerial "élite" does not become so well established as to gain some measure of independence from the Party chiefs. Thus, Krushchev has been concerned to show the members of this group that they remain the creatures of the Party and that their privileges are not permanent but still rest upon their obedience and service to the Party. Those whom Djilas has referred to as the "new class" in Communist society[44] cannot in fact be allowed by the Party leadership to become a class—in the sense of a collectivity which is capable of maintaining its position in society (and that of its children) through its own social power, and which possesses some degree of group consciousness and cohesion. For the emergence of such a class would constitute a serious threat to the Party's totalitarian rule, different only in degree from the threat that would be posed by the emergence of an independent trade union, professional body or political organization. It is awareness of this danger, one would suggest, which chiefly lies behind the recent attacks—verbal as well as material—which have been made upon higher officialdom and the top industrial personnel. For apart from the curtailment of economic rewards in some cases, it is interesting to note that the quasi-military status distinctions of the war decade have now been largely abolished and that the Party has actually encouraged rank and file employees in industry and agriculture to expose inadequacy and inefficiency on the part of their superiors.[45] Furthermore, there has been some weeding out of superfluous posts, and demo-

tions appear to have become much more common.[46] Finally, though, it is probably Krushchev's educational reforms which have been of greatest significance. These were carried through at a time when pressure on the institutions of secondary and higher education was reaching a peak; yet they were designed to make access to these institutions less dependent than previously upon economic resources and the new rules for competitive entry which were introduced seem, if anything, to shift the balance of "social" advantage away from the children of the "élite" and towards candidates from worker or peasant families. As Feldmesser notes, if a "new class"—a "state bourgeoisie"—were in fact in existence in the USSR, then exactly the reverse of this might have been expected; that is, a move to make access to these scarce facilities *more*, rather than less, dependent upon the ability to pay.[47]

It is then not too much to say that in Soviet society hierarchical differentiation is an instrument of the régime. To a significant degree stratification is *organized* in order to suit the political needs of the régime; and, as these needs change, so too may the particular structure of inequality. In other words, the Soviet system of stratification is characterized by an important element of "deliberateness," and it is this which basically distinguishes it from the Western system, in spite of the many apparent similarities. In the industrial societies of the West, one could say, the action of the state sets limits to the extent of social inequalities which derive basically from the operation of a market economy: in Soviet society the pattern of inequality also results in part from "market" forces, but in this case these are subordinated to political control up to the limits set by the requirements of

---

of the Programme itself is printed as an Appendix; note, in particular, Part Two, Sections II, III, V and VII.

[44] Milovan Djilas, *The New Class*, 1957.

[45] Feldmesser, *op. cit.*, pp. 573–575.

[46] Bialer, *op. cit.*, pp. 576–578.

[47] *Op. cit.*, pp. 576–578.

the industrial system.[48] For this reason, one may conclude, Soviet society is not, in the same way as Western society, *class* stratified. As Raymond Aron has observed, class stratification and a monistic political system are to be regarded as incompatibles.[49]

Conclusion

If, then, the foregoing analysis is accepted, it follows that the arguments I earlier outlined on the development of stratification systems can have no general validity. Their underlying rationale, in terms of the exigencies of an advanced industrial technology and economy, is destroyed. The experience of Soviet society can be taken as indicating that the structural and functional imperatives of an industrial order are not so stringent as to prevent quite wide variations in patterns of social stratification, nor to prohibit the systematic manipulation of social inequalities by a régime commanding modern administrative resources and under no constraints from an organized opposition or the rule of law.

The crucial point, in fact, at which the rationale breaks down is in the supposition that industrialism and totalitarianism cannot "in the long run" co-exist; that is, in the idea that with industrial advance a progressive diffusion of political power must of necessity occur. Were this idea valid, then it would become difficult to maintain the claim that differences between the stratification systems of the Western and Communist worlds are of a generic kind. However, it may be said that no serious grounds exist for believing that within Soviet society any such diffusion of power is taking place, or, at least, not so far as the key decision-making processes are concerned.[50] The régime may be compelled to give more consideration to the effect of its decisions on popular morale and to rely increasingly on the expertise of scientists, technicians and professionals of various kinds; it may also find it desirable to decentralize administration and to encourage a high degree of participation in the conduct of public affairs at a local level. But the important point is that all these things can be done, and in recent years *have* been done, without the Party leadership in any way yielding up its position of ultimate authority and control. Indeed, it is far more arguable that since the end of the period of "collective" rule, the power of the Party leadership

---

[48] This assessment is consistent with the more general interpretations of the Soviet social system advanced by writers such as Brzezinski and Daniel Bell, in some opposition to the interpretation of Inkeles and his associates. "The important thing is that those in charge of Soviet society have assumed that economic and social development in all its aspects can be purposefully steered by man in the direction of an ideal solution. This produces consequences that are not only economic but also political, quite different from those induced by other equally technologically advanced economic systems where, to a large extent, economic life is self-directive and ultimate goals, such as plenty and progress, are purposely vague." Zbigniew K. Brzezinski, *Ideology and Power in Soviet Politics* (New York: Frederick A. Praeger, Inc., 1962), p. 31. "The Harvard group . . . shrinks from seeking to specify the motor forces in the social system as they have conceived it. . . . Is it not quite clear, really, that the Soviet system is characterized, essentially, by the centralized control of political power, that it is a *command* system, with few institutional checks. . . . In a society like Russia, where institutional and behaviour patterns are not autonomous, a 'social system' has no meaning unless it can be defined within the context of politics." Daniel Bell, "Ten Theories in Search of Reality: the Prediction of Soviet Behaviour" in *The End of Ideology* (New York: The Free Press, 1961), pp. 340–341.

[49] See his "Social Structure and the Ruling Class," *British Journal of Sociology*, I, (1950).

[50] For recent discussion of the issue of the compatibility of industrialism and totalitarianism from both empirical and theoretical points of view, see Brzezinski, *op. cit.*, Chaps. I and III, and R. Aron, ed., *World Technology and Human Destiny* (1963).

has become still more absolute and unrivalled. This situation, one would suggest, has been brought about as a result of Krushchev's success in reducing the power and independence, relative to the Party machine, of the other major bureaucratic structures within Soviet society—those of the political police, of the military and of government and industry. In some cases, it might be noted, the changes involved here can be seen as aspects of "destalinization"—for example, the mitigation of the terror or the dissolution of a large part of the central state apparatus. Yet at the same time these changes have had the effect of accentuating still further the totalitarian nature of Party rule. As Bialer points out:

The party bureaucracy is at present the only remaining apparatus which is centralized in its organization, which operates at all levels of the society, and which "specializes" in every sphere of societal activity. In its functions of communicating, controlling and to an ever greater degree directly organizing the tasks set forth by the leadership, it influences the operation of the other bureaucratic apparatuses, but is not in turn subject to any outside interference. It is subordinate only to the top leadership and to its own hierarchical line of authority.[51]

It is, I think, significant that Inkeles himself sees the weakest spot in the entire thesis of "declining differentiation" as being in the application of this to the "realm of power" within Communist society. He acknowledges the distinct possibility that here his model of stratification change may have to be revised and the prediction of increased homogenization restricted to realms other than that of power.[52] Moreover, Inkeles has elsewhere stated quite explicitly that

. . . there is no necessary, or even compelling, force in the modern industrial social order which clearly makes it incompatible with totalitarianism.

and again that

. . . the modern industrial order appears to be compatible with either democratic or totalitarian political and social forms.[53]

What one would wish to stress, then, is that if such views as these are sound (as I believe they are), it becomes difficult to see how one can formulate any general and comprehensive propositions concerning stratification change as part of a "logic" of industrial development. For the essential assumption involved in such propositions—that of some necessary "primacy" of the economic system over the political—is no longer a reliable one. It has to be recognized, rather, that stratification systems are not to be understood as mere "reflections" of a certain level of technology and industrial organization but are shaped by a range of other factors, important among which may be that of purposive political action; and further, that the importance of this latter factor in societies in which political power is highly concentrated is such as to create a distinctive type of stratification which is difficult even to discuss in terms of concepts developed in a Western, capitalist context.[54]

---

[51] *Op. cit.*, pp. 48–49. In addition to Bialer's paper, see also on the strengthening of Party rule under Krushchev, Brzezinski, *op. cit.*, Chap. III, and Edward Crankshaw, *Krushchev's Russia*, 1957, pp. 69, 76–79. Crankshaw shows how this process is in no way inconsistent with the widening of opportunities for popular participation in administrative work at a local level via the "public organizations." See pp. 94–98.

[52] "Social Stratification in the Modernization of Russia," *loc. cit.*, pp. 345–347.

[53] Inkeles and Bauer, *op. cit.*, p. 390.

[54] As Feldmesser has indicated, the argument that Soviet society is not "class" stratified in the

To end with, it might be observed that the arguments pursued in the latter part of this paper have negative implications not only for the model of stratification change with which I have been specifically concerned, but also for the kind of general theory of industrialism with which this model may be associated. The rejection of the particular hypotheses on stratification on the grounds that have been suggested obviously entails a rejection too of the idea of the convergent development of advanced societies focussed on "pluralistic industrialism," and equally of the key notion of a rigorous "logic" of industrialism which is the engine of such development.

At least as expressed in the somewhat brash manner of Kerr and his colleagues, these ideas would seem to amount to little more than what might be called an evolutionary para-Marxism; and, as such, one would say, they share certain major flaws with the developmental theories of Marx and of the social evolutionists alike. In the first place, there is the exaggeration of the degree of determinism which is exercised upon social structures by "material" exigencies, and, concomitantly with this, underestimation of the extent to which a social order may be shaped through purposive action within the limits of such exigencies. Secondly, and relatedly, there is the further underestimation of the diversity of values and ideologies which may underlie purposive action; and thus, from these two things together, there results the tendency to envisage a future in which the complex patterns of past development will become increasingly orderly and aligned—the tendency, in fact, to think in terms of "*the* road ahead" rather than in terms of a variety of roads.[55] And then finally, and perhaps most culpably, there is the ethnocentric bias: that failure of the imagination which leads the sociologist to accept his own form of society, or rather some idealized version of this, as the goal towards which all humanity is moving.

---

manner of Western industrial societies can also be supported from the "subjective" point of view. See his paper, "Social Classes and the Political Structure" in Black, ed., *op. cit.*, pp. 235–252. The available evidence suggests that Soviet citizens exhibit a relatively low level of class consciousness in the sense that their class situation is not of fundamental importance in patterning their dominant modes of thought and action. Members of different social strata in Soviet society seem more alike in their social ideologies and attitudes than their counterparts in the West, while the feature of the social structure which is most strongly reflected in their social consciousness at all levels is that of the division between "Party people" and "non-Party people." On this latter point see Inkeles and Bauer, *op. cit.*, Chap. XIII.

[55] More radically, it may be objected that, if a long-run view is to be taken, the very concept of "industrial society" will eventually cease to be useful. As the Spanish social scientist, Luis Diez del Corral, has pointed out, the concept remains of some significance while societies exist in which highest priority is assigned to industrial and economic values generally. During this phase, "this secularization and concentration of values helps explain the lessening of ideological conflicts . . . " But, Del Corral goes on, "This *élan* will only be temporary, and this standardization, this secularization of values which results in economic growth will one day enable all values to flower, all constraints to be forgotten, unless it ends in the apocalyptic destruction of mankind. These two possibilities underline both the grandeur and the misery of our destiny." See R. Aron, ed., *op. cit.*, p. 68.

Social Stratification in a "Classless" Society

Kibutz

EVA ROSENFELD

American sociologists are notoriously unhappy with the state of empirical research in social stratification. Yet, although numerous critical articles have been written, particularly taking to task the most prolific group of modern students of stratification—the Warner school—little, if any, cumulative effect can be detected, in spite of the great overlap in the points of attack. In the impasse which we seem to have reached, with some happily following beaten paths which others bitterly denounce, it seems to the author that a study of social stratification in social systems different from ours while yet belonging to the broad heritage of Western culture, may prove to be more provocative and contribute more to a clarification of some confused issues than another in the long series of theoretical articles.[1]

The social system in question, the collective settlements in Israel, seems to be particularly rewarding in sociological implications, whatever aspect of it might be studied; this is due mainly to its clear-cut cultural structure and to the fact that the collective settlements grew and developed for many years in a social environment which was not unfriendly and not dominant; the institutional dynamics of the collective society are thus, to a large extent, indigenous.

The presentation, which will follow, of social stratification in these collectives will, it is hoped, throw a new light on some of the old problems, and particularly on three moot questions raised by the critics of present-day research on stratification:

1. The disregard of the question of structural-functional reasons for differential prestige rank associated with various social roles, and of the selective process whereby some individuals get into the high rank positions. The forty-year-old history of the Israeli collectives reveals the process whereby social strata emerge out of an initially undifferentiated group of young adults living in an equalitarian and democratic system and bent on preventing the crystallization of fixed social strata. The fact that such strata *did* emerge, makes it imperative to raise the question of the functional importance of some social roles and the question of scarcity of personnel.[2]

Eva Rosenfeld, "Social Stratification in a 'Classless' Society," Reprinted from *American Sociological Review*, XVI, No. 6 (December, 1951), 766–774, by permission of the author and the American Sociological Association.

Revised version of a paper read at the annual meeting of the Eastern Sociological Society held in New Haven, March 31–April 1, 1951. The analysis of social stratification in the agricultural collectives in Israel is a part of a larger study carried out with the help of a research grant from the Social Science Research Council (1947–1950), aimed at discovering the dynamics of institutional changes in these planned communities.

---

[1] Form expressed a similar hope when, deploring the "failure to distinguish conceptually and empirically the types of stratification," he suggested that "One technique for (overcoming) this is to study settlements that obviously differ from the average in amount and type of stratification." William H. Form, "Status Stratification in a Planned Community," *American Sociological Review*, X (October, 1945), 605.

---

[2] For an admirably concise and clear theoretical analysis of these questions, see Kingsley Davis and Wilbert E. Moore, "Some Principles of Stratification," *American Sociological Review*, X (April 1945), 242–249. The findings presented in this paper support some of their generalizations, mainly that the universality of social stratification seems to be related to differential functional importance of social positions and to differential scarcity of personnel. On the other hand, as will appear below, our findings question their proposition that all types of rewards must be differentially dispensed in favor of high rank strata and their assumption that high prestige is always directly derived from high rank positions.

2. Conceptual confusion in the use of the terms "class" (economic rank), "status" (prestige and honor rank) and "power" or "influence."[3] The Israeli collectives fall into the category of "classless" societies (together with the societies of Hutterites, Amanites, the 19th-century Oneida and others). The social stratification which emerged is, therefore, free from the "confusing" economic factor.

3. The seeming bias against raising the question of conflicting interests of the various strata. In the Israeli collectives there are, as we shall see, no economic classes and, consequently, there is no "class struggle." Yet, the various strata that emerged have different vested interests with respect to institutional change, and the roles they play in the actual process of change reveal this conflict of interests. Thus the question of the functional relation between social stratification and social change is forced into the open with great clarity.

Before proceeding to the analysis of social stratification in the Israeli collectives, some general information is in order. The first collective (or "kibutz") was established in 1910. At present, over thirty thousand adult members and another thirty thousand children, old parents and transient groups live in more than two hundred collective agricultural settlements; this comprises about 6 per cent of the settled Jewish population in Israel and over one-third of its settled rural population. The collectives average about 200 members or about 500 souls; there are several large ones with more than 1,500 population. With the exception of a dozen or so religious collectives, all the rest belong to either one of the three large federations of collectives and through them to the socialist and anti-clerical General Federation of Trade Unions (the Histadrut).

With one exception, all collectives are based on farming but, increasingly, industrial branches are being developed. All property, not only the means of production, belongs to the commune, and members who leave have no claim on any part of it. There is no exchange market nor labor market within the collectives, although there is business as usual with the outside world. Members are assigned to work by an elected Work Committee. All administrative officers and branch managers are elected—by the General Meeting or by the workers in the given branch, respectively—for a period of one to two years and, although their nomination may be extended several times, there is a principle of turnover in managerial positions and of rotation of disliked tasks. The manager of the communal factory may be—and is—assigned to kitchen duty in slack season or on holidays.

Furthermore, the members' position in the administrative hierarchy is not related to their life chances for material gratifications: the basic norm is "from everyone according to ability—to everyone according to need." In principle, and in practice as well, it may happen that the manager of an important branch of the collective enterprise lives in a smaller room, has more primitive furniture, worse clothes, and eats less well than some of the unskilled workers who happen to be sickly and need special food and housing. All commodities are distributed centrally and in kind; food is eaten in the communal dining hall. Children are brought up, from birth, in communal children's homes.

Political institutions are democratic and equalitarian. All decisions of general interest are taken by a simple majority vote in the General Meeting, every member having one vote. Minor decisions are made by the Management Committee and other special committees

---

[3] See especially the survey article by Llewellyn Gross, "The Use of Class Concepts in Sociological Research," *American Journal of Sociology*, LIV (March, 1949), 409–421.

elected by all members for one-year terms.

Thus, the social structure of the kibutz prevents the emergence of economic differentiation. Yet, differential social status exists in the kibutz society. Members with high and low status regard each other with a set of stereotype attitudes, and in their relations the awareness of being a distinct social type is clearly expressed. The high and low strata play distinct roles in the process of institutional change and the difference in their Weltanschauungs is well known.

Several questions demand answering:

1. How did the distinct strata emerge out of the equalitarian group of early settlers?
2. What are the criteria for locating members in one of the strata?
3. What are the characteristics of each stratum?
4. What are the relations between them and their attitudes to each other?
5. What special roles do they play in the process of institutional change?
6. What self-perpetuating processes can be observed?

To simplify matters, the following analysis is limited to first-generation full members; transient and marginal groups are excluded; the special problems of the position of the woman in the collective will also be omitted.

As to methodology, the uniformities reported in this paper were first discovered through participant observation in three of the oldest collectives over a period of a year and a half. These uniformities were subsequently checked by (1) short visits to a selected group of the oldest communes, with a systematic observation and interview guide; (2) intensive interviews with the leaders of the two important factions in the current struggle for institutional change: the "conservatives" and the "innovators" and (3) participation in nationwide meetings of the collective movement,

called to discuss the pressure for change in the institutional structure.

The Emergence of Social Strata

Managerial positions of vital importance to the group are quite naturally[4] entrusted to those members whom the group deems most capable and trustworthy. Yet, the association of a high status rank with managerial positions was not a simple process. Neither could it be said of the kibutz society that "the question of . . . why different positions carry different degrees of prestige . . . is logically prior and, in the case of any particular individual or group, factually prior . . . (to the question of) how certain individuals get into these positions."[5] In fact, it would seem that in the Israeli collectives this order of priority was reversed: managerial positions gained high prestige because of the initially high prestige of the persons who became elected to fill them.

Two structural characteristics of the kibutz society must be kept in mind: the glorification of manual "productive" work and the fierce insistence on complete equality, which made all authority unacceptable. The glorification of manual labor grew out of the general scarcity of workers and farmers among the immigrant Jews and their strategic importance in the task of building the nation anew in the deserted land. Since there was a surplus of intellectuals and whitecollar workers among the Jews, the "clean" and "brainy" type of work

---

[4] "Nothing surprised me more in my investigations of the communistic societies than to discover . . . the ease and certainty with which brains come to the top . . ." concluded a 19th-century observer of communistic societies in this country [Charles Nordhoff, *The Communistic Societies of the United States* (New York: Harper & Row, Publishers, 1875), p. 392].

[5] See Davis and Moore, *op. cit.*, p. 242.

was looked down at and the manual worker became the hero of the day. Such attitudes, particularly strong in the early years of settlement, imbued managerial tasks with deep ambiguity. On the one hand the group itself insisted on a turnover in all managerial and administrative positions—even though efficiency might suffer. On the other hand, the members elected to managerial positions felt impelled to insist on going back to "real work" after the end of their first term—even though they might have enjoyed their task. But in this secular society the pressure of the need for efficiency in time won over the cultural considerations.

In a new settlement there is much movement from bottom to top: new branches are being opened, skill and initiative are at a premium and the small group quickly recognizes ability and good judgment. While, at the outset, there is usually only one skilled worker in every branch and he is naturally put in charge of the less skilled, years of work and experience often produce several self-taught capable workers in every branch. Then a system of turnover of managers may be adopted for some years. But again, as years pass, one worker usually becomes recognized as the best among the good workers and the tendency then is to re-elect him as manager for many years. Such men are usually successful in several fields. The collectives, as any pioneering society, suffer from a lack rather than abundance of men and women with talent, initiative and integrity; their scarcity puts them at a premium and gains them general recognition and high esteem. Thus there emerges a group of members whose personal status is so high that their re-election to important managerial positions is a matter of course, the benefit to the group in making best use of them being obvious to all. In the early years of settlement in Palestine, the formalities were observed more than

now: managers would insist upon returning to "real, productive work" after a term in the office; but these periods of "productive work" grew shorter and shorter and the principle of turnover nowadays means, in reality, turnover within a given range of managerial positions. Simultaneously, the exigencies of managing a big enterprise and the scarcity of good managers made for a general shift in valuation from manual to "brainy" work.

In time, these correlates of personal attribute—managerial positions—became fixed in the popular mind and are used, instead of the original criterion of status, to denote the high standing of these members in the community. This substitution of status criteria became complete with the arrival of newcomers to the kibutz, who are faced with the existence of an already stable group of highly respected leaders-managers whose personal background and attributes are hidden by time and social distance. However, within the core of oldtimers, personal attributes remain the true criterion of the esteem they bestow.

As the community grows older and the original group of pioneers becomes ever smaller in the influx of newcomers, seniority also becomes a source of prestige. The oldtimers ("vatikim") are the aristocracy of the kibutz. They are accorded a certain amount of esteem for the attribute of seniority alone. One might call this "the charisma of the pioneering personality." And since, in most cases, the leaders, managers and "responsible workers" are recruited from among the oldtimers (newcomers are not as generously appraised as the oldtimers and they are not given as much opportunity for showing their best abilities) the attribute of seniority comes to denote not only a personal distinction of idealism and pioneering spirit, but also the correlate: the managerial position; and the managerial positions gain in prestige through the charisma of the oldtimers who hold them.

Locating Members in One of the Social Strata

The objective attributes of status are used explicitly whenever a kibutz member is asked to describe or give information about some other member. The highest rank attribute is mentioned first; other, additional and qualifying attributes may then follow.

The highest rank is associated with a designation of "an important personality" (Yish hashoov) which, on closer questioning, reveals one of the top leaders in the kibutz movement or a person highly skilled and specializing in some activity of general importance in the kibutz movement. A qualification: "an important personality in his kibutz" means a local leader or branch manager who is credited for contributing to the success of the communal enterprise or to the high morale of the community. All "important personalities" are oldtimers and no mention of seniority is made, unless the member is one of the very first pioneers, the father of the kibutz movement. The "important personalities" are the living myths of the collective ideology—they exemplify the devotion, the faith, the accomplishment which show that the system really "works."

Second in rank is, simply, "one of the first members" (ahad mihavatikim); this attribute is then followed by a designation of the special work the oldtimer is doing. In many cases, the oldtimers have a managerial position in one of the branches of the farm or specialize in some administrative tasks. If the work position is not managerial, the special branch in which the oldtimer works as a steady and "responsible" worker is stressed: "He is one of the *chief* field workers," or "She is one of the *oldest* workers in the poultry yard"

or, "She is the *head* nurse of infants."

If a member is not an oldtimer and yet not a recent arrival, the length of his stay in the community is not mentioned, only his position at work. Here, again, we find members in managerial and administrative positions who have successfully merged with the oldtimers; members who are simply "good, reliable workers" in a specific branch; and members who simply "work" in a given branch.

"Just an unskilled, moveable worker" (stam pkak) is the lowest designation. In this category one finds newcomers who are still unknown in the community and those of the older members who are not considered responsible or who are sickly, lazy, unpleasant to work with and shunned by all work groups—and who are, therefore, assigned every day to various menial jobs in whatever branch the need may be—usually the vegetable garden, orchards, services and factory (if there is any)

The concept of rank is thus based on objectively defined attributes of seniority and managerial position in work or administration. The informal leaders of the kibutz movement and within the collectives are always members who belong to this upper stratum of oldtimers-managers. The rank and file (amho) are composed of the middle stratum of "responsible workers" (both oldtimers and middlecomers) and of the lowest stratum of "pkaks."

Within the rank and file, the ratio of steady to moveable workers varies greatly from one community to another and, within every collective, over the span of time. But the significant distinction in terms of differential life attitudes, opinions and social role played in the process of change, obtains between the upper, managerial stratum on the one hand, and the whole rank and file on the other. The numerical ratio of the lower to the middle substrata affects the relations between the upper stratum and the rank and file (see section on relations between the two strata).

The Characteristics of the Two Social Strata

Two special life conditions characterize the upper stratum of leaders-managers; one is the immunity from frustrating and humiliating experiences in dealing with central distributive and administrative kibutz institutions, and the second is the greater life chance for emotional gratifications derived from the special, ego-expanding experiences associated with their position of seniority, responsibility and leadership. These two special life conditions revolve around important areas of communal life.

One of the serious problems in collective life is the dependency of the individual, in the satisfaction of his material needs, upon the elected officers who are supposed to distribute commodities centrally, in kind and according to a general (and rather vaguely defined) concept of "need." For several reasons (into which it would be impossible to enter here) the relations between kibutz members and their distributive officers very often place the members in humiliating and frustrating situations. The kibutz "aristocracy" is spontaneously treated with more respect and deference and, therefore, very unlikely to encounter these humiliating situations. Furthermore, a sense of one's importance in the affairs of the community, and the feeling of security it generates, make their behavior in dealing with the distributive officers more poised and self-confident and this, in turn, affects the attitude of the officers so that it is very unlikely that they will release against the upper stratum members whatever irritation or hostility they may feel.

Another serious problem in the kibutz is generated by the fact that the individual does not see directly the results of his work-effort. His energy is pooled, together with that of others, in the communal enterprise and the fruits of his labor are pooled with those of the others; so is the recognition. The sense of personal creation and an opportunity to realize one's sense of workmanship as well as the claim to the group's recognition for one's efforts, all these are lost to most members among the rank and file. Seemingly, in the kibutz, this loss is serious; especially, is the recognition by the group important to the individual.

A woman working in the kibutz dairy complained to me one day that her supervisor snapped at her "What did you do today, anyway?" and she felt very hurt and upset. I asked her, why should such a thing bother her; after all, she is an experienced, responsible worker and if her conscience is at rest, she should not mind the supervisor's remarks. She answered: "Outside, you get your money for your work and that is the main thing and the work relation ends there. Here you get no reward at all. Look at me, after 13 years of hard work in the dairy, what have I got? But we work, because we know that is the right thing to do. The only thing we want is 'iahas'—recognition."

The managers of the branches, who identify themselves with the branch and direct its policy, see the harvest as the product of their own labor. The administrative officers and the oldtimers in general, who direct the policy of the whole community, see the communal enterprise as a whole, can grasp it as a whole and identify with it; they watch the growth and development of the farm and village with pride and interest and receive therefrom emotional gratifications. Since seniority is so highly correlated with managerial and leadership positions, many members of the upper stratum have several sources of opportunities for ego-expanding experiences, while some of the rank and file have none.[6] Furthermore, managers and administrators often have a chance to leave the settlement and go to town on some errand; they enjoy a degree of freedom of movement and the pleasure of some petty cash which they can spend to see a show or to to a café—pleasures which the rank and file are deprived of. On errands in town, the managers again experience the ego-expanding gratifications, as they represent their whole community in the dealings with banks, merchants and government agencies.

These special life conditions tend to create a special "managerial Weltanschauung" among the upper stratum. They experience less of the strain and dependency and more of the pleasures of collective living. "What is all this talk of 'dependency' I hear?" exclaimed one of the top leaders. "Why, we in the kibutz are the only people who are truly free: free from the worry and anxiety of competitive existence. I feel more free than all your Rockefellers. I do what I *really* want!"

The rank and file, on the other hand, see collective life from the disadvantageous point of daily routine, difficult and subordinate work, tensions and conflicts in many institutional relations.

The importance of emotional gratifications in the kibutz society can not be overstressed. The kibutz ideology is that of avant-garde pioneering, and the motivation is essentially that of self-denial. Material rewards for individual effort are nonexistent. The whole motivational system is based on the assumption that the members derive emotional gratifications in the course of communal life. This assumption is in turn based on the existence of identification of the members with their work, the village, the group, the communal future. If the society does not provide any basis for identification, or if the members are not prepared to identify with the community, no emotional gratifications are forthcoming and the whole motivational system collapses.

Relations between the Managerial Stratum and the Rank and File

Social relations among all members are completely informal. Among the older members no overt signs of deference exist. A certain degree of social distance is, however, introduced by newcomers through their spontaneously deferential attitude towards the managerial stratum. One may observe a newcomer stepping aside to let the "big leader" pass through the door; in addressing the "important personalities" the newcomers speak more politely and quietly than with other newcomers. This deferential attitude on their part springs from the fact that they actually are strangers to the oldtimers and are incapable of ever achieving the degree of familiarity obtaining among the oldtimers; their deferential attitude towards the managers is brought from the outside world. The newcomer is faced with a fixed correlate of personal sta-

---

[6] Davis and Moore (*op. cit.*, p. 243) mention three types of rewards that can be used to induce people into desired positions: those that contribute to "sustenance and comfort," to "humor and diversion" and to "self-respect and ego-expansion." They claim also that "In any social system all three kinds of rewards must be dispensed differentially according to positions." The stratification system in the kibutz certainly supports the statement concerning the existence of special rewards, but it shows also that it is not at all necessary for any system to dispense all three kinds of rewards. Special sustenance and comfort are not associated with high prestige positions; neither is there any indication that, all other forces remaining equal, future developments will necessarily lead to preferential treatment of the managerial stratum with regard to the standard of living. To the contrary, a pressure for higher material rewards comes from the rank and file who are underprivileged in "humor and diversion" as well as in "self-respect and ego-expansion." The former type of rewards is sought by them as a compensation for the lack of the latter two.

tus—managerial position—and he often does not sense the initial criterion of status—personal attributes—which, historically and logically, stands behind these occupational correlates. This attitude of restraint and deference on the part of the newcomers tends to increase the gulf between the upper stratum and the rank and file and interferes with the proper functioning of communication and with mutual understanding of each stratum's viewpoints and problems.

In a summer rest-home maintained by the kibutz, a girl newcomer became friendly with one of the oldtimers. "How I enjoy being able to talk with you," she exclaimed once. "Back home, I would never dare to speak to you—you always seemed so formidable and distant." The oldtimer was bewildered at her feeling of distance. He felt that he was always open to approach by anyone in the kibutz.

In reality, the two strata regard each other with a set of stereotype attitudes. The managers-leaders are respected for their contribution to the communal enterprise as leaders, organizers, managers of farm and shops, but they are not loved. (On the part of some insufficiently motivated newcomers, the respect is not even genuine.) The special character of their life conditions is recognized and they are privately—and sometimes publicly—accused of not really knowing "what kibutz life tastes like." "These people don't lead our lives," say the rank and file. The managers and leaders, on the other hand, feel slightly contemptuous of and discouraged with the rank and file for their inadequate enthusiasm, their lack of interest and participation in group life, their demands for a higher standard of living and less self-denial. It seems clear that the managers-leaders do not grasp the difference in the life conditions of the rank and file and the impact it must make on their image of and attitude toward the collective society. An incident in which the author

participated will illustrate the nature of the differences between the two strata and the relations between them:

I was chatting with an oldtimer in the tiny switchboard-post office-armory room where his job was to answer telephone calls and take care of the mail. "Tell me," he said, "you've been around long enough to know what the score is. You know what is bad in our system and I know it too, so let's not talk about that. But tell me, what, in your mind, are the good things in kibutz life?" I started hesitantly but then warmed up and talked about the deep emotional gratifications many people seem to receive from identifying themselves with a big, expanding, to them meaningful enterprise. As I talked, the manager of the local factory stuck his head through the window and listened. His face warmed up with a smile and when I finished he exclaimed: "Let me shake your hand! It is all true, very true, what you just said!" But the first man flared up: "Oh, that's him again," he cried, dismissing the other with an impatient gesture (though not an unfriendly one; they were both oldtimers). "I know your song—and it is not the whole song, my friend. True, people in central positions, who can influence life around them, do feel all that. But most of the people do the dirty work and they feel nothing of the sort. To the contrary, they ask themselves: 'What the hell am I breaking my neck for? What do I get out of this?'"

The Distinctive Roles of the Two Strata in the Dynamics of Institutional Change

The managerial stratum, strongly identified with the communal enterprise and immune from many tensions, acts as a whip for inducing greater effort in work and maintaining the austerity in consumption. The rank and file, on the other hand, press for the elimination of the discomfort and dependency inherent in some of the institutional structures, and for a higher standard of living. The pressure of the rank and file towards readjustments in the institutional structure is strongly opposed by the leadership, who use several means in their effort to restrain the "innovators." Among the means used by them is, first, intimidation through ridicule in the General Meetings; secondly, administrative obstacles put in the way of an initiator who insists on placing an issue on the agenda for a public discussion or wants to publish an article in the kibutz newspaper or periodical (secretaries and editors are members of the "upper" stratum); thirdly, the invitation of top leaders—men who have a charismatic appeal and are experienced "whipperuppers" for a pep talk; more generally, a systematic attempt is being made at strengthening the ideological motivation through special seminars, literature, lectures, etc.

The different roles played by the two strata are clearly visible at the General Meetings where leaders and managers call for ever greater effort and self-sacrifice and the rank and file resist more or less passively. During the informal gathering which always follows after the official meeting is closed, the resentment of the rank and file members is openly voiced: the leader-stratum is labelled "fanatics," "saints" and "conservatives." The only means used by the rank and file are passive resistance in the form of general apathy, loss of interest and refusal to participate in meetings, committee work and other communal activities. It is only when the passive resistance of the rank and file seriously threatens group morale that the leaders reluctantly give in to the pressure from below. Even then, the central secretariat of the kibutz federation may exert its constraining pressure and threaten the "deviating" settlement with expulsion. The innovations are felt to be a retreat from the pure collective system and are feared eventually to lead to a destruction of the very foundations on which this system rests.

Thus the differences in life conditions and the resulting differences in each stratum's image of and attitude toward the collective society create two types of vested interests with regard to the question of institutional change: those more directly exposed to the dysfunctional consequences of the collective system have a stake in the pressure for change, while those experiencing more directly the functional aspects and less exposed to the tensions and strain fight to preserve the system in its entirety; they identify themselves with and act as the guardians of the system as a whole and of the status quo. Thus in these times of "sturm und drang" the leadership is not best qualified to lead in the search for solutions—its function is mainly conservative.

The question arises as to the *self perpetuating forces in the existing social stratification*. It is too early yet to make definite statements in this respect. The oldest of the sons and daughters of the first generation are still in their twenties and all of them are children of the early pioneers—the kibutz aristocracy. Few have become active in communal affairs. Two tendencies may, however, be observed: (1) to sons and daughters of the top leaders and managers, their parents' intelligence and abilities (and often also personal integrity and a very high standard of values) are often transmitted, whether through heredity or through personal contact and influence. Since special training and higher education are offered by the community on the basis of intellectual promise, special ability and loyalty to kibutz values, these sons and daughters of the upper stratum have a better chance to be given additional training and to be placed in positions of trust and responsibility. In some cases two and three children of an "important personality" show great promise and special talent, and all are given special educational opportunities. (2) In addition, some of the "halo effect" of the parents does fall on their children.

The sons and daughters of "big shots" in the kibutz movement are regarded as the aristocracy among the growing crop of second-generation youths. There is a vague aura of prestige clinging to the "big name." They are very desirable as marriage partners and a marriage of children of "big shots" is a popular event in the kibutz society, while marriages of others pass unnoticed. Still, the community applies the initial criteria of status—intelligence, ability, devotion to collective values and good work performance—to the second-generation members, just as it originally did in the small group of pioneers with respect to each other.

Conclusions

The very special type of social stratification in the Israeli collectives is distinguished by the following features which may now be related to the several theoretical questions raised at the beginning of this paper:

1. A distinct relation between the prestige of personality attributes and the prestige of social position. Scarcity puts a premium on capable and trustworthy members with initiative and leadership ability. Functional necessity forces the group to keep these highly valuable and esteemed members within a narrow range of important, managerial positions. Prestige becomes associated with these positions which are, then, used as an index of high social status.

2. A divorce between material and nonmaterial rewards. High status positions do not bring economic rewards. Members in managerial positions enjoy extensive (long range) emotional rewards (some due to their personalities; particularly, an ability to identify with larger entities and with the future of the group; and some due to the tasks they perform) and these rewards make them more satisfied with their lot than the rank and file. The latter, deprived of these emotional gratifications, demand immediate (short range) material gratifications and reduction in institutional strain.

3. A conflict of interests obtains with regard to institutional change, which is not related to economic exploitation or inequality, but to what might be termed "spiritual exploitation" or an unequal distribution of seemingly crucial, emotional gratifications. The managerial stratum upholds the collective ideology and the status quo. Their special life conditions and resulting managerial Weltanschauung, interfere with effective communication between the strata; they are accused of not knowing what collective life "really" is. Their efforts at grappling with the growing demands of the rank and file take the form of "ideological education" which, they hope, will increase the people's emotional gratifications.

These features of social stratification in the kibutz explain the seeming paradox of "class struggle" in a "classless" society.

The Puerto Rican View of Social Class

MELVIN M. TUMIN   ARNOLD FELDMAN

The way in which Puerto Ricans perceive the class structure of their society is now clear.[1] The salient facts are:

1. A *nominal* three-class structure, with the third class just emerging;
2. A *functional* two-class structure, that is, most persons refer only to the middle or bottom of a three-strata order;
3. Almost only the college-educated people mention an "upper class";
4. Virtual exclusive use of income and education as the distinguishing criteria by which the classes are set off from each other;
5. Some readiness, nevertheless, to rank one's occupation and color, in addition to income and education, and to be willing to assess the *total* social position earned by the combination of income, education, occupation, and skin color;
6. An overall realism about one's relative ranking, with a fringe of strikingly unrealistic self-inflations (lower class) and deflations (upper class);
7. A distinctive tendency for the people with 5–8 years of education to identify in the direction of high school and college people

when they locate themselves in the class structure;
8. A sense that the society is open, as parents think additional income and education beyond present levels are within the grasp of their children;
9. A sense that these new opportunities are not something of the remote future, but almost immediately available, so that parents predict substantially different careers and life chances for their younger than for their older children.

Now a rather large generalization may be ventured: *There is very high morale in all segments of the Puerto Rican community. The present inequalities are not perceived as insuperable obstacles. The social order is viewed at all levels of the class structure as a fair and reasonable arrangement. Members of all classes feel well integrated and feel it is worth giving their loyalty to the society and their effort toward its development. In these terms, though they are decidedly unequally equipped with the required skills,[2] people at*

Reprinted from Melvin M. Tumin with Arnold Feldman, *Social Class and Social Change in Puerto Rico* (Princeton, N.J.: Princeton University Press, 1961), Chap. 5, pp. 164–184, by permission of the authors and the publisher.

---

[1] For comparative materials, primarily from the American scene, see W. Lloyd Warner, *et al.*, *Social Class in America* (Chicago: Science Research Associates, 1949); August B. Hollingshead, *Elmtown's Youth* (New York: John Wiley & Sons, Inc., 1949); Herbert Hyman, "The Value Systems of Different Classes: A Social Psychological Contribution to the Analysis of Stratification," in Reinhard Bendix and Seymour M. Lipset, *Class, Status and Power* (New York: The Free Press, 1953), pp. 426–42; and Seymour M. Lipset, *Political Man* (Garden City, N.Y.: Doubleday & Company, Inc., 1960).

---

[2] Despite an earlier indication that we would refrain from any direct consideration of specifically political aspects of stratification in Puerto Rico, many of the attitudes implied by the statements on loyalty and identification have the highest relevance, even if indirect and mediated, for political organization. Implied, for instance, is a sense of how worthwhile and important it is to participate in political processes, such as voting. The relatively high rate of turnout, sometimes surpassing 80 per cent of registered voters, is a reasonably good indication of the existence of this feeling about political processes. No one has suggested that the turnouts are contrived or forced. At the same time, there has always been enough of a vote for minority and opposition parties and candidates to indicate that certain essential democratic ingredients are present and operative both in the political orientations of the citizens and in the structure of the political processes.

all levels are relatively equally equipped for the future with the spirit required.

This is, for the moment, a tentative statement, offered as the generalization which seems most consonant with the data presented so far. We can now examine the extent to which this tentative formulation is true, by seeing how Puerto Ricans feel about their present chances in life, their present well-being, and their future prospects.

To assert that Puerto Ricans are full of hope and morale in spite of the marked inequalities in skills and resources is to say, in effect, that there is no one-to-one relationship between how poor a man is on certain objective measures and how poor he *feels*. We suggest that Puerto Ricans feel far better off than the objective facts of incomes, educations, and occupations show. In short, there is a dissonance between class as objectively structured and class as functionally operative. Puerto Ricans perceive the existing marked inequalities. Yet they do not feel particularly depreciated by them, and certainly not overwhelmed by them; indeed, on some counts, their views of life and how good it is have often seemed to ignore the objective situation.

For instance, all 1,000 people we studied were asked, "Taking the good with the bad, would you say that compared to the majority of people in this country, life has been more fair, as fair, or less fair to you?" Just over 12 per cent say that life has been more fair to them; nearly 79 per cent say that life has been as fair to them as others; slightly more than 14 per cent say that life has been less fair. If those who said "more fair" and those who said "as fair" are considered as one group of people who have positive feelings about the fairness of life, then more than 85 per cent of the people in the country enjoy this positive feeling.[3] Yet we know that more than one third of these people have never gone to school; that more than half of them have not gone beyond the fourth grade; that comparable numbers earn what seems a barely minimal income; and that the majority of them are employed at relatively menial and hard labor.

Two interpretations suggest themselves. One is that when so many people are relatively so poor off, one must expect that the majority will feel about as well off as others. The other is that the differences of education, income and occupation are not taken too seriously into account when the people estimate how fair life has been to them. Nor is it that their expectations of life are pitched so low that only minimum gratifications are needed to induce in them a sense of the fairness of life. To be sure, there is an evident acceptance of their present positions as just about what they have a right to expect. But one cannot ignore the point that on every visible count, these people at all levels are full of hopes for the future. In short, this is not a caste society where one accepts his relatively degraded and unyielding position as a fact of life not subject to alteration. There is here none of the fatalism about inherited social position. These are people who clearly intend to work as hard as they can to change their lives so that their children may benefit from their extra effort.

It is this optimism, this sense that work and effort and education will pay off, that is the saving grace. However much the sense of life's fairness may be based on the realization that so many

---

[3] These striking asymmetries between the facts of objective inequality and the similarities of perceptions of the society and its conduct constitute the central stabilizing features of the Puerto Rican system.

TABLE 1   **Comparison of Own Income with That of "Most People" in the Country**

Years of school completed	More		Same		Less		Total	
	No.	%	No.	%	No.	%	No.	%
0	6	2.5	47	19.7	186	77.8	239	100.0
1–4	13	4.7	86	30.9	179	64.4	278	100.0
5–8	23	10.4	76	34.2	123	55.4	222	100.0
9–12	29	18.5	83	52.9	45	28.7	157	100.0
13+	24	34.8	37	53.6	8	11.6	69	100.0
Total	95	9.8	329	34.1	541	56.1	965	100.0

others are in the same boat, a good deal of another element must be present: that which measures the worth and satisfaction of life in terms other than material; that which sees fairness in things other than relative incomes, occupations, and the number of leisure activities and luxuries available.

Yet one must not carry this line too far. The objective inequalities are not by any means totally inconsequential. They are known, perceived, felt. These facts, too, must be taken into account in estimating the quality of life and feeling in Puerto Rico. These objective inequalities must be especially remembered when we consider how ready the different classes are for effective participation in the future of Puerto Rico. There is no gainsaying the very marked differences in readiness, when readiness is estimated in terms of the skills education can provide. We have seen how fathers of different education have different hopes for their children. And we have also seen how these levels of aspiration result in different school and occupation achievements by the children.[4]

In considering the objective and sub-

jective attitudes, we asked first about incomes. "Would you say," we queried, "that your income is more, the same as, or less than that of most people in the country?" Table 1 gives us the number and per cent in each of the five educational classes who fell into the three different categories of response.

Seventy-seven per cent of the 0-education class say their income is less, 11 per cent of the 13+ class say theirs is less. There may be under- and overestimates in each of these groups, but relative to each other the sharp difference tallies with the objective evidence. Here, on an objectively verifiable issue, the 5–8 people do not refer themselves unrealistically upward. They may have different people in mind than the 1–4 people do when comparing their incomes with those of the "majority." But they have virtually the same per cent as the 1–4 class who say their incomes are about the same as the majority. Curiously, too, the high school and college classes are almost identical in their just-over-50 per cent who feel they earn the same as the majority of others.

---

[4] It should be specially noted that these data suggest that under special conditions, men's ideas and attitudes can change significantly faster than their material conditions, and that these changed ideas and attitudes can and do become important factors in producing new material conditions.

(self-fulfilling prophecy)

Education

As an additional check on how well and truly the Puerto Ricans perceived the facts about their own positions in the society, we asked once again about

TABLE 2   Comparison of Own Education with That of "Most People" in the Country

Years of school completed	More		Same		Less		Total	
	No.	%	No.	%	No.	%	No.	%
0	2	0.8	7	3.0	228	96.2	237	100.0
1–4	5	1.8	27	9.6	250	88.7	282	100.0
5–8	8	3.6	81	36.5	133	59.9	222	100.0
9–12	30	19.7	104	68.4	18	11.8	152	100.0
13+	44	69.8	17	27.0	2	3.2	63	100.0
Total	89	9.3	236	24.7	631	66.0	956	100.0

educational level. "Would you say," we inquired, "that you have gone to more years of school, the same amount, or fewer years than most people in the country?" Put in this form, the query brings responses even more realistic than when the respondents ranked themselves on a three-class ladder. For now, as is seen in Table 2, 96 per cent of the 0-educated class—those who in fact have less than anyone else—say they have less. These people are obviously not comparing themselves to the one fourth to one third of the people in the country who are also without any education. Rather, they are thinking of the two thirds to three fourths of the country who have at least some education.[5]

From the 1 per cent of the 0-educated class to the 70 per cent of the college class who feel they have more education than the majority, the ordering is precisely as one would expect: every increase in class position is accompanied by an increase in the per cent who feel they are better located than the majority of the country. Here, however, the 5–8 class does not perform as in the past. Its percentage of people who say they have more education than the majority is insignificant, and barely

greater than the two lowest classes.

But when the claim is made for having the same education as the majority, the 5–8 class once again shows its sense of well being, since more than one third of its people say thay have same education as the majority; in so doing, they surge far beyond the 10 per cent of the next lowest class who feel this way.

In sum, then, Puerto Ricans clearly perceive that there are sharp differences in education and income, and they are realistic in locating their own positions in relation to the majority of the country.

Now, too, some of the structure of the dissonance between objective facts and subjective perceptions comes more clearly into view. What seems to happen is that whenever and wherever the Puerto Ricans can find some grounds for saying they are as well off or better off than others, they seize the opportunity to do so, even though the opposite opportunity is equally available. Instead of being querulous about what has happened to them and where they are located on the rank orders of privilege and opportunity, they take pleasure, apparently, in reporting some degree of *relative* well being. They are motivated, so far as can be seen, by a perception that the society is open and changing with new opportunities for improvement at even more rapid rates at all class levels. This is the spirit which promoted the earlier remark that, however unequal in skills the Puerto Ricans may be,

[5] We do not know for sure that these are the comparisons these people are making. We put the matter as strongly as we do, however, because we can conceive of no way to make sense of these outcomes except in terms of the reference groups suggested.

TABLE 3 **Comparison of Own Personal Influence in Affairs of the Community with That of "Most People"**

Years of school completed	More		Same		Less		Total	
	No.	%	No.	%	No.	%	No.	%
0	29	12.4	102	43.8	102	43.8	233	100.0
1–4	36	12.9	130	46.8	112	40.3	278	100.0
5–8	30	13.6	126	57.0	65	29.4	221	100.0
9–12	39	20.5	127	66.8	24	12.6	190	100.0
13+	17	24.6	43	62.3	9	13.0	69	100.0
Total	151	15.2	528	53.3	312	31.5	991	100.0

they seem to be relatively more equal in the spirit required for effective participation in the emerging society.

Personal Influence

Now when we turn to more subjective matters, where there is much more room for the play of personal feelings and few or no ways to implement objective facts, we begin to see even more clearly the dissonance between the objective inequalities and the subjective realities to these inequalities. We asked: "In the affairs of the community, would you say that you have more influence, about the same influence, or less influence than most people?"

Table 3 shows the number and per cent in the five educational classes who chose one or the other category of response.

Counting those who feel more and equally powerful as one group, it can be said that at all levels of the Puerto Rican class structure there is a pervasive sense of effective participation and voice in community affairs. This includes:

56 per cent of the 0-educated class;
60 per cent of the 1–4;
71 per cent of the 5–8;
88 per cent of the 9–12; and
87 per cent of the 13+group.

What are the objective facts? This is a most difficult question to answer. If one judges by the per cent of people who vote and whose candidate has been elected, then fully 75 per cent or more of the people in the country can say they have had an effective voice in the affairs of the country. Judged by how often the official policies of the country make formal public acknowledgment of the importance of the poor and humbler people, then, again understandably, a large majority of the people should feel well considered and sympathetically overseen in their interests.

However we measure, and whatever the distribution of power in the community, we confront a most significant fact: over 50 per cent of the poorest illiterates in the country and 60 per cent of the people in the next-to-last class feel they have as much or more influence in community affairs as the majority of people. Against this pervasive sense of effective power must be balanced the still obvious inequalities in the distribution of this sense. For, as the percentages of Table 3 showed us, there are three distinct levels: the 0-educated and 1–4 classes, the 5–8 group, and the high school and college people.

We may record, therefore, an extraordinary widespread feeling of genuine control of affairs at all levels; once again, however, in this most important area of the psychology of citizenship, class differences unmistakably assert themselves.

So we note the dissonance. Ninety-six per cent of the 0-educated class people feel they have less education than the rest of the country; and 77 per cent feel they have less income. But 56 per cent of them feel they have as much power in community affairs.

And we note the class ordering. From 12 per cent up to 25 per cent, for those who feel they have more voice than others; from 44 up to 62 per cent, for those who feel they have as much voice as others.[6]

Prestige of Work

One of the most significant facts against which large percentages of working-class people in the United States appear to react is the low relative prestige-rating of their occupational positions. The adverse reaction is surely due to the fact that in Western European society one of the major prides which men openly assert, and to which public attention is strongly directed, is the pride in position as measured by occupation. Normally we expect that as a society begins to change from a predominantly rural and agricultural to an urban and industrial community, and as it acquires the division of labor usually associated with this change, it also begins to develop a system of invidious ratings of occupations. But here Puerto Rico seems something of an exception. While the largest majority of people are employed at jobs which would ordinarily command little or no prestige, very large percentages of these people nevertheless feel that their work rates as high or higher in prestige than the work of the majority of people in the country. In response to the specific question: "Would you say that your work has more, the same, or less prestige than the work of the majority of people in the country," the Puerto Rican population gave the answers tabulated in Table 4.

Joining those who feel their jobs have

---

[6] Again, here, we encounter certain attitudes and images directly relevant to political structure, though not rendering any objective description of the actual distribution of power. Variable results have been achieved when comparable questions have been put to different groups of American citizens. Comparable questions are asked most frequently when some version of an "anomie" scale refers to the respondent's sense that anyone cares about what persons like himself think and feel, and how worthwhile it is, accordingly, to make his feelings known. In a recent study conducted on a sample of adult white males in North Carolina [Melvin M. Tumin and Ray C. Collins, Jr., "Status, Mobility and Anomie: A Study in Readiness for Desegregation," *The British Journal of Sociology*, X, No. 3 (September, 1959), 253–67], it was discovered that no relationship of any significant dimension could be found between the experience of mobility, either up or down, and anomie. There was some suggestion of a regular relationship between status and anomie, such that the higher the status, the lower the anomie or sense of meaningfulness and promise. But other investigators have found quite different results on other populations. Some of these results, especially as they bear on political behavior, will be found in Chapter 2 of Bendix

and Lipset, *Social Mobility in Industrial Society* (Berkeley and Los Angeles: University of California Press, 1959), and in Lipset, *op. cit.*. It is hard to urge that the comparisons are flush, since it is not alone the status of the Puerto Ricans that is involved but their perceptions of the openness of the society as well. Thus we are not viewing them here as persons with types of mobility characteristics, or with combined status and mobility characteristics, but rather as status occupants with very definite mobility *horizons*. It is the anticipatory character of their mobility experience that makes it difficult to compare the Puerto Ricans with others. At the same time, their high anticipations must be recognized as a very special feature or outcome of the impact of the Puerto Rican system upon these various strata; here we confront the fact that the differences in anticipations of the future and estimations of the present and past are relatively small, compared to the actual inequalities in scarce goods and services that distinguish the strata from each other. Implied here, we recognize, is a certain set of graded expectations on our part and the differences we encounter may seem large only in view of our expectations. There is no evidence on which to rest the scale of expectations we impose.

TABLE 4   Comparison of Prestige of Own Occupation with That of Majority

Years of school completed	More		Same		Less		Total	
	No.	%	No.	%	No.	%	No.	%
0	40	17.4	100	43.5	90	39.1	230	100.0
1–4	48	19.6	139	56.7	58	23.7	245	100.0
5–8	53	21.3	147	59.0	49	19.7	249	100.0
9–12	45	28.7	104	66.2	8	5.1	157	100.0
13+	38	55.9	30	44.1	0	0.0	68	100.0
Total	224	23.6	520	54.8	205	21.6	949	100.0

more prestige with those who feel equally elevated in their work, we find that once again over half the class with no education feels well off. The figures then rise sharply, so that 76 per cent of the 1–4 people feel this way, followed very closely by 80 per cent of the 5–8 group. Once again there is a jump to the upper level, where 95 per cent of the high school people and all of the college people feel this way.

Again, we have found discord between the objective facts and the subjective estimates. Again, too, there is sharp class structuring; and once again, a widespread sense of social adequacy no matter what the level of class.

What can it mean for such large numbers of humble agricultural day laborers to say that their occupation has as much prestige as others'? Surely they cannot mean the same kind of prestige as that accorded to a day laborer in the United States, for this rank is among the lowest if not the lowest in prestige of all occupational categories. Still, there is obvious reference here to the sense that the work is valued highly by the rest of the society;[7] that the tasks performed are considered as important as any of the others; that the frequent references to the jibaro, or peasant, as the central figure in Puerto Rican life are meant by those who utter them. If any single type of social being in Puerto Rico is celebrated above all others, it is the jibaro: the poor, humble peasant. However romantic this celebration may be, the fact remains that there is frequent public affirmation of the importance of the jibaro, of his essential dignity, of the worth of his work, and of the crucial ways in which he symbolizes Puerto Rico. From the earliest days of the present political regime, the jibaro has occupied a prominent place in the thinking and planning for the country's future. And there has been very effective communication of this concern and admiration. That it has been effective is seen in the ways the members of the lowest class rise spiritually far above their material conditions, affirming their own identification with the society and their sense of being well valued.

Respect Received

Perhaps nowhere is this sense of being positively valued so evident as in the responses give to the question: "Would you say that you receive more, the same, or less respect than most people in the country?" The concept of respect, it must be understood, is a central term in the vocabulary of human relations in

[7] We take this and the next several items referring to respect and importance to be perhaps the most significant data in the entire battery of attitudes studied here. It is our notion that the prospects for further development in Puerto Rico crucially depend upon the continuing sense of importance enjoyed by such large percentages of the relatively uneducated and poorest segment of the population.

Puerto Rico. It is closely allied to the concept of dignidad, or worthiness, and the indisputable ideology regarding dignidad is that all men are equally entitled to it. The way one shows that he accords dignidad to others is by acting respectful of them. Negatively, this means that one never claims superiority or acts superior on the grounds of status; that one does not claim more rights to the good things in life than others; that no one more than others can say he is entitled to what life has to offer.

Obviously in a stratified society, where the good things of life are distributed unequally, there will be some strain between the ideology of equal worth and the facts of inequality. Making it possible for this strain to be kept at a relative minimum is the compromise that one does not claim a position of superiority on the basis of his larger share of materials, goods, and services; nor does one claim a right to deferential behavior. One may properly exercise the powers of his superior office in the running of affairs, if need be, but one must always deal with his inferiors as though they too were equally worthy men in the basic sense, however inferior they may be in skills or in the possessions they can manifest and consume.

As Table 5 shows us, virtually nobody in any of the classes says he receives less respect than others. And the people in the class of no education are second only to the college people in the per cent among them who claim to receive more

respect than others. Here the class differences which have been so noticeable on other matters virtually disappear. The sense of being held worthy by others and treated accordingly is spread throughout the population in virtual disregard of the obvious material differences which are so well recognized by the people themselves. The claim to equal worthiness in spite of the temporary facts of material life is asserted by nearly the entire population.

Importance to the Community

Now a note of realism must once again be introduced. The Puerto Ricans claim they feel virtually equally worthy. And they apparently rest this claim on the universally accepted doctrine of the equal worth of all men, regardless of position. But they are not wide-eyed dreamers who refuse to recognize the facts of life. They do not claim equal income or equal education, for they know these facts to be untrue and there is no way of blinking them off. Nor do they attempt to deny that in the conduct of community affairs some men are more important than others, some positions more vital than theirs. Here it is not a question of their equal or unequal worthiness as men. It is a matter of their social functions as social beings in an organized society. So we see from Table 6 that when asked, "Would you say that you are more important, equally im-

TABLE 5   Comparison of Amount of Respect Received with That Received by Majority

Years of school completed	More		Same		Less		Total	
	No.	%	No.	%	No.	%	No.	%
0	74	31.0	161	67.4	4	1.7	239	100.0
1–4	61	21.6	217	77.0	4	1.4	282	100.0
5–8	48	21.6	170	76.6	4	1.8	222	100.0
9–12	37	23.1	122	76.3	1	0.6	160	100.0
13+	28	41.2	39	57.4	1	1.5	68	100.0
Total	248	25.5	709	73.0	14	1.4	971	100.0

TABLE 6   **Comparison of One's Own Importance to the Well-Being of the Country with That of the Majority**

Years of school completed	More		Same		Less		Total	
	No.	%	No.	%	No.	%	No.	%
0	18	7.9	111	48.7	99	43.4	228	100.0
1–4	30	11.0	171	62.6	72	26.4	273	100.0
5–8	24	11.1	150	69.4	42	19.4	216	100.0
9–12	21	13.5	125	80.6	9	5.8	155	100.0
13+	24	34.8	44	63.8	1	1.4	69	100.0
Total	117	12.4	601	63.9	223	23.7	941	100.0

portant, or less important to the well being of the country than the majority of people," Puerto Ricans aver that there is a hierarchy of functions and that as one goes up from blue-collar to white-collar occupations, from agricultural day laborers to the professions, there is a gradation of importance to the well-being of the society.

If it is proper to stress how this sense of importance is distributed differently from the sense of worthiness and respect, it is also proper to indicate that over half of the lowest class feel they are as important or more important than the majority. In short, nothing even faintly resembles the self-denigration which could accompany the inequalities in circumstances. If there is any outstanding tendency, it is that the facts of occupation, income, and general social function do not count as they usually do in a highly rank-conscious society. As the table above shows us, though only among the college people do a substantial per cent claim superior importance, many members of the other four classes are not reluctant to claim equal importance despite unequal rank on other counts.

The balance which has been drawn before must be drawn again. There is marked stratification of the sense of importance. But there is also marked avowal of equal importance at all class levels. The disparities in material conditions are overridden by more than 50 per cent in all classes who assert that

they are as important to the well-being of the country as the majority of people.

Opportunity for the Good Things in Life

The amount of morale a population is likely to exhibit depends in good measure on how much it has had a chance to get from the society the good things of life. Every person strikes a balance between the work he must do and the gratification he receives—between his responsibilities and rewards—in order to arrive at an estimate of how life has treated him. The people of Puerto Rico are not exceptional in these regards. This dimension of the psychology of citizenship was probed first with the question: "Would you say that you have more, the same, or less opportunity than the majority of people in this society to get the good things in life?"

As Table 7 shows us, there are marked class differences in the per cent who feel they have been as fortunate or more fortunate than others in these regards. But it is also evident that nearly 50 per cent of the lowest group feels it has done as well as others.

In view of the confessed inferior position on the ladder of income and education, what can it mean for such a large percentage of the most under-privileged segment of the community to say it has as much opportunity as others to secure the good things in life? Clearly, they

TABLE 7   Comparison of One's Own Opportunity for the Good Things in Life with That of the Majority

Years of school completed	More		Same		Less		Total	
	No.	%	No.	%	No.	%	No.	%
0	16	6.9	91	39.4	124	53.7	231	100.0
1–4	31	11.0	138	49.1	112	39.9	281	100.0
5–8	25	11.4	125	57.1	69	31.5	219	100.0
9–12	29	18.7	113	72.9	13	8.4	155	100.0
13+	30	41.7	36	50.0	6	8.3	72	100.0
Total	131	13.7	503	52.5	324	33.8	958	100.0

cannot mean the things that income can buy nor that high education makes possible, for these things have not been available to them. They must mean other things; health, love of their children, a respected place in their communities, and the chance to work. Their ambitions and desires refer to those good things in life which are theoretically available to everyone, regardless of material condition or social prestige. What about the somewhat more than 50 per cent who do not feel positively about their opportunities? Again we can only guess, as the information available is minimal. It seems as though we have here exemplified—as in the other instances where the low group has divided on its judgment of how fair life has been—the change which is occurring in Puerto Rico, coupled with the different ways in which men in any population tend to view life. Certainly some of the disgruntled persons are referring to the same types of possible gratifications as those who report themselves satisfied. Certainly, however, a large portion of them are referring to the things that money can buy. In so doing, they naturally see themselves at a disadvantage.

By comparison, 92 per cent of the college people—virtually the entire group—reports feeling as well off or better off than most people in the opportunity for the good things in life. And there is a gradation of percentages with positive feeling: a low of 46 per cent in the 0-educated group, 60 per cent of the 1–4 group, 68 per cent of the 5–8 group, and 92 per cent of the high school people and college people. Surely this is testimony that while many lower class people can come to feel that life has treated them decently, even though they have been at the lowest level of resource, they also seem to feel it is possible to improve the material conditions of their lives, alter the character of their desires and values, and arrive at a much higher standard of living with a much higher level of satisfaction.

Achievement of Ambitions

The good things of life show that one has had the chance to reap normal rewards for responsibilities. But to have been able to achieve one's ambitions implies something more, something over and above the normal returns for social responsibility. For here is suggested the notion of striving and desiring. If morale depends, as a minimum, on a sense of having had a chance at the good things of life, some larger amount of morale is likely to be found among those who also say they have been able to achieve their ambitions. At the same time, one ought to expect, among those who have learned to desire and to pitch their ambitions beyond the visibly available and normally due, that there should be a commensurately greater sense of failure

TABLE 8 **Comparison of the Extent of Achievement of Own Ambitions with Achievement by Majority**

Years of school completed	More		Same		Less		Total	
	No.	%	No.	%	No.	%	No.	%
0	19	9.7	105	53.8	71	36.4	195	100.0
1–4	27	9.8	175	63.4	74	26.8	276	100.0
5–8	28	12.7	138	62.7	54	24.5	220	100.0
9–12	37	20.6	121	67.2	22	12.2	180	100.0
13	18	30.5	29	49.2	12	20.3	59	100.0
Total	129	13.9	568	61.1	233	25.1	930	100.0

regarding the achievement of ambitions.

Some of these results appear when we question: "Would you say that you have achieved your ambitions in life to a greater extent, to the same extent, or to a lesser degree than the majority of people?" The data in Table 8 partly support our suppositions, and partly contradict them.

The most underachieving group is the lowest class. The highest degree of achievement is reported by the high school people. It is apparently not true that the disparity between aspiration and achievement is greater for the more educated and advantaged classes. At the same time, the class gradient of frustrated ambitions is not nearly as sharp as in the reports on the chances for the good things of life. The 0-educated class is definitely lowest of all on the per cent who have achieved their ambitions. But the college group's score is very close to that of the 1–4 and 5–8 classes. It is the high school people who report themselves most satisfied.

But the two other comparisons of the tables give us a different slant. In the first three classes, up through the 5–8 people, fewer report they have secured the good things in life than have achieved their ambitions. Among the high school and college people, however, more have secured the good things than have achieved their ambitions. By class, the differences between the positive feelings on the two issues are as follows:

0-educated class	13 per cent more achieved ambitions
1–4	18 per cent more
5–8	7 per cent more
9–12	6 per cent more
13+	14 per cent less

Table 9 gives added insight into the qualities of the feeling that life has been fair. These findings were developed from answers to the question, "Which ambitions are you referring to when you say you have and have not achieved them?"

The class differences have not been reported in the foregoing table, for there are almost none to speak of. For instance, in the matter of family relations or ambitions, the lowest and 1–4 groups are identical with the high school group in the percentages who report they have achieved their ambitions. On economic matters, the lowest group is slightly *higher* than the college group in its percentage of satisfied people. The 0-educated people, too, are higher than the college group on questions of health. Only on "occupational" ambitions is there a class gradient in the expected direction, so that the college group's per cent is just double that of the lowest group, with the intermediate groups showing intermediate scores. But it will also be seen that the total per cent of the responses falling into this category is below 15 per cent on the "achieved" side and below

TABLE 9   Number[a] and Per Cent of Different "Ambitions" Reported as Achieved
and Not Achieved

	Ambitions achieved		Ambitions not achieved	
	No.	%	No.	%
Economic	493	28.7	506	36.0
Family	332	19.4	535	38.1
Occupational	231	13.5	131	9.3
Having children	145	8.5	16	1.1
Health	138	8.0	32	2.3
Children's outcome	80	4.7	36	2.6
Miscellaneous[b]	296	17.9	150	10.7
Total	1715	100.7	1406	100.1

a The percentages are based on a total of all *responses* given, excluding the "don't know" and "no information" responses.

b This category includes social affairs, educational ambitions, maintaining minimum standard of living, being happy, and avoiding trouble.

ten per cent on the "not achieved" side.

In short, we may say that overall and by individual item, the sense that life has been fulfilled, that one's ambitions have come through, is shared quite uniformly throughout the class structure. Once again, it seems certain that the classes have different levels of aspiration and different values that lead to a satisfaction with life. It is equally interesting that the order of major gratifications is about the same as the order of major disappointments. Economic, familial, and occupational matters are the most frequent sources of both satisfaction and dissatisfaction. And, while nearly 20 per cent of the responses on the "achievement" side refer to "having children," "maintaining health," and the "successful careers of children," only 6 per cent report these as unachieved ambitions. The major sources of gratification are thus somewhat more dispersed over a wider range of events than the major sources of the feeling that one's aims are comparatively unrealized.

The pattern now comes clear. Taking as the minimum expectations the per cent positive satisfaction on normal rewards, that is, on the good things in life, the picture is unmistakably one of increased frustration as one goes up the class ladder. Relative to apparent expectations, people in the upper classes sense greater failure; this is true even though by other standards, not clear in the data, their class position seems to matter little. Though their resources have permitted dues hare and more of the good things in life, they have not, contrary to their hopes, achieved much beyond that level. By contrast, the lower classes seem to say that though they have not been in a position to secure as many of the good things, they have nevertheless done reasonably well in achieving their lower-pitched ambitions.

For the lower classes, the ambitions in life clearly represent something *other* than the good things in life. For the upper classes, the ambitions in their lives clearly represent something distinctly *more* than the ordinary good things in life. The lower classes do not aspire as high as the level implied in the phrase "the good things in life." The upper classes aspire significantly higher than that level. As a result, the sense of relative deprivation does not arrange itself neatly by class position as we might have expected.

In the balance, however, if we judge

the quality of life of the different classes by the per cent who feel *better* off than others, then this sense is clearly a class matter. For here, as we saw in Table 8, there is a rise from the ten per cent of the 0-educated class to the 31 per cent of the upper class, without any anomalies along the way.

Fairness of Life

Earlier we noted that fully three fourths of the people questioned said that life had been as fair to them as to others; another 10 per cent or more felt life had been even fairer to them than to others. Only somewhat less than 15 per cent of the population felt that they had not been dealt with fairly. Now when the data are looked at through the eyes of the different classes, one sees very little class-structuring to the sense of life's fairness (see Table 10). Instead, there is a general satisfaction and very little grumbling from anyone. The only distinct class difference is found in the 40 per cent of the college people who feel life has been *more fair* to them. But 83 per cent is the smallest number in any class who feel reasonably positive about life's fairness.

If this overall assessment is any indication of Puerto Ricans' social integration and social morale, then we may say that this is a population whose thoroughgoing devotion to their society can be surely counted upon. No matter at what level of material comfort or hardship, there is present the sense that they have been dealt with fairly.

The data suggest a three-fold psychology of class in Puerto Rico (see Table 11). The first dimension concerns the person's view of his position on certain ladders of status: income, occupation, education, and color. The second perspective revolves around his view of well-being at these positions compared to others in the country: is he better, worse, or the same as the majority in these regards? This constitutes his evaluation of the position at which he locates himself. The third image deals with the individual's evaluation of the consequences of being at his positions.

In a model phrase, the Puerto Ricans studied here were capable of saying they were in the lowest third of the income ladder; that being there, they were relatively as well off as the majority of the country; and that, all matters of position or income aside, they nevertheless enjoyed the respect of their neighbors as much if not more than the majority of the people in the country.

These three aspects of self-image can be termed (1) the ladder position, (2) the positional evaluation, and (3) the personal evaluation. Where am I located? How does that location rank compared to where others are situated? And, in the third aspect, How do I rate as a person, in my social relations, my personal power, the respect accorded me, and my importance to the com-

TABLE 10   How Fair Life Has Been to One, Compared with Fairness of Life for the Majority

Years of school completed	More		Same		Less		Total	
	No.	%	No.	%	No.	%	No.	%
0	26	7.8	262	78.2	47	14.0	335	100.0
1–4	24	8.7	205	74.3	47	17.0	276	100.0
5–8	23	10.4	168	76.0	30	13.6	221	100.0
9–12	23	14.9	118	76.6	13	8.4	154	100.0
13+	28	40.6	35	50.7	6	8.7	69	100.0
Total	124	11.8	788	74.7	143	13.6	1055	100.0

TABLE 11   Distribution of Sense of Well-Being

Item		Per cent who define themselves favorably
Fairness of Life	(PeE)[a]	84.4
Extent Gained Ambitions	(PeE)	72.9
Importance to Community	(PeE)	72.7
Prestige of Work	(PoE)	70.5
Social Position[b]	(PoE)	67.0
Personal Influence	(PeE)	65.2
Color	(L)	63.7
Opportunity for Good Things	(PeE)	60.7
Total Position	(L)	51.3
Occupation	(L)	46.2
Income	(L)	39.8
Income	(PoE)	38.1
Education	(L)	37.5
Education	(PoE)	24.5

[a] *L* is Ladder; *PoE* is position evaluation; *PeE* is personal evaluation. Ladder questions asked individual to locate himself on the top, middle, or bottom; *PoE* and *PeE* questions asked individual to say whether he had more, same, or less than majority. *A favorable rating* on the Ladder questions was scored if the individual said that his position was either on top or in the middle. On the *PoE* and *PeE* questions, a favorable rating was scored if the individual said he was better off or the same as others, or if he had more or the same of the item in question as the majority.

[b] While this item and that on "color" are not analyzed here, they are taken up in subsequent chapters [of *The Puerto Rican View of Social Class* by Tumin and Feldman].

munity; how well I have done in life, and how fairly has life treated me?

An obvious gradient runs throughout ratings: *The more uncertain the landmarks—the less objectively verifiable the judgment or evaluation—the less consonance is there with the actual material conditions.* The model case is the poor, illiterate, landless peasant, who insists that life has been as fair to him as to anyone else and that he enjoys as much respect and wields as much influence in community affairs as anyone else. One can be at the bottom of the ladder in his income, but on top of the ladder in the personal relations he enjoys, say half the poor people of Puerto Rico. This is pictured in the rank orders of per cent of those who say they are as well off or better off than others on the various dimensions.

A two-fold strain in Puerto Rican life confronts us. On one hand, large numbers of rather poor people feel that despite very low material resources they are nevertheless pretty well off in life. Ordinarily such a benign reaction to an underprivileged condition should cut the ground out from under the type of discontent which helps produce social change and its consequent, hopefully, a better material condition of life. Yet the very same people who count themselves fortunate and well off also evidently desire strongly to improve their material conditions, to send their children to school, to acquire the skills and knowledge requisite to that material improvement. How is this striving compatible with the expression of evident satisfaction with the way of life and with the affairs of their society? Several factors seem to make this duality possible. The first is the apparent way in which Puerto Ricans separate one set of good things in life from another, one set of life's ambitions from another. They do not denigrate the worth of income and education and comfort. On the other hand, they do not take these as the sole criteria of the worthiness of life. Thus while they know they do not have enough of the former, they do not deny life's fairness.

Their second utterance refers to things which cannot be purchased with money. Their insistence that they command respect, for example, derives from their unquestioned feeling of essential worthiness; it is a worthiness all men have, *qua* men, as long as they are moral and decent, and it has no other grading or ranking. In this projection of their self-images, they are giving testimony to a set of values which come from the older and more traditional way of life to which they have been accustomed. Here they are not referring to the values ordinarily associated with the market place and the money measures of a man's worth. At the same time, they are not ignorant of how important are these skills for success at the market place ventures by which their society is coming increasingly to be dominated.

Further, the sense of community equality testifies to the fact that they have been told and they believe that the efforts of all men are equally important to the welfare of the society; the voices of all men will count equally, they feel, so far as the present government is concerned, in making social decisions. That many of them, including the most humble, feel they have a nearly-personal relationship with their nearly-personal leader, Governor Muñoz Marín, is reflected in their answers to the question about their relative influence. Widespread throughout all segments of Puerto Rican society—but especially among the jibaros—is the feeling that they have access to the founts of power, that their petitions will be listened to, that their welfare is uppermost in the minds and the plans of those who conduct affairs in the society.

But now we cannot overlook the fact that these observations refer *unequally* to different segments of Puerto Rican society. If it is important that nearly 85 per cent feel that life has been fair to them, it is just as important, in one sense, that 15 per cent feel otherwise. And it is strategic, from the point of view of planned social change, that these 15 per cent are concentrated disproportionate-ly in the lower classes. So, too, with the concentrations of those who feel dissatisfied in unrealized ambitions, in their sense of relative minor importance to the community, of comparatively low prestige and negligible personal influence, and in their feeling that the good things of life have passed them by without their having a chance at them. These are the people—this one fourth to one third of a nation—who sense their relatively depreciated and denigrated positions in life, or who at least feel that their lower material positions necessarily lead to lower positions on the ladders of respect, influence, and importance to the community.

These are the people who by their own lights have been made the victims of material inequalities. Yet, while more than 25 per cent feel they are low down on respect and influence, substantially fewer feel that this is a mark of the unfairness of life in their society. At the minimum, however, 15 per cent feel they have been mistreated. Low as this per cent may be, given the low material condition of a much large prercentage of the people, it must be reckoned with as the core of dissatisfaction present in the society. To the best of available knowledge, these 15 per cent do not differ substantially from their more satisfied different social trends which play off against each other in the society of today? There is, on one hand, the traditional society, with its emphasis on land and property ownership, resulting in a clear-cut two-class society, the wealthy few and the many poor. In this society men can feel worthwhile regardless of sharp material differences between themselves and others. Here the emphasis upon the dignity of man persists as a dominant mode of thought, cutting across and blanketing any other lines of social differentiation which might be pressing for attention.

But side by side with this traditional orientation runs another orientation, which begins to emerge in modern Puerto Rico with greater clarity. It is one in which landownership is no longer the overwhelmingly dominant claim to status. Now new men come to the fore, with power given to them by new political processes, by advanced skills secured in formal educational institutions, by ownership of industrial means of production and favored positions in service industries. Puerto Rico has self-consciously sought to train this new echelon: to create men who value the new enterprises of the Western World, and are gifted in producing and distributing. Participation in the world being created by these men requires literacy. Thus new value systems have unavoidably come to assert themselves, in which men without education, skilled occupation, and the commensurately high income cannot successfully claim a worthy place.

These two societies are obviously in mutual tension. Without the persistence of the more traditional values and their unqualified affirmation of human worth, one might properly have expected wide scale dissatisfaction with the new social processes and their resultant new criteria for social relations. At the same time, the emergence of the new social order is being overseen by a neighbors in the levels of their incomes or educational achievements, yet they react far more adversely to these common facts. It is more than a matter of being more or less dissatisfied. Others are satisfied. These 15 per cent are *not*. The cutting line is sharper than the notion of a gradient of dissatisfaction implies. This sharpness of division may prove to be important in any plan for social change which is aimed at reducing the number of dissatisfied persons and augmenting the currently unfavorable social rewards.

Among these people there must be many who cannot take the double view

of life described earlier: the view by which deprivations of income, education, and other criteria of status in the new world of markets and money are put aside when the individual comes to assess how positive he feels about his life and his society. Instead, these may well be newer discontents: those who have accepted income, education, and occupation as the main marks of a man's worth and the successful passage of his life, and who consequently feel denigrated and passed by in relation to the way life has elevated and paid attention to others. Among these discontents there must also be a number who cannot feel compensated by the promises and reassurances of their peers and their class superiors, nor by the specific attention given to them in official plans and speeches. The apparently decent social relations among the various levels of classes apparently help many of the lower classes to feel reassured about their worth to the society. But at least some of the latter clearly do not find enough reassurance in decent social relations to make up for their sense of comparative deprivation.

May it not be said that these different responses to questions of how one feels about his society, and how he ranks himself on various dimensions of position and social relations, reveal the government which is democratic in important ways and which exhibits a concern for the fate of people at all levels. These new men of power openly and frequently state this concern for the welfare of all classes of people. If there is any one group for whom special concern is expressed, it is the lower class. This concern receives concrete expression in, among other ways, welfare measures designed specifically to improve the lot of the least privileged sections of the community. By such measures the economic gains which accrue from the new industrial modes of production are allocated more equally then in past distribution of the national wealth.

The importance of these welfare measures can hardly be overestimated. Without them the ideological insistence on the worth of the lower skilled and lesser educated men would seem like empty and vain demagoguery. But when the ideology is implemented so concretely, and in ways felt immediately and directly, a series of forces is set up, acting as effective counterbalances against the lower classes' feelings of material deprivation and self-inadequacy in a newly emerging industrial order.

The industrial order which grows by leaps and bounds in Puerto Rico is characterized by the premiums placed upon education and skills, and by the unequal allocation of income according to presumed functional importance. In such an order, naturally, the unskilled illiterate day laborer, whether agricultural or industrial, comes off rather badly on all the rewards offered. The experience of being denigrated on a ladder of prestige, as well as relatively deprived of material wealth, is a new combination for the lower classes of Puerto Rico. Without countervailing forces, these experiences might readily lead to a significantly lower morale and

an attrition in their identification with the society. It is the persisting values of the more traditional society which help such large numbers of men find a sense of their worthiness to themselves and their new society.

It is equally true that while the governors of the island are deliberately trying to maintain some of these traditional values, they are simultaneously, moving rapidly and efficiently to adjust for the new dislocations produced by the introduction of industry and the market-place psychology of social relations.

Could it be that Puerto Rico is evolving the model form of social transition? By this model can an agricultural society be transformed quickly and efficiently into a combined industrial and agricultural community, preserving intact some basic traditional values? And is this possible without paying too much of the inefficiency which is claimed necessary in any attempt to blend the best of the old world with the highly desired things and ways of the new world?

Surely the emphasis upon basic equal worthiness of all men as men, and the insistence on democratic participation in the making of decisions and the sharing of national wealth, contribute significantly at every point in Puerto Rico's social transformation.

life chances

four

Two main sets of consequence seem to flow from differences in the rewards men receive for their stratified positions, whether these be material rewards such as income, or psychic rewards such as prestige life chances and life styles. Life chances refer primarily to the probabilities of realizing "norms" of well-being, including physical and mental health, longevity, educational and occupational achievements, and so on.

Among the traditionally expected differences between social classes and caste has been the size of their respective families. The usual anticipation is that there will be an inverse correlation between class standing and size of family such that the higher up or better off the family, the smaller the number of children in the family.

In his analysis of trends in class fertility in Western nations, Dennis H. Wrong first examines three different periods during which trends have been variable. In the third and latest period, the baby boom after 1940, Wrong shows that the decline in the birth rate which had continued since the second half of the 19th century was reversed in most of the Western world, and that there was a rapid convergence in family size of the various socio-economic strata. This was in significant part due to the "greater participation of the less fertile high-status groups" in the baby boom, and to the increase in the rate of marriage among these less-fertile, later-marrying upper classes. Wrong suggests a number of possible occurrences that might reduce even further the traditional differences in family size of different classes, including an increase in mobility aspirations of low-status groups.

Although it is not usual to think of the probability of divorce as a statistical likelihood that can be predicted, it is nevertheless true, as William Goode shows in his article, that there is a steady and significant difference in the divorce rates among different socio-economic classes in many countries where education or income or occupational prestige is used as an indicator of class membership. Goode hypothesizes that these differences arise from differential values, internal strains, alternatives outside of marriage, supporting pressures from relevant social networks, the wife's economic dependency, and the degree of economic commitment to the future set up early in upper-status marriages. Goode argues that these differences are likely to be reduced in the future as divorces become easier to secure, as the values supporting divorce increase, and as the class differentials are reduced. It may also be true in the future that divorce will be reconceived such that it is seen as part of the "courtship system," i.e., part of the "sifting out" process, analogous to the adolescent dating pattern.

If birth and divorce rates are patterned, to some degree, according to socio-economic class position, so, too, are death rates, as I. M. Moriyama and L. Guralnick show in their article on occupational and social class differences in mortality. They indicate the difficulties involved in attempting to obtain accurate estimates of these class-based differences in mortality, and they then demonstrate, by the use of the best available data, that there have been variable trends over time, although mostly in the direction of higher death rates for lower-class occupations. Yet there is also some evidence that the gap in the mortality among classes is narrowing, partly because of improvements in safety and health standards for all occupations, prevention of deaths from communicable diseases, and declines in mortality among younger people. Data are not available, the authors suggest, for definitive statements on these rates, nor are they available for examining the possible factors that contribute to such differences that may be found.

Trends in Class Fertility

DENNIS H. WRONG

Although the birth-rate has declined in all Western nations since the middle of the nineteenth century, the decline has not been equal among the various groups that compose their population. Measures of fertility for national units conceal differences in the fertility of the many distinct groups in urban-industrial societies. Changes in the pattern of these differences are of particular significance in the later stages of the demographic transition from high to low birth-rates and death-rates which the Western world has undergone in the past century. Changes in the birth rate rather than in the death-rate are the main determinants of growth in societies where mortality has been brought under control by modern medicine and public health practices.

Demographers have often treated differential fertility as a special, virtually autonomous subject instead of viewing it in the broad historical context of the Western demographic transition. In fact, as J. W. Innes has pointed out, few studies have been made of *trends* in differential fertility by comparison with the numerous studies which simply establish the existence of group differences in fertility at a single point in time.[1] The present paper is concerned with class differences—probably the most pervasive of all group differences in advanced societies. The attempt is made to gather together by historical period

Reprinted from Dennis H. Wrong, "Trends in Class Fertility in Western Nations," *The Canadian Journal of Economics and Political Science*, XXIV, No. 2 (May, 1958), 216–229, by permission of the author and the Canadian Political Science Association. This paper is the concluding chapter, somewhat revised, of a larger [unpublished] study in which statistics on socio-economic fertility-differences in Western nations are intensively analysed. I am indebted to Kingsley Davis for valuable advice and to the Canadian Social Science Research Council for financial assistance.

[1] J. W. Innes, *Class Fertility Trends in England and Wales, 1876–1934* (Princeton, N.J: Princeton University Press, 1938), v.

the available data on trends in class differences in fertility for several Western countries in order to present a systematic picture of the way in which these differences have evolved in modern times.

The problem of dividing a population into socio-economic classes that are genuinely distinct from one another in a sociologically meaningful sense has been widely discussed by sociologists. Demographers, however, usually work with official data which provide only limited information on the characteristics of populations. They are, therefore, unable to employ the more refined indices of class developed by sociologists and are forced to use as indices such relatively simple objective attributes as income, occupation, or education. Censuses provide data on the occupational distribution of the population and their ready-made categories can easily be combined to form broad stratified groups. Occupation is by no means a perfect index of class, for within an occupation there is a good deal of variation in income and education, and neither of these attributes can be ignored in arriving at an adequate, objective measure of class. Nevertheless, most contemporary sociologists agree that, if defined with sufficient specificity, occupation is probably the best *single* index which it is feasible to use in large-scale statistical inquiries.

Since different nations use different systems of occupational classification, precise international comparisons are usually impossible. The systems vary widely both with respect to the number of groups distinguished and the criteria on the basis of which the classification is constructed. Moreover, few nations use systems of classification that correspond with classes or with a socio-economic scale of status. Frequently only broad industrial groups are distinguished or the labour force is subdivided solely according to work status—that is, into employers, self-employed, salaried employees, and wage-workers. For all these reasons, changes that may have been taking place are sometimes obscured.

What is true of measures of class is also true of measures of fertility. Current fertility-rates, both crude and refined, fertility-ratios, and cumulative birth-rates based on retrospective reporting of births in response to census questions asking the numbers of children ever born to women in specified categories of the population—all these familiar but different measures have been used in studies of differential fertility. The present study makes greatest use of cumulative rates,[2] particularly for women whose years of childbearing are over. Such rates are especially useful to the student of trends for they permit comparisons of the childbearing performance of successive groups or cohorts of women who were born or married at different dates.

The nations included in the survey have been selected primarily because they possessed the most adequate data on trends in class differences in fertility. Both primary and secondary sources have been used for Great Britain, the United States, Norway, Sweden, France, and Australia. Germany, Switzerland, Denmark, and Canada have been treated more cursorily, reliance being placed largely on secondary sources. The trend and pattern of class differences in fertility are reviewed for each of the three broad periods into which the data have been grouped, and the agencies—delayed marriage, birth control, and so on—that apparently account for group differences in fertility are briefly discussed.

_____

[2] Cumulative birth-rates are the total numbers of births before a specified age or date per 1,000 women surviving to that age or date.

First Period: From the Beginning of the Decline in Birth-Rate to 1910[3]

Before the general decline in the birth-rate, fertility in Western Europe and the United States varied among classes and tended to be inversely correlated with class, but the relative stability of the differences paralleled the stability of national levels of fertility. Fertility began to decline sharply in most Western countries in the 1870's or 1880's and the general trend of class differences from this period until about the First World War is well defined.

As national birth-rates turned downward, class fertility-differentials increased greatly. The inverse association between fertility and socio-economic status which before the downturn of the birth-rate was clear-cut only for groups at the upper and lower ends of the socio-economic scale the higher non-manual urban occupations on the one hand, and agricultural and unskilled industrial workers on the other—became deeper and more consistent as groups

---

[3] The conclusions for this period are based on the following sources. Innes, *Class Fertility Trends in England and Wales*. Great Britain, Census of England and Wales, 1911, XIII, *Fertility of Marriage* (London, 1917). United States Bureau of the Census, Sixteenth Census of the United States (1940), *Population: Differential Fertility, 1940 and 1910* (5 vols., Washington, D.C., 1943–47). Edgar Sydenstricker and Frank W. Notestein, "Differential Fertility According to Social Class," *Journal of the American Statistical Association*, XXV, No. 30 (March, 1930). France, Bureau de la Statistique Générale, *Statistique des familles en 1906* (Paris, 1912); *Statistique des familles en 1911* (Paris, 1918). Joseph J. Spengler, *France Faces Depopulation* (Durham, N.C.: University of North Carolina Press, 1938). *Census of the Commonwealth of Australia*, 1911, II, Part x (Melbourne, 1921). Jacques Bertillon, "La Natalité selon le degré d'aisance," *Bulletin de l'Institut International de Statistique*, XI (1899).

occupying intermediate positions in the class structure began to conform to it as well. Rural-urban and agricultural-nonagricultural differentials also widened in most countries. While all occupational and economic groups were affected by the general decline in fertility, the evidence that the groups of highest socio-economic status were the leaders of the decline is altogether decisive, though the reduced fertility of the more numerous agricultural population and urban lower classes had a greater quantitative effect on the drop in national fertility.

There is very little evidence that the rate of increase in class differentials in England, the United States, or the many European cities for which data on the birth-rates of residential areas are available, or even in France, was slowing down before the First World War, which in this as in so many other features of modern life seems to mark a crucial watershed of historical transition. There is some evidence to suggest that in Australia class fertility-differentials did not begin to increase until the first two decades of the twentieth century rather than in the final decades of the nineteenth, but the evidence is far from conclusive.

The inverse correlation of fertility and socio-economic status was probably more marked in the period considered in this section of the paper than it has ever been before or since in Western civilization. Yet even as the more rapid decline in fertility of the less fertile upper classes enhanced the relation, exceptions to it emerged. Data on the cumulative fertility of women born and married before 1910 in the United States are tabulated by the most detailed socio-economic categories used in studies made during this period; they show that within the infertile, higher occupations, the group composed of clerical, sales, and kindred workers was somewhat less fertile than either the group of professionals and semi-professionals or the group composed of proprietors, managers, and officials, though both these last two groups were generally higher in status than the white-collar employees of the first group.

Differences in income within broad groups of nonmanual occupations may have been to some degree positively correlated with fertility. The lower fertility of wage-earners and salaried employees as compared with employers in Australia, and of salaried employees as compared with proprietors in France, suggests this possibility. Unfortunately, adequate data on differences in fertility by income are not widely available for this period, although data for later periods have indicated that the familiar inverse pattern is, in urban populations, more marked for income groups than for occupational classes. A 1906 study of differences in fertility by income among French salaried employees in the public service showed that above a certain level of income, family size and income were positively correlated,[4] but it is not known whether this same pattern existed in the general population or in other countries at that time. Since fertility began to decline earlier in France than in other Western nations, French differential fertility may have deviated from the inverse pattern before the First World War, resembling the pattern that developed at a later date in other Western countries.

British textile workers, American service workers, Australians engaged in domestic service, and French domestic servants are other occupational groups whose fertility was lower than that of groups of equal or higher socio-economic status. The reason may probably be found in the special circumstances associated with the environment of these occupations—the British textile industry employed large numbers of women, and personal and domestic service necessitates frequent contacts with people of higher status.

A partially positive relation between fertility and status also existed in the farm populations of several Western countries. The American South, Australia, and probably rural French Canada, which as late as 1941 did not exhibit the usual inverse pattern, showed a direct relation between fertility and class within their farm or rural populations before 1910. In all these areas the direct pattern was associated with relatively high levels of fertility. A direct relation between fertility and status has often been observed in the agricultural areas of under-developed countries such as India and China,[5] so good grounds exist for concluding that it is to some degree characteristic of economically backward and semi-industrialized rural populations. Its presence fifty years ago in the American South, rural Australia, and French Canada, therefore, is not surprising.

Differences in age at marriage by class continued to contribute to socio-economic fertility-differentials after the beginning of the general decline in the birth-rate. The average age at marriage in the upper classes was higher than in the lower classes, as it evidently had been for a long time in Western history, and a direct relation between age at marriage and socio-economic status held from the top to the bottom of the

---

[4] France, Bureau de la Statistique Générale, Statistique des familles en 1906, 46.

[5] Kingsley Davis, The Population of India and Pakistan (Princeton, N. J.: Princeton University Press, 1950), 76–79; Herbert D. Lamson, "Differential Reproduction in China." Quarterly Review of Biology, X, No. 3 (September, 1935); Frank W. Notestein, "A Demographic Study of 38,256 Families in China," Milbank Memorial Fund Quarterly, XVI, No. 1 (January, 1938), 68–70; Ta Chen, Population in Modern China (Chicago, 1946), pp. 30–31 and Table 19, p. 93.

social scale.[6] Yet the trend and pattern of class differences in fertility were not substantially altered when cumulative birth-rates were standardized for age at marriage in England and Wales and for duration of marriage in the United States; class differences in the fertility of marriage were evidently the major immediate cause of class differences in average family size. The spread of family limitation throughout the population during this period is strongly indicated, for by the turn of the century all socio-economic groups were declining in fertility in the nations for which data are available. It was, of course, in the last decades of the nineteenth century that public opinion became more receptive to family limitation throughout the Western world.[7]

Class differences in the incidence of celibacy undoubtedly created greater class differences in *total* as distinct from *marital* fertility. A later age at marriage is usually associated with a lower proportion of ultimate marriages,[8] so low-status groups must have exceeded high-status groups in total fertility by an even larger amount than in marital fertility.

Second Period: From 1910 to 1940[9]

Data on class fertility-differentials reveal trends and patterns that are by no means as uniform after 1910, either within or between nations, as in the decades immediately following the downturn of national birth-rates. No doubt this appearance of greater diversity is in part merely a result of the fact that vastly more data are available for the more recent period. The findings of later studies also reflect improvements in the techniques of demographic

in England and Wales. D. V. Glass and E. Grebenik, *The Trend and Pattern of Fertility in Great Britain*, Part I, Papers of the Royal Commission on Population, VI (London, 1954). Great Britain, Census, 1951, *One Per Cent Sample Tables*, Part 2 (London, 1953). U.S. Bureau of the Census, Sixteenth Census, *Population: Differential Fertility, 1940 and 1910*. Frank W. Notestein, "Differential Fertility in the East North Central States," *Milbank Memorial Fund Quarterly*, XVI, No. 2 (April, 1938). Clyde V. Kiser, *Group Differences in Urban Fertility* (Baltimore, 1942). Paul H. Jacobson, "The Trend of the Birth Rate among Persons on Different Economic Levels, City of New York, 1929–1942," *Milbank Memorial Fund Quarterly*, XXIII, No. 2 (April, 1944). Bernard D. Karpinos and Clyde V. Kiser, "The Differential Fertility and Potential Rates of Growth of Various Income and Education Classes of Urban Populations in the United States," *Milbank Memorial Fund Quarterly*, XVII, No. 4 (October, 1939). Evelyn M. Kitagawa, "Differential Fertility in Chicago, 1920–1940," *American Journal of Sociology*, LIII, No. 5 (March, 1953). France, Bureau de la Statistique Générale, *Statistique des familles en 1926* (Paris, 1932); *Statistique des familles en 1936* (Paris, 1946); Resultats statistiques de recensement général de la population, effectué le 10 mars 1946, IV, *Familles* (Paris, 1954). *France Faces Depopulation*. Folketellingen i Norge, 1 (desember 1930), Niende hefte, *Barnetallet i norske ekteskap* (Oslo, 1935), Statistika Centralbyran, Sarskilda Folkrakningen 1935/1936, VI Particlla Folkrakningen Mars 1936, *Barnantal och Doda Barn i Aktenskapen* (Stockholm, 1939), Karl A. Edin and Edward P. Hutchinson, *Studies of Differential Fertility in Sweden* (London, 1935). *Census of the Commonwealth of Australia*, 1921, Part XXVIII (Melbourne, 1927); *Census of the Commonwealth of Australia*, 1947, Part XI (Canberra, 1952). Danmarks Statistik, *Statistik Arbog 1952* (Copenhagen, 1952). Enid Charles, *The Changing Size of the Family in Canada*, Eighth Census of Canada (1942), Census Monograph No. 1 (Ottawa, 1948).

[6] Frank W. Notestein, "Differential Age at Marriage According to Social Class," *American Journal of Sociology*, XXXVII, No. 1 (July, 1931).

[7] A. M. Carr-Saunders, *World Population* (Oxford: Oxford University Press, 1936), Chaps. VIII, IX; D. V. Glass, *Population Policies and Movements* (Oxford: Oxford University Press, 1940), Chap. I; James A. Field, *Essays on Population and Other Papers* (Chicago, 1931), Chaps. VI, XII.

[8] Kingsley Davis, "Statistical Perspective on Marriage and Divorce," *Annals of the American Academy of Political and Social Science*, CCLXXII (November, 1950), 9–17.

[9] The conclusions for this period are based on the following sources: Innes, *Class Fertility Trends*

measurement as well as actual changes in the conditions observed by earlier investigators. More careful control of the demographic variables that influence fertility-rates, the use of a greater number of indices of socio-economic status, and the development of more sociologically meaningful indices, were the chief methodological improvements. Yet certain general features can be discerned which broadly differentiate trends and patterns in the period under consideration from trends and patterns in the earlier period.

Some contraction of the relative differences in fertility among socio-economic groups occurred. This contrasts with the progressive increase in differentials during the latter part of the nineteenth century. The fertility-levels of non-manual groups in Great Britain, the United States, France, and Norway converged. In Great Britain the fertility-differential between manual and non-manual groups remained remarkably stable from the beginning of the century until the 1930's, when it narrowed slightly but unmistakably. The differential also ceased to widen in the United States, although it did not contract to any appreciable degree. It was also fairly stable in France from 1906 to 1946.

Before 1910, the upper classes everywhere led the decline in fertility, but after 1910 intermediate groups assumed the lead. In Great Britain all groups declined more slowly after the turn of the century, but the nonmanual groups of low status declined most rapidly. Small businessmen, farmers and farm managers, and salaried employees were the leaders from 1890 to 1925. After 1925, non-manual wage-earners and manual wage-earners—the manual group of highest status—exhibited higher rates of decline than the high-status non-manual groups and the low-status manual groups. In the United States

between 1910 and 1940, proprietors, managers, and officials showed the greatest decline, but wage-workers of all degrees of skill declined slightly more rapidly than the other non-manual groups and agriculturalists. In Norway, three white-collar salaried groups, factory workers, and small businessmen showed the greatest relative declines in cumulative fertility between 1920 and 1930. In Sweden, where no direct data on trends exist, comparison of the fertility of marriages of different durations indicates that leadership in the decline in fertility had passed by the 1930's to salaried employees and to middle-income groups. In France, a stabilization of average family size in the upper socio-economic strata was apparently reached as early as 1911; the fertility of people engaged in industrial occupations declined most rapidly from 1911 to 1926, and from 1926 to 1936 average family size in all groups except the most fertile (fishermen) remained fairly stable. Australia alone may have been an exception to the general trend; there is no clear evidence that the least fertile occupational groups were declining less rapidly than the more fertile groups from 1911 to 1921. Australian employers, however, declined more rapidly than wage- and salary-earners, although they continued to have larger families.

It can be concluded, then, that leadership in rate of decline tended to pass in this period to the low-status non-manual workers, urban wage-workers, and the middle-income groups. Of those in the non-manual occupations who had previously led the decline, only white-collar workers and small businessmen— those with the lowest socio-economic status in the non-manual group— continued to take the lead in several nations. The relatively rapid decline shown by small businessmen in both Great Britain and Norway suggests that small businessmen in the American "proprietors, managers, and officials" group may have been responsible for that group's leadership in rate of decline in the United States.

The fertility of an occupational class continued on the whole to be inversely correlated with its socio-economic status, but by 1940 a larger number of exceptions to this relation existed than in the late nineteenth and early twentieth centuries. In Great Britain, salaried employees had smaller families than large employers in all marriage cohorts after 1891, and in the 1910–14 cohort they fell below members of the professions in average size of family to become the least fertile class in British society. In the United States, clerical and sales workers continued to be the least fertile occupational group. In Norway in 1930, white-collar clerks in business and commerce had smaller families than factory owners and merchants and factory workers had smaller families than artisans. In Sweden in 1936 employers and entrepreneurs in non-agricultural occupations had larger families than salaried employees and officials. In France, where the census classifications fail to differentiate occupations by socio-economic status, people engaged in personal-service occupations had smaller families than those in the liberal professions in 1926 and 1936, proprietors had by 1936 increased the margin by which their average family size exceeded that of both salaried employees and wage-workers in 1911, and in 1946 white-collar employees in commerce and public service were less fertile than a combined high-status group of large employers, the liberal professions, and high officials. In Denmark, salaried employees in manufacturing, construction, and commerce were less fertile in 1940 than proprietors in these occupations.

Agricultural workers, miners, fisher-men, and unskilled labourers were the most fertile occupational groups in all countries. In Great Britain and France, miners were more fertile than farmers and agricultural workers, but in all the other countries agricultural owners and labourers were more fertile than any of the non-agricultural groups. In the United States in particular, the differential between agricultural and non-agricultural workers was wide and continued to increase from 1910 to 1940.

Clearly the degree to which fertility was inversely correlated with social class diminished between 1900 and 1940. In general, clerical and sales workers, subordinate officials in both government and business, and small businessmen were the least fertile groups in the Western world and constituted the major exceptions to the inverse pattern of fertility and status. Their exceptionally low fertility, which was already evident in some nations shortly after the beginning of the decline in the Western birth-rate, became more conspicuous in the present century. Only in Canada, where a third of the total population is composed of French-speaking Catholics, traditionally highly fertile, was there no evidence of any break in the inverse pattern. In Australia, on the other hand, the inverse pattern may not yet have fully developed: occupational classes seemed in general to conform to it, but employers and workers on their own account had larger families than wage- and salary-earners within most of the occupational groups.

Studies of differences in the birth-rates of urban areas classified by various indices of economic status also showed a reduction of the inverse relation in the 1920's and 1930's. In New York, London, Paris, Edinburgh, Glasgow, Hamburg, and Vienna the differences in birth-rates between upper-class and lower-class city districts diminished, while in Dresden, Königsberg, Stockholm, and Oslo the differences had disappeared by the late 1920's. In Berlin, Bremen, and Zürich lower-class districts still had the highest crude birth-rates in the 1930's, but upper-class districts had higher birth-rates than middle-class districts.[10]

When we examine variations in family size by income rather than by occupation, several variant patterns of differential fertility can be identified.

a. The most common pattern was for family size to decrease as income increased, until a fairly high income was reached, and then family size increased slightly. French public-service employees conformed to this reverse J-shaped pattern in 1906. In the 1930's it was observed in numerous cities and urban areas of the United States, and (using average monthly rental as an index of income), in the urban population of the entire nation in 1940.[11] Most of the American studies showed that only the highest or the two or three highest income groups, amounting to a relatively small percentage of the total population, deviated from the usual inverse pattern. This pattern was also observed in Melbourne, Australia, in 1942, in urban Sweden in 1936 among all occupations and among employers and entrepreneurs not in agriculture for marriages of from fifteen to thirty-five years duration; and in Canada in 1941 in several high educational groups and two urban occupational groups of English-speaking Canadians.[12]

b. In several countries deviation from the inverse correlation of family size to income had developed somewhat further. Among marriages of ten years duration in Greater Oslo in 1930, the highest income group equalled the lowest in average family size.[13] The smallest families were located in the middle of the income range. The distribution of family size by income conformed to a U-shaped curve, suggesting that this pattern represented a later stage of development of the reverse J-shaped curve which was observed in countries and cities where fertility had not yet fallen to the uniformly low level of the Norwegian capital. A somewhat similar pattern also characterized families of less than fifteen years duration in urban Sweden among

---

[10] For New York, see Jacobson, "The Trend of the Birth Rate, City of New York, 1929–1942." For London, see Innes, *Class Fertility Trends in England and Wales*, Chaps. IV, V; Glass, *Population Policies and Movements*, 76–82; Frank Lorimer and Frederick Osborn, *Dynamics of Population* (New York, 1934), 79–82; K. Mitra, "Fertility and Its Relation to Social Conditions," *Journal of Hygiene*, XXXVII, No. 1 (January, 1937). For Paris, see Spengler, *France Faces Depopulation*, 98–100; Adolphe Landry, *Traité de démographie* (Paris, 1945), 307. For Edinburgh, Glasgow, Hamburg, Dresden, Königsberg, and Berlin, see Roderich von Ungern-Sternberg, *The Causes of the Decline of the Birth Rate within The European Sphere of Civilization* (Cold Spring Harbor, N.Y., 1931), 115–116. For Vienna, see Alexander Stevenson, "Some Aspects of Fertility and Population Growth in Vienna," *American Sociological Review*, VII, No. 4 (August, 1942). For Stockholm, see Edin and Hutchinson, *Studies of Differential Fertility in Sweden*. For Oslo, see Folketellingen i Norge, *Barnetallet i norske ekteskap*. For Bremen, see A. Grotjahn, "Differential Birth Rate in Germany" in Margaret Sanger, ed., *Proceedings of the World Population Conference* (London, 1927), 153–154. For Zürich, see Kurt B. Mayer, *The Population of Switzerland* (New York, 1952), 109–110.

[11] U.S. Bureau of the Census, Sixteenth Census, *Population: Differential Fertility 1940 and 1910: Women by Number of Children Ever Born* (1945), Tables 57–62, pp. 173–206.

[12] For Melbourne, see W. D. Borrie, *Population Trends and Policies* (Sydney, 1948), 120. For urban Sweden, see Statistika Centralbyran, *Barnantal och Doda Barn i Aktenskapen*. For Canada, see Charles, *The Changing Size of the Family in Canada*, 112.

[13] Folketellingen i Norge, *Barnetallet i norske ekteskap*, Table 9.

employers and entrepreneurs not in agriculture, and among salaried employees and officials, although the older marriages in these groups conformed more closely to the reverse J-shaped pattern. Among salaried employees and officials, however, an exceptionally infertile group in most Western countries, there was in Sweden no well-defined relation between average family size and income for the majority of both the older and the younger marriages, and group differences were very slight. They had almost vanished in the two groups of shortest marriage-duration and their disappearance may possibly have indicated the completion of a process of transition to a final stage in which differential fertility ceases to exist.

c. However, the studies of Stockholm by Edin and Hutchinson showed that there was a direct relation in the 1920's between family size and income for marriages of incomplete fertility Moberg also found a direct relation between family size and income among students taking the Swedish matriculations in 1910, 1920, and 1930.[14] Several American studies of differences in fertility by income within highly educated groups have also reported a direct pattern.[15]

Possibly these three different types of relation between fertility and income represent different stages in a process of transition from the inverse pattern. The "straight line" inverse pattern

yields first to a reverse J-shaped curve which is then succeeded by a U-shaped pattern. A final equilibrium, characterized either by the complete disappearance of group fertility-differentials or by the emergence of a positive correlation between fertility and status, may ultimately be attained in relatively stationary populations with uniformly low birth- and death-rates. However, there are not enough data on differences in fertility by income and occupation combined to justify a conclusion that class differentials in the Western world as a whole are following such a process of evolution. The possibility that such a trend is occurring may be regarded as a major hypothesis for future investigation arising out of the present study.

The trends and patterns described above are indirect evidence strongly supporting the view that the practice of family limitation has gradually diffused from the upper to the lower socio-economic strata. Indeed, descriptive studies of differential fertility provided the initial empirical support for this view before there was much direct evidence pertaining to class differences in the use of birth control. Alternative explanations can hardly account for the divergence of class fertility-rates followed by their convergence, the low fertility in occupations such as clerical and sales work and minor government employment, which are characterized by a combination of "bourgeois" standards of living with incomes lower than those of professional people, employers, and even some groups of manual workers, and the greater modification of the inverse pattern in the countries of lowest over-all fertility. The study of Indianapolis by Whelpton and Kiser and Lewis-Faning's study of the contraceptive practices of English wives supplied the first massive direct evidence that family planning was both more frequent and more effective in the groups

[14] Sven Moberg, "Marital Status and Family Size among Matriculated Persons in Sweden," *Population Studies*, IV, No. 1 (June, 1950).

[15] John C. Phillips, "Success and the Birth Rate," *Harvard Graduates Magazine*, XXXV, No. 160 (June, 1927); John J. Osborn, "Fertility Differentials among Princeton Alumni," *Journal of Heredity*, XXX, No. 12 (December, 1939); Ernest Havemann and Patricia Salter West, *They Went to College* (New York, 1952), 46; Frederick Osborn, *Preface to Eugenics* (New York, 1952), 175–176.

at the upper end of the socio-economic scale, and had been adopted earliest by these groups.[16] Whelpton's and Kiser's demonstration that socio-economic fertility-differentials are greatly reduced and the inverse pattern modified and partly reversed when only successful users of birth-control in the different classes are compared, strikingly confirms the class-diffusion-gradient theory of the causation of differential fertility.[17]

It is quite apparent, however, that the process of diffusion was not yet complete in the United States by the 1940's or even in Norway and Sweden by the 1930's. It remains uncertain whether its final result will be the disappearance of group fertility-differentials, the persistence of differentials varying in an almost random manner with socio-economic status in a context of universally low fertility, or, as many demographers contend,[18] the emergence of a direct relation completely reversing the former inverse relation. Whatever group differentials do survive will clearly not be as great in populations of uniformly low fertility where all groups successfully limit the size of their families as they were during the period of transition from high to low fertility.

Discussions of the future of differential fertility often overlook the fact that most of the available data deal only with differences in marital fertility. The few studies which take into account group differences in proportions of marriages show larger fertility-differentials and a more consistent inverse correlation of fertility to socio-economic status. In countries such as Norway and Sweden where the rate of illegitimacy is high, the greater frequency of births out of wedlock in the lower classes may help perpetuate the older pattern of differential fertility with respect to differences in total fertility. Later marriage in the upper classes is also likely to persist in view of the time needed for higher education and the later achievement of peak earning-power in high-status occupations. The report on the 1946 family census of Great Britain, however, demonstrates more fully than earlier family censuses that class differences in average age at marriage make only a minor contribution to differences in marital fertility.[19]

Third Period: The Baby Boom after 1940[20]

The main difference between trends in differential fertility before and after 1940 arises from the fact that after 1940 the decline in the birth-rate which had continued since the second half of the

---

[16] P. K. Whelpton and Clyde V. Kiser, *Social and Psychological Factors Affecting Fertility* (3 vols., New York, 1946, 1950, 1953); E. Lewis-Faning, *Family Limitation and Its Influence on Human Fertility During the Past Fifty Years*, Papers of the Royal Commission on Population, I (London, 1949).

[17] Whelpton and Kiser, *Social and Psychological Factors Affecting Fertility*, II, Part IX.

[18] See, e.g., Rudolph Heberle, "Social Factors in Birth Control," *American Sociological Review*, VI, No. 5 (October, 1941), 800; Margaret Jarman Hagood, "Changing Fertility Differentials among Farm-Operator Families in Relation to Economic Size of Farm," *Rural Sociology*, XIII, No. 4 (December, 1948), 373; Charles F. Westoff, "Differential Fertility in the United States: 1900 to 1952," *American Sociological Review*, XIX, No. 5 (October, 1954), 561.

[19] Glass and Grebenik, *The Trend and Pattern of Fertility in Great Britain*, 113–128.

[20] The conclusions for this period are based on the following sources: Glass and Grebenik, *The Trend and Pattern of Fertility in Great Britain*; Great Britain, Census, 1951, *One Per Cent Sample Tables*; Kiser, "Fertility Trends and Differentials in the United States"; Westoff, "Differential Fertility in the United States, 1900 to 1952"; U.S. Bureau of the Census, *Current Population Characteristics*, Series P–20, No. 46 (Washington, D.C., December 31, 1953); John Hajnal, "Differential Changes in Marriage Patterns," *American Sociological Review*, XIX, No. 2 (April, 1954), and "Analysis of Changes in the Marriage Pattern by Economic Groups," *American Sociological Review*, XIX, No. 3 (July, 1954).

nineteenth century was reversed in most of the Western world. Increases in the proportions of marriages, a decline in the average age at marriage, a reduction in the numbers of women remaining childless, and a slight increase in the average size of completed families appear to have been the major demographic trends underlying the general rise in indices of current fertility.[21] The rise has occurred too recently to permit definitive conclusions about its long-range significance. It remains to be seen whether the cohorts who contributed to the wartime and post-war baby boom will have given birth to more children by the time they reach the end of the reproductive period than the cohorts who preceded them. Forecasts made in the 1930's that fertility would continue to decline and that ultimately there would be actual decreases in the populations of Western countries were clearly mistaken, but few demographers today are of the opinion that recent increases in current fertility represent a long-term renewal of rapid growth in the West.

The long-run effects on differential fertility of the rise in birth-rates that occurred after 1940 are even more debatable. Apparently spectacular reversals of earlier trends may turn out to be of transitory significance when rates of cumulative complete fertility for baby-boom mothers are finally available.

Data for Great Britain and the United States indicate that the narrowing of class fertility-differentials already evident in the 1930's was accelerated by the baby boom. Differential rates of increase in fertility replaced the differential rates of decline of the previous period. There is, of course, no reason in principle why different socio-economic groups might not exhibit opposite trends—some increasing in fertility, others declining. But national societies seem to have responded as wholes to new conditions influencing childbearing and this is as true of the period after the Second World War as it was of the previous long period of declining fertility. Just as all intra-national groups participated in the decline, so did all groups contribute to the increase in the 1940's.

In both Great Britain and the United States, the less fertile high-status groups increased their fertility by greater amounts after 1940 than the more fertile low-status groups. The converging of socio-economic fertility-differentials was thus accelerated. In Great Britain non-manual and manual groups were already converging somewhat in the 1940's when fertility was still declining, and Evelyn Kitagawa observes that trends in differential fertility in the city of Chicago point to "the conclusion that the so-called 'post-war' developments in earlier age at marriage and the convergence of fertility differentials may have started about two decades ago. . . ."[22]

Rates of current fertility and of cumulative incomplete fertility for non-manual workers showed a greater increase in the United States than in Great Britain. Moreover, in Great Britain the earlier pattern of greater increases among non-manual workers was reversed towards the end of the 1940's when manual workers showed greater increases at low marriage-durations.

Greater participation of the less

[21] John Hajnal, "The Analysis of Birth Statistics in the Light of the Recent International Recovery of the Birth Rate," *Population Studies*, I, No. 2 (September, 1947); Clyde V. Kiser, "Fertility Trends and Differentials in the United States"; P. K. Whelpton, "Future Fertility of American Women," *Eugenics Quarterly*, I, No. 1 (March, 1954).

[22] Kitagawa, "Differential Fertility in Chicago, 1920–1940," 493.

fertile high-status groups in the baby boom has clearly increased the deviation from the inverse relation of fertility to status. In Great Britain non-manual workers remain less fertile than manual workers, but within these broad groups a direct relation between fertility and social class partially replaced the inverse pattern among marriages of less than fifteen years duration in 1951. Data on cohorts by socio-economic group are not yet available for the United States, but fertility-ratios for married women indicate sharp reversals of the inverse relation; the non-manual occupational groups of highest status show higher ratios than some manual groups.

In the past, planned families have invariably been smaller than unplanned families and continuously declining fertility has been associated with the spread of family planning. No inherent reason exists, however, why social and economic conditions favourable to child-bearing might not induce married couples to decide to have slightly larger families. Certainly the capacity to "move ahead" one's reproductive schedule is a consequence of planning and has played a large part in the recent rise of current fertility-rates for high-status groups and in cumulative rates for cohorts of incomplete fertility. Changes in the scheduling of births may lead to changes in the ultimate size of family desired. Slightly larger families in the middle classes may be a consequence of the baby boom which has been incorporated into the middle-class concept of the standard of living.

The narrowing of class fertility-differentials since 1940 has also been effected by a relatively greater increase in the rate of marriage among the less fertile, later-marrying, upper classes. Greater lowering of the average age at marriage and of the proportions married at given ages in the high-status groups have undoubtedly resulted in as marked a narrowing of socio-economic dif-

ferences in total fertility as in marital fertility.

The Future of Class Fertility-Differences

The view that the trend of class fertility-differences reflects the gradual spread of family limitation to all intra-national population groups does not go much beyond the descriptive level of statement. Some strata exhibit greater susceptibility to family limitation than others, and the studies by Whelpton and Kiser and Lewis-Faning demonstrate the need for more intensive inquiries into the motivational and ideological predispositions towards family limitation and into their class distribution.

American sociologists have given considerable attention to the relative "openness" of class structures, conducting numerous studies of social-mobility rates and of the complex of attitudes associated with mobility aspirations. Demographers since Arsène Dumont have often suggested that the exceptionally low fertility of mobile persons may account for the persistence in Western societies of the inverse correlation of fertility and status. West-off, for example, has advanced the hypothesis that "social class differences in fertility planning and differential fertility itself are related to the differential frequency of socio-economic ambitions and social mobility within and between class levels—the middle classes exhibiting the clearest manifestations of this type of 'atmosphere' and having the lowest fertility."[23] An increase in the frequency of mobility aspirations in low-status groups would, on this assumption, lead to an increase

[23] Charles F. Westoff, "The Changing Focus of Differential Fertility Research: The Social Mobility Hypothesis," *Milbank Memorial Fund Quarterly*, XXXI, No. 1 (January, 1953), 31.

in the practice of family limitation and accelerate the contraction of class fertility-differentials.

Whether or not an actual increase in the amount of upward social mobility in Western urban-industrial societies has taken place in the past two decades is subject to dispute.[24] Certainly, increases in agricultural and industrial productivity have changed the occupational composition of the labour force and reduced the number of low-status occupations in proportion to those of high status.[25] On the other hand, the narrowing of both absolute and relative class fertility-differences restricts upward mobility by reducing the population "surpluses" of the lower classes and rural areas.[26] The recent increases in the fertility of high-status groups enable them to supply a larger number of candidates for high-status occupations than formerly.

Trends in social mobility, however, are not the only or necessarily the most important feature of the class system related to differential fertility. If mobility and mobility aspirations are associated with low fertility, they can hardly be invoked to explain the *increases* in fertility shown by all socio-economic groups since 1940. Changes in mobility between occupational classes on the one hand, and the upgrading of entire classes as a result both of a redistribution of incomes and of a general rise in the standard of living on the other, are two distinct social processes which may affect fertility in different ways.

Significantly, before the baby boom of the 1940's, the contraction of class fertility-differences had proceeded furthest in the Scandinavian countries. They were the first Western nations where trade unions and co-operatives became powerful pressure groups favouring reduction of the economic inequalities of unregulated capitalism and succeeded in electing to power reformist socialist governments by secure majorities. Since 1940 a marked levelling of incomes has taken place in most Western countries, the result of a sustained period of prosperity during which the lower strata have benefited from increases in productivity, steep progressive taxation of income, and the social policies associated with the rise of the welfare state.

What is of crucial importance so far as the effects of these changes on fertility is concerned, is that "middle-class" standards of living have been brought within the reach of the least privileged strata and made popular by the new mass media. Accordingly, it is not surprising to find that class fertility-differences have diminished in the past thirty years or that, since 1940, all intra-national groups have responded similarly to conditions favourable to higher rates of childbearing.

It is the writer's belief that class fertility-differences are destined to disappear as a feature of the demographic structure of Western populations. This seems a more probable outcome of present trends than the emergence of the positive correlation of fertility to status predicted by several demographers. Yet within the general context of a growing uniformity of behaviour on the part of all classes and groups, some significant differences in standards of living and styles of life are likely to persist, and it is

[24] William Petersen, "Is America Still the Land of Opportunity?" *Commentary*, XVI, No. 5 (November, 1953); S. M. Lipset and Natalie Rogoff, "Class and Opportunity in Europe and the U.S." *Commentary*, XVIII, No. 6 (December, 1954); Ely Chinoy, "Social Mobility Trends in the United States," *American Journal of Sociology*, XX, No. 2 (April, 1955); Herbert Luethy, "Social Mobility Again—And Elites," *Commentary*, XX, No. 3 (September, 1955).

[25] Nelson Foote and Paul K. Hatt, "Social Mobility and Economic Advancement," *American Economic Review*, XLIII (May, 1953).

[26] Elbridge Sibley, "Some Demographic Clues to Stratification," *American Sociological Review*, VII, No. 3 (June, 1942).

possible that a positive correlation of family size to income will develop within homogeneous occupational and educational groups which are small enough to serve as psychological reference groups for their members.[27] Indeed, studies of differential fertility within high-status groups in the United States and Sweden indicate that this development has already taken place.

Much research and analysis remains to be done before we shall fully understand the changes in fertility that are now taking place. The most useful type of inquiry into the underlying causes of trends in differential fertility must address itself primarily to the relation between fertility-trends and secular economic growth in Western industrial society, or, more accurately, to the changes in class structure and in the styles of life of the various classes that are a consequence of rapid and sustained economic expansion.[28] Inquiries into the individual psychological attributes associated with high or low fertility, such as the Indianapolis study by Whelpton and Kiser are of undoubted value, but they are supplementary to analysis of the effects on fertility of the historical transformations which have so profoundly altered the class structures and cultural outlooks of Western populations in the past half-century.

---

[27] A similar hypothesis has been advanced by Albert Mayer and Carol Klapprodt, "Fertility Differentials in Detroit: 1920–1950," *Population Studies*, IX, No. 2 (November, 1955), 15.

[28] Heberle ("Social Factors in Birth Control," 805) makes a similar general point, although, writing in 1941, he forecast a continuing decline in fertility to levels below replacement requirements—a trend he regarded as an inevitable result of structural changes in the economic system in the era of "late capitalism."

Marital Satisfaction and Instability: A Cross-Cultural Class Analysis of Divorce Rates

WILLIAM J. GOODE

Because family experiences arouse so much emotion and social philosophers continue to believe that the family is a major element in the social structure, the field has for over two millennia attracted more ideologists than theorists and has been the object of much speculation but little rigorous research. Personal acquaintance with a family system has usually been confused with valid knowledge, and journalistic descriptions of the past have been the main source of information for the analysis of family changes.

The past two decades have witnessed important changes in this situation. We have come to agree that theory is not opposed to fact but is a structure of interrelated empirical propositions.[1] Good theory not only orders known

Reprinted from William J. Goode, "Marital Satisfaction and Instability: A Cross-Cultural Class Analysis of Divorce Rates," *International Social Science Journal*, XIV, No. 3 (1962), 507–526, by permission of the author and UNESCO.

---

[1] See the clear statement of this position by Robert K. Merton, "The Bearing of Sociological Theory on Empirical Research," in *Social Theory and Social Structure*, 2nd ed. (New York: The Free Press, 1957), pp. 85–101.

facts; it also leads to new ones. In this sense, good theoretical work on the family has been rare,[2] and the younger generation of theorists does not enter the field.[3] However, we have at least come to understand the necessity of adequate theory even in this field. In addition, anthropologists—whose work is all too often neglected by sociologists— are no longer content to report that a tribe prefers some type of cross-cousin marriage but attempt to find out how frequently such marriages occur.[4] Moreover, the ideologist who sermonizes for or against some family behaviour, such as egalitarianism for women, is no less free to pursue his taste, but we no longer believe that his value-laden expositions should be given the same respect we pay to responsible research.

These changes do not imply that we should ignore ideological writings about the family. On the contrary, they are phenomena—like political or economic changes or public attitudes about morality—that affect family behaviour, and therefore must be taken seriously without being regarded at all as scientific reports. Moreover, an ideological position may determine a man's choice of the scientific problem he investigates. Nevertheless, we must keep clearly in mind that the ideological bases from which a scientific problem is chosen are essentially irrelevant to the truth of the research findings. We are properly suspicious when the author's aim seems to be to persuade us of his ideology, rather than to demonstrate, by a precise exposition of his methods, the accuracy of his data. On the other hand, the work itself is to be judged, not the motives of the researcher. We evaluate the importance of the research by its fruitfulness, and its validity and reliability by methodological canons; if it is adequately done, it is a contribution to science even if we deplore its policy sources and implications.

Finally, it is obvious that ideological positions can sometimes point to good research problems. For example, egalitarianism is certainly one motive for investigating how culture determines sex roles.[5] In general, however, ideology is a poorer compass than good theory for discovering important facts, and is at times successful only because it may happen (in the social sciences at least) that what is at the centre of ideological debate is also a key to understanding how a social pattern operates.

In any event, we are now better able to distinguish what is from what ought to be, and even the ideologist may gradually understand that without good science, policy is inevitably misguided.

[2] Three serious monograph attempts may be noted here: George P. Murdock, *Social Structures* (New York: The Macmillan Company, 1949); Claude Levi-Strauss, *Les Structures Elémentaires de la Parenté* (Paris: Presses Universitaires de France, 1949); and William J. Goode, *After Divorce* (New York: The Free Press, 1956). Various reviews of the research over the past decade are now available: Robert F. Winch, "Marriage and the Family," in Joseph B. Gittler, ed., *Review of Sociology, (1945–55)* (New York: John Wiley & Sons, Inc., 1957); Reuben Hill and Richard L. Simpson, "Marriage and Family Sociology, 1945–55," in Hans L. Zetterberg, ed., *Sociology in the United States* (Paris: Unesco, 1956), pp. 93–101; and Nelson Foote and Leonard S. Cottrell, *Identity and Interpersonal Competence* (Chicago: University of Chicago Press, 1955). See also William J. Goode, "Horizons in Family Theory," in Robert K. Merton, Leonard Broom and Leonard S. Cottrell, eds., *Sociology Today* (New York: Basic Books, Inc., 1959).
[3] Theorists of the rank of Talcott Parsons, Kingsley Davis, Robert K. Merton, and George C. Homans have all written theoretical papers on the family, however.
[4] See Meyer Fortes, "Kinship and Marriage among the Ashanti," in A. R. Radcliffe-Brown and Daryll Forde, eds., *African Systems of Kinship and Marriage* (London: Oxford University Press, 1956), p. 282.

[5] See Margaret Mead, "Sex and Temperament," in *From the South Seas* (New York: William Morrow & Co., Inc., 1939).

a cross-cultural class analysis of divorce rates **155**

Marital Adjustment and Happiness

Salon sociologists have talked and written much about the modern "right to marital happiness," but it is not clear that spouses even in the United States really accept such a norm. Society does not seek to create the conditions which would assure its achievement, or punish anyone who fails to make others happy. On the other hand, all societies recognize the desirability of marital contentment and the intimate misery of marital discontent. The scientific problem of studies in marital adjustment was to try to predict whether certain types of couples were more or less likely to be content in their marriages. The ideological impulse was simply, as in the field of medicine, that it would be good to advise couples beforehand not to marry if they seemed ill-suited to one another. The pragmatic basis was simply that the wisdom of elders, who have in all societies made such predictions, might be systematized, standardized, and made more precise. The first published predictive instrument in this country was developed by Jessie Bernard,[6] but at that time Burgess and Cottrell had already begun (1931) their larger study, growing out of Burgess, creation of an instrument for parole prediction. The psychologist Lewis M. Terman utilized some of their findings in a similar study, but the Burgess-Cottrell work remained the most sophisticated attempt at developing a marital prediction instrument until the Burgess-Wallin study in 1953. Locke tested its discriminative power, and various men have tried the instrument in one form or another on other popula-

tions (Chinese, Swedes, Southern Negroes).[7] Unfortunately, this line of research seems to have come to a dead end. Widely used by marital counsellors in this country, the instrument has not improved so as to achieve greater predictive power and its power was never great. Successive studies have confirmed the relevance of only a few items: for example, most show that if the couple's parents' marriages were happy, if the couple have been acquainted for a long time, and if the engagement was long, there is greater chance for marital success; but most other items are not confirmed by various researches. Most of the variance is not accounted for by the items that have been singled out as important.[8] In short, no new, and only few corroborating, findings have emerged in recent years.

The Theory of Complementarity

The primary key to this sterility can be found in the picture of the contented couple which emerges from these studies; it is the conventional bourgeois couple, meeting for the first time under

---

[6] "An Instrument for Measurement of Success in Marriage," *Publications of the American Sociological Society*, No. 27 (1933), 94–106.

[7] The major publications noted here are Ernest W. Burgess and Leonard S. Cottrell, *Predicting Success or Failure in Marriage* (Englewood Cliffs, N. J.: Prentice-Hall, Inc., 1939); Lewis M. Terman *et al.*, *Psychological Factors in Marital Happiness* (New York: McGraw-Hill Book Company, 1939); Harvey J. Locke, *Predicting Adjustment in Marriage* (New York: Holt, Rinehart & Winston, Inc., 1951); Ernest W. Burgess and Paul W. Wallin, *Engagement and Marriage*; and Georg Karlsson, *Adaptability and Communication in Marriage* (Uppsala, Sweden: Almqvist & Wiksells, 1951). For a convenient summary of the meaning of various parts of the instrument, see Ernest W. Burgess and Harvey J. Locke, *The Family*, 2nd ed. (New York: American Book Company, 1953), Chap. 14, 15.

[8] For a summary of the main findings, see *ibid.*, pp. 408–429, and Clifford Kirkpatrick, *What Science says About Happiness in Marriage* (Minneapolis: Burgess Publishing Co., 1947).

respectable auspices, coming from non-divorcing families, not venturing far toward intimacy during acquaintance-ship, holding steady jobs, enjoying a relatively higher education, and so on. Since, to a perhaps increasing degree, modern couples do not always come from such backgrounds, the instrument cannot estimate their future success relative to one another. To a considerable extent, the instrument in its various forms merely discriminates the old-fashioned from the modern couple, but does not discriminate from within the population of modern couples those who will be more or less successful.

One line of theory has emerged which might be helpful in gauging which men and women might live in harmony with one another, after granting that "modern" couples are less prone to be happy in marriage. The "Theory of Complementarity" was developed by Robert F. Winch to explain why, within a given pool of marital eligibles (leading to homogamy), certain people fall in love with one another and marry.[9] No one, unfortunately, has attempted either to verify this theory on a substantial random population, or even to extend it to other areas of courtship and marriage.[10]

This theory, developed with considerable rigour, accepts the wide range of findings which show that couples who marry are usually of the same religion, ethnic group, occupational background, education, and so on. However, the specific attraction between socially homogamous couples[11] is the heterogamy

of their basic psychological needs.[12] For example, those who need to show deference are attracted by those who wish to achieve; those who seek abasement by those who seek dominance, and so on. Whether X falls in love with Y seems a trivial enough scientific issue, but precisely because this is a theory, it has further implications, pragmatic, sociological and psychological. It suggests, for example, why some divorcees continue to marry precisely the kind of spouses who will make them unhappy. It points to the structurally determined misperceptions of others in the courtship situation—the Western male should, for example, exhibit a relatively dominant personality, seeking achievement and autonomy, but the woman who is attracted to him may find later that he is quite different in his real needs. Winch himself denies that the theory applies to marital happiness,[13] but such an application seems worthwhile. Essentially, it is the pleasure that the young man and woman give to one another by the mutual satisfaction of their basic personality needs which determines their serious emotional involvement and commitment. To the extent that this need-satisfaction continues after marriage, the union should have greater stability and happiness (other things being equal). That is, if need-satisfaction continues, then so should the attraction between spouses. A further implication is that the new situational elements of marriage may be very different from those of courtship, and thus frustrate (or perhaps enhance) the satisfaction of each other's needs. In addition, it is of psychological importance to ask, with reference to both courtship and marriage, just how much need-satisfaction of what kind

---

[9] Robert F. Winch, *Mate Selection* (New York: Harper & Row, Publishers, 1958).

[10] Several studies claim to have tested it, but they have not used the same measures for each important factor, or an appropriate population.

[11] Burgess and Locke, op. cit., p. 369, note that over one hundred studies exist to show that married couples are homogamous with respect to a wide variety of traits.

[12] Winch developed his categories from the work of Henry A. Murray, *Explorations in Personality* (New York: Oxford University Press, Inc., 1938).

[13] Personal communication, 22 July 1961.

(abasement, autonomy, deference, achievement, etc.) may outweigh a failure to get satisfaction of other needs. Next, one or the other spouse may eventually obtain some of these satisfactions outside marriage, e.g., in his or her work, thus posing a new set of questions to be answered.[14] Finally, the theory seems to elucidate to some extent the attraction between very close friends.

Marital Instability

I have suggested elsewhere that happiness is probably not a strategic variable in the analysis of marital institutions. Marital strain and instability, however, or the stability of the family as a boundary-maintaining social unit, may well be because at such points the individual has an option and must decide among several sets of consequences (mostly difficult for him to predict) on the basis of a complex set of value and situational elements. By contrast, there can be no problem of moral choice as between happiness and unhappiness, or "happiness and duty." Happiness would always win. Moreover, happiness cannot be built into the structure of any marriage and kinship system as a statistical likelihood or a moral norm. Again by contrast, the stability of the family unit can be, and often is.

As fruitful as the view that marital instability is the failure of boundary-maintaining forces, is the view that the family is made up of role relations. Then instability can be defined as the failure of one or more individuals to perform their role obligations. The major forms of instability or disorganization could thereby be classified as follows:[15]

1. The uncompleted family unit: illegitimacy. Here, the family unit did not come into existence. However, the missing individual obviously fails in his "father-husband" role-obligations as defined by society, mother, or child. Moreover, a major indirect cause of the illegitimacy is likely to be the role-failure of both mother and father.

2. Instability when one spouse wilfully departs: annulment, separation, divorce, and desertion. Instances of "job desertion" might also be included here, when the individual stays away from home for a long period of time on the excuse of a distant job.

3. The "empty-shell" family: in which individuals interact instrumentally, but fail essentially in the role-obligation to give emotional support to one another. Here, of course, there is no public dissolution or instability but the unit is in effect dissolved.

4. The crisis and strain caused by "external" events such as the temporary or permanent unwilled absence of one of the spouses because of death, imprisonment, or some impersonal catastrophe such as flood, war or depression.

5. Internal crises which create "unwilled" major role-failures: mental, emotional, or physical pathologies; severe mental retardation of a child, psychoses, chronic and incurable physical conditions.

---

[14] Winch has commented on this point in *Mate Selection*, op. cit., pp. 202–210, 300–303. For some of the consequences of such actions in general terms, see the author's two related papers, "Norm Commitment and Conformity to Role-Status Obligations," *American Journal of Sociology*, LXV (November, 1960), 246–258; and "A Theory of Role Strain," *American Sociological Review*, XXV (August, 1960), 483–496, as well as the use of this theory in "Illegitimacy in the Caribbean Social Structure," *American Sociological Review*, XXV (February, 1960), 21–30.

---

[15] This classification is developed and applied in my article, "Family Disorganization," in Robert K. Merton and Robert A. Nisbet, eds., *Contemporary Social Problems* (New York: Harcourt, Brace & World, Inc., 1961), pp. 390ff.

Such a conception poses nearly impossible problems of data collection under present conditions, but does offer one way of conceptualizing the strains and options in certain kinds of marital instability. Indeed, precisely because at the present time we have no way of knowing, in any country, how many families fall into one or another of these categories at a given time, I shall in a moment limit my perspective somewhat and consider only certain problems of divorce rates.

For the moment, however, it is at least useful to keep in mind certain distinctions in this area of analysis. A primary distinction is that between the instability of the family unit and the instability of the family system in a given society. Both of these in turn must be distinguished from social change in the family system, as well as from disorganization. With respect to the first distinction, it is evident that all families do end, but this need not affect the family system. It is likely that high divorce rates have been common in Arab countries for many generations, as they are now, but there is no evidence that this has been until recently a changing family system. That is, the Arab family system creates—and, within limits, copes with—the problems of a high divorce rate and its essential structure remains unchanged. As we shall note in a moment, this may be also said of the Japanese Tokugawa family system. With respect to change, it is evident that if the rates of occurrence of major family happenings such as the percentage eventually marrying, percentage married at certain ages, divorce rates, fertility patterns and so on, are changing, then it may be that the family system is also changing and that at least some parts of it are dissolving or undergoing disorganization. On the other hand, some of these changes may actually reduce the rates of occurrence of some phenomena classically called "disorganization," such as divorce, separation, illegitimacy or desertion. Thus, for example, the rate of desertion has been dropping in the United States. In Latin American countries in process of industrialization with all its predictable *anomie*, the rate of illegitimacy has been dropping. Japan's family system has been undergoing great changes over the past generation and thus by definition certain parts of it must have been "dissolving," but the divorce rate has steadily dropped. Finally, even though the old family patterns may be dissolving, they may be replaced by new ones which control as determinately as the old.

Returning for the moment to a publicly recognized form of marital instability, divorce, we ought at least to ask the ideological question of whether a high divorce rate is "good" or "bad." Doubtless, there is more marital disharmony in a period of great social change than in periods of stability (assuming one can find such periods). However, marital disharmony is probably ubiquitous, and one may ask the sociological question: what are the institutional patterns that cope with that potential or real strain? All family systems include some mechanisms for keeping the hostilities between spouses within limits. A primary pattern is, of course, to lower expectations of emotional performance on both sides, so that neither side expects great happiness or love but does expect a minimal set of behavioural performances. A second obvious pattern noted by many is to place the greatest social value on the kin network and to reduce the importance of the husband-wife relation. As a consequence the tensions between the two are less likely to build to an intolerable level. Thirdly, all groups have patterns of avoiding marital tensions, by suppression, by defining certain types of disagreements as unimportant, and by seeing to it that husbands and wives have similar social backgrounds so that the areas of disagreement will be fewer.

Nevertheless, despite such mechanisms of prevention, disharmony is bound to arise. Societies differ, however, as to how much strain should be tolerated, just as they also differ in their solutions of problems when the level of tension seems intolerable.

Of course, divorce is one of the major solutions for an intense degree of marital disharmony and is to be found in most societies and nations. Yet I know of no contemporary society, primitive or industrialized, in which divorce is actually valued.[16] Divorce has its consequences for the society, the kin networks and the individual; and these are tedious when not awkward, and burdensome when not destructive. On the other hand, we cannot say as yet why one society develops the pattern of divorce rather than separation or taking on an additional wife or concubine. Its primary difference is that it permits both partners to remarry. In societies without divorce, it is ordinarily only the man who is permitted to enter a new union. Thus in Western nations such as Brazil, Italy, Spain, and Portugal, the public attitudes opposing a wife's entering an unsanctioned public union are very strong while the husband is usually permitted to have a mistress outside his household. Viewing these alternatives, it seems false to speak of divorce as a "more extreme" solution than other patterns. We do not know at present whether the introduction of a concubine into a Japanese or Chinese household

created more unhappiness than a divorce might have done. And whatever the answer might be, the judgement as to its desirability would still remain a matter of personal or social evaluation.

The Objective and Ideological Evaluation of Marital Instability

One's ideological position primarily determines the evaluation of marital instability, and evidently the "rising tide" of divorce in Western nations arouses dismay even among objective social scientists—the dismay arising mainly from the peculiar historical place of divorce in Church dogma. Adequate assessment of the costs of marital instability, by any ideological standards, is hampered by the lack of a good measure of "total marital instability" in even the most statistically sophisticated countries, if we are to include in such a rate all the five major types of instability listed above. In fact, we know neither the total rate nor the psychological social costs of any one of the five types.

We do not even know the effects of divorce although more analysts have busied themselves with this than with any other form of marital instability.[17] Moreover, such costs must always be assessed by reference to the genuine alternatives open to the participants. For example, children of divorce suffer many disadvantages compared to those who live in a happy home. But the divorcing couple cannot choose between creating a happy home and getting a divorce. They can will a divorce or not; they cannot will (and achieve) marital harmony. And, unfortunately, at least in the United States, the best opinion

---

[16] George P. Murdoch notes that among the Crow a man might be ridiculed if he stayed too long with one woman ["Family Stability in Non-European Cultures," in *Annals*, CCLXXII (November, 1950), 198].

[17] For example, I have been unable to locate in any Western country a monograph study comparable to my own *After Divorce*, dealing with the consequences of divorce in the lives of 425 young urban mothers.

and data insist that children of discord or separation suffer greater disadvantages than those whose parents actually divorce.[18]

Divorce Differentials

Lacking a total rate of marital instability, I should like to explore further a question which I dealt with some years ago and which seems to relate the family in several interesting ways to the larger social structure: class differentials in the divorce rate. A fuller inquiry would be introduced by an analysis, which I am attempting elsewhere, of the broader social-structural concomitants of divorce rates. At present, we have no good study of the problem. Instead, current writers seem to be guided by the clichés, partly wrong in important theoretical and empirical respects, that urbanization and industrialization necessarily increase the divorce rates and that low divorce rates are only to be found in pious, peasant, patriarchical family systems. In addition, a good inference from anthropological data may be noted, that matrilineal societies are prone to a high divorce rate.[19]

---

[18] See Sheldon and Eleanor Glueck, *Unraveling Juvenile Delinquency* (Cambridge, Mass.: Harvard University Press, 1950), Table VIII–19, p. 91; Paul H. Landis, *The Broken Home in Teenage Adjustment* (Pullman, Wash.: Institute of Agricultural Sciences, State College of Washington, 1953), p. 10 (*Rural Sociology Theories on The Family*, No. 4); and Raymond Ilsey and Barbara Thompson, "Women from Broken Homes," *Sociological Review*, IX (March, 1961), 27–53.

[19] Although in earlier drafts he does not deal systematically with the problem of divorce, David L. Schneider in his excellent analysis of matriliny shows some of the inherent strains in such a system. See "The Distinctive Features of Matrilineal Descent Groups," Chap. 1 of his larger book, *Matrilineal Descent Groups* (Palo Alto, Calif.: Center for Advanced Study in the Social Sciences, 1959), mimeographed. See also his "A Note on Bridewealth and the Stability of Marriage," in *Man*, LXXV (April, 1953).

Class Differentials: United States

Postponing such a necessarily extended discussion of the structural conditions creating high divorce rates, let us confine ourselves instead to class differentials in the divorce rate, beginning with the United States which seems to foreshadow so many of the changes which later take place in other countries.

Prior to the first world war, social analyses had guessed that the social relations of certain occupations created a greater proneness to divorce: the travelling salesman because he lived much of the time away from the social control of his neighbours; the bartender and entertainers because of the temptations to which their lives exposed them; the physician because of the emotional responses ("transference phenomenon" in the modern psychodynamic vocabulary) he aroused; and so on. Occupational data were indeed collected at that time although registration procedures were poor.[20] Most American textbooks that dealt with the topic in succeeding decades repeated these findings in one form or another. But though predictions could be made from a few specific occupations, (clergymen, physicians, teachers, dancers) our knowledge of most occupations permitted no prediction at all, and occupation was soon dropped from most records.

By contrast, it seems likely that class position, with its concomitant patterning of social relations and styles of life, might affect divorce rates in at least a rough fashion. Popular belief, and to some extent that of social scientists, supposed until recently that United States divorce rates were higher among the

---

[20] *Marriage and Divorce*, 1867–1906 (Washington, D. C.: Bureau of the Census, 1909). See my critique of these items in *After Divorce* (New York: The Free Press, 1956), pp. 52 ff.

upper strata and lower among the lower strata, where desertion was and is a common occurrence. However, a summary of the available data extending over half a century, together with new calculations from national surveys and censuses, shows that in fact there was an inverse correlation between class position and divorce rates. These findings may be summarized briefly:

Class and a Model of Divorce Decision

If we avoid the pitfall of attempting to analyse divorce through so-called "cause" and focus instead on rates, a simple model of divorce decision clarifies the inverse correlation between class and divorce. We would need at least these items:

1. Predispositions in the economic and social stratum in favour of or against divorce: values and attitudes.
2. Internal strains in, or satisfactions from, the marriage.
3. Alternatives outside marriage.
4. Supporting or dissolving pressures on the part of relevant social networks.

It seems likely that ideologically the upper strata in the United States are more tolerant of divorce than the lower strata. However, the following factors would seem to create a somewhat lesser propensity to divorce toward the upper socio-economic strata:

1. The network of social relations and of kin relations is more extended, more tightly organized, and exercises greater control over the individual.
2. The income differentials between the wife and husband in the upper strata are greater than in the lower strata; consequently the wife has more reason to maintain the marriage if she can.
3. Toward the upper strata, far more of the husband's income is committed to long-term expenditures, from which he cannot easily withdraw to support an independent existence.
4. The husband in the lower strata can more

easily escape the child-support payments and other post-divorce expenditures because his life is more anonymous and legal controls are less effective.
5. The strains internal to the marriage are greater toward the lower strata: marital satisfaction scores are lower, romantic attachment between spouses is less common, the husband is less willing to share household tasks when the wife is working, and so on.

Class Differentials in Other Societies; Phases of Development

The relationship between social structure and divorce seems general enough to apply to other societies. Let us explore the matter. Where there is a well-developed stratification system it would seem likely that the lower class does not count on the stability of the marriage, that the marriage itself costs less, less is invested in it than in the upper strata, the kin ties are less important and therefore the ambiguity created by divorce would not be taken so seriously as in the upper strata.

In the past, on the other hand, without any question the divorce rate (as distinguished from the general rate of instability) was higher in the upper strata of the United States. In some states' jurisdictions, an act of the legislature was necessary to obtain a divorce and generally divorce was costly. Consequently at some unknown point in American history, the lower strata began to surpass the upper strata in the divorce rate, just as happened with respect to the Negro-White divorce differential. Thus a fuller exploration must at some point introduce the notion of phase in these considerations. In other words, the lower strata may generally have a higher rate of marital instability, but their divorce rate may not always be higher until some stage of development in the marriage and divorce system occurs.

This general theory of the relationship between the larger social structure and class divorce rates may correctly apply to the Western culture complex where Church dogma with respect to the family was translated into State laws in every nation, and where the administration of these restrictive laws was until recently in the hands of the *élite*. However, those laws have been altered greatly over the past half-century in most Western States. Moreover, if the theory is to be generalized, it must be modified to fit those cultures such as China, India, Japan and Arab Islam where marriage and divorce were not generally under the jurisdiction of State officials (except for extreme cases) and where marriage was not primarily a sacred affair (Japan, China).

Finally, the use of occupation as a class index, perhaps the best in view of the necessarily crude data available for cross-national comparisons, may at times introduce a new variable into the analysis, the peculiar style of life of certain occupations. For example, clergymen and teachers (in the West) will have low divorce rates but physicians and artists will have high ones— yet in most national tabulations of divorce these will all be classified together. In the West, farmers have lower divorce rates, but in Japan a special pattern of "trial marriage" creates high divorce rates among agriculturists—though many of these are never recorded.

If these necessary modifications are integrated, several inferences can be tested. (1) In the pre-industrial or early industrialization period of Western nations the upper classes will have higher divorce rates. Indeed, there may be almost no lower class divorces. (2) As a Western nation industrializes, its divorce procedures are gradually made available to all classes. Since family strain toward the lower strata is greater, the proportion of lower strata divorces will increase, and eventually there should be an inverse relation between class and divorce rate, as in the United States. (3)

In China, India, Japan and Arab Islam, where the power to divorce remained in the hands of the groom's family, no such set of phases will occur. Indeed—though very likely precise data do not exist—I hypothesize that the relation between class and divorce rate moves in the opposite direction: that is though the lower strata will continue to furnish more than their "share" of the divorces, the class differential will narrow somewhat as the upper strata begin to divorce more. (4) Finally (though here again the data will very likely never become available) since the dominant pattern of respectability was set by the urban *élite*, and rural marriage and divorce patterns seem to have been looser, it is likely that in China, Japan, India and Arab Islam any modern changes would be toward a decline in the divorce rate of agriculturists.

Let us look at the data that bear on the first of these three hypotheses.

New Zealand. The ratio of divorced to married by income distribution shows clearly that toward the lower strata the divorce rate is higher.

Ratio of Percentage of Divorced to Percentage of Married, within Income Groups

Income group	Ratio[a]	Income group	Ratio[a]
Under £100	1.79	£100–£449	.67
£100–£149	1.84	£450–£549	.58
£150–£199	1.86	£550–£649	.56
£200–£249	1.50	£650–£749	.48
£250–£299	1.10	£750 and over	.34
£300–£349	.96	Not specified	2.01
£350–£399	.87		

a Figures higher than 1.00 indicate that the income group concerned contributes more than its numerical "share" to the total number of divorces.

Source: A. J. Dixon, *Divorce in New Zealand*, Auckland, Auckland University College Bulletin No. 46 (1954), 42 (Sociology Series No. 1).

The same relationship shows by occupation; the ratio of comparative frequency of divorce to numbers in each of various occupational groups being:

Proneness to Divorce by Occupation, New Zealand

Occupation	Ratio[a]	Occupation	Ratio[a]
Architect, dentist, lawyer, lecturer, doctor	.07	Mechanic	.96
		Railway employee	.80
Engineer	.72	Clerk	.55
Farmer	.17	Salesman	1.17
Manager (not company)	.32	Barman	4.73
Carpenter	.78	Labourer	2.30
Butcher	1.05		

[a] Figures higher than 1.00 indicate that the occupation concerned contributes more divorces than its numerically proportionate "share" within all occupations.
SOURCE: *ibid.*

United States. Although an extensive summary of the relevant data is available for the United States,[21] it may be relevant to note that a more recent summary has corroborated these findings, and from one of these the following table has been taken.

Ratio of Divorced to 1,000 of Ever-Married Men by Occupation of Civilian Labor Force, 14 Years and Over, 1950 United States Census

Occupations	Number divorced per 1,000 ever-married men
Professional technical and kindred workers	18.49
Managers, officials and proprietors (excluding farm)	16.59
Clerical and kindred workers	25.70
Craftsmen, foremen and kindred workers	24.15
Operatives and kindred workers	26.18
Farm labourers and foremen	40.76

SOURCE: Karen G. Hillman, *Marital Instability and Its Relation to Education, Income and Occupation: An Analysis Based on Census Data* (Evanston, Ill.: Northwestern University, 1961), p. 19, mimeographed.

Australia. In Australia, too, the relationship holds:

[21] *Ibid.*, pp. 52ff. *et passim.*

164 life chances

Ratio of Divorced to 1,000 Married Males by Occupational Class, 1947 Census of Australia[a]

Occupational level	Number divorced per 1,000 married males
Employer	9
Self-employed	9
Employee (on wage)	15
Helper (not on wage)	23

[a] Calculated from: *Census of the Commonwealth of Australia, 30 June 1947. Statistician's Report*, Canberra, 1952, p. 268.

Sweden. A similar ratio may be found in the 1950 Swedish census.

Ratio of Divorced per 1,000 Married Men, by Occupational Category[a]

Category	Number divorced per 1,000 married men
Employers	12
Salaried employees	21
Wage-earners	28

[a] Calculated from: Personal correspondence, Central Bureau of Statistics, Sweden. Statistiska Centralbyran, Folkräkningen, Den 31 December 1950, V, VI, Totala Räkningen, Folkmängden Efter Yrke. Hushall, Utrikes Födda Och Utlänningar: Tab. 8., "Förvärvsarbetande befolkning efter naringsgren (huvudoch undergrupper) och yrkesstallning i kombination med kön, alter och civilstand den 31 december 1950" (Economically active population by industry [divisions and major groups] and occupational status, and by sex, age and marital status), pp. 162–163 (Males only).

Belgium.

Ratio of Divorced per 1,000 Married Men, by Occupational Category (excluding Agriculture, Farming and Fishing)[a]

Category	Number divorced per 1,000 married men
Employers	13
Salaried workers	14
Skilled and unskilled workers	15
Auxiliary personnel	31

[a] Calculated from: Institut national de Statistique, *Recensement Général de la Population, de l' Industrie et du Commerce au 31 Décembre 1941*. Vol. 8: *Répartition de la Population d'après l'Activité et la Profession*. Tableau 18—Répartition de la population active masculine de nationalité belge d'après l'État Civil, l'État Social et les Sections d'Activité, pp. 34–35.

In the preceding table calculated from the 1947 Belgian census, a similar relation appears, although here the differences are very small.

France. The relationship also holds here.

Ratio of Divorced per 1,000 Married Men, by Occupational Category[a]

Category	Number divorced per 1,000 married men
Liberal professions and senior cadres	17
Intermediate cadres	20
Salaried workers	21
Skilled and unskilled workers	24
Domestic servants	78

    a Calculated from: *Résultats du sondage au 1/20e*, Institut National de la Statistique et des Études économiques, Presses Universitaires de France, 1960 (Recensement général de la Population de Mai, 1954), pp. 61–63.

England. A special study of the occupational structure of the divorcing and the "continued married relations population" in England and Wales in 1951 reveals that the proportions of the divorcing population in the selected occupational categories were almost exactly those of the proportions in the continued married population. Thus the "professional and managerial class" accounted for 13.5 per cent of the divorcing sample and 13.9 per cent of the continuing married.

Much more instructive, however, and strongly confirming our second hypothesis is the change in the distribution of the husband's occupation at divorce. Such a comparison is presented below, showing how the "gentry, professional and managerial workers" dropped from 41.4 per cent of the total divorcing population, to 11.4 per cent between 1871 and 1951. During the same period, the proportion furnished by the manual workers increased from 16.8 to 58.5 per cent.

South Africa. Up to the time of writing, I have been unable to make a similar comparison for South Africa because the categories used for occupation and divorce do not correspond to one another in the sources available to me.[22]

Netherlands. The data from the Netherlands do not fit the hypothesis because of the extremely high divorce ratio among the free professions, which include both the established professions of medicine and law, and such occupations as musician, artist, writer and so on. Teaching is separate and of course has a low ratio. Unfortunately, skilled workers seem to be classified with manual labourers. Thus, although the extreme categories in the Netherlands do fit our thesis, the "free professions" do not fit.

    [22] See the table on divorce and occupation in *Egskeiding in Suid-Afrika* by Hendrik Johannes Piek (unpublished doctoral dissertation, University of Pretoria, 1959). p. 262.

Husband's Occupation at Divorce, 1871 and 1951, England and Wales[a]

Year	Gentry, professional and managerial workers %	Farmers and shopkeepers %	Black-coated workers %	Manual %	Unknown occupations %	Total of occupation
1871	41.4	12.7	6.3	16.8	22.8	285
1951	11.4	6.7	7.6	58.5	15.8	1,813

    a Calculated from: Griselda Rowntree and Norman H. Carrier, "The Resort to Divorce in England and Wales, 1858–1957," in: *Population Studies*, No. 11 (March 1958), p. 222.

a cross-cultural class analysis of divorce rates   **165**

Ratio of Divorce per 1,000 Married Male Heads of Households, Netherlands 1955–57 (excluding Agriculture)[a]

Categories	Number of divorces per 1,000 male household heads
Heads of enterprises	48
Free professions	50
Civil Service and office employees	21
Teaching	15
Other bureaucrats	37
Manual workers	30

[a] Calculated from: Number of households taken as of 30 June 1956; divorces as of 1955–57.

SOURCE: *Echtscheidingen in Nederland*, 1900–57, Central Bureau Voor De Statistiek Zeist, W. de Haan, 1958, Appendix II, Table D, p. 63.

Yugoslavia. Yugoslavia has recently begun to industrialize, and our hypothesis would suggest that the divorce ratio would be higher towards the upper strata. If education is used as an index, this appears to be so as of 1959.

Ratio of Divorce to 1,000 Married Males, by Education

School achievement of husband	Number of divorced per 1,000 married
Without school	124
Primary school	124
Secondary school (incomplete)	144
Secondary school (completed)	148
Faculty, high and higher school	144

SOURCE: *Statistical Yearbook of the Federal People's Republic of Yugoslavia*, Federal People's Republic of Yugoslavia Federal Statistical Institute, Belgrade, August 1961. Calculated from: Table 202–23—Contracted Marriages by School Qualifications of Bridegroom and Bride in 1959 (preliminary data), p. 83; Table 202–27—Divorces by School Qualifications of Husband and Wife in 1959 (preliminary data), p. 85.

However, the ratios by occupation are puzzling. Here the technical problem of the ratio itself is important: if the ratio used is actual divorces and marriages in one given year, the result may be an anomaly: e.g., a high divorce-marriage

ratio among pensioners because they do experience some divorces, but very few marriages on account of their age. However, this result is a function of age level rather than of a high propensity to divorce.

In any event, with this warning, the following table presents data comparable in part to the previous tables.

Ratio of Divorces to Marriages by Occupation of Husband[a]

Occupation of husband	Number of divorces per 1,000 marriages
Unskilled	144
Workers in manufacturing industries, arts, crafts	140
Administrative and managing personnel	256
Professional and technical occupations and artists	132

[a] Calculated from: *Statistical Yearbook of the Federal People's Republic of Yugoslavia*, Federal Statistical Institute, Belgrade, August 1961. Data calculated from: Table 202–21—Contracted Marriages by Occupation of Bridegroom and Bride in 1959 (preliminary data), p. 83; Table 202–28—Divorces by Occupation of Husband and Wife in 1959 (preliminary data), p. 85.

These figures are also somewhat different from those which Milic has calculated, apparently from the same sources.[23]

Egypt. Egyptian data on such a matter raises the problem, common to all countries in which divorce has been a limited concern of the State, of how adequate the coverage of divorces is, and whether the more literate or better educated couples who divorce are more likely to record their divorces. As can be seen in the succeeding table, the divorce/married ratio predicted holds good primarily for the distinction between

[23] Vojin Milič, "Sklapanje I Razvod Braka Prema Zanimanju," in: *Statisticka Revija*, No. 7 (March, 1957), 19–44, esp. p. 38.

employers on the one hand and all other occupations on the other.

Ratio of Divorces to Marriages by Occupation of Husband (excluding Agriculture, Fishing and Hunting)[a]

Categories	Number of divorces per 1,000 marriages
Employers	9
On own account	18
Directors and sub-directors	12
Employees	11
Labourers and artisans	18
Unemployed	117

[a] Calculated from: *Population Census of Egypt*, 1947, General Tables, Ministry of Finance and Economy, Statistical and Census Department, Government Press, Cairo, 1954. Table XXIX (concluded)—Working Status for Persons engaged in Industries by Sex, Age Group and Civil Status (excluding children below 5 years). Table refers to males and excludes occupations in agriculture, fishing, and hunting, pp. 362–363.

However, one comparison of illiteracy and divorce shows no difference in the literacy of bridegrooms and divorced males in 1956 (47 and 45 per cent).[24]

Ratios calculated for those engaged in agriculture, fishing and hunting in Egypt follow the pattern presented above for occupations outside these categories.[25]

Jordan. Corresponding data do not exist for Jordan, but it is at least possible to calculate that in 1959 75 per cent of the males who married were literate, but only 59 per cent of those who divorced; and 25 per cent of the females who married were literate, but only 5 per cent of the divorcees.[26] Therefore we can conclude that the better educated divorced less than the less educated. This general conclusion also emerges from many non-quantitative analyses of divorce in Arabic Islam. Specifically, it is sometimes asserted that divorce and remarriage are the "poor man's polygyny."[27]

Finland. Allardt found that in 1947 the divorce rate per 100,000 of the main supporters of the family was higher toward the upper strata, which would fit our first hypothesis. Using these three classes, labouring, middle, and upper, he found rates of 527, 543 and 1,022.

However, most of the élite are to be found in Helsinki, where the divorce rates are higher than elsewhere in Finland and a comparison of the divorce applications in different classes in 1945–46 showed no statistically significant differences among them, i.e., in the more industrialized areas, the older class pattern had already changed. Allardt notes that the differences among the classes were greater at the beginning of the century but that there is now very little difference (second hypothesis).[28]

Hungary. As a newly industrializing nation, Hungary would be expected to

---

[24] United Arab Republic (Egypt), Presidency of the Republic, Statistics and Census Department, *Vital Statistics, 1956*, Vol. II, Table XXIII, p. 340—Classification of Divorced Males by Locality according to Literacy for year 1956; Table VI, pp. 274–275—Classification of Bridegrooms by Locality according to Literacy (and Marital Condition) for the year 1956. Perhaps the literate are more likely to record their divorces officially.

[25] Population Census of Egypt, 1947, General Tables, op. cit., Table XXIX,—Working Status for Persons engaged in Industries by Sex, Age Group and Civil Status (excluding children under 5 years). This table refers to those engaged in agriculture, fishing and hunting only.

[26] *Statistical Yearbook*, 1959, Hashemite Kingdom of Jordan, Jerusalem, pp. 45–50.

[27] Lester Mboria, *La Population de l'Égypte*, University of Paris Faculty of Law Thesis (Cairo: Procaccia, 1938), p. 63.

[28] Erik Allardt, *The Influence of Different Systems of Social Norms on Divorce Rates in Finland* (New York: Columbia University Press, 1954), mimeographed. These data are taken from Allardt's *Miljobetingade differenser i skilsmässofrekvensen i Finland 1891–1950* (Heisingfors: Finska Vetenskaps-Societeten, 1953).

have a somewhat lower divorce rate toward the lower strata. Our data suggest caution but do conform.

Ratio of Divorces to Marriages, 1958

Occupation	Number of divorces	Number of marriages	Number of divorces per 1,000
Agricultural workers	1,827	25,154	72
Manual workers	9,133	51,017	179
Intellectuals	3,481	15,156	223

SOURCE: *Statisztikai Evkonyv, 1958*, Kozponti Statisztikai Hivatal, Budapest, 1960. Table 20—Marriages by the Professional Status of Husband and Wife, p. 20; Table 26—Divorces by Professional Status of Husband and Wife, p. 22.

India. The Indian pattern is, of course, very well known though no quantitative data exist. Divorce has been impossible for Brahmans until very recently (1955). On the other hand, the lower castes and the outcasts, as well as tribal groups, have long permitted divorce. As a consequence there is no doubt that the general relationship presented earlier fits at least the observed differences among the strata—though in this instance it is perhaps not possible to make a strong case for differential strain.[29]

China. The case of China is similar to that of Japan. Though China has permitted divorce from at least the T'ang period, divorce has not been a respectable step in Chinese culture and thus would tend to be more common towards the lower strata. Indeed among the *élite*,

other solutions were open to the dissatisfied husband.[30]

Japan. The divorce rate in Japan has been dropping over the past half century, though at the same time divorce has been much more completely recorded than formerly. Again, our hypothesis is confirmed.

The Ratio of Divorce per 1,000 Married Male Workers 15 Years and Over, Japan, July 1957[a]

Occupation	Number divorced per 1,000 male workers
Technicians and engineers	7
Professors and teachers	3
Medical and public health technicians	5
Managers and officials	4
Clerical and related workers	8
Farmers, lumbermen, fishermen and related workers	10
Workers in mining and quarrying	18
Craftsmen, production process workers, and labourers not elsewhere included	18
Domestic	238

[a] Calculated from: Japan, Bureau of Statistics, Office of the Prime Minister, *1955 Population Census of Japan*, Vol. II: *One Percent Sample Tabulation*, Part III, "Occupation, July 1957," Table 3—Occupation (Intermediate Group) of Employed Persons 15 Years Old and Over by Marital Status and Sex, for all Japan, all *Shi* and all *Gun*, pp. 136–137 (males only).

The "Easy Divorce" Phase: Further Inferences

Fully to resolve all of these irregularities would require an institutional analysis of each country. Our earlier analysis seems to be correct, that there is likely to be more marital instability towards the lower strata than towards the upper. But whether this set of forces is exhibited in actual divorce proceedings depends on the extent to which divorce itself has become easy, that is, has come to "cost"

[29] See *India: Sociological Background*, HRAF–44 Cornell 8, Vol. 1, M. Opler, ed. (New Haven: Yale University Press, 1958), p. 25; P. V. Kane, *Hindu Custom and Modern Law* (Bombay: University of Bombay Press, 1950), p. 82; Mohindar Singh, *The Depressed Classes* (Bombay: Hind Kitebs, 1947), p. 168.

[30] A good historical analysis of divorce in China is Wang Tse-Tsiu, *Le Divorce en Chine* (Paris: Lovitow, 1930).

little—these costs being calculated necessarily by reference to the available resources of the family, and including both monetary and social costs. We also noted that in a country with "easy" divorce (Japan, Arab Islam), industrialization would reduce the divorce rate of the lower strata relative to the upper. In a country moving toward the easy divorce phase, the upper strata begin to furnish a smaller proportion of total divorces. Let us consider the further implications of these notions.

First, where divorce costs little, there will be a high divorce rate. This is a reciprocal and reinforcing relationship. Easy divorce means in effect that there are fewer strong factors to maintain the boundaries of the family unit. Moreover, in that type of situation, the peers of any individual are likely to have had similar experiences, that is, divorce, and therefore have less basis on which to chide or deprecate anyone who gets a divorce. And the ubiquitous strains in all marriage systems will ensure a high number of individuals who seek this way out and who are also available as potential mates.

Where divorce is difficult and costly, it is primarily an upper-class privilege. There are rarely special laws for the lower classes, other than those which prevent the lower classes from attacking the privileges of the *élite*. On the other hand, if and when there are upper-class family difficulties that have to be solved in a social structure posing barriers against divorce, there must be at least a few mechanisms for handling them, such as annulment and migratory divorce. The property stakes and problems of lineage are too important to permit the merely informal solutions which the lower classes may enjoy.

In a family system permitting easy divorce and thus having a high divorce rate, there will also be a very high rate of remarriage.[31] In the United States, this rate of eventual remarriage among divorcees is roughly as high as that for the unmarried population, about nine in ten. No such figures exist for Arab Islam, but the few data available, including observations made in specific studies, suggest that there is an extremely high rate of marital turnover. The percentage married in the upper age groups in Japan has been over 95 per cent for decades, while the divorce rate was extremely high, thus showing that the rate of remarriage was high. Irene Taeuber has in addition used demographic techniques to show that the divorced as well as the widowed "disappear" in successive age groups.[32] In such a high-divorce system, divorce creates no social stigma, there are many available divorcees to marry, and divorce is no longer likely to be a deviant in many psychological or social respects.

Indeed the divorce system then becomes in effect part of the courtship and marriage system: that is, it is part of the "sifting out" process, analogous to the adolescent dating pattern. Individuals marry, but there is a free market both in getting a first spouse, and in getting a second spouse should the individual not be able to create a harmonious life with the first one. Indeed, to the extent that marriage becomes a personal bond between husband and wife, and they marry after they are formed psychologically, there would seem to be at least some ideological arguments for their being free to shift about in order to find someone who fits better.

Finally, as such a system becomes established, heavy investments in brideprice or dowry will decline. These are

---

[31] Jesse Bernard, *Remarriage* (New York: Dryden, 1956), Chap. 2, 3.

[32] Irene Taeuber, *The Population of Japan* (Princeton, N. J.: Princeton University Press, 1958), pp. 226ff.

never individual investments in any family system, but represent the commitment of an extended family network to the marriage. Where the likelihood is great that the marriage will be unstable, and undoing it expensive, then neither side is likely to be willing to make a large, long-term investment in it.

Some but not all of these hypotheses can be tested by available data, and in some of my current research I am attempting to assemble such materials from many countries—a formidable task! The present paper has aimed at presenting a small theoretical perspective, developing hypotheses from that theoretical position and then testing them.

Occupational and Social Class Differences in Mortality

I. M. MORIYAMA   L. GURALNICK

Occupation and socio-economic status are generally recognized to have an important influence on health. Yet, as Daric's review (1) of studies on occupational mortality up to 1949 shows, there is a surprising lack of information in this area of study. The Registrar General's decennial supplements on mortality by occupation for England and Wales constitute the only continuous series of national data available (2). These decennial compilations were started by William Farr for 1851 and were made around every census year except for the war year of 1941. Currently, questionnaire responses on file in the United Nations Statistical Office indicate that fourteen other countries have tabulated mortality by occupation for a recent year, but these areas cannot be compared readily with the United States or the United Kingdom. Inquiries directed to the various countries of low mortality brought negative or no response on the availability of current

Reprinted from *Trends and Differentials in Mortality*, proceedings of a round table at the 1955 Annual Conference, Milbank Memorial Fund (New York: Milbank Memorial Fund, 1956), pp. 61–73, by permission of the authors and the publisher.

data. Therefore, this review of occupational and social class differences in mortality will be, by necessity, limited to the preliminary figures just tabulated for the United States, and to data for England and Wales.

In the United States mortality tabulations by occupation were made beginning in 1890 for each census year with the exception of 1940. However, tables were published only for 1890 (3), 1900 (4), and 1930 (5). Complete tabulations were made for 1910 and 1920 and death rates computed by occupation, age, race, and sex, but these data were not released. The vital statistics volumes for these years do not show why the figures were not published. According to an unpublished evaluation entitled "The Adequacy of Occupational Returns on Death Certificates" prepared by Mary V. Dempsey in 1929, the data contained certain defects which related primarily to differences in the general accuracy of the occupational information returned on death certificates as compared with that on the population schedules. This and other studies led to an intensive campaign for the improvement of the occupational returns on the death certificates for

1930. When the data for that year were examined, a large proportion of unknown and unspecific occupations were noted. Published data were therefore limited to an area of ten states for which the occupation returns were judged to be reasonably good.

With the approach of the 1940 census, an evaluation of the comparability of death certificates and census returns for the same individuals was made. This study showed a serious lack of correspondence between the information from the two sources, owing chiefly to the large proportion of decedents returned as "retired" in the census. Occupation was not enumerated for retired persons on the census schedule, while a report of usual occupation was given on the death certificate. On the basis of this study, plans for a mortality study by occupation were dropped.

In considering plans for the 1950 census period, the evaluation study made previously was reviewed. It was noted that if a cut-off was made in the tabulations at age 60 or 65, the problem caused by the retired population would be largely eliminated. Plans were made to code occupation and industry for deaths of men between the ages of 20 and 65 years, and the State vital statistics offices were encouraged to improve the returns on the occupation and industry items. The study has now reached the stage where some provisional figures are available, but even this limited accomplishment would not have been possible without the strong support of the National Cancer Institute.

From the outset, it was recognized that most of the defects noted in the studies for earlier years still existed in the data for 1950. These problems could cause serious distortions in the measures describing occupational mortality risks for certain specific occupations. By combining the various occupations into broad groups, and by selecting particular occupations for detailed study, it was felt that much valuable information could still be obtained.

In the early part of the century, interest in the actual risks in occupations, such as those encountered by the coal miner, the bricklayer and the blast-furnace blower appears to have been the only recognized purpose of the study of occupational mortality. The industrial environment of today is far different from that of fifty years ago. Although occupational diseases are still problems of some magnitude, it is becoming increasingly difficult to identify large numbers of deaths attributable solely to occupational exposure. However, mortality rates by occupation still show large differentials. For example, the standardized mortality ratio in 1950 for physicians is 92, for miners, 180, and for mailcarriers, 69. Part of the difference in these ratios must certainly be due to the hazards of particular occupations although not necessarily to their physical environment. On the other hand, these differentials are not free of the effects of social and economic status, factors which are highly correlated with occupation. Measurement of the differences in death rates that can be attributed to levels of living may be as important a part of occupational mortality studies today as the computation of rates by occupation.

The British have long recognized the use of occupation data as a guide to social variables, rather than as a measure of risk in itself. The Registrar General's decennial supplements for 1921, 1931, and 1951 describe mortality rates in terms of five social classes which are determined by the occupation to which a person is classified. A similar approach was made to the 1950 data for the United States. Occupations were classified into five groups, but without regard to the contents of the social classes used by the General Register Office because there was no reason to assume that the combination of economic, educational, and social status that determine the levels in this country correspond exactly with those of the British.

Each of the occupations, or groups of occupations, in the Intermediate Occupational Classification of the Bureau of the Census (6) was assigned, on the basis of "expert" judgment, to one of five levels. Farmers and farm managers were assigned to occupation level II, and farm foremen and farm laborers to V. It has been noted, however, that farm laborers seemed to be grossly underreported on the death certificates, and farmers apparently overreported, particularly at younger ages. Examination of death rates that were obtained when farmers were included in occupation level II and farm laborers in V served to confirm

TABLE 1   **Estimated Number of Men 20 to 64 Years Old with Previous Work Experience, by Occupation Level, Age, and Race, United States, 1950[a]**

Age and race	Total	Occupation level					Agri-cultural workers
		I	II	III	IV	V	
All races							
Total							
20–64 years	40,224,242	1,568,064	3,795,962	14,898,037	9,859,072	4,111,342	5,316,318
20–24	4,524,932	83,453	222,088	1,419,394	1,428,439	645,893	596,515
25–29	5,414,615	241,930	414,317	1,997,522	1,509,646	554,433	591,810
30–34	5,281,782	246,504	479,217	2,019,838	1,394,617	477,010	585,169
35–44	10,197,274	454,158	1,065,526	3,863,081	2,494,699	913,375	1,263,692
45–54	8,360,560	327,586	937,555	3,245,831	1,770,304	798,364	1,157,581
55–59	3,502,339	119,701	377,769	1,303,915	700,902	371,693	576,929
60–64	2,942,740	94,732	299,490	1,048,456	560,465	350,574	544,622
Nonwhite							
Total							
20–64 Years	3,922,598	19,851	118,508	556,243	1,168,891	1,233,419	742,361
20–24	531,712	1,367	9,318	61,832	167,317	170,401	104,711
25–29	568,079	2,787	12,760	81,396	178,946	180,684	96,782
30–34	511,394	2,870	14,253	75,079	160,651	162,474	85,353
35–44	1,027,136	5,881	33,315	150,312	327,917	312,278	178,036
45–54	804,928	4,773	30,847	121,546	217,523	259,521	156,354
55–59	272,707	1,463	10,506	38,532	66,674	84,991	66,353
60–64	206,642	710	7,509	27,546	49,863	63,070	54,772
		Per cent distribution					
All races							
Total							
20–64 Years	100.0	3.9	9.4	37.0	24.5	10.2	13.2
20–24	100.0	1.8	4.9	31.4	31.6	14.3	13.2
25–29	100.0	4.5	7.7	36.9	27.9	10.2	10.9
30–34	100.0	4.7	9.1	38.2	26.4	9.0	11.1
35–44	100.0	4.5	10.4	37.9	24.5	9.0	12.4
45–54	100.0	3.9	11.2	38.8	21.2	9.5	13.8
55–59	100.0	3.4	10.8	37.2	20.0	10.6	16.5
60–64	100.0	3.2	10.2	35.6	19.0	11.9	18.5
Nonwhite							
Total,							
20–64 Years	100.0	0.5	3.0	14.2	29.8	31.4	18.9
20–24	100.0	0.3	1.8	11.6	31.5	32.0	19.7
25–29	100.0	0.5	2.2	14.3	31.5	31.8	17.0
30–34	100.0	0.6	2.8	14.7	31.4	31.8	16.7
35–44	100.0	0.6	3.2	14.6	31.9	30.4	17.3
45–54	100.0	0.6	3.8	15.1	27.0	32.2	19.4
55–59	100.0	0.5	3.9	14.1	24.4	31.2	24.3
60–64	100.0	0.3	3.6	13.3	24.1	30.5	26.5

[a] Excludes students, members of the armed forces, and persons who never worked.

these observations. It was decided to form a separate group for agricultural workers, and to exclude these occupations from their respective occupation level classes.

Some of the groups of the Intermediate Occupational Classification, particularly residual groups, are not homogeneous. Consequently, the occupation levels made up from the Intermediate List include some arbitrary combinations. The classes, and the proportion of the male population with previous work experience at ages 20–64 (Table 1) assigned to each class are as follows:

Occupation level	Per cent
I Professional Worker	4
II Technical, Administrative, and Managerial Workers	9
III Proprietors, Clerical, Sales, and Skilled Workers	37
IV Semiskilled Workers	25
V Laborers, except Farm and Mine	10
Agricultural Workers	13

Age-specific and age-adjusted death rates were computed for the six groups. Within these broad groups, it is not likely that lack of detailed correspondence between occupation reported in the census schedule and that reported on the death certificate will bias the rates. Another perennial problem in interpreting occupational mortality—the length of time spent by an individual in his so-called usual occupation—is mostly eliminated when analyses are made according to large groupings. There is probably some mobility between these classes but less than would be found between specific occupations.

Even with the study limited to ages under 65 years, some special adjustments were required for the retired population. In the 1950 Census of Population about 10 per cent of the men aged 55–59, and 18 per cent of the men 60–64 years old were numerated as not in the labor force. Since an occupation is requested on the death certificates for all persons

TABLE 2   Provisional Death Rates for Men 20 to 64 Years Old, by Occupation Level, Age, and Race, United States, 1950[a]

Age and race	Occupation level					Agricultural workers
	I	II	III	IV	V	
All races						
20–24	95.9	146.8	139.6	176.1	372.4	257.5
25–29	92.6	141.7	144.2	190.1	438.1	257.7
30–34	135.1	168.4	183.6	242.3	575.5	284.5
35–44	288.9	333.4	379.0	451.0	954.6	400.3
45–54	946.9	944.2	1,036.0	1,116.2	1,944.6	916.3
55–59	1,922.3	1,858.5	2,081.3	2,015.1	2,993.6	1,716.2
60–64	2,886.0	2,844.8	3,137.2	2,905.4	3,824.6	2,539.4
Standardized mortality ratio	84	87	96	100	165	88
Nonwhite						
20–24	0	268.3	177.9	224.1	608.0	410.7
25–29	b	329.2	223.6	304.0	704.5	473.2
30–34	b	329.8	322.3	416.4	938.6	617.4
35–44	b	672.4	539.9	621.5	1,443.6	784.7
45–54	b	1,458.8	1,316.4	1,366.3	2,790.9	1,778.7
55–59	b	3,398.1	2,473.3	2,315.7	4,815.8	3,149.8
60–64	b	4,767.6	3,521.4	2,679.3	5,874.4	4,445.7
Standardized mortality ratio	101	151	120	123	263	167

a Rates per 100,000 population in each specified group. Excludes students, members of the armed forces, and persons who never worked.

b Frequencies too small for rate computation.

occupational and social class differences   **173**

who have worked, it was necessary to estimate the population by occupation for men not in the labor force in these age groups and add these populations to the corresponding labor force groups. Data obtained in a monthly Current Population Survey conducted by the Bureau of the Census on the usual occupation of men not in the labor force served as a basis for these estimates.

The standardized mortality ratio, which is an age-adjusted rate shown as a ratio to the average death rate for all men 20–64, ranges for the five occupation levels from 84 for the professions to 165 for laborers (Table 2). The ratios for the first four groups are relatively close together, the figures being 84, 87, 96, and 100 respectively. Examination of age-specific rates also shows some clustering for the rates for the first four occupation levels, all differing sharply from the rates found for laborers (V). (See figure.) There is, in general, a regular increase in death rates with occupation level at the younger ages. For ages 45–64, the curves for the first four groups overlap considerably. For example, the lowest mortality rates are found in the professions (Occupation Level I) until age 45; at ages 45–54, the rate is about the same as for group II, and at older ages, the figures exceed those for group II. The death rates for the semi-skilled workers (IV) are lower than the

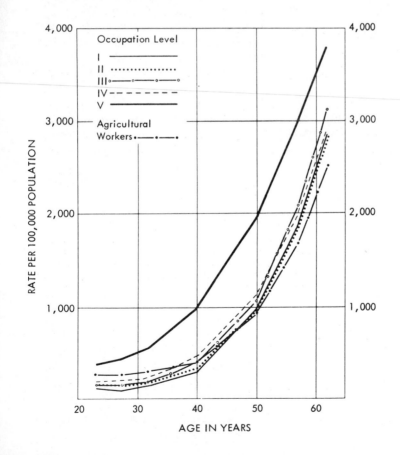

Provisional death rates for men by occupation level and age: United States, 1950.

skilled, clerical, and sales workers (III) after age 55.

The death rates for agricultural workers are lower than those for laborers at every age, but higher than the figures for occupation levels I–IV in the age groups under 35 years. The death rate for agricultural workers at ages 35–44 falls below that for the same age group in occupation level IV, and at older ages, rates for agricultural workers are below those for any other group.

Some men may be reported on the death certificate as "laborers" with no industry stated rather than as farm laborers. Such an error would result in an overstatement of death rates for occupation level V, and an understatement for the agricultural workers. The direction of error in returns for agricultural workers may be clarified by the study now being made by the Scripps Foundation for Research in Population Problems, in which occupation returns on death certificates for a sample of the male population who died in 1950 will be matched against the data given in the 1950 census.

It would be of interest to compare death rates for the social classes of England and Wales in 1950 with those for the United States, but there are many differences in the assignments of occupations to the classes. By reducing the five groups to three for both sets of data, better comparability is achieved. Social class, or occupation level I, is made up chiefly of the traditional professions in both countries. There seems to be little difficulty in identifying laborers (V); and bringing together classes II, III, and IV disposes of the greatest distinctions in assignments in the two countries. A separate group was set up for agricultural workers in both areas.

The comparison of rates for the two areas is further complicated by the fact that mortality among adult males for the United States is higher at every age than that for England and Wales. In order to remove this factor from the comparison, the death rates at each age in the United States and in England and Wales were assumed to be 100, and the ratio of the rate for a particular occupation class for the country to that for the total population in that age group was computed. These figures are shown in Table 3. In every age group, the range of ratios is greater for the United States than for England and Wales. Occupation level I for the United States is below the mean, and occupation level V above the average in every age group. For England and Wales, the differences from the average

TABLE 3 **Ratios of Death Rates by Occupation Level to Total Death Rates, by Age, for Men 20 to 64 Years Old, United States and England and Wales, 1950**

Occupation level	20–24 years	25–34 years	35–44 years	45–54 years	55–59 years	60–64 years
United States	100	100	100	100	100	100
England and Wales	100	100	100	100	100	100
Occupation level I:						
United States	49	53	66	87	94	97
England and Wales	102	90	83	98	99	100
Occupation levels II, III, and IV:						
United States	80	84	91	96	99	101
England and Wales	94	95	96	97	99	101
Occupation level V:						
United States	190	232	219	178	146	128
England and Wales	122	138	143	129	115	106
Agricultural workers:						
United States	132	125	92	84	84	85
England and Wales	139	104	87	75	75	72

are smaller throughout the age scale. The ratio for social class I is actually equal to or higher than the average at ages 20–24 and 60–64. In both countries the dispersion in the ratios decreases with increasing age, the maximum differences occurring between the ages of 25 and 44. Relatively, the professional workers of the United States have a more favorable mortality than their peers in England, while the laborers are at a relative disadvantage.

The comparison between the death rates for the United States and England and Wales has been made from the experience of the total male population of each country. It is only on this basis that the entire range of socio-economic strata in both areas can be included. For the United States, rates for the nonwhite population are of especial interest because of the high correlation between race and socio-economic status. Figures for the nonwhite population similar to those described for the total population are shown in Tables 1 and 2. According to the population distribution shown in Table 1, 31 per cent of the nonwhite males between 20 and 64 years of age are laborers, 30 per cent are semiskilled workers, and 14 per cent retail proprietors, clerical and skilled workers. The death rates for nonwhite men (Table 2) in occupation levels II, III, IV, and V (with one exception) are higher at every age than those for the comparable groups of the total population. The pattern of rates for the nonwhite population in groups III, IV, and V is somewhat similar to that for the total, with the differences between the rates for laborers (V) and for occupation level IV being much larger than the differences between the rates for groups III and IV.

The rates for occupation level II for the nonwhite population do not fall into the general pattern observed for the total population. The selection of occupations that make up group II for the

nonwhites differs considerably from the distribution for the total population, and this may account for the observed rates. Figures for the agricultural workers shown in Table 2 differ also from those for the total population. For the nonwhites, the death rates of agricultural workers fall between groups IV and V at every age.

These figures suggest that the occupation levels for the nonwhites are not necessarily comparable with the same group for the total population. Within each group, the nonwhites may represent the lower end of the socio-economic scale. On the other hand, factors other than those described by occupation may contribute to higher mortality for all nonwhites.

It should be possible soon to complete additional tabulations of the occupational mortality data. These tables may indicate whether there are particular occupations or particular causes of death which are chiefly responsible for the large differences in rates between laborers (V) and the remainder of the population. It may also be possible to attempt some assessment of the importance of factors directly connected with an occupation; and those that are chiefly economic.

One method of evaluating the force of socio-economic levels, isolated from occupation, is to examine mortality rates for wives and families of men of known occupations. The socio-economic circumstances would be similar for the household, while the risks on the job will be suffered only by the husband. The General Register Office of England and Wales has developed this approach. In this country there is not enough information on the death certificate to permit such a study. But, in large cities, the existence of other methods of measuring economic status has made possible studies of mortality rates for all members of the family, according to class. Deaths have been grouped according to residence of the deceased by census tract, a subdivision of the city into a small relatively homogeneous neighborhood. In census years, the median monthly rental, or median income can be determined for each tract. The tracts may be arrayed in a frequency distribution by median income or median rental, and grouped into suitable classes which represent economic strata of the population. Comparison of age-adjusted and age-specific death rates for each economic stratum of the cities in which such data have been accumulated may permit better understanding of the part economic status plays in mortality. Intensive studies have been made in many cities, including Chicago, Buffalo, Cincinnati, Cleveland, Baltimore, and New York, but it has not yet been possible to relate the findings to those of the present study.

Daric concluded from his study of occupational mortality data that the large mortality differentials by social class are attributable more to socio-economic factors than to direct occupational risks. (1) The experience for England and Wales between 1921 and 1931 is taken as a clear indication of a narrowing of the gap in mortality between social classes resulting from improvements in mortality experience of the poorer classes. Daric interprets this to be the effect of social and medical advances which have benefited the poorer classes relatively more than those in better economic circumstances.

The age-specific death rates for England and Wales for 1950 (2) do not show the convergence of death rates as noted by Daric for an earlier period. In fact, the reduction in the death rate for social class V between 1930 and 1950 was the lowest at every age up to 65 years compared with the change in rates for the other social classes. Similarly, the improvement in the infant mortality rate for the neo-natal and post-neonatal periods was least for social class V. A more complete analysis covering the period 1949–1953 may cause a revision of these findings. However, at the present time, there does not appear to be a clear cut indication of convergence of death rates due to greater improvements in mortality in the poorer classes.

The pattern of decline in the death rates in the United States would seem to support the suggestion of the narrowing of the gap in mortality between socio-economic groups. Great strides have been made in the prevention of deaths from the communicable diseases. Significant declines in mortality among younger people have been recorded, the death rate for nonwhites has been dropping faster than for the whites, and the once large differentials among states are closing. However, data on differences in mortality for the various economic strata have been compiled only for scattered segments of the population, and have never been studied as a whole.

The data presented here show high mortality rates for laborers. Also significant is the lack of great differentiation in the rates for the occupation levels other than laborers in the older age groups, 55 to 64 years. It is in these age groups that the accumulated effects of direct occupational risks, or for that matter of socio-economic forces, would be expected to be greatest.

The few preliminary statistics presented here give some indication of mortality differentials by occupation level in the United States. They also serve to stimulate but do not answer a number of questions. For example, are the differences in mortality in the younger age groups the result of selection of entrants into various occupations, or is economic position more important at these ages? Is there an optimum economic status level for survival under present conditions? Is the convergence of rates at the older ages due to mobility between occupation levels? What conditions in our way of living or working produce a wider range of death rates in the United States than in England and Wales? It is hoped that further analyses of the occupational mortality data will either provide an answer of these questions or lead to other studies which will.

Bibliography

1. DARIC, JEAN, "*Mortality, Occupation and Socio-Economic Status*," National Office of Vital Statistics, *Vital Statistics—Special Reports*, XXXIII, No. 10 (1951).
2. GREAT BRITAIN REGISTRAR GENERAL, *Decennial Supplement, England and Wales, 1951, Part 1: Occupational Mortality.* London, Her Majesty's Stationery Office, 1954.
3. UNITED STATES CENSUS OFFICE, *Eleventh Decennial Census:* 1890. Vol. IV: Report on Vital and Social Statistics in the United States, Part 1. Washington, D.C.: United States Government Printing Office, 1896.
4. UNITED STATES CENSUS OFFICE, *Twelfth Census of the United States, 1900.* Census Reports, Volume III, Vital Statistics, Part I. 1902.
5. WHITNEY, J. S., *Death Rates by Occupation Based on Data of the United States Census Bureau, 1930.* New York, National Tuberculosis Association, 1934.
6. UNITED STATES BUREAU OF THE CENSUS, *United States Census of Population, 1950. Volume II. Characteristics of the Population, Part I, United States Summary, Chapter C.* Washington, D. C.: U. S. Government Printing Office, 1953.

life styles

five

Max Weber used the term "life styles" to refer to those modes of conduct, dress, speech, thought, and attitudes, that defined various "honor" groups and that in turn served as models of behavior for those who aspired to be members of these groups. By extension, the term is often used now to include the range of distinctive behavior patterns, including institutional patterns such as family styles, value orientations to the world in general, and patterns of interpersonal and intergroup conduct.

Three different aspects of "life styles" are considered in this section. Alex Inkeles examines the distribution of the feeling of happiness and well-being among different classes; Herbert H. Hyman searches for basic value patterns that might be said to be distinctive; and Urie Bronfenbrenner examines the data available on patterns of child-rearing in different classes.

Inkeles finds that there are indeed class differences, and in the expectable direction—in the reported feeling of happiness such that the better off you are economically, the more likely you are to have laughed recently and the less likely to have cried out of sadness. So, too, the classes respond as expected with regard to their reported feelings of satisfaction with the progress of life in general, the occupations they optimistically expect to achieve, and the attendant sense of mastery over their fates and careers.

Hyman looks at related things, including the emphasis placed on college education and its assigned importance for advancement, the kinds of occupations chosen for youth, and the rationales offered for these choices, and the beliefs in the possibilities of economic achievement and advancement. He finds in these and other instances that the general and expected correlation of class and well-being holds here: the better off the group is economically, the higher its aspirations for its children, the greater its expectations of success and advancement, and the stronger its beliefs in the openness of the system of opportunity.

Bronfenbrenner, in turn, is concerned with the general assumption that there are significant differences in the patterns of child rearing among different classes. He examines a range of data carefully, specifying the difficulties in securing sensibly comparative data, and discovers that there have been shifting styles of child-rearing over time. He feels that some of the shift is due to the exposure of middle-class mothers to a body of persuasive literature such as the Children's Bureau bulletins on child care, and, of course, the ubiquitous and powerful books of Benjamin Spock. Because of the greater susceptibility to literature of middle-class women and because of the greater shift in the pediatric trends recommended over the years in this literature, Bronfenbrenner concludes that these women are likely to change their practices more often. Thus, he notes a significant shift toward greater permissiveness in feeding and toilet-training practices in the first two years of the child's life.

Bronfenbrenner extends his analysis to other aspects of child-rearing and finds that there has been a decisive convergence between the different classes, one that may, in fact, have existed for some time, but that was obscured by the traditional view of the impulsivity of the lower class as opposed to the imputed rationality and control of the middle class. Yet some significant differences persist, especially in degree of permissiveness, degree of expectations for children, modes of discipline employed, and degree of acceptance and egalitarianism in parent-child relationships.

Class and Happiness

ALEX INKELES

Granted that happiness is a very elusive thing, we may yet make so bold as to study it and to do so through so crude a device as a public-opinion poll. Of course we should not naively accept what man says when we ask him, "Are you happy?" But neither is it reasonable to assume that whatever he says means the opposite. That would be all too regular and a sure key to the truth. Some men will be truly cheerful but suspect our purpose; fear of the "evil eye," or a trait of personality, may lead them to deny publicly their true feeling. If everyone answered the question in a random and, in that sense, meaningless way, we would expect by chance that 50 per cent in any population would say "Yes," 50 per cent "No." and that no control variable such as age, sex, or income would reveal anything but this 50/50 division.

Reprinted from Alex Inkeles, "Industrial Man: The Relation of Status to Experience, Perception, and Value," *The American Journal of Sociology*, LXVI, No. 1 (July, 1960), 13–18, by permission of the author and the University of Chicago Press, Copyright © 1960 by the University of Chicago.

Common sense tells us that some groups produce more people who feel they are happy than do others, and with reason. Those about to commit suicide tell their friends, doctors, or diaries that they are miserable; those who are about to get divorced are likely to report their marriage is unhappy. Admittedly, where there are pressures which make people disguise their true feelings, their more or less public report of how they feel will certainly reduce the clarity of the relationship between the objective situation and their true inner feeling. If, despite this built-in and essentially uncontrollable distortion, we still find strong and meaningful connections between a man's situation and what he says about his happiness, then we must assume that the "real" connection is, if anything, not weaker but stronger than the one which emerges in our data.

Both direct and indirect questions have been used in an effort to assess individual happiness. An identical direct question was put to people in the U.S., England, France, and Canada during 1946. By contrast to the Anglo-Saxon trio, the French emerge as dour indeed: in the other countries a third or more were "very happy," but in France only

8 per cent. Forty per cent of the French said they were "not very happy," as against a maximum of 10 per cent elsewhere.[1] Much the same question was asked in 1949 by at least six of the Gallup affiliates, with similar results. Only 11 per cent of the French were "very happy," as against a range of from 26 per cent in Norway to 52 per cent in Australia.[2] Unfortunately, we do not have cross-tabulations by stratification variables for either of these two studies, but comparable data from Italy and Britain leave little doubt that, when these are made, we will find in each society that such happiness as anyone cares to admit will be found oftenest among those in the more advantaged strata of society.

In the British study men were asked: "In the last twenty-four hours, have you had a hearty laugh?" Women were asked whether they had had a "good cry," an effort being made to disarm them by prefacing the question with the statement: "Many doctors say it is good to give vent to your feelings by crying once in a while." Although the questions do not deal directly with happiness, they very probably measure much the same thing. The proportion who had laughed in the last twenty-four hours decreased, and the proportion who had cried increased, as one descended the socio-economic scale (Table 1). The differentiation was sharp, however, only in the case of the very poor, who had laughed only half as often and had cried twice as often as did those in the middle and upper economic classes.

I have asked many people, including several large audiences, to predict the outcome of this poll. The great majority

TABLE 1   Laughing and Crying in England by Class and Sex[a]

Economic class	Percentage who laughed in last 24 hours (men only)	Percentage who cried in last 24 hours (women only)
Well-to-do	47	12
Average	50	11
Below average	41	16
Poor	26	27

[a] Reported in *Doxa Bolletino*, V, No. 6 (April, 1956).

invariably expected the working class to laugh more often. They express surprise at the findings and generally question me closely as to the time and country involved.[3] On learning the study was done in England, they invariably offer an *ad hoc* explanation, based on assumptions about the character of English society, and regularly volunteer the opinion that certainly in Italy the results would be different. Unfortunately the same question seems not to have been asked in sunny Italy. But its smiling workers and singing peasants have been asked two other questions which should serve our purpose. The first was simple and straightforward: "Just now do you feel happy or unhappy?" The second was more complex: "Could you summarize in a few words the state (or balance) of your life today?" The respondents were then offered a choice of six sentences suggesting various combinations and degrees of pain and joy ranging from "Life has given me only joys and satisfactions," to "Life has given me only pain and disillusionment."

The results are fairly unambiguous

---

[1] Hadley W. Cantril, ed., *Public Opinion, 1935–1946* (Princeton, N. J.: Princeton University Press, 1951), p. 281.

[2] AGP, Nos. 569–78 (February-March, 1949). The other countries were Holland (43 per cent), the United States (43 per cent), and the United Kingdom (39 per cent).

[3] These audiences were generally composed of faculty and students, supplemented by people in the college or university community who attend lectures "open to the public"—safely characterized as solidly middle class. Despite their high average level of education, they seemed to harbor a stereotype of the working class which in important respects is strikingly analogous to that held by southern whites about the poor, irresponsible, but "happy" Negro.

but, as is so often true of such data, by no means completely so. For example, on the first, "test" the lowest proportion of happy people is found among one of the more favored groups—the managers (*dirigente*), a category which seems to include free professionals. On the other hand, this group is quite "normal" on the second test, reporting life to be full of pain and disillusionment less often than any other group. Leaving aside such complications, however, we may conclude that on the whole, in Italy no less than in Britain, happiness is much more commonly reported by the advantaged strata of society, while sadness and despair are more standard in the manual and depressed classes. Of course, the well-to-do have no monopoly on happiness, nor does a majority of the working class report itself miserable. In all classes the central tendency is toward some mixture of happiness and pain. But at the extremes the general pattern we have found elsewhere is manifested here as well. As we ascend the occupational ladder, the proportion who are "very" or "fairly" happy rises from 29 per cent among farm laborers and ordinary workers to 47 per cent among employers.[4] Similarly, at the other extreme, workers report themselves as unhappy two-and-a-half times as often as do employers and managers. Among the manual classes the ratio of the happy to the unhappy is as low as 1:1, whereas in the more advantaged groups it is almost 5:1.

Much the same pattern is shown in the second test. The life of much pain and little joy is claimed by about 50 per cent of workers and farm laborers, by as few as 23 per cent of the managers and professionals, and by about one-third of employers and farm owners (Table 2).

---

[4] There is, however, not much to choose between the lowest categories who are clustered around the 30 per cent level (cf. *Doxa*, No. 12 [April, 1948]).

To assess happiness in a number of countries simultaneously we must, unfortunately, use a question which can at best be taken as only a rough approximation of those dealing directly with happiness, namely, one inquiring about "satisfaction." What happiness is may be somewhat ambiguous, but we are generally clear that it deals with an *emotional* state. "Satisfaction" is a much more ambiguous term, and, when not further specified, it can mean satisfaction with one's financial situation, social or political advancement, family life, or any one of a number of things. Furthermore, "happiness" may be translated fairly well from one language to another, but "satisfaction" changes its meaning. In addition, in the available comparative study the question on satisfaction came immediately after one on security, and this probably led people more often to respond in terms of financial criteria rather than of general satisfaction in life. Consequently, to check the reasonableness of using the question on satisfaction in life as an index of happiness, I compared the results (for Italy) of two different polls, one asking directly about happiness (described above), the other using the question on satisfaction from the available cross-national study. The structure of the answers was very similar (Table 3). On both questions, business and farm owners and managers reported themselves either dissatisfied or unhappy only half as often as did manual and farm workers, with clerks and artisans falling in between. The correlation was not perfect, but there was quite close association.

Allowing, then, for many necessary reservations, let us look at the responses to the question, "How satisfied are you with the way you are getting on now?" which was asked simultaneously in nine countries. The results (Table 4) are certainly less sharp and clear-cut than those obtained for job satisfaction. There are

TABLE 2   Balance of Joy and Pain in Life in Italy, in Percentages by Occupation[a]

Occupation	More pain than joy[b]	More joy than pain[c]	A balance of joy and pain[d]	No answer
Employer	32	20	45	3
Manager	23	23	56	—
Farm owner and operator	33	20	46	1
White collar	28	15	55	2
Artisan	36	12	51	1
Worker	48	11	41	—
Farm laborer	51	11	38	1

a *Doxa Bolletino*, No. 12 (April, 1948).

b Includes the response: "Life has given *only* pains and disillusion."

c Includes: "Life has given me *only* joys and satisfactions."

d Includes: "Many pains but also many joys" and "Few pains and few joys." Among workers and farm laborers and employees the choice of "few joys" predominated markedly; among managers, the reverse; and by the remainder the two alternatives were equally chosen.

TABLE 3   Comparison of Italian Results on Questions of "Happiness" and "Satisfaction with Situation" (Per Cent)

Occupation	"Dissatisfied" with present situation[a]	Occupation	"Unhappy" at this moment[b]
Business owners	31	Employers	10
Salaried managers	35	Managers	10
Farm owners	32	Farm owners	10
Artisans	43	Artisans	16
Clerks	55	Employees	14
Manual workers	64	Workers	26
Farm workers	63	Farm laborers	20

a From William Buchanan and Hadley Cantril, *How Nations See Each Other* (Urbana: University of Illinois Press, 1953), p. 170. The question was the same as that reported in Table 4 for nine countries including Italy.

b From *Doxa Bolletino*, No. 12 (April, 1948).

TABLE 4   Percentage Dissatisfied with How They Are "Getting On" by Country and Occupation[a]

Country	Occupation						
	Owners	Managers	Professionals	White collar	Artisans	Workers	Farm labor
Australia	11	18	15	22	31	17	17
Britain	41	21	14	36	40	36	26
France	38	29	55	56	56	67	63
Germany	46	39	50	35	37	48	52
Italy	31	35	46	55	43	64	63
Mexico	58	57	50	55	67	65	75
Netherlands	26	15	22	23	37	43	41
Norway	7	4	2	11	12	11	22
United States	20	22	26	24	28	31	39

a Adapted from data in Appendix D of William Buchanan and Hadley Cantril, *How Nations See Each Other* (Urbana, Ill.: University of Illinois Press, 1953), pp. 125–216.

numerous irregularities and ambiguities. For example, Germany produces not our familiar step pattern but a U-shaped curve, and Australia yields, if anything, an inverted U. These cases suggest what the table as a whole hints, namely, that the question is ambiguous and people respond to it in terms of different criteria. Nevertheless, there seems to be an underlying cross-national pattern. The higher non-manual positions hold at least rank 1 (lowest proportion dissatisfied), 2, or 3 in seven of nine countries, whereas the workers held so high a rank in no country and the farm laborers in one. The occupations were originally listed in a rough approximation of their standing in the hierarchy of power and rewards. It is interesting, therefore, that when we sum the rank orders for each occupation we emerge with a regular progression which follows the original ordering. Except for the owners, whose score of 27 is strongly affected by their extremely deviant response in Britain, there is a steady increase from managers (20), through professionals (24), white collar (33), artisans and skilled workers (45), and workers (50), to farm laborers (53). That a comparable cross-national pattern emerges when either socioeconomic status or education is used as the independent variable strengthens our conviction that the underlying structure is real. The fact that the relationship holds more firmly when occupation or economic status rather than education are the independent variables suggests that, as we anticipated, the answers more strongly reflect satisfaction with economic than with spiritual welfare.

Whatever their weakness as a guide to the cross-national pattern we seek, these data also point to the usefulness of our procedure for identifying groups with special problems or distinctive responses to more general problems. It is striking, for example, that in Britain the owners formed the group whose members were *most* often dissatisfied with the way they were "getting on." But this was 1948, when they were threatened by the highest level reached by the wave of nationalization sentiment in England, and so the result is not surprising.

Some of the difficulty raised by the question on "satisfaction with getting on" could be avoided if the respondent were asked to disregard his financial condition. An international poll meeting this requirement is, unfortunately, not at hand. We should, however, examine an International Research Associate study in which the wording of the question and its location in the questionnaire may have somewhat reduced the role of economic referents. The question was: "Do you feel that you have gotten as far ahead as you should at this stage of your life, or are you dissatisfied with the progress you have made so far?" Here again, unfortunately, the question would probably be understood by many to mean mainly economic or material "getting ahead" or "progress." This assumption is greatly strengthened by the fact that the responses are more regular and the differences sharper when socioeconomic status rather than occupation is used (Table 5). Using socioeconomic status to classify the respondents, we find the step structure present in eight of eleven cases, markedly so in four. There is no instance in which the result is the complete reverse of our expectation, but in three countries the group classified as "middle" has the lowest proportion satisfied. Using occupation as the independent variable, we again have four strong cases and a fifth which is up to standard, but now six fail to qualify. In five of these instances the difficulty arises again from the fact that a higher proportion of the middle level of white-collar workers are dissatisfied than is the case among workers. If we compare the executive-professional and worker groups

TABLE 5   Percentage Satisfied with Progress in Life, by Country and Status[a]

Country	Occupation			Socioeconomic group		
	Executive, professional	White collar	Wage earner	Upper	Middle	Lower
Australia	70	64	66	73	70	65
Austria	61	60	47	64	59	60
Belgium	37	36	21	43	41	34
Brazil[b]	74	60	63	81	71	54
Britain	79	66	70	73	68	71
Denmark	77	78	68	81	75	64
Germany	73	71	68	73	72	65
Japan	52	42	33	50	40	13
Netherlands	61	57	59	67	58	66
Norway	89	79	70	87	71	60
Sweden	71	58	67	80	67	60

[a] Tabulations from a study conducted by International Research Associates.
[b] Rio de Janeiro and São Paulo only.

alone, the pattern is clear-cut in all eleven cases.[5]

In sum, no very "pure" measure of feelings of happiness or of spiritual or psychic (as against material) well-being, applied cross-nationally and fully reported, is at hand. Taking the available evidence together, however, we cannot entertain any other hypothesis but that the feeling of happiness or of psychic well-being is unevenly distributed in most, perhaps all, countries. Those who are economically well off, those with more education or whose jobs require more training and skill, more often report themselves happy, joyous, laughing, free of sorrow, satisfied with life's progress. Even though the pattern is weak or ambiguous in some cases, there has not been a single case of a *reversal* of the pattern, that is, a case where measures of happiness are inversely related to measures of status, in studies involving fifteen different countries—at least six of which were studied on two different oc-

casions, through the use of somewhat different questions. There is, then, good reason to challenge the image of the "carefree but happy poor." As one angry man wrote to me, after he had read a news report of a speech I had made reporting the relation of laughter to social status: "And what the hell do you think the poor have to laugh about, anyway?"

Plausible as this contention may be on the surface, it is obviously not the end but only the beginning of a study. If those who are better placed and more fortunate more often report they are happy, can we test the validity of this report by such other measures as their rates of suicide, homicide, and mental illness?[6] If the proportion satisfied rises with income, will better-paid workers in any country be happier than those less well paid at the same occupational level?

[5] A twelfth case, France, was a strong instance of the expected relationship. Since socioeconomic status classifications were not not available for France, it was excluded from Table 5 to make both parts strictly comparable.

[6] Suicide rates rise with socioeconomic status, but their absolute frequency is quite low in all groups. Homicides, many times more common than suicide, and psychopathic illness, which is incomparably more frequent, are both markedly commoner in the lower classes. Insofar as these rates, when combined, provide an index of misery, the pattern observed would be congruent with that already described.

Will raising the incomes of all increase the happiness of all, or does it require an unequal gain to bring happiness to some? What of the man who is well educated but poorly paid, or rich but poorly educated? Some questions of this kind can be answered by further cross-tabulation of the original IBM cards, which it is hoped will be possible at a later date.[7] Some will require new cross-national studies clearly focused on these issues.

[7] The Roper Center for Public Opinion Research at Williams College plans to collect the IBM cards from studies conducted since World War II in some twenty countries. If this objective is achieved, it will open exceptional opportunities for comparative research.

The Value Systems of Different Classes: A Social Psychological Contribution to the Analysis of Stratification

HERBERT H. HYMAN

Introduction

The existence of stratification in American society is well known. The corollary fact—that individuals from lower strata are not likely to climb far up the economic ladder is also known. However, what requires additional analysis are the factors that account for this lack of mobility. Many of these factors of an objective nature have been studied. Opportunity in the society is differential; higher education or specialized training, which might provide access to a high position, must be bought with money— the very commodity which the lower classes lack. Such objective factors help maintain the existing structure. But there are other factors of a more subtle psychological nature which have not been illuminated and which may also work to perpetuate the existing order. It is our assumption that an intervening variable mediating the relationship between low position and lack of upward mobility is a system of beliefs and values

Reprinted from *Class, Status, and Power,* eds. Reinhard Bendix and Seymour Martin Lipset, 2nd ed., (New York: The Free Press, 1966), pp. 488–499, by permission of the author, the editors, and the publisher.

within the lower classes which in turn reduces the very *voluntary* actions which would ameliorate their low position.

The components of this value system, in our judgment, involve less emphasis upon the traditional high success goals, increased awareness of the lack of opportunity to achieve success, and less emphasis upon the achievement of goals which in turn would be instrumental for success. To put it simply the lower class individual doesn't want as much success, knows he couldn't get it even if he wanted to, and doesn't want what might help him get success. Of course, an individual's value system is only one among many factors on which his position in the social hierarchy depends. Some of these factors may be external and arbitrary, quite beyond the control of even a highly motivated individual. However, within the bounds of the freedom available to individuals, this value system would create a *self-imposed* barrier to an improved position.

Presumably this value system arises out of a realistic appraisal of reality and in turn softens for the individual the impact of low status. Unfortunately, we have at the moment little information on its genesis. However, we aim to document in this paper the presence of these values as a contemporary factor to be considered in discussions of the larger problems of stratification and mobility.

There are implications in such an analysis that go far beyond the specific problem of understanding the lack of upward mobility. The study of the psychological correlates of the objective class structure is in itself a problem to which social psychologists have [addressed] and continue to address themselves for its relevance to the larger theoretical problem of attitude formation. And the study of values specific to the economic realm contributes much to the social psychological analysis of adjustment and deviant behavior. Thus in Merton's influential paper, *Social Structure and Anomie*, deviant behavior is analyzed as a phenomenon concentrated in certain strata and emerging out of strains that differentially burden those lower in the social structure.[1] For example, one type of deviance is hypothesized as resulting from the frustration of the lower class individual's desire to achieve the cultural goal of economic success because the access to the means for such success is less available to him. "This syndrome of lofty aspirations and limited realistic opportunities. . . is precisely the pattern which invites deviant behavior." (p. 148). It is clear that Merton's analysis assumes that the cultural goal of success is in actuality internalized by lower class individuals. Perhaps it also requires that the lower class individual *recognize* that the means to success are not available to him. It is certainly true *at a given point in time* that an individual frustrated in his goals because access to means is not open to him, will experience the incident as frustrating *whether or not he realizes* that the means are beyond his grasp. But it seems also true in the larger time perspective that if he continues to think that the means for a *future* success are available to him that the frustration will be milder and that deviance might not occur.[2] Conversely, if the individual regarded his chances to achieve his goal of success as negligible, when in reality they were good, there would be a psychologically produced strain toward deviance.

What is obviously required is empirical evidence on the degree to which individuals in different strata value the culturally prescribed goal of success, believe that opportunity is available to them, and hold other values which would aid or hinder them in their attempts to move towards their goal. This paper, in a preliminary way, is thus complementary to Merton's theoretical analysis.

While there is considerable literature on the beliefs and attitudes of the different economic classes, the specific realm that concerns us seems to have been generally neglected. Kornhauser's early writings come close to our problem and we shall allude to his findings in considerable detail. While Centers gives considerable attention to such values, he concentrates much more on the problem of the politico-economic ideology of individuals in different positions in the class structure. These studies provide the only quantitative evidence predicated on representative samples of large universes. Knupfer's study, while concerned with the problem and guided by the explicit hypothesis that there are "psychological restrictions which reinforce the economic," is essentially a characterology of the lower class individual describing in qualitative terms a diversity of attitudes, behaviors, and values. Similarly, Davis, Gardner and Gardner

---

[1] R. K. Merton, *Social Structure and Anomie*, reprinted as Chap. IV, *Social Theory and Social Structure* (New York: The Free Press, 1949).

[2] Farber has demonstrated that the experience of suffering as a consequence of some objective frustration is dependent on the time perspective of the individual. See M. L. Farber, "Suffering and Time Perspective of the Prisoner," *University of Iowa Studies in Child Welfare*, XX (1944), 155–227.

give some evidence on the way in which the class structure is experienced by individuals in different objective positions, but the reports are qualitative and literary in character. A number of quantitative studies are relevant but are limited in scope to specialized samples. Chinoy's study deals directly with our problem but is confined to a homogeneous group of 62 industrial workers in one automobile plant. Similarly, Hollingshead provides information on one aspect of the problem, the occupational goals of youth in different classes, but the study is limited to one community of about 6,000 people in the Middle West. Form presents data on occupational and educational aspirations for contrasted groups of white collar and manual workers living in the relatively homogeneous planned community of Greenbelt, Maryland. Galler also presents information on the occupational goals of children in two contrasted classes for a sample limited to Chicago.[3]

A variety of other psychological concomitants of objective class position have been explored. The political ideology of the different classes is a classic realm for research by social scientists. Aesthetic values such as tastes and preferences have been mapped for the different classes by communication research specialists. Attitudes towards child rearing in the different classes have been studied by Allison Davis and Erickson.[4]

In seeking additional information in the realm of values, we shall avail ourselves of the accumulated findings of public opinion surveys, and use a procedure of secondary analysis. It is our belief that public opinion surveys have much rich information on many social science problems, such information often being an accidental by-product of the continuing inquiry into the characteristics of the public which opinion polls have been conducting for the past 15 years. While these inquiries often deal with applied problems of a transitory and insignificant character, from the great mass of data available much can be extracted by re-analysis which bears on problems of fundamental theoretical interest. We shall limit this analysis to the United States, but it should be noted that surveys parallel in content have been conducted in other countries, for example, Germany and England. Ultimately the analyses of these studies would permit us to examine the psychological variations between the classes as a function of the larger societal setting.

[3] See Arthur W. Kornhauser, Analysis of "Class Structure" of Contemporary American Society—Psychological Bases of Class Divisions, in *Industrial Conflict*, G. W. Hartmann and T. Newcomb, ed. (New York: Dryden Press, 1939); A. Davis, B. B. Gardner and M. Gardner, *Deep South, A Social Anthropological Study of Caste and Class* (Chicago: University of Chicago Press, 1941); R. Centers, *The Psychology of Social Classes* (Princeton, N. J.: Princeton University Press, 1949), see esp. Chap. IX for a treatment of other values; also see his paper, "Motivational Aspects of Occupational Stratification," *Journal of Social Psychology*, XXVIII (1948), 196–197; G. Knupfer, "Portrait of the Underdog," *Publishers Opinion Quarterly*, XI (1947), 103–114; E. Chinoy, "The Tradition of Opportunity and the Aspirations of Automobile Workers," *American Journal of Sociology*, LVII (1952), 453–459; A. B. Hollingshead, *Elmtown's Youth* (New York: John Wiley & Sons, Inc., 1949); William H. Form, "Toward an Occupational Social Psychology," *Journal of Social Psychology*, XXIV (1946), 85–99; E. H. Galler, "Influence of Social Class on Children's Choices of Occupations," *Elementary School Journal*, LI (1951), 439–445.

[4] For summaries of literature on attitudes as related to objective class position the reader is referred to H. Hyman, "The Psychology of Status," *Archives of Psychology*, CCLXIX (1942), esp. Chap. VI; for summaries of aesthetic values as related to class factors, the reader is referred to J. T. Klapper, *The Effects of Mass Media* (New York: Columbia University, Bureau of Applied Social Research, 1950) (mimeo); for studies in the child-rearing realm, see M. C. Erickson, "Social Status and Child-Rearing Practices," in T. Newcomb and E. L. Hartley, eds., *Readings in Social Psychology* (New York: Holt, Rinehart & Winston, Inc., 1947); Allison Davis, *Social-Class Influences Upon Learning* (Cambridge, Mass.: Harvard University Press, 1951).

Most such inquiries also have the usual advantage of being conducted on the basis of scientific sampling of the national population, and therefore permit more precise and generalized inferences than is usually the case in academic research. By contrast, Erickson's analysis of class and child rearing practices was based on 100 families in the Chicago area and the major study by Havighurst and Davis on differences in child rearing was based on 100 white and 100 Negro families living in Chicago.[5]

Such studies while pioneering in character were limited in size by lack of resources. We are suggesting that even with minimal resources, academicians can fall heir to massive data collected at considerable expense for other purposes, and achieve greater generality in their findings.

Limitations are present, of course. The area of inquiry that interests us may have been touched only tangentially in the original survey, and possibilities for analysis may be scanty. Particularly, where the published account of the survey has to be used rather than the original data, the re-analysis is gravely limited. However, what we sacrifice in these respects is compensated for by the efficiency of the procedure and the great gain in generality. The sections to follow seek to demonstrate that secondary analyses are worthwhile, and that implicit in many surveys are data of great theoretical significance.[6]

Achievement in any realm is dependent upon two factors: the possession of both the necessary ability and the motivation to reach the goal. Ability is of course limited by *socially imposed* barriers to training and lack of channels to given types of positions. However, ability may also be retarded by lack of individual striving to obtain whatever training in turn is instrumental to economic advancement.

Consequently if we find that both motivation to advance to high positions and to obtain the training which is instrumental in achieving such positions are reduced in the lower class individual we shall have established our hypothesis. The same formula as applies to achievement, with minor modification, is relevant to Merton's theory. We need evidence here on the acceptance of success goals and on the belief in the accessibility of such goals.

The Value Placed on Formal Education

Part of the ideology of American life is that important positions are not simply inherited by virtue of the wealth of one's parents, but can be achieved. Such achievement, however, requires for many types of important positions considerable formal education. One cannot, for example, become a physician or a lawyer or an engineer without advanced education. Consequently, insofar as the lower classes placed less value on higher education, this would constitute an aspect of a larger value system which would work detrimental to their advancement. That such is really the case is evidenced in data collected by the National Opinion Research Center in a nationwide survey in 1947.[7] Within the total sample of approximately 2,500 adults and 500 youths about half indicated that they regarded "some college training" as their answer to the question: "About how much schooling do you

---

[5] *Ibid.*

[6] The basic source for such analyses is now available in H. Cantril and M. Strunk, *Public Opinion* (Princeton, N. J.: Princeton University Press, 1935–1946).

[7] For a summary report of this survey, the reader is referred to *Opinion News*, September 1, 1947, National Opinion Research Center, University of Chicago. The survey was conducted in conjunction with Ohio State University; Profs. Hatt and North representing that institution and Don Cahalan of the Center acting as Study Director.

think most young men need these days to get along well in the world?" That this value is not equally shared by the lower groups is clear from the data presented in Table 1 where the value is distributed by various stratification measures.

It is clear that whatever measure of stratification is employed the lower groups emphasize college training much less.[8] Insofar as such training is one avenue to upward movement, this value would operate to maintain the present system.

These data emphasize the difference in the belief in the value of higher education. A related finding is available from a survey done by Roper in 1945 in which a more direct question was put to adults on their desire for their own children to go on to college. The exact question and the data are presented in Table 2.

In terms of the perpetuation of the present system of stratification, however, these values as measured among adults only take on relevance insofar as they would be passed on to the children.[9] As a possible contribution to a more precise treatment of the consequences of this

---

[8] On the basis of a variety of studies, Havighurst and Rodgers confirm these findings. They remark "the motivational reasons for not going to college may be summarized as follows: Practically all of the superior youths who do not continue their education beyond high school are children of people who have had less than a high school education. These families participate in a culture which has little personal contact with higher education. They value a job and an earning career highly for their young people. . . . While these people have come to look favorably on a high school education for their children they do not regard colleges really within the reach of their aspirations or their financial means." Havighurst and Rodgers do, however, point to the interesting phenomenon of the deviant case, and note that a substantial *minority* of the working class do view higher education for their children in favorable terms. They attribute this to exposure to "upper middle class culture." See *Who Should Go to College* (New York: Columbia University Press, 1952.), p. 162.

[9] Merton similarly calls attention to the role of parents as central to his analysis: *op. cit.*, p. 148.

TABLE 1   The Differential Emphasis among Economic Classes upon College Education as an Essential to Advancement

Interviewer's rating of economic level	Per cent recommending college education	N
Wealthy and prosperous	68	512
Middle class	52	1,531
Lower class	39	856
Occupation		
Professional	74	301
Businessmen and proprietors	62	421
White collar workers	65	457
Skilled labor	53	392
Semiskilled	49	416
Domestic and personal service workers	42	194
Farmers	47	417
Non-farm laborers	35	132
Highest education achieved		
Attended college	72	564
Attended high school	55	1,411
Attended grammar school	36	926
Among renters, monthy rental		
Above $60	70	327[a]
$40–$60	64	666
$20–$40	54	990
Below $20	37	403

[a] The numbers do not add to the total sample because farm respondents and certain other groups are excluded from the rental question.

TABLE 2   Preference for a College Education for the Children of the Different Classes

"After the war, if you had a son (daughter) graduating from high school would you prefer that he (she) go on to college, or would you rather have him (her) do something else, or wouldn't you care one way or the other?"

	Per cent preferring college[a]
Prosperous	91
Upper middle	91
Lower middle	83
Poor	68

[a] Taken from H. Cantril and M. Strunk, *Public Opinion* (Princeton, N. J.: Princeton University Press, 1935–1946), p. 186. The number of cases in the different classes is unfortunately not given. The measure of stratification is presumably an interviewer's rating of standard of living. A parallel question asked by the Fortune Poll in 1949 yielded essentially similar differences by class. See *Public Opinion Quarterly*, XIII (1949), 714–715. Confirmatory data are also available in Centers, "Motivational Aspects," *op. cit.*, p. 202.

adult value we present in Table 3 the same datum for groups varying in age and sex. Thus, if one were to hypothesize that American mothers are more important in the indoctrination of children than fathers, and that this value becomes crucial among those who would have children of college age, one could determine from the table below whether this reduced emphasis on college education impinges at the most crucial points in the developmental process. Incidental to

TABLE 3 **The Emphasis upon the Need for College Education as Related to the Sex and Age Composition of the Classes**

	Per cent recommending college education	N
Males over 40		
Wealthy and prosperous[a]	58	147
Middle class	47	312
Lower class	29	202
Difference between wealthy and poor +29%[b]		
Females over 40		
Wealthy and prosperous	73	139
Middle class	63	330
Lower class	41	189
Difference between wealthy and poor +32%		
Males between 21–39 years of age		
Wealthy and prosperous	56	66
Middle class	54	334
Lower class	35	143
Difference between wealthy and poor +21%		
Females between 21–39 years of age		
Wealthy and prosperous	72	78
Middle class	64	327
Lower class	43	187
Difference between wealthy and poor +36%		

a Plus sign will be used to denote the fact that the difference is in the direction of greater endorsement of the value by the upper class.

b In a national survey of high school youth conducted in 1942 by Elmo Roper, all students were asked "what do you expect to do when you finish high school?" "Continuing with education is the first choice of every occupational group, including the children of laboring and farming families." However, Roper reports that this choice "is . . . outranked by the idea of going to work among the poor and the Negroes." Thus, not only is there a difference in the value attached to education among the different classes, there is also a difference in the expectation or aspiration for higher education among the different classes. See *Fortune*, XXVI, No. 6 (1942), 9.

this analysis, one can note whether or not the major finding of a differential value system by class continues to be demonstrated even when one controls factors of age and sex simultaneously.

It is clear that even when factors of age and sex composition are controlled the differential emphasis upon education persists. There is a suggestion that women, presumably the more significant group in the rearing of children than men, are more likely to vary in their values as their class position changes. While women thus appear to be more conscious of their class, it can also be noted that women emphasize the value of education more than their male counterparts *for every age and class* group in the table, i.e., women in general place greater premium on formal education. Such phenomena of sex differences *per se* can also be observed in other findings yet to be presented. Parenthetically, it might be noted in the data of both Tables 1 and 3 that the middle class groups approximate closer to the value system of the prosperous, rather than being a kind of halfway group between lower and upper.

While we cannot clearly establish any major differences within the family structure of the different classes with respect to the distribution of this value, it is clear from additional data that the children of the different classes show value systems parallel to their parents.[10] In this survey, a sample of youths between the ages of 14 and 20 were studied in addition to the regular sample of the

10 A variety of measures of objective class could be used in this and subsequent tables. The interviewer's rating of economic level will be used wherever possible since it is the most efficient for our purposes. However, the correlations among all these different indices are high so that the particular index chosen makes little difference. Thus the relation between interviewer's rating and monthly rental as expressed by a contingency coefficient is .74 and between the rating and education is .55.

adult population. Table 4 presents the distribution of this value for youths of the different classes. The data are presented separately for males and females.

TABLE 4 **The Differential Emphasis upon the Need for College Education among Youths of the Different Classes**

	Per cent recommending college education	N
Males between 14–20		
Wealthy and prosperous families	74	39
Middle class	63	100
Lower class	42	62
Difference between wealthy and lower classes +32%		
Females between 14–20		
Wealthy and prosperous families	85	45
Middle class	71	128
Lower class	49	73
Difference between wealthy and lower classes +36%		

In addition to demonstrating the persistence of the difference when sex is controlled, this breakdown would permit us again to examine whether the differential value of the classes is most prominent in the very place in the social structure where it would have greatest significance. Insofar as male youth are the major future participants in economic life, the difference between upper and lower groups would have most social consequences if it were greater in males. It is interesting to note that the youth of both sexes and all classes are closer in their values to adult women than to adult men. This can be noted by comparing Tables 3 and 4 and it is suggestive of the greater influence of mothers in the transmission of values.

Motivation to Advance in the Economic Structure

Achievement in any realm is as previously noted a function of motivation.

Of course, *motivation* is only one of the factors leading toward success; the other being *ability* to succeed which would be dependent on degree of competence or training or barriers imposed on those of lowly position. Given the strongest motivation, a man might still be incapable of advancement if other factors reduced his ability to advance. A variety of data suggest that the lower class individual holds values of such a nature as to reduce his striving towards those ends which would result in his moving up the class structure.

In the same study where values with respect to higher education were ascertained, the respondents were asked a question which provided evidence on the desiderata the different classes considered in choosing an occupation. The findings show that lower class individuals emphasize those factors which would lead them to strive for careers which would be less high in the economic structure. The sample was asked, "what do you think is the most important *single* thing for a young man to consider when he is choosing his life's work?" The major considerations fell into two groups, 49 per cent of the total sample answering in terms of the congeniality of the career pattern to the individual's personality, interests, and individual qualifications, and 32 per cent answering in terms of direct economic considerations such as security, wages or subsidiary economic benefits, the steadiness of employment, etc. It can be clearly shown that the lower classes emphasize the latter desiderata, and the upper classes the more personal aspects of the work.[11] It is our belief that this difference in what would be sought in a

---

[11] Similar findings are reported by Centers. When his samples were shown a card and asked which kind of job they would choose, if they had the choice, the middle class emphasized "self-expression" and the working class emphasized "security" as the basis for choice. *Op. cit.*, pp. 151–158.

career would lead the lower class individuals into occupations that would be less likely to enhance their position. Such desiderata will be achieved in a "good job" but not in such positions as managerial or professional jobs. These latter careers have greater elements of risk and are the very ones that would not mesh with the desire for stability, security and immediate economic benefits, but would mesh with the goal of congeniality to the individual's interests. Admittedly, this is only inferential but it will be clear from related questions to be presented shortly that interpreting these respective orientations in the above terms is warranted. The data for adults of the different classes, separated by age and sex, are presented in Table 5.

It can be noted that the influence of class position on the desiderata mentioned declines with age. This might appear paradoxical, in that one would expect the younger poor still to have their illusions whereas the older individuals among the poor would have confronted reality longer and any illusions they might have would have been dissipated. Therefore, one might expect among the old a greater difference among the classes. However, what seems to be the case is that with age *all* individuals regardless of class give greater emphasis to such factors as stability and security, and therefore the differences while sizeable are somewhat reduced.

Findings of a parallel nature are found for the sample of youth. The data are presented in Table 6.[12]

We have some confirmatory data on the desiderata in choice of an occupation from surveys conducted by Roper. In 1942 a national sample of high school students were asked to express their

---

[12] In a comparison of children between the ages of 10–14 from a "lower class school" with children from an "upper middle class school" in Chicago, Galler obtained parallel findings. The resons the lower class children gave for their choice of an occupation emphasized extrinsic rewards whereas the upper class children emphasized interest of the job, *op. cit.*

TABLE 5   The Desiderata in Choosing an Occupation as Related to Class Position

| | Per cent mentioning the factor of | | | |
	Congeniality to person	Economic benefit	Ratio of congeniality to economic answers	N
Males between 21–39				
Wealthy or prosperous	72	17	4.2	66
Middle class	55	20	2.7	334
Lower class	37	31	1.2	143
Difference between upper and lower classes +35% −15%				
Females between 21–39				
Wealthy or prosperous	72	7	10.0	78
Middle class	53	24	2.2	327
Lower class	37	30	1.2	187
Difference between upper and lower classes +35% −23%				
Males over 40				
Wealthy or prosperous	58	22	2.7	147
Middle class	49	21	2.3	312
Lower class	32	31	1.0	202
Difference between upper and lower classes +26% −9%				
Females over 40				
Wealthy or prosperous	51	14	4.3	137
Middle class	48	19	2.5	330
Lower class	32	33	1.0	189
Difference between upper and lower classes +29% −19%				

| | Per cent mentioning the factor of | | | |
	Congeniality to person	Economic benefit	Ratio of congeniality to economic answers	N
Males between 14–20				
Wealthy or prosperous	61	15	4.1	39
Middle class	57	17	3.4	100
Lower class	42	29	1.4	62
Difference between upper and lower classes +19% −14%				
Females between 14–20				
Wealthy or prosperous	60	14	4.3	45
Middle class	55	19	2.9	128
Lower class	45	27	1.7	73
Difference between upper and lower classes +15% −13%				

preference for one of three types of jobs: a low income but secure job, a job with good pay but with a 50–50 risk of losing it, or a job with extremely high income and great risk. Data are presented for the different classes in Table 7. . . .

The poor youth cannot accept the risk involved in becoming less poor. Similar data are available for adults from surveys conducted by Roper. In 1947, in answer to the identical question, one obtains a similar pattern by class. Thus, for example, a low income but secure job is chosen by 60 per cent of factory workers but only by 20 per cent of professional and executive persons. In 1949, a question presenting a similar choice situation between a secure job and a risky but promising career in one's own business yielded parallel results.[13]

The inference that the desideratum of economic benefit rather than congeniality of work would lead the lower class individual to prefer occupations which are lower in the hierarchy can be supported by other data from a more direct question in this same NORC survey.[14]

TABLE 7   Type of Occupation Chosen by Youth of the Different Classes[a]

Among high school youth	Per cent preferring job that offers all-or-nothing opulence
Poor	14
Prosperous, upper middle	29
From laboring parents	16
From executive and professional parents	31

[a] The youth data are from *Fortune*, XXVI, No. 6 (1942). Unfortunately the number of cases in the different groups is not given. In 1948, the Fortune Poll repeated an almost identical question of a sample of youths aged 18–25. The stratification measure available in the published report was formal-education which correlates highly with other measures. The all-or-nothing opulent job was chosen by 33 per cent of the college educated but only by 11 per cent of those with grade school education. See *Public Opinion Quarterly*, XIII (1949), 168.

[13] *Fortune* (1947), 10; *Public Opinion Quarterly*, XIV (1950), 182.

[14] In a study by Lipset and Bendix based on a probability sample of 1,000 cases representing the city of Oakland, exclusive of highest and lowest socio-economic segments, somewhat contradictory data are reported. They note that a considerable majority of manual workers have had aspirations to own their own businesses, and that a sizeable minority have actually attempted such a career. Moreover, differences between various grades of manual workers are negligible. These data certainly do not conform to our picture of reduced aspirations among the lower groups, and increased emphasis upon desiderata such as security. However, apart from the restriction of the findings to the city of Oakland, it should also be noted, as the authors point out, that they are based on a somewhat truncated economic distribution. S. M. Lipset and R. Bendix, "Social Mobility and Occupational Career Patterns, II, Social Mobility," *American*

TABLE 8   Types of Occupations Recommended by the Different Classes

| | Per cent recommending | | |
	Professional occupation	Skilled manual work	N
Males between 21–39			
Wealthy and prosperous	45	5	66
Middle class	49	13	334
Lower class	38	22	143
Difference between wealthy and poor +7% −17%			
Females between 21–39			
Wealthy and prosperous	51	3	78
Middle class	55	7	327
Lower class	44	17	187
Difference between wealthy and poor +7% −14%			
Males over 40			
Wealthy and prosperous	49	9	147
Middle class	43	20	312
Lower class	27	22	202
Difference between wealthy and poor +22% −13%			
Females over 40			
Wealthy and prosperous	54	3	139
Middle class	49	13	330
Lower class	32	15	189
Difference between wealthy and poor +22% −12%			

The respondents were asked: "Suppose some outstanding young man asked your advice on what would be one of the best occupations to aim toward. What *one* occupation do you think you would advise him to aim toward?" Partial data for the different classes are presented in Table 8, where it can be noted that the upper classes are more likely to stress professional careers whereas the lower groups emphasize skilled manual occupations.

Parallel data are presented for youths of the different classes in Table 9.

That the occupational goals of the lower classes are limited is evidenced by other data in the area of personal income aspirations. In a number of different surveys, respondents have been asked to indicate the level of future income they would like to have, or expect to be earning. The exact question varies from survey to survey in terms of the time perspective involved and the level of reality emphasized. Correspondingly the measure obtained is expressive variously of an aspiration that is geared either to realistic expectations or to rather wild hopes and remote strivings. In general, these data show for the lower class a pat-

TABLE 9   Types of Occupations Recommended by Youth of the Different Classes

| | Per cent recommending | | |
	Professional occupation	Skilled manual work	N
Males between 14–20			
Wealthy or prosperous	76	5	39
Middle class	52	6	100
Lower class	21	27	62
Difference between wealthy and poor +55% −22%			
Females between 14–20			
Wealthy or prosperous	81	4	45
Middle class	64	5	128
Lower class	42	18	73
Difference between wealthy and poor +39% −14%			

Journal of Sociology, LVII (1952), 494–504. By contrast, Centers found sizeable differences between various grades of workers with respect to the hope or expectation of owning one's own business. See "Motivational Aspects," *op. cit.*, pp. 199–201.

the value systems of different classes   **195**

tern of more limited expectations and/or strivings.[15] Thus, in 1942 in Roper's national survey of youth, the question was put: "How much a week do you think you should be earning about ten years from now?" The average for the entire sample was $49.81 but the children of the prosperous and middle classes gave a figure of $58.94, whereas the children of the poor gave an average estimate of $40.26.[16]

Centers and Cantril report in 1946 on a survey conducted with a national sample of about 1200 adults. The question that was asked was: "About how much more money than that (the current income) do you think your family would need to have the things that might make your family happier or more comfortable than it is now?" As one goes up in the economic ladder, the increment of income desired decreases.

Relatively speaking the wealthier need and want less of an increase.[17] However, in terms of *absolute aspiration* level, the situation is quite different. The poor do not aspire to achieve the same dollar level as the wealthier. Thus, the absolute increase in dollars among those with a current income of less than $20 is only $16.20 on the average, whereas for those with a weekly income between $60 and $100, the absolute increase wanted is

$41.60. As Centers and Cantril remark, "Individuals in the lowest income group do want a great deal more than they are now getting, but, in comparison to the sums wanted by those above them, theirs is a modest want indeed. An individual's present earnings obviously provide him with a frame of reference by means of which he sets his aspirations and judges his needs."[18]

Similar data are available from a study involving the sampling of male college students conducted by NORC in 1947.

The students were asked the weekly income they expected to be earning five years out of college. Among those students who come from families where the father is in a professional or managerial occupation, the median expectation was $119 a week whereas among those students whose fathers are in semi-skilled or skilled jobs the median figure was $103. Thus, the aspirations vary with the class origins of the student. However, this particular study bears on certain interesting subtle aspects of reference group processes. The very fact that some children from lower class families entered college implies that they deviated in their behavior from the modal pattern of this class. A similar interpretation is made of this phenomenon of lower class college attendance by Havighurst and Rogers and was alluded to earlier. Consequently, one might expect such individuals to show the lower class motivational pattern but in an attenuated form. That it is somewhat attenuated is suggested by the fact that the difference between the students of different classes is not as striking in magnitude as the differences we have just reported from other studies. In an early study by Gould there is some evidence of an even more

---

[15] Hollingshead presents similar findings for Elmtown. Each youth "was asked to name the occupation he would like to follow when he reached maturity." As one goes down in the class structure, the per cent choosing a profession or business declines from 77 per cent to 7 per cent and indecision or lower occupational choices increases. *Op. cit.*, p. 286. Galler presents similar findings for her youth group in Chicago, *op. cit.*

[16] *Fortune* (1942), *op. cit.*

[17] Merton remarks on a study conducted by H. F. Clark which appears to contradict the Centers-Cantril finding. He states that Clark indicates a constant increment of 25 per cent for each income level. However, it is not clear on what kind of sample or research procedure these data are based. *Op. cit.*

[18] R. Centers and H. Cantril, "Income Satisfaction and Income Aspiration," *Journal of Abnormal Social Psychology*, XLI (1946), 64–69.

extreme form of deviant value system among lower class college students.[19] In an experimental study of levels of aspirations among 81 male college students, two groups contrasted with respect to the size of their discrepancy score on six experimental tasks were studied. The group whose aspiration far exceeded their achievement were of predominantly *lower* class backgrounds and from minority ethnic groups. This appears to contradict our findings that lower class individuals set their goals lower than upper class groups. However, the apparent contradiction may imply the very interesting fact—that among those lower class individuals who do orient themselves to upper class patterns, i.e., enter college, their goal striving can be even more extreme.

In the NORC study of college students, one other datum suggests the attenuation of the expected pattern in the lower class college student. The students indicated those items within a list which were the three major desiderata in their choosing a job. It can be noted that this question corresponds very closely to the question previously analyzed in Table 5 for a national sample of adults. If we analyze these answers in terms of the differential emphasis upon factors of "economic benefit" vs. factors of "congeniality" for the different classes the differences by occupation of father are generally in the expected direction, but are of much smaller magnitude than those previously reported. They are presented in Table 10.

Beliefs in Opportunity

This pattern of reduced personal aspirations and reduced appeal or valence

---

[19] See R. Gould, "Some Sociological Determinants of Goal Strivings," *Journal of Social Psychology*, XIII (1941), 461–473.

TABLE 10   The Desiderata in Choosing an Occupation among College Students of Different Class Origins

Per cent mentioning desideratum of:[a]	Per cent among students whose fathers are	
	Professional or managerial	Skilled or semi-skilled
Adventure—excitement	7	8
Being one's own boss	27	18
Congenial atmosphere	31	23
Intellectual challenge	55	42
Advancement	50	55
Money	26	30
Security	58	58
N =	301	106

[a] The per cents add to much more than 100 per cent since each respondent was asked to name the *three* most important desiderata.

of given occupations among the lower classes seems to derive from the perception of reality that the lower classes have. The goals of *all* individuals are governed to some extent by the appraisal of reality. Since a variety of data indicate that the poor are more aware of their lack of opportunity, presumably they would set their goals in the light of such beliefs.[20]

---

[20] Chinoy makes the same general point on the basis of his study of automobile workers. "The aspirations of the automobile workers . . . represent a constant balancing of hope and desire against the objective circumstances in which they find themselves. . . . By and large they confine their aims to those limited alternatives which seem possible for men with their skills and resources." *Op. cit.*, p. 454. The statistical data in support of this conclusion are that: only 8 out of his 62 subjects felt they had a promising future outside of the factory; only five felt they had any real hope of becoming foremen within the factory; only 3 of the semi-skilled group felt it might be possible to move up to skilled levels. The remaining 46 subjects could see little in the way of opportunity and hence reduced their goals. However, Kornhauser in his original analysis of class differences in attitudes and values disagrees with our interpretation. He remarks that people at the lower income levels "cling devotedly to the American belief in individual opportunity." He predicates this interpretation

In a national survey in 1947 by Roper, a series of questions dramatically demonstrate the difference in the beliefs of the lower classes about opportunity. The data are presented in Table 11.

A parallel finding is available from 1937 when Roper asked a national sample of adults the question: "Do you think that today any young man with thrift, ability, and ambition has the opportunity to rise in the world, own his own home, and earn $5,000 a year?" Among the prosperous 53 per cent indicated categorically that such an aspiration was realistic, whereas among the poor only 31 per cent indicated their belief in this possibility.

Evidence from a variety of psychological studies sheds further light on the way in which the person's own expectations and striving for a goal are affected by his social position. These are all based on the analysis of levels of aspiration with respect to experimental tasks.[21] Although these tasks do not have a direct relevance to behavior in the economic sphere and constitute mere analogies, the analysis of the process of setting of goals may contribute much to our problem.

In one experimental level of aspira-

TABLE 11   Beliefs in Economic Opportunity among the Different Classes[a]

	Among employees who are	
	Professional or executives	Factory workers
Per cent believing that years ahead hold good chance for advancement over present position[b]	63	48
Per cent believing that following factor is important consideration in job advancement:[c]		
Quality of work	64	43
Energy and willingness	56	42
Getting along well with boss	12	19
Friend or relative of boss	3	8
Being a politician	6	4
Per cent believing that harder work would net them personally a promotion	58	40

[a] *Fortune* (1947). Unfortunately the size of the different groups is not reported. For the exact questions asked, the reader is referred to the original table.

[b] The identical question asked seven years before shows approximately the same pattern of findings for the different classes. See Cantril and M. Strunk, *Public Opinion* (Princeton, N. J.: Princeton University Press, 1935–1946), p. 830. Parallel findings are reported by R. Centers. See "Motivational Aspects of Occupational Stratification," *Journal of Social Psychology*, XXVIII (1948), 196–197.

[c] Chinoy confirms this general picture in his study of automobile workers. His subjects stressed as criteria for achieving promotion such considerations as "pull," "connections," and various personal techniques for gaining favor—"The Tradition of Opportunity and the Aspirations of Automobile Workers," *American Journal of Sociology*, LVII (1952), 455. In 1948 the Fortune Poll queried a sample of youth aged 18–25 with a similar question and obtained parallel results by class. See *Public Opinion Quarterly*, XIII (1949), 174. Also Centers reports similar findings from a national sample of adults. See *Journal of Social Psychology*, XXVII (1948), 168–169.

on a number of questions asked in his survey of attitudes in Chicago in which differences were small between income groups, and in which the majority of the lowest group endorsed the view that they and their children can get ahead. Yet, in certain other questions he asked in the realm of satisfaction with the opportunities for their children and satisfaction with their own life chances, differences between income groups were large and in the direction of our hypothesis. Admittedly, the wide variety of data that exists, some of it contradictory, permits of some qualification of the conclusions we have drawn. See A. W. Kornhauser, *op. cit.*, pp. 241–242.

[21] For a discussion of the level of aspiration experiment, and a summary of the literature, the reader is referred to K. Lewin, T. Dembo, L. Festinger and P. Sears, "Level of Aspiration," Chap. X, in J. McV. Hunt, *Personality and the Behavior Disorders* (New York: The Ronald Press, 1944).

tion study, there is a graphic demonstration of the way in which the socially defined opportunity of a group affects specific aspirations, and specific responses to past success. Adams matched groups of white and Negro subjects on a series of characteristics and compared successive aspirations in an experimental task involving dart throwing. Among the white college subjects, achievement of their aspiration on the task was followed by raising of the aspiration level on the next trial, whereas for the matched Negro college group past success on the task was less likely to result in their raising their goal on the next trial.[22]

In a series of other experiments, beginning with the work of Chapman and Volkmann individuals alter their level of aspiration on experimental tasks when informed of the achievement on that task of some other social group. When this fictitious standard represents a group ostensibly superior in standing to the individual, he reduces his estimate of his own future performance.[23] Implicitly, these findings demonstrate that the individual in lowly position sets his strivings and expectancies for success in the light of the established social hierarchy of groups and a belief in differential opportunities within the hierarchy.

Two illustrative experiments show this process graphically for groups with well defined social positions. Preston and Bayton found that an experimental group of Negro college students reduced their aspiration levels when informed that white college students had achieved a certain level in the task more than the control group of Negro students informed that the same fictitious standard of achievement had been achieved by other Negroes. The mirror image of this experiment was conducted by Mac-Intosh who used white college students as subjects and presented them with the fictitious standard of performance of a Negro group. In the case of the white students, they orient themselves to the knowledge of Negro achievement by raising their estimates.[24]

Altered Forms of Striving for Success

Thus far the data presented show clearly that there is reduced striving for success among the lower classes, an awareness of lack of opportunity, and a lack of valuation of education, normally the major avenue to achievement of high status. However, there may well be subtle ways in which the lower class individual shows the effect of the cultural emphasis on success. Conceivably, our data might be interpreted to indicate that the person *really* wants to achieve the goal of great success, but that he has merely accommodated himself to his lesser opportunities and reduced his aspirations so as to guard against the experience of frustration and failure. Yet, the fact that the data for the sample of youth parallel so closely the findings on adults suggests that this explanation is not generally tenable. Such a dynamic readjustment of goals in relation to reality would be expected to come later. Youth seem to have internalized differentiated goals dependent on their class at an age too early to represent a kind of secondary resetting of their sights.[25]

Similarly, one might argue that adults would have accommodated *themselves* to reality, but that the cultural emphasis

---

ferential Effect of the Status of the Competing Group upon the Levels of Aspiration," *American Journal of Psychology*, LV (1942), 546–554. Minor differences in the findings in these two experiments on minimum and maximum aspirations do not concern us in this context.

[25] Yet it is conceivable that even in the case of youth the limited occupational goals of the lower class represents a readjustment to reality occurring at a very early age. Hollingshead notes among his lower class youth *who are already employed* that the frequency of choice of professional or business careers is less than such choices among youth of the *same classes who are still in school*. He concluded that they have adjusted their hopes, in most cases, to the reality of the work world. *Op. cit.*, pp. 382–383.

---

[22] D. K. Adams, "Age, Race, and Responsiveness of Levels of Aspiration to Success and Failure," *Psychological Bulletin*, XXXVI (1939), 573 (abstract).

[23] K. Lewin, *et al.*, *op. cit.*, pp. 341–342.

[24] Preston and Bayton, J., "Differential Effect of a Social Variable upon Three Levels of Aspiration," *Journal of Experimental Psychology*, XXIX (1941), 351–369. A. MacIntosh, "Dif-

upon success would be reflected by a vicarious aspiration for their children to achieve high success. Chinoy, for example, remarks on the existence of this pattern among his automobile workers. He notes that everyone of his 26 subjects with young children had greater hopes for them and believed in better opportunities for their children.[26] Merton notes the same process, and reports preliminary data from his housing studies. He notes that the lower the occupational level of the parent, the larger the proportion having aspirations for a professional career for their children.[27]

Yet, if such were *generally* the case, we would expect our youth sample to reflect such a pattern of indoctrination. They seem instead to show the pattern of aspirations of the adult members of their class.

Another possibility that presents itself is that the cultural emphasis upon success is reflected in the lower class groups in substitute forms. They cannot achieve occupational success, and so substitute other goals more readily achieved, and regard these symbolically as equivalents. Chinoy remarks on such a "shift in the context of advancement from the occupational to the consumption sphere."[28] We have no data on the problem unfortunately for large samples.

We have some data, however, on one substitute form of motivation for success in the economic sphere.

Deviant Occupational Goals

In general, it has been shown that the lower class individual has less opportunity and less motivation to advance in the hierarchy. However, there are certain occupations in America which provide wealth and benefits to which he might have singular access. These would be occupations which the more genteel classes might regard with disdain and consequently, the lower class person would have less competition. Insofar as the lower class person would have a value system which would endorse the pursuit of such occupations, this would provide a deviant and "sheltered" avenue to success. Such occupations might, for example, exist in the entertainment realm, the realm of politics, and in certain specialized jobs which appear distasteful in character.[29]

Inferential evidence in support of such a pattern is available from a series of measures of the prestige accorded by the different classes to certain selected types of occupations.

Each individual in the sample related the prestige of a series of occupations. We shall assume that according high prestige to an occupation would so-to-speak correspond to that occupation having a strong positive valence for the individual, i.e., he would be more likely to direct his strivings toward occupations he regards as prestigious and not towards occupations he regards as non-prestigious. The hierarchy of prestige has been found in past investigations to be uniform among different occupational groups and, among groups geographically diverse, to be stable over long periods of time.[30] In the national sample

---

[26] Chinoy, *op. cit.*, p. 459.
[27] Merton, *op. cit.*, p. 148.
[28] Chinoy, *op. cit.*

[29] Certain kinds of professional athletics might also fall into this grouping. For evidence on the way the occupation of boxer provides such an avenue to high status to ethnic minorities and lower socio-economic individuals, see S. K. Weinberg and H. Arond, "The Occupational Culture of the Boxer," *American Journal of Sociology*, LVII (1952), 460–469.
[30] See G. S. Counts, "Social Status of Occupations," *School Review*, XXXIII (1925), 16–27; M. E. Deeg and D. G. Paterson, "Changes in Social Status of Occupations," *Occupations*, XXV (1947), 205–208; J. Tuckman, "Social Status of Occupations in Canada," *Canadian Journal of Psychology*, I, No. 2 (1947), 71–75; "Jobs and Occupations, Soldiers' Evaluation," *Opinion News* (*NORC*) (June 15, 1948).

studied by NORC, there was, similarly, a general uniformity to the prestige accorded to different occupations by persons in widely different groups. However, despite this cultural norm, we note certain interesting differences in the prestige accorded by the different classes to occupations which we have labelled deviant. County Judge is used in this analysis as exemplifying a political career goal; singer in a night club as exemplifying an entertainment career goal, and undertaker as exemplifying a distasteful but lucrative occupation. It will be noted from Table 12 below that the lower classes are more likely to accord high prestige to these careers. Conceivably the judge and singer could be regarded as positions of respectability in the judiciary and cultural world or the reactions could be predicated on the intrinsic content of the work. Therefore in the table we present results for two "control" occupations, Supreme Court Justice and musician in a symphony orchestra. Insofar as the responses of the different classes were to the intrinsic contents and the respectability of the occupation, one would expect a similar pattern to the two judicial posts and the two musical positions. However, it can be noted that the classes reverse themselves for the control occupation. In other words, a judicial post of respectability is differentially favored by the upper classes; a judicial post of a *political* nature is favored by the lower classes. Similarly, a *long haired* musical post is favored by the upper classes, and a popular musical position by the lower classes.

It can be noted that there is one inversion in the table which violates the general hypothesis. However, among the 20 possible regressions by class in the table, this is the only inversion found.

TABLE 12   **The Prestige Accorded to Deviant Occupations by the Different Classes**

| | Per cent giving the rating of excellent standing to: | | | | | |
	Supreme Court Justice	Musician in symphony orchestra	County judge	Singer in night club	Undertaker	N
Males between 21–39						
Wealthy or prosperous	88	31	32	0	12	66
Middle class	85	25	42	1	10	334
Lower class	82	21	44	6	16	143
Difference between upper and lower classes	+6%	+10%	−12%	−6%	−4%	
Females between 21–39						
Wealthy or prosperous	95	37	41	3	8	78
Middle class	83	31	44	1	13	327
Lower class	72	30	55	5	22	187
Difference between upper and lower classes	+23%	+7%	−14%	−2%	−14%	
Males over 40						
Wealthy or prosperous	84	25	48	0	12	147
Middle class	81	26	49	2	14	312
Lower class	79	23	52	4	17	202
Difference between upper and lower classes	+5%	+2%	−4%	−4%	−5%	
Females over 40						
Wealthy or prosperous	92	37	52	0	11	139
Middle class	81	36	55	2	18	330
Lower class	72	29	49	6	20	189
Difference between upper and lower classes	+20%	+8%	+3%	−6%	−9%	

Evidence of a more direct nature supports the conclusions just presented. In 1944, the NORC asked a national sample of 2,500 cases, "If you had a son just getting out of school, would you like to see him go into politics as a life work?" About two-thirds of the total sample disapproved of such a career, but the disapproval was much more characteristic of the upper classes (see Table 13).

(see Table 13)

TABLE 13 **Disapproval of a Career in Politics by the Different Classes**

Economic level	Per cent disapproving[a]
Wealthy or prosperous	78
Middle class	73
Lower class	54

[a] Unfortunately, the number of cases in each of the economic groups was not available in the published report.

Reference Group Processes and the Deviant Case

While the evidence thus far presented provides consistent and strong evidence that lower class individuals *as a group* have a value system that reduces the likelihood of individual advancement, it is also clear from the data that there is a sizeable proportion of the lower group who do not incorporate this value system. Similarly, there are individuals in the upper classes who do not show the modal tendency of their group. In part, such deviant instances can be accounted for in terms of the crudity of the measurements used. In part, one must recognize that the members of these classes have much heterogeneity in such other social respects as their ethnic, religious, and other memberships and have been exposed to a variety of idiosyncratic experiences.

The value systems would be correspondingly diverse. However, one systematic factor that can be shown to account for the deviant cases which confirms at *a more subtle psychological level* the influence of class factors is that of the reference group of the individual. Some of our lower class individuals may well be identifying themselves with upper groups, and absorbing the value system of another class to which they refer themselves. Some of our upper class individuals may for a variety of reasons refer themselves psychologically to other classes. That the reference group of the individual affects his value system, was suggested by data presented earlier on lower class college students and can be shown inferentially from additional data

TABLE 14 **Reference Group Processes as Revealed in the Influence of the Class History of the Individual on His Values**

Per cent who—	Among respondents whose occupations are			
	Professional or business		Skilled or semi-skilled	
	Father prof. or bus.	Father skilled or semi	Father prof. or bus.	Father skilled or semi
Recommend college education	71	60	57	50
Recommend as best occupation:				
Professional work	44	29	31	25
Skilled manual work	10	29	23	44
Mention the desideratum in choosing an occupation of:				
Congeniality	65	62	52	46
Economic benefit	15	19	23	27
N =	(377)	(140)	(298)	(397)

collected in the NORC survey. Evidence was available on the occupation of the parent of each respondent. If we classify each individual in a lower class occupation in terms of whether his parental background is that of a lower or higher occupation group, we presumably have a contrast between individuals of objectively identical class, but who differ in the class with which they might identify. We shall assume that those with upper class origins would not think so much in lower class terms and would continue to reflect their more prestigious origins. If we, similarly, take individuals who are now objectively in upper class occupations and divide them in terms of parental occupation we shall presumably be classifying respondents in more psychological terms. For these four groups we shall contrast their values in each of the realms previously analyzed purely by *current* objective class membership.[31]

The patterning of the findings is presented in Table 14. It can be noted that the values are a resultant of both the "class history" of the individual and his current position. Individuals of equal current position reflect the values of their parents' class. This can be noted by comparing Col. 1 with Col. 2 of the table and Col. 3 with Col. 4. It is also true, however, that individuals with the same class origins have different values depending on their current position. This requires the comparison of Col. 1 with Col. 3 and Col. 2 with Col. 4. Where the two sets of class factors combine in an additive way, the effect on the value system is maximal as seen in the comparison of Col. 1 with Col. 4. The residues of earlier class experiences in some manner are present suggesting that reference group processes are at work.

---

[31] Lipset and Bendix on the basis of noting the large amount of "temporary" mobility, or shifting of jobs within the careers or workers, make the basic point that such changes contribute much to reference group selection and to beliefs about mobility. Thus, they remark: "Those in the middle and upper brackets of the occupational hierarchy may continue to insist that ready opportunities for social and economic advancement exist, because from 40 to 80 per cent of their numbers have at one time or another worked in the manual occupations. While this is not the place to explore the subjective aspects of mobility, we want to emphasize the importance of considering the impact of casual job experiences on the subjective appraisals of opportunities and on the presence or absence of subjective class identifications." By extension, the same theory can be generalized from mobility within the life history of the individual to mobility between generations. See S. M. Lipset and R. Bendix, "Social Mobility and Occupational Career Patterns, II, Social Mobility," *American Journal of Sociology*, LVII (1952), 494–504.

Socialization and Social Class through Time and Space

URIE BRONFENBRENNER

I. Background and Resources

During the past dozen years, a class struggle has been taking place in American social psychology—a struggle, fortunately, not *between* but *about* social classes. In the best social revolutionary tradition the issue was joined with a manifesto challenging the assumed superiority of the upper and middle classes and extolling the neglected virtues of the working class. There followed a successful revolution with an overthrow of the established order in favor of the victorious proletariat, which then reigned supreme—at least for a time. These dramatic changes had, as always, their prophets and precursors, but they reached a climax in 1946 with the publication of Davis and Havighurst's influential paper on "Social Class and Color Differences in Child Rearing."[1] The

Reprinted from *Readings in Social Psychology*, eds. E. E. Maccoby, T. M. Newcomb, and E. L. Hartley, 3rd ed. (New York: Holt, Rinehart & Winston, Inc., 1958), pp. 400–425, by permission of the author, The Society for the Psychological Study of Social Issues, and the publisher. This article was made possible only by the work of others; for, in effect, it is a synthesis of the contribution of a score of investigators over a score of years. The author is particularly grateful to Nancy Bayley, Melvin L. Kohn, Richard A. Littman, Daniel R. Miller, Fred L. Strodtbeck, Guy E. Swanson, and Martha S. White, who made available copies of their research reports prior to publication. For their invaluable suggestions, he is also indebted to John E. Anderson, Wesley Allinsmith, Alfred L. Baldwin, John A. Clausen, Robert J. Havighurst, Harry Levin, Eleanor E. Maccoby, and Theodore M. Newcomb.

paper cited impressive statistical evidence in support of the thesis that middle-class parents "place their children under a stricter regimen, with more frustration of their impulses than do lower-class parents." For the next eight years, the Davis-Havighurst conclusion was taken as the definitive statement of class differences in socialization. Then, in 1954, came the counter revolution: Maccoby and Gibbs published the first report[2] of a study of child-rearing practices in the Boston area which, by and large, contradicted the Chicago findings: in general, middle-class parents were found to be "more permissive" than those in the lower class.

In response, one year later, Havighurst and Davis[3] presented a reanalysis of their data for a subsample more comparable in age to the subjects of the Boston study. On the basis of a careful comparison of the two sets of results, they concluded that "the disagreements between the findings of the two studies are substantial and large" and speculated that these differences might be attributable either to genuine changes in child-rearing practices over time or to technical difficulties of sampling and item equivalence.

A somewhat different view, however, was taken by Sears, Maccoby, and

[1] A. Davis and R. J. Havighurst, "Social Class and Color Differences in Child Rearing," *American Sociological Review*, XI (1948), 698–710.

[2] E. E. Maccoby, P. K. Gibbs, and the staff of the Laboratory of Human Development at Harvard University, "Methods of Child Rearing in Two Social Classes," in W. E. Martin and C. B. Standler, eds., *Readings in Child Development* (New York: Harcourt, Brace & World, Inc., 1954).

[3] Havighurst and Davis, "A Comparison of the Chicago and Harvard Studies of Social Class Differences in Child Rearing," *American Sociological Review*, XX (1955), 438–442.

Levin[4] in their final report of the Boston study. They argued that Davis and Havighurst's interpretation of the Chicago data as reflecting greater permissiveness for the working-class parent was unwarranted on two counts. First, they cited the somewhat contrasting results of still another research—that of Klatskin[5] in support of the view that class differences in feeding, weaning, scheduling, and toilet training "are not very stable or customary." Second, they contended that the Chicago findings of greater freedom of movement for the lower-class child were more properly interpreted not as "permissiveness" but as "a reflection of rejection, a pushing of the child out of the way." Such considerations led the Boston investigators to conclude:

This re-examination of the Chicago findings suggests quite clearly the same conclusion that must be reached from Klatskin's study and from our own: the middle-class mothers were generally more permissive and less punitive toward their young children than were working-class mothers. Unfortunately, the opposite interpretation, as presented by Davis and Havighurst, has been widely accepted in education circles during the past decade. This notion of working-class permissiveness has been attractive for various reasons. It has provided an easy explanation of why working-class children have lower academic achievement motivation than do middle-class children—their mothers place less restrictive pressure on them. It has also provided a kind of compensatory comfort for those educators who have been working hard toward the goal of improving educational experiences for the noncollege-oriented part of the school population. In effect, one could say, lower-class children may lack the so highly desirable academic motivation, but the lack stems from a "good" reason—the children were permissively reared.[6]

It would appear that there are a number of unresolved issues between the protagonists of the principal points of view—issues both as to the facts and their interpretation. At such times it is not unusual for some third party to attempt a reappraisal of events in a broader historical perspective with the aid of documents and information previously not available. It is this which the present writer hopes to do. He is fortunate in having at his disposal materials not only from the past and present, but also seven manuscripts at the time of this writing, which report class differences in childrearing practices at four different places and five points in time. To begin with, Bayley and Schaefer[7] have reanalyzed data from the Berkeley Growth Study to provide information on class differences in maternal-behavior ratings made from 1928 to 1932, when the children in the study were under three years old, and again from 1939 to 1942, when most of them were about ten years old. Information on maternal behavior in this same locale as of 1953 comes from a recent report by Martha Sturm White[8] of class differences in childrearing practices for a sample of preschoolers in Palo Alto and environs. Miller and Swanson have made available relevant data from their two comprehensive studies of families in Detroit, one based on a stratified sample of families with children up to 19 years

---

[4] R. R. Sears, E. Maccoby, and H. Levin, *Patterns of Child Rearing* (New York: Harper & Row, Publishers, 1957).

[5] E. H. Klatskin, "Shifts in Child Care Practices in Three Social Classes under an Infant Care Program of Flexible Methodology," *American Journal of Orthopsychiatry*, XXII (1952), 52–61.

[6] Sears, Maccoby, and Levin, *op. cit.*, pp. 446–447.

[7] N. Bayley and E. S. Schaefer, "Relationships between Socioeconomic Variables and the Behavior of Mothers towards Young Children," unpublished manuscript, 1957.

[8] M. S. White, "Social Class, Child Rearing Practices, and Child Behavior," *American Sociological Review*, XXII (1957), 704–712.

of age,[9] the other a specially selected sample of boys, ages 12 to 14 years.[10] Limited information on another sample of adolescent boys comes from Strodtbeck's investigation of "Family Interaction, Values, and Achievement".[11] Also Littman, Moore, and Pierce-Jones[12] have recently completed a survey of child-rearing practices in Eugene, Oregon for a random sample of parents with children from two weeks to 14 years of age. Finally, Kohn[13] reports a comparison of child-training values among working and middle-class mothers in Washington, D.C.

The writer has made use of nine additional published researches.[14] In some instances—notably for the monumental regrettably neglected Anderson report —data were reanalyzed and significance tests computed in order to permit closer comparison with the results of other investigation. A full list and summary description of all the studies utilized in the present review appear in Table 1 [on pp. 208–9]. Starred items designate the researches which, because they contain reasonably comparable data, are used as the principal bases for analysis.

II. Establishing Comparable Social-Class Groupings

Although in most of the studies under consideration the investigators have based their classification of socioeconomic status (SES) explicitly or implicitly on the criteria proposed by Warner,[15] there was considerable variation in the number of social class categories employed. Thus, in the Anderson report data were analyzed in terms of seven SES levels, the New York survey distinguished five, the second Chicago and the two Detroit studies each had four, and Klatskin used three. The majority, however, following the precedent of Havighurst and Davis, differentiated two levels only—middle vs. lower or working class. Moreover, all of these last studies have been reanalyzed or deliberately designed to facilitate comparison with each other. We have already mentioned Havighurst and Davis' efforts in this regard, to which the Boston group contributed by recalculating their data in terms of medians rather

[9] D. R. Miller and G. E. Swanson, *The Changing American Parent* (New York: John Wiley & Sons, Inc., 1958).

[10] Miller and Swanson, *Inner Conflict and Defense* (New York: Holt, Rinehart & Winston, Inc., 1960).

[11] F. L. Strodtbeck, "Family Interaction, Values, and Achievement," in A. L. Baldwin, Urie Bronfenbrenner, D. C. McClelland, and F. L. Strodtbeck, *Talent and Society* (Princeton, N.J.: D. Van Nostrand Co., Inc., 1958).

[12] R. A. Littman, R. A. Moore, and J. Pierce-Jones, "Social Class Differences in Child Rearing: A Third Community for Comparison with Chicago and Newton, Massachusetts," *American Sociological Review*, XXII (1957), 694–704.

[13] M. L. Kohn, "Social Class and Parental Values," paper read at the Annual Meeting of the American Sociological Society, Washington, D.C., August, 27–29, 1957.

[14] H. E. Anderson (Chrmn.), *The Young Child in the Home*, report of the Committee on the Infant and Preschool Child, White House

Conference on Child Health and Protection (New York: Appleton-Century-Crofts, 1936); A. L. Baldwin, J. Kalhorn, and F. H. Breese, *Patterns of Parent Behavior*, Psychological Monographs, LVIII, No. 3 (1945), (Whole No. 268): W. E. Boek, E. D. Lawson, A. Yankhauer, and M. B. Sussman, *Social Class, Maternal Health, and Child Care* (Albany, N. Y.: New York State Department of Health, 1957); Davis and Havighurst, *op. cit.*; E. M. Duvall, "Conceptions of Parenthood," *American Journal of Sociology*, LII (1946–1947), 190–192; Klatskin, *op. cit.*; E. E. Maccoby and P. K. Gibbs, *op. cit.*; D. C. McClelland, A. Rindlisbacher, and R. DeCharms, "Religious and Other Sources of Parental Attitudes toward Independence Training," in McClelland, ed., *Studies in Motivation* (New York: Appleton-Century-Crofts, 1955); Sears, Maccoby, and Levin, *op. cit.*

[15] W. L. Warner, M. Meeker, and others, *Social Class in America* (Chicago: Science Research Associates, 1949).

than means.[16] Both White and Littman *et al.* were interested in clarifying the contradictions posed by the Chicago and Boston studies and hence have employed many of the same indices. As a result, both necessity and wisdom call for dropping to the lowest common denominator and reanalyzing the results of the remaining researches in terms of a two-level classification of socioeconomic status.

In most instances, the delicate question of where to establish the cutting point was readily resolved. The crux of the distinction between middle and working class in all four of the studies employing this dichotomous break lies in the separation between white-and blue-collar workers. Fortunately, this same differentiation was made at some point along the scale in each of the other researches included in the basic analysis. Thus, for the several studies[17] using four levels of classification (upper and lower middle, upper and lower lower), the split occurred, as might be expected, between the two middle categories. For the New York State sample an examination of the occupations occurring at each of the five class levels used pointed to a cutting point between Classes III and IV. Klatskin, in comparing the social-class groupings of the New Haven study with the middle and lower classes of the original Chicago research, proposed a division between the first and second of her three SES levels, and we have followed her recommendation. Finally, for the seven-step scale of the Anderson report, the break was made between Classes III and IV, placing major clerical workers, skilled mechanics and retail business men in the middle class, and farmers, minor clerical positions, and semiskilled occupations in the working class.

In all of the above instances it was, of course, necessary to compute anew percentages and average scores for the two class levels and to calculate tests of significance (almost invariably x^2, two-tailed test, with Fisher-Yates correction for continuity). These computations, the results of which appear in the tables to follow, were performed for the following samples: National I–IV, New Haven I, Detroit I and II, and Upstate New York. All other figures and significance tests cited are taken from the original reports.

The effort to make the division between middle and working class at similar points for the basic samples, however successful it may have been, does not eliminate many other important sources of difference among the several researches. We now turn briefly to a consideration of these.

III. Problems of Comparability

The difficulties involved in comparing the results of more than a dozen studies conducted at different times and places for somewhat different purposes are at once formidable, delicate, and perilous. First of all, even when similar areas are explored in the interview, there is the problem of variation in the wording of questions. Indeed, however marked the changes may be in child-rearing practices over time, they are not likely to be any more dramatic than the contrasts in the content and, above all, connotation of the queries put to mothers by social scientists from one decade to the next. Thus, the comprehensive report from the first White House Conference, which covered the gamut from the number of children having rattles and changing their underwear to the number of toothbrushes by age, and the times the child was frightened by storms (analyzed by seven SES levels), says not a murmur about masturbation or sex play. Ten years later, in Chicago, six questions were devoted to this topic, including such items as: "How did you frighten them out of the habit?" and "What

---

[16] Sears, Maccoby, and Levin, *op. cit.*, p. 427.

[17] Duvall, *op. cit.*, Miller and Swanson, *Inner Conflict and Defense* and *The Changing American Parent*, *op. cit.*

TABLE 1   **Description of Samples**

Sample	Principal investigator source	Date of field work	Age	Number of cases			Description of sample
				Total	Middle class	Working class	
National cross section,[a] I, II, III, IV	Anderson	1932	0–1 1–5 6–12 1–12	494 2420 865 3285	217 1131 391 1522	277 1289 474 1763	National sample of white families "having child between 1 and 5 years of age" and "representing each major geographic area, each size of community and socio-economic class in the United States." About equal number of males and females. SES (seven classes) based on Minnesota Scale for Occupational Classification.
Berkeley, Cal., I–II	Bayley and Schaefer	1928–32 1939–42	1–3 9–11	31 31	Information not available		Subjects of both sexes from Berkeley Growth Study, "primarily middle class but range from unskilled laborer, relief, and three-years education to professional, $10,000 income and doctoral degrees." SES measures include education, occupation (Taussig Scale), income, home and neighborhood rating, and composite scale.
Yellow Springs, Ohio	Baldwin	1940	3–12	124	Information not available		Families enrolled in Fels Research Institute Home Visiting Program. "Above average" in socioeconomic status but include "a number of uneducated parents and from the lower economic levels." No SES index computed but graphs show relationships by education and income.
Chicago, I[a]	Davis and Havighurst	1943	5 (approx.)	100	48	32	Middle-class sample "mainly" from mothers of nursery-school children; lower class from "areas of poor housing." All mothers native born. Two-level classification SES following Warner based on occupation, education, residential area, type of home, etc.
Chicago, II	Duvall	1943–44	5 (approx.)	433	230	203	Negro and white (Jewish and non-Jewish) mothers. Data collected at "regular meetings of mothers' groups." SES classification (four levels) following Warner.
New Haven, Conn., I[a]	Klatskin	1949–50	1 (approx.)	222	114	108	Mothers in Yale Rooming-in Project returning for evaluation of baby at one year of age. SES classification (three levels) by Hollingshead, following Warner.
Boston, Mass.[a]	Sears, et al.	1951–52	4–6	372	198	174	Kindergarten children in two suburbs. Parents American born, living together. Twins, adoptions, handicapped children, and other special cases eliminated. Two-level SES classification follows Warner.
New Haven, Conn., II	Strodtbeck	1951–53	14–17	48	24	24	Third-generation Jewish and Italian boys representing extremes of under- and over-achievement in school. Classified into three SES levels on basis of occupation.

Sample	Principal investigator source	Date of field work	Age	Number of cases			Description of sample
				Total	Middle class	Working class	
Detroit, Mich., I[a]	Miller and Swanson	1953	12–14	112	59	53	Boys in grades 7–8 above border-line intelligence within one year of age for grade, all at least third-generation Americans, Christian, from unbroken, nonmobile families of Northwest European stock. SES (four levels) assigned on basis of education and occupation.
Detroit, Mich., II[a]	Miller and Swanson	1953	0–18	479	Information not available		Random sample of white mothers with child under 19 and living with husband. Step-children and adoptions eliminated. SES (four levels) based primarily on U.S. census occupation categories.
Palo Alto, Cal.[a]	White	1953	$2\frac{1}{2}$–$5\frac{1}{2}$	74	36	38	Native-born mothers of only one child, the majority expecting another. Unbroken homes in suburban area SES (two levels) rated on Warner scale.
Urban Connecticut	McClelland et al.	1953–54	6–18	152	Information not available		Parents between 30–60 having at least one child between six and eighteen and representing four religious groups. "Rough check on class status" obtained from educational level achieved by parent.
Upstate New York	Boek, et al.	1955–56	3–7 months	1432	595	837	Representative sample of N.Y. state mothers of newborn children, exclusive of unmarried mothers. SES classification (five levels) as given on Warner scale.
Eugene, Oregon[a]	Littman, et al.	1955–56	0–14	206	86	120	Random sample of children from preschool classes and school rolls. Two SES levels assigned on same basis as in Boston study.
Washington, D.C.	Kohn and Clausen	1956–57	10–11	339	174	165	Representative samples of working- and middle-class mothers classified by Hollingshead's index of social position.

[a] Denotes studies used as principal bases for the analysis.

physical methods did you use (such as tight diaper, whipping them, tying their hands, and so forth)?" In the next decade the interviewer in the Boston study (perhaps only a proper Bostonian) was more restrained, or simply less interested. He asked only two questions: first, whether the mother noticed the child playing with himself, then, "How important do you feel it is to prevent this in a child?" Nor is the difficulty completely eliminated in those all-too-few instances when a similar wording is employed in two or more studies, for there is the very real possibility that in different contexts the same words have different meanings.

Serious problems arise from the lack of comparability not only in the questions asked but also in the character of the samples employed. Havighurst and Davis, for example, point out that the Chicago and Boston samples had different proportions of cases in the two bottom categories of the Warner scale of occupations. According to the investigators' reports, the Palo Alto and Eugene studies deviated even further in both directions, with the former containing few families from the lowest occupational categories, and the Oregon group exceeding previous studies in representation from these same bottom levels. The authors of several studies also call attention to the potential importance of existing differences in ethnicity, religious background, suburban vs. urban residence, and strength of mobility strivings.

A source of variation perhaps not sufficiently emphasized in these and other reports is the manner in which cases were selected. As Davis and Havighurst properly pointed out in their original publication, their sample was subject to possible bias "in the direction of getting a middle-class group which had been subjected to the kind of teaching about child rearing which is prevalent among the middle-class people who send their children to nursery schools." Equally important may be the relatively high proportion in the Chicago lower-class sample of mothers coming from East European and Irish background, or the four-year discrepancy in the average ages of the mothers at the two-class levels. The first New Haven sample consisted entirely of mothers enrolled in the Yale Rooming-in Project who were sufficiently interested to bring the baby back for a check-up a year after mother and child had left the hospital. As Klatskin recognized, this selectivity probably resulted in a "sample composed of the families most sympathetic to rooming-in ideology," a fact which, as she noted, was reflected in her research results. White's Palo Alto group consisted solely of mothers of only one child, most of whom were expecting a second offspring; cases were recruited from a variety of sources including friends, neighbors, personnel managers, nursery school teachers, Public Health nurses, and maternal prenatal exercises classes. In short, virtually every sample had its special eccentricities. For some of these, one could guess at the extent and direction of bias; in others, the importance or effect of the selective features remains a mystery. Our difficulties, then, derive as much from ignorance as from knowledge—a fact which is underscored by the absence, for many of the samples, of such basic demographic information as the distribution of subjects by age and sex.

It is clear that many factors, some known and many more unknown, may operate to produce differences in results from one sample to the next. It is hardly likely, however, that these manifold influences will operate in a consistent direction over time or space. The possibility of obtaining interpretable findings, therefore, rests on the long chance that major trends, if they exist, will be sufficiently marked to override the effects of bias arising from variations in sampling and method. This is a rash and optimistic hope, but—somewhat to our own surprise—it seems to have been realized, at least in part, in the analyses that follow.

IV. Social Class Differences in Infant Care, 1930–1955

In interpreting reports of child-rearing practices it is essential to distinguish between the date at which the information was obtained and the actual period to which the information refers. This caution is particularly relevant in dealing with descriptions of infant care for children who (as in the Eugene or Detroit studies) may be as old as 12, 14, or 18 at the time of the interview. In such instances it is possible only to guess at the probable time at which the practice occurred by making due allowances for the age of the child. The problem is further complicated by the fact that none of the studies reports SES differences by age. The best one can do, therefore, is to estimate the median age of the group and from this approximate the period at which the practice may have taken place. For example, the second Detroit sample, which ranged in age from birth to 18 years, would have a median age of about nine. Since the field work was done in 1953, we estimate the data of feeding and weaning practices as about 1944.[18] It should be recognized, however, that the practices reported range over a considerable period extending from as far back as 1935 to the time of the interview in 1953. Any marked variation in child-rearing practices over this period could produce an average figure which would in point of fact be atypical for the middle year 1944. We shall have occasion to point to the possible operation of this effect in some of the data to follow.

If dates of practices are estimated by

---

[18] It is true that because of the rising birth rate after World War II the sample probably included more younger than older children, but without knowledge of the actual distribution by age we have hesitated to make further speculative adjustments.

the method outlined above, we find that the available data describe social-class differences in feeding, weaning, and toilet training for a period from about 1930 to 1955. The relevant information appears in Tables 2 through 4.

It is reasonable to suppose that a mother's reports of whether or not she employed a particular practice would be somewhat more reliable than her estimate of when she began or discontinued that practice. This expectation is borne out by the larger number of statistically significant differences in tables presenting data on prevalence (Tables 2 and 3) rather than on the timing of a particular practice (Tables 4–6). On the plausible assumption that the former data are more reliable, we shall begin our discussion by considering the results on frequency of breast feeding and scheduled feeding, which appear in Tables 2 and 3.

General Trends

We may begin by looking at general trends over time irrespective of social-class level. These appear in column 6 of Tables 2 and 3. The data for breast feeding are highly irregular, but there is some suggestion of decrease in this practice

TABLE 2   Frequency of Breast Feeding

		Number of cases reporting			Percentage breast fed			
1	2	3	4	5	6	7	8	9
Sample	Approx. date of practice	Total sample	Middle class	Working class	Total sample	Middle class	Working class	Difference[a]
National I	1930	1856	842	1014	80	78	82	− 4[b]
National II	1932	445	201	244	40	29	49	−20[b]
Chicago I	1939	100	48	52	83	83	83	0
Detroit I	1941	112	59	53	62	54	70	− 16
Detroit II	1944	200	70	130	Percentages not given			+
Eugene	1946–47	206	84	122	46	40	50	− 10
Boston	1947–48	372	198	174	40	43	37	+ 6
New Haven I	1949–50	222	114	108	80	85	74	+11[b]
Palo Alto	1950	74	36	38	66	70	63	+ 7[b]
Upstate New York	1955	1432	594	838	24	27	21	+ 6[b]

a Minus sign denotes lower incidence for middle class than for working class.
b Denotes difference significant at 5-per cent level of confidence or better.

TABLE 3   Scheduled versus Self-demand Feeding

1	2	Number of cases reporting			Percentage fed on demand			9
	Approx. date of	3	4	5	6	7	8	
		Total	Middle	Working	Total	Middle	Working	
Sample	practice	sample	class	class	sample	class	class	Difference[a]
National I	1932	470	208	262	16	7	23	−16[b]
Chicago I	1939	100	48	52	25	4	44	−40[b]
Detroit I	1941	297	52	45	21	12	53	−41[b]
Detroit II	1944	205	73	132	55	51	58	− 7
Boston	1947–48	372	198	174	Percentages not given			—
New Haven I	1949–50	191	117	74	65	71	54	+17
Palo Alto	1950	74	36	38	59	64	55	+ 9

a Minus sign denotes lower incidence of self-demand feeding in middle class.

b Denotes difference significant at 5-per cent level of confidence or better.

TABLE 4   Duration of Breast Feeding (for Those Breast Fed)

	Approx.	Number of cases[a]			Median duration in months			
	date of	Total	Middle	Working	Total	Middle	Working	
Sample	practice	sample	class	class	sample	class	class	Difference[b]
National II[c]	1930	1488	654	834	6.6	6.2	7.5	−1.3[d]
Chicago I	1939	83	40	43	3.5	3.4	3.5	− .1
Detroit I[c]	1941	69	32	37	3.3	2.8	5.3	−2.5
Eugene	1946–47	95	34	61	3.4	3.2	3.5	− .3
Boston	1947–48	149	85	64	2.3	2.4	2.1	+ .3
New Haven I[c]	1949–50	177	97	80	3.6	4.3	3.0	+1.3
Upstate New York	1955	299	145	154	1.2	1.3	1.2	+ .1

a Number of cases for Chicago, Eugene, Boston, and Upstate New York estimated from percentages cited.

b Minus sign denotes shorter duration for middle class than for working class.

c Medians not given in original report but estimated from data cited.

b Denotes difference significant at 5-per cent level of confidence or better.

over the years.[19] In contrast, self-demand feeding is becoming more common. In both instances the trend is more marked (column 8) in the middle class; in other words, it is they especially who are doing the changing. This fact is reflected even more sharply in column 9 which highlights a noteworthy shift. Here we see that in the earlier period— roughly before the end of World War II —both breast feeding and demand feeding were less common among the middle class than among the working class. In the later period, however, the direction is reversed; it is now the middle-class mother who more often gives her child the breast and feeds him on demand.

The data on duration of breast feeding (Table 4) and on the timing of weaning and bowel training (Tables 5 and 6) simply confirm, somewhat less reliably, all of the above trends. There is a general tendency in both social classes to wean the child earlier from the breast but, apparently, to allow him to suck from a bottle till a somewhat later age. Since no uniform reference points were used for securing information on toilet training

_____

[19] As indicated below, we believe that these irregularities are largely attributable to the highly selective character of a number of the samples (notably, New Haven I and Palo Alto) and that the downward trend in frequency and duration of breast feeding is probably more reliable than is reflected in the data of Tables 2 and 4.

TABLE 5   Age at Completion of Weaning (either Breast or Bottle)

Sample	Approx. date of practice	Number of cases Total sample	Middle class	Working class	Median age in months Total group	Middle class	Working class	Difference[a]
Chicago I	1940	100	48	52	11.3	10.3	12.3	−2.0[b]
Detroit I	1942	69	32	37	11.2	10.6	12.0	−1.4[b]
Detroit II	1945	190	62	128	—Under 12 months—			—
Eugene	1947-48	206	85	121	13.6	13.2	14.1	−.9
Boston	1948-49	372	198	174	12.3	12.0	12.6	−.6
New Haven I	1949-50	222	114	108	—Over 12 months—			—
Palo Alto	1951	68	32	36	13.1	14.4	12.6	+1.8

a Minus sign denotes earlier weaning for middle than for working class.
b Denotes difference significant at 5-per cent level of confidence or better.

TABLE 6   Toilet Training

Sample	Approx. date practice begun	Number of Cases Bowel training	Bladder training	Direction of Relationship Beginning bowel training	End bowel training	Beginning bladder training	End bladder training
National II	1931	2375	2375		—[a]		—[b]
National I	1932	494	494		—	—	
Chicago I	1940	100	220[a]	—[a]	—	—[a,c]	+[a]
Detroit I	1942	110	102	—	—	+	—
Detroit II	1945	216	200	+[a]	—	+	—
Eugene	1947-48	206	206	+	—	+	+
Boston	1948-49	372		—	+[a]		
New Haven I	1950-51	214		+[a]			
Palo Alto	1951	73		+[a]			

a Denotes difference significant at 5-per cent level of confidence or better.
b Minus sign indicates that middle class began or completed training earlier than lower class.
c Based on data from 1946 report.

in the several studies (i.e., some investigators report percentage training at six months, others at ten months, still others at 12 or 18 months), Table 6 shows only the direction of the difference between the two social classes. All these figures on timing point to the same generalization. In the earlier period, middle-class mothers were exerting more pressure; they weaned their children from the breast and bottle and carried out bowel and bladder training before their working-class counterparts. But in the last ten years the trend has been reversed—it is now the middle-class mother who trains later.

These consistent trends take on richer significance in the light of Wolfenstein's impressive analysis[20] of the content of successive editions of the United States Children's Bureau bulletin on *Infant Care*. She describes the period 1929–38 (which corresponds to the earlier time span covered by our data) as characterized by

. . . a pervasive emphasis on regularity, doing everything by the clock. Weaning and intro-

[20] M. Wolfenstein, "Trends in Infant Care," *American Journal of Orthopsychiatry*, XXIII (1953), 120–130. Similar conclusions were drawn in an earlier report by Stendler surveying 60 years of child-training practices as advocated in three popular women's magazines. *Cf.* C. B. Stendler, "Sixty Years of Child Training Practices," *Journal of Pediatrics*, XXXVI (1950), 122–134.

duction of solid foods are to be accomplished with great firmness, never yielding for a moment to the baby's resistance . . . bowel training . . . must be carried out with great determination as early as possible . . . . The main danger which the baby presented at this time was that of dominating the parents. Successful child training meant winning out against the child in the struggle for domination.

In the succeeding period, however,

. . . all this was changed. The child became remarkably harmless. . . . His main active aim was to explore his world. . . . When not engaged in exploratory undertakings, the baby needs care and attention; and giving these when he demands them, far from making him a tyrant, will make him less demanding later on. At this time mildness is advocated in all areas: thumbsucking and masturbation are not to be interfered with; weaning and toilet training are to be accomplished later and more gently.[21]

The parallelism between preachment and practice is apparent also in the use of breast feeding. Up until 1945, "breast feeding was emphatically recommended," with "warnings against early weaning." By 1951 "the long-term intransigence about breast feeding is relaxed." States the bulletin edition of that year: "Mothers who find bottle feeding easier should feel comfortable about doing it that way."

One more link in the chain of information completes the story. There is ample evidence that, both in the early and the later period, middle-class mothers were much more likely than working-class mothers to be exposed to current information on child care. Thus Anderson cites table after table showing that parents from higher SES levels read more books, pamphlets, and magazines, and listen to more radio talks on child care and related subjects. This in 1932. Similarly, in the last five years, White, in California, and Bock, in New York, report that middle-class mothers are much more likely than those in the working class to read Spock's best-seller, Baby and Child Care[22] and similar publications.

Our analysis suggests that the mothers not only read these books but take them seriously, and that their treatment of the child is affected accordingly. Moreover, middle-class mothers not only read more but are also more responsive; they alter their behavior earlier and faster than their working-class counterparts.

In view of the remarkably close parallelism in changes over time revealed by Wolfenstein's analysis and our own, we should perhaps not overlook a more recent trend clearly indicated in Wolfenstein's report and vaguely discernible as well in the data we have assembled. Wolfenstein asserts that, since 1950, a conservative note has crept into the child-training literature; "there is an attempt to continue . . . mildness, but not without some conflicts and misgivings. . . . May not continued gratification lead to addiction and increasingly intensified demands?"[23] In this connection it is perhaps no mere coincidence that the differences in the last column of Tables 2 to 4 show a slight drop after about 1950; the middle class is still more "relaxed" than the working class, but the differences are not so large as earlier. Once again, practice may be following preachment—in the direction of introducing more limits and demands—still within a permissive framework. We shall return to a consideration of this possibility in our discussion of class differences in the training of children beyond two years of age.

Taken as a whole, the correspondence between Wolfenstein's data and our own suggests a general hypothesis extending beyond the confines of social class as

[21] Wolfenstein, op. cit., p. 121.

[22] Benjamin Spock, Baby and Child Care (New York: Pocket Books, Inc., 1957).

[23] Wolfenstein, op. cit., p. 121.

such: *child-rearing practices are likely to change most quickly in those segments of society which have closest access and are most receptive to the agencies or agents of change (e.g., public media, clinics, physicians, and counselors).* From this point of view, one additional trend suggested by the available data is worthy of note: rural families appear to "lag behind the times" somewhat in their practices of infant care. For example, in Anderson's beautifully detailed report, there is evidence that in 1932 farm families (Class IV in his sample) were still breast feeding their children more frequently but being less flexible in scheduling and toilet training than non-farm families of roughly comparable socioeconomic status. Similarly, there are indications from Miller and Swanson's second Detroit study that, with SES held constant, mothers with parents of rural background adhere to more rigid techniques of socialization than their urban counterparts. Finally, the two samples in our data most likely to contain a relatively high proportion of rural families—Eugene, Oregon and Upstate New York—are also the ones which are slightly out of line in showing smaller differences in favor of middle-class permissiveness.

The above observations call attention to the fact that the major time trends discerned in our data, while impressive, are by no means uniform. There are several marked exceptions to the rule. True, some of these can be "explained" in terms of special features of the samples employed. A case in point is the New Haven study, which—in keeping with the rooming-in ideology and all that this implies—shows the highest frequency and duration of breast feeding for the postwar period, as well as the greatest prevalence of feeding on demand reported in all the surveys examined. Other discrepancies may be accounted for, at least in part, by variations in time span encompassed by the data (National 1930 *vs.* 1932), the demonstrated differ-

ential rate in breast feeding for first *vs.* later children (Palo Alto *vs.* National 1930 or Boston), ethnic differences (Boston *vs.* Chicago), contrasting ages of mothers in middle- *vs.* working-class samples (Chicago), etc. All of these explanations, however, are "after the fact" and must therefore be viewed with suspicion.

Summary

Despite our inability to account with any confidence for all departures from the general trend, we feel reasonably secure in our inferences about the nature of this trend. To recapitulate, over the last 25 years, even though breast feeding appears to have become less popular, American mothers—especially in the middle class—are becoming increasingly permissive in their feeding and toilet-training practices during the first two years of the child's life. The question remains whether this tendency is equally apparent in the training of the child as he becomes older. We turn next to a consideration of this issue.

V. Class Differences in the Training of Children Beyond the Age of Two

Once we leave the stage of infancy, data from different studies of child training become even more difficult to compare. There are still greater variations in the questions asked from one research to the next, and results are reported in different types of units (e.g., relating scales with varying numbers of steps diversely defined). In some instances (as in the Chicago, Detroit II, and, apparently, Eugene surveys) the questions referred not to past or current practices but to the mother's judgment about what she would do at some later period when her child would be older. Also, when the samples include children of widely varying ages, it is often difficult to determine at what period the behavior described by the mother actually took place. Sometimes a particular age was specified in the interviewer's question and when this occurred, we have made use of that fact in estimating the approximate date of the practice. More often, however, such information was lacking. Accordingly, our time estimates must be regarded as subject to considerable error. Finally, even though we deal with substantially the same researches considered in the analysis of infant care, the total period encompassed by the data

TABLE 7   Permissiveness toward Impulse Expression

Sample	Approx. date of practice	No. of cases reported	Direction of trend for middle class			
			Oral behavior	Toilet accidents	Sex	Aggression
National I	1932	470			More infants allowed to play on bed unclothed.[a]	
Chicago	1943	100		Treated by ignoring,[a] reasoning or talking, rather than slapping,[a] scolding, or showing disgust.[a]		More children allowed to "fight so long as they don't hurt each other badly."[a]
Detroit II	1946	70–88	Less often disciplined for thumb sucking.		Less often disciplined for touching sex organs.	
New Haven	1949–50	216	Less often disapproved for thumb sucking, eating habits, mannerisms, etc.[a]			
Eugene	1950	206		Less often treated by spanking or scolding.	More permissive toward child's sexual behavior.[a]	Fewer children allowed "to fight so long as they don't hurt each other badly." More permissiveness toward general aggression.
Boston	1951–52	372	Less restriction on use of fingers for eating.[a]	Less severe toilet training.[a]	Higher sex permissiveness (general index).[a]	More permissive of aggression toward parents,[a] children[b] and siblings. Less punishment of aggression toward parents.[a]
Palo Alto	1953	73		Less severe toilet training.[a]		More permissive of aggression toward parents.[a] Less severe punishment of aggression toward parents.

[a] Indicates difference between classes significant at the 5-per cent level or better.
[b] The difference between percentages is not significant but the difference between ratings is significant at the 5-per cent level or better.

is appreciably shorter. This is so because the mothers are no longer being asked to recall how they handled their child in infancy; instead they are reporting behavior which is contemporary, or at least not far removed, from the time of the interview.

All of these considerations combine to restrict severely our ability to identify changes in practices over time. Accordingly, the absence of evidence for such changes in some of the data is perhaps more properly attributed to the limitations of our measures than to the actual course of events.

Permissiveness and Restriction on Freedom of Movement

The areas of impulse expression documented in Table 7 reflect a continuity in treatment from babyhood into early childhood. With only one minor, statistically insignificant exception, the results depict the middle-class parent as more permissive in all four spheres of activity: oral behavior, toilet accidents, sex and aggression. There is no suggestion of a shift over the somewhat truncated time span. The now-familiar trend reappears, however, in the data on restriction of freedom of movement shown in Table 8.

In Table 8 we see a gradual shift over time with the middle class being more restrictive in the 1930's and early 1940's but becoming more permissive during the last decade.

Training for Independence and Achievement

Thus far the trends that have appeared point predominantly in one direction—increasing leniency on the part of middle-class parents. At the same time, careful consideration of the nature of these data reveals that they are, in a sense, one-sided: they have been concerned almost entirely with the parents'

TABLE 8   Restriction on Freedom of Movement

Sample	Approx. date of practice	No. of cases reported	Age	Item	Direction of relationship[a]
National II	1932	2289	1–5	Play restricted to home yard	—
				Play restricted to block	+
				Play restricted to neighborhood	+[b]
				No restriction on place of play	+[b]
National III	1932	669	6–12	Child goes to movie with parents	+
				Child goes to movie with other children	+
National IV	1932	2414	1–12	Child goes to bed earlier	+
Chicago	1943	100	5	Age at which child is allowed to go to movie alone or with other children	+[b]
				Age at which child is allowed to go downtown	—[b]
				Time at which children are expected in at night	+[b]
New Haven I	1949–50	211	1	Definite bed time	—[b]
Boston	1951–52	372	5	Restriction on how far child may go from home	—
				Frequency of checking on child's whereabouts	—[c]
				Strictness about bed time	[b]
				Amount of care taken by persons other than parents	—[b]
Detroit II	1953	136	0–18	Child supervised closely after 12 years of age	—[b]
Palo Alto	1953	74	2½–5½	Extent of keeping track of child	0

a Plus sign denotes greater restriction for middle class.

b Denotes difference significant at 5-per cent level or better.

c The difference between percentages is not significant but the difference between mean ratings is significant at the 5-per cent level or better.

response to the expressed needs and wishes of the child. What about the child's response to the needs and wishes of the parent, and the nature of these parental demands? The results presented in Table 9 are of especial interest since they shed light on all three aspects of the problem. What is more, they signal a dramatic departure from the hitherto unchallenged trend toward permissiveness.

Three types of questions have been asked with respect to independence training. The first is of the kind we have been dealing with thus far; for example, the Boston investigators inquired about the mother's reaction to the child's expression of dependence (hanging on to the mother's skirt, demanding attention, etc.). The results for this sort of query, shown in column 6 of Table 9, are consistent with previous findings for the postwar period; middle-class mothers are more tolerant of the child's expressed needs than are working-class mothers. The second type of question deals with the child's progress in taking care of himself and assuming responsibility (column 7). Here no clear trend is apparent, although there is some suggestion of greater solicitousness on the part of the middle-class mother. For example, in the 1932 material the middle-class child excelled in dressing and feeding himself only "partially," not "completely." In the 1935 Palo Alto study, the middle-class mother viewed her child as more dependent even though he was rated less so by the outside observer. It would appear that middle-class mothers may be on the alert for signs of dependency and anxious lest they push too fast.

Yet, as the data of column 8 clearly indicate, they push nevertheless. By and large, the middle-class mother expects more of her child than her working-class counterpart. All five of the statistically significant differences support this tendency and most of the remaining results point in the same direction. The conclusion is further underscored by the finding on class differences in parental aspirations for the child's academic progress, shown in column 9. The only exception to the highly reliable trend is in itself noteworthy. In the Boston study, more middle-class mothers expected their children to go to college, but they were less likely to say that it was important for their child to do well in school. Are these mothers merely giving what they consider to be the socially acceptable response, or do they really, as Sears and his colleagues suggest, have less cause for concern because their children are living up to expectations?

The preceding question raises an even broader and more significant issue. Our data indicate that middle-class parents are becoming increasingly permissive in response to the child's expressed needs and desires. Yet, these same parents have not relaxed their high levels of expectations for ultimate performance. Do we have here a typical instance of Benedict's "discontinuity in cultural conditioning,"[24] with the child first being encouraged in one pattern of response and then expected to perform in a very different fashion? If so, there are days of disappointment ahead for middle-class fathers and mothers. Or, are there other elements in the parent-child relationship of the middle-class family which impel the child to effort despite, or, perhaps, even because of, his early experiences of relatively uninhibited gratification? The data on class differences in techniques of discipline shed some light on this question.

Techniques of Discipline

The most consistent finding documented in Table 10 is the more frequent

[24] R. Benedict, "Continuities and Discontinuities in Cultural Conditioning," *Psychiatry*, I (1938), 161–167.

TABLE 9   Training for Independence and Academic Achievement

1 Sample	2 Approx. date of practice	3 No. of cases reported	4 Age	5 Item	Direction of relationship			
					6 Parents' reponse to child's dependency	7 Child's behavior[a]	8 Parental demands and expectations	9 Academic aspirations for child[a]
National II	1932	2380	1–5	Dress self not at all		+		
				Dress self partially		|		
				Dress self completely		−		
		2391		Feed self not at all		−		
				Feed self partially		+		
				Feed self completely		−		
		2301		Children read to by parents				+
National III	1932	865	6–12	Runs errands		0		
				Earns money		−		
				Receive outside lessons in music, art, etc.				+[b]
National IV	1932	2695	1–12	Books in the home				+[b]
Chicago I	1943	100	5	Age child expected to dress self			0	
				Expected to help at home by age 5			+[b]	
				Expected to help with younger children			+[b]	
				Girls expected to begin to cook			+	
				Girls expected to help with dishes			+	
				Child expected to finish high school only				+[b]
				Child expected to finish college				+[b]
				Father teaches and reads to children				+[b]
Detroit II	1946		0–18	All right to leave three-year-old with sitter			0	
	1947	128		Expected to pick up own toys			+	
	1948	127		Expected to dress self by age 5			+	
	1948	126		Expected to put away clothes by age 5			+[b]	
				Children requested to run errands at age 7			0	
				Agree child should be on his own as early as possible			+	
Urban Connecticut	1950	152	6–18	Age of expected mastery (Winterbottom scale)			+[b]	
Eugene	1950	206	0–18	Household rules and chores expected of children			+	
Boston	1951–52	372	5	Parent permissive of child dependency	−[b]			
				Punishment, irritation for dependency	−[b]			
				Parents give child regular job around house			0	
				Importance of child's doing well at school				−[b]
				Expected to go to college				+[b]
New Haven II	1951–53	48	14–17	Father subscribes to values of independence and mastery			+[b]	
		1151[c]	14–17	Expected to go to college				+[b]
				Family checks over homework				+[b]
Palo Alto	1953	74	2½–5½	M's report of child's dependency	−			
				Amount of attention child wants		+		
				Child objects to separation	−			
				Judge's rating of dependency		+		
Upstate New York	1955	1433	0–1	Mother's educational aspirations for child				+[b]

[a] Plus sign denotes greater independence or achievement required for middle-class child.

[b] Difference between classes significant at the 5-per cent level or better.

[c] This is the entire high-school sample which Strodtbeck surveyed in order to select his experimental and control group.

TABLE 10   Techniques of Discipline

Sample	Approx. date of practice	No. of cases reporting	Age	Direction of relationship[a]				Nature of love-oriented technique	Other significant trends for middle class
				Physical punishment	Reasoning	Isolation	Love-oriented technique		
National II	1932	1947	1–5	—b					
National III	1932	839	6–12			+b			
National IV	1932	3130	1–12		+b				Infractions more often ignored b More children deprived of pleasure as punishment
Chicago I	1943	100	5	+		—	+b	Praise for good behavior	Soiling child more often ignored,b rather than spankedb or shown disgust
Detroit I	1950	115	12–14	—b			+b	Mother expresses disappointment or appeals to guilt	
Detroit II	1950	222	0–19	—			+	Mother uses symbolic rather than direct rewards and punishments	
Eugene	1950	206	0–18	—		0	+b		
Boston	1951–52	372	5	—b	+	+	0	No difference in overall use of praise or withdrawal of love	Less use of ridicule,b deprivation of privilegesc or praise for no trouble at the tableb

a Plus sign indicates practice was more common in middle class than in working class.

b Denotes difference between classes significant at 5-per cent level or better.

c The difference between percentages is not significant but the difference between mean ratings is significant at the 5-per cent level or better.

use of physical punishment by working-class parents. The middle class, in contrast, resort to reasoning, isolation, and what Sears and his colleagues have referred to as "love-oriented" discipline techniques.[25] These are methods which rely for their effect on the child's fear of loss of love. Miller and Swanson referred to substantially the same class of phenomena by the term "psychological discipline," which for them covers such parental behaviors as appeals to guilt, expressions of disappointment, and the use of symbolic rather than direct rewards and punishments. Table 10 shows all available data on class differences in the use of corporal punishment, reasoning, isolation, and "love-oriented" techniques. Also, in order to avoid the risks, however small, involved in wearing theoretical blinders, we have listed in the last column of the table all other significant class differences in techniques of discipline reported in the studies we have examined.

From one point of view, these results highlight once again the more lenient policies and practices of middle-class families. Such parents are, in the first place, more likely to overlook offenses, and when they do punish, they are less likely to ridicule or inflict physical pain. Instead, they reason with the youngster, isolate him, appeal to guilt, show disap-

[25] These investigators also classify "isolation" as a love-oriented technique, but since this specific method is reported on in several other studies as well, we have tabulated the results separately to facilitate comparison.

pointment—in short, convey in a variety of ways, on the one hand, the kind of behavior that is expected of the child; on the other, the realization that transgression means the interruption of a mutually valued relationship.

These consistent class differences take on added significance in the light of the finding, arrived at independently both by the Boston and Detroit investigators, that "love-oriented" or "psychological" techniques are more effective than other methods for bringing about desired behavior. Indeed, both groups of researchers concluded on the basis of their data that physical punishment for aggression tends to increase rather than decrease aggressive behavior. From the point of view of our interest, these findings mean that middle-class parents, though in one sense more lenient in their discipline techniques, are using methods that are actually more compelling. Moreover, the compelling power of these practices, rather than being reduced, is probably enhanced by the more permissive treatment accorded to middle-class children in the early years of life. The successful use of withdrawal of love as a discipline technique implies the prior existence of a gratifying relationship; the more love present in the first instance, the greater the threat implied in its withdrawal.

In sum, to return to the issue posed in the preceding section, our analysis suggests that middle-class parents are in fact using techniques of discipline which are likely to be effective in evoking the behavior desired in the child. Whether the high levels of expectation held by such parents are actually achieved is another matter. At least, there would seem to be some measure of functional continuity in the way in which middle-class parents currently treat their children from infancy through childhood.

Before we leave consideration of the data of Table 10, one additional feature of the results deserves comment. In the most recent study reported, the Boston research, there were three departures from the earlier general trend. First, no class difference was found in the over-all use of praise. Second, working-class parents actually exceeded those of the middle class in praising good behavior at the table. Third, in contrast to earlier findings, the working-class mother more frequently punished by withdrawing privileges. Although Sears et al. did not classify "withdrawal of privileges" as a love-oriented technique, the shift does represent a change in the direction of what was previously a method characteristic of the middle-class parent. Finally, there is no clear trend in the differential use of love-oriented techniques by the two social classes. If we view the Boston study as reflecting the most recent trends in methods of discipline, then either middle-class mothers are beginning to make less use of techniques they previously relied upon, or the working class is starting to adopt them. We are inclined toward the latter hypothesis in the belief that the working class, as a function of increasing income and education, is gradually reducing its "cultural lag." Evidence from subsequent studies, of course, would be necessary to confirm this speculative interpretation, since the results cited may merely be a function of features peculiar to the Boston study and not typical of the general trend.

Overall Character of the Parent-Child Relationship

The material considered so far has focused on specific practices employed by the parent. A number of researches document class differences as well in variables of a more molar sort—for example, the emotional quality of the parent-child relationship as a whole. These investigations have the additional advantage of reaching somewhat further back in time, but they also have their shortcomings. First of all, the results are not usually reported in the conventional form of percentages or means for specific social-class levels. In some studies the findings are given in terms of correlation coefficients. In others, social status can only be estimated from educational level. In others still, the data are presented in the form of graphs from which no significance tests can be computed. Partly to compensate for this lack of precision and comparability, partly to complete the picture of available data on class-differences in child rearing, we cite in Table 11 not only the results from these additional studies of molar variables but also all other statistically significant findings from researches considered previously which might have bearing on the problem at hand. In this way, we hope as well to avoid the bias which occasionally arises from looking only at those variables in which one has a direct theoretical interest.

The data of Table 11 are noteworthy in a number of respects. First, we have clear confirmation that, over the entire 25-year period, middle-class parents have had a more acceptant, equalitarian relationship with their children. In many ways, the contrast is epitomized in Duvall's distinction between the "developmental" and "traditional" conceptions of mother and child. Duvall asked the mothers in her sample to list the "five things that a good mother does" and the "five things that a good child does." Middle-class mothers tended to emphasize such themes as "guiding and understanding," "relating herself lovingly to the child," and making sure that he "is happy and contented," "shares and cooperates with others," and "is eager to learn." In contrast, working-class mothers stressed the importance of keeping house and child "neat and clean," "training the child to regularity," and getting the child "to obey and respect adults."

What is more, this polarity in the value orientation of the two social classes

appears to have endured. In data secured as recently as 1957, Kohn[26] reports that working-class mothers differ from those of the middle-class in their choice of characteristics most desired in a child; the former emphasize "neatness, cleanliness, and obedience," while the latter stress "happiness, considerateness, and self-control."

Yet, once again, it would be a mistake to conclude that the middle-class parent is exerting less pressure on his children. As the data of Table 11 also show, a higher percentage of middle-class children are punished in some manner, and there is more "necessary" discipline to prevent injury or danger. In addition, though the middle-class father typically has a warmer relationship with the child, he is also likely to have more authority and status in family affairs.

Although shifts over time are difficult to appraise when the data are so variable in specific content, one trend is sufficiently salient to deserve comment. In the early Berkeley data the working-class parent is more expressive of affection than his middle-class counterpart. But in the follow-up study of the same children eight years later the trend is reversed. Perhaps the same mothers behave differently toward younger and older children. Still, the item "Baby picked up when cries" yields a significant difference in favor of the working-class mother in 1932 and a reliable shift in the opposite direction in 1953. *Sic transit gloria Watsoniensis!*

Especially with terms as heavily value laden as those which appear in Table 11, one must be concerned with the possibility that the data in the studies examined document primarily not actual behavior but the middle-class mother's superior knowledge of the socially acceptable response. Undoubtedly, this factor operates to inflate the reported relationships.

---

[26] Kohn, *op. cit.*

TABLE 11   Overall Character of Parent-Child Relationship

Sample	Approx. date of practice	No. of cases reported	Age	Middle-class trend	Working-class trend
Berkeley I	1928–32	31	1–3	Grants autonomy Cooperative Equalitarian	Expresses affection Excessive contact Intrusive Irritable Punitive Ignores child
National I	1932	494	0–1		Baby picked up when cries[a]
National IV	1932	3239	1–12	Higher percentage of children punished[a]	Nothing done to allay child's fears[a]
Yellow Springs, Ohio	1940	124	3–12	Acceptant-democratic	Indulgent Active-rejectant
Berkeley II	1939–42	31	9–11	Grants autonomy Cooperative Equalitarian Expresses affection	Excessive contact Intrusive Irritable Punitive Ignores child
Chicago I	1943	100	5		Father plays with child more[a]
Chicago II	1943–44	433	1–5	"Developmental" conception of "good mother" and "good child."[a]	"Traditional" conception of "good mother" and "good child."[a]
New Haven I	1949–50	219	1	More necessary discipline to prevent injury or danger[a]	More prohibitive discipline beyond risk of danger or injury
Boston	1951–52	372	5	Mother warmer toward child[a] Father warmer toward child[b] Father exercises more authority[b] Mother has higher esteem for father[a] Mother delighted about pregnancy[a] Both parents more often share authority[b]	Father demands instant obedience[a] Child ridiculed[a] Greater rejection of child[a] Emphasis on neatness, cleanliness, and order[a] Parents disagree more on child-rearing policy[b]
New Haven II	1951–53	48	14–17	Fathers have more power in family decisions[a] Parents agree in value orientations[a]	
Palo Alto	1953	73	2½–5½	Baby picked up when cries[a]	Mother carries through demands rather than dropping the subject[a]
Eugene	1955–56	206	0–18	Better relationship between father and child[a]	
Washington, D.C.	1956–57	400	10–11	Desirable qualities are happiness,[b] considerateness,[b] curiosity,[b] self-control[b]	Desirable qualities are neatness, cleanliness,[b] obedience[b]

[a] The difference between percentages is not significant but the difference between mean ratings is significant at the 5-per cent level or better.

[b] Trend significant at 5-per cent level or better.

But there are several reassuring considerations. First, although the items investigated vary widely in the intensity of their value connotations, all show substantially the same trends. Second, four of the studies reported in Table 11 (Berkeley I and II, Yellow Springs, and New Haven II) are based not on the mother's responses to an interview but on observation of actual interaction among family members. It seems highly unlikely, therefore, that the conclusions we have reached apply only to professed opinions and not to real behavior as well.

VI. Retrospect and Prospect

It is interesting to compare the results of our analysis with the traditional view of the differences between the middle- and lower-class styles of life, as documented in the classic descriptions of Warner,[27] Davis,[28] Dollard,[29] and the more recent accounts of Spinley,[30] Clausen,[31] and Miller and Swanson.[32] In all these sources the working class is typically characterized as impulsive and uninhibited, the middle class as more rational, controlled and guided by a broader perspective in time. Thus Clausen writes:

The lower class pattern of life . . . puts a high premium on physical gratification, on free expression of aggression, on spending and sharing. Cleanliness, respect for property, sexual control, educational achievement—all are highly valued by middle class Americans—are of less importance to the lower class family or are phrased differently.[33]

To the extent that our data even approach this picture, it is for the period before World War II rather than for the present day. The modern middle class has, if anything, extended its time perspective so that the tasks of child training are now accomplished on a more leisurely schedule. As for the lower class the fit is far better for the actual behavior of parents rather than for the values they seek to instill in their children. As reflected in the data of Tables 10 and 11, the lower-class parent—though he demands compliance and control in his child—is himself more aggressive, expressive, and impulsive than his middle-class counterpart. Even so, the picture is a far cry from the traditional image of the casual and carefree lower class. Perhaps the classic portrait is yet to be seen along the skid rows and Tobacco Roads of the nation, but these do not lie along the well-trodden paths of the survey researcher. He is busy ringing doorbells, no less, in the main section of the lower-class district, where most of the husbands have steady jobs and, what is more important, the wife is willing to answer the door and the interviewer's questions. In this modern working-class world there may be greater freedom of emotional expression, but there is no laxity or vagueness with respect to goals of child training. Consistently over the past 25 years, the parent in this group has emphasized what are usually regarded as the traditional middle-class virtues of cleanliness, conformity, and control, and although his methods are not so effective as those of his middle-class neighbors, they are perhaps more desperate.

Perhaps this very desperation, enhanced by early exposure to impulse and aggression, leads working-class parents to pursue new goals with old techniques of discipline. While accepting middle-class levels of aspiration he has not yet internalized sufficiently the modes of response which make these standards readily achievable for himself or his children. He has still to learn to wait, to explain, and to give and withhold his affection as the reward and price of performance.

[27] W. L. Warner and P. S. Lunt, *The Social Life of a Modern Community* (New Haven: Yale University Press, 1942); Warner, Meeker, *et al.*, *op. cit.*

[28] A. Davis, B. Gardner, and M. R. Gardner, *Deep South* (Chicago: University of Chicago Press, 1941).

[29] J. Dollard, *Caste and Class in a Southern Town* (New Haven: Yale University Press, 1937).

[30] B. M. Spinley, *The Deprived and the Privileged: Personality Development in English Society* (London: Routledge & Kegan Paul, Ltd., 1953).

[31] J. A. Clausen, "Social and Psychological Factors in Narcotics Addiction," *Law and Contemporary Problems*, XXII (1957), 34–51.

[32] Miller and Swanson, *The Changing American Parent, op. cit.*

[33] Clausen, *op. cit.*, p. 42.

As of 1957, there are suggestions that the cultural gap may be narrowing. Spock has joined the Bible on the working-class shelf. If we wish to see the shape of the future, we can perhaps do no better than to look at the pages of the newly revised edition of this ubiquitous guidebook. Here is a typical example of the new look—a passage not found in the earlier version:

> If the parent can determine in which respects she may be too permissive and can firm up her discipline, she may, if she is on the right track, be delighted to find that her child becomes not only better behaved but much happier. Then she can really love him better, and he in turn responds to this.[34]

Apparently "love" and "limits" are both watchwords for the coming generation of parents. As Mrs. Johnson, down in the flats, puts away the hairbrush and decides to have a talk with her unruly youngster "like the book says," Mrs. Thomas, on the hill, is dutifully striving to overcome her guilt at the thought of giving John the punishment she now admits he deserves. If both ladies are successful, the social scientist may eventually have to look elsewhere in his search for ever larger F's and t's.

Such speculations carry us beyond the territory yet surveyed by the social scientist. Perhaps the most important implication for the future from our present analysis lies in the sphere of method rather than substance. Our attempt to compare the work of a score of investigators over a score of years will have been worth the labor if it but convinces future researchers of the wastefulness of such uncoordinated efforts. Our best hope for an understanding of the differences in child rearing in various segments of our society and the effects of these differences on personality formation lies in the development of a systematic long-range plan for gathering com-

parable data at regular intervals on large samples of families at different positions in the social structure. We now have survey organizations with the scientific competence and adequate technical facilities to perform the task. With such hopes in mind, the author looks ahead to the day when the present analysis becomes obsolete, in method as well as substance.

VII. Recapitulation and Coda

A comparative analysis of the results of studies of social-class differences in child rearing over a 25-year period points to the following conclusions.

A. Trends in Infant Care

1. Over the past quarter of a century, American mothers at all social-class levels have become more flexible with respect to infant feeding and weaning. Although fewer infants may be breast fed, especially over long periods of time, mothers are increasingly more likely to feed their children on demand and to wean them later from the bottle.

2. Class differences in feeding, weaning, and toilet training show a clear and consistent trend. From about 1930 till the end of World War II, working-class mothers were uniformly more permissive than those of the middle class. They were more likely to breast feed, to follow a self-demand schedule, to wean the child later both from breast and bottle, and to begin and complete both bowel and bladder training at a later age. After World War II, however, there has been a definite reversal in direction; now it is the middle-class mother who is the more permissive in each of the above areas.

3. Shifts in the pattern of infant care—especially on the part of middle-class mothers—show a striking correspondence to the changes in practices advocated in successive editions of U.S.

[34] Spock, op. cit., p. 326.

Children's Bureau bulletins and similar sources of expert opinion.

4. In addition to varying with social-class level, methods of infant care appear to differ as a function of cultural background, urban vs. rural upbringing, and exposure to particular ideologies of child rearing.

5. Taken together, the findings on changes in infant care lead to the generalization that socialization practices are most likely to be altered in those segments of society which have most ready access to the agencies or agents of change (e.g., books, pamphlets, physicians, and counselors).

B. Trends in Child Training

6. The data on the training of the young child show middle-class mothers, especially in the postwar period, to be consistently more permissive toward the child's expressed needs and wishes. The generalization applies in such diverse areas as oral behavior, toilet accidents, dependency, sex, aggressiveness, and freedom of movement outside the home.

7. Though more tolerant of expressed impulses and desires, the middle-class parent, throughout the period covered by this survey, has higher expectations for the child. The middle-class youngster is expected to learn to take care of himself earlier, to accept more responsibilities about the home, and—above all—to progress further in school.

8. In matters of discipline, working-class parents are consistently more likely to employ physical punishment, while middle-class families rely more on reasoning, isolation, appeals to guilt, and other methods involving the threat of loss of love. At least two independent lines of evidence suggest that the techniques preferred by middle-class parents are more likely to bring about the development of internalized values and controls. Moreover, the effectiveness of such methods should, at least on theoretical grounds, be enhanced by the more acceptant atmosphere experienced by middle-class children in their early years.

9. Over the entire 25-year period studied, parent-child relationships in the middle class are consistently reported as more acceptant and equalitarian, while those in the working class are oriented toward maintaining order and obedience. Within this context, the middle class has shown a shift away from emotional control toward freer expression of affection and greater tolerance of the child's impulses and desires.

In the past few years, there have been indications that the gap between the social classes may be narrowing. Whatever trend the future holds in store, let us hope that the social scientist will no longer be content to look at them piecemeal but will utilize all the technical resources now at his command to obtain a systematic picture of the changes, through still more extended space and time, in the way in which humanity brings up its children.

methods

six

It is a well-recognized fact that what one finds in scientific research depends in large part on the methods employed to secure data. In turn, the methods employed depend upon, or should flow from, the basic notions one has as to what is important to study, what questions ought to be asked, and what are the boundary limits of the phenomena one is investigating.

These considerations are especially pertinent to the study of stratification, since various students define the phenomena of stratification differently and hence are led by these definitions to investigate different phenomena. For instance, if stratification is said to consist primarily of differential ranking of individuals on some scale of value or honor, and the differential patterns of grouping and intimate association they form on the basis of these rankings, then, as with W. Lloyd Warner, the study of stratification will focus primarily on discovering the rankings men assign each other. If one further assumes that the differences in objective features such as income and education are important primarily for their influence on these rankings, then, again as with Warner, one will not be concerned with the impact of ranking on differences in objective resources.

Warner's methods, which have tended to be adopted by numerous investigators in American society studies, and even in studies abroad, come under severe criticism by Harold W. Pfautz and Otis Dudley Duncan in the article reprinted here. The latter raise questions about (1) the techniques used for assigning individuals in a community to given places on the class ladder, (2) the validation of the indices of social class used by Warner, (3) the sampling procedures Warner employs, (4) the generalizability of the data from any given community study, (5) the limited phenomena embraced by Warner's conception of stratification, and (6) the theory offered by Warner to account for the empirical findings of various community studies.

Thomas E. Lasswell pays explicit attention to the problem of defining class and stratification and other allied terms, indicating that confusion or diversity in usages often leads us to false arguments. He distinguishes seven different types of concepts, each of which refers to a somewhat different body of social behavior and social aggregation. The clarification of the conceptual "muddle," as Lasswell terms it, is essential if we are to secure comparative data from one study to another, and from one society to another, about the forms and functions of social inequality.

In dealing with people's own ideas about the class structure of their society, investigators find they obtain very different views from respondents of that class structure depending on the questions they ask. A central aim of all such questions is to discover the respondent's views with regard to whom he considers his equal and whom he does not. Here, too, however, "equal" is a vague term, and people who are equals in one sense may be viewed as unequals in another. The different possible responses to such questions are illustrated in Melvin M. Tumin's report from Puerto Rico, where he asked each respondent to identify places on a three-class ladder occupied by those whom the respondent felt were in the same class as he, by those with whom he felt most comfortable, by those who most respected him, by those who led the kind of life he would like his children to enjoy, and so on. The diverse responses to these questions illustrate the range of differing "reference groups" to whom respondents orient themselves and the different contexts in which the focal reference groups are changed. This procedure illustrates how different the "data" about social class can be, depending on the questions one asks, and how different, therefore, the form and function of stratification can appear to be from one study to another.

The Study of Social Stratification

W. LLOYD WARNER

The Problem

The contemporary study of the several varieties of social stratification is blessed (although at times confused) by an increasing use of evidence directly derived from field researches on human behavior and by the steady accumulation and use of statistical facts. These test theory, develop methods and techniques, and help establish the empirical foundations for understanding how the varying orders of rank operate in the lives of individuals in all types of society. Territorially, these studies range throughout the world, through the literate and nonliterate societies. The present chapter gives considerable attention to some of these studies but cannot cover

Reprinted from *Review of Sociology*, ed. Joseph B. Gittler (New York: John Wiley & Sons, Inc., 1957), pp. 221–258, by permission of the author, the editor, and the publisher.

them sufficiently for systematic comparison, something that is now possible and very much needed for the advancement of a balanced understanding of the scientific problem of rank, as well as to put the study of our own forms of social stratification in their proper perspective (114, 138, 153, 251). Conceptually these works vary from doctrinaire Marxism and other forms of economic determinism to structural analysis and psychological interpretations of behavior (16, 154, 173, 192, 242).

Disciplines and methods involved represent greatest diversity. In sociology occupational and organizational approaches predominate. The community research approach is essentially a methodological device to use present (structural) procedures for the study of the structure of status in contemporary society. Methodologically, the occupational approach can disregard the values and organization of the local community (60, 104, 198, 199, 211, 212). But in so doing it delimits the field of interest and understanding of what the human behavior, beliefs, and values are which compose some of the more important aspects of status research. Obviously both approaches and their integrated combinations are necessary (52, 125, 256, 261).

In social anthropology work now being published about Africa (20, 32, 174, 175), China (85, 86, 87, 166, 171), India (188, 189), Ceylon (228), Burma (165), and elsewhere greatly contributes to our knowledge about stratification.[1]

Reference group theory and method have contributed to more effective collaboration among social psychologists, psychologists, and "organizational" sociologists on the problems about the meaning of class. The use of the small group and the clique by the individual in social-class contexts to identify and place himself and communicate to others about what it is that he is, has been, and wishes to be or not be, has been studied with notable advances (36, 149, 209).

Some of the more interesting studies of communication concern the use of mass media in small groups as they are related to class levels (95, 96).

The reference group approach is but one of the many contributions by social psychology to our understanding of rank (8, 9, 52, 94).

Several varieties of psychology, including stimulus-response and psychoanalysis, have also contributed to the study of social stratification (11, 53, 58, 117). The latter comes particularly through the use of projective techniques (133). The earlier studies of John Dollard and Allison Davis gave us many of the leads now being exploited (252).

Other disciplines which have made major contributions are economics (19, 74, 115, 194, 195), political science and history (14, 22, 73, 112, 185), and education (67, 130, 131).

The behavior examined and the parts of society studied range from social-class systems,[2] castes,[3] occupations (21, 123, 125), occupational and social mobility,[4] age and sex divisions (32, 220), political, economic, educational, and ecclesiastical and other institutional hierarchies to the relations of these institutions to the general social structure (218, 255, 262). For example, voluntary associations, as organizations operating in American

---

[1] I wish to thank McKim Marriott and Yung-Teh Chow for their expert assistance.

[2] Class studies are being pursued throughout most of the western world, particularly in the United States (7, 18, 47, 49, 75, 106, 128, 136, 159, 176, 221, 248, 249, 261) and in England and the Commonwealth (100, 215). Other areas that might be mentioned are Burma (165), Africa (174), India (188, 189, 228), and Latin America (23).

The recent literature on social mobility and stratification on China and Japan provides valuable comparative material. Several studies on social mobility and the play of such factors as education, the acquisition of property, political achievement, and personality have been examined (87, 145, 147). Studies of the gentry, peasantry, and other ranks now make it possible to substitute evidence for speculation and doctrine for the comparative analysis of stratification (56, 268). Social change, conflict, and co-operation have been treated (235).

[3] The study of the varieties of caste ranges over major areas of the earth and many of the major civilizations. In the United States, Hill and McCall have recently published a study of color caste and class in Georgia (15, 61, 93, 136, 138). The differences between the systems in the South and North and the effects of social change and urban life are reported on (77). Tumin has provided a detailed study from Latin America (246). The whole body of knowledge about Indian caste is now being re-examined, indicating that what has been called Indian caste varies enormously and ranges through a great variety of forms, most not conforming to the classical definitions (188, 189). The larger comparative perspective for literate and nonliterate societies is given by Murdock (206).

[4] Some of the principal issues about vertical mobility in the United States are argued in the recent studies of Warner and Abegglen (252, 253), Sjoberg (237), Rogoff (222), Hatt (125, 127), Centers (48, 51), Adams (5), and many others (10, 57, 190, 267). Those for England are (100, 101, 102, 120, 123, 201, 202, 203, 215).

life that both close mobility for many and open and encourage it for others, have been studied indicating how they validate the status claims of some and refuse them to others. Research on associations shows how they help structure the class alignments and regulate participation, how they organize some of the ethnic and interest groups of various levels, as well as how they function to relate other hierarchies into the larger community (for example, factories, churches, and schools). See (55, 76, 193).

Present studies also include the personalities sometimes found at different status levels (126, 141, 254), the effects of status on the mental life of individuals at different status levels, the social psychological processes of the socialization of the young by the old into the status order (129, 132, 141), thus often giving precedence to the roles of family members (1, 80, 82, 191) and the school (2, 67, 68). The relations of status systems to problems of communication and the use of sacred and secular symbols have been given considerable attention (46, 103, 251).

The depth and lasting psychological effects of rank in American life are nowhere more clearly demonstrable than in the studies of illness and the psychobiological effects on the individual (224, 225, 226, 227). Unfulfilled status aspirations, blocked mobility, the overstriving of the very successful, the feelings of rejection of family members by those who are mobile appear as factors in the psychosomatic effects of social class (227). Many of these studies further document Durkheim's social psychological thesis having to do with *anomie*.

Any casual inventory of the recent literature also reveals theoretical interest and research on problems of power and prestige (64, 73, 105, 161, 162), on leadership (260), on social and status change. The problem of change and of

change as class conflict is central to the Marxian thesis, where the structuralists are accused of being blind to the significance of change (28, 173). It is perhaps true that the structuralists have understated the role of change, yet even this is debatable. The chart showing the relations of caste and class, originally published in 1941, and used in many other recent studies (77, 251), is based on a time dimension (caste and class changing through time and in conflict as a consequence). The study of class conflict in a strike (255) and ethnic and class and ethnic changes (259), as well as other writings, all emphasize social change.

There is also concern about the advantages and disadvantages of the several methods for the study of the various aspects of stratification. The technical and methodological literature is very great, perhaps too much so, in proportion to the amount of space given to understanding the different systems of rank, the role they play in collective life, and the functions they perform. Characteristically, our understanding of the nature of such systems in certain other societies (where less attention is given to what the investigator is doing and more to learning about the nature of the system) is clearer (26, 45, 54, 111, 144, 154, 233, 234, 250).

Some of the methods used for stratifying the members of a community include the use of interviews, participant observation, and structural analyses (54, 79, 136, 257). Hollingshead uses both structural and informed panels of judges (142) for class stratification.

Occupation has been one of the principal and, at times, the only criterion used for ranking (9, 50).

Education, house typing, source and amount of income, the social register, residential area, rent, and other so-called "objective" criteria have been used (17, 35, 80).

Some have been used in combination, such as the present writer's Index of Status Characteristics (255, 257). This instrument allows for characteristics to be used other than the original ones (1, 80, 183).

Although Centers' (52) method is referred to as subjective because it uses the informant's own conception and evaluation of his class, actually, since the method is dependent on the use of objective occupations previously chosen by the researcher, it is a combination of subjective and objective methods. Except for purposes of rough classification, this division into objective and subjective is misleading. Hatt's studies of occupational ranking and class (125) clearly indicate this as do those of Warner (257).

Clearly it will be impossible to so much as pretend to cover such a vast amount of material in the brief limits of this essay. Rather, the task as defined by the writer will be to state some of the broader generalizations that now seem possible because of the recent research advances in the whole area of social stratification. These will be given in terms of descriptive and explanatory principles to advance a general theoretical and methodological framework for relating many varieties of status research to one conceptual scheme. The body of the text ordinarily will be used for this purpose. Since many will be interested in the more limited generalizations or issues that are confined to particular researches, these have been treated in extensive footnotes that follow the continuity of the text. It is hoped that this form of presentation will not allow the treatment of the general or particular to interfere with each other. Finally, the text and footnotes are referred to a selected bibliography at the end. There are thus three levels of abstraction, the most abstract being the text, the footnotes next, followed by the references indicating where the reader may go for more evidence.

The Marxian writings will not be treated here. Although the Marxians continue to develop a vast body of literature, the Communists with their variety, the Socialists with theirs, more often than not they are less research-minded and more given to the exposition of doctrine where concrete facts are illustrations. Moreover, they have their own eager compilers, commentators, and polemicists. Such writings, having been dealt with elsewhere, will be largely eliminated from the present statement.

The non-Marxian economic determinists have their own theories of rank. Lineal descendants from earlier English and American theorists, in making assumptions about men as social beings they tend to see the whole problem of status and rank in purely economic terms. Moreover, following the assumptions of their progenitors, they often view *social and group* behavior in *individual* terms (5, 10, 48, 222). Individuals are not seen as interconnected parts of a social web of super- and subordinate relations, but as separate economic units to be reassembled by the investigator into economic categories which are evaluated as superior or inferior. Such studies are valuable and necessary, but they are not sufficient. They do not cover the whole area of man's group life in a status order, although many try to make them do so. Economic stratification is of first importance in any complex social system, and understanding it as such is of equal importance, but such behavior must also be examined as *one* part of the larger system of rank. Occupational studies can be treated separately, but ultimately to understand their social place they must be related by structural studies to the structure of collective life.

Although there have been a number of recent investigations of the social and status structures of communities[5] (136, 249, 260) and still others on the hierarchies of institutions in this and other societies (86, 87, 268), there has been no general statement about the assumptions, the methodology and theory of *structural* and comparative analysis of the forms of social stratification or of its relation to the study of occupational stratification. With the results of present and previous research on which to build, it is now possible to present some of the basic principles involved. While examining the results of contemporary research, the present enterprise will do no more than make a beginning at such an undertaking.

We may say briefly what is meant by structural studies and comparative analysis. The work of the structural analyst is similar to that of the biologist. The biologist studies the characteristics of an animal species as they are found in the animals themselves; he observes the relations of the characteristics to each other (taxonomy). He examines the genetic relations of the generations of animals and learns about the modifications and persistence of the several forms. The structural student of rank does likewise. He investigates the words and acts of men in relation to each other and observes uniformities and differences in these relations. He determines norms and modalities of behavior about what does happen and "ideally" what "ought" to happen, while learning the extent of the variations. Where possible he studies persistence and change (214).

For the structural analyst, "status is

---

[5] The limitations of community analysis are numerous, including the difficulty of determining how representative the communities are of the national community (77, 79, 251, 259). Occupational studies are more easily used for national analysis, but this raises other problems, since they lose or disregard much of the significant life of the people at all levels of rank (163).

the most general term used to refer to the location of the behavior of individuals or the social positions of individuals themselves in the structure of any group. It is a defined social position located in a social universe. The term is synonymous with social position, social place, or social location. Statuses may or may not be ranked as superior or inferior." Therefore, they fall into two general types—the ranked and nonranked (251). We are dealing with the former only.

The form of a particular status in a rank order is defined operationally by answering the following questions: What are the rights and privileges enjoyed by those who occupy it? What are the rights and privileges of members of *other* statuses that are directly or indirectly related to it? What are the duties and obligations of those who occupy a given status and what are the duties and obligations of others who are in statuses which are related to it? To restate this in somewhat different terms, we need to know the rules of conduct and the appropriate symbols used by those who are in, or implicated with, a given status.

Status always implies and implicates the larger social universe in which it has its place. It is definable in large part explicitly or implicitly by reference to its relations with other parts of the social system. Ultimately, full understanding of a particular status can be gained not only by knowing what it is as a social object and how it is interrelated with other statuses but by understanding its relation to, and place in, the whole society (40, 108, 148, 218, 253, 256).

The comparison of particular status systems studied by this method reveals general types (class, for example), varieties of the type (open and "closed" varieties of class systems), and particular instances (the class system of a community). The latter can be "broken down" into the observed acts of behavior out of which the status norms were built by the researcher. Thus, type, variety, the particular case and the observed acts of behavior, represent various levels of abstraction and generality. In discussions about status, not recognizing this fact has caused much difficulty and several needless controversies. If a *type* of status system such as caste is taken to mean, and is equated with, a *variety* or an *instance* or one observed bit of behavior, erroneous and improper comparisons are certain to be made. For example, if American Negro–white status relations are *typed* as caste (65, 77), it does not mean that they are necessarily the same as the several varieties of Indian or African caste (39, 63) or the classical type of Indian caste,[6] any more than when the biologist calls St. Bernards and Pomeranians dogs, he is saying they are identical. They are alike by the criteria of taxonomy.

Each of the several forms to which social stratification or the term rank refers is composed of interconnected statuses in relations of superordination and subordination and of superiority and inferiority. Power or prestige, or power and prestige are unequally distributed among the several statuses whose entirety comprises any given system (105, 162). All orders of rank distribute unequally the highly valued material and immaterial social objects as facts of power and symbols of prestige among the superior and inferior statuses.

These systems persist and are modified through time, incorporating the members of each generation into their orderings of status. The methods by which forms of rank are transferred or not from generation to generation and the rules governing the relations of the generations constitute important parts of any of these orders.[7] The processes which accomplish the task of socializing the young by the older with the status belief, values, and behavior of any given status system provide one of many places where structural and psychological analysis works effectively. The studies of the psychological effects of status on the learning adilities of the young and the research on performance by students at the different grade levels from different social classes have added much to our knowledge of how social class in America and Britain affects the lives of individuals and functions as a system of rank.

The public school as a structural system, its control, the place of the school in the life of the community, the recruitment of teachers in grade and high schools, the treatment of children

---

[6] The study of caste in India is being pursued by the several social sciences. Some of the problems examined and the issues now in debate are: What the roles of economic and ritual factors are in caste as a system of Indian ranking (188); how far social and economic class rather than caste determine a man's prestige and power; the degree to which tradition and social and economic change influence contemporary caste organization and behavior (189); what similarities and differences exist between Indian and other forms of caste (138). The comparative study of caste as a *type* of rank and all of its varieties has also been given attention (251).

---

[7] The many researches in the relation of status and class to mental performance in school clearly demonstrate the living reality of the differential effects of class levels on the individuals of the new generations. The effects of class on performance in school and the I.Q .have been well documented (42, 43, 81, 119).

The child training and infant care on the several levels show how their children are inducted into the system and by experience learn their place (83). On the other hand, the differential effects of class on individuals' learning and aspirations also have been examined and valuable results obtained, showing how some become ambitious and socially mobile and others remain "stable and immobile" (251).

Adolescence and its place in the school system as related to social class and age grading have been well documented. All studies show how previous training in childhood and infancy affect the adolescent (151) and how present experiences of the young person are greatly influenced by status (180, 207, 262).

of "higher and lower" families, and the performance and achievement of children in the schoolroom and playgrounds at different grade levels have had noteworthy treatment as partial products of class influence (15, 205, 230, 238). Perhaps no two social scientists have done more to advance our knowledge than Allison Davis and Robert Havighurst (69, 132). Hollingshead (141), McGuire (181, 183), Neugarten (208), Taba (132), Eells (81), Stendler (241), White (262), as well as Haggard (119), Becker (25), Himmelweit (137), Kahl (153), and many others have contributed to a solid body of knowledge on class, mentality, and learning.

Since the varieties of rank differ in form (28, 29, 38, 109, 168) and function (23, 245, 246), and in their relations to the larger social systems in which they exist, all can be profitably compared and classified, and inferences drawn about the nature of the forms studied and the values they express. Fortunately a solid body of literature is now developing about the workings of status systems throughout the "civilized" and "primitive" societies of the world. The descriptive and explanatory generalizations about rank in the present chapter are built upon it.

Social stratification is a *type* of subsystem which exists in most, if not all, literate and nonliterate societies, whether in all or not is largely a matter of definition. Since the distinctions involved in the differences in definition are important, they need to be examined to help us better understand the principles involved in stratification. Stern's (242) recent paper (following similar distinctions of Hobhouse, Wheeler, and Ginsberg), as well as the publications of most anthropologists and sociologists, is not in accord with the position taken by writers like Sorokin. The latter includes such social systems as age and sex divisions among the forms of social stratification; the others do not. He declares in *Social Mobility* that "Any organized social group is always a stratified social body. There has not been and does not exist any permanent social group which is 'flat,' and in which all members are equal. Unstratified society, with a real equality of its members, is a myth which has never been realized in the history of mankind" (240, p. 12).

Stratified society is manifested in various forms: "First, in the existence of the sex and age groups with quite different privileges and duties..." (240, p. 13).

While it is true that age divisions place their members in super- and subordinate positions (32, 143, 220), the rules and principles involved are quite different from such forms of rank as social and economic class, or political, military, or ecclesiastical hierarchies, and others. Although they are socially defined and evaluated, age categories are essentially biologically founded and "fit *everyone* during lifetime, the grades of age being statuses through which *all* maturing individuals must pass. There are no necessary invidious discriminations; age is a form that can be *commonly* shared at least by all those of the same sex. During their life development, members of the other systems of rank do not move inevitably through the higher and lower levels.

Because age grades do place people in orders of prestige and power, for our purposes they are treated as a major subtype of rank, rudimentary and nonspecialized, to be distinguished from all specialized and developed forms. They divide clearly into two basic varieties, those age divisions which are based entirely on social definitions of the aging processes and those which include other evaluative principles, such as economic, political, and birth distinctions. The second type of system is of particular importance in Africa which, with other status systems, is now being studied.

The literature on hierarchies and stratification in Africa grows rapidly. Studies of political and social systems and their relation to power and stratification have been reported (20, 32, 174). A large number of excellent monographs and papers on status systems among the different groups are regularly appearing (too numerous for discussion here). The changing stratification caused by culture contact with European systems and indigenous developments have been well studied.

This literature and the older studies of such systems as caste in East Africa need to be comparatively analyzed. Comparative studies of political hierarchies (see above) and of age grades have been successfully undertaken.[8]

Criteria for the Study of Rank

Since the diversity of the forms of rank, even when limited to the specialized ones, is very great and, when taken on a world-wide basis, bewilderingly so, the question arises whether it is possible to make scientific sense out of the diversity and establish valid uniformities by use of classifications founded on criteria and principles basic to the behavior of men living in groups. Since all humans live in societies and since the societies are diverse in range and type, criteria adequate for this culture may not be so for others. The criteria used necessarily must be relevant to all systems of social stratification; they must be "culture free." Such criteria can only be said to be scientifically valid when founded on basic principles of human behavior and applicable at all times and places, including the *known* past of our own and other societies.

The *tests* for such guiding criteria are

1. They should be founded primarily on human adaptive behavior necessary everywhere for the maintenance and persistence of the social and biological life of all men in all groups.
2. They should be of vital significance to the life careers of individuals.
3. They should apply to all societies and all forms of rank.
4. They should come from, and be subject to, the evidence of actual observed behavior and not the armchair theories of ideologists or those primarily interested in constructing abstract philosophical theories.
5. From them and the evidence it should be possible and scientifically necessary to establish types of rank capable of testing by further evidence and analysis, which thus begin to assume a general and more abstract and less individual and unique conceptual character and are therefore subject to further analysis and testing.
6. From the several types it should be possible to build a coherent system incorporating the uniformities and the varieties into a conception of rank that comprehends the whole diversity yet refers to and places each individual form.
7. The taxonomic system of rank, consisting of interdependent logical categories referring to empirically derived individual systems, must be capable of yielding propositions about the nature of rank, its several forms, the conditions under which they exist, and the relations between the diverse forms and their surrounding conditions.

Two *kinds* of basic questions about the access to each other of the members of the species of any given group help us meet the demands of the several tests: First, are the statuses (or a status) within a system of rank open to movement to and from them so that those who might

---

[8] I am particularly indebted for guidance and information about African status systems to Alfred Harris, of the University of Cambridge, who has done research in the area and on these problems.

seek access or seek to leave them may do so? Is the system of assignment of status such that each individual's position is free so that he can move vertically or horizontally toward others and they to him? Can he and they compete for higher status or strive to maintain their own? Or is the status system closed so that men cannot move from status to status, their own individual positions thus being so fixed that their careers are confined to one status (or level of rank) and competition for any other status not possible? Some systems of rank conform to the first and some to the second type. In the first, individuals, families, and other groups through time move up or down from one status to another. Vertical mobility, social and occupational, are forms of this movement. Such a type can be called an open status system, subject to free competition. The second type is a system of closed status with the individual's life chances controlled by the rules governing the status he was assigned at birth. The principles of open and restricted competition for individuals and families and of free movement as well as social control over ingress and egress from ranked statuses are involved. Obviously these two are extreme polar forms; numerous mixed types intervene along the range between the two.

The second kind of basic question may be stated: To what extent is the life of a society and the activities of each individual controlled by any order of rank? Is the order's province *limited* to certain activities and not others? Is it limited to particular periods and times? Is it limited to certain individuals and not others? Does it regulate part of the lives of some people for part of the time but not all of it? What and how much does it control? In brief, and to apply terms, is it a *limited* hierarchy segmenting the membership and activities of the group, or is it inclusive, generally comprising everyone and all or most of the activities

that make up the round of life of the group and each individual?

These two principles when used as criteria, the restriction of movement to and from statuses and the limitation and extent of the social and individual activities, are applicable to all systems and are of significance to each. Since systems of rank conforming to them order the several varieties of *status* which function to control the basic activities of man and determine who shall have or not have access to them, who shall have power and prestige or not, they clearly meet the demands of the tests previously set.

The Several Types of Rank

When the two polar types of status control, the closed form (not accessible to free competition) and the open (accessible to movement into it and allowing movement out) are combined with the two polar types of hierarchy (the general and all-inclusive one, which covers most or all of the activities of the individual and the society, and the segmentary or limited one whose controls are confined to a limited part of the society and its behavior) four basic forms of rank are logically recognizable. Each of the four logical types is now satisfied by empirical reality, there being numerous documented cases from contemporary research on civilizations and on the unlettered cultures of primitive society. Many varieties exist in the middle distances which can be arranged scientifically according to the two principles, the amount of control exercised over the free movement of peoples, and the extent of the control exercised over the total social activities.

The four extreme types are:

1. The inclusive (or general) system with open statuses where free competition prevails among individuals (and families)

for position. Social class in the United States is but one variety.[9] Successful competition is expressed in social mobility (31, 48, 123, 202, 204).

2. The limited (segmentary) system within which the ranked statuses are open to free competition and there is movement in and out of the available statuses.

3. The inclusive (general) system whose statuses are closed and not open to competition. The position of the individual is fixed.

4. The limited (segmentary) system closed to free competition where, for the purposes of the hierarchy, the position of the individual is fixed and there is no movement from status to status.

The several types range from a high degree of freedom for the individual, with great fluidity of status, to a rigid, inflexible system with fixed life chances for the individual and his family.[10] The intermediate distances, ranging between the two extremes of the extent of the control of the variety of activities and

<hr>

[9] Several issues about social and occupational mobility are now being profitably debated. Some of the principal ones are: How much movement is there (5, 17, 237)? Is there more or less than previously (252, 253)? Is American society becoming less or more rigid (134)? What are the factors involved in contemporary mobility: education, acquisition of skill, social and occupational imitation and modeling? Or are they personal and psychological (66, 133)? Do members of certain classes, the middle as compared with the upper or lower, move more (251)?

[10] Since in all or most societies there is a variety of ranked statuses, each with its own power and prestige, the same individual may be ranked differently. In some hierarchies he may have high status (a Brahmin) and in others low or high (economically or politically). For a discussion of the relation of an individual's status ratings in India see Marriott (188). By a careful study of the ratings of men of several castes by members of the community, he shows that different criteria are used by the villagers who evaluate them. Caste is but *one* system of rating. There was more disagreement about the prestige of the different men among the raters than among the members of the New York village studied by Kaufman (156, 157). *The Status System of a Modern Community* attacked the same problem (256).

the degree of closure of status, make it possible to recognize and place a number of intermediate or subtypes corresponding with the variations found by research in this and other societies. However, for our present purposes, only one intermediate type for each dimension will be introduced.

Each system may be in a state of equilibrium, with opposition between the ranks organized or in a state of conflict. Partly as a result of the long reign of Marxian ideology among social scientists, the literature on class conflict is far greater than that on the study of cooperation among all levels on the common tasks of society, or than on organized opposition (in Simmel's sense) among those who collaborate. In fact, some writers would define the task of the analyst of rank as the study of the history of class conflict. Structural analysis disagrees; the histories of class and other forms of rank necessarily record periods of conflict and the nature of it, but such studies will be founded on the larger problem of status opposition where cooperation is an essential part of the class relations.

Inspection of Table 1 shows that the degrees of inclusion of activities have been arranged horizontally and the degrees of closure or openness of status vertically. The general and more inclusive type is at the upper left combined with free competition and the other extreme types (so numbered in one of the four corners) at the right; the mixed types are between them.

It will be noted that social class, which allows competition for the more prestigeful and powerful positions, is in the upper left (1) and that color caste, at the other extreme in status closure, which prohibits movement and competition, is in the lower left (2). The position of the individual and his family is *not* fixed in social class, for his life chances and those of the family can be (by the nature of the system) improved by competing

The degree of the inclusion of activities controlled by a rank order

<table>
<tr><td rowspan="2" colspan="2"></td><td rowspan="2">General
and
Inclusive</td><td colspan="2">Mixed</td><td rowspan="2">Limited
and
Segmentary</td></tr>
<tr><td>To
General</td><td>To
Limited</td></tr>
<tr><td colspan="2">Open With Free
Competition</td><td>General and free
(certain social
classes and age
grades)

1</td><td>Neither inclusive nor
entirely limited, but
free competition (eth-
nic group, certain oc-
cupations and profes-
sions)
8</td><td>Segmentary and free
(certain factories, vari-
ous military hierarch-
ies, churches, etc., po-
litical)

3</td></tr>
<tr><td rowspan="4">Mixed

Neither
Open
nor
Closed</td><td rowspan="2">Open</td><td>General extension and
with intermediate
rules of closure</td><td>Neither inclusive nor
limited, partly open</td><td>Segmentary, partly
open</td></tr>
<tr><td rowspan="2">(Certain ethnic
groups. The middle
classes more open, up-
per more closed)

5</td><td rowspan="2">(Certain occupations
and professions; cer-
tain ethnic groups; de-
gree of assimilation)

6</td><td rowspan="2">(Certain ethnic groups;
degree of assimilation;
certain factories, un-
ions, associations,
churches, etc.)
7</td></tr>
<tr><td rowspan="2">Closed</td></tr>
<tr></tr>
<tr><td colspan="2">Status Closure
With No Status
Competition</td><td>General with status
closure, no competi-
tion (color caste, cer-
tain castes in India, sex
divisions)
2</td><td>Neither inclusive nor
limited. Closed to
competition (certain
occupations and pro-
fessions)
9</td><td>Segmentary with status
closure. No competi-
tion (certain factories,
unions, associations,
etc.)
4</td></tr>
</table>

The degree of openness or closure of the status controls

freely (51) for higher position. The position of the individual and his family in a (classical) caste system is fixed and determined by birth. He is not free to compete for all or some of the prestige and power of the higher caste. His life chances (so far as caste is involved) are limited. The two forms of rank, however, are alike inasmuch as each covers the whole or most of the activities of those who are members of either system (246, 247, 266).

The literature on American, English,[11] and European[12] social class and the issues being debated are endless. Some of them are methodological (4, 71, 109, 110, 118, 191, 217, 236). Is American class no more than a statistical construct? Or is it a reality in group life (167, 239, 257)? The number of classes (109) has been discussed (251). The degree to which they exist and how they do (142) in great metropolitan centers and the smaller cities and rural areas have been issues (79, 217). Research on the varying meanings of words, objects, and symbols as they are used in the different media by dif-

[11] English sociologists are rapidly developing a large body of literature on social class, social mobility, and other aspects of social stratification. The several classes and their composition have been recently reported on (3, 11, 37, 88, 89, 100, 169, 170). Occupational grading and succession are now being studied (52, 253). The relation of recent political, economic, and social change to changes in the status structure has been treated

(215). The broad generalities of occupational grading in English-speaking culture now seem clear (59, 152, 186).

[12] Studies of stratification and social mobility in other European countries, including France, Italy, Russia, the Netherlands, and the several Scandinavian countries, are being conducted and published (99, 120, 150, 177, 245).

ferent kinds of people at the several status levels in a mass society has led to many fruitful results and leads for future work (34, 35, 160). The newspapers, books (113), magazines, television, and radio (254), motion pictures, as well as rumor and gossip (229) have been given considerable attention. All show the strong influence of status in giving multiple meanings to common symbols and increasing the problem of communication within a total group. Questions about the objective and subjective aspects of class and the methodological problems involved are problems of concern to many (216). Others see the subjective and objective characteristics class as parts of one system and possibly a false dichotomy (249, 261).

How sharply delineated or not the several levels are and the number involved in fact are interrelated problems. The present writer and those colleagues he has had the satisfaction of working with have at no time believed they were sharp and clearly distinct (251, 257). Nor has it been believed that everyone in a community sees them alike (251). In fact, the structural type of analysis (like the occupational one) depends on the analyst's examining his data and judging where the breakpoints are (for purposes of analysis and scientific representation of communicable reality). The technique of "matched agreement" (251) clearly indicates that the scientific class construct refers to the norms of social reality. The class variations in an *open* system (with social mobility) necessarily make class "boundaries" indistinct. Only a classically defined caste system sharply separates two or more levels of rank.

The issue on the exact number of social classes existing in American (or English) society seems a false one. For some purposes there may be only three recognized by the participant or the informant, for example, the "Common Man Level" and those above and below it. The participant-informant may then redivide them in four, five, or six levels, running from upper down through the middle levels to the lowest class. Or he may see them as simply upper, middle, and working classes. Each system of classification exists in his mental life (beliefs and values) and behavior and among other members of the society. Analogous to these several divisions of class are those of age grades. The old, mature, and the young may be further divided or collapsed into the adult and subadult levels. Each is a reality.

The interrelations of the social classes have not had sufficient and proper attention. If they had, many of the false problems about the nature of American class would disappear. McCall's paper showing the amount of interaction of people in small groups among different class levels is most important (179). It indicates that for some purposes members of different classes are sometimes closer than those of the same level. This follows the approach set forth in the second volume of the Yankee City Series (256) where the interactions and relations of the six classes were meaured for family, clique, and association.[18]

Forms of rank in the segmentary

---

[18] Unfortunately for purposes of sensible debate of the real issues, this volume has not been given the same attention as Volume I. On page 12 of the second volume it is said, "When the several internal structures of the community of Yankee City had been analyzed to determine the number and kind of positions [statuses] and relations, we sought to convert all the relations and positions of the separate structures into one general positional [status] system. If this were possible [as it was] we could dispense with the older class and structural analysis and depend entirely on the positional and relational system."

In brief, each class becomes a series of multiple statuses, and they are part of an interactive totality of statuses. All of them, for the individuals who participate in them, are as contexts of behavior "reference groups."

positions are quite different from the general types (see chart, Positions 3 and 4). They are alike in so far as the control is limited; they are different since in the one the system is open, and in the other, closed to competition. The segmentary hierarchies, including political,[14] economic,[15] ecclesiastical,[16] military, and the like, in America (70, 78, 107) and many parts of Europe (231) may be open for competition for power and prestige to all those who enter them, or they may be partly closed or entirely so. The *accessibility* to the highly valued things and symbols of a society may be

controlled by the rules governing such hierarchies. Salaries, wages, and other economic differences can be determined by such social rules governing movement. The distribution of goods and services and wealth is partly a function of position in the segmentary and general hierarchies.

An inspection of the cases of rank in the mixed types is revealing. The American ethnic groups are not found in any of the polar types, but primarily in the three mixed types, according to their degree of assimilation (259, 266). They are not in Position 1 with social class because, although for a brief time the ethnic subsystem covers almost all or most of the activities of the individual and his family as does class, the system itself is a subsystem that does not include everyone in the society or all its activities. Only part of the society is involved. Yet, except in the broadest sense of the term, an ethnic group cannot be typed as segmentary since (unlike a job in a segmentary factory) most of the individual's and family's activities are ordered by it. Although in some respects certain American ethnic systems are like a caste (Position 2) in regard to closure, in fact there is always some movement and the group's ambivalent values partly encourage movement up and out. Consequently by *extent* it belongs in the mixed types. Most ethnic groups of two or three generations belong in the central position (6). They are partly general in their application of control but not entirely; they are partly open, yet there is a degree of closure beyond the rule of social class and the position of an individual is more often fixed than in an (open) social class. As an ethnic group such as the Irish Catholic becomes more assimilated, its members largely enter the general social system and confine their remaining ethnic activities (if any) to the hierarchy of the church (Position 7). Some of the members of ethnic groups who refuse to

---

[14] Political hierarchies have their own separate bodies of literature. However, certain of them in the past have been of great influence in sociology and some in the present are of direct sociological significance. The nature of power in the hierarchy with its relation to community and individual affairs is one of them (27, 158, 185, 187, 223). The relation of the different kinds of personality to political behavior in hierarchical structures is another (161, 162). The study of the meaning of voting behavior, political parties, political attitudes, and socioeconomic and class levels and their significance for understanding national and community life is yielding valuable knowledge on which the sciences having to do with status can now depend (6, 12, 23, 30, 33, 84, 164).

[15] The literature on industrial hierarchies, including factories, corporations, and industries, as well as unions and other employer and employee groups, is exceedingly large and beyond the compass of this chapter. However, certain writers have emphasized the structural as well as the economic characteristics of these organizations. A few must be mentioned (19, 97, 98, 116, 196, 197, 244, 264). Others have stressed the personality as it functions in business enterprise (252).

The literature on industrial conflict has been examined in the history of structural change (115, 255).

[16] The varying ideologies of the church (218), the membership of the church (40, 41, 219, 266), and the place of churches in the class structure in the United States (219) have been studied. All show strong status relations, but they indicate that the effects of the entire community and democratic values are strongly felt by this institution (249). However, certain churches are heavily class-defined and are "store front," "middle-class," or "society" (77).

assimilate may become sects and develop a closed system (266).

When the two basic types of rank are combined, the rudimentary, universal one to which age grading belongs and the differentiated, specialized type in which social and economic class are varieties, it is then possible to cover all forms of rank existing in this and all societies. They all distribute power and prestige through the controls of the statuses which compose them.

The nature of power and its sources are concerns of fundamental importance and of necessary interest to contemporary students of rank. We need now to turn our attention to them.

Power, Prestige, and the Human Adaptive Controls

Power may be simply defined for our immediate purposes as the possession of control over other beings and objects in the social and natural environments, making it possible to act on them to achieve outcomes that would not take place if control were not exerted. Prestige is the kind and amount of value socially attributed to objects, activities, persons, and statuses (135, 155). The two are usually interrelated; power can derive from prestige and prestige from power. However, a man may have power with little prestige or high prestige with little power.[17] The kinds and amount of power and prestige vary from one territorial group to another. They also

differ among the several forms of rank and status. The problem of how forms of rank are related to prestige and power as well as the nature of sources of power and prestige must be considered.

The Marxians and others have founded their system of class analysis on the assumption that power is *only* a product of *one* kind of status control over *one* kind of environment; that the statuses which control the means of production and the distribution of their products hold the power and are thus given the prestige which determine class alignments (61, 172); it is argued that since the technological adjustments to the natural environment are moving in a given, predetermined direction, the dependent society, its mental and cultural life, the class forms, their composition and relations are perforce moving in a predictable sequence to a classless society (28).

Clearly such economic determinists are correct in pointing out the importance of the statuses which control the natural environment and the real power inherent in such statuses or those superordinate statuses which control them. They are wrong, however, in assuming that technological control is the *only* source of power. The sources of power are *multiple*, not one. To properly understand the problems of power and prestige we must use the knowledge of sociology, social anthropology, and the psychological sciences that has accumulated since Marx and Engels. We must re-examine the whole question of the relation of power to the human adaptive controls of the several environments, and man's dependence on them.

Human survival universally *depends* on two and, it is believed, three environments. The first is the so-called natural environment which in varying degrees is controlled by the technology; the second, the human species environment which is controlled by (part of) the moral order, a system of social

---

[17] The problem of power and rank is of almost obsessive concern to Marxians. The followers of Max Weber are also greatly concerned with it, but conceive it more broadly and are less inclined to derive it entirely from one source (62, 187, 213, 214, 231). Others view it more in classical, political terms and with the ultimate use of force (73).

Lasswell, influenced by Freud and Pareto, as well as other psychologies and sociologies, views power broadly; but essentially he is concerned with the moral aspects of power as they are felt and expressed in the rewards and deprivations of the organism living in society (161, 162).

organization; and the third, real or not, the supernatural environment, ordered and controlled, it is believed, by the "myths" and rituals of religion and magic, a system of sacred symbols.

The very presence of these adaptive controls demonstrates: (1) that men are *dependent* on an adequate use of them for survival, each having the power of life and death over them; (2) that the controls exercised over the environments to reduce their control *over* men involve the use of several forms of power by individuals and groups; and (3) that, in exercising control, each adaptive mechanism employs real power. The tools and skills of the technology transform the natural world sufficiently to aid men in acquiring and producing food, shelter, and the other creature needs and comforts which increase the life chances (Weber's term more broadly used) of the adult individual, of the young to grow into maturity, and in a given group of the species to survive.

The second, the control over the species, by imposing the pressures of moral forms on animal behavior, regulates the discharge of species energy; it controls the interactions of individuals and structures their access to each other. Thus it orders the basic life-flow of the species and of each individual, including the procreative processes and the relations of the adult and immature; it orders the expression of hostility, aggression, and violence, the disposition of prized objects, and the imposition of unpleasant tasks among the members of the group. Control over the species environment means an exercise of real power; it also means the presence of power in every socially organized species group and a *sense* of social power (in Durkheim's sense) within the group among those who live in it. The meanings and social representations of what social power is vary from group to group; the forms by which it is utilized and expressed also vary enormously. The

violent, not to say explosive, power of the emotions generated by the moral order's control over sexuality, individual growth and development, adult deterioration, and senility among the several family statuses has been given much attention. This focus, under the conceptual schemes of the psychoanalyst, has helped us understand emotion's great force but has tended to lose some of its deserved strength for status and power analysis because of too great reliance on individual psychology rather than on group and species foundations.

The *supernatural* adaptations controlling, it is believed, man's ultimate fate, govern those activities and outcomes over which the other two have insufficient power. Sickness, death, obliteration of the self, social disaster, and the ill or well being of man are in its compass. Each society has fashioned its own adaptive controls to meet as best "it" can the terrible and absolute power of this other world and thereby reduce human anxiety and dread.

Statuses function to order and coordinate the multiple activities involved in the control of each environment. They assign tasks and socially locate activities; they include and exclude the members of the society while placing them in a social universe. The statuses directly involved in the several adaptive activities, as integral parts of their ordering, possess, or are attributed, varying power and prestige according to the members of the society who feel their beneficial or harmful effects. Those with a high degree of adaptive control are likely to have high ranking; those believed to exercise low control are often given lower ranking.

Those statuses *not* directly involved in the mechanics of the adaptive processes, but which control those statuses that are, *share* some of their power with them, or they *remove* and *hold* it for themselves. Thus statuses are hierarchically arranged. The problem becomes why these secondary statuses in a rank order exercise control over the others and often accumulate more power and prestige than the primary ones directly involved in the adaptive tasks? This question is closely allied to another. Why do some societies possess specialized and developed rank orders of prestige and power and others only the rudimentary types? These questions will be dealt with in the following section.

The power of an adaptive status, or hierarchy of statuses, may be *intrinsic* and directly applied or *extrinsic* to its activities and functions. In other words, the force it possesses and applies may be an integral and necessary part of its adaptive activity, or it may be ("given") attributed to it by all, or some, members of the society. The power to kill a kangaroo with a spear by a hunter (who does or does not keep its meat for himself, his family, and clan) is at least partly intrinsic, but the man may also be accorded by his group increased power beyond his ability to kill and keep. The first is an intrinsic and integral part of his technical status as a hunter and of his moral status as a member of his family and clan; the latter power, not necessary for the execution of his technical and moral acts, is of course attributed to him.

The prestige of a status, the esteem in which it is held, or the derogation, is attributable and extrinsic. The values of the group, or some part of it, are projected upon the status and determine its social worth. Much of what are popularly and scientifically termed prestige and power are products of the larger group's feelings. The facts of the adaptive actions of a status become evaluated symbols which accumulate and attract other negative or positive social values that may have little to do with the activities of the status.

Since the statuses of adaptation are integral parts of a social system, they are in a position of mutual influence. No one system of adaptation is entirely free from the others. No one at *all* times and *all* places will necessarily dominate the others, the technological, the moral, or the social system, the other two. When the technology is complex the kinds and number of statuses (occupations, for example) are necessarily numerous and highly diverse. Such economic status systems may be scientifically classified into types and arranged along a continuum of simple to complex. In many primitive societies, occupations are largely undifferentiated. Each man performs many productive functions which are not classifiable occupationally. Occupational ranking is therefore not possible. In such a society as ours where the division of labor is exceedingly great, ranking of occupations is one of the principal forms of stratification; and the accumulation of wealth and the sources of wealth are also ranked in "separate" systems (257).

The several economic status orders found in different societies may be closed or open; they may be limited or general rank orders. In any given society the statuses associated with the technology may dominate the whole status order and all other types of status be subordinate to one or more orders of technological status. On the contrary, they may be under the control of, and subordinate to, the statuses which control the species or the myths and rituals which regulate the power of the supernatural and the unknown (32, 123, 165). Or the three may be in conflict (Russia seems to be a case in point).

The moral order's family, age, and sex statuses control and regulate some of the most powerful activities and energies of the species environment. The status of the parent, the father particularly, subordinates the statuses of the sons and daughters. The foundations of authority, its use by the one and submission to it by the other, are in this universal relation. The usual super-ordination of males and subordination of females and the similar relation of the mature to the young are forms of authority where social power is exercised. Rudimentary systems of rank are part of all family, kinship, and age grade systems (13, 139, 140, 178, 200, 263).

By extension or limitation of the usual rules of descent and marriage, the control of sexual accessibility or its prohibition and of descent of the offspring (together with economic controls) provides the powerful foundations for many general systems of rank. Crucial questions for understanding this problem of the relation of the moral statuses which control the species environment and rank order are: Are all unmarried males and females of mature sexuality potential mates, unfettered by any rules other than those of incest prohibitions (70, 71, 251, 253)? Or is the choice of mates bounded by, and limited to, sharply defined ranked categories? The general (inclusive) closed statuses which fix the position of the individual sharply divide the biological group by social prohibitions and boundaries. Full access between all members of the sexes for marriage purposes is forbidden. The physical life of the individual is confined within narrow boundaries; mates do not come from diverse but from socially similar statuses (138). The open, inclusive type provides a "mating" system where the two members of the marriage pair may come from most diverse or very similar backgrounds.

Since the children are identified with the social status of the parents, both the closed and open general systems initially place the child's status in this system of rank. In the closed system like color caste the child remains by moral rule at the parents' and his ancestors' level; in the open he may stay or move out of it.

If the general inclusive type is an open system, the parent-child relation and the sibling relations often assume most diverse forms and are subject to great stress and distortion (68, 182). The son may move to superior position, or the daughter marry into one, thus subordinating the parent and placing the family's superior adult in an inferior position of rank. Some of the siblings may move up, others down, and still others remain at the parents' level. Open systems with free competition disperse the members of many families over distant parts of the rank order. Ordinarily they must if the systems are to continue. Closed fixed systems tend to hold the members of the family together and add their influence to maintaining family solidarity. In an open system the family of orientation quickly yields its maturing young to the larger world and to their own families of procreation; in a closed system the older generations are more likely to be related to the younger ones. The two families, often forming into a *grosse* family, hold together in primary interaction biologically, territorially, and socially. They provide the hard core of fixed position for their members and closure for movement beyond their limits (138).

The families of orientation and procreation are necessary and integral parts of the general, inclusive types of system (251). Their moral power, too, is an integral part of the power of these rank orders. It may be contained and held within the closed ranks of a caste or spread over the several ranks of a class system where there is freedom of movement.

The family may or may not be related to segmentary systems of rank. Political and ecclesiastical and other differentiated forms may derive part or most of their power and their structural form from the family, but such hierarchies can and do exist without the direct use of the family. Certain African political hierarchies are elaborations of superordinate heads of families; ecclesiastical hierarchies may be a scalar system of "fathers," but they may be built without direct use of family relations.

The statuses associated with the control of the unknown which reduce human anxieties about their life chances by the use of myth and ritual are religious and magical. They are ordinarily centered in the church. They include such ritual statuses as priests, magicians, some doctors and psychiatrists, and occasionally other statuses to which such power is attributed.

They, too, may be simple or complex. They, too, may be in societies where the religious life dominates, or is subordinate to, the technological or secular organization. In the simpler societies there may be no more than a temporary ritual leader with little power and prestige, his tenure being only during the ceremony. In many of the complex societies there may be a hierarchy of statuses from local ones up through a hierarchy that integrates and controls the supernatural activities of a whole nation or those of many nations. The vertical height may be exceedingly great or not, the area of social activity limited, or in a theocracy it may include the whole society.

The powers of the supernatural environment which can harm or benefit men are often dualistically conceived. The problem confronting the statuses related to these beings and the forces of sacred good and evil is to control them and to adapt their power to man's ends. The forces of good must be harnessed to assist men; the forces of evil must be diverted, quarantined, or weakened. When it is believed that the statuses manipulating myth and ritual accomplish these ends and they "control" the uncontrollable, the statuses of magicians, priests, and others like them are attributed some of the power of the environment they control. They and their statuses derive power and prestige both from their knowledge and ability to use the symbols effectively and from

the power that comes from the sacred world itself. As Durkheim pointed out, supernatural forces are comparable to physical forces;[18] the words and objects of the rites of religion have social force and strength attached to them. They have the power to kill or cure. The priest or magician can benefit man or the sorcerer can cause sickness and death in his victim. They control the forces that can take or give life. The power that the sacred statuses possess tends to be absolute.

The generations of individuals arrive and disappear "but (spiritual) *force* [mana] always remains. . . . This force is an expression of the social power of the clan [the society]."[19] It awakens in all those who feel its force, all individuals in each society, an idea of an external force. According to Durkheim, the sign of the totem (the emblem of God) is a substitute for this abstract social force, allowing the sentiments of the group to be easily expressed. Since all religious symbols are signs expressing, and referring to, the forces of group life, the statuses which control (and manipulate) them exercise their power.

Since all men incorporate some of the society into their persons and since mana is power socially derived, all men necessarily possess some mana or social power. Weber's *charisma* seems to be little more than one form of personal mana. Charisma and mana, as parts of the value and meaning of objects and

---

[18] The ethnologists early recognized these significant "sacred forces." Durkheim took his lead from Codrington, who identified and defined *mana* as he found it among the Melanesians. "There is," Codrington said, "a belief in a force altogether distinct from physical power, which acts in all ways for good and evil. . . . It is a power or influence . . . it shows itself . . . in any kind of power or excellence which a man possesses." (Robert H. Codrington, *The Melanesians* [Oxford: Clarendon Press, 1891], p. 118).

[19] Chapter VI of Emile Durkheim, *The Elementary Forms of the Religious Life* (New York: The Macmillan Company, 1915), pp. 188, 204.

people, can be forms of attributed power. Ordinarily those in the more lowly statuses have less opportunity to acquire or express power than those advantageously placed in superior statuses. If *mana* (we use this term broadly as applicable to all societies) is largely a felt force deriving from the dominant values of the group being expressed in persons, objects, and actions, then in each society those possessing high mana are likely to be men and women who occupy one or more high-ranking statuses or, if the system be open and free, they will be candidates for achieved higher status. In a fixed and closed system there will be little or no legitimate opportunity (within that system) for those of low status to acquire high mana.

In a society where power primarily is *ritually derived* (attributed to ritual sources), if all men have access to sacred sources it is possible for men of high or low status to gain ritual mana (power and prestige). If the general systems of rank are closed and not open for vertical status movement, then the possessor of such power born to low status may become a very holy man of high spiritual worth, but remain in his same lowly *social* status. He may achieve high status in a formal or informal segmentary hierarchy of sacred significance; at times his increased prestige and power may have such strong social influence that they will threaten the rules and sanctions of the social order. If the status order is open and free the spiritual power may be translated into vertical movement in one or more segmental or general hierarchies (church and association). If the ritual values are ascetic, it may be that lowly organizational and economic status (poor, deprived, and despised) may contribute to the conditions necessary for the acquisition of ritual power (a form of mana).

Since in the simple societies the degree of differentiation among the adaptive statuses is very low, and in the complex ones differentiation is exceedingly great, the powers of the technology and of the moral and sacred orders are accordingly combined and felt as one in the simple societies, and in the more advanced ones they divide into various political, economic, and religious categories and are felt to be many. Among the latter, including Western Europe and America, mana or social power takes on a rational as well as nonrational character. Superordinate statuses appear which often possess great power but which are not directly involved in the immediate adaptive activities.

The sources of power and prestige accordingly are multiple. They derive from all powerful environments and from their adaptive controls. The statuses which function to organize the activities of these controls possess their power. In all societies social power expressed in secular or sacred terms is present and distributed among statuses, persons, and things. Power, like prestige, may not be intrinsic to the activities of the status but attributed by the group to the status and its activities.

Social Stratification, Social Change, and Structural Condition

All present research on the very simple societies confirms previous study that stratification there is largely confined to the universal, unspecialized types. However, earlier as well as more recent studies demonstrate that age and sex divisions unequally distribute property, sacred symbols, and other goods and services, and that power and prestige are attributed to certain and not other levels (32). The "advanced" forms of rank more often appear in the complex heterogeneous societies. It is in them that the adaptive statuses are reordered and placed in lincations of super- and subordination and inferiority and superiority (24, 72, 74, 90, 91, 92,

121, 122, 146, 253, 255). Social evolution in its broad sweep moves away from the nonspecialized forms of rank toward the specialized ones which place individuals and families in superior and inferior social orders.

The question is why are these empirically founded generalizations true? Why does rank grow and luxuriate in the heterogeneous societies? We must analyze comparatively the conditions in the several societies which prohibit or contribute to the functioning and presence of rank orders. To do this we must examine within a time perspective the functional statuses, the environments they control, and the societies in which they are found. To guide our inquiry we shall offer an explanation founded on the established fact that greater specialization, heterogeneity, and higher division of labor are associated with a greater development of rank orders. Through the broad, long-term social changes, the emergent complexity of the social parts makes the use of rank orders necessary. If the highly differentiated statuses and activities of contemporary societies are to function properly for the common good, if the necessary social labor is to be performed, and if disorder is to be avoided and unified action among the necessary diverse statuses is to be maintained, hierarchies of segmentary and general types must be present to order and coordinate their diverse activities (257). The superordinate and subordinate levels exert power which serves common ends and achieves integration. As the number and variety of statuses among each of the three adaptive types increase and the relations among them become more numerous and complex, the total effect is to produce a society of hierarchies which coordinate the variety of statuses and their activities. The need for coordination in all complex societies produces rank orders which differentially distribute power and prestige (98).

For the social labor of the society to be performed, ordering by coordination of the diverse activities must take place. The coordinating functions are hierarchically located in positions of power to direct and sanction activity. These positions accumulate actual and attributed power and prestige. Back of many of them is the sanctioned use of force (73). Those which coordinate the primary adaptive statuses are re-ordered by superior and superordinate levels (97, 264). Through time, vast hierarchies are often developed. Each may have its own province, political, economic, or ecclesiastical (223, 258).

When the family with its rules of marriage and descent is related to such hierarchies or is an integral part of their development, general types of stratification, open or closed, appear (77, 246). The controls of the family serve to broaden the range of the hierarchy, as well as move the locus of power from the several adaptive primary statuses to one or more superior ones. Power is here inherent; those being controlled have their freedom of choice reduced, and those who control extend the social area of their own choice-making. The ordering of the relations of the statuses of the controlled and controlling takes the form of subordination and superordination (255).

The effect of coordination of complex statuses is not only (1) to produce superordinate statuses and subordinate position and (2) to distribute power differentially between them, but (3) to reduce the number of statuses which exercise control within the society, thereby creating a few statuses with more power than the others. This ordering of statuses produces an exclusive few in superordinate relations to an inclusive many. When the *few* exercise power over the many, they establish the foundations for the development of elites and aristocracies with lower rankings beneath them. When social change occurs rapidly the general closed types of rank are not adaptive, since they do not easily accommodate to the movement of individuals vertically or horizontally that is a necessary part of such change. The open system does (251). Color caste and all "fixed" forms are nonadaptive and likely to disappear.

Future research developments on rank, of course, will follow the interests of the investigators. It is certain if important advances are to be made and if we are to use present evidence more fruitfully and future knowledge more purposefully, we must follow MacRae's suggestion. He declares, "The most necessary and I believe the most valuable research open to us in the field of social stratification is synthetic, comparative and genetic" (186).

Many of the obsessive discussions of method, often betraying personal fears rather than scientific acumen, are likely to disappear when the several forms of American rank can be viewed by their investigators without the fear (or presence) of ethnocentrism.

Bibliography

1. ABERLE, D. F., and K. D. NAEGELE, "Middle-Class Father's Occupational Role and Attitudes Towards Children," *American Journal of Orthopsychiatry*, XXII (1952), 366–378.
2. ABRAHAMSON, STEPHEN, "Our Status System and Scholastic Rewards," *Journal of Educational Sociology*, XXV (1952), 441–450.
3. ABRAMS, M., *The Condition of the British People*. London: Gollancz, 1945.
4. ADAMS, S., "Fact and Myth in Social Class Theory," *Ohio Journal of Science*, LI (1951), 313–319.
5. ———, "Regional Differences in Vertical Mobility in a High-Status Occupation," *American Sociological Review*, XV (1950), 228–235.
6. ALMOND, G., "The Political Attitudes of Wealth," *Journal of Politics*, VII (1945), 213–256.
7. AMORY, C., *The Proper Bostonians*, New York: E. P. Dutton & Co., Inc., 1947.
8. ANASTASI, A., and J. P. FOLEY, *Differential Psychology: Individual and Group Differences in Behavior*, rev. ed. New York: The Macmillan Company, 1949.
9. ANASTASI, A., and S. MILLER, "Adolescent 'Prestige Factors' in Relation to Scholastic and Socio-economic Variables," *Journal of Social Psychology*, XXIX (1949), 43–50.
10. ANDERSON, C. A., S. C. BROWN, and M. J. BARMAN, "Intelligence and Occupational Mobility," *Journal of Political Economy*, LX (1952), 218–239.
11. ANDERSON, C. A., and M. SCHAPNER, *School and Society in England: Social Backgrounds of Oxford and Cambridge Students*. Washington: Public Affairs Press, 1952.
12. ANDERSON, H. D., and P. E. DAVIDSON, *Ballots and the Democratic Class Struggle*, Stanford, Calif.: Stanford University Press, 1943.
13. ANDERSON, W. A., "Family Social Participation and Social Status Self-Ratings," *American Sociological Review*, XI (1946), 253–258.
14. ARON, R., "Social Structure and the Ruling Class," *British Journal of Sociology*, I (1950), 1–17.
15. ASHMORE, HARRY S., *The Negro and the Schools*. New York: Van Rees Press, 1954 (copyright 1954 by the University of North Carolina Press).
16. BAILEY, W. C., N. FOOTE, P. K. HATT, R. HESS, R. T. MORRIS, M. SEEMAN, and G. SYKES, *Bibliography on Status and Stratification*. New York: Social Science Research Council, 1952.
17. BALTZELL, E. DIGBY, " 'Who's Who in America' and 'The Social Register': Elite and Upper Class Indexes in Metropolitan American," in Reinhard Bendix, ed., *Class, Status and Power*. New York: The Free Press, 1953, pp. 172–184.
18. BARBER, B., and L. S. LOBEL, "Fashion in Women's Clothes and the American Social System," *Social Forces*, XXXI (1952), 124–132.
19. BARNARD, C. I., "Functions and Pathology of Status Systems," in W. F. Whyte, *et al.*, *Industry and Society*. New York:

McGraw-Hill Book Company, 1946.

20. BASCOM, WILLIAM R., "Social Status, Wealth, and Individual Differences among the Yoruba," *American Anthropologist*, LIII (1951), 490–506.

21. BAUDLER, LUCILLE, and D. G. PATTERSON, "Social Status of Women's Occupations," *Occupations*, XXVI (1947–1948), 421–424.

22. BEALES, H. L., "The Labour Party in Its Social Context," *Political Quarterly*, XXIV (1953), 90–98.

23. BEALS, R. L., "Social Stratification in Latin America," *American Jounal of Sociology*, LVIII (1952–1953), 327–340.

24. BECKER, H., "Changes in Social Stratification in Germany," *American Sociological Review*, XV (1950), 333–342.

25. BECKER, HOWARD S., "Social-Class Variations in the Teacher-Pupil Relationship," *Journal of Educational Sociology*, XXV (1952), 451–465.

26. BELCHER, J. C., "Evaluation and Restandardization of Sewell's Socioeconomic Scale," *Rural Sociology*, XVI (1951), 246–255.

27. BENDIX, R., *Higher Civil Servants in American Society*, University of Colorado Studies, Series in Sociology No. 2. Boulder: University of Colorado Press, 1949.

28. ———, and SEYMOUR MARTIN LIPSET, *Class, Status and Power: A Reader in Social Stratification*. New York: The Free Press, 1953.

29. BENNETT, J. W., and M. M. TUMIN, *Social Life*. New York: Alfred A. Knopf, Inc., 1948.

30. BENNEY, M., and P. GEISS, "Social Class and Politics in Greenwich," *British Journal of Sociology*, I (1950), 310–327.

31. BERENT, J., "Fertility and Social Mobility," *Population Studies*, V (1952), 224–261.

32. BERNARDI, B., "The Age-System of the Nilo-Hamitic Peoples," *Africa*, XXII (1952), 316–333.

33. BONHAM, J., "The Middle Class Elector," *British Journal of Sociology*, III (1952), 222–231.

34. BOSSARD, J. H. S., "Ritual in Family Living," *American Sociological Review*, XIV (1949), 463–469.

35. ———, and E. S. BOLL, "Rite of Passage—a Contemporary Study," *Social Forces*, Vol. 26 (1948), pp. 247–255.

36. BOTT, ELIZABETH, "The Concept of Class as a Reference Group," *Human Relations*, VII (1954), 259–285.

37. BOTTOMORE, THOMAS, "Social Stratification in Voluntary Organizations," in D. V. Glass, ed., *Social Mobility in Britain*, New York: The Free Press, 1954, pp. 349–382.

38. BOURIEZ-GREGG, FRANÇOISE, *Les Classes Sociales aux États-Unis*. Paris: Librairie Armand Colin, 1954.

39. BROOKS, M. R., "American Class and Caste: An Appraisal," *Social Forces*, XXV (1946), 201–211.

40. BROWN, J. S., "Social Class, Intermarriage and Church Membership in a Kentucky Community," *American Journal of Sociology*, LVII (1951–1952), 232–242.

41. BULTENA, LOUIS, "Church Membership and Church Attendance in Madison, Wis.," *American Sociological Review*, XIV (1949), 384–389.

42. BURT, C., "Family Size, Intelligence and Social Class," *Population Studies*, (1947), 177–187.

43. ———, "The Trend of National Intelligence," *British Journal of Sociology*, I (1950), 154–168.

44. CANTRIL, II., "Identification with Social and Economic Class," *Journal of Abnormal Social Psychology*, XXXVIII (1943), 574–580.

45. CASE, H. M., "An Independent Test of the Interest-Group Theory of Social Class," *American Sociological Review*, XVII (1952), 751–754.

46. CAUTER, T., and J. D. DOWNHAM, *The Communication of Ideas*. London: Chatto & Windus Ltd., 1954.

47. CENTERS, R., "Class Consciousness of the American Woman," *International Journal of Opinion and Attitude Res.*, III (1949), 399–408.

48. ———, "Educational and Occupational Mobility," *American Sociological Review*, XIV (1949), 143–147.

49. ———, "Marital Selection and Occupational Strata," *American Journal of Sociology*, LIV (1948–1949), 530–535.

50. ———, "Motivational Aspects of

Occupational Stratification," *Journal of Social Psychology*, XXVIII (1948), 187–217.

51. ———, "Occupational Mobility of Urban Occupational Strata," *American Sociological Review*, XIII (1948), 197–203.

52. ———, *The Psychology of Social Classes: A Study of Class Consciousness*. Princeton, N. J.: Princeton University Press, 1949.

53. ———, "Social Class, Occupation, and Imputed Belief," *American Journal of Sociology*, LVIII (1952–1953), 543–555.

54. ———, "Towards an Articulation of Two Approaches to Social Class Phenomena," *International Journal of Opinion and Attitude Res.*, IV (1950), 499–514.

55. CHAMBERS, ROSALIND C., "A Study of Three Voluntary Organizations," in D. V. Glass, ed., *Social Mobility in Britain*, New York: The Free Press, 1954, pp. 383–406.

56. CHEN, T. A., "Basic Problems of the Chinese Working Classes," *American Journal of Sociology*, LIII (1947–1948), 184–191.

57. CHINOY E., "The Traditions of Opportunity and the Aspirations of Automobile Workers," *American Journal of Sociology*, LVII (1951–1952), 453–459.

58. CLARK, R. E., "Psychoses, Income, and Occupational Prestige," *American Journal of Sociology*, LIV (1948–1949), 433–435.

59. COLE, G. D. H., "The Conception of the Middle Classes," *British Journal of Sociology*, I (1950), 275–291.

60. CONGALTON, A. A., "Social Grading of Occupations in New Zealand," *British Journal of Sociology*, IV (1953), 45–60.

61. COX, O. C., *Caste, Class and Race: A Study in Social Dynamics*. Garden City, N.Y.: Doubleday & Company, Inc., 1948.

62. ———, "Max Weber on Social Stratification: A Critique," *American Sociological Review*, XV (1950), 223–227.

63. ———, "Race and Caste: A Distinction," *American Journal of Sociology*, L (1944–1945), 360–368.

64. DAVIES, A. F., "Prestige of Occupa-

tions," *British Journal of Sociology*, III (1952), 134–147.

65. DAVIS, A., "Caste, Economy and Violence," *American Journal of Sociology*, LI (1945–1946), 7–15.

66. ———, "The Motivation of Underprivileged Workers," in W. F. Whyte et al., *Industry and Society*. New York: McGraw-Hill Book Company, 1946, pp. 84–106.

67. ———, *Social-Class Influences Upon Learning*. Cambridge, Mass.: Harvard University Press, 1948.

68. ———, and R. J. Havighurst, *Father of the Man*. Boston: Houghton Mifflin Company, 1947.

69. ———, "Social Class and Color Differences in Child Rearing," *American Sociological Review*, XI (1946), 698–710.

70. DAVIS, K., *Human Society*, New York: The Macmillan Company, 1949.

71. ———, and W. E. Moore, "Some Principles of Stratification," *American Sociological Review*, X (1945), 242–249.

72. DEEG, M. E., and D. G. PATERSON, "Changes in Social Status of Occupations," *Occupations*, XXV (1947), 205–208.

73. DE JOUVENAL, BERTRAND, *Power: The National History of Its Growth*. London: Batchworth, 1952.

74. DOBB, M., *Studies in the Development of Capitalism*. London: Routledge & Kegan Paul Ltd., 1946.

75. DOLLARD, JOHN, "Drinking Mores of the Social Classes," in *Alcohol, Science and Society*. New Haven: Yale University Press, 1945, pp. 95–104.

76. DOTSON, F., "Patterns of Voluntary Association among Urban Working-Class Families," *American Sociological Review*, XVI (1951), 687–693.

77. DRAKE, St. C., and H. CAYTON, *Black Metropolis*. New York: Harcourt, Brace & World, Inc., 1945.

78. DRUCKER, P. F., *The New Society*. New York: Harper & Row, Publishers, 1949.

79. DUNCAN, O. D., "A Critical Evaluation of Warner's Work in Community Stratification," *American Sociological Review*, XV (1950), 205–215.

80. DUVALL, E. M., "Conceptions of Parenthood," *American Journal of*

Sociology, LII (1946), 193–203.

81. EELLS, K., et al., *Intelligence and Cutural Differences.* Chicago: University of Chicago Press, 1951.

82. ERICSON, M. C., "Child-rearing and Social Status," *American Journal of Sociology*, LII (1946–1947), 190–192.

83. ———, "Social Status and Child-rearing Practices," in T. M. Newcomb and E. L. Hartley, eds., *Readings in Social Psychology.* New York: Holt, Rinehart & Winston, Inc., 1947.

84. EYSENCK, H. J., "Primary Social Attitudes as Related to Social Class and Political Party," *American Journal of Sociology*, LVII (1951–1952), 222–231.

85. FEI,HSIAO-TUNG, "Peasantry and Gentry: An Interpretation of Chinese Social Structure and Its Changes," *American Journal of Sociology*, LII (1946–1947), 1–17.

86. ———, and CHIH-I CHANG, *Earthbound China: A Study of Rural Economy in Yunnan.* Chicago: University of Chicago Press, 1945.

87. FEI, HSIAO-TUNG, and YUNG-TEH CHOW, *China's Gentry: Essays in Rural-Urban Relations* by Fei with Six Life-Histories of Chinese Gentry Families Collected by Chow. Chicago: University of Chicago Press, 1953.

88. FLOUD, J., "The Educational Experience of the Adult Population of England and Wales as at July 1949," in D. V. Glass, ed., *Social Mobility in Britain.* New York: The Free Press, 1954, pp. 98–140.

89. ———, "Educational Opportunity and Social Mobility," *Year Book of Education.* London: Evan Brothers, 1950, pp. 117–136.

90. FOOTE, N. N., "Destratification and Restratification," *American Journal of Sociology*, LVIII (1952–1953), 325–326.

91. ———, "The Professionalization of Labor in Detroit," *American Journal of Sociology*, LVIII (1952–1953), 371.

92. ———, and Paul K. Hatt, "Social Mobility and Economic Advancement," *American Economic Review*, XLIII, Supplement (May, 1953), 364–378.

93. FOREMAN, P. B., and M. C. HILL, "The Negro in the United States: A Bibliography," *Oklahoma A. and M. College Bulletin*, XLIV (Stillwater, Okla., 1947).

94. FORM, W. H., "Toward an Occupational Social Pyschology," *Journal of Social Psychology*, XXIV (1946), 85–99.

95. FRIEDSON, E., "Relation of Social Situation of Contact to the Media in Mass Communication," *Public Opinion Quarterly*, XVII (1953), 230–239.

96. ———, "Communications Research and the Concept of the Mass," *American Sociological Review*, XVIII (1953), 313–317.

97. GARDNER, BURLEIGH B., "The Factory as a Social System" in William Foote Whyte, ed., *Industry and Society.* New York: McGraw-Hill Book Company, 1946.

98. ———, and DAVID MOORE, *Human Relations in Industry.* Homewood, Ill.: Richard D. Irwin, Inc., 1955.

99. GEIGER, T., "An Historical Study of the Origins and Structure of the Danish Intelligentsia," *British Journal of Sociology*, I (1950), 209–220.

100. GLASS, D. V., ed., *Social Mobility in Britain.* New York: The Free Press, 1954.

101. ———, and J. R. HALL, "A Description of a Sample Inquiry into Social Mobility in Great Britain," in D. V. Glass, ed., *Social Mobility in Britain.* New York: The Free Press, 1954, pp. 79–97.

102. ———, "Social Mobility in Britain: A Study of Inter-Generation Changes in Status," in D. V. Glass, ed., *Social Mobility in Britain.* New York: The Free Press, 1954, pp. 177–265.

103. GOFFMAN, ERVING, "Symbols of Class Status," *British Journal of Sociology*, II (1951), 294–305.

104. GOLD, RAY, "Janitors versus Tenants: A Status-Income Dilemma," *American Journal of Sociology*, LVII (1951–1952), 486–493.

105. GOLDHAMMER, HERBERT, and EDWARD A. SHILS, "Types of Power and Status," *American Journal of Sociology*, XLV (1939–1940), 171–182.

106. GOLDSCHMIDT, W. R., "America's Social Classes: Is Equality a Myth?" *Commentary*, X (1950), 175–181.

107. ——, *As You Sow*. New York: Harcourt, Brace & World, Inc., 1947.

108. ——, "Class Denominationalism in Rural California Churches," *American Journal of Sociology*, XLIX (1943–1944), 348–356.

109. ——, "Social Class in America: A Critical Review," *American Anthropology*, LII (1950), 483–499.

110. ——, "Social Class in American Sociology," *American Journal of Sociology*, LV (1949–1950), 262–268.

111. ——, "A System of Social Class Analysis" (Drew University Studies, No. 2). Madison, N. J.: Drew University Bulletin, 1951.

112. GOODWIN, A., ed., *The European Nobility in the Eighteenth Century*. London: Adam and Charles Black, 1953.

113. GORDON, M. M., "Kitty Foyle and the Concept of Class Culture," *American Journal of Sociology*, LIII (1947–1948), 210–217.

114. ——, "Social Class in American Sociology," *American Journal of Sociology*, LV (1949–1950), 262–269.

115. GOULDNER, ALVIN, *The Wildcat Strike*. London: Routledge & Kegan Paul Ltd., 1955.

116. ——, *Patterns of Industrial Bureaucracy*. London: Routledge & Kegan Paul Ltd., 1955.

117. GREEN A., "The Middle Class Male Child and Neurosis," *American Sociological Review*, XII (1946), 31–41.

118. GROSS, L., "The Use of Class Concepts in Sociological Research," *American Journal of Sociology*, LIV (1948–1949), 409–422.

119. HAGGARD, E. A., "Social-Status and Intelligence: An Experimental Study of Certain Cultural Determinants of Measured Intelligence," *Genetic Psychology Monographs*, XLIX (1954), 141–186.

120. HALL, J. R., and W. ZIEGEL, "A Comparison of Social Mobility Data for England and Wales, Italy, France and the U.S.A.," in D. V. Glass, ed., *Social Mobility in Britain*. New York: The Free Press, 1954, pp. 260–265.

121. HALL, J. R., "A Comparison of the Degree of Social Endogamy in England and Wales and the U.S.A.," in D. V. Glass, ed., *Social Mobility in Britain*. New York: The Free Press, 1954, pp. 344–346.

122. ——, and D. CARADOG JONES, "Social Grading of Occupations," *British Journal of Sociology*, I (1950), 31–55.

123. HALL, J. R., and D. V. GLASS, "Education and Social Mobility," in D. V. Glass, ed., *Social Mobility in Britain*. New York: The Free Press, 1954, pp. 291–307.

124. HATT, P. K., "Class and Ethnic Attitudes," *American Sociological Review*, XIII (1948), 36–43.

125. ——, "Occupation and Social Stratification," *American Journal of Sociology*, LV (1950), 533–544.

126. ——, "Social Class and Basic Personality Structure," *Sociology and Social Research*, XXXVI (1952), 355–363.

127. ——, "Stratification in Mass Society," *American Sociological Review*, XV (1950), 216–222.

128. ——, and V. KTSANES, "Patterns of American Stratification as Reflected in Selected Social Literature," *American Sociological Review*, XVII (1952), 670–679.

129. HAVIGHURST, R. J., "Child Development in Relation to Community Social Structure," *Child Development*, XVII (1946), 85–89.

130. ——, and F. H. BREESE, "The Relation between Ability and Social Status in a Midwestern Community: III. Primary Mental Abilities," *Journal of Educational Psychology*, XXXVIII (1947), 241–247.

131. HAVIGHURST, R. J., and R. R. RODGERS, "The Role of Motivation in Attendance at Post-High School Educational Institutions," in *Who Should Go to College*, B. S. Hollingshead, ed. New York: Columbia University Press, 1952.

132. HAVIGHURST, R. J., and HILDA TABA, *Adolescent Character and Personality*. New York: John Wiley & Sons, Inc., 1949.

133. HENRY, W., "The Business Executive: Psychodynamics of a Social Role," *American Journal of Sociology*, LIV (1948–1949), 286–291.

134. HERTZLER, J. O., "Some Tendencies Toward a Closed Class System in the

United States," *Social Forces*, XXX (1952), 313–323.

135. HILDEBRAND, GEORGE H., "American Unionism, Social Stratification, and Power," *American Journal of Sociology*, LVIII (1952–1953), 381–390.

136. HILL, M. C., and B. C. MCCALL, "Social Stratification in a Georgia Town," *American Sociological Review*, XV (1950), 721–730.

137. HIMMELWEIT, H. T., "Social Status and Secondary Education since the 1944 Act: Some Data for London," in D. V. Glass, ed., *Social Mobility in Britain*. New York: The Free Press, 1954, pp. 141–159.

138. HOGART, A. M., *Caste: A Comparative Study*. London: Methuen & Co. Ltd., 1950.

139. HOLLINGSHEAD, A. B., "Class and Kinship in a Middle Western Community," *American Sociological Review*, XXIV (1949), 469–475.

140. ———, "Class Differences in Family Stability," *Annals of the American Academy of Political and Social Science*, CCLXXII (1950), 39–46.

141. ———, *Elmtown's Youth: The Impact of Social Classes on Adolescents*. New York: John Wiley & Sons, Inc., 1949.

142. ———, "Selected Characteristics of Classes in a Middle Western Community," *American Sociological Review*, XII (1947), 385–395.

143. ———, "Status in the High School," in W. Lloyd Warner, ed., *Democracy in Jonesville*. New York: Harper & Row, Publishers, 1949, pp. 193–213.

144. ———, "Trends in Social Stratification: A Case Study," *American Sociological Review*, XVII (1952), 264–285.

145. HSIAO-T'UNG FEI, "Peasantry and Gentry in China," *American Journal of Sociology*, LII (1946–1947), 1–17.

146. HSI-EN CHEN, THEODORE, "The Marxist Remolding of Chinese Society," *American Journal of Sociology*, LVIII (1952–1953), 340–346.

147. HSU, FRANCIS L. K., "Social Mobility in China," *American Sociological Review*, XIV (1949), 764–771.

148. HUGHES, E. C., "Dilemmas and Contradictions of Status," *American Journal of Sociology*, L (1944–1945), 353–360.

149. HYMAN, H. H., "The Psychology of Status," *Archives of Psychology*, CCLXIX (1942), 1–94.

150. INKELES, A., "Social Stratification and Mobility in the Soviet Union," *American Sociological Review*, XV (1950), 465–480.

151. JANKE, L. L., and R. J. HAVIGHURST, "Relations Between Ability and Social Status in a Midwestern Community: 11. 16-year-old Boys and Girls," *Journal of Educational Psychology*, XXXVI (1946), 499–509.

152. JENKINS, H., and D. CARADOG JONES, "Social Class of Cambridge Alumni of the 18th and 19th Centuries," *British Journal of Sociology*, I (1950), 93–116.

153. KAHL, JOSEPH A., "Education and Occupational Aspirations of 'Common Man' Boys," *Harvard Educational Review*, XVIII (1953), 186–203.

154. KAUFMAN, H. F., "An Approach to the Study of Urban Stratification," *American Sociological Review*, XVII (1952), 430–437.

155. ———, *Defining Prestige in a Rural Community* ("Sociometry Monographs," No. 10), New York: Beacon House, 1946.

156. ———, "Members of a Rural Community as Judges of Prestige Rank," *Sociometry*, IX (1946), 71–86.

157. ———, *Prestige Classes in a New York Rural Community*. Ithaca, N. Y.: Cornell University Agricultural Experiment Station Memoir No. 260, 1944.

158. KELSALL, R. K., *Higher Civil Servants in Britain*. London: Routledge & Kegan Paul Ltd., 1955.

159. KINSEY, A. C., *et al.*, *Sexual Behavior in the Human Male*. Philadelphia: W. B. Saunders Co., 1948.

160. KLUCKHOHN, C., and F. KLUCKHOHN, "American Culture: General Orientations and Class Patterns," in L. Bryson, L. Finkelstein, and R. M. MacIver, eds., *Approaches to Group Understanding*. New York: Harper & Row, Publishers, 1947.

161. LASSWELL, H. D., *Power and Society: A Framework for Political Inquiry*. New Haven: Yale University Press, 1950.

162. ———, D. Lerner, and C. E. Rothwell, *The Comparative Study of Elites: An*

Introduction and Bibliography. Stanford, Calif.: Stanford University Press, 1952.

163. LASTRUCCI, C. L., "The Status and Significance of Occupational Research," *American Sociological Review.* XI (1946), 78–84.

164. LAZARSFIELD, P. F., B. BERELSON, and H. GOUDIT, *The People's Choice.* New York: Columbia University Press, 1948.

165. LEACH, E. R., *Political Systems of Highland Burma: A Study of Kachin Social Structure.* London: G. Bell & Sons Ltd., 1954.

166. LEE, SHU-CHING, "Intelligentsia of China," *American Journal of Sociology,* LII (1946–1947), 489–497.

167. LENSKI, G. E., "American Social Classes: Statistical Strata or Social Groups?" *American Journal of Sociology,* LVIII (1952–1953), 139–144.

168. LERNER, MAX, *America as a Civilization.* New York: Simon & Schuster, 1957.

169. LEWIS, R., and A. MAUDE, *The English Middle Classes.* London: Phoenix House, 1949.

170. ———, *The English.* London: Phoenix House, 1949.

171. LIN, YUEH-HWA, *The Golden Wing: A Sociological Study of Chinese Familism.* London: Routledge & Kegan Paul Ltd., 1947.

172. LIPSET, S. M., and R. BENDIX, "Social Mobility and Occupational Career Patterns: 1. Stability of Jobholding," *American Journal of Sociology,* LVII (1952), 366–374.

173. ———, "Social Status and Social Structure," *British Journal of Sociology,* II (1951), 150–168, 230–257.

174. LITTLE, K. L., "Social Change and Social Class in the Sierra Leone Protectorate," *American Journal of Sociology,* LIV (1948–1949), 10–21.

175. ———, "The Study of 'Social Change' in British West Africa," *Africa,* XXIII (1953), 274–284.

176. LOOMIS, C. P., J. A. BEAGLE, and T. W. LONGMORE, "Critique of Class as Related to Social Stratification," *Sociometry,* X (1947), 319–337.

177. LOWIE, R. H., *The German People.* New York: Holt, Rinehart & Winston, Inc., 1945.

178. MAAS, HENRY, "Some Social Class Differences in the Family Systems and Group Relations of Pre- and Early Adolescents," *Child Development,* XXII (1951), 145–152.

179. MCCALL, BEVODE, "Social Status and Social Interaction: A Case Study." Unpublished manuscript.

180. MACDONALD, M., C. McGUIRE, and R. HAVIGHURST, "Leisure Activities and the Socio-Economic Status of Children," *American Journal of Sociology,* LIV (1948–1949), 505–520.

181. McGUIRE, C., "Family Life in Lower and Middle Class Homes," *Marriage and Family Living,* XIV (1952), 1–6.

182. ———, "Social Mobility: The Rise and Fall of Families," in *Democracy in Jonesville.* New York: Harper & Row, Publishers, 1949, pp. 55–76.

183. ———, "Social Status, Peer Status and Social Mobility" (Memorandum for the Committee on Human Development). Chicago: University of Chicago, Committee on Human Development, 1949.

184. ———, "Social Stratification and Mobility Patterns," *American Sociological Review,* XV (1950), 195–204.

185. MacIVER, R. M., *The Web of Government.* New York: The Macmillan Company, 1947.

186. MacRAE, D. G., "Social Stratification: A Trend Report," *Current Sociology,* II (1953–1954), 5–74.

187. MANNHEIM, KARL, *Freedom, Power and Democratic Planning.* New York: Oxford University Press, Inc., 1950.

188. MARRIOTT, McKIM, "Individual Prestige *versus* Caste Ranking in Some Hindu Villages," Unpublished paper read at the AAA meetings, Tucson, 1953.

189. ———, ed., *Village India.* Chicago: University of Chicago Press, 1955.

190. MARSHALL, T. H., *Citizenship and Social Class.* Cambridge: Cambridge University Press, 1950.

191. ———, "The Nature and Determinants of Social Status," *The Year Book of Education.* London: Evan Brothers, 1953, pp. 30–50.

192. MARTIN, F. M., "An Inquiry into Parents' Preferences in Secondary

Education," in D. V. Glass, ed., *Social Mobility in Britain*. New York: The Free Press, 1954, pp. 160–174.

193. MEEKER, MARCHIA, "Status Aspirations and the Social Club," in W. Lloyd Warner, ed., *Democracy in Jonesville*. New York: Harper & Row, Publishers, 1949, pp. 130–148.

194. MILLER, W., "The Business Elite in Business Bureaucracies," in W. Miller, ed., *Men in Business*. Cambridge, Mass.: Harvard University Press, 1952, pp. 286–305.

195. ———, "The Recruitment of the American Business Elite," *Quarterly Journal of Economics*, LIV (1950), 242–253.

196. MILLS, C. W., "The American Business Elite: A Collective Portrait," *Journal of Economic History*, V (suppl. 5) (1945), 20–45.

197. ———, *The New Men of Power: America's Labor Leaders*. New York: Harcourt, Brace & World, Inc., 1948.

198. ———, *White Collar: The American Middle Classes*. New York: Columbia University Press, 1951.

199. MOSER, C. A., and J. R. HALL, "The Social Grading of Occupations," in D. V. Glass, ed., *Social Mobility in Britain*. New York: The Free Press, 1954, pp. 29–50.

200. MOTZ, A. B., "Conceptions of Marital Roles by Status Groups," *Marriage and Family Living*, XII (1950), 136–162.

201. MUKHERJEE, RAMKRISHNA, "A Study of Social Mobility between Three Generations," in *Social Mobility in Britain*. London: Routledge and Kegan Paul, Ltd., 1954, Vol. 9. pp. 266–290.

202. ———, "A Further Note on the Analysis of Data on Social Mobility," in D. V. Glass, ed., *Social Mobility in Britain*. New York: The Free Press, 1954, pp. 242–259.

203. ———, and J. R. HALL, "A Note on the Analysis of Data on Social Mobility," in D. V. Glass, ed., *Social Mobility in Britain*. New York: The Free Press, 1954, pp. 218–241.

204. MULLIGAN, R. A., "Social Mobility and Higher Education," *Journal of Educational Sociology*, XXV (1952), 476–487.

205. ———, "Socio-Economic Background and College Enrollment," *American Sociological Review*, XVI (1951), 188–196.

206. MURDOCK, G. P., *Social Structure*. New York: The Macmillan Company, 1949.

207. NEUGARTEN, B., "The Democracy of Childhood," in W. Lloyd Warner, ed., *Democracy in Jonesville*. New York: Harper & Row, Publishers, 1949, pp. 77–88.

208. ———, "Social Class and Friendship among School Children," *American Journal of Sociology*, LI (1945–1946), 305–314.

209. NEWCOMB, T. M., *Social Psychology*. New York: Dryden Press, 1950.

210. ———, and E. T. HARTLEY, eds., *Readings in Social Psychology*. New York: Holt, Rinehart & Winston, Inc., 1947.

211. NORTH, C. C., and P. K. HATT, "Jobs and Occupations: A Popular Evaluation," *Opinion News*, I (1947), 3–13.

212. PARSONS, T., "The Professions and Social Structure," *Social Forces*, XVII (1939), 457–467, reprinted in T. Parsons, ed., *Essays in Sociological Theory: Pure and Applied*. New York: The Free Press, 1949.

213. ———, "Social Classes and Class Conflict in the Light of Recent Sociological Theory," *American Economic Review*, XXXIV (1949), 16–26.

214. ———, *The Social System*. New York: The Free Press, 1951, pp. 132, 172.

215. PEAR, T. H., *English Social Differences*. London: George Allen & Unwin, Ltd., 1955.

216. PFAUTZ, H. W., "The Current Literature on Social Stratification: Critique and Bibliography," *American Journal of Sociology*, LVIII (1952–1953), 391–418.

217. ———, and O. P. DUNCAN, "A Critical Evaluation of Warner's Work in Social Stratification," *American Sociological Review*, XV (1950), 205–215.

218. POPE, L., *Millhands and Preachers* (Studies in Religious Education, No. 15). New Haven: Yale University Press, 1943.

219. ———, "Religion and Class Structure," *Annals of the American Academy*

of *Political and Social Science*, CCLVI (1948), 84–91.

220. PRINS, A. H. J., *East African Age-Class Systems: An Inquiry into the Social Order of Galla, Kipsigis, and Kikuyu.* Groningen: J. B. Wolters, 1953.

221. RIESMAN, D., *The Lonely Crowd: A Study of the Changing American Character.* New Haven: Yale University Press, 1950.

222. ROGOFF, N., "Recent Trends in Urban Mobility," in P. Hatt and A. Reiss, eds., *Reader in Urban Sociology.* New York: The Free Press, 1951, pp. 406–420.

223. ROSENSTEIN, JOSEPH, "Party Politics: Unequal Contests," in W. Lloyd Warner, ed., *Democracy in Jonesville.* New York: Harper & Row, Publishers, 1949, pp. 213–235.

224. RUESCH, J., *Chronic Disease and Psychological Invalidism*, Psychosomatic Medicine Monographs, New York: Paul Hoeker, 1946.

225. ———, "Social Technique, Social Status, and Social Change in Illness," in H. A. Murray and C. Kluckhohn, eds., *Personality in Nature, Society and Culture.* New York: Alfred A. Knopf, Inc., 1948, pp. 117–130.

226. ———, A. JACOBSON, and M. B. LOEB, "Acculturation and Illness," *Psychological Monographs: General and Applied,* LXII No. 292 (1948).

227. RUESCH, J., *et al.*, *Duodenal Ulcer: A Sociopsychological Study of Naval Enlisted Personnel and Civilians.* Berkeley, Calif.: University of California Press, 1948.

228. RYAN, B. F., *Caste in Modern Ceylon.* New Brunswick, N. J.: Rutgers University Press, 1953.

229. SCHATZMAN, LEONARD, and ANSELM STRAUSS, "Social Class and Modes of Communication," *American Journal of Sociology,* LX (1954–1955), 329–338.

230. SCHLESINGER, A. M., *Learning How to Behave.* New York: The Macmillan Company, 1946.

231. SCHUMPETER, J. A., *Imperialism and Social Classes.* New York: Kelley, 1951.

232. SELLARS, R. W., V. J. McGILL, and M. FABER, *Philosophy for the Future.* New York: Macmillan Company, 1949.

233. SEWELL, W. H., *The Construction and Standardization of a Scale for the Measurement of the Socio-Economic Status of Oklahoma Farm Families*, Oklahoma A. and M. College Technical Bulletin No. 9 (1940).

234. ———, and B. L. ELLENBOGEN, "Social Status and the Measured Intelligence of Small City and Rural Children," *American Sociological Review,* XVII (1952), 612–616.

235. SHIH, KUO-HENG, eds. and trans. Hsiao-tung Fei and Francis L. K. Hsu, *China Enters the Machine Age.* Cambridge, Mass.: Harvard University Press, 1944.

236. SHILS, E., *The Present State of American Sociology.* New York: The Free Press, 1948.

237. SJOBERG, G., "Are Social Classes in America Becoming More Rigid?" *American Sociological Review,* XVI (1951), 775–783.

238. SMITH, BENJAMIN F., "Wishes of Negro High School Seniors and Social Class Status," *Journal of Educational Sociology,* XXV (1952), 466–475.

239. SOROKIN, PITIRIM, *Society, Culture, and Personality.* New York: Harper & Row, Publishers, 1947, pp. 277–278.

240. ———, *Social Mobility.* New York: Harper & Row, Publishers, 1927.

241. STENDLER, CELIA BURNS, *Children of Brasstown,* (*University of Illinois Bulletin,* XLVI, No. 59). Urbana, Ill.: Bureau of Research and Service of the College of Education, 1949.

242. STERN, BERNHARD J., "Some Aspects of Historical Materialism," in R. W. Sellars, ed., *Philosophy for the Future.* New York: The Macmillan Company, 1949.

243. STONE, GREGORY, "City Shoppers and Urban Stratification: Observations on the Social Psychology of City Life," *American Journal of Sociology,* LX (1954–1955), 36–45.

244. TAFT, P., *The Structure and Government of Labour Unions.* London: Geoffrey Cumberlege, and Cambridge, Mass.: Harvard University Press, 1955.

245. TIMASHEFF, N. S., "Vertical Social Mobility in Communist Society," *American Journal of Sociology,* XLIX (1943–1944), 9–22.

246. TUMIN, M. M., *Caste in a Peasant Society.* Princeton, N. J.: Princeton University Press, 1952.

247. VOGT, E. Z., Jr., "Social Stratification in the Rural Middle West: A Structural Analysis," *Rural Sociology*, XII (1947), 364–375.

248. ———, "Town and Country: The Structure of Rural Life," in W. Lloyd Warner, ed., *Democracy in Jonesville*, New York: Harper & Row, Publishers, 1949, pp. 236–265.

249. WARNER, W. LLOYD, ed., *Democracy in Jonesville*. New York: Harper & Row, Publishers, 1949.

250. ———, "A Methodological Note," in St. Clair Drake and Horace R. Cayton, eds., *Black Metropolis*. New York: Harcourt, Brace & World, Inc., 1945.

251. ———, *Structure of American Life.* Edinburgh: The University Press, 1952. (American title: *American Life: Dream and Reality*. Chicago: University of Chicago Press, 1953.)

252. ———, and J. ABEGGLEN, *Big Business Leaders in America*. New York: Harper & Row, Publishers, 1955.

253. ———, *Occupational Mobility in American Business and Industry, 1928–1952.* St. Paul, Minn.: University of Minnesota Press, 1955.

254. WARNER, W. LLOYD, and WILLIAM E. HENRY, "The Radio Daytime Serial: A Symbolic Analysis," *Genetic Psychology Monographs*, XXXVII (1948), 3–72.

255. WARNER, W. LLOYD, and J. O. LOW, *The Social System of the Modern Factory.* New Haven: Yale University Press, 1947.

256. WARNER, W. LLOYD, and P. S. LUNT, *The Status System of a Modern Community*. New Haven: Yale University Press, 1947.

257. WARNER, W. LLOYD, M. MEEKER, and K. EELLS, *Social Class in America.* Chicago: Science Research Associates, 1949.

258. WARNER, W. LLOYD, and MARCHIA MEEKER, "The Mill: Its Economy and Moral Structure," in W. Lloyd Warner, ed., *Democracy in Jonesville.* New York: Harper & Row, Publishers, 1949.

259. WARNER, W. LLOYD, and LEO SROLE, *The Social Systems of American Ethnic Groups*, Vol. III, Yankee City Series. New Haven: Yale University Press, 1945.

260. WARRINER, CHARLES K., "Leadership in the Small Group," *American Journal of Sociology*, LX (1955), 361–369.

261. WEST, J., *Plainville, U.S.A.* New York: Columbia University Press, 1945.

262. WHITE, CLYDE, *These Will Go to College.* Cleveland: Western Reserve University Press, 1952.

263. WHYTE, W. F., "A Slum Sex Code," *American Journal of Sociology*, XLIX (1943), 24–31.

264. ———, "The Social Structure of the Restaurant," *American Journal of Sociology*, LIV (1949), 302–310.

265. WILLIAMS, ROBIN M., Jr., *American Society: A Sociological Interpretation.* New York: Alfred A. Knopf, Inc., 1951, pp. 78–135.

266. WRAY, D., "The Norwegians: Sect and Ethnic Group," in W. Lloyd Warner *et al.*, *Democracy in Jonesville.* New York: Harper & Row, Publishers, 1949, pp. 168–192.

267. WOHL, R. RICHARD, "The Rags to Riches Story: An Episode of Secular Idealism," *Class Status and Power*. New York: The Free Press, 1953.

268. YANG, MARTIN C., *A Chinese Village: Taiton, Shantung Province.* New York: Columbia University Press, 1943.

Variable Meanings of Social Class

THOMAS E. LASSWELL

Stratification

The area of social class and social stratification at present seems to be a conceptual muddle. Yet, as a potential researcher in the area, the reader is entitled to at least a glimpse of some of the concepts in current and recent use. The vista is admittedly depressing. We find it peopled by those who insist that social class is indistinguishable from social stratification; by those who insist that social class is real and social stratification is a fiction; by others who insist that social stratification is real and social class is a fiction; and by still others who insist that neither social class nor social stratification has any real referent. The only universal elements seem to be that all the writers are, to a lesser or greater extent, sure they are right and often intolerant of those who feel differently. Let us examine some of the more recent conceptions of "social class":

We are suggesting the possibility that the concept of social class as used by a number of writers is lacking in identifiable empirical content.[1]

... the term social class ... is nearly valueless for the clarification of the data of wealth, power, and social status in [the] contemporary United States. . . . In some,

Reprinted from Thomas E. Lasswell, *Class and Stratum* (Boston: Houghton Mifflin Company, 1965), pp. 53–66, by permission of the author and the publisher. Copyright © 1965 by Thomas E. Lasswell.

[1] Llewellyn Gross, "The Use of Class Concepts in Sociological Research," *American Journal of Sociology*, LIV (March, 1949), 419.

the concept of social class has been an important, and probably inevitable, first step in the study of differential power and status in society; admittedly, there are non-Western areas of civilization, as well as ages of the past, where the class concept is indispensable to an understanding of power and status; but so far as the bulk of Western society is concerned, and especially in the United States, the concept of class is largely obsolete.[2]

In the light of modern research knowledge . . . is there any justification for employing such an expression as "the class system" of this country? . . . To such questions we should at last be ready to answer a flat "no." It is now time to search for new, objective, accurate terms to describe the ways in which our population varies in terms of money, power, prestige, and occupational way of life.[3]

Any discussion of social stratification has to cope with the difficulty that the term "social class" is not definitely fixed and uniformly understood in sociological literature. How can we rid it of ambiguities?

1. The term should not be used as a synonym for related concepts which have assumed a univocal meaning. Income classes, occupational strata, races, interest groups or other clearly definable groupings should not be called social classes. . . .
2. . . . No theory which proceeds from a particular objective criterion or set of criteria can do more than describe social stratification in a particular system: it must fail to explain the phenomenon of social class as such. . . .
3. . . . All theories of stratification hold that similarity of behavior and of social

[2] Robert A. Nisbet, "The Decline and Fall of Social Class," *Pacific Sociological Review*, II (Spring, 1959), 11, 17.

[3] Robert E. L. Faris, *Social Disorganization*, 2nd ed. (New York: The Ronald Press Company, 1955), p. 83.

TABLE 1   **Some Ways of Ranking People in Contemporary American Society**

Income	Occupation	Education	Family descent	Racial descent	Ethnic descent
1. Wealthy	1. Big-business executives	1. Graduate and professional school	1. Leading old families	1. Whites	1. English, Scottish
2. Comfortable income	2. Professional people, independent businessmen	2. College graduates	2. Other—often in terms of residence in community	2. Orientals	2. Germanic peoples
3. Modest income	3. White-collar employees; small shop-keepers	3. Attendance at but not completion of college		3. Negroes	3. Other nationalities from Northern and Western Europe
4. Low income	4. Skilled workers	4. High-school graduate			4. Nationalities from Southern and Eastern Europe
5. Dependent on public support	5. Semiskilled workers	5. Attendance at high school			5. Orientals
	6. Unskilled workers	6. Elementary school only			

Source : Kimball Young, *Social Psychology* (New York : Appleton-Century-Crofts, 1956). Copyright © 1956 by Appleton-Century-Crofts. Reproduced by permission of Appleton-Century-Crofts.

relationship is a criterion of social class, much as opinions differ as to the forces which make for this similarity. Yet almost all of these analyses fail to dissociate the general theory of behavior from the special theory of social stratification. The frame of reference which consists in behavior in general is too wide for a definition of class. *The specific characteristic of the relation between social classes is hierarchy.* . . .[4]

Wherever classes are defined by factors which permit the construction of a hierarchical continuum, they are wrongly defined; i.e., the term has been applied wrongly. Status, ranking by others, self-ranking, style of life, similar economic conditions, and income level are all factors which define social strata but not social classes.[5]

I have no objection to using the term "class" to speak of arbitrary divisions in the United States, on any continuum—occupation, education, status or prestige, power, or one of the many other bases of significant social differentiation—provided it is recognized that class is a different phenomenon in Europe. But I suspect that it is too difficult to keep this distinction clear. Nor would finding a new word improve matters greatly, because social differentiation in the United States does not lend itself to realistic treatment in terms of arbitrary and blanket concepts.[6]

The subject of social stratification is currently in a truly paradoxical state. On the one hand social class or socio-economic status, as the more cautious sociologists often prefer to call it, has become the most widely used variable in empirical sociological research. . . . Stratification concepts are now part and parcel of the intellectual baggage, and indeed of the everyday vocabulary of the educated layman. This is surely a handsome tribute to the efficiency of sociological teaching and research.

Yet at the same time, and this is the

---

[4] Hans Speier, *Social Order and the Risks of War*, cited in Lewis A. Coser and Bernard Rosenberg, *Sociological Theory: A Book of Readings* (New York: The Macmillan Company, 1957), pp. 398–399.

[5] Ralf Dahrendorf, *Class and Class Conflict in Industrial Society* (Stanford, Calif.: Stanford University Press, 1959), p. 76.

---

[6] Arnold M. Rose, "The Concept of Class in American Sociology," *Social Research*, XXV (Spring, 1958), 65.

paradox, the conceptual confusion which has long characterized this field shows no signs of abating. . . . Indeed sociologists find it increasingly necessary to devote entire sessions at their national and international professional meetings not only to the presentation of findings from stratification research but to the clarification of basic theoretical and conceptual issues.[7]

It is both remarkable and slightly ludicrous that it should prove necessary to carry out the most elaborate research in order to discover what the shape of the class structure is in modern society.[8]

Stratification is the objective result of rating. It indicates the order of rating, the relative position of ranks, and their distribution within a rating system. If a system rates persons regardless of group membership, we speak of individual stratification. If groups are rated as units, we speak of group stratification. . . .

In many instances the rating in the various systems of individual stratification is of no "status" relevance and has no bearing on class membership in a system of group stratification. But there is one important exception: some achievements and some positions imply assignment to certain social classes.[9]

Rather than continue a recitation of the controversy, let us attempt to separate the various concepts of social class and social stratification into a series of categories for easier recognition and handling. Seven categories seem indicated:

1. The "single structure" concept
2. The plural structure concept

---

[7] Kurt B. Mayer, "The Changing Shape of the American Class Structure," *Social Research*, XXX (Winter, 1963), 458.

[8] T. H. Marshall, "General Survey of Changes in Social Stratification in the Twentieth Century," *Transactions of the Third World Congress of Sociology*, cited in Mayer, *ibid.*, p. 459.

[9] Egon Ernest Bergel, *Social Stratification* (New York: McGraw-Hill Book Company, 1962), pp. 4, 6.

3. The functional concept
4. The continuum concept
5. The class boundary concept
6. The interest-group concept
7. The interactional concept

The "Single Structure" Concept

One of the most common ideas of social class is that the classes together form a single social structure which can be fitted to a mathematical model whose graphic presentation is in the form of a triangle, a diamond, a rectangle, or the solid form of a pyramid, with horizontal lines or planes indicating the boundaries between classes. The vertical dimension of the model represents the "height" of each of the social classes, and the horizontal dimension(s) represents numbers of people, except in the rectangular model, where members are represented vertically, and the height of social classes by order.

An excellent recent description of such a model comes from Mayer:

To sum it up, America's social structure today and in the proximate future can be perceived as a diamond where the top and bottom are still pretty rigidly fixed, inhabited by upper and lower classes. A working class of the traditional sort also persists but comprises nowadays only a part of the manual workers. Between the extremes, however, classes are disappearing. To be sure, prestige, power and economic differentials persist here too, of course, and prestige differentials tend even to become accentuated as crude economic differences diminish and lose their visibility. But these differentials are no longer the hallmarks of social classes. In the middle ranges of the various rank orders we are witnessing the beginnings of a classless society in a modern industrial economy. It readily involves roughly one half of our population and may well involve more than that in the future although there are no signs that the top and bottom classes are likely to disappear altogether. This is a somewhat different classless society from that envisaged by

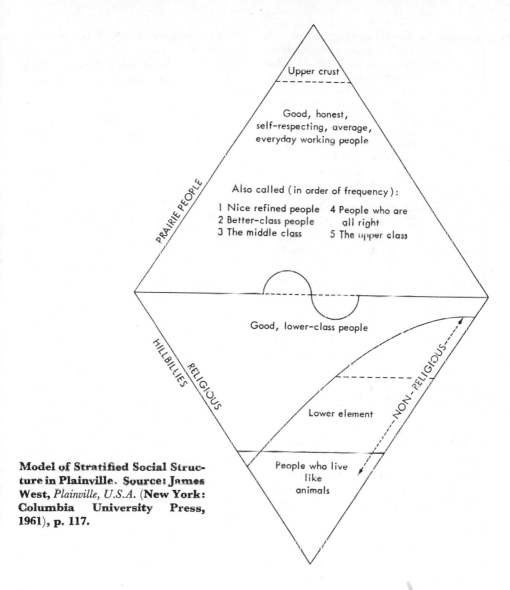

Upper crust

Good, honest,
self-respecting, average,
everyday working people

Also called (in order of frequency):

1 Nice refined people   4 People who are
2 Better-class people   all right
3 The middle class   5 The upper class

PRAIRIE PEOPLE

HILLBILLIES

RELIGIOUS

NON-RELIGIOUS

Good, lower-class people

Lower element

People who live
like
animals

**Model of Stratified Social Struc-
ture in Plainville. Source: James
West,** *Plainville, U.S.A.* **(New York:
Columbia University Press,
1961), p. 117.**

Marx a century ago, but it is at least a partially classless society nevertheless.[10]

Mayer's model, a diamond, is easy to conceptualize. Unfortunately, it is also easy for the superficial reader to make an analogy between this model and a population pyramid, and to think of the diagram as representing a population

rather than a social structure. The view of the "social structure" as a demographic phenomenon would certainly be inconsistent with Merton's definition of the social structure; indeed, it would not only be irrelevant, but also quite likely very confusing. Merton says:

The patterned arrangement of role-sets, status-sets and status-sequences can be held to comprise the social structure. The concepts

---

[10] Mayer, *op. cit.*, p. 468.

remind us, in the unlikely event that we need to be reminded of this insistent and obstinant fact, that even a seemingly simple social structure is extremely complex. For operating social structures must somehow manage to organize these sets and sequences of statuses and roles so that an appreciable degree of social order obtains, sufficient to enable most of the people most of the time to go about their business of social life without having to improvise adjustments anew in each newly confronted situation.[11]

Writers such as Warner and West (see figure on p. 261) make it clear that the social structure is perceived differentially by different categories of people in the population, but the notion is still conveyed that a monolithic structure— probably comprised of people rather than concepts of relationships between people—*is* there to be perceived.

It is interesting to speculate about the impulse to reify one's concept of a social structure. Among more primitive peoples it might take the form of mana or a totem animal. Among more literate peoples, the eight-fold path of Buddhism, the *jen* and *li* of Confucianism, or simply the "we" spoken by a monarch might be considered ways of reifying the social structure. Some evidence for the existence of *the* social structure of a society is found in the existence of mass stereotypes and what Lee has called "societal culture."[12] Closer investigation reveals that this is *a* structure, that it is a cognitive and most certainly not a demographic phenomenon, and that it is not found alone, but is coincident with a number of "group cultures"[13] and personal images of significant individuals.

Gordon reflects the difficulties into which the single-structure conceptualizers fall:

One of the important questions in social stratification analysis is whether the social class system is to be considered a function of the local community or the national, or "mass" society. This question factors into a number of subquestions: (1) Are there different ranges of income, power, and prestige in various American communities? (2) Are the relative status levels or positions uncovered in various communities comparable and thus determined presumably by values common to the mass society, or are they separately unique to the local situation? (3) Are there power and status systems which function on an inter-community or national level and which cannot therefore be adequately studied by research into one community?[14]

The single structure concept as a model of society seems to run into the most theoretical difficulty at the construct level; this, as noted earlier, ordinarily has an adverse effect on the testability of hypotheses for research and theory construction.

The Plural Structure Concept

In less common usage is a concept of social class which allows for the validity of Lee's observation mentioned above. This concept recognizes the existence of a number of social structures in at least *some* communities and relegates the possibility of a single structure to a special case.

Polsby's study of power distribution in New Haven and his review of eight widely accepted stratification-based studies of social power led him to the con-

---

[11] Robert K. Merton, *Social Theory and Social Structure* (New York: The Free Press, 1957), p. 370.

[12] Cf. Thomas E. Lasswell, "Orientations Toward Social Classes," *American Journal of Sociology*, LXV (May, 1960), 585–587.

[13] Alfred McClung Lee, "Attitudinal Multivalence in Relation to Culture and Personality," *American Journal of Sociology*, LX (November, 1954), 294–299.

---

[14] Milton M. Gordon, *Social Class in American Sociology* (Durham, N.C.: Duke University Press, 1958), p. 202.

clusion that not only did a single "power elite" appear not to exist in New Haven, but no single power hierarchy was indicated.[15] In a summary of "the various ways in which the authors [of the eight stratification studies of community power] have tried to save stratification theory," he concluded that "in all we have found reasons to mistrust [their] findings. . . ."[16] Conservatively stating that no single group *necessarily* constitutes *the* power structure in every community, he commented further that ". . . no properly documented instance of communities where hierarchy predominates have come to light."[17]

Vidich and Bensman offered a somewhat broader statement:

. . . even in a relatively "simple" rural community there is no single standard for social stratification. That is, social stratification in this type of situation represents a plurality of unrelated dimensions, often in conflict or not even coherent, in the midst of which groups of individuals may exist as congeries. This has been pointed out in the literature of urban stratification, but it has always been assumed that the small-scale rural society could be stratified from top to bottom, an hypothesis which this observation suggests is not the case. A major reason why a single standard of stratification cannot be used is that a single standard presupposes knowledge which makes assessments possible. The Springdaler does not have the knowledge of the complex industrial commerical processes of modern society to be able to locate individuals in these processes.[18]

It is interesting to note that Vidich and Bensman, in explaining the lack of a single structure in Springdale, turned to a cognitive approach. Such an approach would be equally applicable to an explanation of Polsby's findings. We shall see this approach recur in the interactional concept of social stratification. But "cognitive" explanations must not be confused with "rational" explanations which more nearly fit the functional concept of social stratification and social class as discussed below.

The Functional Concept

Spencer's organic analogy likened evolving society to a developing embryo; by differentiation he referred to the analog of tissue differentiation—not only a "becoming different," but changing from a generalized to a specialized function in the process. Durkheim suggested a similar explanation for the evolution of society by means of the "division of labor." And Sorokin has commented that if specialization and the division of labor have not promoted the evolution of society, they have at least permitted its survival. Society is, in short, *functional*.

Two separate economic principles appear to be at work in the functional society. One is that of rewarding those who contribute to the general welfare or, conversely, penalizing those who fail to contribute. The other is the impulse to share goods and privileges with other persons—from dependent infants to all mankind—or, conversely, the wish to prevent certain others from sharing goods or privileges. According to the functionalist, a social system is functional when it provides persons with goods or privileges proportionate to their contributions to the welfare of the valued group or society, and is dysfunctional when it provides goods or services to persons who are not contributing to the welfare of the valued social entity or are in fact working against its welfare.

---

[15] Nelson W. Polsby, *Community Power and Political Theory* (New Haven: Yale University Press, 1963).

[16] *Ibid.*, p. 67.

[17] *Ibid.*, p. 138.

[18] Arthur J. Vidich and Joseph Bensman, *Small Town in Mass Society: Class, Power and Religion in a Rural Community* (Princeton, N.J.: Princeton University Press, 1958), pp. 94–95.

The functionalist concept of social stratification is an extension of the single-structure concept. The index of general social status or of social class most likely to be used in conjunction with the functionalist concept is, of course, occupation. The relics of feudalism in the form of prestige accorded to property-holders or, at the other extreme, of taxes on land and other property rather than entirely on income, are socially dysfunctional in contemporary industrial society. The distribution of the population into positions whose prestige and rewards are commensurate with their contributions to social welfare and their scarcity in the population comprises the basic structure of society.[19]

Critics of the functionalist concept of social stratification have been numerous, and the literature on the subject has become quite voluminous, with four articles on the topic appearing in one issue of the *American Sociological Review*.[20] Tumin alone has contributed more than half a dozen articles to the controversy.

Among the criticisms of the functionalist concept are its failure to incorporate provisions for mobility,[21] "its assumption that members of a social system rationally calculate an individual's contribution to the system and then impartially and accurately appraise status in terms of these calcula-

tions,[22] and its "unwarranted assumption of a well integrated social system."[23]

The functionalist concept of social structure is apparently a model of all the positions in a society, arranged in something like a gigantic corporation chart. It assumes the massive, monolithic social structure discussed above, and adds that it is rational as well as historical in its ordering.

The Continuum Concept

The geometric model for an ordered or metric scale is usually a straight line extending from a point representing the lowest-ordered case or possibility to a point representing the highest-ordered case or possibility. Such a model is called a *continuum* and the end-points are called its *poles*.

Cuber and Kenkel observed that in American society "there are several privilege, power, and status ranges, more or less continuous from top to bottom, with no clear lines of demarcation."[24] They continue:

As everyone knows, students of differential rank have "discovered" that the possession of wealth and income, family background, education, ownership of status-giving goods, and prestige give a person or family ranking in the local community or even in the nation. However, when we *measure* each of these attributes, a *continuous series of data emerges*. . . the alleged bases or criteria for ranking (whether prestige or power or privilege is focused upon) mostly do not show significant *correlations* with one another. . . . It seems for these and other reasons that we are on more sound theoretical ground as social scientists if we proceed on the assumption that the American ranking system is more

[19] See Kingsley Davis and Wilbert E. Moore, "Some Principles of Stratification," *American Sociological Review*, X (April, 1945), 242–249, for the original statement of the functionalist position.

[20] Harold Fallding, "Functional Analysis in Sociology"; Wilbert E. Moore, "But Some Are More Equal than Others"; Melvin Tumin, "On Inequality"; and Wilbert E. Moore "Rejoinder," *American Sociological Review*, XXVIII (February, 1963).

[21] Dennis H. Wrong, "The Functional Theory of Stratification: Some Neglected Considerations," *American Sociological Review*, XXIV (December, 1959), 772–782.

[22] Robert A. Ellis and Thomas C. Keedy, Jr., "Three Dimensions of Status: A Study of Academic Prestige," *Pacific Sociological Review*, III (Spring, 1950), 23–28.

[23] Werner Cohn, "Social Status and the Ambivalence Hypothesis," *American Sociological Review*, XXV (August, 1960), 508–509.

[24] John F. Cuber and William F. Kenkel, *Social Stratification in the United States* (New York: Appleton-Century-Crofts, 1954), p. 25.

accurately conceived of as a continuum than as a set of discrete categories.[25]

Critics of the continuum concept of social class and social stratification argue that status categories may be indexes of social class, but they do not comprise social class or social strata.[26] Although he addressed his remarks to those who hold the functional concept, Buckley spoke also to the supporters of the continuum concept when he said, "The current functional theory of stratification is not a theory of stratification at all but something that more closely resembles a theory of certain aspects of social differentiation and hierarchical organization—a distinction, our argument insists, that is not merely one of arbitrary terminology."[27]

Cuber and Kenkel answer such critics by saying, "The authors reject the pedantry which holds that for the sake of consistency we should now not use the term *social class* and should recommend that others do not. We see no objection to the use of the verbal convention *social class*, so long as the reader and the listener are aware of the proximate nature of the reference and of the essentially statistical character of the construct."[28]

It is clear from the material cited here that the continuum concept of social class and social stratification is distinct from some, if not all, of the other concepts presented.

The Class Boundary Concept

Landecker felt that neither a strictly structural concept of social class nor a continuum concept is adequate by itself to deal with the description of a community. Implicit in his work is his view of classes or strata as population categories with characteristic attributes. To this concept, however, he adds the notion that different ranking systems may distribute the population into differently ordered categories. In his empirical study of Detroit these ranking systems were occupational, income, educational, and ethnic-racial. Thus persons in the highest category in one rank system can be preponderantly in the second highest category in another rank system. Where a congruency of rank occurs or where there is a break at the same point in all four rank systems, so that all individuals in every system fall into a cluster of ranks entirely above or entirely below the break, Landecker says a class boundary exists.[29] In Detroit, Landecker found that:

The measurement of class boundaries attempted in this investigation reveal the presence of one major class boundary, by which the topmost strata are divided from the bulk of the population. Below this elite boundary, the dominant feature is a status gradation of considerable continuity, aside from a few minor indentations. The view suggested by these findings is that neither the class structure nor the status continuum hypothesis takes precedence over the other, but rather that each is appropriate to a different portion of the total system of stratification.[30]

The most obvious criticism of Landecker's work is that his concept is in reality a structural one and that his empirical findings revealed the presence of two classes with differential status distributions in each. Thus his findings could readily be interpreted to support the Marxian concept of classes as economic conflict groups, or Sjoberg's empirical observation that a two-class system has been the rule throughout most of history.

[25] *Ibid.*, pp. 26–27.
[26] Cf. Robert A. Ellis, "The Continuum Theory of Social Stratification: A Critical Note," *Sociology and Social Research*, XLII (March-April, 1958), 269–273.
[27] Walter Buckley, "Social Stratification and the Functional Theory of Social Differentiation," *American Sociological Review*, XXIII (August, 1958), 370.
[28] Cuber and Kenkel, *op. cit.*, pp. 307–308.
[29] Werner S. Landecker, "Class Boundaries," *American Sociological Review*, XXV (December, 1960), 868–877.
[30] *Ibid.*, p. 877.

The Interest-Group Concept

This concept is generally identified with Marxian thought. When defined accordingly, social classes are diffuse collectivities of people, related to one another by their common interests. Such an interest may be positive; that is, it may be a goal or value (or set of goals or values) the collectivity shares because the goals or values are such an integral part of the way of life or shared sentiment structure of the members that they are intertwined with their philosophy of life itself. The term "interest" seems mild as a label for such a powerful tie. The interest of such a collectivity may also be defensive. That is, it may exist in the impulse to conserve and protect the values—and, according to Marx, subsistence and even life itself—of the collectivity from exploitation or destruction by others.

Interest groups are viewed as more basically integrated with the life patterns of collectivities than political parties. They are a definite part of the sentiment structure of the members of the collectivity.[31] Nor does interest have as its object values such human universals as survival and sex, or even tribal or national philosophies or attitudes. An interest group in this sense is never a completely self-sufficient entity. It invariably requires the presence of other interest groups, or at least a social host for its parasitic or symbiotic nurture.

The interest-group concept of social class has both similarities to and differences from some of the other concepts mentioned. The reader should not misunderstand the presentation of these concepts by inferring that they are mutually exclusive. Rather, they are orientations toward, or perspectives of, terms that have been widely used for a long period of time.

The Interactional Concept

The interactional concept of social class sees social class as one aspect of interpersonal relationships. Encounters of the person with others must involve some categorizing of both self and others if they are to have any definition or any cognitive referent.

In the interpersonal concept, social class is a situational phenomenon. It is possible for a person to see himself as identified with one social class when he is in interaction with one group of persons, and of another social class when interacting with another group. To the interactionist, it is not only impossible to interpret, but ridiculous to try to interpret the social behavior of a human being except as it relates to the behavior of some other human being. The construction of an "objective" person is not possible, although this does not prevent generalization based on the statements of a number of observers. The only *truths* about Person A are the "truths" upon which Person B operates. This concept is vaguely reminiscent of and analogous to the notion of physical relativity. Russell remarked that "measurements of distances and times do not directly reveal properties of the things measured, but relations of the things to the measurer."[32]

To the interactionist, whatever "structures" may appear in society, whatever systems may exist in social phenomena, are the result of the behaviors, habits, and understandings— not to overlook the memories and feelings—of particular persons. Skinner hypothesizes that:

... It is only because the behavior of the individual is important to society that society in turn makes it important to the individual. The individual becomes aware of what he is doing only after society has

---

[31] "Sentiment" is used here in the strongest sense of the term. Cf. Alexander H. Leighton, *My Name is Legion: Foundations for a Theory of*

Man in Relation to Culture (New York: Basic Books, Inc., 1959), pp. 395–415.

[32] Bertrand Russell, *The ABC of Relativity* (New York: New American Library, 1959), p. 76.

UPPER-UPPER CLASS / LOWER-UPPER CLASS

UPPER-UPPER CLASS		LOWER-UPPER CLASS
"Old aristocracy"	UU	"Old aristocracy"
"Aristocracy," but not "old"	LU	"Aristocracy," but not "old"
"Nice, respectable people"	UM	"Nice, respectable people"
"Good people, but 'nobody'"	LM	"Good people, but 'nobody'"
	UL	
"Po' whites"	LL	"Po' whites"

UPPER-MIDDLE CLASS / LOWER-MIDDLE CLASS

UPPER-MIDDLE CLASS		LOWER-MIDDLE CLASS
"Society" — "Old families"	UU	"Old aristocracy" (older) — "Broken-down aristocracy" (younger)
"Society" but not "old families"	LU	
"People who should be upper class"	UM	"People who think they are somebody"
"People who don't have much money"	LM	"We poor folk"
	UL	"People poorer than us"
"No' count lot"	LL	"No' count lot"

UPPER-LOWER CLASS / LOWER-LOWER CLASS

UPPER-LOWER CLASS		LOWER-LOWER CLASS
	UU	
	LU	
"Society" or the "folks with money"	UM	"Society" or the "folks with money"
"People who are up because they have a little money"	LM	"Way-high-ups," but not "Society"
"Poor but honest folk"	UL	"Snobs trying to push up"
"Shiftless people"	LL	"People just as good as anybody"

The social perspectives of the social classes. In this diagram, Davis and the Gardners illustrate the way in which definitions of the social classes and the number of classes conceptualized vary with categories of conceptualizers. Source: Allison Davis, Burleigh B. Gardner, and Mary R. Gardner, *Deep South* (Chicago: The University of Chicago Press, 1941), p. 65. Copyright 1941 by The University of Chicago.

reinforced verbal responses with respect to his behavior as the source of discriminative stimuli. The behavior to be described (the behavior of which one is to be aware) may later recede to the covert level, and (to add a crowning difficulty) so may the verbal response. It is an ironic twist, considering the history of the behavioristic revolution, that as we develop a more effective vocabu- lary for the analysis of behavior we also enlarge the possibilities of awareness, so defined. The psychology of the other one is, after all, a direct approach to "knowing thyself."[33]

[33] B. F. Skinner, "The Operational Analysis of Psychological Terms," *Cumulative Record* (New York: The Macmillan Company, 1959), p. 281.

A Critical Evaluation of Warner's Work in Community Stratification

HAROLD W. PFAUTZ

OTIS DUDLEY DUNCAN

Approximately two decades ago W. L. Warner and his associates went into "Yankee City" to apply the methods of social anthropology to the study of a modern community. In the interim, numerous researches of the Warner school have been reported. With the recent appearance of *Social Class in America*,[1] which purports to clarify the research operations and theoretical position of the group, along with a substantive volume[2] concerning the latest town studied in this tradition, a re-examination of the Warner group's objectives, methods and results is in order.

Previous articles and reviews have evaluated specific researches of this prolific school.[3] This paper raises ques-

Reprinted from Harold W. Pfautz and Otis Dudley Duncan, "A Critical Evaluation of Warner's Work in Community Stratification," *American Sociological Review*, XV, No. 2 (April, 1950), 205–215, by permission of the authors and the American Sociological Association.

---

[1] W. Lloyd Warner, Marchia Meeker, and Kenneth Eells, *Social Class in America* (Chicago: Science Research Associates, 1949).

[2] W. Lloyd Warner *et al.*, *Democracy in Jonesville* (New York: Harper & Row, Publishers, 1949).

[3] See reviews by C. Wright Mills, *American Sociological Review*, VII (April, 1942), 263–271; Kingsley Davis, *American Journal of Sociology*, XLVIII (January, 1943), 511–513; and Helen M. Wolfle, *Science*, CX (October 28, 1949), 456; Warner's formulations on caste have been adequately dealt with in the critical literature, and are not considered here; see Oliver C. Cox, "Race and Caste: A Distinction," *American Journal of Sociology*, L (March, 1945), 360–368; and Maxwell R. Brooks, "American Class and Caste: An Appraisal," *Social Forces*, XXV (December, 1946), 207–211.

tions about the endeavor as a whole, particularly the treatment of social stratification, which has been the central problem in all of the studies. The first question we wish to raise is that of the *relevance* of the work of Warner and his associates to the objectives they have set themselves. Second, we wish to consider the reliability, validity, and pertinence of their methodological operations. And finally, we propose to assess the adequacy of their conceptual formulations, in terms of the significance and implications of the questions they have asked of the data.

On the Objectives of the Warner Researches

Warner has described the *Yankee City Series* as a "practical attempt to use the techniques and ideas which have been developed by social anthropologists in primitive society in order to obtain a more accurate understanding of an American community."[4] The ultimate success of the venture would seem to rest on the validity of the explicit assumption that studies of preliterate communities are a prerequisite for the understanding of modern communities, and the implicit assumption that the methods employed to study the former are equally applicable to the latter. But this program did not only aspire to an

---

[4] W. Lloyd Warner and Paul S. Lunt, *The Social Life of a Modern Community*, Yankee City Series, Vol. 1 (New Haven: Yale University Press, 1941), p. 14.

enrichment of the methodology of community analysis and the multiplication of discrete monographic studies. Rather it was conceived as providing a basis for substantive *generalizations* of two kinds. In the first place, Warner looked toward a "comparative sociology" of a sort made familiar by the work of Hobhouse, Wheeler, and Ginsberg. Thus Warner's early articles refer to "types of societies" relative to such analytic dimensions as "degree of complexity" and type of "integrating structure."[5] This presumably involves the observation of a considerable number of communities in the hope that a subsequent comparative analysis will eventuate in "laws or principles" of social behavior and structure.

The second type of generalization from anthropological community studies which Warner proposed was no less than to "see and understand the larger design of American life." The specific community is but a "laboratory" in which it is proposed to study "the social structure governing American capitalism."[6]

As to the first objective—the contribution of further materials for a comparative study of communities—there can be little question about the theoretical relevance of the researches, provided that the projected "comparative sociology" will be concerned with those same dimensions of social structure which the several studies have emphasized. Here the pertinent question is merely that of the efficacy of the methology advanced.

But much more serious demands are placed on the data in connection with the second objective, i.e., when the level of abstraction becomes that of American communities in general, or the whole pattern of "American thought and action." Viewed in this light, the Warner researches are proceeding on the basis of assumptions as to the nature of modern society which are directly incompatible with the actual character of that society, as revealed by some of its most eminent students.[7] It is difficult on the basis of the available evidence to square Warner's lyric observation that "All Americans are in Jonesville" with the picture of the urban way of life which modern sociology has built up. Whereas in an urbanized society social contacts are depicted by sociologists as typically impersonal, anonymous, and rational, the community studied by Warner has been described by another observer in terms more appropriate to the rural pole of the rural-urban typology:

In a town of 6,000 people, everything that is done, or not done, and then talked about tends to be personalized. One person does something at some time; other persons know about it, find out about it, and above all, gossip about it, and then pass judgment on it.[8]

More is involved here than the tendency shared with many American sociologists to confine studies to the local community level for the sake of ease in gathering data.[9] The traditional anthropological perspective of the

[5] W. Lloyd Warner and Allison Davis, "A Comparative Study of American Caste," Ch. VIII in *Race Relations and the Race Problem*, ed. Edgar T. Thompson (Durham, N. C.: Duke University Press, 1939).

[6] *Democracy in Jonesville, op. cit.*, pp. xiv–xv.

[7] Cf. Robert E. Park, Ernest W. Burgess, and Roderick D. McKenzie, *The City* (Chicago: University of Chicago Press, 1925); Louis Wirth, "The Urban Society and Civilization," in *Eleven Twenty-Six*, ed. Louis Wirth (Chicago: University of Chicago Press, 1940); and Georg Simmel, "The Metropolis and Mental Life" in *Contemporary Society; Selected Readings*, 8th ed. (Chicago: University of Chicago Bookstore, 1939).

[8] August B. Hollingshead, *Elmtown's Youth* (New York: John Wiley & Sons, Inc., 1949), p. 44.

[9] Cf. Edward Shils, *The Present State of American Sociology* (New York: The Free Press, 1948).

Warner group together with their studied indifference to previous sociological literature leads to a failure to distinguish between "community" on the one hand and "society" on the other. American society—a vastly complex ecological, political, and economic entity—cannot be described adequately, in Sumner's formula, as comprised of "small groups scattered over a territory." Yet this is what is implied in an effort to derive an account of the larger unity, either by way of a comparative analysis of Jonesville and other small communities, or by direct extrapolation of the Jonesville findings.[10]

On Some Methodological Problems of the Warner Researches

In prosecuting the major interest in the social stratification of the community, Warner has developed two techniques, both of which are used for the basic research tasks of ascertaining the "social class configuration" and placing individuals within the social class system. The first technique is termed "evaluated participation" (EP). It involves the content analysis of "indirect interviews" to "discover" the social class system, as well as to get at the "social participation" and "status reputation" of community members to whom references are made in the body of the interviews. Data from this source are summarized on "status personality cards" and form the basis for an "estimate of class position." The second technique, an objective "index of status characteristics" (ISC), is described as a "measure of socio-economic status." This index is the weighted sum of the individual's scores on four seven-point rating scales de-

signed to evaluate, respectively, occupation, source of income, house type, and dwelling area. EP is thought to be the most valid and reliable method for identifying the social classes in a community and for placing community members in them. The ISC is considered only an approximate method if employed alone. However, if EP has previously been used on an "adequate" (sic) sample, a conversion table can be constructed to obtain the "social class equivalents" of ISC scores.

Despite a plethora of materials illustrating these techniques, some very basic points are left entirely opaque: What are the actual criteria for summarizing the interview data on the "social personality cards" (which are the basis for class placement by EP)? What use is made of the several rating scales for the "social levels" of participation by family, clique, church, and association? Do these rating procedures really represent the evaluations of "those who interact in the social system of the community?"[11]—or are they rather the subject judgments of the analyst?—and if the latter, what criteria are used for placing individuals on these scales? The fact is that these basic steps in arriving at EP are never clarified. No independent investigator could use or apply the technique with confidence that his results would approximate those that Warner would get with the same materials.

Since no reliability coefficients are presented, and the problem is not referred to, we do not even know whether the initiated adept at these techniques get reliable results. This problem is perhaps rather less serious for ISC than for EP—though even the ISC formula requires the establishment of subjective rating categories by the investigator for two of its four

[10] Cf. Robert Bierstedt, "The Limitations of Anthropological Methods in Sociology," *American Journal of Sociology*, LIV (July, 1948), 22–30.

[11] *Social Class in America, op. cit.*, p. 35.

component scales, i.e., house type and dwelling area. But the reliability problem must be quite serious for EP, which is not even claimed to be an "objective" method.

There is likewise no technical discussion of the validity of these two indices of social class. This is perhaps not a serious criticism, since in any case the utmost in validity that could be claimed for either index is that it yields an operational definition of social class. The validity problem enters obliquely in the extended treatment (over one-third of the methodological volume) of the predictive relationship between ISC and EP. In deriving EP the analyst is warned "to be sure that mention of the characteristics of the ISC are eliminated in order to guarantee that only Evaluated Participation is being considered."[12] The import of this procedural injunction is not clear. It is presumably offered as a device to prevent spurious correlation from entering into the establishment of a predictive relationship between ISC and EP. But such independence in the operational sense is factitious, for we have Warner's own evidence that members of the community "evaluate" each other, in part, on the basis of such "status characteristics" as dwelling area. Actually, it is never clear whether Warner regards ISC and EP as two different orders of data, or simply two different techniques for getting at an operational definition of social class. The problem of the validity of either index is therefore bound up with the whole conceptualization of the research, which we discuss below.

Perhaps the most serious methodological criticisms that can be leveled at the Warner researches arise in connection with the problem of sampl-

ing. Despite the statistical orientation of many of the studies, this problem has in no sense been adequately treated.[13] The obvious gap in the reporting of the researches can perhaps be blamed on the anthropological background of the Warner group—as Wirth has pointed out, in very few instances do anthropological monographs even take the trouble to delimit the universe on which they are reporting.[14] Even "rural" Jonesville, however, is relatively complex in comparison to the typical primitive community; this necessitates considerably more circumspection in case selection than has been exhibited in the Warner researches. Inasmuch as EP, which necessarily depends on interview materials, is considered the most valid method, it is incumbent on the investigator to be quite specific regarding the sampling problem. Yet at no point in either study are the relative sizes, the methods of selection, or the characteristics of the samples referred to or discussed.

All the results in the methodological volume are derived from a study of 339 cases, which cover about one-sixth of Jonesville's 2,095 families. The major criterion for the selection of these cases seems to have been merely that data on both EP and ISC were available for the individuals concerned. A second criterion was the certainty of the EP estimate of social class position, although there is no indication of how "certainty" was defined or measured. Though the report does not try to

---

[13] Sampling instructions and information given about the samples merely state the problem; for example: "Establish class levels by Social-Class Configuration from a number of interviews with several people." (*Social Class in America, op. cit.*, p. 116.)

[14] For Wirth's observation, see Herbert Blumer, *An Appraisal of Thomas and Znaniecki's The Polish Peasant in Europe and America,* Social Science Research Council Bulletin 44 (1939), p. 129.

---

[12] *Ibid.,* p. 115.

evaluate the representative character of this sample, a few stray bits of data appear which strongly indicate that it is *not* representative, and is in fact seriously biased toward the upper reaches of the stratification structure. Thus, the "upper" class comprises 13 per cent of the 339 sample cases (or 21 per cent of the 209 Old American cases), but only 3 per cent of the total population of Jonesville. Income data are given for only 108 cases, but of these 63 per cent have incomes classed as "above average" or higher. Finally, a total of 53 per cent of 208 cases on whom occupational ratings are given falls into the upper three categories of professionals and proprietors of large businesses, semi-professionals and smaller officials of large businesses, and clerks and kindred workers. Whereas Census figures for "Jonesville"[15] for 1940 show that 35 per cent of employed persons are classified as professional workers; semi-professional workers; proprietors, managers and officials (except farm); and clerical, sales and kindred workers. This figure, while not exactly comparable with Warner's, is comparable enough to disclose a wide discrepancy between sample and population.

This demonstrated bias in the sample raises serious questions about the conclusions on the accuracy of predicting EP from ISC, when the latter is applied to the whole population, rather than just within the sample. These suspicions are at least partially justified by a study of class differences in the errors of prediction. The discussion and analysis of prediction errors certainly is one of the most important aspects of the research, yet it is treated with the least imagination of any topic. It would seem patent that the major interest should be centered here, not only because the whole area of social stratification is shot through with complicated relativities, but also because the ultimate interest is in correctly identifying the members of each class, as well as minimizing errors of class placement for the community as a whole. Warner, however, virtually neglects the discussion of prediction errors by class, and instead devotes the bulk of the discussion to errors of placements by "grades" *within* classes.[16] In a brief paragraph devoted to class errors, it is simply reported that the greatest percentage error occurred in the upper-lower class. Though the authors give no table of prediction errors by social class, such information can be compiled from data given at two different places in the monograph. The column, "percentage error," in Table 1 is our own computation, and represents,

TABLE 1   **Errors in Predicting Class Level (as Determined by EP) from ISC Scores, for the Sample of Old Americans**

Social class (as determined by EP)	Number in sample	Number of errors[a]	Per- centage error
Upper	44	8	18
Upper-middle	50	11	22
Lower-middle	44	3	7
Upper-lower	28	9	32
Lower-lower	43	2	5
All Classes	209	33	16

a The number of errors is given for only 200 of the 209 cases in the sample.

SOURCE: Data abstracted from W. Lloyd Warner, M. Meeker, and K. Eell, *Social Class in America*, (Cicago: Science Research Associates, 1949), Tables 10 and 30.

[15] The actual name of Jonesville has been stated in print, though not in any of the research reports.

[16] The concept of "grade" seems to be purely operational and arbitrary, being introduced, apparently, to get the data in a form amenable to correlation analysis. Warner seems to recognize the largely factitious character of the "grades": "The grades assigned by evaluated participation do not always prove valid, but they are useful in training the status analyst to exercise care (*sic*) and continually to refine his analysis" (*Social Class in America, op. cit.*, p. 97.)

if anything, an understatement of the errors, since the 33 cases incorrectly predicted are drawn from only 200 of the 209 cases for which the class distribution is given. While Warner gives considerable favorable attention to the over-all error of 16 per cent, it is obvious that such an average is misleading since the error is not at all evenly distributed by class. For three of the five classes the percentage error exceeds this average figure, and it is twice the average in the case of the "upper-lower" class.[17] Incidentally, the "upper-lower" is the most numerous class in the total population, though not in this unrepresentative sample. The over-all error of prediction would, therfore, be substantially greater than the reported 16 per cent, if the total population were considered rather than the sample alone. It might also be noted that the monograph makes the barest reference to another crucial aspect of the sampling problem—namely the almost invariable loss in predictive accuracy involved in applying an instrument developed on one sample to another.[18] Altogether it would appear that unscientific sampling practice vitiates to a considerable extent the claims made for the ISC as an instrument for determining class level by the criterion of EP.

A final observation along methodological lines concerns the feasibility of the techniques recommended in the situations for which they are prescribed. It is claimed that both the methods, EP and ISC, "can be used in any kind of community."[19] But imagine the plight of an investigator starting out, manual in hand, to do a study of stratification in, say Detroit. He would find the problem of sampling left largely to his own imagination, given only the erroneous guidance that "city directories are excellent sources."[20] Supposing his sample were "well distributed throughout the city," how would he fare with "rating by matched agreements" which presumes that "many of the same names appear in two or more informants' interviews?"[21] (Incidentally, this is the only method for which comparable ratings by two or more persons are presented in the text.) While these and other difficulties in applying the methods to metropolitan areas are patent, it is curious that no exposition of them is given, despite the experience with "systematic studies from coast to coast, in cities large and small. . . ."[22] While "segments of the Chicago population"[23] have been studied with ISC, yielding results of admittedly problematical value, no such experience is mentioned for EP—and on the face of the matter, the latter technique is obviously impractical and impossible except in a community of restricted size and with predominantly primary contacts.

On the Conceptualization of the Warner Researches

The concept of class has been one of the most ambiguous in the sociologist's vocabulary. There are two major reasons for the present lack of consensus on its definition. On the one hand, it is a generic term, covering a wide variety of phenomena, operations, and

---

[17] Hollingshead likewise reports the greatest percentage of disagreements on the ratings of individuals in "Class IV" (*Elmtown's Youth, op. cit.*, pp. 39, 41.)

[18] Cf. Lloyd E. Ohlin and Otis Dudley Duncan, "The Efficiency of Prediction in Criminology," *American Journal of Sociology*, LIV (March, 1949), 441–451; Paul Horst *et al.*, *The Prediction of Personal Adjustment*, Social Science Research Council Bulletin 48 (1941), pp. 104–106.

[19] *Social Class in America, op. cit.*, p. 36.
[20] *Ibid.*, p. 227.
[21] *Ibid.*, p. 37.
[22] *Ibid.*, p. 24.
[23] *Ibid.*, p. 201.

purposes for different writers. On the other hand, it is also a term which is shot through with historical, political, and social connotations which often have served to make it more of a slogan than a research tool. Warner's formulations of the nature and significance of the concept reflect both these difficulties.

His position is an excellent example of a most unfortunate trend in contemporary stratification research—that of making a particular definition, specific in its *denotative* properties, serve a more general purpose in its *connotative* usages. Thus Warner employs the term in the very restricted sense of "social" class, locating individuals primarily with reference to a prestige hierarchy ("social reputation"), but in discussing the significance of the findings he implies that its use in this sense covers the ground generally. This is exemplified in the effort to discount Marxian analysis on the basis of the conceptualization and findings in Yankee City and Jonesville.

There can be no quarrel with the explicit use of the concept "social class" to refer to hierarchical status levels relative to such criteria as "social participation" and "social reputation." However, there are obviously other alternatives for "classifying" a population— there is class and class. And the "social" classes with which Warner is concerned are not necessarily the same phenomena with which Mosca, or Marx, or Veblen, for example, were concerned. In this connection the effort to discount other students' work makes us suspicious of the possible ideological implications of the whole endeavor. It is certainly true that one's social class (in Warner's sense), plays an important part in one's life; further, that such classes are an important functional aspect of local community structure. It may be said, however, just as T. H. Marshall re-marked of Marx's formulation, "This does not exhaust the topic of stratification."

Even a superficial examination of the literature on social stratification provides a basis for characterizing two quite different approaches to the problem of class. On the one hand there exists a tendency for many theorists to consider class relative to the distribution of *power* in the economic and/or political sense. On the other hand, much stratification theory and research centers on the phenomenon of *prestige*, classes being located relative to a hierarchy of esteem rather than power. That a fundamental distinction as regards *types* of classes is involved can be seen from certain other correlative facets of these two perspectives. Thus, whereas research on power classes seems to be done on the more abstract national level,[24] prestige class data are usually obtained from and referred to local communities.[25] Again, the power type of class is usually pictured as a mass phenomenon—an unorganized aggregate— while the prestige type is usually thought of as associational in character, having the attributes of a society. Power classes are generally assumed to come into existence on the basis of identity of economic and/or political "interests," and interclass relations are studied pri-

---

[24] E.g., Richard Centers, *The Psychology of Social Classes* (Princeton, N.J.: Princeton University Press, 1949); Goetz A. Briefs, *The Proletariat* (New York: McGraw-Hill Book Company, 1937); Robert Marjolin, "The Middle Classes in the United States," *Inventories*, Vol. III, ed. C. Bouglé (Paris: Alcan, 1939) mimeo, translated by S. L. Thrupp for use at the University of Chicago.)

[25] E.g., Charles Booth, *Life and Labor of the People in London*, 17 vols. (London: Macmillan, 1902–4); Harold F. Kaufman, "Defining Prestige Rank in a Rural Community," *Sociometry*, VIII (May, 1945), 199–207; John Useem, Pierre Tangent, and Ruth Useem, "Stratification in a Prairie Town," *American Sociological Review*, (June, 1942), 331–342.

marily in terms of conflict. Prestige classes usually are assumed to involve shared attitudes held in common—not simply like attitudes held by individuals. Further, such interclass relations are viewed as essentially accommodative in quality.[26] Finally, whereas homogeneity of social origins is irrelevant in the case of power classes, such homogeneity is regarded as the *sine qua non* of prestige classes. While both approaches seem valuable for their respective insights, the limited relevancies of each should be recognized. A confusion enters in when the protagonists of the prestige class define their concept on the basis of such criteria as intimate association, culture, family, way of life, etc., and then, because they fail to find group closure and intimate participation on the national level, conclude that power classes just do not exist[27]—or, as in the case of Warner, assume that the study of prestige classes encompasses the whole field. Undoubtedly there are relationships between the two types of classes, but this is an empirical question—in fact, a crucial question—yet to be answered by research.

Not only is the substantive character of Warner's classes of limited relevance, but, in the final analysis, since he provides no consistent conceptual scheme, it is also difficult to draw conclusions as to their logical character. At times his social classes are considered real entities; at other times they become simply heuristic constructs; and, at one point in the Jonesville volume, the class structure seems to be regarded as a continuum. As mentioned above (in connection with the use of the seven-point "status level" scale to arrive at EP), there is even some question as to

whether his "social classes" represent the community's or the analyst's evaluations.

There are numerous indications that the principal motivation of many crucial points of the analysis is more a matter of the imposition of a set of categories and the manipulation of a technique than the understanding of what is at stake—the social structure. This point is evidenced by a general tendency to regard any anomalies encountered as being problematic only in a methodological light, rather than from the standpoint of the theory of class structure. There is often a failure to consider the meaning of negative instances, or to consider alternative hypotheses.

For example, it is pointed out that the upper-lower class is least sharply defined and least rigorously related to the status characteristics:—"The upper-lower class, least differentiated from the adjacent levels and hardest to distinguish in the hierarchy, but clearly present [*sic*]."[28] Just how "clearly present" is defined remains a mystery. We suggest, however, that its "visibility"— or the visibility of any class—is not solely a methodological issue. Rather, alternative hypotheses should be considered in the light of the data at this point.

On the one hand, it is theoretically and empirically possible that such a category as "upper-lower" does not, in fact, exist in the sense that the middle, upper, or lower classes do. Halbwachs' study of the standards of living of the working classes offers a basis of just such an interpretation! On the basis of an examination of family budgets, Halbwachs notes the relative lack of development of the "housing need" among the working classes, which is a characteristic setting it off from the upper classes.

---

[26] See especially, Useem *et al.*, *op. cit.*

[27] Dewey Anderson and Percy E. Davidson, *Ballots and the Democratic Class Struggle* (Stanford, Calif.: Stanford University Press, 1943), pp. 250–255.

[28] *Social Class in America, op. cit.*, p. 14.

He concludes that "within the working class sub-divisions of a social character do not appear and the unity of this class remains complete."[29] Whereas with regard to the upper classes,

rather clear intervals separate the prices of lodging [and] to each figure for rental expense are found associated, in the social mind, definite figures for each one of the other expenses [food and clothing]. To these determined standards of living correspond distinct social strata.[30]

On the other hand, the indeterminacy of the "upper-lower" class might be significant in and of itself! It can rather be interpreted as evidence in favor of Parsons' hypothesis as to the vagueness of the "actual scale of stratification" in this country, and further, the functional character of this indeterminacy as a "cushioning mechanism."[31]

That the inspiration of the study is often merely operational and manipulative is indicated by the treatment of findings such as the following:

Symbolic Placement is almost equally sure as a placement technique, but unfortunately (sic), Symbolic Placements are less often used for the lower-middle and upper-lower classes than for the top and bottom levels.[32]

Two points should be made with reference to this sort of data and its interpretation by Warner. In the first place, the material is, in fact, of considerable significance in getting at differential social class perspectives. Therefore it should not be seen as representing simply a methodological impasse. Secondly, such data are evidence for other propositions which might be call-

ed to mind relative to the nature of the phenomena Warner and his people are studying.

Thus, the fact that Symbolic Placements are used primarily for the extremes of the social class hierarchy might lead one to conclude that the "upper-upper" and "lower-lower" classes are more nearly, in Weber's terms, "status groups" than "social classes."[33] The concept of "closure," which is crucial for the structure of status groups, would seem to have little meaning relative to the "middle" classes; whereas the estate-tendencies at the extremes of the social class configuration as well as the "communal" character of the upper-uppers and lower-lowers are obvious from the data at hand.

Another illustration for our argument is the passing off of the reported failure of the ISC to discriminate between upper-uppers and lower-uppers on the basis of the "numerical insignificance" of the upper-upper social class.[34] Obviously the relatively small numbers involved will have little effect from the standpoint of statistics on "overall placement error." On the other hand, if the analysts are primarily concerned (as they insist) with the understanding of the social structure of the community, the importance of the upper-uppers is, of course, in no way proportionate to their relative numbers.[35]

The significance of the general area of Warner's interest and the value of

[29] Maurice Halbwachs, *La Classe Ouvriere et les Niveaux de Vie* (Paris: Alcan, 1913), p. 450.

[30] *Ibid.*, p. 451.

[31] Talcott Parsons, *Essays in Sociological Theory* (New York: The Free Press, 1949), pp. 180–182.

[32] *Social Class in America, op. cit.*, p. 114.

[33] It has already been pointed out by C. Wright Mills (*op. cit.*) that Warner's conceptualization involves a failure to distinguish between status groups and classes; our point is somewhat different.

[34] *Social Class in America, op. cit.*, p. 125.

[35] The failure of the ISC in this connection is further evidence for our proposition as to the status group character of the upper-upper as opposed to the class character of the intermediate categories.

much of his data should not be underestimated. At the same time it is quite obvious that the lack of an insightful set of interrelated questions with which to face the materials makes the final results disappointing. As Speier has pointed out, a theory of social stratification should so define its objective that it may be distinguished from a general theory of the influence of society on behavior.[36] No such distinction is attempted in the Warner volumes, with the result that important facets of the phenomenon of stratification are not brought into focus. As a matter of fact, insofar as social classes are conceived primarily as microscopic societies with distinctive cultures, the general outcome of the studies would seem to be merely a variety of cultural determinism. Thus, in *The Social Life of a Modern Community* there are whole chapters which are nothing but catalogs of culture traits descriptive of each of the several classes, with no attempt to distinguish the structurally crucial from the more or less incidental traits. The net impression is simply that social classes are important in many areas of social life. If the interest is in the phenomenon of stratification, however, of equal importance is information concerning areas in which social classes are not determinative. Only in connection with the bearing of sex on social class does Warner give any evidence of the lack of relevance of social class as "the fundamental integrating structure." He observes that in the case of clique behavior where the exercise of skill is the primary motive, social class is *not* determinative of the associational pattern: —"If social participation is outside the home away from their families the class differences of the participants are more

varied."[37] Since in metropolitan centers a large proportion of male contacts are of this character, this only raises again the question as to the adequacy of the Warner formulation for understanding large and important aspects of our social structure.

The failure to come to grips with the nature of the stratification phenomenon and the lack of interest in developing a coherent body of theory are nowhere more clearly brought out than in regard to the problem of mobility, which is admittedly of central concern. The conclusions (though singularly unstudied) of both the Yankee City and Jonesville researches are that in spite of the existance of social class lines (1) there is, in fact, mobility; and (2) popular belief in the possibility of mobility performs an important function in stabilizing our social organization. Yet it is amazing that we find—in spite of the vast amount of funds expended, time consumed, and materials gathered—not a single figure in any of the studies which bears on the crucial empirical questions of (1) how much mobility in fact takes place, and (2) at what points in the social class system it occurs. Except for some partly inferential data on the assimilation of ethnic groups, the only data cited on mobility are the fictionalized case histories.

In view of the importance of answers to these critical questions, the failure adequately to deal with them indicates inherent weaknesses in the theoretical equipment brought into play in the analysis of the materials. That this question is left unexamined hangs together, of course, with the focus on prestige rather than power classes. The amount and location of mobility is significant primarily as it bears on the probability of certain types of class ac-

[36] Hans Speier, "Social Stratification in the Urban Community," *American Sociological Review*, I (April, 1936), 193–202.

[37] *Social Class in America, op. cit.*, p. 88.

tion,[38] a problem which is relevant in the theoretical context of power classes, but which can scarcely even be formulated in terms of prestige classes. The ideological biases of the Warner enterprises are further revealed in the discussions of the purposes of the methodological volume. Thus it is declared that the status system is being investigated in order that people may learn "where they fit in" and how they may "improve" or "make more tolerable" (*sic*) their present positions. Such techniques are regarded as a prerequisite for "adjustment"—a vacuum value of the first order![39]

Yet to live successfully and *adaptively*, in America, every one of us must *adjust* his life to each of these contradictions. . . . It is the hope of the authors that this book will provide a corrective instrument which will permit men and women better to evaluate their social situations and thereby better to *adapt themselves to social reality* and fit their dreams and aspirations to what is possible.[40]

The crucial question at this point in the analysis is, of course, *whose reality?*

Here again, the data are informative if significant questions are asked of them. One of the major problems in class theory is the relation of objective position to subjective perspective. And Warner's data do, in fact, show that as one's social class differs, the image of the social structure one has also varies. Even fairly simple Jonesville is heter-

ogeneous enough to exhibit a lack of consensus as to the number of classes and the criteria of status. But, the "reality" which Warner has chosen to abstract and the criteria which he uses for ranking purposes can be shown to be biased toward the upper reaches of the social class system. For example, while the materials from the upper and middle ranges clearly stress the criteria of social participation and acceptance, Warner himself says the following of the upper-lower image:

He sees class as purely a matter of income and power. . . . He draws a distinction between powerful land owners and wealthy industrialists and professional people, but he puts all of them at the top. . . . His class lines are less clearly drawn than those of the other.[41]

Interestingly enough, Lundberg makes the same sort of incidental observation in an experimental study of alternate rating techniques:

The large disagreement between the janitor and the banker on the last four cases appears to have been largely due to an admitted tendency on the part of the janitor to consider primarily *income and property* in his rating, whereas the banker gave more weight to the instruction which emphasizes "how comfortably people live in their homes and in their community."[42]

Obviously the janitor's criteria for rating people in the community are *different* from those of the banker. Observations of this sort should suggest a problematization of the question of social class in terms of its relativities, rather that an attempt to impose a monolithic "class structure" on the data. Both Warner and Lundberg, however, regard the disagreement among raters as purely a methodological problem and

---

[38] Cf. Francis D. Wormuth, "Class Struggle," Indiana University Publication, Social Science Series No. 4, 1946; Elbridge Sibley, "Some Demographic Clues to Stratification," *American Sociological Review*, VII (June, 1942), 322–30; John W. Bennett and Melvin M. Tumin, *Social Life* (New York: Alfred A. Knopf, Inc., 1948), Chap. 29.

[39] A characterization proposed in William L. Kolb, "Sociologically Established Family Norms and Democratic Values," *Social Forces*, XXVI (May, 1948), 451–456.

[40] *Social Class in America, op. cit.*, p. 5 (emphasis added).

[41] *Ibid.*, p. 57.

[42] George A. Lundberg, "The Measurement of Socioeconomic Status," *American Sociological Review*, V (February, 1940), p. 32 (emphasis added).

fail to perceive its theoretical relevance.

A bias toward upper and middle class criteria of status is also evident in *Deep South* where the "structure" of a class is defined in terms of "the interrelationships between . . . families and cliques, in such informal activities as visiting, dances [*sic*], receptions [*sic*], teas [*sic*], and larger informal affairs [*sic*]."[43]

Or consider Warner's use of "house type" as a measure of social status. Halbwachs' materials are again pertinent. We have already mentioned the significant conclusion on the lack of development of the "housing need" among members of the working class. On the other hand, regarding the upper class, he points out that "with respect to external indices of wealth, the housing expense is most often in the foreground." While not denying that variations exist in the quality of housing among the working class, Halbwachs contends that the working class "has not yet become conscious of the social importance of lodging."[44] This discrepancy between upper and working class is further discussed in reference to differential culture patterns involving family organization, relations among families, and family expenditures. While this argument can be extended only tentatively to American society at present, the presence of such a strong hypothesis in the literature should suggest the relativity of "status symbols" and the necessity of empirical inquiry into their discriminatory character at all levels of stratification. Warner's procedure bypasses this whole problematization, and in effect, by arbitrarily taking "house type" as a criterion of rank, he chooses to regard the upper class view as "real"

rather than as class determined. This matter of the class-bias of the central conceptual apparatus is, of course, a much more serious weakness of the Warner researches than the statistical bias in case selection, which we noted above.

Conclusion

In summary, we believe we have demonstrated (1) that the type of study which Warner and his associates have developed is to a considerable degree not relevant to their announced objective of portraying the stratification structure of American society; (2) that technical deficiencies in the execution of their studies considerably weaken the support claimed for their findings; that their methods are not yet proved to satisfy scientific requirements of reliability and communicability and are, further, patently inapplicable in some of the situations they are recommended for; and (3) that their conceptual formulations are inadequate to account even for their own findings, are theoretically uninformed in relation to the existing literature on social stratification, and further, are ideologically suspect.

That the Warner researches fall short in these respects is in some degree attributable to the general weaknesses of of the "anthropological approach" to contemporary complex societies, which have been elsewhere called to the attention of sociologists.[45] The seeming sufficiency of this approach has served to keep the Warner group isolated from a considerable body of relevant speculation and research on contemporary social stratification, and has led to a failure to discern the crucial problems which these studies have raised. This same one-sidedness probably accounts

---

[43] Allison Davis, Burleigh B. Gardner, and Mary R. Gardner, *Deep South* (Chicago: The University of Chicago Press, 1941), p. 59.

[44] Halbwachs, *op. cit.*, pp. 451–452.

[45] Cf. Bierstedt, *op. cit.*

also for the defective standards of scientific reporting which mar all the published monographs.

Despite the obvious character of our critical remarks, we are somewhat concerned to note that Warner's formulations have by and large been accepted uncritically into a great many sociological texts (as being, apparently, very "teachable") and into the everyday patois of practicing sociologists. There are notable, but seemingly uninfluential, exceptions. While sociologists have reacted quite unfavorably to the zoological approach to sex (Kinsey), they have apparently not exercised equal acumen with regard to the materials under review. We look hopefully, therefore, to the improvement of standards in this regard—even more hopefully, of course, to the execution of superior research in this area on the part of sociologists who can certainly profit by thoughtful examination of the Warner efforts.

Reference Groups and Class Orientations

MELVIN M. TUMIN   ARNOLD FELDMAN

There are widespread inequalities in Puerto Rico. These range from the most objectively measurable items, such as income, to the most subjective issues, such as how much one enjoys the good opinion of one's neighbor. While the objective inequalities are more uniformly recognized and admitted, there is some persistent denial of inequality on the subjective matters. The subjective denial takes the form of an expressed sense of the fairness of the society; it is also indicated by a strong identification of persons in all classes with the present policies and future plans of the society. There is discontent, to be sure, and a substantial amount by any system of reckoning. But not much of this discontent takes the form of a desire or demand for revolutionary changes in the present organization of the society or its leadership.

One of the surest signs that the discontent does not take this form is the vigor with which lower class adults express their intentions to do what they can in the existing society to allow their children more school, and hence better jobs and income and more comfortable lives than they themselves have had. In short, there is striving *within* the existing and emerging network of social institutions, focused primarily on parents' hopes for their children.

The foregoing facts taken alone may give one a picture of a thoroughly harmonious society, where there is a minimum of ill will, where sharp differences in life chances and levels of comfort do not overly perturb anyone, and where the majority of men admire and respect each other. This is obviously an unbalanced and hence untrue picture. Social relations and the different views of life among Puerto Ricans are by no means uniformly benign and agreeable. Indeed, considering the numerous reasons men could find to disagree with each other and be discontent with their fates, there is an extraordinary amount of mutual give and take. But there is undeniably, as well, a pervasive awareness that men

Reprinted from Melvin M. Tumin with Arnold S. Feldman, *Social Class and Social Change in Puerto Rico* (Princeton, N.J.: Princeton University Press, 1961), pp. 185–201, by permission of the authors and the publisher.

are grouped into social units which are sharply distinguishable from each other by, and often in basic competition for, the rewards the society has to offer. The evidence for these statements comes from the answers given by Puerto Ricans to the following series of questions.

"Who are the people," we asked,

1. "Who are in the same social class as you;
2. With whom you feel most comfortable;
3. Who lead the same kind of life as you;
4. To whom you can most easily confide intimate matters;
5. Who most respect you;
6. Whose opinions about your character you most value;
7. Whose opinions and ideas you most respect;
8. Whom you most distrust;
9. Who most disrespect you;
10. Who lead the kind of life you would like your children to enjoy?"

Five possible answers to each question were allowed. The identified group could be located in the upper, middle or lower part of the three-part class ladder; or, the respondent could say that *all people* liked him, or that *no one* liked him. We call the first three responses "class-oriented," in the sense that one social stratum or another is used as the reference; we call the two last answers (all or none) "nonclass oriented." With these terms, we can see from Table 1 what per cent of the people in each of the five educational strata gave class-oriented responses to these questions.

Two things are clear. The majority of each class gives class-oriented responses with virtually no differences among them in this regard. Defining class consciousness as the frequency with which class-oriented responses are preferred to others, the strong suggestion here is that about an equal amount of class consciousness exists at all class levels in Puerto Rico.

TABLE 1   Frequency of "Class-Oriented" Responses Given by Members of Five Different Educational Strata to Ten Questions Concerning Reference Groups

Years of school completed	Total responses	Total class-oriented responses	Per cent of class-oriented responses
0	2390	1810	75.73
1–4	2860	2090	73.07
5–8	2230	1677	75.20
9–12	1650	1201	72.79
13+	700	492	70.28

Because of the way in which the questions and possible answers were constructed, some discount must be made of the total per cent in each class who gave class-oriented responses. But the fact that almost one fourth of each class denied the significance of class as a point of reference in social relations signifies that it was not at all difficult or impossible to give nonclass answers. Moreover, that the percentage is about the same in each class shows decisively that the ability to think in terms of "class" was not dependent on the kind of verbal abilities or sophistication one might attribute only to the better educated people.

Who Are the People in the Same Social Class?

With whom does the respondent feel he is a class equal? Who are his class peers? A majority of the two lowest classes prefer to identify themselves as low class, with about a fourth of each class preferring to think of themselves as middle class. By contrast, the transitional 5–8 group moves decisively toward a middle class identification, though a little more than one third still think of themselves as lower class. Finally, the high school and college people plump solidly for a middle class identification, with the latter having a slight edge in the per cent who prefer to think of themselves as upper class. See Table 2.

Who Are the People with Whom Respondent Feels Most Comfortable?

One of the surest marks of class feeling is the capacity to relax with one's peers in the assurance that they share the same standards, employ the same modes of judgment, and have the same expectations in social intercourse. But as Table 3 reveals, there is some tendency among Puerto Ricans of all classes to feel comfortable with all people, regardless of class. It is a small tendency—ranging from the nearly nine per cent among the 5–8 people to the 14

per cent among the college people—but it is noticeable.

These responses inform us that there is definite class identification, about as might be expected: the higher the class, the higher the frequency of identification with the upper classes.

Who Are the People Who Lead the Same Kind of Life?

This question probes whether Puerto Ricans define class peership by a common style of life. Is this style of life what they mean when they say that others are in the same class? From previous evidence it is clear that persons are allocated to a given class primarily on the basis of income and secondarily of education. Now it can be seen from

TABLE 2   Class Location on a Three-Class Ladder of Persons Whom Respondent Considers in His Own Class

Class	Years of School Completed											
	0		1–4		5–8		9–12		13+		Total	
	No.	%	No.	%	No.	%	No.	%	No.	%	No.	%
High	13	5.4	13	4.5	7	3.1	6	3.6	7	9.9	46	4.6
Middle	60	24.8	80	27.8	103	45.4	114	68.7	50	70.4	407	40.9
Low	142	58.7	153	53.1	84	37.0	24	14.5	1	1.4	404	40.6
All	11	4.5	14	4.9	10	4.4	6	3.6	2	2.8	43	4.3
None	0	0.0	1	0.4	0	0.0	0	0.0	0	0.0	1	0.1
Mixed responses	13	5.4	24	8.3	19	8.4	15	9.0	10	14.1	81	8.1
Don't know	0	0.0	1	0.4	0	0.0	0	0.0	0	0.0	1	0.1
No information	3	1.2	2	0.7	4	1.8	1	0.6	1	1.4	11	1.1
Total	242	100.0	288	100.0	227	100.0	166	100.0	71	100.0	994	100.0

TABLE 3   Class Location on a Three-Class Ladder of Persons with Whom Respondent Feels Most Comfortable

Class	Years of school completed											
	0		1–4		5–8		9–12		13+		Total	
	No.	%	No.	%	No.	%	No.	%	No.	%	No.	%
High	25	10.3	23	8.0	11	4.8	5	3.0	3	4.2	67	6.7
Middle	59	24.0	79	27.4	91	40.1	90	54.2	41	57.8	359	36.1
Low	113	46.7	123	42.7	70	30.8	27	16.3	7	9.9	340	34.2
All	28	11.6	37	12.9	20	8.8	19	11.4	10	14.9	114	11.5
None	0	0.0	0	0.0	0	0.0	1	0.6	0	0.0	1	0.1
Mixed responses	13	5.4	24	8.3	33	4.6	22	13.3	10	14.1	102	10.3
Don't know	1	0.4	0	0.0	0	0.0	0	0.0	0	0.0	1	0.1
No information	4	1.7	2	0.7	2	0.9	2	1.2	0	0.0	10	1.0
Total	242	100.0	288	100.0	227	100.0	166	100.0	71	100.0	994	100.0

Table 4 that class membership and common style of life are virtually synonymous. The responses to this question are distributed about the same way as those given to the question on social class itself. There are some shifts in percentages but in each case they are minor.

To Whom Can He Most Easily Confide Intimate Personal Matters?

There is little in the literature of research to guide us on what we ought to expect in the patterns of confidence and intimate trust. A good *a priori* argument would be that the most probable reference is to one's own class peers, or to anyone but a member of own class. For, while friendship lines tend to develop most frequently and naturally among class peers, it is precisely those at one's own level who can most effectively gossip and must be most distrusted.

The Puerto Rican responses, shown in Table 5, do not decisively settle the issue. There is definite class stratification of responses: the higher the class, the higher the frequency of reference to high classes, for confidantes. But there are other patterns as well. Over 20 per cent of the lowest class feel they can confide best in members of the upper class. Some per cent of each group feel they can confide in no one. Between 7 and 10 per cent of each group feel that class is irrelevant—they can confide in people at all class levels. As usual, the

TABLE 4   **Class Location on a Three-Class Ladder of Persons Who Lead Same Kind of Life as Respondent**

Class	Years of school completed											
	0		1–4		5–8		9–12		13+		Total	
	No.	%	No.	%	No.	%	No.	%	No.	%	No.	%
High	7	2.9	7	2.4	4	1.8	6	3.6	6	8.5	30	3.0
Middle	62	25.6	86	29.9	111	48.9	123	74.1	60	84.5	442	44.5
Low	161	66.5	168	58.3	91	40.1	27	16.3	1	1.4	448	45.1
All	3	1.2	6	2.1	3	1.3	1	0.6	0	0.0	13	1.3
None	0	0.0	0	0.0	0	0.0	1	0.6	0	0.0	1	0.1
Mixed responses	7	2.9	18	6.3	15	6.6	8	4.8	4	5.6	52	5.2
Don't know	0	0.0	2	0.7	1	0.4	0	0.0	0	0.0	3	0.3
No information	2	0.8	1	0.4	2	0.9	0	0.0	0	0.0	5	0.5
Total	242	100.0	288	100.0	227	100.0	166	100.0	71	100.0	994	100.0

TABLE 5   **Class Location on a Three-Class Ladder of Persons to Whom Head of Family Can Confide His Personal Affairs**

Class	Years of school completed											
	0		1–4		5–8		9–12		13+		Total	
	No.	%	No.	%	No.	%	No.	%	No.	%	No.	%
High	49	20.2	49	17.0	33	14.5	23	13.9	9	12.7	163	16.4
Middle	60	24.8	76	26.4	91	40.1	84	50.6	38	53.5	349	35.1
Low	82	33.9	103	35.8	48	21.2	14	8.4	6	8.5	253	25.5
All	18	7.4	21	7.3	19	8.4	15	9.0	7	9.9	80	8.0
None	12	5.0	15	5.2	9	4.0	16	9.6	2	2.8	54	5.4
Mixed responses	17	7.0	18	6.3	22	9.7	13	7.8	8	11.3	78	7.8
Don't know	1	0.4	2	0.7	2	0.9	1	0.6	0	0.0	6	0.6
No information	3	1.2	4	1.4	3	1.3	0	0.0	1	1.4	11	1.1
Total	242	100.0	288	100.0	227	100.0	166	100.0	71	100.0	994	100.0

reference groups and class orientations   **283**

people in the 5–8 group are almost squarely in the middle.

The 20 per cent of the lowest class who trust upper class members as confidantes must include a significant number of those persons found in every society who develop a dependency-intimacy relationship with those far above them in social rank. There is the suggestion of a patron type relationship, where the lower class person counts strongly on the upper class confidante for support, though there is little or no reciprocity.

In sum, the class structure asserts itself strongly on the issue of intimacy, though not nearly as strongly as previously. There is also here a substantial amount of disregard for class affiliation.

From Whom Does He Receive the Most Respect?

On the issue of respect in personal and social relations, it will be recalled, Puerto Ricans are extremely sensitive and yet rather sure of themselves. Only a small per cent at any class level have encountered what they would term disrespect, even though, in a sense, they would be among the first in the world to detect any. In previous questions about respect, Puerto Ricans have told us that most people in the society are rather decent. Now we find this judgment repeated and reaffirmed in the responses to the question, "Who are the people who most respect you?" As Table 6 shows, only five people say that they receive respect from no one. Just over one third of each class insists it receives respect from everyone. We may say, therefore, that neither the *locus* nor the *frequence* of respect follows class lines. If there is any class bias involved, it is in the curious and inverted fact that the lower classes excel the upper classes and all others in the percentage who claim they receive the most respect from the upper classes.

Whatever other indications of inter-class antagonism and intra-class solidarity in our data, the distribution of the sense of being respected will not bear out the class theme.

Whose Opinions about His Character Are Most Important?

The conditions for true class conflict may exist when the members of any given class do not care what members of other classes think about them. Not to care what one's class superiors or inferiors think or feel marks a true separation; it implies that classes have different standards of judgment norms of behavior, and criteria of worth.

TABLE 6   Class Location on a Three-Class Ladder of Persons from Whom Respondent Feels He Receives Most Respect

| | Years of school completed | | | | | | | | | | |
| | 0 | | 1–4 | | 5–8 | | 9–12 | | 13+ | | Total | |
Class	No.	%	No.	%	No.	%	No.	%	No.	%	No.	%
High	39	16.1	36	12.5	27	11.9	14	8.4	6	8.5	122	12.3
Middle	43	17.8	50	17.4	51	22.5	45	27.1	15	21.1	204	20.5
Low	55	22.7	77	26.7	47	20.7	23	13.9	10	14.1	212	21.3
All	86	35.5	107	37.2	84	37.0	64	38.6	26	36.6	367	36.9
None	3	1.2	0	0.0	0	0.0	2	1.2	0	0.0	5	0.5
Mixed responses	11	4.6	14	4.9	14	6.1	17	10.2	12	16.9	68	6.8
Don't know	2	0.8	3	1.0	1	0.4	1	0.6	0	0.0	7	0.7
No information	3	1.2	1	0.4	3	1.3	0	0.0	2	2.8	9	0.9
Total	242	100.0	288	100.0	227	100.0	166	100.0	71	100.0	994	100.0

Under such circumstances, true hostility is eminently likely. *Stratification* of the social order has led to *fragmentation* of that order when this hostility exists.

Is this the case in Puerto Rico? Do the classes insulate themselves from each other by rejecting each others' standards? Or are they sensitive to the opinions of each other? Do the lower class people care what others think about them, only to find that upper class people are disdainful of their opinions? Or is there reciprocity of concern for each other's judgements? We asked the Puerto Ricans whose opinions of their character they valued most.

Table 7 reveals some most interesting facts on class feeling about others' opinions of them.

1. Virtually no one is indifferent to the opinions of others.
2. About 25 per cent in each class care most what the upper class thinks of their character.
3. The higher the class, generally, the smaller the per cent who care about what everyone, regardless of class, thinks of their character. Still, as many as 18 per cent of the upper class feel this way.
4. Only 3 per cent of the college people and 7 per cent of the high-school people care most for the opinion of the lower class people. They care much more about the opinions of their class peers.
5. By contrast, the lower classes care some-

what more about the opinions of people outside their own classes than of those in their own brackets.
6. The 5–8 people incline more toward the higher class patterns than to those of the people with less education.

How can we summarize these diverse trends? There is, on one hand, a generalized strain toward democratic society, in view of the fourth of each class who say they are concerned about what everyone thinks of their character. Their sense of self-esteem depends, in short, if we are to believe them, on receiving favorable resonance from people at all class levels. On the other hand, as many if not more in each class pick out the high or upper class people as those whose opinions about their character they most value. This means that many Puerto Ricans at virtually all class levels are sensitive to the views which their class superiors take of them.

Can this be interpreted as a form of class-courting? Class self-denial? Are men saying, in effect, that the standards of judgment of people at their own social levels are inferior? Or are they expressing a sense of dependency upon the good opinion of people who command positions of prominence and power? Whichever of the many possible interpretations one prefers, it is sure that we are again dealing in Puerto Rico with an open class structure, one

TABLE 7   **Class Location on a Three-Class Ladder of Persons Whose Opinions about His Character the Respondent Most Values**

| | Years of school completed | | | | | | | | | | |
| | 0 | | 1–4 | | 5–8 | | 9–12 | | 13+ | | Total |
Class	No.	%	No.	%	No.	%	No.	%	No.	%	No.	%
High	68	28.1	75	26.0	59	26.0	43	25.9	18	25.4	263	26.5
Middle	49	20.3	51	17.7	63	27.8	54	32.5	25	35.2	242	24.3
Low	43	17.8	57	19.8	33	14.5	11	6.6	2	2.8	146	14.7
All	59	24.4	75	26.0	44	19.4	37	22.3	13	18.3	228	22.9
None	2	0.8	3	1.0	4	1.8	3	1.8	3	4.2	15	1.5
Mixed responses	13	5.4	21	7.3	22	9.7	16	9.6	9	12.7	81	8.1
Don't know	2	0.8	2	0.7	0	0.0	1	0.6	0	0.0	5	0.5
No information	6	2.5	4	1.4	2	0.9	1	0.6	1	1.4	14	1.4
Total	242	100.0	288	100.0	227	100.0	166	100.0	71	100.0	994	100.0

reference groups and class orientations   **285**

in which there is much contact between people at all class levels, and in which status lines, though important, are not the sole or even the preponderant lines along which the search for esteem is conducted. That nearly as many college people as illiterates should care about what everyone thinks of them—or that they should say so, no matter what they may truly feel—indicates that there is present a considerable pressure not to close class ranks. The pressure, to the contrary, seems to be to express a generalized human feeling, rather than a sharply class-oriented feeling. Could this be, once again, an expression of the ideology of *dignidad*: the ideology which insists that all men are equally worthy, as men, and that differences in social and economic position are temporary and accidental phenomena which are irrelevant in judging a man's worth?

May it not properly be said, then, that Puerto Ricans at all class levels care about the opinions of others at all class levels? They are not indifferent to each other. They share many of the same standards of judgment and evaluation, with little hostility of the kind which flows from the rejection of others as unworthy people. The social order is differentiated and stratified, but by no means fragmented.

Whose Ideas and Opinions Does the Respondent Most Respect?

Many of the same observations must now be made for the responses to this question.

Table 8 shows the same tendencies to concentrate upon the "All" category or upon the "upper class" as the people whose ideas are most respected. But now, substantially more than a third of each group have most respect for the ideas and opinions of the upper class. Somewhat smaller percentages insist they respect the ideas and opinions of everyone, that is, class affiliation is not important to the question of whose ideas one ought to respect most. Once again, a two-way orientation is evident: toward those who occupy the prominent positions in the society, and toward good ideas and opinions wherever they may be. It is as though Puerto Ricans were saying that everyone has a right to have his ideas and opinions respected, if they are worthy of this respect, and there is no reason why people at all class levels cannot have such worthy ideas and opinions. On the other hand, we shall most likely find such good ideas and opinions among people in the most prominent positions, the men of edu-

TABLE 8 **Class Location on a Three-Class Ladder of Persons Whose Ideas and Opinions the Respondent Most Respects**

Class	Years of school completed											
	0		1–4		5–8		9–12		13+		Total	
	No.	%	No.	%	No.	%	No.	%	No.	%	No.	%
High	101	41.7	118	41.0	94	41.4	69	41.6	25	35.2	407	40.9
Middle	32	13.2	32	11.1	39	17.2	31	18.7	14	19.7	148	14.9
Low	15	6.2	12	4.2	9	4.0	2	1.2	1	1.4	39	3.9
All	81	33.5	109	37.8	66	29.1	53	31.9	17	24.0	326	32.8
None	1	0.4	0	0.0	0	0.0	1	0.6	0	0.0	2	0.2
Mixed responses	8	3.3	14	4.9	17	7.5	10	6.0	14	19.7	63	6.3
Don't know	1	0.4	1	0.4	0	0.0	0	0.0	0	0.0	2	0.2
No information	3	1.2	2	0.7	2	0.9	0	0.0	0	0.0	7	0.7
Total	242	100.0	288	100.0	227	100.0	166	100.0	71	100.0	994	100.0

cation, who occupy the jobs of most prestige and are in charge of the affairs of the society.

In short, there seems to be a clear-cut expression of willingness to accept leadership from men in prominent positions, but always with the reservation that men of all origins and at all social positions are likely to have ideas which deserve attention. Even one fourth of the college people attach this reservation.

Whom Does the Respondent Most Distrust?

Now the patterns of response undergo some noteworthy changes. Roughly ten per cent of each class say they distrust everyone. Roughly 20 per cent of each class say they distrust no one. And all classes, including the lower class, most distrust people in the lower classes. As Table 9 shows, there are more people in the 0-educated group than in the high school group who say they distrust lower class people. And, while over 20 per cent of the lower class distrust upper class people most, nearly 13 per cent of the college people and over 17 per cent of the high school people also distrust the upper classes most.

For the first time, lines of hostility come out, showing very little class patterning. Of what patterns can we sensibly talk when as many illiterates as college people distrust lower class persons, and nearly as many high school as illiterate persons distrust members of the upper classes.

Whatever sense we may have developed from previous responses that Puerto Ricans generally feel confident in each other, and kindly toward each other, must now be modified in light of the clear cut evidence that considerable distrust runs throughout the population. Just as patterns of trust and confidence tend to focus either on all people or on the upper classes, now, patterns of distrust and lack of confidence single out the lower classes for their primary target, with the upper classes as the secondary focus. But all the classes tend to locate their major class antagonisms in about the same way.

In short, "class" is a useful concept in identifying the objects of trust and distrust, but is not nearly as useful in identifying the sources from whom trust and distrust emanate. Classes are targets; but they are as frequently targets for their own members as for persons at other class levels.

Surely this is the best evidence yet that while there is a clear cut and crystallized class structure by objective

TABLE 9 **Class Location on a Three-Class Ladder of Persons Whom Respondent Most Distrusts**

| Class | Years of school completed | | | | | | | | | | | |
| | 0 | | 1–4 | | 5–8 | | 9–12 | | 13+ | | Total | |
	No.	%	No.	%	No.	%	No.	%	No.	%	No.	%
High	49	20.2	70	24.3	58	25.6	29	18.0	9	12.7	215	21.6
Middle	20	8.3	15	5.2	8	3.5	12	7.3	11	15.5	66	6.6
Low	92	38.0	99	34.4	92	40.5	59	36.6	29	40.9	371	37.5
All	22	9.1	28	9.7	22	9.7	24	14.9	6	8.5	102	10.3
None	48	19.8	61	21.2	34	15.0	34	21.1	12	16.9	189	19.0
Mixed responses	4	1.7	9	3.1	9	4.0	1	0.6	3	4.2	13	1.3
Don't know	2	0.8	2	0.7	2	0.9	1	0.6	0	0.0	7	0.7
No information	5	2.1	4	1.4	2	0.9	1	0.6	1	1.4	26	2.6
Total	242	100.0	288	100.0	227	100.0	161	100.0	71	100.0	989	100.0

indices of position and life-chances, and equally clear cut class identification of those for whom various sentiments are felt, there is very little class patterning in the distribution of these sentiments. Most importantly, there is considerable inter-class confidence, and relatively very little inter-class hostility

Who Are Those Who Most Depreciate the Respondent?

The above generalizations now require some modification in light of the responses to this question. As Table 10 shows, the higher the class, the fewer the people who feel depreciated.

Twenty-one and one-half per cent of the lowest group and 35.2 per cent of the college people say they are depreciated by no one. Similarly, the higher the class, the fewer the people who refer to the upper class as the main locus of their depreciation. Here, however, the pattern is not so neat. Almost as many high school as 0-years people feel the upper classes are those who most depreciate them. By contrast, the per cent of college people who feel depreciated by upper class persons is just about one half of the high school percentage, and even smaller by comparison with the lower classes.

To balance this class distribution of the sense of depreciation, there is the surprising fact that nearly the same percentages in each class say they are most depreciated by lower class people. The high school people sense this lower class depreciation most. But the college and 0-years people differ by less than half a percentage point on this issue.

By contrast with the responses to the issue of distrust, these answers show a more definite class arrangement. The upper classes are felt to be the chief depreciators, in inverse proportion to one's own class position. And the sense of being generally appreciated by all and depreciated by none is distributed in direct proportion to one's own class position. Only in some senses may one say that men allocate their trust and distrust to those by whom they feel most appreciated and depreciated. There is some of this tendency present among Puerto Ricans, but not nearly as much as one might expect. Trust and distrust seem to be assigned with considerable less regard to class affiliation than one would predict from the more clear-cut class distribution of the sense of depreciation.

One may not overlook the fact, however, that both upper and lower class people feel depreciated about equally by lower class people. Nor may we

TABLE 10   **Class Location on a Three-Class Ladder of Persons Who Most Depreciate the Respondent**

	Years of school completed											
	0		1–4		5–8		9–12		13+		Total	
Class	No.	%	No.	%	No.	%	No.	%	No.	%	No.	%
High	87	36.0	99	34.4	72	31.7	45	27.1	11	15.5	314	31.6
Middle	16	6.6	17	5.9	17	7.5	10	6.0	9	12.7	69	6.9
Low	51	21.1	58	20.1	54	23.8	44	26.5	14	19.7	221	22.2
All	21	8.7	21	7.3	10	4.4	8	4.8	7	9.9	67	6.7
None	52	21.5	74	25.7	62	27.3	50	30.1	25	35.2	263	26.5
Mixed Responses	8	3.3	10	3.5	9	4.0	4	2.4	4	5.6	35	3.5
Don't know	1	0.4	6	2.1	0	0.0	4	2.4	1	1.4	12	1.2
No information	6	2.5	3	1.1	3	1.3	1	0.6	0	0.0	13	1.3
Total	242	100.0	288	100.0	227	100.0	166	100.0	71	100.0	994	100.0

safely disregard the fact that almost as many upper class people feel depreciated by their own peers as by lower class people. In brief, whatever *inter*class hostilities the data bespeak, they also give strong testimony to the presence of *intra*class distrust and depreciation.

If, now, on the basis of this new evidence, we were to try once again to answer the questions raised earlier regarding class patterns of hostility, we would answer as follows: *(Summary)*

1. When men in Puerto Rico come to identify their location in a class structure, they tend generally to avoid the extremes and to place themselves in the middle. More upper class people prefer to think of themselves as members of the middle class than of the upper class. But the lower class people, as expected, tend to distribute themselves mostly through the middle and lower class categories. There is some apparent modesty about what one claims for his class position.
2. When Puerto Ricans assess their rating with other persons in the society, they accept a class structure as a reasonable frame of reference, and tend generally to expect more favorable rating from members of their own classes than from others. But there is also a noticeable tendency to insist on the irrelevance of class when it is a question of according respect.
3. When questioned about whose judgments of themselves they tend to value most, Puerto Ricans generally tend to avoid the middle class range, and to express a concern for the good opinion either of everyone or of the people in the upper class echelons. This tendency is even more pronounced when the issue at stake is whose ideas and opinions deserve most respect. Here the double tendency—on one hand, to insist that all men are capable of having respectable ideas and on the other, that most worthy ideas will come from men in the most prominent positions—is most noticeable.
4. When the people of Puerto Rico assess whom they most distrust and who they feel most depreciates them, between one fourth and one third of the members of each class deny that they are depreciated by anyone or that they distrust anyone. Among the other two thirds to three fourths of the population there is an evident awareness of being depreciated and a ready response of distrust toward others.

Once again class identifications are accepted in these issues, but not as much as one might expect. The lower classes do not distrust upper classes more than their own class peers, and the upper classes show the same tendency. If there is any clear cut pattern of inter-class hostility, it is in the percentages of people at all levels through high school, larger on this issue than the upper class people, who feel depreciated by the class. And if there is any one strong point of evidence for the proposition that class position determines one's sense of his own worth, it is in the fact that the higher the class, the larger the percentage of those who feel they are appreciated by all people. In short, the lower the class, the more difficult it is apparently to feel generally esteemed by everyone.

Again, we are aware of a very fluid and open class structure, where class identification is useful and relevant, but where the class lines of felt hostility and separation have hardly formed. Making the best possible estimate from the data, one would say that the classes in Puerto Rico are generally aware of each other, concerned about each other and about the good opinion of each other; they feel respected by each other and respectful of each other, and there is mutual trust and value for others' opinions and ideas. There is much more inter-class amity than hostility. *Sum:*

These findings have important implications both for the present qualities of Puerto Rican society and for its probable future. Some can be seen more clearly if they are recast slightly in terms of the sociological concept of "reference groups."[1] As this term has come to be used, it means that humans almost always shape their conduct in response to the norms of their groups. But some groups are more important than others. Feelings of affiliation, loyalty, and membership are unequal. Some groups we belong to command these sentiments from us more than do others. The groups to which we refer ourselves for guidance, support, and solidarity are our reference groups. In effect, the reference groups are those which are most important to us.

What the previous data of this chapter have shown is that one's class is generally an important reference group for Puerto Ricans in some regards, but not in others, or much less so in others. For purposes of self-identification, Puerto Ricans most frequently refer to people at their own levels of income and education. But at this point one's own class tends to become less and less

[1] The standard reference work here is the article, "Contributions to the Theory of Reference Group Behavior" by Robert K. Merton and Alice S. Kitt, in *Studies in the Scope and Method of "The American Soldier,"* eds. Robert K. Merton and Paul F. Lazarsfeld (New York: The Free Press, 1950), pp. 40–105.

Perhaps the single most relevant observation in that article, for clarifying certain tendencies observed in Puerto Rican responses, is the statement that "positive orientation toward the norms of a non-membership group is precipitated by a passage between membership groups, either in fact or fantasy, and that the functional or dysfunctional consequences evidently depend upon the relatively open or closed character of the social structure in which this occurs" (pp. 88–89). This formulation helps considerably in succinctly systematizing some of the major factors in the abilities of low-ranked Puerto Ricans to define the overall system as fair and responsive to their needs; it was this way, too, in the case of low-ranked soldiers, some of whom were willing to estimate the army system of promotion as fair. This statement is followed, in the Merton and Kitt article, by some observations to the effect that this form of anticipatory socialization (that is, referring oneself to standards observed in groups of which one is not yet a member) may be functional for the individual in an open system but dysfunctional for the solidarity of his group or stratum. In the army case, the authors then observe that the in-group or stratum interprets this benign attitude as defection from the mores of the in-group and "responds by putting all manner of social restraints upon such positive orientations to certain out-group norms" (p. 89). We do not for a moment suggest that this was not the case in the army situation. But, so far as our evidence indicates, this is not the case in Puerto Rico, not in the lower class or stratum nor in any of the strata. The anticipatory socialization into non lower-class group life appears to function to invigorate individual morale and energy in the various strata; at the same time, it provides an extra margin of morale for use by the total collectivity. Merton and Kitt are right in stating that the openness of the system makes this nonmembership reference group behavior possible and viable, and in the sense that the ability to so identify and to be rewarded for doing so prevents the development of an intransigent kind of militant class consciousness in the lower strata. But the curious and unexpected thing in the Puerto Rican case is that the issue is not between competing membership groups: it is between solidarity with a membership subgroup of the society— and hence some hostility toward other membership subgroups—and a reciprocally supporting pair of memberships, one within one's subgroup or stratum and the other within the membership group defined by the total society. It is, in short, not a matter of competition for loyalty between lower and middle class, but between some intransigent version of *any* class identification and that kind of class identification which can coexist with and reciprocally support identification with the total society. In the Puerto Rican case, it seems eminently possible for a person to maintain on some counts an identification with a particular stratum and, at the same time, to have an equally strong and nonconflicting identification with the total society. It is suggested that this is perhaps a very good index of an open class system. Mobility is desired and approved, without any necessary implication that this involves changing one's class identity, or that this prevents or impedes the same kind and amount of mobility for everyone else in every other stratum.

In their essay, Merton and Kitt have also properly called attention to the phenomenon of shifting reference groups. They raise questions concerning the factors at work here, especially with regard to the "*dynamic processes* involved in the theoretically supposed counter-tendencies induced by multiple reference groups." Our data

important as a reference group, especially for the lower classes. They are just as likely to have in mind the middle and upper segments of society when they identify the people for whose good opinion they care the most, from whom they receive the most respect, and whom they themselves most respect.

The middle and upper segments of Puerto Rican class structure, unlike the lower classes, tend more frequently to stay within their own class lines for their reference groups. For them the lower classes are not important reference points. The single most important invocation of the lower class group comes when the upper and middle classes identify those who most depreciate them and whom they most "distrust."

A third prevalent tendency competes with the concept of one class as the most important reference group. It denies the importance of any single or several classes and to insist instead that the good opinion and the ideas and beliefs of people at all levels are most important. To this extent one may say that the *total society* constitutes a reference group for large numbers of Puerto Ricans on many important matters concerning behavior, self-esteem, and conduct of social affairs. In some sense, this is testimony to a great deal of social unity and harmony, in spite of the abundant evidence that social stratification is pervasive in many sectors of social life.

These ways of thinking and feeling have implications for the Island's future. First, class distinctions do not isolate people into hardened, hostile groups working at cross purposes with each other. Whatever the inequalities in education and income, the fact remains that Puerto Ricans do not tend to blame nor depreciate each other nearly as much as one might expect in

---

concern certain suggestions relevant to these problems. The openness of the class system must first be taken into account as a prime factor in preventing the formation of rigid, self-enclosing frames of reference; to the contrary, an open class system induces a type of fluidity and ease of psychological access to a wider range of reference groups than might ordinarily be supposed available. The particular kinds of groups chosen for self-reference seem to be a function, at least in part, of the interplay between two factors. One is the issue or criterion under judgment, that is, "Whose opinion about your character matters to you?" as against some more restrictive item such as, "Who are those who lead lives most similar to yours?" The nature of the question—the particular matter up for judgment—seems to set broad or narrow limits upon the possible choices.

The second factor, intersecting with the issue in question, has most to do with the communications network. That is, in such questions as, "Compared to most people in the country, would you say that you are doing better, worse or the same?" we expect and receive two types of responses. One is obviously and unqualifiedly unrealistic: the judgment rendered is so far removed from the facts, as measured by certain objective indices (income, education, and so forth), that we can conclude either that the individual is simply distorting beyond recognition his condition of well-being, or that he has invoked certain criteria of comparison that are simply not relevant to the question (for example, he is comparing his subjective feelings of happiness with what he imagines those of others to be).

This response is found in only a minority of the cases. The more frequent response is more realistic, as measured by correspondence with the objective facts. It shows two main tendencies: (1) a slight and expected euphorization, so that the individual seems to be somewhat badly informed about how much better a designated reference group is actually doing; and (2) a corollary condensation of the actual ladders or hierarchies of distribution of the goods in question (income, jobs, and so forth), so that the range of possible choices is narrowed from the three or four offered, to only two, one of which is too distant and obviously too different for the individual to refer himself to. This leaves him only the proximately higher group about which he is also somewhat badly informed. Again, this latter process of selecting a reference group at the proximately higher level seems to be characteristic of actors who perceive that their system is fundamentally open and promising. The Puerto Rican respondents show a standard tendency to condense or reduce any array of possibilities offered to them, when a model structure of hypothetical strata are presented as choices of possible reference groups.

reference groups and class orientations   **291**

a society with such marked inequalities. They express, it seems, a sense of common tie to a common unity, and they find people on many important levels whom they respect and trust.

To the extent that plans for future development are likely to depend on such social harmony for their success, Puerto Rico has today a solid basis for that success. As long as the conditions which now promote interclass harmony continue to hold force, the relative advantages of one segment or class are not likely to be viewed as evidence of class favoritism nor to be responded to with bitterness and resentment.

Yet in all the social harmony there is considerable awareness of class differences in the critical matters of education and income. And the present levels and standards of the middle and upper classes are offered by the lower class Puerto Ricans as models of the kinds of life they want for their children in the proximate future. More than that, virtually every segment of the class structure—middle and upper as well as the lower—expresses hopes for future improvement.

This is borne out clearly by the materials in Table 11, where responses to the following question are recorded: "In what part of the class ladder are the persons who lead the kind of life

you hope your sons will be able to have?"

As the frequencies in the column labeled "low" show us, every step up in the class ladder involves a decrease in the per cent of people who want the same life for their sons as they themselves now have. Over half of each of the five groups look toward a middle class level for their sons.

But the real differences in own class locations vs. that desired or hoped for one's son do not come clear until we juxtapose the two sets of reports. Taking the materials from Table 11 and laying them side by side with the data from Table 7 of Chapter 8 [of *Social Class and Social Change in Puerto Rico* by Tumin and Feldman], we get Table 12.

Now the pattern emerges clearly. There is very little difference in the "middle class" column. Actually the changes represent a depletion of "middle class" as an aspired level for one's son, as these hopes are expressed by people. The two lower classes hold nearly constant their percentages in the middle class bracket.

The real changes occur in the depletion of the "low" class category and the swelling of the "upper." The 0-years people halve their membership in the low class, and the 1–4 group reduces its membership to almost one

TABLE 11   Class Location on a Three-Class Ladder of Persons Who Lead the Kind of Life the Respondent Hopes His Sons Will Be Able to Lead

| | Years of school completed | | | | | | | | | | | |
| | 0 | | 1–4 | | 5–8 | | 9–12 | | 13+ | | Total | |
Class	No.	%	No.	%	No.	%	No.	%	No.	%	No.	%
High	42	17.4	67	23.3	73	32.2	53	31.9	21	29.6	256	25.8
Middle	125	51.7	166	57.6	120	52.9	102	61.5	43	60.6	556	55.9
Low	51	21.1	31	10.8	17	7.5	2	1.2	0	0.0	101	10.2
All	4	1.7	5	1.7	3	1.3	2	1.2	0	0.0	14	1.4
None	1	0.4	0	0.0	0	0.0	0	0.0	0	0.0	1	0.1
Mixed responses	5	2.1	11	3.8	9	4.1	4	2.4	4	5.6	33	3.3
Don't know	3	1.2	3	1.0	1	0.4	1	0.6	0	0.0	8	0.8
No information	11	4.6	5	1.7	4	1.8	2	1.2	3	4.2	25	2.5
Total	242	100.0	288	100.0	227	100.0	166	100.0	71	100.0	994	100.0

TABLE 12

TABLE 12   **Own Class Location vs.
Class Desired for Son (in
Percentages)**

Years of school completed	Upper		Middle		Low	
	Self %	Son %	Self %	Son %	Self %	Son %
0	8.9	17.4	50.5	51.7	40.5	21.1
1–4	3.8	23.3	57.6	57.6	38.6	10.8
5–8	5.6	32.2	60.7	52.9	33.8	7.5
9–12	7.6	31.9	71.7	61.5	20.8	1.2
13+	17.9	29.6	65.7	60.6	16.4	0.0

fourth of its present constituency. The three highest classes reduce their membership even more drastically. By contrast, the 0-years people double their upper class membership; the 1–4 people multiply by a factor of 7; the 5–8 group swells its upper class ranks five times or more beyond its present condition; the high school group quadruples its membership; and the college people have an increase by about 50 per cent or more of their going state.

What seems to have occurred is that numerous people in all classes who ranked themselves as low class aspired for middle class for their sons; in turn, significant numbers of those who rated themselves as middle class moved on to the upper class level in their aspirations for their children. About the same numbers flowed out of the mid-

dle class as came in, thereby maintaining the numerical strength of that class at its present par.

In sum, there is hope and aspiration at all levels, proportionate to present class position. If the aspirations are realized, relatively few people in the society will be in what is now the "low" class when today's children come to their maturity.

Withal, one dour note must be sounded. It is the fact that somewhat over 20 per cent of the people in the lowest group and ten per cent in the 1–4 people seem willing to settle for the likelihood that their sons will not go beyond their present levels of existence. Can this 20 per cent of one group and 10 per cent of another be the hard core of resistance to change in Puerto Rico? Are these the people who have not been able to lift their eyes off the ground long enough to hope and aspire for something more for their children? Will these people be a drag upon social change? Whatever the answer to these questions, it is clear that any planning for change must take account of the fact that a fifth of the most underprivileged group in Puerto Rico does not aspire for very much more, in the lives of their children, than they themselves now have.

mobility I:
patterns and structures

seven

The opposite of stratification is mobility, that is, just as stratification is the study of the unequal placement and reward of members of a society in the various available positions, so is mobility the study of the movement in and out of these positions. Moreover, mobility may be seen as the other "moral" side of stratification, for insofar as inequality is considered to be "unfair," at least to some degree, mobility—or the chance to improve one's position (and disimprove it as well)—is seen as the counterbalancing moral weight.

These views are especially pertinent in societies such as those of the United States and England, where there is considerable emphasis on the "positive" value of mobility and its possibilities. Ralph H. Turner provides us with a very useful distinction between "sponsored" and "contest" types of mobility. The distinction refers not to the *amount* of mobility (which is the most frequent concern of students comparing two countries), but rather to the *type* of mobility characteristic of social systems. As Turner puts it,

contest mobility is a system in which elite status is the prize in an open contest and is taken by the aspirants' own efforts. There are rules of fair play, but the contestants have wide latitude in the strategies they employ. By contrast, sponsored mobility is a system in which elite recruits are chosen by the established elites or their agents and elite status is given on the basis of some criterion of supposed merit and cannot be taken by any amount of effort or strategy.

These two terms, Turner feels, are useful in comparing not only the American and British systems, but in comparing other societies as well. In his article, reproduced here, he analyzes (1) the complexities of the premises and assumptions underlying the two systems, (2) the connections with the types of social control in the two countries, (3) the detailed reflections of these two sets of "norms" in the educational systems of the countries, and (4) the effects of mobility under each of the systems on the personalities of the individuals involved.

Thomas Fox and S. M. Miller are also concerned with international comparisons, especially the variety of possible measures of the amount of mobility in the countries they compare: the United States, Great Britain, Japan, and the Netherlands. They point out quite correctly that the ability to compare mobility rates across nations depends on the availability of comparable data, for example, the occupational categories—movement in and out of which constitutes the focus of study—should be the same in each of the countries under comparison. But these conditions are not easily met in the available data. For this reason, and others, numerous students compress various categories of occupations into one set of manual and one set of nonmanual occupations and compare countries in terms of the movement in and out of these two sets of categories. As a result, movement to and from categories *within* each set is ignored, and one can therefore get a picture of a country that is very different from that secured when *internal* details are attended to.

Fox and Miller illustrate some of these problems by a series of comparisons they make among the four countries chosen for special study. In spite of the many pitfalls involved in such comparisons, the authors feel that the study of mobility is a fruitful area of research, especially, perhaps, when it is connected with the study of political stability and instability.

Because the family is the social unit from which the individual members acquire their primary social identity and status, and because the family unit exercises such a great impact on the fate of any individual member, it becomes a focal point for the study of stratification and mobility. As William J. Goode puts it in the excerpts from his monograph printed here,

> To inquire into the confusing web of relations between family and stratification is therefore to seek an understanding of the core processes of any society and its changes, at once of prime importance and difficulty. The family is the keystone of the stratification system, and this in turn is made up of the rewards granted by the society for filling its posts. How rigidly the family system enforces its rules determines how rigidly people are kept in the positions ascribed to them at birth.

By the same token, the family is a crucial unit in social mobility. As Goode says, we are concerned with the factors that facilitate upward or downward movement of families and individuals and the consequences for family structure when families rise or fall.

Among the factors concerning the family that may affect rates of mobility are rules of inheritance (here considered in the contrast between unigeniture and equal division of property) and heterogamy vs. homogamy as these practices reflect rules of legitimacy of marriage partners and the possibilities of the inclusion of persons from various strata in one family group. And among the mobility factors that the family can influence are the orientations of the children to achievement. The selection from Goode's monograph focuses on these three sets of relationships.

Sponsored and Contest Mobility and the School System

RALPH H. TURNER

This paper suggests a framework for relating certain differences between American and English systems of education to the prevailing norms of upward mobility in each country. Others have noted the tendency of educational systems to support prevailing schemes of stratification, but this discussion concerns specifically the manner in which the *accepted mode of upward mobility* shapes the school system directly and indirectly through its effects on the values which implement social controls.

Two ideal-typical normative patterns of upward mobility are described and their ramifications in the general patterns of stratification and social control are suggested. In addition to showing relationships among a number of differences between American and English schooling, the ideal-types have broader implications than those developed in this paper: they suggest a major dimension of stratification which might be profitably incorporated into a variety of studies in social class; and they readily can be applied in further comparisons between other countries.

Reprinted from *American Sociological Review*, XXV, No. 6 (December, 1960), 855–867, by permission of the author and the American Sociological Association. This is an expanded version of a paper presented at the Fourth World Congress of Sociology, 1959, and abstracted in the *Transactions* of the Congress. Special indebtedness should be expressed to Jean Floud and Hilde Himmelweit for helping to acquaint the author with the English school system.

The Nature of Organizing Norms

Many investigators have concerned themselves with rates of upward mobility in specific countries or internationally,[1] and with the manner in which school systems facilitate or impede such mobility.[2] But preoccupation with the *extent* of mobility has precluded equal attention to the predominant *modes* of mobility. The central assumption underlying this paper is that within a formally open class system that provides for mass education the organizing folk norm which defines the accepted mode of upward mobility is a crucial factor in shaping the school system, and may be even more crucial than the extent of upward mobility. In England and the United States there appear to be different organizing folk norms, here termed *sponsored* mobility and *contest* mobility, respectively. *Contest* mobility is a system in which elite[3] status is the prize in an

[1] A comprehensive summary of such studies appears in Seymour M. Lipset and Reinhard Bendix, *Social Mobility in Industrial Society* (Berkeley and Los Angeles, Calif.: University of California Press, 1959).

[2] *Cf.* C. A. Anderson, "The Social Status of University Students in Relation to Type of Economy: An International Comparison," *Transactions of the Third World Congress of Sociology,* (London, 1956), Vol. V, pp. 51–63; J. E. Floud, *Social Class and Educational Opportunity* (London: William Heinemann Ltd., 1956; W. L. Warner, R. J. Havighurst, and M. B. Loeb, *Who Shall Be Educated?* (New York: Harper & Row, Publishers, 1944).

[3] Reference is made throughout the paper to

open contest and is taken by the aspirants' own efforts. While the "contest" is governed by some rules of fair play, the contestants have wide latitude in the strategies they may employ. Since the "prize" of successful upward mobility is not in the hands of an established elite to give out, the latter cannot determine who shall attain it and who shall not. Under *sponsored* mobility elite recruits are chosen, and elite status is *given* on the basis of some criterion of supposed merit and cannot be *taken* by any amount of effort or strategy. Upward mobility is like entry into a private club where each candidate must be "sponsored" by one or more of the members. Ultimately the members grant or deny upward mobility on the basis of whether they judge the candidate to have those qualities they wish to see in fellow members.

Before elaborating this distinction, it should be noted that these systems of mobility are ideal types designed to clarify observed differences in the predominantly similar English and American systems of stratification and education. But as organizing norms these principles are assumed to be present at least implicitly in people's thinking, guiding their judgments of what is appropriate on many specific matters. Such organizing norms do not correspond perfectly with the objective characteristics of the societies in which they exist, nor are they completely independent of them. From the complex interplay of social and economic conditions and ideologies people in a society develop a highly simplified conception of the way in which events take place. This conception of the "natural" is translated into a norm—the "natural" becomes what "ought" to be—and in turn imposes a strain toward consistency upon relevant aspects of the society. Thus the norm acts back upon the objective conditions to which it refers and has ramifying effects upon directly and indirectly related features of the society.[4]

In brief, the conception of an ideal-typical organizing norm involves the following propositions:

1. The ideal types are not fully exemplified in practice since they are normative systems, and no normative system can be devised so as to cope with all empirical exigencies.
2. Predominant norms usually compete with less ascendant norms engendered by changes and inconsistencies in the underlying social structure.
3. Though not fully explicit, organizing folk norms are reflected in specific value judgments. Those judgments which the relevant people regard as having a convincing ring to them, irrespective of the logic expressed, or which seem to require no extended argumentation may be presumed to reflect the prevailing folk norms.
4. The predominant organizing norms in one segment of society are functionally related to those in other segments.

"elite" and "masses." The generalizations, however, are intended to apply throughout the stratification continuum to relations between members of a given class and the class or classes above it. Statements about mobility are intended in general to apply to mobility from manual to middle-class levels, lower-middle to upper-middle class, and so on, as well as into the strictly elite groups. The simplified expressions avoid the repeated use of cumbersome and involved statements which might otherwise be required.

[4] The normative element in an organizing norm goes beyond Max Weber's *ideal type*, conveying more of the sense of Durkheim's *collective representation; cf.* Ralph H. Turner, "The Normative Coherence of Folk Concepts," *Research Studies of the State College of Washington*, XXV (1957), 127–136. Charles Wagley has developed a similar concept which he calls "ideal pattern" in his as yet unpublished work on Brazilian kinship. See also Howard Becker, "Constructive Typology in the Social Sciences," *American Sociological Review*, V (February, 1940) 40–55.

Two final qualifications concerning the scope of this paper: First, the organizing folk norm of upward mobility affects the school system because one of the latter's functions is the facilitation of mobility. Since this is only one of several social functions of the school, and not the most important function in the societies under examination, only a very partial accounting of the whole set of forces making for similarities and differences in the school systems of United States and England is possible here. Only those differences which directly or indirectly reflect the performance of the mobility function are noted. Second, the concern of this paper is with the current dynamics of the situation in the two countries rather than with their historical development.

Distinctions between the Two Norms

Contest mobility is like a sporting event in which many compete for a few recognized prizes. The contest is judged to be fair only if all the players compete on an equal footing. Victory must be won solely by one's own efforts. The most satisfactory outcome is not necessarily a victory of the most able, but of the most deserving. The tortoise who defeats the hare is a folk-prototype of the deserving sportsman. Enterprise, initiative, perseverance, and craft are admirable qualities if they allow the person who is initially at a disadvantage to triumph. Even clever manipulation of the rules may be admired if it helps the contestant who is smaller or less muscular or less rapid to win. Applied to mobility, the contest norm means that victory by a person of moderate intelligence accomplished through the use of common sense, craft, enterprise, daring, and successful risk-taking[5] is

more appreciated than victory by the most intelligent or the best educated.

Sponsored mobility, in contrast, rejects the pattern of the contest and favors a controlled selection process. In this process the elite or their agents, deemed to be best qualified to judge merit, choose individuals for elite status who have the appropriate qualities. Individuals do not win or seize elite status; mobility is rather a process of sponsored induction into the elite.

Pareto had this sort of mobility in mind when he suggested that a governing class might dispose of persons potentially dangerous to it by admitting them to elite membership, provided that the recruits change character by adopting elite atitudes and interests.[6] Danger to the ruling class would seldom be the major criterion for choice of elite recruits. But Pareto assumed that the established elite would select whom they wished to enter their ranks and would inculcate the attitudes and interests of the established elite in the recruits.

The governing objective of contest mobility is to give elite status to those who earn it, while the goal of sponsored mobility is to make the best use of the talents in society by sorting persons into their proper niches. In different societies the conditions of competitive struggle may reward quite different attributes, and sponsored mobility may select individuals on the basis of such diverse qualities as intelligence or visionary

---

[5] Geoffrey Gorer remarks on the favorable evaluation of the successful gamble in American culture: "Gambling is also a respected and important component in many business ventures. Conspicuous improvement in a man's financial position is generally attributed to a lucky combination of industry, skill, and gambling, though the successful gambler prefers to refer to his gambling as 'vision.' " See *The American People* (New York: W. W. Norton & Company, Inc., 1948), p. 178.

[6] Vilfredo Pareto, *The Mind and Society* (New York: Harcourt, Brace & World, Inc., 1935), Vol. 4, p. 1796.

capability, but the difference in principle remains the same.[7]

Under the contest system society at large establishes and interprets the criteria of elite status. If one wishes to have his status recognized he must display certain credentials which identify his class to those about him. The credentials must be highly visible and require no special skill for their assessment, since credentials are presented to the masses. Material possession and mass popularity are altogether appropriate credentials in this respect, and any special skill which produces a tangible product and which can easily by assessed by the untrained will do. The nature of sponsored mobility precludes these procedures, but assigns to credentials instead the function of identifying elite members to one another.[8] Accordingly, the ideal credentials are special skills that require the trained discrimination of the elite for their recognition. In this case, intellectual, literary, or artistic excellencies, which can be appraised only by those trained to appreciate them, are fully suitable credentials. Concentration on such skills lessens the likelihood that an interloper will succeed in claiming the right to elite membership on grounds of the popular evaluation of his competence.

In the sporting event there is special admiration for the slow starter who makes a dramatic finish, and many of the rules are designed to insure that the race should not be declared over until it has run its full course. Contest mobility incorporates this disapproval of premature judgments and of anything that gives special advantage to those who are ahead at any point in the race. Under sponsored mobility, fairly early selection of only the number of persons necessary to fill anticipated vacancies in the elite is desirable. Early selection allows time to prepare the recruits for their elite position. Aptitudes, inherent capacities, and spiritual gifts can be assessed fairly early in life by techniques ranging from divination to the most sophisticated psychological test, and the more naive the subjects at the time of selection the less likely are their talents to be blurred by differential learning or conspiracy to defeat the test. Since elitists take the initiative in training recruits, they are more interested in the latters' capabilities than in what they will do with them on their own, and they are concerned that no one else should first have an opportunity to train the recruits' talents in the wrong direction. Contest mobility tends to delay the final award as long as practicable to permit a fair race; sponsored mobility tends to place the time of recruitment as early in life as practicable to insure control over selection and training.

Systems of sponsored mobility develop most readily in societies with but a single elite or with a recognized elite hierarchy. When multiple elites compete among themselves the mobility process tends to take the contest pattern, since no group is able to command control of recruitment. Sponsored mobility further depends upon a social structure that fosters monopoly of elite

---

[7] Many writers have noted that different kinds of societies facilitate the rise of different kinds of personalities, either in the stratification hierarchy or in other ways. *Cf.* Jessie Bernard, *American Community Behavior* (New York: Dryden, 1949), p. 205. A particularly interesting statement is Martindale's exploration of "favored personality" types in sacred and secular societies. Don Martindale and Elio Monachesi, *Elements of Sociology* (New York: Harper & Row, Publishers, 1951), pp. 312–378.

[8] At one time in the United States a good many owners of expensive British Jaguar automobiles carried large signs on the cars identifying the make. Such a display would have been unthinkable under a sponsored mobility system since the Jaguar owner would not care for the esteem of persons too uninformed to tell a Jaguar from a less prestigious automobile.

credentials. Lack of such monopoly undercuts sponsorship and control of the recruitment process. Monopoly of credentials in turn is typically a product of societies with well-entrenched traditional aristocracies employing such credentials as family line and bestowable title which are intrinsically subject to monopoly, or of societies organized on large-scale bureaucratic lines permitting centralized control of upward social movement.

English society has been described as the juxtaposition of two systems of stratification, the urban industrial class system and the surviving aristocratic system. While the sponsored mobility pattern reflects the logic of the latter, our impression is that it pervades popular thinking rather than merely coexisting with the logic of industrial stratification. Patterns imported into an established culture tend to be reshaped, as they are assimilated, into consistency with the established culture. Thus it may be that changes in stratification associated with industrialization have led to alterations in the rates, the specific means, and the rules of mobility, but that these changes have been guided by the but lightly challenged organizing norm of sponsored mobility.

Social Control and the Two Norms

Every society must cope with the problem of maintaining loyalty to its social system and does so in part through norms and values, only some of which vary by class position. Norms and values especially prevalent within a given class must direct behavior into channels that support the total system, while those that transcend strata must support the general class differential. The way in which upward mobility takes place determines in part the kinds of norms and values that serve the indicated purposes of social control in each class and throughout the society.

The most conspicuous control problem is that of ensuring loyalty in the disadvantaged classes toward a system in which their members receive less than a proportional share of society's goods. In a system of contest mobility this is accomplished by a combination of futuristic orientation, the norm of ambition, and a general sense of fellowship with the elite. Each individual is encouraged to think of himself as competing for an elite position so that loyalty to the system and conventional attitudes are cultivated in the process of preparation for this possibility. It is essential that this futuristic orientation be kept alive by delaying a sense of final irreparable failure to reach elite status until attitudes are well established. By thinking of himself in the successful future the elite aspirant forms considerable identification with elitists, and evidence that they are merely ordinary human beings like himself helps to reinforce this identification as well as to keep alive the conviction that he himself may some day succeed in like manner. To forestall rebellion among the disadvantaged majority, then, a contest system must avoid absolute points of selection for mobility and immobility and must delay clear recognition of the realities of the situation until the individual is too committed to the system to change radically. A futuristic orientation cannot, of course, be inculcated successfully in all members of lower strata, but sufficient internalization of a norm of ambition tends to leave the unambitious as individual deviants and to forestall the latters' formation of a genuine subcultural group able to offer collective threat to the established system. Where this kind of control system operates rather effectively it is notable that organized or gang deviancy is more likely to take the form of an attack upon the conventional or moral order rather than upon the class system itself. Thus the United States has its "beatniks"[9] who repudiate ambition and most worldly values and its delinquent and criminal gangs who try to evade the limitations imposed by conventional means,[10] but very few active revolutionaries.

These social controls are inappropriate in a system of sponsorship since the elite recruits are chosen from above. The principal threat to the system would lie in the existence of a strong group the members of whom sought to *take* elite positions themselves. Control under this system is maintained by training the "masses" to regard themselves as relatively incompetent to manage society, by restricting access to the skills and manners of the elite, and by cultivating belief in the superior competence of the elite. The earlier that selection of the elite recruits is made the sooner others can be taught to accept their inferiority and to make "realistic" rather than phantasy plans. Early selection prevents raising the hopes of large numbers of people who might otherwise become the discontented leaders of a class challenging the sovereignty of the established elite. If it is assumed that the difference in competence between masses and elite is seldom so great as to support the usual differences in the advantages accruing to each,[11] then the differences must be artificially augmented by discouraging acquisition of elite skills by the masses. Thus a sense of mystery about the elite is a common device for supporting in the masses the illusion of a much greater hiatus of competence than in fact exists.

While elitists are unlikely to reject a system that benefits them they must still be restrained from taking such advantage of their favorable situation as to jeopardize the entire elite. Under the sponsorship system the elite recruits—who are selected early, freed from the strain of competitive struggle, and kept under close supervision—may be thoroughly indoctrinated in elite culture. A norm of paternalism toward inferiors may be inculcated, a heightened sensitivity to the good opinion of fellow elitists and elite recruits may be cultivated, and the appreciation of the more complex forms of aesthetic, literary, intellectual, and sporting activities may be taught. Norms of courtesy and altruism easily can be maintained under sponsorship since elite recruits are not required to compete for their standing and since the elite may deny high standing to those who strive for position by "unseemly" methods. The system of sponsorship provides an almost perfect setting for the development of an elite culture characterized by a sense of responsibility for "inferiors" and for preservation of the "finer things" of life.

Elite control in the contest system is more difficult since there is no controlled induction and apprenticeship. The principal regulation seems to lie in the insecurity of elite position. In a sense there is no "final arrival" because each person may be displaced by newcomers throughout his life. The limited control of high standing from above prevents the clear delimitation of levels in the class system, so that success itself becomes relative: each success, rather than an accomplishment, serves to qualify the participant for competition at the next higher level.[12] The restraints upon the behavior of a person of high standing, therefore, are principally those applicable to a contestant who

[9] See, e.g., Lawrence Lipton, *The Holy Barbarians* (New York: Messner, 1959).

[10] *Cf.* Albert K. Cohen, *Delinquent Boys: The Culture of the Gang* (New York: The Free Press, 1955).

[11] D. V. Glass, ed., *Social Mobility in Britain* (New York: The Free Press, 1954), pp. 144–145, reports studies showing only small variations in intelligence between occupational levels.

[12] Gorer, *op. cit.*, pp. 172–187.

must not risk the "ganging up" of other contestants, and who must pay some attention to the masses who are frequently in a position to impose penalties upon him. But any special norm of paternalism is hard to establish since there is no dependable procedure for examining the means by which one achieves elite credentials. While mass esteem is an effective brake upon over-exploitation of position, it rewards scrupulously ethical and altruistic behavior much less than evidence of fellow-feeling with the masses themselves.

Under both systems, unscrupulous or disreputable persons may become or remain members of the elite, but for different reasons. In contest mobility, popular tolerance of a little craftiness in the successful newcomer, together with the fact that he does not have to undergo the close scrutiny of the old elite, leaves considerable leeway for unscrupulous success. In sponsored mobility, the unpromising recruit re-reflects unfavorably on the judgments of his sponsors and threatens the myth of elite omniscience; consequently he may be tolerated and others may "cover up" for his deficiencies in order to protect the unified front of the elite to the outer world.

Certain of the general values and norms of any society reflect emulation of elite values by the masses. Under sponsored mobility, a good deal of the protective attitudes toward and interest in classical subjects percolates to the masses. Under contest mobility, however, there is not the same degree of homogeneity of moral, aesthetic, and intellectual values to be emulated, so that the conspicuous attribute of the elite is its high level of material consumption—emulation itself follows this course. There is neither effective incentive nor punishment for the elitist who fails to interest himself in promoting the arts or literary excellence, or who continues to maintain the vulgar manners and mode of speech of his class origin. The elite has relatively less power and the masses relatively more power to punish or reward a man for his adoption or disregard of any special elite culture. The great importance of accent and of grammatical excellence in the attainment of high status in England as contrasted with the twangs and drawls and grammatical ineptitude among American elites is the most striking example of this difference. In a contest system, the class order does not function to support the *quality* of aesthetic, literary, and intellectual activities; only those well versed in such matters are qualified to distinguish authentic products from cheap imitations. Unless those who claim superiority in these areas are forced to submit their credentials to the elite for evaluation, poor quality is often honored equally with high quality and class prestige does not serve to maintain an effective norm of high quality.

This is not to imply that there are no groups in a "contest" society devoted to the protection and fostering of high standards in art, music, literature, and intellectual pursuits, but that such standards lack the support of the class system which is frequently found when sponsored mobility prevails. In California, the selection by official welcoming committees of a torch singer to entertain a visiting king and queen and "cancan" dancers to entertain Mr. Khrushchev illustrates how American elites can assume that high prestige and popular taste go together.

Formal Education

Returning to the conception of an organizing ideal norm, we assume that to the extent to which one such norm of upward mobility is prevalent in a society there are constant strains to shape the educational system into conformity with that norm. These strains operate in two fashions: directly, by blinding people to alternatives and coloring their judgments of successful and unsuccessful solutions to recurring educational problems; indirectly, through the functional interrelationships between school systems and the class structure, systems of social control, and other features of the social structure which are neglected in this paper.

The most obvious application of the distinction between sponsored and contest mobility norms affords a partial explanation for the different policies of student selection in the English and American secondary schools. Although American high school students follow different courses of study and a few attend specialized schools, a major educational preoccupation has been to avoid any sharp social separation between the superior and inferior students and to keep the channels of movement between courses of study as open as possible. Recent criticisms of the way in which superior students may be thereby held back in their development usually are nevertheless qualified by the insistence that these students must not be withdrawn from the mainstream of student life.[13] Such segregation offends the sense of fairness implicit in the contest norm and also arouses the fear that the elite and future elite will lose their sense of fellowship with the masses. Perhaps the most important point, however, is that schooling is presented as an opportunity, and making use of it depends primarily on the student's own initiative and enterprise.

The English system has undergone a succession of liberalizing changes during this century, but all of them have retained the attempt to sort out early

in the educational program the promising from the unpromising so that the former may be segregated and given a special form of training to fit them for higher standing in their adult years. Under the Education Act of 1944, a minority of students has been selected each year by means of a battery of examinations popularly known as "eleven plus," supplemented in varying degrees by grade school records and personal interviews, for admission to grammar schools.[14] The remaining students attend secondary modern or technical schools in which the opportunities to prepare for college or to train for the more prestigeful occupations are minimal. The grammar schools supply what by comparative standards is a high quality of college preparatory education. Of course, such a scheme embodies the logic of sponsorship, with early selection of those destined for middle-class and higher-status occupations, and specialized training to prepare each group for its destined class position. This plan facilitates considerable mobility, and recent research reveals surprisingly little bias against children from manual laboring-class families in the selection for grammar school, when related to measured intelligence.[15] It is altogether possible that adequate comparative study would show a closer correlation of school success with measured intelligence and a lesser correlation between school success and family background in England

[14] The nature and operation of the "eleven plus" system are fully reviewed in a report by a committee of the British Psychological Society and in a report of extensive research into the adequacy of selection methods. See P.E. Vernon, editor, *Secondary School Selection: A British Psychological Inquiry* (London: Methuen & Co. Ltd., 1957); and Alfred Yates and D. A. Pidgeon, *Admission to Grammar Schools* (London: Newnes Educational Publishing Co., 1957).

[15] J. E. Floud, A. H. Halsey, and F. M. Martin, *Social Class and Educational Opportunity* (London: William Heinemann Ltd., 1956).

[13] See, e.g., *Los Angeles Times*, May 4. 1959, Part I, p. 24.

than in the United States. While selection of superior students for mobility opportunity is probably more efficient under such a system the obstacles for persons not so selected of "making the grade" on the basis of their own initiative or enterprise are probably correspondingly greater.

That the contrasting effects of the two systems accord with the social control patterns under the two mobility norms is indicated by studies of student ambitions in the United States and in England. Researches in the United States consistently show that the general level of occupational aspiration reported by high school students is quite unrealistic in relation to the actual distribution of job opportunities. Comparative study in England shows much less "phantasy" aspiration, and specifically indicates a reduction in aspirations among students not selected following the "eleven-plus" examination.[16] One of the by-products of the sponsorship system is the fact that at least some students from middle-class families whose parents cannot afford to send them to private schools suffer severe personal adjustment problems when they are assigned to secondary modern schools on the basis of this selection procedure.[17]

This well-known difference between the British sorting at an early age of students into grammar and modern schools and the American comprehensive high school and junior college is the clearest application of the distinction under discussion. But the organizing norms penetrate more deeply into the school systems than is initially apparent. The most telling observation regarding the direct normative operation of these principles would be evidence to support the author's impression that major critics of educational procedures within each country do not usually transcend the logic of their respective mobility norms. Thus the British debate about the best method for getting people sorted according to ability, without proposing that elite station should be open to whosoever can ascend to it. Although fear of "sputnik" in the United States introduced a flurry of suggestions for sponsored mobility schemes, the long-standing concern of school critics has been the failure to motivate students adequately. Preoccupation with motivation appears to be an intellectual application of the folk idea that people should *win* their station in society by personal enterprise.

The functional operation of a strain toward consistency with the organizing norms of upward mobility may be illustrated by several other features of the school systems in the two countries. First, the value placed upon education itself differs under the two norms. Under sponsored mobility, schooling is valued for its cultivation of elite culture, and those forms of schooling directed toward such cultivation are more highly valued than others. Education of the non-elite is difficult to justify clearly and tends to be half-hearted, while maximum educational resources are concentrated on "those who can benefit most from them"—in practice, this means those who can learn the elite culture. The secondary modern schools in England have regularly suffered from less adequate financial provision, a higher student-teacher ratio, fewer well trained teachers, and a general

---

[16] Mary D. Wilson documents the reduction in aspirations characterizing students in British secondary modern schools and notes the contrast with American studies revealing much more "unrealistic" aspirations; see "The Vocational Preferences of Secondary Modern Schoolchildren," *British Journal of Educational Psychology*, XXIII (1953), 97–113. See also Ralph H. Turner, "The Changing Ideology of Success," *Transactions of the Third World Congress of Sociology, 1956* (London), Vol. V, esp. p. 37.

[17] Pointed out by Hide Himmelweit in private communication.

lack of prestige in comparison with the grammar schools.[18]

Under contest mobility in the United States, education is valued as a means of getting ahead, but the contents of education are not highly valued in their own right. Over a century ago Tocqueville commented on the absence of an hereditary class "by which the labors of the intellect are held in honor." He remarked that consequently a "middling standard is fixed in America for human knowledge."[19] And there persists in some measure the suspicion of the educated man as one who may have gotten ahead without really earning his position. In spite of recent criticisms of lax standards in American schools, it is in keeping with the general mobility pattern that a Gallup Poll taken in April, 1958, reports that school principals are much more likely to make such criticisms than parents. While 90 per cent of the principals thought that ". . . our schools today demand too little work from the students," only 51 per cent of the parents thought so, with 33 per cent saying that the work was about right and 6 per cent that schools demanded too much work.[20]

Second, the logic of preparation for a contest prevails in United States schools, and emphasizes keeping everyone in the running until the final stages. In primary and secondary schools the assumption tends to be made that those who are learning satisfactorily need little special attention while the less successful require help to be sure that they remain in the contest and may compete for the final stakes. As recently as December, 1958, a nationwide Gallup Poll gave evidence that this attitude had not been radically altered by the international situation. When asked whether or not teachers should devote extra time to the bright students, 26 per cent of the respondents replied "yes" and 67 per cent, "no." But the responses changed to 86 per cent "yes" and only 9 per cent "no" when the question was asked concerning "slow students."[21]

In western states the junior college offers many students a "second chance" to qualify for university, and all state universities have some provision for substandard high school students to earn admission.

The university itself is run like the true contest: standards are set competitively, students are forced to pass a series of trials each semester, and only a minority of the entrants achieve the prize of graduation. This pattern contrasts sharply with the English system in which selection is supposed to be relatively complete before entrance to university, and students may be subject to no testing whatsoever for the first year or more of university study. Although university completion rates have not been estimated accurately in either country, some figures are indicative of the contrast. In American institutions of higher learning in 1957–1958, the ratio of bachelor's and first-professional degrees to the number of first-time de-

[18] Less adequate financial provision and a higher student-teacher ratio are mentioned as obstacles to parity of secondary modern schools with grammar schools in *The Times Educational Supplement*, February 22, 1957, p. 241. On difficulties in achieving prestige comparable with grammar schools, see G. Baron, "Secondary Education in Britain: Some Present-Day Trends," *Teachers College Record*, LVII (January, 1956), 211–221; and O. Banks, *Parity and Prestige in English Secondary Education* (London: Routledge & Kegan Paul Ltd., 1955). See also Vernon, *op. cit.*, pp. 19–22.

[19] Alexis de Tocqueville, *Democracy in America* (New York: Alfred A. Knopf, Inc., 1945), Vol. I, p. 52.

[20] An earlier Gallup Poll had disclosed that 62 per cent of the parents opposed stiffened college entrance requirements while only 27 per cent favored them. Reported in *Time* (April 14, 1958), 45.

[21] Reported in the *Los Angeles Times*, December 17, 1958, Part I, p. 16.

gree-credit enrollments in the fall four years earlier was reported to be .610 for men and .488 for women.[22] The indicated 39 and 51 per cent drop-out rates are probably underestimates because transfers from two-year junior colleges swell the number of degrees without being included in first-time enrollments. In England, a study of the careers of individual students reports that in University College, London, almost 82 per cent of entering students between 1948 and 1951 eventually graduated with a degree. A similar study a few years earlier at the University of Liverpool shows a comparative figure of almost 87 per cent.[23] Under contest mobility, the object is to train as many as possible in the skills necessary for elite status so as to give everyone a chance to maintain competition at the highest pitch. Under sponsored mobility, the objective is to indoctrinate elite culture in only those presumably who will enter the elite, lest there grow a dangerous number of "angry young men" who have elite skills without elite station.

Third, systems of mobility significantly affect educational content. Induction into elite culture under sponsored mobility is consistent with an emphasis on school *esprit de corps* which is employed to cultivate norms of intraclass loyalty and elite tastes and manners. Similarly, formal schooling built about highly specialized study in fields wholly of intellectual or aesthetic concern and of no "practical" value serves the purpose of elite culture. Under contest mobility in the United States, in spite of frequent faculty endorsement of "liberal education," schooling tends to be evaluated in terms of its practical benefits and to become, beyond the elementary level, chiefly vocational. Education does not so much provide what is good in itself as those skills, especially vocational skills, presumed to be necessary in the competition for the real prizes of life.

These contrasts are reflected in the different national attitudes toward university students who are gainfully employed while in school. More students in the United States than in Britain are employed part-time, and relatively fewer of the American students receive subsidies toward subsistence and living expenses. The most generous programs of state aid in the United States, except those applying to veterans and other special groups, do not normally cover expenses other than tuition and institutional fees. British maintenance grants are designed to cover full living expenses, taking into account parental ability to pay.[24] Under sponsored mobility, gainful employment serves no apprenticeship or testing function, and is thought merely to prevent students from gaining the full benefit of their schooling. L. J. Parry speaks of the general opposition to student employment and asserts that English university authorities almost unanimously hold that ". . . if a person must work for financial reasons, he should never spend more than four weeks on such work during the whole year."[25]

Under contest mobility, success in school work is not viewed as a sufficient test of practical merit, but must be supplemented by a test in the world of prac-

---

[22] U. S. Department of Health, Education, and Welfare, Office of Education, *Earned Degrees Conferred by Higher Education Institutions, 1957–1958* (Washington, D. C.: Government Printing Office, 1959), p. 3.

[23] Nicholas Malleson, "Student Performance at University College, London, 1948–1951," *Universities Quarterly*, XII (May, 1958), 288-319.

[24] See, e.g., C. A. Quattlebaum, *Federal Aid to Students for Higher Education* (Washington, D.C.: Government Printing Office, 1956); and "Grants to Students: University and Training Colleges," *The Times Educational Supplement*, May 6, 1955, p. 446.

[25] "Students' Expenses," *The Times Educational Supplement*, May 6, 1955, p. 447.

tical affairs. Thus in didactic folk tales the professional engineer also proves himself to be a superior mechanic, the business tycoon a skillfull behind-the-counter salesman. By "working his way through school" the enterprising student "earns" his education in the fullest sense, keeps in touch with the practical world, and gains an apprenticeship into vocational life. Students are often urged to seek part-time employment, even when there is no financial need, and in some instances schools include paid employment as a requirement for graduation. As one observer describes the typical American view, a student willing to work part-time is a "better bet" than "the equally bright student who receives all of his financial support from others."[26]

Finally, training in "social adjustment" is peculiar to the system of contest mobility. The reason for this emphasis is clear when it is understood that adjustment training presumably prepares students to cope with situations for which there are no rules of intercourse or for which the rules are unknown, but in which the good opinions of others cannot be wholly ignored. Under sponsored mobility, elite recruits are inducted into a homogeneous stratum within which there is consensus regarding the rules, and within which they succeed socially by mastering these rules. Under contest mobility, the elite aspirant must relate himself both to the established elite and to the masses, who follow different rules, and the elite itself is not sufficiently homogeneous to evolve consensual rules of intercourse. Furthermore, in the contest the rules may vary according to the background of the competitor, so that each aspirant must successfully deal with persons playing the game with slightly different rules. Consequently, adjust-

ment training is increasingly considered to be one of the important skills imparted by the school system.[27] That the emphasis on such training has had genuine popular support is indicated by a 1945 *Fortune* poll in which a national sample of adults was asked to select the one or two things that would be very important for a son of theirs to get out of college. Over 87 per cent chose "Ability to get along with and understand people;" and this answer was the second most frequently chosen as the *very* most important thing to get out of college.[28] In this respect, British education may provide better preparation for participation in an orderly and controlled world, while American education may prepare students more adequately for a less ordered situation. The reputedly superior ability of "Yankees" to get things done seems to imply such ability.

To this point the discussion has centered on the tax supported school systems in both countries, but the different place and emphasis of the privately supported secondary schools can also be related to the distinction between sponsored and contest mobility. Since private secondary schools in both countries are principally vehicles for transmitting the marks of high family status, their mobility function is quite tangential. Under contest mobility, the private schools presumably should have little or no mobility function. On the other hand, if there is to be mobility in a sponsored system, the privately controlled school populated largely with the children of elite parents would be the ideal device

---

[26] R. H. Eckelberry, "College Jobs for College Students," *Journal of Higher Education*, XXVII (March, 1956), 174.

[27] Adjustment training is not a necessary accompaniment of contest mobility. The shift during the last half century toward the increased importance of social acceptability as an elite credential has brought such training into correspondingly greater prominence.
[28] Reported in Hadley Cantril, ed., *Public Opinion 1935–1946* (Princeton, N. J.: Princeton University Press, 1951), p. 186.

through which to induct selectees from lower levels into elite status. By means of a scholarship program, promising members of lesser classes could be chosen early for recruitment. The English "public" schools, in fact, have incorporated into their charters provisions to insure that a few boys from lesser classes will enter each year. Getting one's child into a "public" school, or even into one of the less prestigeful private schools, assumes an importance in England relatively unknown in the United States. If the children cannot win scholarships the parents often make extreme financial sacrifices in order to pay the cost of this relatively exclusive education.[29]

How much of a role private secondary schools have played in mobility in either country is difficult to determine. American studies of social mobility usually omit information on private *versus* tax-supported secondary school attendance, and English studies showing the advantage of "public" school attendance generally fail to distinguish between the mobile and the nonmobile in this respect. However, during the nineteenth century the English "public" schools were used by *nouveaux riches* members of the manufacturing classes to enable their sons to achieve unqualified elite status.[30] In one sense, the rise of the manufacturing classes through free enterprise introduced a large measure of contest mobility which threatened to destroy the traditional sponsorship system. But by using the "public" schools in this fashion they bowed to the legitimacy of the traditional system—an implicit acknowledgement that upward mobility was not complete without sponsored induction. Dennis Brogan speaks of the task of the "public" schools in the nineteenth century as "the job of marrying the old English social order to to the new."[31]

With respect to mobility, the parallel between the tax-supported grammar schools and the "public" schools in England is of interest. The former in important respects have been patterned after the latter, adopting their view of mobility but making it a much larger part of their total function. Generally the grammar schools are the vehicle for sponsored mobility throughout the middle ranges of the class system, modelled after the pattern of the "public" schools which remain the agencies for sponsored mobility into the elite.

Effects of Mobility on Personality

Brief note may be made of the importance of the distinction between sponsored and contest mobility with relation to the supposed effects of upward mobility on personality development. Not a great deal is yet known about the "mobile personality" nor about the specific features of importance to the personality in the mobility experience.[32] However, today three aspects of this experience are most frequently stressed: first, the stress or tension involved in striving for status higher than that of others under more difficult conditions than they; second, the complication of interpersonal relations introduced by the necessity to abandon lower-level friends in favor of uncertain acceptance into higher-level circles; third, the problem of working out an adequate personal scheme of values in the face of movement between classes marked by somewhat variant or even contradictory value systems.[33] The

---

[29] For one account of the place of "public" schools in the English educational system, see Dennis Brogen, *The English People* (New York: Alfred A. Knopf, Inc., 1943), pp. 18–56.

[30] A. H. Halsey of Birmingham University has called my attention to the importance of this fact.

[31] *Op. cit.*, pp. 24–25.

[32] *Cf.* Lipset and Bendix, *op. cit.*, pp. 250 ff.

[33] See, e.g., August B. Hollingshead and Frederick C. Redlich, *Social Class and Mental Illness* (New York: John Wiley & Sons, Inc.,

impact of each of those three mobility problems, it is suggested, differ depending upon whether the pattern is that of the contest or of sponsorship.

Under the sponsorship system, recruits are selected early, segregated from their class peers, grouped with other recruits and with youth from the class to which they are moving, and trained specifically for membership in this class. Since the selection is made early, the mobility experience should be relatively free from the strain that comes with a series of elimination tests and long-extended uncertainty of success. The segregation and the integrated group life of the "public" school or grammar school should help to clarify the mobile person's social ties. (One investigator failed to discover clique formation along lines of social class in a sociometric study of a number of grammar schools.[34]) The problem of a system of values may be largely met when the elite recruit is taken from his parents and peers to be placed in a boarding school, though it may be less well clarified for the grammar school boy who returns each evening to his working-class family. Undoubtedly this latter limitation has something to do with the observed failure of working-class boys to continue through the last years of grammar school and into the universities.[35] In general, then, the factors stressed as affecting personality formation among the upwardly mobile probably are rather specific to the contest system, or to incompletely functioning sponsorship system.

It is often taken for granted that there is convincing evidence to show that mobility-oriented students in American secondary schools suffer from the tendency for cliques to form along lines predetermined by family background. These tendencies are statistically quite moderate, however, leaving much room for individual exceptions. Furthermore, mobility-oriented students usually have not been studied separately to discover whether or not they are incorporated into higher-level cliques in contrast to the general rule. Nor is it adequately demonstrated that the purported working-class value system, at odds with middle-class values, is as pervasive and constraining throughout the working class as it is conspicuous in many delinquent gangs. The model of contest mobility suggests, then, that there is more serious and continuing strain over the uncertainty of attaining mobility, more explicit and continued preoccupation with the problem of changing friendships, and more contradictory learning to inhibit the acquisition of value system appropriate to the class of aspiration than under sponsored mobility. But the extent and implications of these differences require fuller understanding of the American class system. A search for personality-forming experiences specific to a sponsorship system, such as the British, has yet to be made.

Conclusion: Suggestions for Research

The foregoing discussion is broadly impressionistic and speculative, reflecting more the general impression of an observer of both countries than a systematic exploration of data. Relevant data of a variety of sorts are cited above, but

1958); W. Lloyd Warner and James C. Abegglen, *Big Business Leaders in America* (New York: Harper & Row, Publishers, 1955; Warner *et al.*, *Who Shall Be Educated?*, op. cit., Peter M. Blau, "Social Mobility and Interpersonal Relations," *American Sociological Review*, XXI (June, 1956), 290–300.

[34] A. N. Oppenheim, "Social Status and Clique Formation among Grammar School Boys," *British Journal of Sociology*, VI (September, 1955), 228–245. Oppenheim's findings may be compared with A. B. Hollingshead, *Elmtown's Youth* (New York: John Wiley & Sons, Inc., 1949), pp. 204–242. See also Joseph A. Kahl, *The American Class Structure* (New York: Holt, Rinehart & Winston, Inc., 1957), pp. 129–138.

[35] Floud *et al.*, *op. cit.*, pp. 115 ff.

their use is more illustrative than demonstrative. However, several lines of research are suggested by this tentative analysis. One of these is an exploration of different channels of mobility in both England and the United States in an attempt to discover the extent to which mobility corresponds to the mobility types. Recruitment to the Catholic priesthood, for example, probably strictly follows a sponsorship norm regardless of the dominant contest norm in the United States.

The effect of changes in the major avenues of upward mobility upon the dominant norms requires investigation. The increasing importance of promotion through corporation hierarchies and the declining importance of the entrepreneurial path of upward mobility undoubtedly compromise the ideal pattern of contest mobility. The growing insistence that higher education is a prerequisite to more and more occupations is a similar modification. Yet, there is little evidence of a tendency to follow the logic of sponsorship beyond the bureaucratic selection process. The prospect of a surplus of college-educated persons in relation to jobs requiring college education may tend to restore the contest situation at a higher level, and the further possibility that completion of higher education may be more determined by motivational factors than by capacity suggests that the contest pattern continues within the school.

In England, on the other hand, two developments may weaken the sponsorship system. One is positive response to popular demand to allow more children to secure the grammar school type of training, particularly by including such a program in the secondary modern schools. The other is introduction of the comprehensive secondary school, relatively uncommon at present but a major plank in the labour party's education platform. It remains to be determined whether the comprehensive school in England will take a distinctive form and serve a distinctive function, which preserves the pattern of sponsorship, or will approximate the present American system.

Finally, the assertion that these types of mobility are embedded in genuine folk norms requires specific investigation. Here, a combination of direct study of popular attitudes and content analysis of popular responses to crucial issues would be useful. Perhaps the most significant search would be for evidence showing what courses of action require no special justification or explanation because they are altogether "natural" and "right," and what courses of action, whether approved or not, require special justification and explanation. Such evidence, appropriately used, would show the extent to which the patterns described are genuine folk norms rather than mere by-products of particular structural factors. It would also permit determination of the extent to which acceptance of the folk norms is diffused among the different segments of the populations.

Intra-Country Variations:
Occupational Stratification and Mobility

THOMAS FOX   S. M. MILLER

The Study of Social Mobility

The sociological study of social mobility is almost exclusively concerned with occupational mobility. Changes in the distribution of citizenship rights or in social acceptance are not likely to be in the forefront of study of social mobility. Within the investigation of occupational social mobility, primary emphasis is on ranking occupations by prestige levels rather than by indicators of skill, income, or span of control. Occupational prestige indicators, based on surveys of attitudes of a national cross section, are assumed to be adequate summaries of the other dimensions of job positions. The emphasis in present day studies is still chiefly on intergenerational mobility (the relation of son's occupation to father's) rather than on intragenerational mobility (the course of job movement in one individual's career) or of stratum mobility (the movement of one stratum relative to other strata along the relevant dimensions). Thus, the definition of social mobility and the indicators employed to measure it provide only a limited slice of the phenomena commonly regarded

as social mobility by other social scientists.[1]

In making comparisons among nations, a leap of courage must be made. Many of the difficulties of individual studies are compounded in comparative perspective. Some national studies are of poor technical quality, but we have no choice of substitutes if we wish to include a particular nation in a comparison. Time periods differ in various studies; occupational titles and ratings are not fully comparable. Consequently, it is important to recognize that *any comparisons are at best only approximations.*

The usual comparison in mobility studies is the movement of sons of manual families into nonmanual occupations.[2] The concern is with vertical mobility, though downward mobility from nonmanual strata into manual strata has been widely neglected. Cross-national studies of manual-nonmanual mobility make the heroic assumption that the manual-nonmanual divide has equal importance in all nations at all times. This assumption is obviously untrue but it is difficult to make comparisons without it. The manual-nonmanual comparison also suffers from a neglect of intra-stratum mobility, e.g., the movement from unskilled to skilled; from the lower levels of the middle class to elite posi-

Reprinted from "Intra-Country Variations: Occupational Stratification and Mobility," *Studies in Comparative International Development*, I, No. 1 (1965), 3–10, by permission of the authors and the Social Science Institute. Originally presented at an International Conference on the Use of Quantitative Political, Social and Cultural Data in Cross-National Comparison. This study has been supported by project 6-25-124 of the National Science Foundation.

---

[1] *Cf.* S. M. Miller, "Comparative Social Mobility: A Trend Report, "*Current Sociology*, IX, No. 1 (1960), 1–5.

[2] We are interchangeably and loosely using terms like stratum, occupations, and categories.

occupational stratification and mobility   **311**

tions. This kind of movement can be substantial and important but is not caught when the manual-nonmanual divide is the focus of attention.

A number of technical problems intrude in international comparisons. The number of strata employed in a study affects the amount of mobility: the more strata, the more mobility. Therefore, for comparative purposes it is necessary to compress categories into a similar number of groupings. This technical need encourages the utilization of manual-nonmanual compressions. Another difficulty is that while we speak of a sons' generation and of a fathers' generation, we do not in actuality have such pure categories. There are fathers and sons in each occupational category but we treat our data as though each could be factored out.

A number of different types of comparisons are possible with the same data. Movement can be viewed from different perspectives and it is easy to become dizzy with perspectives and over-produce results. In the standard mobility matrix, the rows represent the outflow: "What is the occupational distribution of sons born of fathers in a given stratum?" This type of analysis is the usual one. But we can look across the principal diagonal of the matrix and note the degree of inheritance by sons of fathers' occupations. The columns provide inflow data. "What are the social origins of individuals presently in a given occupational stratum?" Now, the same sons are involved in outflow and inflow analyses; the difference is in what base they are related to in computing rates or percentages. For example, an outflow analysis can show that of 1,000 nonmanual sons 250, or 25 per cent, move into manual strata. From the point of view of manual strata which are larger than the nonmanual strata say, 2,500 sons, the extent of inflow is only 10 per cent. The same movement can have different implications from varying perspectives.

Despite myriad difficulties, comparative studies of social mobility have endured. Sorokin, in his classical study of *Social Mobility* in 1927, amassed a great deal of data but it was not subjected to careful, systematic analysis. Yet, his work was prescient in many ways. For almost two decades comparatively little work was done that referred to nations as a whole. David Glass and Theodore Geiger, in their own work and in the work they fostered in the Research Sub-Committee on Social Stratification and Social Mobility, emphasized in the fifties national studies executed with similar concerns and well-developed methodologies. As a result, we now have many more studies of national rates of social mobility. Seymour Martin Lipset and his collaborators, Reinhard Bendix, Hans Zetterberg and Natalie Rogoff Ramsoy, attempted to make sense out of the array of national mobility data by suggesting a basic similarity in the rates of advanced industrial nations. Miller, in his appraisal of the data, emphasized the neglect of downward mobility in most generalizations about mobility, the varied contours of mobility (e.g., knowledge of manual-nonmanual movement is not revealing about manual-elite movement), and the value of developing typologies of mobility. The work of Peter Blau and Otis Dudley Duncan in making a careful analysis of mobility patterns in the United States based on fresh data in a comparative perspective, may have great significance. At the moment, though, there seems to be a standstill in developing international comparisons of mobility.

The present paper illustrates a few of the various ways of utilizing mobility data. It does not question the international comparability of the data but attempts to improve comparability by restricting analysis to four nations. The concern is with both outflow and inflow. Its particular contribution is that it introduces a new measure which facilitates statements comparing the degree of equality and inequality of mobility among nations.

The Manual-Nonmanual Dichotomy

The conventional profile of social mobility is projected by the manual-nonmanual dichotomy. Table 1 presents profiles for the four nations by way of passage into (inflow mobility) and away from (outflow mobility) the manual and nonmanual strata. Our analysis encompasses both upward and downward mobility in contrast to the more frequent solitary emphasis on upward mobility.[3] Manual inflow and nonmanual outflow illustrate *downward* mobility for sons of nonmanual origins from two points of views—the manual stratum and the nonmanual stratum. Conversely, manual outflow and nonmanual inflow record the *upward* mobility of sons of manual origin into the nonmanual stratum. The importance of qualifying statements about mobility rates by specifying a particular point of reference (inflow or outflow for a particular stratum) is exemplified by studying Table 1.

Beginning with the data on outflow mobility we see that in Great Britain the rate of outflow is greater for the nonmanual stratum than for the manual. Downward movement is greater than upward movement: this description also applies to Japan and the Netherlands but not the United States where upward mobility predominates.

A comparison of the nations on the outflow indicators shows that the United States has the highest rate of upward movement, i.e., manual to nonmanual. It also has the lowest rate of downward movement from the nonmanual stratum.

TABLE 1   Comparative Manual and Nonmanual Inflow and Outflow Mobility (in Percentages)

Nation	Manual mobility		Nonmanual mobility	
	Inflow	Outflow	Inflow	Outflow
Great Britain	24.83	24.73	42.01	42.14
Japan	12.43	23.70	48.00	29.66
Netherlands	18.73	19.77	44.84	43.20
United States	18.06	30.38	32.49	19.55

SOURCE: Data sources for computations are D. V. Glass, et. al., *Social Mobility in Britain* (London: Routledge & Kegan Paul, Ltd., 1954), p. 183; Special tabulations of Johannes van Tulder based on the Survey of the Institute for Social Research in the Netherlands; Sigeki Nishihira, "Cross-National Comparative Study on Social Stratification and Social Mobility," (Japan), *Annuls of the Institute of Statistical Mathematics*, VIII, No. 3 (1957), 187; Richard Centers, "Occupational Mobility of Urban Occupational Strata," *American Sociological Review*, XIII, No. 2 (April, 1948), 138 (limited to sons of urban whites). These social mobility matrices are given in appendix of S. M. Miller, "Comparative Social Mobility," *Current Sociology*, IX, No. 1 (1960), 1ff. (Note: in Center's data for the U.S. as cited by Miller above, categories VIII [farm owners or managers] and IX [farm tenants or laborers] which appear only in the sons' generation have been omitted.)

Great Britain has the most downward movement and is second in terms of upward mobility.

Downward mobility may be more indicative of social fluidity than upward mobility. To illustrate, we are well aware that the process of industrialization has been associated with a decline in the size of the manual stratum, relative to the nonmanual—a phenomenon contributing to upward intergenerational mobility. Downward movement on the other hand may be evidence that sons are not always entitled to their fathers' social position as heir apparent but must be able in their own right or suffer displacement by more capable individuals from lower social strata.[4] If this argument is

[3] *Cf.* Seymour M. Lipset and Reinhard Bendix, *Social Mobility in Industrial Society* (Berkeley, Calif.: University of California Press, 1959).

[4] But the possibility of downward mobility by choice cannot be denied. In this case the son simply prefers an occupation and "way-of-life" that differs from that of his "origin."

valid, then the social structures of Great Britain and the Netherlands are less congealed in some respects than in the United States and Japan—contrary to popular opinion.

The inflow patterns pertain to mobility into a stratum. All four nations are characterized by more heterogeneity of social origins in the nonmanual stratum than in the manual. Heterogeneity is measured by the extent to which sons born into another stratum become members of a given stratum. With Herrington C. Bryce, we have elsewhere dealt in depth with the concepts of heterogeneity-homogeneity that are used here.[5] Britain has the highest heterogeneity in the manual stratum as we would expect from its nonmanual pattern of outflow. But the Netherlands with a similar percentage of nonmanual outflow has less heterogeneity in the manual stratum. Even though nonmanual outflow is high in the Netherlands, its compositional effect on Dutch manual inflow is less than in Great Britain because of the relatively larger proportion of manual sons in the Netherlands.

[5] Herrington J. Bryce, S. M. Miller, and Thomas Fox, "The Heterogeneity of Social Classes in Industrial Societies: A Study in Social Mobility," paper presented at the Spring meetings of the Eastern Sociological Associations, New York City, April, 1963.

Japan and the United States are similar in their changing occupational patterns. Japan has a lower rate of movement out of the manual stratum than the United States but an even higher degree of nonmanual heterogeneity: almost half the nonmanual workers originated in manual families. The United States has an expanding nonmanual stratum which absorbs many from manual homes and, as the nonmanual outflow figure (19 per cent) shows, has the highest level of inheritance of the nonmanual strata.

The data for Great Britain and the Netherlands show little change in the in the contours of the occupational structure between generations: a contour map which *only approximates* reality is presented in Table 2. In the British manual stratum (Table 1), about 25 per cent are of nonmanual backgrounds, "replacing" the 25 per cent born in manual families who have moved up into nonmanual occupations. The corresponding Dutch occupational interchange is about 19 per cent. The inference is that a virtual exchange of social position occurred between the manual sons moving up and an equal *absolute* number of nonmanual sons moving down.

As we have seen, the nonmanual strata are characterized by higher rates of both inflow and outflow mobility than the manual strata in these countries. Interestingly without a deep-seated

TABLE 2   **Percentage Distribution of Strata by Fathers' Generation and Sons' Generation**

	Great Britain		Japan		Netherlands		United States	
	Fathers'	Sons'	Fathers'	Sons'	Fathers'	Sons'	Fathers'	Sons'
Nonmanual	37.11	37.02	26.74	36.17	29.98	30.87	43.97	52.40
Manual	62.89	62.98	73.26	63.82	70.02	69.13	56.03	47.60
Total	100.00	100.00	100.00	99.99	100.00	100.00	100.00	100.00
Elite	7.98	7.49	11.15	11.74	7.18	11.08	8.92	16.86
Middle class	29.13	29.53	15.59	24.45	22.80	19.79	35.04	35.54
Skilled	38.74	33.91	8.52	12.06	32.65	34.22	29.59	19.50
Semiskilled	13.09	16.95	4.02	7.50	26.41	27.39	20.16	20.33
Unskilled	11.06	12.12	60.72	44.26	10.96	7.52	6.28	7.77
Total	100.00	100.00	100.00	100.01	100.00	100.00	99.99	100.00

SOURCE: See Table 1.

change in the occupational distributions among generations, Great Britain and the Netherlands have considerable interchange among social strata. For Japan and the United States, the relative growth of the nonmanual stratum (see Table 2) can account for much of the observed upward mobility. But in Britain and the Netherlands with relatively constant occupational distributions, technological or demand induced mobility fails to explain the fluidity of their respective social structures.

The lower portion of Table 2 pictures changes in occupational structures between generations in greater detail. The elite and middle class were formerly subsumed under the nonmanual category; the skilled, semiskilled, and unskilled collectively composed the manual stratum.

In Great Britain, little change is evident in the sizes of either the elite or middle-class groups—little mobility can be attributed to variations in the relative number of positions within the nonmanual stratum. However the structure within the manual category has altered between generations. The data suggest a decrease in the level of manual skills: the relative size of the skilled substratum has diminished while the semiskilled and unskilled groups have expanded in the sons' generation.

Japan shows little change in the relative size of elites between generations, but a large increase in the middle class. The quality of the manual stratum has shifted upward; the proportion of unskilled declined while both the skilled and semiskilled proportions have increased. Use of the manual classification blankets considerable intra-stratum mobility due to structural changes over time.

The compositional change within the Dutch nonmanual stratum is unusual. Here we note that the relative size of the elite increases, but accompanied by a shrinking middle class. (The other countries portray, at minimum, a moderate middle-class expansion.) Within the manual category, the qualitative trend parallels that in Japan; the unskilled proportion diminishes while that of the skilled and semiskilled increases.

The trend for the elite in the United States shows a large increase, but little change for the middle class. A sharp decline is evident for the skilled group. The semiskilled and unskilled substrata have moderate increments in proportions in the sons' generation. Over half the sons are in the nonmanual stratum, which, as in Japan, is characterized by a large increase in the relative number of nonmanual positions between generations.

Skilled, Semiskilled and Unskilled Outflow into the Nonmanual Stratum

Table 3 breaks down the manual stratum into integral parts, skilled, semiskilled, and unskilled, for a closer look at the sources of upward mobility into the nonmanual category.

In Great Britain, the chances of sons of skilled workers entering the nonmanual stratum are less than two times that of semiskilled sons. Unskilled sons have the greatest disadvantage for such movement but not strikingly less than the semiskilled. The data for the Netherlands and the United States roughly parallels that of the British case: all three nations are characterized by a large gap

TABLE 3   Outflow of Sons of Skilled, Semiskilled and Unskilled Origins into the Nonmanual Stratum (in Percentages)

Social origin	Great Britain	Japan	Netherlands	United States
Skilled	29.08	30.19	26.92	38.55
Semiskilled	18.78	29.33	14.79	21.31
Unskilled	16.54	22.42	10.47	21.05

Source: See Table 1.

between the skilled and semiskilled components of the manual stratum with a relatively smaller gap between the semiskilled and unskilled substrata.

In Japan there is little difference between the skilled and semiskilled movement into nonmanual occupations although intuitively one would expect the skilled to enjoy a relative advantage over the unskilled for upward mobility; both have considerably better opportunities than the unskilled.

Great Britain, the Netherlands and Japan have quite similar percentages of skilled sons entering the nonmanual stratum, but considerably less than in the United States. Inter-country similarities are less pronounced as we turn to the semiskilled and unskilled groups. Semiskilled outflow in Japan is greater than skilled outflow in the Netherlands and has an 8-percentage-point edge on United States semiskilled outflow, which in turn is less than 3 points greater than Great Britain and almost 7 points over the Netherlands. Unskilled outflow is similar in Japan and the United States, followed at some distance by Great Britain, and at a much larger interval by the Netherlands.

This table demonstrates the importance of compositional effects. Despite the highest rate of overall manual movement into the nonmanual stratum, the United States ranks but second in terms of semiskilled and unskilled movement into the top stratum. The United States overall manual rank as highest is primarily due to a considerably larger degree of skilled outflow than that observed in the other nations, and to the numerical importance of the skilled component within the manual stratum.

Sources of Nonmanual Heterogeneity

Table 4 shows the contribution of skilled, semiskilled and unskilled mobility to the composition of the nonmanual

TABLE 4   Sources of Nonmanual Heterogeneity (in Percentages)

Social origin	Great Britain	Japan	Netherlands	United States
Skilled	30.42	7.11	28.47	21.77
Semiskilled	6.64	3.26	12.65	8.20
Unskilled	4.94	37.63	3.71	2.52
Total non-manual inflow	42.00	48.00	44.83	32.49

Source: See Table 1.

stratum. We are now looking at the sources of heterogeneity in social origins among the nonmanual occupations.

In Great Britain, almost three-quarters of the heterogeneity of the nonmanual stratum is due to the mobility of sons of skilled workers. The semiskilled contribution to nonmanual heterogeneity is slightly higher than the unskilled, but considerably less than the skilled. In the Netherlands, the entry of skilled sons accounts for somewhat less than two-thirds of the nonmanual heterogeneity; the semiskilled sons are decidedly more important than the unskilled. Two-thirds of United States nonmanual heterogeneity is due to the movement of skilled sons; semiskilled sons are three times as numerous in the nonmanual stratum as are unskilled. Japan is an anomaly: unskilled sons are the predominant source of nonmanual heterogeneity. This is largely but not fully due to the high percentage of the Japanese labor force which is classified as unskilled. Except for Japan, the skilled category is the greatest contributor to nonmanual heterogeneity. Movement of the semiskilled is greatest in the Netherlands and the United States.

Elite and Middle-Class Movement into the Manual Stratum

A breakdown of the nonmanual stratum into the elite and middle class permits a closer look at the sources of manual heterogeneity. Taking the outflow mobility dimension first, Table 5 gives the percentages of *downward* elite and middle-class mobility.

The United States and Great Britain have low rates of elite outflow. The low figure for the United States was anticipated from prior observations where we noted nonmanual inheritance to be high. Given the extremely high rate of nonmanual outflow in Great Britain (42.1 per cent), a much greater rate of elite outflow would be expected if this substratum is almost as congealed as in the United States. Elite inheritance is lowest in Japan and is similar to the Netherlands in terms of elite outflow.

Middle-class outflow in Great Britain and the Netherlands are similar and high, 50 per cent higher than in Japan and more than double that of the United States. The difference between elite and middle-class outflow rates into the manual stratum is greatest in Great Britain, lowest in Japan.

Table 6 shows the impact on manual

heterogeneity by the *downwardly* mobile sons of elite and middle-class origins. For all countries the elite contribution to the composition of the manual stratum is relatively small, less than 5 per cent (less than 3 per cent if Japan is excepted.) Most of the heterogeneity results from the downward movement of the middle-class origins. Middle-class origins in the manual stratum account for over 20 per cent of the sons in this category in Great Britain and over 15 per cent for the other countries. The four nations each have a noticeable middle class origin effect on the composition of the manual stratum but elite representation is almost nil.

Intra-Country Equality of Mobility Opportunity

Within each country, the distribution of opportunities of sons of other social origins entering any given stratum can be studied with the aid of Feldmesser's index of equality of opportunity.[6] This index takes the proportion of sons remaining in their stratum of origin (e.g., nonmanual sons of nonmanual fathers) in each country as 100. The proportions of sons of other origins entering the given stratum are expressed as ratios to 100. If the proportions or frequencies of sons of all social origins entering any given stratum are equal, all ratios will have the value of 100. In other words, this index examines the proportional representation of all social strata in any given stratum. The further any ratio is from 100, the less opportunity that group has for entering any given stratum than do the sons who inherit the status.

Table 7 presents the indices of intra-country equality of opportunity for the elite, middle class, skilled, semiskilled,

TABLE 5   **Outflow of Sons of Elite and Middle-Class Origins into the Manual Stratum (in Percentages)**

Social origin	Great Britain	Japan	Netherlands	United States
Elite	17.92	26.92	24.26	11.01
Middle Class	47.62	31.62	49.16	20.75

SOURCE: See Table 1.

TABLE 6   **Sources of Manual Heterogeneity (in Percentages)**

Social origin	Great Britain	Japan	Netherlands	United States
Elite	2.27	4.70	2.52	2.78
Middle class	22.56	15.28	16.22	15.28
Total manual inflow	24.83	18.06	18.74	18.06

SOURCE: See Table 1.

[6] Robert A. Feldmesser, *Aspects of Social Mobility in the Soviet Union* (unpublished doctoral dissertation, Harvard University, 1955), pp. 223–225.

TABLE 7   Indices of Equality of
               Opportunity for Entry into
               Elite, Middle Class, Skilled,
               Semiskilled, and Unskilled
               Strata

Equality of opportunity for:				
Elite	Great Britain	Japan	Nether-lands	United States
Elite	100	100	100	100
Middle class	19	39	22	37
Skilled	7	21	20	22
Semiskilled	3	17	6	6
Unskilled	2	18	5	9
X̄	26.2	39.0	30.6	34.8
Middle class				
Middle class	100	100	100	100
Elite	88	65	57	51
Skilled	61	41	41	45
Semiskilled	39	43	29	31
Unskilled	36	29	20	27
X̄	64.8	55.6	49.4	50.8
Skilled				
Skilled	100	100	100	100
Semiskilled	84	53	64	70
Unskilled	80	18	62	56
Middle class	76	20	68	28
Elite	29	20	39	27
X̄	73.8	42.2	66.6	56.2
Semiskilled				
Semiskilled	100	100	100	100
Unskilled	75	23	89	47
Skilled	54	50	46	47
Middle class	36	29	31	21
Elite	16	25	13	8
X̄	56.2	45.4	55.8	44.6
Unskilled				
Unskilled	100	100	100	100
Semiskilled	57	33	48	27
Skilled	48	19	28	18
Middle class	23	24	18	6
Elite	7	18	3	5
X̄	47.0	38.8	39.4	31.2

and unskilled strata for each of the four nations.

Equality of Opportunity in Entering the Elite and Middle-Class Strata

In Great Britain, sons of middle-class fathers enjoy a distinct advantage over sons of skilled, semiskilled and unskilled in securing membership in the elite stratum. The middle-class sons have almost three times the opportunities of the semi-

skilled sons (19/7) of entering the elite, six times the opportunities of the semiskilled (19/3), and nine times the chances of the unskilled (19/2). But the son of an elite father has the best opportunity to become an elite himself—his chances are five times greater than for the son of a middle-class father (100/19) and fifty times that for the son of an unskilled father (100/2). Thus equality of opportunity for movement into the elite category appears extremely limited in Great Britain.

The son of a middle-class father in Japan enjoys almost twice the opportunity of a skilled son (39/21) for gaining admission to elite status, and only slightly more than twice the advantages of the semiskilled and unskilled (respectively, 39/17 and 39/18). Japanese sons of middle-class origins are more than one-third of the way toward achieving elite entry equality with the sons of elite fathers (100/39).

In the Netherlands, sons of middle-class origins have very little advantage over the sons of skilled origins in securing elite status, their chances are almost equal (22/20). But skilled and middle-class sons have considerably better chances of entering the elite than the semiskilled sons. The close proximity of the opportunities of the middle-class and skilled for elite entry suggest, as a possibility, that these groups are more closely related to each other than to the elite category.

Turning now to the United States, we find that here, as in Japan, the sons of middle-class fathers have traveled more than a third of the route leading to equality of opportunity with sons of elite fathers (100/37). Middle-class advantage over offspring of the skilled exists but is less than double the chances of the latter (37/22). The son of a skilled father has almost four times the opportunity of a semiskilled to reach the elite stratum (22/6). (Although the index for equality of opportunity for entry into the elite in the United States is greater for the un-skilled than for the semiskilled, its valid-ity may be questioned and perhaps at-tributed to weaknesses in the original study.)

An average value for the index is given below the last stratum for equality of opportunity of movement into the elite (and for each strata below) but can only be compared within countries, not be-tween them. The data in Table 7 then, do not say that equality of opportunity is greatest in Japan and least in Great Britain.

Equality of Opportunity in Entering the Skilled, Semiskilled, and Unskilled Strata

One of the most striking findings, with the exception of Japan, is that the aver-ages of the indices of equality of oppor-tunity are largest within each country for entry into the skilled stratum, not the middle class, which might be expected. Lloyd Reynolds has recently argued (with respect to the manual stratum) that there is a tendency for the skilled category to become more of a closed group, with the opportunities of move-ment from unskilled and semiskilled oc-cupations into the skilled stratum declin-ing.[7] Although our data are not appro-priate for directly questioning this hy-pothesis, our calculations for Great Bri-tain, Netherlands and the United States show that the skilled stratum is _the group_ in which equality of opportunity is greatest.

Turning to the other end of the social spectrum from the elites—the unskilled —we find an interesting pattern in the USA. The USA shows a relatively lower

degree of equality of access to this occu-pational substratum than do the other nations. At this end of the occupational ladder, low access has different impli-cations than it does at the other end. At the high end, it shows the inability of those below the elite to overcome the barriers. For at the low end, it represents the pooling of the unskilled, their low ability to leave and the relative invulner-ability of the higher strata to such drastic falls in position.[8]

Inter-Country Equality of Opportunity

Feldmesser's index of equality of op-portunity for each of the four nations can be made directly comparable by select-ing the proportion of occupational in-heritance within any given country as the base of the index for each stratum. This measure, developed by Fox, gives the inter-country equality of opportu-nity indices for all countries, relative to the nation selected as the base. Great Britain has been used as the base nation for this paper. If the index for, say, elite inheritance is above 100 in the United States, occupational inheritance would be greater in the United States than in Great Britain with the difference be-tween the respective index values indi-cating how much greater. (The values of the comparative indices for the base-country Great Britain in Table 8 are the same as in Table 7.)

Elite Stratum Comparisons

Table 8 clearly shows that the ability of sons of elite fathers to inherit their fathers' socioeconomic status is greatest in the United States, 24 per cent greater than in Great Britain. The proportion of elite inheritance is second greatest in the

[7] Lloyd G. Reynolds, "Economics of Labor," p. 277 in Howard S. Ellis, ed., _A Survey of Con-temporary Economics_ (Philadelphia: American Economic-Assoc., Blakiston Co., 1948), pp. 255–287.

[8] _Cf._ Lipset and Bendix, _op. cit._, pp. 57–58 and 64–68.

TABLE 8   **Comparative Indices of Equality of Opportunity for Entry into Elite, Middle Class, Skilled, Semiskilled and Unskilled Strata (Base=Great Britain)**

Equality of opportunity for:	Great Britain	Japan	Netherlands	United States
Elite				
Elite	100	86	119	124
Middle class	19	34	26	46
Skilled	7	18	24	27
Semiskilled	3	15	7	7
Unskilled	2	15	6	12
X̄	26.2	33.6	36.4	43.2
Middle class				
Middle class	100	143	92	137
Elite	88	93	53	70
Skilled	61	59	38	62
Semiskilled	39	61	27	42
Unskilled	36	42	18	37
X̄	64.8	79.6	45.6	69.6
Skilled				
Skilled	100	111	112	81
Semiskilled	84	59	72	56
Unskilled	80	19	69	45
Middle class	76	22	77	22
Elite	29	22	43	23
X̄	73.8	46.6	74.6	45.4
Semiskilled				
Semiskilled	100	81	148	144
Unskilled	75	19	132	67
Skilled	54	40	69	68
Middle class	36	23	45	30
Elite	16	20	19	12
X̄	56.2	36.6	82.6	64.2
Unskilled				
Unskilled	100	233	74	144
Semiskilled	57	78	35	39
Skilled	48	44	21	26
Middle class	23	56	14	9
Elite	7	42	2	7
X̄	47.0	90.6	29.2	45.0

entry in the Netherlands is about three and one-half that of the skilled in Great Britain—one and one-fourth that in Japan. The Japanese semiskilled and unskilled have the advantage over their contemporaries in Great Britain, the Netherlands, and the United States in terms of their chances of becoming elites —almost the opportunities of the middle class in Great Britain.

Strikingly, the averages of the indices for elite entry show opportunity to be greatest in the United States (more than one and a half that in Great Britain), followed at some distance by the Netherlands, then Japan and Great Britain. When we examined the intracountry equality of opportunity in Table 7 (within countries), Japan had the highest rate of intra-country elite equality, followed by the United States. This means that in Japan, there is less difference between the proportions of various strata entering the elite and the proportion of elite inheritance. But in the United States (with its expanding elite) the *actual* proportions of the different strata entering the elite are greater than those in Japan. In other words, relatively larger proportions of nonelite and elite origin sons tend to become members of the elite stratum in the United States than in Japan.

Middle-Class Comparisons

Middle-class stratum inheritance is proportionally highest in Japan, then the United States, both with a degree of middle-class inheritance at least 35 per cent greater than in Great Britain. The Netherlands has the lowest proportion of inheritance. Sons of elite fathers have the highest relative chance of falling into the middle class in Japan and England. This might be expected since elite inheritance was lowest in Japan and England, therefore, relatively more sons of

Netherlands—least in Japan. Middle-class and skilled sons in the United States also have better chances of becoming elites than their counterparts in the other three nations. The USA has high inheritance and high accessibility. The middle class in Japan has almost double the opportunity of the British middle class of gaining elite membership and 30 per cent better than the Netherlands middle class. Skilled opportunity for elite

elites experience downward mobility of one step to the middle class.

Strikingly, although United States elite inheritance was the highest, then closely followed by the Netherlands, United States sons of elite fathers have considerably greater relative likelihood of entering the middle class than in the Netherlands.

There is little difference between the proportion of skilled entering the middle class in the United States and Great Britain, with Japan in close proximity. But much less opportunity for skilled movement into the middle class exists in the Netherlands.

Semiskilled and unskilled opportunity for middle-class movement is greatest in Japan and the United States, then Great Britain. The opportunity for unskilled entry into the middle class in Japan is about two and a half times as great as in the Netherlands.

Skilled Comparisons

When the focus of attention shifts to comparison of equality of opportunity for entry into the skilled category, the United States loses much of its former prominence, showing considerably less skilled inheritance than the base-country Great Britain and the other two nations. Dutch skilled inheritance is slightly greater than Japan; both are about 10 per cent greater than in Great Britain. The proportion of semiskilled entering the skilled category is highest in Great Britain, strangely enough, with this holding also for sons of unskilled origins. In the Netherlands, the opportunity of semiskilled and unskilled movement into the skilled stratum is considerably less than in Great Britain but well above that in the United States and Japan. Japanese sons of semiskilled fathers have but a slight advantage over those in the United States. The Japanese unskilled are the most disadvantaged, having but

about one-half the chances of the United States unskilled to enter the skilled stratum and one-third the Dutch unskilled chances. The unskilled in Great Britain have four times the proportion of sons in the skilled categories as in Japan.

Overall, averages of the indices show the chance to become a member of the skilled stratum is highest in the Netherlands and Great Britain, with both countries ranking well above Japan and the United States.

Semiskilled Comparisons

The Netherlands and the United States have considerably greater semiskilled inheritance than Great Britain. In turn, Japan has about 20 per cent less than Great Britain. The proportion of unskilled entering the semiskilled stratum in the Netherlands is double that in the United States, less than twice that in Great Britain. Skilled and unskilled chances for semiskilled stratum entry are about equal in the United States. The middle classes and elites are less represented in the semiskilled stratum.

Unskilled Comparisons

Unskilled socioeconomic inheritance in Japan is two and one-third that in Great Britain—significantly greater than in the United States, the second highest nation on unskilled inheritance. Dutch unskilled inheritance is but about one-half that in the United States. Japanese unskilled inheritance of such astronomical proportions is in part explained by the tremendous size of this group in the Japanese social structure. But the most astounding index value for the unskilled stratum occurs for the elite chance in Japan of becoming a member of the unskilled. Elite entry into the unskilled in Japan is six times greater than in the United States and Great Britain, twenty times that in the Netherlands. The unskilled entry values in Japan for skilled, middle-class and elite movement are similar within a limited range, whereas the spread between these social strata is considerably greater for the other three countries. In the case of Great Britain, we find, however, that the proportion of the skilled entering the unskilled is somewhat greater than in Japan, but around twice that in the United States and Netherlands.

Conclusions?

We wish that we could offer a concise and parsimonious explanation of the variations in the rates of social mobility both within and between the countries. But we cannot. The following fragmentary observations are substitutes for all-encompassing empirical generalizations or explanatory theorems.

There are a host of different ways of measuring mobility. And mobility has many varied contours. Mobility statements, as we have said elsewhere,[9] must be specific—indicative of a particular frame of reference, e.g., only manual into nonmanual; or the degree of heterogeneity of the elite substratum. As a corol-

---

[9] Miller, *op. cit.*, p. 5; Bryce, Miller, and Fox, *loc. cit.*

lary, patterns of mobility seem to differ in different parts of the class structure. A statement of accessiblity to elite status is inadequate for describing (let alone understanding) accessibility to the unskilled stratum. Inheritance and accessibility are different dimensions of similar phenomena.

Aware of the pitfalls inherent in mobility analysis, we still find it a fruitful area of research. We think it can be further extended, as we plan to do, attempting to see under what conditions of social mobility, political stability is greatest. If political scientists and others would give us indicators of political stability, it would be helpful.

Mobility analysis is not an "open sesame" to understanding everything—studies of fertility have shown this. We think American sociologists have a dreadful predilection to explain *everything* in terms of status panic or reward, instability or stability. This status concern may be more revealing about sociologists than about societies! But we believe that the study of social mobility, especially if broadly conceived, gives us a picture, though not complete, of changes taking place in socio-occupational patterns. And it gives snapshots of different periods of time, which if used judiciously, should be illuminating.

Family and Mobility

WILLAM J. GOODE

It seems useful . . . at this time to sketch some of the central structural points at which family variables seem to affect the mobility process in general, or the specific rise and fall of individuals.

Excerpted from *Family and Mobility*, A Report to the Institute of Life Insurance (New York: Institute of Life Insurance, 1963), pp. 32–41 and 61–72, by permission of the author and the publisher.

Unigeniture versus Equal Division of Property

All family systems have two conflicting aims, (1) to maintain intact the family property as it descends, from one generation to the next; and (2) to provide for all its children adequately. Since property is limited, a division of property each generation will mean that the children in the first generation will very likely not have as much individually as the parents have enjoyed together—and of course in successive generations the property is dissipated into holdings that become financially trivial. On the other hand, to give all the property to one child only, whether the first child or the last child, means that the others will not be properly provided for. Even where there is only one son, it is likely that the dowry system will require a substantial amount of family property to leave with the daughter who marries. Some evidence now suggests that the single-heir or unigeniture system of inheritance may effect economic and social mobility patterns. Since the data remain fragmentary, as yet, it seems useful merely to offer the following speculations.

First, with regard to population growth itself, where a single heir inherited all the property, this landowner himself had little reason to limit the number of his children, but his own brothers and sisters often could not marry at all, or had to remain unmarried for many years. Where there was an equal division of property, almost everyone could marry, even at a low level of subsistence, but in turn the lower level of subsistence may have motivated some to limit the number of their own offspring. It seems likely that the regions of equal division of property had in general a higher rate of population growth.

With respect to geographical and social mobility, two types of processes are visible. In all the agricultural regions of Europe in the 19th century, there was considerable short term or seasonal geographical mobility, in which the basic occupation did not change. An individual might have a small landholding from which he worked with his kinsmen, but during the harvest season he might move a short distance in order to earn wages.[1]

As for geographic mobility over a greater distance, permanent migration, and change of occupation, it seems likely that the single-heir system facilitated all three far more than the equal division of property. This system created more unmarried males, who at best were given some small financial settlement, but no hope of any substantial amount of family property. The system of equal inheritance gave little to each individual, but each person thereby had some stake in keeping his own holding, and supplementing his small income with wages for hired labor in the locality.

This last factor created another difference. Since people in the regions of equal division were somewhat more tied to their locality, if industry was to develop at all it had to come to the population, and this would happen only if the region possessed some advantage in natural resource. However, in regions of countries of single-heir inheritance, the population could go to the area in which industry was being established, usually in areas where natural resources facilitated its development. By contrast, in equal-division areas, small local industries could develop. Thus the theoretical speculation seems warranted that at least one factor in the industrial development of both England and Germany was a relatively greater preponderance of single-heir inheritance, which also thrust more of the sons of any given generation into new occupations some distance from home.

Heterogamy and Homogamy

As more than one analyst has noted, marriage and courtship systems may be

---

[1] H. J. Habakkuk, "Family Structure and Economic Change in 19th Century Europe," *Journal of Economic History*, XV, No. 1 (1955), 7.

viewed as market systems. In some societies it is the elders who do the haggling, while in Western countries generally it is the young people themselves who select one another, but in either case, the most common result is that people at any given social level usually marry others at that same level. In a free market system such as our own, where the woman does not typically rise in social position through her occupation, she must seek a mobile husband if she wishes to be mobile herself. Because a man loses esteem in our society if he does not work for a living, very few men can solve their personal problem of support by marrying a woman with sufficient wealth, but this fact must not disguise the possibility that he may be helped in his upward movement by marrying into a family that will afford him additional opportunities.

Although the pattern of homogamy—"like marries like"—is found in all societies, it is more than an expression of preference for a mate similar to oneself or one's family. It is the resultant of a market process in which either elders or courting young people attempt to locate the most desirable mate, just as a seller attempts to obtain the very best price for his commodities. However, since others in marriageable ages are doing precisely the same thing, the net resultant is that in general those who marry will actually be able to choose a spouse who has roughly the same market value. Even in the romance-laden system of the United States, young people are highly aware of the potential advantages that this or that possible spouse might offer, and peers are quick to point out to an individual that he "can do better than that."

Homogamy, then, is not merely ethnocentricism. It is also the blind result of many individuals who in seeking the very best possible spouses for their children or for themselves, and by virtue of the types of offers made or rejections re-

ceived, come to find spouses of their own social and economic level. This process however opens the possibility, again universally found in all societies, of exchanging desirable characteristics *other* than those of simple social rank, and of making a bargain in which there is rough equality of exchange, but very different things exchanged. Perhaps at all times in the history of the world it has been possible for some women to exchange their beauty for a man's social rank or power. Many men whom years have carried beyond youth and beauty must throw into the scales some of their achievements in the market place or in family lineage, in order to obtain the charm and loveliness of a young woman as wife. Women of social position may also exchange it for *potential achievement;* that is, a talented young man may, even without much income, obtain a wife above him in the social scale, simply because his future worth is worth a good deal on the present marriage market. Note however that *what* may be exchanged is defined by the society itself. Thus in the Jewish ghetto, a poor young man devoted to learning could count to some extent on his intellectual achievement as a basis for obtaining a wife with money, and this was at least an ideal in Imperial China. On the other hand, our society disapproves of a marriage exchange in which it is the woman who has the brains and talent, and the young man has great beauty; or the woman has social position and money, and the man has youth. In such cases it becomes clear that the society requires the man to achieve some part of his position with his own work and ability. A young man is not disapproved, for example, if he marries the boss's daughter, *but also* works hard to make a success of the company.

From the considerable mass of data demonstrating that generally people marry within the same class, ethnic group, economic level, religion, and age, (or at least that they are far more likely to marry within those categories than could occur by chance alone) two major processes ought to be noted here. One is, that though young people in our society insist on making this important family decision, while their elders are somewhat dubious of their ability to make wise choices, the sifting process actually begins at the earliest years of association among children. That is, marriage is the final point in a long process, and since young people will fall in love with and marry only the people they meet, their parents attempt to control whom they meet.

This process is reflected in the data in Hollingshead's research in Elmtown, where he recorded 1,258 clique ties. Three out of five of these ties were between boys or girls at the same class level, and nearly two out of five between boys and girls only one class removed. In the few instances when a clique tie included a child two classes removed, the child was usually an outstanding one. When boys and girls noted who was their "best friend," 70 per cent were with class equals. Somewhat similar patterns were found in dating.

Sussman's analysis of about one hundred middle class families showed that even in the young adult years before marriage, parents attempt to control their social contacts by inviting marital prospects to the home for a weekend, supervising their parties, choosing schools and so on. Indeed, when these young people expressed some intention of marrying an "inappropriate" person, in 81 per cent of the cases the parents used extended persuasion or threats of economic withdrawals in order to break up the relationship.

It is not surprising, then, that in the United States about half of all marriages occur between people who live no more than one mile from one another, and toward the upper strata the distances are much greater—but this means only that those with social and economic advantages can more easily travel longer distances to find similar spouses.

This large process, coupled with the process of market sifting, points to a second pattern, which is that in spite of the research data suggesting an increasing number of marriages between people of different classes, in fact such unions are likely to take place between young people of different class *origins*, but very similar life styles. That is, one of the spouses is socially mobile, and has taken on the cultural patterns, attitudes, and even aspirations common in the class of the potential spouse.

This reflects indeed the pattern of class mobility in many societies in the past. Perhaps the two most striking instances are those of China and 18th-century France.[2] In France, the amount of dowry necessary for achieving an upward marriage between the young daughter of a merchant family and a noble family was quite widely known, the amount necessary rising with each successive layer in the hierarchy of nobility. However, it cannot be supposed that such marriages occurred between an uneducated merchant's daughter and an elegant courtier. Rather, the merchant's family began to live "nobly" before such a marriage took place, and might well be interacting socially on fairly intimate terms with noble families, while the young women themselves were of course being educated in all the graces necessary for a high born lady.

In both France and China one may say that the typical process of upward mobility consisted in the family obtaining its wealth in business or manufacturing, but then moving from such activities

---

[2] For an excellent description of the French process, see Elinor Barber, *The Bourgeoise in 18th-Century France* (Princeton, N. J.: Princeton University Press, 1955).

into official position and a life style common to the elite of the society. For China, the evidence seems to be that maintenance of a mandarin's status over generations was relatively difficult, once the source of wealth in business had been abandoned.

In any event it seems fairly clear that the upper class family must maintain a higher control over its young members, especially in the choice of spouse, if the family is not to lose its position.

Choices in marriage seem not to be a major source of upward or downward mobility in any society although any society seems to exhibit some degree of upward movement of this type. We may however present here a few of the major findings now available.

1. Since women depend far more than men upon their mate choice as a basis for their future social position, they tend to be more objective in weighing the characteristics of their potential spouses.
2. Since men derive less benefit from marrying upward socially, they have a wider range of permitted mates; i.e., they can marry downward without losing in prestige. At the same time, the higher their social position, the more they are worth on the marriage market.
3. Consequently, far more men marry downward than upward, whether the index used is education, income, or prestige. Moreover, in the higher social strata, a higher percentage of men marry eventually, but a lower percentage of women.
4. The average ages at marriage are higher toward the upper social strata, although the differences are not great. However, both men and women who marry upward are likely to marry earlier than those who marry at the same class level.[3]
5. In general, the occupational career of women has little effect on the direction

of movement when they marry. However, Danish data suggest that working women who marry downward had experienced some downward occupational mobility before that marriage; and women who move upward occupationally before marriage are more likely to marry upward as well.

Perhaps a parallel association is that the higher a man's father-in-law's social status is, relative to the groom himself, the more likely is the man to be occupationally upwardly mobile.[4]

6. Women who marry upward socially are more likely to have higher than average I.Q. scores than women who marry within their own stratum; and those who marry within their own social stratum have higher scores than those who marry downward.[5]

Achievement, Aspiration, and Family Structure

Let us first begin with some simple distinctions in order to clarify the phenomenon we wish to examine. The major distinctions may be stated as follows:

1. The psychological need for achievement may not always be expressed in *action*, but may instead occur primarily in fantasy, and result in little more than self-dissatisfaction.
2. Similarly, mobility *values*, or aspirations, may not be supported by a psychological need for achievement, or by any effective drive.
3. A high score on an I.Q. test does not necessarily mean a high level of *creativity*; the high score may merely

---

[3] Ramkrishna Mukherjee, "Social Mobility and Age at Marriage," in D. V. Glass, ed., *Social Mobility in Britain* (London: Routledge & Kegan Paul Ltd., 1954), p. 342.

[4] Kaare Svalastoga, "The Family in the Mobility Process," in *Recherches sur la Famille*, ed. Nels Anderson, Vol. III (Göttingen: Vandenhoeck and Ruprecht, 1958), pp. 302–4.

[5] Eileen M. Scott, R. Illsley, and A. M. Thompson, "A Psychological Investigation of Primigravidae." II—Maternal Social Class, Age, Physique, and Intelligence," *Journal of Obstetrics and Gynaecology of the British Empire*, LXIII (June, 1956), 339–40.

mean that the individual learns quickly.

4. Neither high I.Q. scores nor creativity necessarily means that the individual will be impelled to move upward in the social system.

5. The most likely theories of psychodynamics of our time do not suggest that the creative or mobile person is more neurotic, or that the neurotic person is either more mobile or creative.

Let us now begin with an apparently anomalous finding, that is, a finding that somehow seems not to fit common experience: Numerous studies have reported that eminent scientists, scholars, and men of letters are more likely to be first *born* or only children, than they are to be later born children. Ordinal position in the family seems to have some consequences for achievement and mobility. It is not necessary to summarize the wide array of data that have been recorded here and there since Francis Galton's *English Men of Science: Their Nature and Nurture* in 1871. A recent attempt by Stanley Schachter to explain this peculiarity has both summarized the data, and arrived at no conclusive explanation.[6]

Some have attempted to explain this phenomenon by asserting that the first child or the only child lives in a different kind of intellectual environment, in that he is required to manipulate verbal symbols far more, to engage in more abstract thinking, and thus acquires adult thinking patterns earlier, including of course linguistic skills.[7]

Indeed, such a finding is somewhat in harmony with other data, which Nisbet also cites. The finding is also in accord with the general finding, from many nations, that I.Q. level drops with size of family.[8] The fact that youngest children are only slightly behind first born or only children in achievement would also follow from such an interpretation.

Since this finding is upheld even when size of family is kept constant, some have also attempted a psychodynamic interpretation, and with this interpretation we must enter still more complex theories and data. The suggestion has been offered that the first born child is more likely to be *dependent* psychologically, to have greater anxiety with reference to the problems of controlling *others*, inhibited aggression, and also a greater strength of total *drive*.[9]

It should be emphasized that social psychologists have spent much intellectual energy on this point not because of its intrinsic significance, but because they have suspected that underlying it is some set of important processes that may generate achievement, mobility, or perhaps even creativity. In technical terms, the percentage of first born in any population of eminent people is far greater than chance, but this variable does not explain much of the *variance*. That is, one cannot predict eminence from being first born; one can only assert that among the eminent a higher percentage than expected will be first born. Thus, Cattell and Brimhall found in their 1920 study that though one might expect one-third of the men born in three-child families would be first born, one-third

[6] "Birth Order, Eminence, and Higher Education," *American Sociological Review*, XXVIII (October, 1963), 757–768. See also the numerous references in his *The Psychology of Affiliation* (Stanford, Calif.: Stanford University Press, 1959), esp. Chaps. 5 and 6.

[7] John Nisbet, "Family Environment and Intelligence," in A. H. Halsey, Jean Floud, and C. Arnold Anderson, eds., *Education, Economy, and Society* (New York: The Free Press, 1961), pp. 273–287.

[8] See the summary of materials in Seymour M. Lipset and Reinhard Bendix, *Social Mobility in Industrial Society* (Berkeley and Los Angeles: University of California Press, 1960), pp. 238 ff.

[9] Robert R. Sears, "Ordinal Position in the Family as a Psychological Variable," *American Sociological Review*, XV (June, 1950), 400–401.

second born and one-third born third in order, in fact, some 44 per cent of these starred scientists from three-child families were first born.[10]

This is 10 per cent more than expected. The greater dependence of the first child on his *mother*, and the supposed ensuing greater anxiety and drive, raise many questions, but point to one important line of research. It is not immediately evident why dependency and anxiety might lead to high achievement, but an increasing body of evidence has suggested that the relationship of the child to his mother may be crucial in achievement motivation. Moreover, the research which bears out this general hypothesis is partly inconsistent with other findings of an essentially sociological nature. A precise statement of exactly how much of what is needed to create maximum motivation is not to be found anywhere in the literature. The main thrust of this hypothesis is that somewhere between six and eight years of age the son should have a relatively close relationship with his mother, and in his interaction with a somewhat weak or ineffectual father should have the general experience of "winning" against the father, but in coalition with his mother. Similarly, maximum need for motivation does not occur when the mother is merely indulgent; she must insist on meeting performance norms that are not beyond his capacity.[11]

In a somewhat more speculative use of such psychodynamic explanation, Hagen has suggested that they are the source of not merely individual mobility and achievement, but economic growth and development as well.[12]

Data from many civilizations past and present have been unearthed in support of this very rough hypothesis. One research in Brazil, for example, noted that in middle class circles the mother is indulgent but not insistent upon the boy meeting performance standards rigorously; and the boy in turn cannot win against the very strong Brazilian father. He thus does not become accustomed to thinking of the world as something that he can master.[13]

Similarly a recent article on the influence of dormitory roommates upon one another ties both achievement motivation and ordinal position together. This rather ingenious and complex experiment shuffled the allocation of rooms to students upon their arrival at college, so that various combinations of high and low ability room mate pairs were created. They found that though in general the high ability student influences others, by developing ideas, by giving help, or setting an example for study, any substantial amount of influence occurred only when the high ability roommate is *later* born than the other student. That is to say the *first-born* student (whether or not he has high ability) responds more vigorously to the influence of the high ability roommate. Thus the first-born student might be called more "dependent"; but at the same time he is highly motivated to achieve, and responds to the high per-

---

[10] Schachter, "Birth Order, Eminence, and Higher Education, *op. cit.*, pp. 758–759. See also James McK. Cattell and Dean R. Brimhall, *American Men of Science*, 3rd ed. (Garrison, N.Y.: Science Press, 1921).

[11] A wide range of research material has been summarized in David C. McClelland, *The Achieving Society* (Princeton, N. J.: D. Van Nostrand Co., Inc., 1961), esp. Chap. 9.

A statement that discriminates better between achievement *values* and motivation may be found in F. L. Strodtbeck, "Family Interaction, Values, and Achievement," in McClelland, *et al.*, *Talent and Society* (Princeton, N. J.: D. Van Nostrand Co., Inc., 1958), pp. 135–194.

[12] Everett E. Hagen, *On the Theory of Social Change* (Homewood, Ill.: Richard D. Irwin, Inc., 1962).

[13] Bernard C. Rosen, "Socialization and Achievement Motivation in Brazil," *American Sociological Review*, XXVII (December, 1962), 612ff.

formance of his high ability roommate by moving his own performance upward.[14]

Some further implications of this approach should be noted. We should not be surprised for example that children reared in primitive societies would have a relatively low motivation toward achievement. In most of them, the child is reared extremely permissively, but is also taught to stay within very narrow boundaries of action, thought and attitude. The father or (in matrilineal societies) the mother's brother has a firm hand and the boy may not challenge authority in any serious way. He does not have the experiences of winning against outside forces. Some cross-cultural study of the achievement motivation in a few societies has been carried out, but with inconclusive results, since the primary materials used were simply the various themes of struggle and strife used in folk tales within the society rather than the actual behavior patterns.[15] Moreover, some societies with a fairly high rating in achievement motivation are actually societies which are extremely group oriented, and do not approve individual achievement.

This general approach also derives some support from the fact that when the mother's or the father's education is higher than the average for their occupational stratum, then sons are more likely to be mobile; and if the father is downwardly mobile, sons are more likely to be upwardly mobile. For if the mother's education is higher than that of the people in her stratum, she is more likely to press the son to meet standards of competition and performance, since it is only through his efforts that she can enjoy a sense of accomplishment. And if the father is downwardly mobile, or has more education than others in his occupation, and thus apparently has not been a success, then it seems more likely that he would not be a strong figure in the eyes of his son.

Locating this source of striving in the parent-child relationship and thus de-emphasizing the peer group runs counter to much popular journalism of our time, but all studies of adolescence show that their attitudes and values, their aspirations and plans, are highly consonant with those of their parents. The adolescent rebellion is a superficial one. Moreover, where lower class boys are strongly oriented towards college, in almost all cases the pressure comes from the parents—whatever other sources there may be.[16]

Some foundation for this type of exploration may also be found from a study of families with highly gifted children, in which the *mother* or *grandmother* played a vital role in family life, emphasizing educational skills and planning the non-school activities of the children.[17] Looking for motivational sources of upward mobility seems worthwhile in part because (as noted earlier) a substantial percentage of the abler young people in our society do *not* go to college; because there is often a discrepancy between aspiration *values* and the *motivation* to achieve. In the middle classes, a higher

[14] Robert M. Hall and Ben Willerman, "The Educational Influence of Dormitory Room Mates," *Sociometry*, XXVI (September, 1963), 294–318. The authors do not, however, introduce achievement motivation as a factor; I am pointing out this connection.

[15] David C. McClelland and G. A. Friedman, "A Cross-Cultural Study of the Relationship Between Child-Training Practices and Achievement Motivation Appearing in Folk Tales," in *Readings in Social Psychology*, eds. Guy E. Swanson, Theodore Newcomb, and Eugene L. Hartley (New York: Holt, Rinehart & Winston, Inc., 1952), pp. 243–249.

[16] Joseph A. Kahl, "Educational and Occupational Aspirations of 'Common Man' Boys," *Harvard Educational Review*, XXIII (Summer, 1953), 186–203.

[17] Paul M. Sheldon, "The Families of Highly Gifted Children," *Marriage and Family Living*, XVI (February, 1954), 59–60, 67.

proportion of both children and parents express aspiration values; that is, they believe it would be good to move upward, that it is good to work hard, and so on. However, this does not mean that they attempt to *live by* those values, and psychological exploration of their motivation suggests that they may *express* such values without at all being highly motivated to achieve.

Indeed—and here common observation may bear out some exploratory research—the more the father subscribes to achievement values, the less his son's power in the family is likely to be.[18]

Of some relevance, though not directly in support, is the finding of Sewell and others that parents toward the lower classes do require a certain type of autonomy from their children, but upon examination it turns out not to be any encouragement towards self-directed activities, with a close watch over performance and applause for going past the boundaries successfully; but it is rather a type of *rejection*, a demand that the youngster be able to take care of himself. That is, he is encouraged to have a high degree of skill in "caretaker activities" rather than in achievement activities.

It is perhaps worth remarking, as a mere passing comment on this exploratory research, the people who have a high need for achievement prefer certain types of odds in their gains—and perhaps in their occupational lives as well. They do not gravitate towards easy tasks with very little payoff; or towards extremely difficult tasks with a high payoff but a low chance of success. They seem rather to seek out odds and chances (when given the option) in which they may have about a fifty-fifty chance of winning, and the task is a rather difficult one. Perhaps one might phrase this in a crude way by saying that the person with a high need for achievement seeks tasks that will strain him somewhat; but which he can conquer or master with extra effort (and an ensuing good payoff).[19]

Nevertheless, the careful reader will have already felt some small doubts about both the theory and the facts of this line of speculation. We do not believe that at present it is possible to clarify all of these. As a way of presenting some of the discrepancies and the difficulties in this set of relationships, the following list of findings is presented. They have been taken from different samples, with research techniques of doubtful validity; and the problems of measurement are great in all of them. They do offer a challenge to the society that wishes to utilize its human potential more effectively, and to the sociologist who wishes to understand better how family relations interact with mobility processes.

1. Striving for achievement is more frequent among boys who felt their relationship with their parents was *un*-satisfying.
2. Lower-class men who later become business leaders often show a pattern of strong mothers and weak fathers, and an emotionally unsatisfying family life.
3. Boys who aspire upward are more likely to share their leisure activities with their parents and to come from warm, permissive family backgrounds.
4. Middle class parental values emphasize self-direction, consideration for others, and curiosity, while putting somewhat less stress on obedience to parental commands than do working class parents.
5. Men from middle class backgrounds are

---

[18] And thus the son may have a much less frequent experience of winning over powerful forces: Jerome K. Myers and Bertram H. Roberts, eds., *Family and Class Dynamics in Mental Illness* (New York: John Wiley & Sons, Inc., 1959), p. 182.

[19] Additional support for these assertions may be found in Robert A. Ellis and W. Clayton Lane, "Structural Supports for Upward Mobility," *American Sociological Review*, XXVIII (October, 1963), 748–756.

more likely to strive upward, and are also more likely to be work-oriented while rejecting strong family ties or strong ties with their fathers; on the other hand men from upper class families are still more successful but are less oriented towards work as a field of accomplishment while having stronger family feelings and more respect for their father.

6. A lower satisfaction with family relationships is positively related to a willingness to sacrifice in order to achieve a higher level of occupation.

7. Toward the lower strata, and especially among Negroes, the mother is likely to be stronger and the father somewhat weaker, than in the middle and upper classes, but children from these backgrounds strive upwards much less vigorously, both in school and occupation.

6. Those who have a high level of aspiration are more likely to feel that they were not much wanted by either father or mother, or both. Middle class fathers do not in general approve of a career for their daughters, and unmarried *mobile* career women in the middle classes are more likely to have felt that they were partially rejected in favor of one of the siblings, than the *non*-mobile women.

9. Children who rate their parents as very dominant and low in affection toward them were judged least favorably by their classmates.

10. The lack of a strong father figure with whom to identify may create in the son a weak masculine ego.

11. Mental illness is more likely to occur if an individual's brothers or sisters are seen as having been more successful.

12. Mental disorders are more common among people who see a great discrepancy between their aspirations and what they are actually achieving.[20]

13. At similar levels of occupational achievement, the higher the level of education, the higher the rate of schizophrenia (that is, the greater the *discrepancy* between the level of training and the level of achievement).

---

[20] With reference to the general problem of striving for goals and emotional or mental difficulties, the following book analyzes this set of relationships: Seymour Parker and Robert J Kleiner, *Goal Striving and Mental Disorder* (New York: The Free Press, 1964).

mobility II:
reactions to evaluation

eight

    Because mobility from previously "lower" positions is generally viewed as something "positive" within the value system of a democratic and mobility-minded society, there is a tendency to overlook those consequences of mobility which may have negative influences upon other valued social states or conditions.

    Melvin M. Tumin has considered some of those consequences in "Some Unapplauded Consequences. . . ." He is concerned here with (1) the fragmentation of the social order that may occur in periods of rapid social mobility, (2) the extent to which the idea of doing well, economically speaking, can become of paramount value and thereby lead to a denial of the worth of work and to the corollary development of a cult of the "quick buck," (3) the tendency for people who have experienced mobility to forget the difficult conditions from which they moved, the amount of social criticism they endured, and the number of social changes they made in order to make their movement possible, and, finally, (4) the extent to which the displacement of persons through social mobility may lead to a generalized diffusion of insecurity and anxiety regarding place and worth.

    Dorothy L. Meier and Wendell Bell look at some of the same phenomena in greater detail in their consideration of "anomia" (also called "anomie"), as it may arise from one's lack of access to the achievement of life goals. The authors examine data collected from a sample of the population of San Francisco, to whom they administered Srole's scale for the measurement of anomie. They are concered with the possible effects, individually, of the factors of socioeconomic status, age, class-identification, and social isolation, and then with the combined effects of these factors, when combined in one index of access to life chances. They also examine some of the influence of religious preference and marital status. They conclude that there may be important connections between lack of access to means of achievement of life goals and the feeling of anomie.

    Implications for the study of mobility are important because much of the research on anomie suggests that it is the rapid *change* of position, rather than the *occupancy* of degraded positions, that may be critical. It may very well be that the apparent disagreement of these findings is due to different meanings attributed to anomie. For Meier and Bell, anomie is primarily a measure of despair. Other researchers tend more to see anomie as a measure of rootlessness or a feeling of being unanchored and insecure, or devoid of steady normative guides.

Reactions to degradation and despair, especially among Negroes, are among the primary interests of Abram Kardiner and Lionel Ovesey in the selection from their book presented here. Their model of reactions to degradation starts with the formation of low self-esteem, which leads to anxiety and unreal aspirations as well as cautious and apologetic behavior. When combined with aggression, the feeling of low self-esteem may produce ingratiating behavior or a fear of looking too deeply into anything, or a denial of aggression, coupled with false affability and good humor; and these in turn yield passivity and resigned acceptance, or reduction of affect altogether, and a fear of loss of control.

The authors sensitively analyze the possible reaction-formations of different classes of Negroes, and offer some penetrating suggestions about the impact of low position on the development of the Negro child. The role of drugs, alcohol, gambling, magic, and other forms of withdrawal or avoidance are placed in the context of the demeaned position occupied by and perceived by the Negro. Although this analysis was written in the early 1950's, it is extraordinarily relevant to race relations today as seen in the context of a caste-stratified social order.

Some Unapplauded Consequences of Social Mobility in a Mass Society

MELVIN M. TUMIN

The process of getting to be better-off than one used to be does not ordinarily make one sit and reflectively balance what he may have lost against the advantages gained. For, if being reasonably well-off is a novel experience as is implied when we talk of mobility—it may take a long time for the novelty to wear off. One begins to spend time and energy in cultivating the new habits of consumption and the new modes of living appropriate to his new position. And, perhaps one's most ardent wish is that no one should rock the boat, or raise questions about other dimensions of life on which this experience of mobility may be having an impact.

But this is what I propose to do here,

briefly, and, in large part, impressionistically, since while much attention has been given to measuring mobility and to comparing the mobility rates of various groups in various societies,[1] relatively little attention has been paid to the range of consequences generated.

I

In the broadest sense, any economic improvement of heretofore disadvantaged persons strikes us as valuable.[2]

Reprinted from Melvin M. Tumin, "Some Unapplauded Consequences of Social Mobility in a Mass Society," *Social Forces*, XXXVI, No. 1 (October, 1957), 32–37, by permission of the author and the University of North Carolina Press.

[1] See, for instance, three book length studies: N. Rogoff, *Recent Trends in Occupational Mobility* (New York: The Free Press, 1954); W. L. Warner and J. C. Abegglen, *Occupational Mobility in American Business and Industry, 1928–1952* (Minneapolis: University of Minnesota Press, 1955); D. V. Glass, ed., *Social Mobility in Britain* (New York: The Free Press, 1954); also, an earlier review of the literature in P. Sorokin, *Social Mobility* (New York: Harper & Row, Publishers, 1927).

[2] Robin Williams, Jr., *American Society: A Sociological Interpretation* (New York: Alfred A. Knopf, Inc., 1951) on the dominant values of American society.

This is true whether we start with a Marxist orientation toward the factors which determine man's fate, or a twentieth century liberal's version of what constitutes the good life; or the most conservative of political orientations, which, ultimately, joins with a version of Marxism in insisting that the economic welfare of the society is the basis of the total welfare of that society.

Even a smattering of sociological sophistication, however, informs us that economic changes do not occur in a vacuum;[3] that other conditions precede, accompany and follow; that a range of values is affected; and that general social change, and not simply economic change, is necessarily implied. Surely, then, the consequences of any phenomenon as broadsweeping as socio-economic mobility are likely to be diverse and mixed—diverse in their institutional ramifications and mixed in their implications for other values.

The same bit of sociological sophistication will also inform us that mobility is too broad a term to allow for more than vague generalizations, unless we further specify the kinds of mobility, the rates or occurrence, the conditions under which it transpires, and the segments of the population affected.[4]

With these requirements in mind I wish now to specify more closely the mobility about which I am here talking. I refer first to the current American scene, and, within that, to the improvement in the standard of living, both relative and absolute, of large numbers of members of various ethnic minority groups. This improvement is preceded and accompanied by a reallocation of persons to high-er-rated occupational groups, in which these higher incomes are earned.[5] I refer secondly to the fact that much of this has occurred within the last fifty years, or less than two demographic generations; and that a very substantial portion of the change is attributable to the opportunities presented by the Second World War and the Korean incident. I cite these specific events only as convenient indicators of the time periods involved.

These transformations have occurred in a contest of what we are now wont to call a "mass society." The referents of that term are numerous and mixed.[6] For our purposes here, as a minimum, when we speak of a "mass society" we shall have reference to the following things:

1. There are media for rapid interchange and transfer of ideas, persons, incentives and styles.
2. Economic motives include specific intents to produce for and distribute to all available segments of the population.
3. Inexpensive duplication of elite items of consumption is a dominant theme in production and consumption.
4. Traditional criteria of prestige, such as membership in exclusive kinship groups, are rapidly vanishing. First appraisals and apprisals of status-rank are made increasingly on the basis of apparent income, as manifested in items openly consumed.
5. The "ideal" values insist that existing lines of social differentiation, including class and caste barriers, are temporary, and in the long run, insignificant; that all men are ultimately equal, some temporarily more equal than others; but that in some way we take turns at being more equal, since this is a condition which is theoretically available to everyone under the right happenstances.
6. It is theoretically permissible and even

[3] See Wilbert Moore, *Economy and Society* (Garden City, N. Y.: Doubleday & Company, Inc., 1955), especially Chap. 2.
[4] Melvin Tumin and Arnold Feldman, "Theory and Measurement of Occupational Mobility in Puerto Rico," *American Sociological Review*, XXII, No. 3 (June, 1957).

[5] See H. P. Miller, *Income of the American People* (New York: John Wiley & Sons, Inc., 1955).
[6] Daniel Bell, "The Theory of the Mass Society," *Commentary*, XXII, No. 1 (July, 1956), 75–83, presents an historical survey of the meanings ascribed to the term "mass society."

well-mannered to compete with everyone, no matter what his rank.

Running through this type of social order is a major theme of status striving which, for our present purposes, we need not try to explain, but rather will take as given. Sometimes and some places this motif is at bottom a search for some token by which to assure oneself of the rightness of self-esteem. Other times and other places it is egregiously insistent upon formal and overt recognition by others of one's right to an elevated place and a differentiated set of powers. Whatever the motive to which status-rivalry can be reduced, and whatever the forms it may assume, it is an intense focus of social activity and interpersonal relations, especially among mobile-minded Americans.[7]

These features then roughly and approximately describe the types, conditions, rates, and participants in social mobility to which we have reference.

A further word of caution needs to be inserted before we proceed to the main analysis in hand. Some of the consequences to be cited will refer only to some of the most mobile segments of the population; some of them and those with whom they come in contact during their movement or at their temporary resting places; some to the relations between them and their kin; some have to do with phenomena which emerge in the interplay between strains toward mobility and those toward stability; some are only dimly visible while others are already well-developed. In short, the sweep, coverage, intensity, and importance of the consequences we are about to specify are as mixed as the conditions which give rise to them.

---

[7] In Melvin Tumin, "Some Disfunctions of Institutional Imbalance," *Behavioral Science*, I, No. 2 (July, 1956), the consequences of heavy emphasis upon status as measured by economic achievement are argued in some detail.

II

1. The Fragmentation of the Social Order

I have reference here in general to the numerous ways in which rapid social mobility, in a mass society in which status rivalry is a dominant theme, leads to the proliferation of interest groups, associations and temporary social congeries, all oriented toward the accumulation and symbolization of prestige.

This proliferation is set in motion when status-mobiles, with full credentials in hand, knock upon the doors of elite membership groups, demanding acceptance and recognition, and are then denied the final bestowals of grace on grounds quite irrelevant to those which presumably determine one's right to such recognition. Even though sufficient income, education, occupational rank, commodiousness of residence, and auxiliary criteria have been met, the occupants of the top statuses invoke other criteria, such as kinship, ethnic origin, table and bar manners, and coldness of emotional toning, in order to justify the denial to the status-mobiles of access to intimacy with them in their own highly-ranked associations.

These criteria—precious and refined —are not only irrelevant to the major themes in the culture, but essentially hostile to democratic values. Their invocation, in denying admission to aspirants, leads to actions on the part of the mobiles which intensify certain anti-democratic and anti-open-society tendencies.

Thus, for instance, one finds the rejected aspirants creating dual and triple sets of elite facilities such as social clubs, country clubs, recreational facilities, residential sites, and even colleges and universities. These tend to be justified on the grounds that where opportunity has been illegitimately cut off, it is proper to create such facilities. Whatever pleasures and properties these dual facilities may insure for the participants and whatever pleasure of restricted intimacy this may residually grant to the older elite, the creation of such facilities, along lines of ethnic, racial, and religious distinctions, gives further strength to these anti-democratic distinctions. Moreover, because the *elites* of various ethnic and religious persuasions engage in such distinctions, these styles of social intercourse are likely to be emulated at other class levels.

Within these separate hierarchies status-rivalry becomes heightened and intensified, and there is sharper insistence on class-oriented behavior. This intensification of class distinctions within ethnico-religious status-hierarchies is not unmixed in its implications for a democratic, open society.

Under these circumstances, one may expect some loss of faith in the fairness of the social process and in the democratic quality of the culture. For if the major criteria of equal status have been satisfied, but personal recognition is nevertheless withheld, there is good ground to disbelieve the value-themes which emphasize the equality of all men and the worthwhileness of supporting the society in general, without reference to ethnic or religious origin.

Still another consequence may be cited. Highly mobile members of ethnic and religious groups tend to impose upon their less mobile co-ethnics the same criteria of disability with which they were earlier afflicted. Thus, Negroes use color as bases of distinction within their groups; Jews use Jewish folk-characteristics of language, gesture, and food. In short, denigrated minority groups absorb, accept, and apply to themselves the very anti-democratic criteria which their status-superiors earlier imposed upon them. In the extreme cases, the ethnics tend to blame their own rejection upon the persistence of these identifying traits of origin among their less mobile co-ethnics. The phenomenon of Negro and Jewish self-hatred has often been partially and correctly explained on these grounds.

The implications for self-esteem and mental health of such self-depreciation are obvious. What may not be quite so obvious is the way in which this shift of focus misplaces the responsibility for the existing barriers to social mobility, redirecting it mistakenly from the institutional restraints and anti-democratic tendencies in the older elites where it properly belongs.

2. The Denial of Work

A good deal of the social energy and drive which have made mobility possible for many of the heretofore underprivileged groups in America derived from the belief that hard work pays off. This belief was tied in and compatible with prior value commitments to the inherent virtue of work.

But now the emphasis has shifted from the importance of work and striving to the urgency of appearing to be successful. In at least some important elite circles, the social productivity of one's occupation, the social value of products which one distributes, and the skill required to produce these items are systematically ignored. Instead, almost exclusive preference is given to the open portrayal of *being* successful, as measured by the power and property which one openly consumes.

No one in any society has more quickly oriented himself to what is the right way to succeed in our status-conscious society than the new-mobile. Being a mobile and seeking further mobility makes it imperative that one adopt the standards which rule the market. In adopting those standards, and playing the game by them, he helps institutionalize them and make them the themes into which the next generations are socialized and indoctrinated. In this manner, the fact of rapid social mobility contributes importantly to the loss of a theme of the instrumental importance and the inherent dignity of work. In their place has been substituted the cult of the quick buck, with its theme that nothing succeeds like success.

Most of the major consequences of the triumph of the cult of the quick buck are well known. Some of the less obvious but equally important consequences bear scrutiny for a moment.

We may note, in the first place, the development of a Cult of Opportunity, Unlimited. That is, there has spread through the younger members of the more mobile groups in our population a sense that only success is in store for them; that the paths to this success are pretty clearly indicated; that no downward turns of the economy are possible; and that the insistence upon a horizon of despair is simply a neurotic hankering for the past on the part of those who have not quite made the grade.

This set of attitudes leads to an uncritical acceptance of the strength and durability of those economic and social arrangements which have recently yielded such high standards of living. In turn, this makes any ideas regarding the need for checks, controls, and contingency mechanisms, designed to cushion cyclical downturns, seem like morbid, gloomy, and radical prophecies of doom. Such policies and legislation as may be required to provide just these contingency cushions and provisions for possible economic disaster, fail to receive at least the kind of attention which our past history has indicated they merit. It would be one thing to reject them after scrutiny, on the grounds that the fears for the possible future are pointless. It is quite another to dismiss them out of hand as undeserving of consideration. Nothing is likely to contribute so much to the possibility of a bust as the denial, during the boom, of that possibility.

The denial of work also has consequences for social integration. For the only system of social recognition which makes it possible for all men in a society to achieve a sense of their worthiness to that social order, and thus to be integrated within it, must contain important reference to the dignity of work, *at any level*, and to the worthiness of conscientiousness regardless of the level of skill or income associated with the work. Any tendency which denies the dignity of work and which, in turn, insists upon consumption of high income as a criterion of social worth, undermines the possibility of widespread social integration. For, thereby, large numbers of men are deprived of the only basis on which they can achieve a sense of their equality. It is extremely difficult for a democratic ideology to have vital meaning at all levels of skill and income when we denigrate work and applaud income.

9. The Loss of Social Criticism

I have reference here at the outset to the numerous ways in which the ranks of social critics and the ideas of social criticism are being depleted under the impact of the illusions and fantasies which social mobility for large numbers has generated.

There are evident signs of the emergence of "a cult of gratitude" among significant sections of the mobile population. Members of this cult tend to lose sight of the history of effort and struggle which have been required for past mobility. They engage in a type of euphoric wallowing in present comforts. They organize their perspectives around a sense of gratitude to the social order for making the present pleasures possible.

A prime case in point concerns some intellectuals. Perhaps never before has there been so much room in the well-paying portions of the occupational ladder for the skills and talents of intellectuals. Again it may be inconsequential that ideas now become commodities, or gain much of their value from their marketability. It is consequential, however, for the total society, that many of the ablest critics of the social order, whose criticism and ideas were important in making past mobility and present comfort possible, have been in a sense, bought off by the social order. This reference is not alone to political critics operating directly in the field of political ideology, but also to men of creative imagination and ideas operating in the fields of literature, mass entertainment and the media of mass-know-how-enlightenment.

Any social order stands in danger when it becomes smug regarding its past and even smugger about its future. The presence of an alert, critical-minded and creatively-oriented group of men of ideas is an indispensable antidote to such smugness. The mobility of the society in general has made creative criticism highly undesired and unpopular. And the mobility of prior critics has made significant numbers of them deny their histories and the value of their prior criticism. Those denials have helped them move quickly and surely into the ranks of those who feel it important to applaud. The active pursuit of open and sharp debate—an indispensable condition for the maintenance of an open society—is thus seriously endangered.

4. The Diffusion of Insecurity

Anomie spreads through any social order when its personnel moves rapidly through a series of statuses and roles, whose definitions or rights and responsibilities are constantly shifting. This is generally what occurs in any society when much of the population experiences rapid social mobility, and when styles of behavior are oriented primarily toward status-acceptance and prestige-ranking, rather than some persistent and assured sense of what the social welfare requires.

In its simplest terms one sees this process occurring when the primary orientation is upon moving out of given levels into others as rapidly as possible; and when each of the major roles at any of these levels—whether parental, occupational, or community-member role—is defined in accordance with the class level. There is neither time nor inclination to become absorbed in a set of traditional responsibilities and to cultivate the expectations of traditional rights. The stability of bearing and the security deriving from adequate role-playing are thereby surrendered in preference for the constant readaptation of oneself and his role performances to the requirements of the next income level.[8]

Insecurity is also spread under such conditions, when, in addition, one takes his bearings on his worth to himself and his social order by his position on the prestige-ladder, and when that position is primarily defined by income and its correlates. For in a society with differentiated income-classes, almost everyone is outranked by someone else who, by his own criteria, is more worthy.

Moreover, no source or criterion of prestige is quite so shaky and unstable as wealth, especially when that wealth flows from commerce rather than from proprietary estates based on land. Many of the very same persons who today are wealthy and therefore prestigeful have known in their own life-times what it has meant to be poor, therefore low-ranking, to become wealthy and improve their ranking, to become impoverished once again and lose their ranking, and finally, now once again, to be wealthy and be back in the high ranks. It is difficult to see how there could be any deeply built-

---

[8] See Melvin Tumin, "Rewards and Task Orientation," *American Sociological Review*, XX (August, 1955).

in sense of security under such circumstances. It is easy to see how a gnawing, though perforce, concealed, sense of the ephemerality and impermanence of their present conditions might permeate such a population.

Rapid social mobility of the type we have experienced, and under the circumstances which have prevailed, has led to an extreme emphasis upon income-accumulation and consumption as the basis of ranking. Thus, there has tended to diffuse throughout significant portions of the population at all levels an insecurity regarding place and position. An illustration in point is the intense demand for reassurance that we are loved. This is exemplified in its most unself-conscious form in the cult of "palship" among café society habitués. To insist that a true friend is one who sticks by one through all varying economic fortunes, and, in turn, to place the value of that kind of friend above all other values except money, is to testify to the instability of money as a measure of worth in general, and the uncertainty regarding one's personal worth, so measured, in particular.

III

Time forbids the detailed analysis of any other set of consequences of social mobility. Yet a number of these may be mentioned in passing, to indicate how truly mixed are those consequences, in contrast to the general bland assumption that social mobility is eminently and predominantly a benign process.

5. We must recognize, therefore, that rapid social mobility, under the conditions stated, leads to a severe imbalance of institutions, insofar as it encourages the invasion of such institutions as family, religion, and education by criteria derived from the market place. The success of role-performances in these institutions tends to be measured by some income yardstick, thus endangering seriously the major functions they have traditionally performed.[9]

6. Comparably, the possibilities of genuine cultural pluralism in our society are seriously diminished by some results of the process of rapid social mobility. For in leading to the creation of dual and triple hierarchies on new class levels, ethnic groups become converted into status-competing hierarchies rather than the culture-contributing peer groups which a theory of the pluralist society envisions.

7. Along with the loss of social critics and criticism, goes the depreciation of taste and culture which occurs in a highly mobile society when marketability becomes the criterion of aesthetic worth, and when one consumes such products as the taste-merchants assure us that the elite are presently enjoying.

8. Finally, it may be observed that rapid social mobility generates in the older portions of the population a cranky and bitter conservatism and worship of the past; and in the new-mobile segments a vituperative contempt for traditions. If it is true that the age of a custom is no guarantee of its contemporary fitness, it is equally true that the age of a custom is no guarantee of its inadequacy. Any society will be the loser which either wallows in its past indiscriminately or, equally indiscriminately, rejects it.

IV

Marx somewhere says that the philosopher with his eyes upon the stars is betrayed by his lower parts into a ditch. Without being silly enough to try to improve upon that formulation, I would try to adapt it to the present situation, by

---

[9] Melvin Tumin, "Some Disfunctions of Institutional Imbalance," *loc. cit.*

noting that the mobiles, with their eyes upon the higher reaches of the social ladder, are betrayed into their ditches by their overly careful devotion to how and where they might next move.

Anomia and Differential Access to the Achievement of Life Goals

In an earlier paper Bell reported that anomia, as defined by the Srole scale, was related inversely to each of the following variables: the economic status of the neighborhood within which a respondent lived; individual economic status as measured by occupation, income, and education; and amount of informal and formal group participation. He also reported that older respondents were more likely to be anomic, in this psychological sense, than were younger respondents.[1]

Reprinted from Dorothy L. Meier and Wendell Bell, "Anomia and Differential Access to the Achievement of Life Goals," *American Sociological Review*, XXIV, No. 2 (April, 1959), 189–202, by permission of the authors and the American Sociological Association. A revised version of a paper read at the annual meeting of the American Sociological Society, August, 1958. For their helpful comments and criticisms of an earlier version of this paper we wish to thank Henry W. Bruck, Metropolitan Community Studies, Inc., Dayton, Ohio, John I. Kitsuse, Northwestern University, and Ralph H. Turner and Charles R. Wright, University of California, Los Angeles. We thank Frank J. Massey, University of California, Los Angeles for statistical counsel. The second author wishes to thank the Carnegie Corporation of New York and the Stanford University Committee for Research in the Social Sciences for the financial assistance which made this study possible.

The present paper is a continuation of the analysis of the cause or causes of anomia, also based upon data from the San Francisco Study of Social Participation, but in this case more independent variables have been introduced into the analysis. We introduce the variables *simultaneously* and thereby approach the logic of the controlled experiment to a greater extent than in the earlier paper. Admittedly, the measures utilized are crude, the techniques—mostly dichotomies and percentages—are rudimentary, and therefore the results are only approximate.

However, the interpretation of our data has led us to a single, but of course tentative, generalization which constitutes the thesis of this paper. The evidence argues fairly consistently that in American society *anomia results when individuals lack access to means for the achievement of life goals.* Such lack of opportunity follows largely as a result of the individual's position in the social structure as determined by such factors as type of occupation, amount of education, income, age, sex, ethnicity, marital status,

[1] Wendell Bell, "Anomie, Social Isolation, and the Class Structure," *Sociometry*, XX (June, 1957), 105–116. Following Srole's suggestion, we use the term "anomia" to refer to the phenomenon measured by his scale so as to distinguish the psychological concept from the sociological concept of anomie; the former refers to the state of an individual and the latter to the condition of a group or a society. See Leo Srole, "Social Integration and Certain Corollaries: An Exploratory Study," *American Sociological Review*, XXI (December, 1956), 709–716.

the type and amount of association in both formal organizations and in informal groups of friends, work associates, neighbors, and relatives, and the degree of commitment to particular beliefs, attitudes, and values. That differences with respect to many of these factors result in discrepancies in access to the means for the achievement of life goals has long been recognized in such notions, to name but a few examples, as differential life chances, power differentials, and varying opportunities to participate as an effective and meaningful member of society.[2] Our hypothesis is that socially structured limitations in access to the means for the achievement of life goals produce anomia in the individuals so affected.

In this paper, first, we discuss Srole's scale and suggest that despair is a major part of what it measures. Second, we try to show that a number of variables are *independently* related to anomia, that each adds to predictive power. And, finally, we attempt to demonstrate how each of the independent variables may be interpreted as a measure of structural access to the means for the achievement of life goals; we construct, and relate to anomia, a multi dimensional index which reflects this higher abstraction.

Srole's Anomia Scale

Srole's anomia scale contains five items, and in this study the response cate-

gories offered were "Strongly agree," "Agree," "Undecided," "Disagree," and "Strongly disagree." The Cornell scaling technique was applied to the sample described below, the coefficient of reproducibility being .90 and the coefficient of scalability being .65.[3] Collapsing the response categories during the scaling procedure resulted in two trichotomies and three dichotomies. The scale scores ranged from a possible low of zero to a possible high of 10. The questions comprising the scale as used in this study and the scores assigned to the various response categories ordered from the fewest to the most "agree" responses are the following:

1. In spite of what some people say, the lot of the average man is getting worse.
   2 Strongly agree and Agree.
   0 Undecided, Disagree, and Strongly disagree.
2. It's hardly fair to bring children into the world with the way things look for the future.
   2 Strongly agree and Agree.
   0 Undecided, Disagree, and Strongly disagree.
3. Nowadays a person has to live pretty much for today and let tomorrow take care of itself.
   2 Strongly agree, Agree and Undecided.
   1 Disagree.
   0 Strongly disagree.

[2] See, e.g., Bernard Barber, *Social Stratification* (New York: Harcourt, Brace & World, Inc., 1957); Reinhard Bendix and Seymour Martin Lipset, eds., *Class, Status and Power* (New York: The Free Press, 1953); Joseph Kahl, *The American Class Structure* (New York: Holt, Rinehart & Winston, Inc., 1957); Kurt B. Mayer, *Class and Society* (New York: Random House, Inc., 1955); Talcott Parsons, *Essays in Sociological Theory* (New York: The Free Press, 1949), pp. 166–184.

[3] Standard scaling procedures were used. See Louis Guttman, "The Cornell Technique for Scale and Intensity Analysis," in C. West Churchman, Russell L. Ackoff, and Murray Wax, eds., *Measurement of Consumer Interest* (Philadelphia: University of Pennsylvania Press, 1947), pp. 60–84; and Samuel A. Stouffer *et al.*, *Measurement and Prediction*, Studies in Social Psychology in World War II, Vol. IV (Princeton, N. J.: Princeton University Press, 1950), Chap. 3. For a discussion of the coefficient of scalability see Herbert Menzel, "A New Coefficient for Scalogram Analysis," *Public Opinion Quarterly*, XVII (Summer, 1953), 268–280.

4. These days a person doesn't really know who he can count on.

    2 Strongly agree and Agree.

    0 Undecided, Disagree, and Strongly disagree.

5. There's little use writing to public officials because often they aren't really interested in the problems of the average man.

    2 Strongly agree and Agree.

    1 Undecided and Disagree.

    0 Strongly disagree.

According to Srole this scale measures the socio-psychological concept of anomie, which he refers to as the individual eunomia-anomia continuum so as to distinguish it from the sociological concept of anomie; the latter refers not to individuals as such, but to the degree of normlessness of social systems or subsystems.[4] Also, in this account of his work Srole emphasizes that he had attempted to "devise a measure of interpersonal alienation . . . ,"[5] stating that

. . . the immediate analytical objective would be to place individuals on a eunomia-anomia continuum representing variations in interpersonal integration with their particular social fields as "global entities." More concretely, this variable is conceived as referring to the individual's generalized, pervasive sense of "self-to-others belongingness" at one extreme compared with "self-

others distance" and "self-to-others alienation" at the other pole of the continuum.[6]

It is beyond the scope of this paper to attempt a detailed conceptual analysis of anomie. However, several writers have extended the concept to refer to a condition of individuals rather than of groups or societies.[7] Although there is no precise agreement about the psychological or socio-psychological concept of anomie (anomia), there are encouraging convergences and partial agreements.

For example, Gwynn Nettler has recently constructed a scale to measure feelings of estrangement which he designates as alienation, and which he correlates with the Srole anomia scale.[8] The Pearsonian coefficient is $+.309$; although Nettler concludes that his measure of alienation is related to Srole's anomia, he argues that they are not identical and has suggested in a personal communication that Srole's scale may most likely be measuring *despair*.

We emphasize the notion of despair in the interpretation of our findings, although alienation appears to be measured in some degree as well. In order of the listing of the Srole questions given above, the first item is said to measure "the individual's view, beyond abdication of future life goals, that he and people like him are retrogressing from the goals they have already reached." The second question measures "the deflation or loss of internalized social norms and values, reflected in extreme form in the individual's sense of the meaning-

---

[4] Srole, *op. cit.* Unfortunately, the semantic difficulty here may not be easily solved. Although most sociologists would agree that we need two different terms, one to refer to social disorganization and another to refer to personal disorganization, they may not agree with Srole's suggestion. Divergences in his usage already exist in the literature. For example, see Harry Alpert, *Emile Durkheim and His Sociology* (New York: Columbia University Press, 1939). Alpert uses the term "anomia" to refer to social disorganization. Lacking consensus in the field, we have arbitrarily adopted Srole's usage. (On this matter, *cf.* the exchange between Isabel Cary-Lundberg and Elwin H. Powell in *American Sociological Review*, XXIV, No. 2 [April, 1959], 250ff.

[5] Srole, *op. cit.*, p. 712.

---

[6] *Ibid.*, p. 711.

[7] In addition to the references in Srole's paper, see, e.g., those in Robert K. Merton, "Continuities in the Theory of Social Structure and Anomie," *Social Theory and Social Structure* (New York: The Free Press, 1957), pp. 161–194.

[8] Gwynn Nettler, "A Measure of Alienation," *American Sociological Review*, XXII (December, 1957), 670–677.

lessness of life itself." The third question is intended to measure "individual's perception of the social order as essentially fickle and unpredictable, i.e., orderless, inducing the sense that under such conditions he can accomplish little toward realizing future life goals." The fourth and fifth questions were constructed to measure respectively "the individual's perception that his framework of immediate personal relationships, the very rock of his social existence, was no longer predictive or supportive" and "the individual's sense that community leaders are detached from and indifferent to his needs."[9]

We are convinced that these questions for the most part measure despair, that is, utter hopelessness and discouragement. A person agreeing strongly with each of these questions is beyond simple apathy; his is a condition of sadness and distress in which he is unable to exercise any confidence or trust that his desires or wishes may be realized, and in the extreme may reach the point described by MacIver as "unquiet introspection and self-torture."[10] At the very least, despondency, and, at worst, abject despair characterizes such a person. It is despair, however, which is in part turned toward one's fellows and the social order with the particular implication that no one is bound by any effective norms of responsibility toward others.

We have adopted the term, "anomia," to refer to the Srole scale, but other terms such as "despair," "hopelessness," "discouragement," "personal disorganization," "demoralization" (especially in the sense of disheartenment), and other terms might be used at this point in our understanding of the phe-nomenon being measured. In the remainder of the paper the use of such terms will refer specifically to the Srole scale.[11]

Elaboration of Generalization

Life Goals

In hypothesizing that frustration of an individual's attempts to achieve his life goals results in anomia, we assume, of course, that his goals are for the most part culturally acceptable, if not preferred or prescribed. We say "life" goals rather than "cultural" goals, however, because we are trying to explain anomia in an individual member of the society, not anomie in the society itself, nor rates of deviant behavior, nor rates of anomia—although we can make predictions about these latter abstractions once we know the place in the cultural values of the particular life goals being blocked and the range of applicability of the complementary cultural goals for various members of the society. Nonetheless, in explaining a specific individual's despair we can not ignore the fact that *his* goals and *his* lack of opportunities to achieve them produce *his* despair. Of course, this is not to deny the fact that in the smoothly functioning society an individual's life goals usually correspond to some configuration of cultural values;

---

[9] Srole, *op. cit.*, pp. 712–713.

[10] R. M. MacIver, *The Ramparts We Guard* (New York: The Macmillan Company, 1950), p. 87.

[11] Just as the Srole scale appears to be related somewhat to Nettler's alienation scale it may also be related in some measure to what Koos describes as narcotization. Koos reports finding two families who experienced unemployment, death, and disorganization due to other troubles to the point where they appeared to be unconcerned about them. Their attitude had become apathetic, but apparently did not contain the element of hostility which seems to be contained in the Srole scale. Earl Loman Koos, *Families in Trouble* (New York: King's Crown, 1946).

indeed this assumption is central to our analysis.

Here, we cannot discuss life goals in American society at length, but it should be noted that the whole range of relatively long-term, value-laden life objectives are included. Many writers have discussed these objectives, emphasizing, perhaps too much so, the goal of material success. In this vein, Max Lerner recently described the pattern of life aims characteristic of twentieth-century Americans: success, prestige, money, power, and security.[12] Lerner loosely terms this pattern the "success system," but the inclusion of security, as well as his later reference to "the good life" and "the pursuit of happiness," clearly points to life goals other than achievement of prestige, power, and property. Discussions of social choice and life styles in modern American society are relevant to the variety of life goals, some of them mutually exclusive for many persons. Riesman, for example, has argued that consumer preferences and tastes embody purposes other than monetary success and occupational mobility,[13] and Bell has demonstrated the different patterns of living involved in the goals of familism, consumership, and career (upward mobility).[14] However, whether his major life goal is career advancement or a happy family life, effortless living or power, the pursuit of constant satisfaction or freedom, or some combination of several of these, that individual will suf-fer from anomia, we predict, if he is prevented from achieving his goal. The degree of anomia is dependent, we suggest, on the importance to the individual of the life goal being blocked, the degree to which its achievement is blocked, and the availability of substitute goals. Unfortunately, in this paper, because the data do not bear directly upon them, our statements concerning life goals are strictly inferential, although they appear to constitute a reasonable and plausible explanation of our findings.

Future research in this area could profitably focus on (1) the life goals of different segments of the population, (2) their structure in relation to each other with respect to a hierarchy of importance, (3) differential opportunities to achieve different goals for different segments of the population, (4) substitution rates of some goals for others, and (5) degrees of anomia resulting from failure to achieve *specific* life goals. These subjects are now being investigated by one of the authors.

Differential Access

We have generalized that anomia results when an individual lacks access to means for the achievement of life goals. Such access, for the most part, is *socially structured*. The relative opportunities to obtain particular social statuses and the relative control over resources characteristic of them, as embedded in their rights and duties, are most important in evaluating the degree to which a person can achieve or has achieved his major life goals. The achievement of a particular status—occupational or marital, for example—may itself be the attainment of a life goal. The differential control over people and things which adhere in the rights and duties of particular statuses may be the means by which other goals are achieved.

We do not exclude from consideration, however, nonsocial factors associat-

---

[12] Max Lerner, *America as a Civilization* (New York: Simon and Shuster, 1957), p. 689.

[13] David Riesman, Nathan Glazer, and Reuel Denney, *The Lonely Crowd* (New Haven: Yale University Press, 1951). See also Riesman and Howard Roseborough, "Careers and Consumer Behavior," in Lincoln H. Clark, ed., *Consumer Behavior*, Vol. II (New York: New York University Press, 1955), pp. 1–18.

[14] Wendell Bell, "Social Choice, Life Styles, and Suburban Residence," in William M. Dobriner, ed., *The Suburban Community* (New York: G. P. Putnam's Sons, 1958), pp. 225–247.

ed with biological or physiological conditions as they limit the achievement of life goals. For example, the person who is accidentally blinded may despair and maintain little hope for the future. The social meaning of his new handicaps, the reactions of others to him as a blind person, may greatly facilitate or impair his opportunities to achieve his life goals, but the blind person *is* physically handicapped and is "not capable of doing everything, as some fanciful and romantic propaganda would have us believe."[15]

Description of the Data

The data presented in this paper were collected in four San Francisco census tracts during the spring of 1953. The tracts had been selected according to their scores on the Shevky-Bell typology so that they would vary widely with respect to economic and family characteristics, but would contain few non-whites or foreign-born whites from certain countries.[16] Within each of the four tracts probability area samples were selected from a complete list of all the dwelling units in each area. The respondents were men aged 21 or over, whose response rate was in excess of 85 per cent. A total of 701 interviews were obtained.[17]

For the purposes of this analysis the neighborhood distinction was dropped and the cases lumped together to comprise an analytic sample with respect to individual economic and family characteristics.[18] Although we predict that our generalization holds for American society in general, strictly speaking these findings are applicable only to the four census tract populations from which our samples were drawn. Nor are the findings necessarily representative of the entire San Francisco population.

Throughout most of the analysis to follow the responses to Srole's Anomia Scale have been simply dichotomized into high and low scores. Those persons with anomia scores of 5 or more are classified as being anomic, as having high anomia scores; those with scores of 4 or less as being eunomic, as having low anomia scores.

The independent variables for the most part also have been dichotomized in the presentation of data, although in tables not shown we have broken down the variables into finer divisions in order

---

[15] Edwin M. Lemert, *Social Pathology* (New York: McGraw-Hill Book Company, 1951), p. 131.

[16] Eshref Shevky and Wendell Bell, *Social Area Analysis* (Stanford, Calif.: Stanford University Press, 1955). See also Wendell Bell, "Social Areas: A Typology of Urban Neighborhoods," in Marvin Sussman, ed., *Community Structure and Analysis* (New York: Thomas Y. Crowell, 1959).

[17] Other reports from the San Francisco Study of Social Participation include Bell, "Anomie, Social Isolation, and the Class Structure," *op. cit.*; Wendell Bell "The Utility of the Shevky Typology for the Design of Urban Subarea Field Studies," *The Journal of Social Psychology*, XLVII (February, 1958), 71–83; Bell and

Marion D. Boat, "Urban Neighborhoods and Informal Social Relations," *American Journal of Sociology*, LXII (January, 1957), 391–398; Bell and Maryanne T. Force, "Religious Preference, Familism and the Class Structure," *Midwest Sociologist*, XIX (May, 1957), 79–86; Bell and Force, "Social Structure and Participation in Different Types of Formal Associations," *Social Forces*, XXXIV (May, 1956), 345–350; Bell and Force, "Urban Neighborhood Types and Participation in Formal Associations," *American Sociological Review*, XXI (February, 1956), 25–34; and Dorothy L. Meier, *Anomie and Structural Accessibility to Achievement*, M.A. thesis, Northwestern University, 1957.

[18] For similar uses of analytic sampling see H. J. Eysenck, "Social Attitude and Social Class," *British Journal of Sociology*, I (March, 1950), 57–58; Neal Gross, "Social Class Identification in the Urban Community," *American Sociological Review*, XVIII (August, 1953), 398–404; William H. Form and Gregory P. Stone, "Urbanism, Anonymity, and Status Symbolism," *American Journal of Sociology*, LXIII, (March, 1957), 504–514; and Peter Rossi, *Why Families Move* (New York: The Free Press, 1955).

to make certain that the relationship between anomia and a specific variable is not U-shaped, for example. The variables were dichotomized with due regard for a sufficiency of cases in each sub-category as well as their realistic relationship to the desired theoretical meaning of the sub-category. For example, the division into participants and isolates reflects the fact that we considered a person to be an isolate in fact only if he had informal contacts twice a month or less *and* if he belonged to no formal associations or was an inactive member of such groups.

The Findings

Socio-Economic Status, Class Identification, Age, and Social Isolation

Table 1 shows the percentage of males having high anomia scores by socio-economic status, class identification, age, and social isolation.[19] Each of these independent variables may limit opportunity so achieve life goals. Socio-economic status, measured by occupation, income, and education, is itself a life goal for most persons in American society. It is also a measure of the control over resources necessary to achieve other goals. A person of low socio-economic status, lacking in education, capital, and occupational training, has relatively little opportunity to improve his life chances, to achieve prestige and power in the society. As Hyman says,

the existence of stratification in American society is well known. The corollary fact— that individuals from lower strata are not likely to climb far up the economic ladder— is also known. . . . Opportunity in the society is differential: higher education or specialized training, which might provide access to a high position, must be bought with money —the very commodity which the lower classes lack.[20]

Consequently, the member of the lower classes may view the structure as not

---

[19] See the Appendix for complete definitions of socio-economic status and social isolation.

[20] Herbert Hyman, "The Value Systems of Different Classes: A Social Psychological Contribution to the Analysis of Stratification," in Bendix and Lipset, *op. cit.*, p. 426.

TABLE 1   **Percentage of Males Having High Anomia Scores by Socio-Economic Status, Class Identification, Age, and Social Isolation**[a]

| | Socio-economic status | | | |
| | Low age *(status)* | | Middle and high age *(status)* | |
Class identification	Young (%) >50	Old (%) 50+	Young (%)	Old (%)
Participants				
Lower and working	48	56	24	24
	(83)[b]	(43)	(38)	(17)
Middle and upper	23	22	8	25
	(14)	(18)	(98)	(111)
Isolates				
Lower and Working	23	63	37	43
	(39)	(60)	(27)	(14)
Middle and Upper	40	39	17	16
	(10)	(18)	(52)	(44)

[a] Chi-square equals 44.28, p<.001, with 15 degrees of freedom. (Based on an elaboration of the method given in Alexander M. Mood, *Introduction to the Theory of Statistics* [New York: McGraw-Hill Book Company, 1950], pp. 280-281.)
[b] The number of cases on which the percentages are based is given in parentheses in each case.

legitimate, the prescribed goals as impossible of achievement, and thus, the norms and values of society as false or meaningless. The social order may be seen as non-supportive. This interpretation is supported by a comparison of the percentage of men with high anomia scores by socio-economic status, with class identification, age, and social isolation controlled, as shown in Table 1. Comparing the low to high socio-economic status men, the percentages having high anomia scores are 48 to 24, 56 to 24, 43 to 8, 44 to 21, 23 to 37, 63 to 43, 40 to 17, and 39 to 16. All but one comparison, to be discussed below, is in the direction consistent with our generalization.[21]

Class identification, as measured by Centers' subjective self-placement question,[22] is inversely related to anomia even with socio-economic status, age, and social isolation controlled (see Table 1). In seven of the eight possible comparisons relatively more men who claim membership in the lower or working classes have high anomia scores than do men who claim membership in the middle or upper classes.

Apparently, the person of lower or working class identification, perceiving himself as being at the bottom of the class hierarchy and thus lacking the advantages, qualifications, and opportunities for achievement regards his chances for the attainment of his life goals—especially those having to do with monetary success, power, and prestige—as being very slight. Our assumption here is that these individuals hold values, attitudes, and outlooks similar to the members of the classes with which they identify. Hyman describes lower class values in this connection as "a *self-imposed* barrier to an improved position" in that they tend to prevent the "very *voluntary* actions which would ameliorate the individual's low position."[23] Thus, class identification, as something more than just another measure of socio-economic level, may also be an indicator of a belief system which limits access to opportunity for the achievement of life goals for certain segments of the population.

Bell, in reporting a positive relationship between age and anomia, with neighborhood economic status controlled, has suggested that the explanation may be found in a "tendency for older aged persons to evaluate their present situation and future prospects in terms of some idealized conception of their past situation."[24] The generalization offered in this paper, however, leads us to examine more specifically the character of age statuses in American society, particularly the degree of access to means for the achievement of life goals available to the aged.

It is well known that in our society many life goals become increasingly difficult to reach for older aged persons. The goals may be monetary success, prestige, and power—or merely regular employment. They may be marriage and a family or "youthful living" or

<hr/>

[21] In an article, "Anomie, Authoritarianism, and Prejudice: A Replication," *American Journal of Sociology*, LXI (January, 1956), 355–358, A. H. Roberts and M. Rokeach report data which they interpret as showing that education, not income, is truly related to Srole's anomia scale. Our data do not support them. We intercorrelated occupation, income, education, and anomia, and then computed partial and multiple correlations. Although the zero order correlation between any one of the measures of socio-economic status and anomia was reduced when the others were introduced into the relationship, it was never reduced to zero.

[22] Richard Centers, *The Psychology of Social Classes* (Princeton, N. J.: Princeton University Press, 1949).

<hr/>

[23] Hyman, *op. cit.*, pp. 426–427.
[24] Bell, "Anomie, Social Isolation, and the Class Structure," *op. cit.*, pp. 111–112.
[25] Lerner, *op. cit.*, p. 611.

personal expressiveness. Lerner notes that the "most difficult years in American life are the middle years, when the first bleak intimation comes to a man that he has fallen short of the standards of the culture and his own life goals."[25] However, it is not simply that the aged may realize that they have thus failed, but also—and perhaps more importantly—that they have little opportunity of ever succeeding. They are literally running out of time, energy, health, and other resources essential to achieving their life goals. Not the least among these resources is the fact that the old are rarely treated with reverence and respect and are seldom given the opportunities a younger man receives, even though these middle and older aged persons may be completely capable physically and emotionally. Lerner quite rightly says that the aged are treated "like the fag end of what was once good material."[26] But this general devaluation of old age is not equally operative in all segments of the society, as Clinard points out:

The tendency for older persons to play a reduced status role is undoubtedly greater among the lower socio-economic groups than among the upper classes, whose position and wealth continue to give them status even into advanced age. Likewise, in certain professions, such as law and medicine, an elderly person may even have increased status.[27]

In sum, older age status appears to be accompanied by decreasing opportunity to function as an effective and influential member of the society—and therefore, by an inability to achieve many life goals. Consequently, hopelessness, discouragement, despair, and demoralization are more characteristic of older than younger aged persons in American society, and more so among the aged

who are of lower socio-economic status.[28]

For our sample as a whole the older men are significantly more anomic than the younger men. A detailed breakdown, however, reveals that age makes no difference in anomia until after the age of about 50. (From 21 to 49 there is little difference in the percentage of men with high anomia scores by age).

Table 1 presents the percentage of men with high anomia scores by age, not for the sample as a whole, but for subgroups classified according to socioeconomic status, class identification, and social isolation. The comparisons between the young (under age 50) and old (over age 50) men show that four of the eight are relatively large and in the direction consistent with our formulation, the other four being negligible. The largest difference is found between the young and old men of low socio-economic status, lower or working class identified, and socially isolated, the percentages having high anomia scores being 23 and 63 respectively.

When controls are introduced for socio-economic status, class identification, and age, as in Table 1, the relationship between participation and anomia is not consistent (four of the eight comparisons being in the hypothesized direction). But it does appear under

---

[26] Ibid., p. 613.

[27] Marshall Clinard, Sociology of Deviant Behavior (New York: Holt, Rinehart & Winston, Inc., 1957), p. 403.

---

[28] A recent discussion of adolescence, however, by Kitsuse and Dietrick leads us to predict that adolescents, particularly among the lower and working classes, may be more anomic than young adults in that they occupy a "defective status" in our society. The "efforts of the adolescent to assume adult status [are], on the one hand, culturally induced and reinforced, but on the other are thwarted and impeded by a systematically imposed status of social, economic, and legal dependency." John I. Kitsuse and David C. Dietrick, "Delinquency and Delinquent Subculture: An Alternative Formulation," paper read at the annual meetings of the Pacific Sociological Society, April, 1958. See also John I. Kitsuse, "Differential Perceptions of Adolescent Status," unpublished Ph.D. dissertation, University of California, Los Angeles, 1958.

certain conditions. Participation in formal and informal activities seems to be a factor in causing anomia when the individual identifies with the lower or working classes, but it does not relate to anomia in a consistent direction. The young person of low socio-economic status who realistically assesses his position in the class system is less likely to be anomic *if he is socially isolated* than if he is an active participant. The remainder of the individuals who identify with the lower or working classes are anomic if they are socially isolated, and are not anomic if they have frequent formal and informal contacts. Unfortunately, our indexes of social isolation do not fully delimit the individual's social position as to the availability of communication channels and lines of influence, since his associations with members of his family with whom he may live and with persons on the job are not included.

Accounting for many of the differences in Table 1 which are not in the hypothesized direction is the subcategory containing the young, low socio-economic status, and lower or working class identified isolates. These men are much less anomic than our generalization would lead us to believe. As expected, they are less anomic than the comparable group of old persons, but contrary to our expectation, they are also less anomic than the comparable groups of participants, middle and upper class claimants, and middle and high socio-economic status men. Three of the four possible comparisons are in the "wrong" direction for this group, and it appears to constitute the major exception to our generalization.

Although it is sheer conjecture, we suggest that for the low socio-economic status, lower or working class identified, young men social isolation is not an obstacle to the achievement of life goals, but a condition under which life goals are more easily achieved. For this to be plausible we must assume that such young men are working largely for the goals of the larger culture—especially the middle class aims of career achievement and family life—and that the lower or working class sub-culture, from which they are isolated, contains elements inimical to the achievement of these goals. The handicaps associated with the culture of the lower classes for young men seeking success in the "American status game" are well known.[29] The young, lower and working class identified, low socio-economic status isolate may be less anomic than his counterpart among the participants because the very fact of his lack of participation with kin, peers, and neighbors makes him less susceptible to the limitations to achievement contained in lower or working class beliefs, attitudes, and values. He may be less anomic than the isolates among the middle and high socio-economic status men and the middle or upper class identified men because his social isolation is a clear-cut, unmixed advantage to him while their social isolation may be in part an isolation from functional, helpful support toward the achievement of their life goals which are provided in the subculture of the middle or upper social classes.

Comparison of Theoretically Extreme Categories

According to the measures of access to means for the achievement of life goals presented above, the most anomic persons should be those with low socio-economic status, who identify with the lower or working class, who are old, and are socially isolated. Table 1 shows that among such men 63 per cent, the table's largest entry, have high anomia scores.

[29] See, e.g., Hyman, *op. cit.*; Albert K. Cohen, *Delinquent Boys: The Culture of the Gang* (New York: The Free Press, 1955); and William Foote Whyte, *Street Corner Society* (Chicago: The University of Chicago Press, 1943).

On the other hand, the least anomic should be those of middle or high socio-economic status, who identify with the middle or upper class, who are young, and participants. Again, Table 1 shows this sub-category to contain the smallest percentage (8 per cent) of anomic men.

Table 2 presents the difference, in the percentage of men with high anomia scores, between theoretically extreme categories as each independent variable is introduced. The last entry, 55 per cent, represents the 63 per cent minus the 8 per cent, noted in the preceding paragraph. The first entry is the percentage difference between the percentage of men with high anomia scores by socio-economic status alone. The second entry is the difference between the theoretically extreme categories after class identification has been introduced into the relationship; the third entry is the difference after age has been introduced. Table 2 indicates, that as each new variable is introduced, the percentage difference increases between the cate-gory which should, according our to generalization, contain the most anomic men and the category which should contain the least. A rough measure, to be sure, each independent variable nevertheless adds to the cumulative predictive power of the independent variables in terms of their interpretation as measures of access to means for the achievement of life goals.

Importance of Each Independent Variable

Table 3 is based entirely upon Table 1, giving a rough approximation of the relative importance of each of the independent variables as predictors of anomia, with each of the other independent variables controlled. For example, the eight possible comparisons of the percentages of men with high anomia scores by socio-economic status were averaged to get the mean difference (24 per cent), disregarding sign between low and high socio-economic status men. The same procedure was used for the comparisons involving differences in class identification, social isolation, and age. Although this is only a crude measure, it shows that socio-economic status is the most important predictor of anomia, followed by class identification, social isolation, and age.

TABLE 2   **Difference in Percentage of Men with High Anomia Scores between the Theoretically Extreme Categories as Each Independent Variable Is Introduced**[a]

Theoretically extreme categories compared	Difference (%)
Low SES *versus* Middle and High SES	29
Low SES, Lower and Working CI *versus* Middle and High SES, Middle and Upper CI	34
Low SES, Lower and Working CI, Old *versus* Middle-High SES, Middle and Upper CI, Young	49
Low SES, Lower and Working CI, Old, Isolate *versus* Middle and High SES, Middle and Upper CI, Young, Participant	55

SES = Socio-Economic Status
CI = Class Identification
[a] Except for the final entry, based on tables which are not given in this paper.

TABLE 3   **Mean Differences in Percentage of Men with High Anomia Scores by Each Independent Variable, Holding the Other Independent Variables Constant**[a]

Independent variable	Mean difference (%)
Socio-Economic Status	24
Class Identification	15
Social Isolation	11
Age	9

[a] Based on Table 1.

The Index of Access to Means for the Achievement of Life Goals

Our central hypothesis justifies, we believe, the construction of a multi-dimensional index to measure differential access to means for the achievement of life goals. The variables we have selected for this purpose for the most part operate empirically in the direction predicted by the hypothesis. Implicit in our formulation is the notion that there are *degrees* of access to such means. The degree of access is a function of the varying combinations of the factors which circumscribe an individual's position in the social structure.

Hyman describes the procedure that we use to combine the independent variables into a single index. This procedure begins with the examination of various independent variables as they relate to a particular phenomenon. With the introduction of simultaneous controls, these variables are "manipulated to a stage of greater complexity." The resulting configuration need not be unidimensional or one frequently occurring in nature. In order to test its explanatory power, the analyst "then *pools* information from several of these variables and forms an index which represents the more complex and *synthetic* configuration."[30]

Our procedure follows Hyman's description up to the point of the index formation. The next step is to construct a multi-dimensional index composed of various independent variables, which, in this study, are combined as follows: Each independent variable is dichotomized (as in Table 1), and scores of 0 or 1 are assigned to the dichotomies. The "0" categories represent low socio-economic status, lower or working class identification, old age, and isolation from informal and formal group participation; the "1" categories indicate high or middle socio-economic status, middle or upper class identification, young age, and participation in informal and formal group activities. These scores are then summed to form composite scores on the *Index of Access to Means for the Achievement of Life Goals* or, more simply, the *Index of Life Chances*. Scores on this index range theoretically from 0 (very little access) to 4 (a great deal of access).

The percentage of men with high anomia scores by the Index of Life Chances is shown in Table 4. This percentage *decreases* at every step of increased access to means for the achievement of life goals.

TABLE 4   Percentage of Men with High Anomia Scores by the Index[a] of Life Chances[b]

Index scores of access to means for the achievement of life goals (high score equals relatively much access)	% having high anomia scores	Number of cases
4	8	98
3	22	215
2	37	199
1	40	114
0	63	60

[a] Index is based upon measures of socio-economic status, class identification, age, and social isolation.

[b] More exactly: The Index of Access to Means for the Achievement of Life Goals.

Occupational Mobility, Marital Status, and Religious Preference

These variables, data for which are available in the San Francisco study, should be related to anomia because they appear to be measures of life chances or direct measures of achievement.

Occupational mobility may be a measure of actual achievement. It may

---

[30] Herbert Hyman, *Survey Design and Analysis* (New York: The Free Press, 1955), pp. 271–272.

also be a measure of opportunity to greater achievement due to the increased control over resources made possible by the higher occupational position and, perhaps, by the psychology of successful achievement. From our generalization, it follows that upwardly mobile persons will be less anomic than those who are stable, and much less anomic than individuals who have been downwardly mobile.[31] This prediction is somewhat at odds with the view that anomia results from changes in status—especially rapid, extensive, or unanticipated changes—as expressed by Durkheim[32] and recently discussed by Merton.[33] Thus, occupational mobility, whether upward or downward, might be expected to result in anomia.

Using both a career and an intergenerational measure of mobility and controlling for socio-economic status, class identification, and age, we find some evidence in support of our prediction. The upwardly mobile men of low socio-economic status are less likely to be anomic than the stable or downwardly mobile men, but the stable men of high socio-economic status are generally less anomic than the upwardly mobile men;—perhaps occupational mobility should be interpreted as an additional dimension of socio-economic status, the upwardly mobile men are better off than either the stable or the downwardly mobile. However, among those of high socio-economic status the stable men are better off than both the downwardly mobile (who have lost some degree of socio-economic status) and the upwardly mobile (who have *recently reached* their new positions).

Marriage and family living being almost universal goals in American society, on the basis of our general hypothesis we would predict that single, and especially widowed, separated, and divorced, men would be more likely to be anomic than the married. The simple relationship between marital status and anomia clearly supports this prediction, but when additional variables are introduced, the findings are not altogether consistent. In general, however, the large differences in anomia scores show the married men as less anomic than the single, widowed, separated, and divorced—and this is particularly true among the older aged men.

Bell reported earlier that comparisons of principal religious preferences—none, Protestant, Catholic, and Jewish—show no significant differences in anomia when neighborhood economic status is held constant.[34] However, we have further examined this relationship. Our general hypothesis leads to the specific prediction that Protestants should be less anomic than Catholics, Jews, agnostics, atheists, and independents, since in all likelihood, in American society, religious preferences other than Protestant generally limit access to opportunities to achieve life goals.[35]

Table 5 presents the percentage of men with high anomia scores by religious preference. Jews and Protestants are the least likely to show high scores, followed by Catholics and those of no religious preference, and men indicating

---

[31] For an analysis of this group, see "The Skidder" by Harold L. Wilensky and Hugh Edwards, *American Sociological Review*, XXIV (April, 1959), 215ff.

[32] Emile Durkheim, *Suicide*, trans. John A. Spaulding and George Simpson (New York: The Free Press, 1951), pp. 252–253.

[33] Merton, *op. cit.*, p. 188.

---

[34] Bell, "Anomie, Social Isolation, and the Class Structure," *op. cit.*

[35] Of course, among some sub-groups and for certain kinds of statuses Protestants may have limited access to opportunities. Moreover, denominational distinctions, which are not taken into account here, may obscure some of the differences between the broader religious groups. For a brief discussion related to this point, see T. C. Keedy, Jr., "Anomie and Religious Orthodoxy," *Sociology and Social Research*, XLIII (September-October, 1958), 34–47.

TABLE 5   **Percentage of Men with High Anomia Scores by Religious Preference**

Religious preference	% having high anomia scores	Number of cases
Jewish	21	52
Protestant	23	287
Catholic	38	267
None	38	72
Other	53	19

still other religious preferences score most highly. The relationship between anomia and religious preference is about what we expected except for the case of the Jews showing no more anomia than Protestants; the Jews may not represent a deviant case if they achieve their life goals in spite of the discrimination directed against them either by "clannishly" helping each other or by exerting concentrated individual effort.

Introducing socio-economic status and age into the analysis should test whether or not the relationship shown in Table 5 is spurious. (The introduction of other variables is of little value because of the small number of cases in some of the religious preference categories.) In general, the relationship is more obscure when socio-economic status and age are introduced, but the Protestants generally show lower anomic scores than the other religious groups. Among young men of high socio-economic status, however, there are no significant differences by religious preference, all religious groups having less than 12 per cent of their number classified as anomic. Another exception consists of the old, low socio-economic status Jews who have much lower anomia scores than any other group among the old, low socio-economic status men.

Notwithstanding these exceptions, the evidence confirms the deduction from our central hypothesis that non-Protestants have less opportunity in general than do Protestants to achieve their life goals, other things being equal. The relative social cohesion of these religious groups is not in question here. We contend only that membership in non-Protestant groups is a religious or perhaps ethnic status which limits access to the means for the achievement of life goals, as culturally defined in the larger American society.

The Revised Index of Access to Means for the Achievement of Life Goals

Given the small number of cases in many of the subcategories, it is of no particular use to construct a table showing high anomia scores simultaneously by socio-economic status, class identification, age, social isolation, occupational mobility, marital status, and religious preference. However, because each of these variables appears to be an indicator of access to the means for the achievement of life goals and because, as far as the empirical tests show, each contributes some additional predictive power of anomia in the individual under certain conditions, we have reconstructed the Index of Life Chances so as to include all of the independent variables used in this study.[36]

Employing this revised index, the percentage of men with high anomia scores is given in Table 6, along with the scoring procedure used in each of its component measures. Table 6 shows that the Revised Index of Life Chances is a better predictor of anomia than the simpler Index of Table 4. At the extreme of good life chances, the percentage of men with high anomia scores is about the same in Tables 6 and 4, 10 and 8 per cent, respectively. Perhaps these measures reflect the upper limits of hope and encouragement and personal morale. At

---

[36] See the Appendix for a full definition of the mobility measure used in the Revised Index of Life Chances.

TABLE 6 Percentage of Men with High Anomia Scores by the Revised Index[a] of Life Chances[b]

Revised index scores of access to means for the achievement of life goals (high score equals relatively much access)	% having high anomia scores	Number of cases
7	10	40
6	9	130
5	28	166
4	38	174
3	43	119
2	60	42
1	83	6
0	100	2

[a] The following scores are added for each of the variables composing the Revised Index:

Socio-economic status		Social isolation	
Low	0	Isolate	0
High	1	Participant	1
Class identification		Social mobility	
Lower and working	0	Down	0
Middle and upper	1	Stable and up	1
Age		Religious preference	
Old	0	Non-protestants	0
Young	1	Protestants	1
Marital status			
Single, widowed, separated, divorced (old)			0
Single, widowed, separated, divorced (young)			1
Married (old and young)			1

[b] More exactly: The Revised Index of Access to Means for the Achievement of Life Goals.

the extreme of poor life chances, the percentage of men with high anomia scores is greater in Table 6 than 4, reflecting perhaps extreme despair, anguish, and personal disorganization. Apologies are in order for computing percentages of such small numbers. But to see that two out of two men who are of low socio-economic status, lower or working classid entified old, isolated, downwardly mobile, non-Protestant, and single widowed, separated or divorced are anomic, and that five out of six men who rank only 1 on the Index of Life Chances are also anomic, is of importance to our general hypothesis.

Conclusion

We have argued that anomia results when an individual is prevented from achieving his life goals, and that the character of the goals and the obstacles to their achievement are rooted in social and cultural conditions. We have illustrated this hypothesis by showing the very high negative correlation between anomia, as measured by the Srole scale, and structural access to the means for the achievement of life goals, as measured by a multi-dimensional index.

For this generalization to be accepted additional research is required. Our analysis is largely *post factum:* our findings are "explained" by a single formulation after the results were known. Consequently, the data given do not provide a test of the hypothesis, serving merely as illustrative material which give plausibility to our formulation.

Moreover, there are alternative interpretations for our findings, involving other inferences concerning the nature of the causal chain. We have inferred that socio-economic status, class indentification, age, social isolation, occupational mobility, marital status, and religious preference, all indicators of life chances, precede in time and cause anomia. Yet all of these variables, except age, conceivably could be a consequence of anomia. An individual who despairs might become socially isolated, move down the social and economic scale, identify himself with the working or lower classes, get divorced or separated, and reject religion. The possible ordering of these variables in "reasonable" ways is manifold. Nonetheless the consistency of our findings should not be discounted.

Additional variables, of course, can be expected to limit opportunities to achieve life goals, and therefore from our hypothesis, to produce anomia. In American society opportunity is narrowed by race and nationality, physical handicaps, and sex, among other conditions.

A number of well-established areas of inquiry are related to the thesis of this paper, including studies of reactions to frustration, levels of aspiration—especially research by Lewin and his associates, personal esprit and morale, mental disorders, deviant behavior, and suicide. It is beyond the scope of this paper to discuss the implications of those studies for our hypothesis, but preliminary work suggests that they contain highly relevant materials.

In a moment of whimsy and perhaps wisdom, Scott Greer and Ella Kube recently said that "sociology, like the French generals, typically fights the last war describing a world that existed thirty or forty years ago."[37] They were explaining the discrepancy between the isolation and anomia of the lost urban person, which have been emphasized by so many writers, and recent data indicating that the vast majority of urbanites are not socially isolated, seldom anomic, and rarely lost. They point out, quite rightly, that urbanism as a way of life has been often confused with poverty or wealth or ethnicity as a way of life.

Anomia is not necessarily confined to the city dweller, it should be stressed, if our generalization is correct. Nor for that matter is it restricted to urban societies (at least as these are defined by demographic variables). In fact, we may expect considerable despair in the near future among members of agricultural, nonindustrial, nonurbanized populations with low living standards—the densely settled "underdeveloped areas." For these people increasingly accept configurations of life goals involving political freedom and economic advancement—while facing severe obstacles as they attempt to achieve these goals. This is precisely the breeding ground of anomia.[38]

APPENDIX

Measurement of Socio-Economic Status, Social Isolation, and Career Mobility

Social-Economic Status

This was determined by a composite score based on a simple average of scores given for each respondent's occupation, education, and income. The scores for each of the components are given below. The range on the composite index of socio-economic status is 24 with a lowest possible score of 3 and a highest of 27. For the purpose of this paper, this index was dichotomized by grouping together persons with scores from 3 to 17 into one category (low socio-economic status) and those with scores from 18 to 27 into another (high socio economic status).

Income	Score
Under $1,000	1
$1,000–1,999	2
2,000–2,999	3
3,000–3,999	4
4,000–5,999	5
6,000–9,999	6
10,000–16,999	7
17,000–29,999	8
30,000 and over	9

---

[37] Scott Greer and Ella Kube, "Urbanism and Social Structure: A Los Angeles Study," in Sussman, *op. cit.*

[38] A more extensive statement of the empirical relations reported in this paper can be found in Meier, *op. cit.*

Occupation	Score
Laborers	1
Service Workers	2
Operatives & Kindred Workers	3
Farmers and Farm Managers	4
Craftsmen, Foremen & Kindred Workers	5
Sales, Clerical & Kindred Workers	6
Managers, Officials & Proprietors	7
Semi-Professionals	8
Professionals	9

Education	Score
No School	1
Some Elementary	2
Elementary Completed	3
Some High School	4
Completed High School	5
Some College	6
Completed College	7
Some Graduate Work	8
Completed Graduate Work	9

Social Isolation

This index was constructed from combined measures of formal organizational membership and annual attendance plus a measure of informal social participation with neighbors, co-workers outside of work, relatives other than those living with the respondent, and other friends. This index was simply dichotomized as follows: the isolate is an individual who belongs to no formal organizations or, if he belongs, who attends meetings only once a month or less, and who gets together with friends, neighbors, relatives, or co-workers once or twice a month or less. The participant is one who belongs to at least one formal organization and who attends meetings several times a month or more, or who gets together informally with friends, neighbors, relatives, or co-workers several times a month or more, or both.

Career Mobility

An individual's career social mobility was determined by comparing his present job or occupation with his *first* full-time job. The downwardly mobile person is one whose present job is more than one occupational ranking below that of his first job (see occupational scale given above). The individual whose social mobility is considered stable holds a present job which is ranked either the same, one step below, or one step above the occupational ranking of his first job. The upwardly mobile person has moved more than one occupation ranking above his first job or occupation.

Psychodynamic Inventory of Negro Personality

ABRAM KARDINER, M. D.   LIONEL OVESEY, M. D.

It is a consistent feature of human personality that it tends to become organized about the main problems of adaptation, and this main problem tends to polarize all other aspects of adaptation toward itself. This central problem of Negro adaptation is oriented toward the discrimination he suffers and the consequences of this discrimination for the self-referential aspects of his social orientation. In simple words, it means that his self-esteem suffers (which is self-referential) because he is constantly receiving an unpleasant image of himself from the behavior of others to him. This is the subjective impact of social discrimination, and it sounds as though its effects ought to be localized and limited in influence. This is not the case. It seems to be an ever-present and unrelieved ir-

Reprinted from Abram Kardiner and Lionel Ovesey, *The Mark of Oppression* (Cleveland: The World Publishing Company, Meridian Books, 1962), pp. 302–317, by permission of the authors. Copyright 1951 by Abram Kardiner and Lionel Ovesey.

ritant. Its influence is not alone due to the fact that it is painful in its intensity, but also because the individual, in order to maintain internal balance and to protect himself from being overwhelmed by it, must initiate restitutive maneuvers in order to keep functioning—all quite automatic and unconscious. In addition to maintaining an internal balance, the individual must continue to maintain a social façade and some kind of adaptation to the offending stimuli so that he can preserve some social effectiveness. All of this requires a constant preoccupation, notwithstanding the fact that these adaptational processes all take place on a low order of awareness. The following is a diagram of a typical parallelogram of forces:

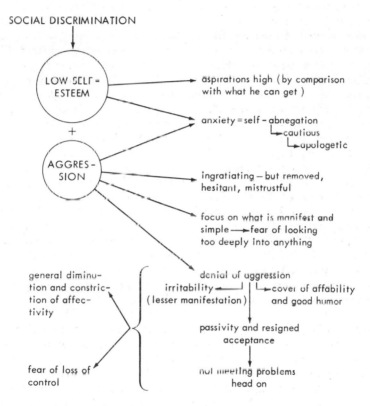

In the center of this adaptational scheme stand the low self-esteem (the self-referential part) and the aggression (the reactive part). The rest are maneuvers with these main constellations, to prevent their manifestation, to deny them and the sources from which they come, to make things look different from what they are, to replace aggressive activity which would be socially disastrous with more acceptable ingratiation and passivity. Keeping this system going means, however, being constantly ill at ease, mistrustful, and lacking in confidence. The entire system prevents the affectivity of the individual that might otherwise be available from asserting itself.

This is the adaptational range that is prescribed by the caste situation. This is, however, only a skeletal outline. Many types of elaboration are possible, particularly along projective or compensatory lines. For example, the low self-esteem can be projected as follows:

Low self-esteem = self-contempt ⟶ idealization of the white ⟶

frantic efforts to be white = unattainable ⟨ hostility to whites

introjected white ideal ⟶

self-hatred ⟶ projected on to other Negroes = hatred of Negroes

The low self-esteem can also mobilize compensations in several forms: (1) apathy, (2) hedonism, (3) living for the moment, (4) criminality.

The disposition of aggression is similarly susceptible to elaboration. The conspicuous feature of rage lies in the fact that it is an emotion that primes the organism for motor expression. Hate is an attenuated form of rage, and is the emotion toward those who inspire fear and rage. The difficult problem for those who are constantly subject to frustration is how to contain this emotion and prevent its motor expression. The chief motive for the latter is to avoid setting in motion retaliatory aggression.

The most immediate effect of rage is, therefore, to set up a fear of its consequences. Fear and rage become almost interchangeable. When the manifestations of rage are continually suppressed, ultimately the individual may cease to be aware of the emotion. In some subjects the *only* manifestation of rage may be fear.

The techniques for disposing of rage are varied. The simplest disposition is to suppress it and replace it with another emotional attitude—submission or compliance. The greater the rage, the more abject the submission. Thus, scraping and bowing, compliance and ingratiation may actually be indicators of suppressed rage and sustained hatred. Rage can be kept under control but replaced with an attenuated but sustained feeling—resentment. It may be kept under control, but ineffectively, and show itself in irritability. It may be kept under sustained control for long periods, and then become explosive. Rage may show itself in subtle forms of ingratiation for

purposes of exploitation. It may finally be denied altogether (by an automatic process) and replaced by an entirely different kind of expression, like laughter, gaiety, or flippancy.

Rage may ricochet back on its author, as it does in some types of pain-dependent behavior (masochism). This is only likely to happen when rage is directed toward an object that is loved; the rage is then accompanied by strong guilt feelings. In this case the only manifestation of rage may be depression.

The tensions caused by suppressed or repressed aggression often express themselves through psychosomatic channels. Headaches of the migrainous variety are often the expression of rage which is completely repressed. These are usually not accompanied by amorphous anxiety —though the latter may be the sole vehicle for this aggression. Hypertension is another psychosomatic expression of the same, but predominantly suppressive, process.

In the case histories, we found all these varieties of the expression and control of rage. All kinds of combinations are possible. The two commonest end products of sustained attempts to contain and control aggression were low self-esteem and depression. These are merely the results of the continuous failure of a form of self-assertion.

The adaptational scheme we have charted above takes in the impact of discrimination but does not account for the integrative systems due to other conditions operative in the process of growth. This division is purely arbitrary for actually both series run concomitantly. There is no time in the life of the Negro that he is not actively in contact with the caste situation. The other personality traits derive, however, from the disturbances in his family life. This source gives rise to the following constellations: the affectivity range, the capacity for idealization and ideal formation, the traits derived from reactions to discipline, and conscience mechanisms. In these categories there is some difference as we proceed from the lower to the upper-class Negro. Let us take up the lower-class Negro first.

Affectivity range means the range of emotional potential. In appraising the role of emotion in personal and social adaptation, we have both quantitative and qualitative features to take into account. The total adaptation of the individual will depend on how much and what kind of emotion he has in a given situation. Emotion in man's adaptation tends to operate on a mass action principle. That is, the predominance of one emotion tends to stifle all others.

Emotion has the function of orientation toward objects in the outer world that can be the source of frustration or gratifications. The individual responds to a frustrating object with the emergency emotions of fear and rage, and their derivatives of hate, suspicion, distrust, apprehensive anticipation, and the like. These functions are self-preservative in intent and gear the organism for defensive action. The feeling toward objects which are the source of gratifications is the wish to be near, to perpetuate the influence of, to love, to desire, to have anticipations of continued gratifications, to trust, to have confidence, to cooperate with.

We must stress the point from this inventory that the emotions most conducive to social cohesion are those that pertain to the categories of love, trust, and confidence. All creatures are natively endowed with the capacity for fear and rage. The positively toned feelings of love, trust, and confidence, however,

must largely be cultivated by experience. Hence, when we refer to the affectivity potential of an individual, we do not mean the emergency functions of fear and rage. We mean rather the capacity for cooperative and affectionate relatedness to others.

None of these emotions functions in isolation; they have a continuous adaptive interplay during the entire process of growth and living. What counts in the individual are the types of emotional response that become habitual and automatic. These fixed patterns of emotion are not only adaptive, in the sense that they are reaction types to actual situations; they also play a dominant role in shaping anticipations and to a degree, therefore, influence how events will shape up. For example, a person trained to be suspicious will shape the actual events of his life in such a way that his suspicions appear warranted.

The emotions play a decisive role in determining the sociability (peaceful cooperation with others) of the individual through the development of conscience mechanisms and the formation of ideals. The desire on the part of the child to be loved and protected is the dominant incentive for child to be obedient to his protectors. He needs this because he is helpless himself. The child thus becomes socialized in order to continue the boons of love and protection. He learns to anticipate the requirements for these returns by internalizing them and making them automatic. He also learns the methods of escaping blame and of devising techniques for reinstatement. Thus, the fear of punishment and the withdrawal of love exert a powerful restraining influence against antisocial behavior. The reward for conformity is a sense of pride in the social recognition of "good" behavior, while the fear of detection and punishment leads to guilty fear and either an anticipation of punishment or self-punishment.

However, in order for these positive emotional feelings and the functions of conscience to be instituted, certain behavior by the parents toward the child is required. Thus, we cannot expect the child to develop affection and dependence on the parent who is not constant in his care, who does not love in return for obedience, whose punishments are either disproportionate, or have no relation to the offense. In this instance, conformity is of no adaptive value at all. A child who is constantly abused by the parent cannot be expected to have pleasant anticipations or to idealize the parent or wish to be like him. A child exposed to this kind of behavior from the parent will not love, trust, or cooperate. It can take flight from the hostile environment and try to seek another more friendly one. Or it can stay and hate the parent, and suppress all the hostile feeling.

On the institutional side, the family structure of the lower class Negro is the same as the white. However, in the actual process of living, the vicissitudes of the lower-class family are greater and its stability much less. This is where the broken family through early death of parents, abandonment or divorce, takes a heavy toll on the opportunities for developing strong affective ties to the parents. First, the needs for dependency are frustrated. This makes the mother a frustrating object, rather than one the child can depend on. This does not mean that it is the intention of the mothers to neglect or mistreat their children. Quite the contrary, the intention is the usual one, and many lower-class Negro mothers have strong maternal feelings, are exceedingly protective, and try to be good providers. This is not, however, what one hears from the subjects. They tell chiefly the story of frustration and of arbitrary discipline by mothers. Not infrequently there is also the constant story of beating and cursing as disciplinary reinforcements. The rivalry situation between siblings in the lower classes is greatly enhanced by the general scarcity in which they live. This situation, of course, is greatly magnified when the child is given to some other relative for custody, as a consequence of a broken home. These children fare worse than any of the others. They are the ones who, because of mistreatment, decide at the age of 10 or 12 to run away and shift for themselves. In these children, some of whom we studied, the premature independence hardly works to the advantage of the personality in the long run. They become shrewd and adjustable, but at the cost of complete mistrust in everyone.

The result of the continuous frustrations in childhood is to create a personality devoid of confidence in human relations, of an eternal vigilance and distrust of others. This is a purely defensive maneuver which purports to protect the individual against the repeatedly traumatic effects of disappointment and frustration. He must operate on the assumption that the world is hostile. The self-referential aspect of this is contained in the formula "I am not a lovable creature." This, together with the same idea drawn from the caste situation, leads to a reinforcement of the basic destruction of self-esteem.

Thus, many of the efforts of the lower-class Negro at emotional relatedness are canceled out by the inner mistrust in others, the conviction that no one can love him for his own sake, that he is not lovable. Under these conditions, not much real social relatedness is possible. It is, however, very significant that the lower-class Negro is an inveterate "joiner" in one kind of social voluntary organization or another, of clubs and cliques with high sounding names and with much ritualism in initiation rites. In these organizations, which have a very short life span, there is continuous discord, jockeying for position and prestige, and insistence that each member must have his own way. In other words, through these clubs and associations, the Negro tries to compensate for his lack of relatedness. But for the greater part, he fails. The intrapsychic mistrust and need for dominance destroy the effectiveness of these compensatory efforts. This is a noteworthy feature of Negro life, because the social organizations are supposed to facilitate cooperative endeavor and to give the members the satisfaction of belonging to something, to diminish their isolation. This end is not accomplished because most of the energy of these "associations" is taken up with overcoming mutual distrust and very little energy goes into the mutual supportive aspects of the organization.

Closely related to the question of the affectivity potential is the capacity for idealization. This trait is a general human characteristic, and is rooted in the biological make-up of man. It is the most powerful vehicle for the transmission of culture. During his helpless state man must place his trust in the parent who is his support. If this support and affection aid the individual in his adjustment, the natural tendency is to magnify the powers of the parent to magical proportions. This projection of magical attributes on the parent is the most powerful implement the parent has in enforcing discipline, because the threat of withdrawal of this support creates anxiety in the child. It follows, therefore, that the idealized parent is the satisfying parent whose authority is less enforced than it is delegated, and the acquiescence to discipline is a method the child has for perpetuating those boons he has already enjoyed in the past and hence expects to enjoy in the future.

The formation of ideals to pursue is a corollary of the idealization of the parent. It is easy to identify oneself with the idealized parent if the expectations from him have been realized. If these expectations are frustrated, then there may develop a reactive ideal or the opposite to the one experienced. This is generally a rare phenomenon, where a mistreated child becomes an ideal parent by living the opposite of what he has experienced. It does indeed happen. But it is far from the rule. The commonest outcome of this situation is that despite the hatred to the parent, the child takes on and identifies himself with the hated and frustrating attributes and becomes the replica of the frustrating parent. Here one must draw the line between an activating ideal and the unconscious identification. The activating ideal may be "I will be a provident parent"; the unconscious identification, however, may be with the frustrating parent. In some instances, the mistreated child when it becomes the parent is actuated by the idea: "Why should I give you what I never had myself?" These are the cases in which the frustrated dependency cravings interfere with the protective parental role.

The question of Negro-ideal formation is hardly limited to the parental role. The "ideal" answers the question: "Whom do I want to be like?" This is where the Negro encounters a great deal of difficulty. The parent is a member of a despised and discriminated-against group. Hence, this ideal is already spoiled because it carries with it a guarantee of external and reflected hatred. No one can embrace such an ideal. Furthermore, until very recently the Negro has had no real culture heroes (like Joe Louis and Jackie Robinson) with whom he could identify. It is therefore quite natural that the Negro ideal should be *white*. However, accepting the white ideal is a recipe for perpetual self-hatred, frustration, and for tying one's life to unattainable goals. It is a formula for living life on the delusional basis of "as if." The acceptance of the white ideal has acted on the Negro as a slow but cumulative and fatal psychological poison. Its disastrous effects were due to the fact that the more completely he accepted the white ideal, the greater his intrapsychic discomfort had to become. For he could never become *white*. He had, therefore, to settle for the delusion of whiteness through an affectation of white attributes or those that most closely resembled them. This also means the destruction of such native traits as are susceptible of change (kinky hair, etc.). In its most regressive form, this ideal becomes the frantic wish to be reborn white. . . . Pride in oneself could not, therefore, be vested in attributes one had, but in attributes one aspired to have, that is to say, on borrowed ideals. This maneuver, calculated as a restitutive one, ends by being destructive of self-esteem.

The reactions to discipline and the dynamics of conscience mechanisms are closely interrelated, and these in turn are related to the general affectivity potential and ideal formation.

In general, there are several factors operating on the parental side of the induction of disciplines which differ from the situation among whites. The Negro parent has no authority in the social world in which he lives. It is, therefore, a strong temptation for the Negro parent to tend to be authoritative in the only place where he can exercise it, namely in his own home. Hence, we get repeated stories of children being subjected to disciplines that are both arbitrary, instantaneous, and inconsistent, depending often on whim, and at the same time without the ability to offer the child the appropriate rewards for obedience and conformity. Children recognize these rewards chiefly in terms of need satisfactions. These the parent, more often than not, cannot implement. They often fail on the sheer subsistence level. Such a parent cannot have much

delegated authority or inspire much dependence. Hence, the authority of the parent is destroyed. A second factor occurs especially in those cases where the mother works. She has no time to be the careful and provident mother. After a day's work, during which time the child often shifts for itself, she is inclined to be tired and irritable which accounts for much of her impatience and insistence on immediate and unqualified obedience.

As between mother and father, many factors conspire to make the mother the chief object of such dependency as is possible under the circumstances. The male as provider and protector definitely suffers disparagement. The mother's objective—since she has so little time—is to make the child as little nuisance as possible. This makes her both an object to be feared and at the same time the only one that can be relied upon.

In passing, we must mention here the place of street life for the Negro child and adolescent. In many ways this street life is no different from corresponding street life in lower-class whites. The crowded home is not a happy place for the growing child, especially when parents are so often away. Since the family does not implement its disciplines with appropriate rewards, the children tend to get their ideals and pattern their amusements on the opportunities of the street, with its values, its heroism, its ideals, and its factionalism. They differ from corresponding white groups in the quantity of the savagery of their mutual aggression, in which the boys get seriously hurt and in some instances killed. Part of this street life pattern is the result of sheer boredom and the irrelevancy of education. Hence, they cannot be attentive at school or get the feeling that they are engaged in a meaningful and ego-enhancing activity. Many of these high school boys have been to bed with women the age of their female teachers and the disciplines and obligations of school life make no sense to them. In consequence, school is treated as a meaningless routine. The street, on the other hand, offers adventure, struggle for dominance, mock and real hostilities. It is, in other words, a better training for life—according to their sights—than education. Delinquency among adolescents runs high for very good reasons.

In this general setting we can evaluate the effects of the socializing disciplines.

We have seen but little evidence of rigid anal training in childhood. There is no serious contest of will between parent and child over this aspect of socialization. It is largely neglected, and in those who came from the South, there was little emphasis on order, neatness, or systematization. Hence, in this group we would not expect much adventitious use of the anal zone for elaborate constellations about expulsion and retention. If there are any compulsive traits in the Negro of this group, they do not derive from this source.

A more important aspect of socializing discipline is in the sexual domain. Here the picture is very confused. In the lower classes, the sex morality taught is of the Victorian variety. However, there is but little effort made to implement it. There is, on the whole, much less anxiety introduced into sexual disciplines than is the case with the white middle classes. The result is actually more sexual freedom among lower-class Negro children than among whites. And it is by no means unusual for boys and girls to be inducted into sexual activity quite early (7 to 13). It is therefore highly unlikely that potency troubles in both males and females of this group derive from anxieties introduced into the picture by parental threats. In those cases observed these difficulties usually arose from another source. They came from the confusion in the sociosexual roles of male and female. The male derives these difficulties from his inability to assume the effective masculine role according to white ideals, as against the dominant position of the female, first in the dominant mother and later in the dominant wife. The economic independence of the female plays havoc with the conventional male-female roles, and this in turn influences the potency of the males. In the case of the female, her sociosexual role is reversed. She is dominant, and rebels against the passive and dependent role. Thus, the sexuality of the Negro in the lower classes is confused by the sexual significance of the social role.

Contrary to expectations, the sexual drive of the adult Negro is relatively in abeyance. We saw no evidence of the sex-craved and abandoned Negro. This playing down of sex is the result of the socioeconomic hardship and the confusion in the sexual roles.

What kind of conscience mechanisms can be integrated under these conditions? This situation is, if anything, more complex than in the white. Basically, the tonicity of the conscience mechanisms depend on the ability of the parent to act as provider of satisfactions. Hence, in the lower-class Negro, we cannot expect strong internalized conscience. If we add to this the disastrous effects of the caste system, then the lower-class Negro, in his hatred for the white, is robbed of any incentive for developing a strong conscience. However, the effects of the caste system are such that they inspire a great deal of fear. Therefore, antisocial tendencies would be held in rigid check by fear of detection. In fact, we can say that conscience in the lower-class Negro is held in tow by his general vigilance over his hatred and aggression, and that the fear of detection of his aggression and antisocial tendencies are both governed by the same control mechanisms. The great danger for the lower-class Negro is that these control devices may occasionally and impulsively be overwhelmed—a factor that is of enormous concern to every lower-class Negro.

This group of constellations sets up in

the Negro a strong need for compensatory activities, to help establish some semblance of internal harmony. These compensatory activities have the function of (1) bolstering self-esteem, (2) narcotizing the individual against traumatic impact, (3) disparaging the other fellow, (4) getting magical aid for status improvement.

Among the activities for bolstering self-esteem are flashy and flamboyant dressing, especially in the male, and the denial of Negro attributes, such as doing away with kinky hair.

Narcotizing the individual against traumatic influences is effected largely through alcohol and drugs. In these activities, the males predominate. Alcoholic psychoses in Negroes occur with twice the frequency that they do in whites.[1] Narcotics have a wide use among Negroes, but their high cost makes alcohol much more available.

Disparaging the other fellow is widespread among urban Negroes. It is of a vindictive and vituperative kind and derives largely from the status strivings. The street corner and candy store are favorite places for malicious gossip.

In the domain of magical aid to self-esteem, gambling takes a high place. This takes the form of card playing but more often of participation in the numbers racket. Here everyone has a chance at beating fate, of being the favored one, if only for a day. The lure of this tantalizing game must be very high, judging from the vast fortune spent annually by the bulk of the Negro population.

In addition to these, there are occasional outlets, chiefly by males, which stem from their inability to plan or have any confidence in a future. Since the general tendency is to live from day to day, explosive spending when they have money is not infrequent. An occasional illusion of plenty and luxury can thus be created, even if to do so means to mortgage one's energy for months ahead to pay for the luxury.

This psychological picture is to some extent changed in the middle and upper classes. Here the family organization corresponds more closely to the middle-class white group. The emphasis shifts from subsistence problems to status problems. There is also a shift from female to male dominance in the family. The chief conflict area is that concerned with status. In general, the benefits derived from better parental care, better induction of affectivity, better ideal formation and more tonic conscience mechanisms are to a large extent canceled out by the enormous increase in status conflict caused by the caste situation.

In appraising the adaptation of the middle- and upper-class Negro, we encountered a good deal of difficulty in differentiating the real from the apparent. For example, the affectivity potential is much better in this group than in the lower-class. But against this we must discount the fact that the representations of better affectivity rest largely on a formal basis. Their marriages are more stable, they induct affectivity more appropriately, etc. But these features are due largely to the fact that the upper-and middle-class Negroes strive hardest to live and feel like the whites. They are more conventional, have more rigid sex mores, set more store by "respectability" than do lower-class Negroes. They know what the "right" feelings are for a given situation and they try very hard to have them. But whether they do or not depends on the quantity of the conflicts they have on the issues of skin color and status strivings, all of which tend to detract from the freedom of feeling.

---

[1] See Malzberg, Benjamin, "Mental Disease Among American Negroes: A Statistical Analysis," in Klineberg, Otto, ed., *Characteristics of the American Negro* (New York: Harper & Row, Publishers, 1944).

In the specific integrative areas this group approximates the white. Parental care is good in the same sense and with the same incompatibilities as with whites. The affectivity potential is apparently higher than in lower-class Negroes and they have more capacity for relatedness. They have a high capacity for idealization, but what is idealized is white and not Negro. Here again the ideal formation in the Negro has two layers. The natural figure to idealize is the provident parent; but he is a disparaged figure. Introjecting this object means to hate it to the accompaniment of perpetual guilt. The substitution of a white object as the source of the ideal does not solve the problem. It, too, is hated and likewise must give rise to guilt. The Negro cannot win in either case. As one upper-class Negro observed: "The only thing black that I like is myself." Their ideal formation is of a high order, but founders on the rock of unattainable ideals. The fact that these ideals are relatively more capable of achievement than in the lower classes renders the conflict sharper. Thus, they tend to drive themselves harder, make greater demands on themselves for accomplishment, and are obligated to refuse the compensatory activities open to lower-class Negroes. This greatly augments the internal self-hatred and makes it more difficult to accept the Negro status. I could love myself "if" is all the more tantalizing because they can almost make the grade, but for skin color. They are therefore more vulnerable to depressed self-esteem than the lower class.

The need to conform to white standards of middle-class respectability gives the upper classes a harder time with their control of aggression. And this in turn has a constricting effect on all their affectivity.

In view of the good parental care, one would expect that their tendencies to passivity would be accentuated. But this is countered by the strong pressure against any form of passivity or subordination especially to other Negroes— since they cannot avoid subordination to the white. This constellation would be very valuable to follow through in Negro homosexuals. . . .

The points where the intrapsychic conflicts are sharpened for the middle- and upper-class Negro, then, are in the disposition and compensations for lowered self-esteem, the disposition of aggression, and in the uncompromising acceptance of white ideals.

The self-hatred of this group takes the usual form of projection on both white and on Negroes lower than themselves. However, they have more guilt about their Negro hatred than is the case with lower classes. To the whites, the formula is hatred + control = disguise; to the Negro the formula is hatred + guilt = anxiety of retaliation. Thus, every middle- and upper-class Negro has increased competitiveness with whites, but his psychological task is merely one of control and concealment. The hatred to the Negro has a way of ricocheting back on its source. Every Negro who is higher than lower class has a sense of guilt to other Negroes because he considers success a betrayal of his group and a piece of aggression against them. Hence, he has frequently what might be called a "success phobia," and occasionally cannot enjoy the fruits of his achievements.

In his acceptance of white ideals, the Negro often overshoots the mark. He overdoes the sex mores so that the incidence of frigidity in the women is very high. In his acceptance of the white man's cleanliness obsession, the Negro ends by identifying himself with feces, and becomes extraordinarily clean and meticulous. However, the obstructions to the accomplishments of white ideals lead to increase in aggression, anxiety, depression of self-esteem, and self-hatred. This compels him to push harder against the social barriers, to drive himself harder, and ends with more frustration and more self-hatred. This vicious circle never ends.

Thus, as we stated above, it is difficult to appraise the advantages and disadvantages of the upper classes as regards their intrapsychic effects. The shift from female to male orientation at least saves this group from the confusion of social and sexual roles. It is one of male dominance and clear definition of sexual role. However, they overdo the rigidity of sexual restrictions, and this affects the female more than the male. The marriages are more stable, but the importance of conventionality is very high, hence the impression remains that as an average the marriages are not more happy. Affectivity is better, but its betterment is largely on the formal side.

The chief outcome of the psychological picture is that the upper classes of Negro society have so much controlling to do of their psychic life, that they must be extremely cramped and constricted and unspontaneous. There is too little self-contentment for true abandonment, and too much self-hatred and mutual mistrust for effective social relatedness. They must constantly choose the lesser evil between spontaneity and getting hurt by retaliation. Hence, they prefer not to see things as they are, or to enter too deeply into anything to the accompaniment of apathy and resignation.

Is there such a thing as a basic personality for the Negro? This work proves decidedly that there is. Though he lives in American culture, the Negro lives under special conditions which give this personality a distinctive configuration. Taking as our base line the white middle class, the conditions of life for the Negro are so distinctive that there is an actual alteration of the pressures to which he must adapt. Hence, he develops a distinctive personality. This basic Negro personality is, however, a caricature of the corresponding white personality, because the Negro must adapt to the same culture, must accept the same social goals, but without the ability to achieve them. This limitation in social opportunities accounts for the difference in personality configuration.

theory

nine

A large number of important theoretical issues in the study of stratification and mobility remain moot at this point in the development of the field. Among these are: (1) Is stratification inevitable? (2) If so, for what reasons? (3) Are all forms and amounts of inequality, as presently found, or as have historically occurred, also to be judged inevitable? (4) What functions, positive and negative, may one assign to stratification? (5) To what extent do the amount and the form of inequality in a society represent temporary and culturally-specific themes as opposed to universal social needs and features? (6) How can one account for the persistence, ubiquity, and antiquity of stratification in terms other than some universal social needs or requirements?

These are among the issues to which the writers whose works are reproduced here have addressed themselves. By and large, Kingsley Davis and Wilbert E. Moore incline toward a notion of the inevitability and positive functionality of stratification, although each has some special reservations and qualifications. On the other hand, Melvin Tumin inclines toward a notion of the dispensability and negative functionality of social inequality, especially those aspects defined by unequal rewards and unequal prestige.

These two sets of arguments, addressed by Davis, Moore, and Tumin in a continuing debate in the sociological literature, provide the student with a brief overview of some of the crucial theoretical issues.

In his article, George A. Huaco attempts to present the essential elements in these arguments, and he includes additional material from the work of other sociologists who have joined in the dispute.

Melvin Tumin's selection, "Dissonance and Dissensus in Evaluation," taken from his book on Puerto Rico, raises still another theoretical issue by proposing that the requirement of consensus on values is a condition of a stable social system. He asks whether the assumption of such value-consensus is as fruitful as alternative assumptions, and whether it might not be better for sociological analysis to begin with a model of a social system which assumes the existence of significant value-disagreement among the stratified segments of a society.

The Puerto Rican materials are used to illustrate how, in spite of severe inequalities in property, power, and prestige, there is nevertheless a remarkable amount of morale and value-consensus among Puerto Ricans. The principal causes, as Tumin sees them, are the regular and frequent public avowals and demonstrations of the importance and social worth of even the most humble people of Puerto Rico. This, plus the persisting sense of the fairness of the society, and of its open possibilities for improvement, seems to contribute much toward reducing such inter-stratum dissensus and conflict as might otherwise be expected.

Seymour M. Lipset and Hans L. Zetterberg focus on constructing some basic theoretical propositions regarding mobility. After considering the diversity of possible dimensions of mobility that might be measured, they then examine a range of causes of mobility and of political consequences of mobility. A major assumption that guides their analysis of consequences is that "many of the major political problems facing contemporary society are, in part, a consequence of the conflict and tensions resulting from the contradictions inherent in the need for both aristocracy and equality." Using comparative data, against this background, Lipset and Zetterberg examine the distribution of left- and right-wing voting in a number of countries, as seen as reflections of reactions to both low position and to mobility experiences of the voters.

Some Principles of Stratification

KINGSLEY DAVIS   **WILBERT E. MOORE**

In a previous paper some concepts for handling the phenomena of social inequality were presented.[1] In the present paper a further step in stratification theory is undertaken—an attempt to show the relationship between stratification and the rest of the social order.[2] Starting from the proposition that no society is "classless," or unstratified, an effort is made to explain, in functional terms, the universal necessity which calls forth stratification in any social system.

Reprinted from Kingsley Davis and Wilbert E. Moore, "Some Principles of Stratification," *American Sociological Review*, X, No. 2 (April, 1945), 242–249, by permission of the authors and the American Sociological Association.

---

[1] Kingsley Davis, "A Conceptual Analysis of Stratification," *American Sociological Review*, VII (June, 1942), 309–321.

[2] The writers regret (and beg indulgence) that the present essay, a condensation of a longer study, covers so much in such short space that adequate evidence and qualification cannot be given and that as a result what is actually very tentative is presented in an unfortunately dogmatic manner.

Next, an attempt is made to explain the roughly uniform distribution of prestige as between the major types of positions in every society. Since, however, there occur between one society and another great differences in the degree and kind of stratification, some attention is also given to the varieties of social inequality and the variable factors that give rise to them.

Clearly, the present task requires two different lines of analysis—one to understand the universal, the other to understand the variable features of stratification. Naturally each line of inquiry aids the other and is indispensable, and in the treatment that follows the two will be interwoven, although, because of space limitations, the emphasis will be on the universals.

Throughout, it will be necessary to keep in mind one thing—namely, that the discussion relates to the system of positions, not to the individuals occupying those positions. It is one thing to ask why different positions carry different degrees of prestige, and quite another to ask how certain individuals get into those positions. Although, as the argument will try to show, both questions are related, it is essential to keep them separate in our thinking. Most of the literature on stratification has tried to answer the second question (particularly with regard to the ease or difficulty of mobility between strata) without tackling the first. The first question, however, is logically prior and, in the case of any particular individual or group, factually prior.

The Functional Necessity of Stratification

Curiously, however, the main functional necessity explaining the universal presence of stratification is precisely the requirement faced by any society of placing and motivating individuals in the social structure. As a functioning mechanism a society must somehow distribute its members in social positions and induce them to perform the duties of these positions. It must thus concern itself with motivation at two different levels: to instill in the proper individuals the desire to fill certain positions, and, once in these positions, the desire to perform the duties attached to them. Even though the social order may be relatively static in form, there is a continuous process of metabolism as new individuals are born into it, shift with age, and die off. Their absorption into the positional system must somehow be arranged and motivated. This is true whether the system is competitive or non-competitive. A competitive system gives greater importance to the motivation to achieve positions, whereas a non-competitive system gives perhaps greater importance to the motivation to perform the duties of the positions; but in any system both types of motivation are required.

If the duties associated with the various positions were all equally pleasant to the human organism, all equally important to societal survival, and all equally in need of the same ability or talent, it would make no difference who got into which positions, and the problem of social placement would be greatly reduced. But actually it does make a great deal of difference who gets into which positions, not only because some positions are inherently more agreeable than others, but also because some require special talents or training and some are functionally more important than others. Also, it is essential that the duties of the positions be performed with the diligence that their importance requires. Inevitably, then, a society must have, first, some kind of rewards that it can use as inducements, and second, some way of distributing these rewards differentially according to positions. The rewards and their distribution become a part of the social order, and thus give rise to stratification.

One may ask what kind of rewards a society has at its disposal in distributing its personnel and securing essential services. It has, first of all, the things that contribute to sustenance and comfort. It has, second, the things that contribute to humor and diversion. And it has, finally, the things that contribute to self-respect and ego expansion. The last, because of the peculiarly social character of the self, is largely a function of the opinion of others, but it nonetheless ranks in importance with the first two. In any social system three kinds of rewards must be dispensed differentially according to positions.

In a sense the rewards are "built into" the position. They consist in the "rights" associated with the position, plus what may be called its accompaniments or perquisites. Often the rights, and sometimes the accompaniments, are functionally related to the duties of the position. (Rights as viewed by the incumbent are usually duties as viewed by other members of the community.) However, there may be a host of subsidiary rights and perquisites that are not essential to the function of the position and have only an indirect and symbolic connection with its duties, but which still may be of considerable importance in inducing people to seek the positions and fulfil the essential duties.

If the rights and perquisites of different positions in a society must be unequal, then the society must be stratified, because that is precisely what stratification means. Social inequality is thus an unconsciously evolved device by which societies insure that the most important positions are conscientiously filled by the most qualified persons. Hence every society, no matter how simple or complex, must differentiate persons in terms of both prestige and esteem, and must therefore possess a certain amount of institutionalized inequality.

It does not follow that the amount or type of inequality need be the same in all societies. This is largely a function of factors that will be discussed presently.

The Two Determinants of Positional Rank

Granting the general function that inequality subserves, one can specify the two factors that determine the relative rank of different positions. In general those positions convey the best reward, and hence have the highest rank, which (a) have the greatest importance for the society and (b) require the greatest training or talent. The first factor concerns function and is a matter of relative significance; the second concerns means and is a matter of scarcity.

Differential Functional Importance

Actually a society does not need to reward positions in proportion to their functional importance. It merely needs to give sufficient reward to them to insure that they will be filled competently. In other words, it must see that less essential positions do not compete successfully with more essential ones. If a position is easily filled, it need not be heavily rewarded, even though important. On the other hand, if it is important but hard to fill, the reward must be high enough to get it filled anyway. Functional importance is therefore a necessary but not a sufficient cause of high rank being assigned to a position.[3]

Differential Scarcity of Personnel

Practically all positions, no matter how acquired, require some form of skill or capacity for performance. This is implicit in the very notion of position, which implies that the incumbent must, by virtue of his incumbency, accomplish certain things.

There are, ultimately, only two ways

---

[3] Unfortunately, functional importance is difficult to establish. To use the position's prestige to establish it, as is often unconsciously done, constitutes circular reasoning from our point of view. There are, however, two independent clues: (1) the degree to which a position is functionally unique, there being no other positions that can perform the same function satisfactorily; (2) the degree to which other positions are dependent on the one in question. Both clues are best exemplified in organized systems of positions built around one major function. Thus, in most complex societies the religious, political, economic, and educational functions are handled by distinct structures not easily interchangeable. In addition, each structure possesses many different positions, some clearly dependent on, if not subordinate to, others. In sum, when an institutional nucleus becomes differentiated around one main function, and at the same time organizes a large portion of the population into its relationships, the *key* positions in it are of the highest functional importance. The absence of such specialization does not prove functional unimportance, for the whole society may be relatively unspecialized; but it is safe to assume that the more important functions receive the first and clearest structural differentiation.

in which a person's qualifications come about: through inherent capacity or through training. Obviously, in concrete activities both are always necessary, but from a practical standpoint the scarcity may lie primarily in one or the other, as well as in both. Some positions require innate talents of such high degree that persons who fill them are bound to be rare. In many cases, however, talent is fairly abundant in the population but the training process is so long, costly, and elaborate that relatively few can qualify. Modern medicine, for example, is within the mental capacity of most individuals, but a medical education is so burdensome and expensive that virtually none would undertake it if the position of the M.D. did not carry a reward commensurate with the sacrifice.

If the talents required for a position are abundant and the training easy, the method of acquiring the position may have little to do with its duties. There may be, in fact, a virtually accidental relationship. But if the skills required are scarce by reason of the rarity of talent or the costliness of training, the position, if functionally important, must have an attractive power that will draw the necessary skills in competition with other positions. This means, in effect, that the position must be high in the social scale—must command great prestige, high salary, ample leisure, and the like.

How Variations Are to Be Understood

In so far as there is a difference between one system of stratification and another, it is attributable to whatever factors affect the two determinants of differential reward—namely, functional importance and scarcity of personnel. Positions important in one society may not be important in another, because the conditions faced by the societies, or their degree of internal development, may be different. The same conditions,

in turn, may affect the question of scarcity; for in some societies the stage of development, or the external situation, may wholly obviate the necessity of certain kinds of skill or talent. Any particular system of stratification, then, can be understood as a product of the special conditions affecting the two aforementioned grounds of differential reward.

Major Societal Functions and Stratification

Religion

The reason why religion is necessary is apparently to be found in the fact that human society achieves its unity primarily through the possession by its members of certain ultimate values and ends in common. Although these values and ends are subjective, they influence behavior, and their integration enables the society to operate as a system. Derived neither from inherited nor from external nature, they have evolved as a part of culture by communication and moral pressure. They must, however, appear to the members of the society to have some reality, and it is the role of religious belief and ritual to supply and reinforce this appearance of reality. Through belief and ritual the common ends and values are connected with an imaginary world symbolized by concrete sacred objects, which world in turn is related in a meaningful way to the facts and trials of the individual's life. Through the worship of the sacred objects and the beings they symbolize, and the acceptance of supernatural prescriptions that are at the same time codes of behavior, a powerful control over human conduct is exercised, guiding it along lines sustaining the institutional structure and conforming to the ultimate ends and values.

If this conception of the role of religion is true, one can understand why in every known society the religious activities tend to be under the charge of particular persons, who tend thereby to enjoy greater rewards than the ordinary societal member. Certain of the rewards and special privileges may attach to only the highest religious functionaries, but others usually apply, if such exists, to the entire sacerdotal class.

Moreover, there is a peculiar relation between the duties of the religious official and the special privileges he enjoys. If the supernatural world governs the destinies of men more ultimately than does the real world, its earthly representative, the person through whom one may communicate with the supernatural, must be a powerful individual. He is a keeper of sacred tradition, a skilled performer of the ritual, and an interpreter of lore and myth. He is in such close contact with the gods that he is viewed as possessing some of their characteristics. He is, in short, a bit sacred, and hence free from some of the more vulgar necessities and controls.

It is no accident, therefore, that religious functionaries have been associated with the very highest positions of power, as in theocratic regimes. Indeed, looking at it from this point of view, one may wonder why it is that they do not get *entire* control over their societies. The factors that prevent this are worthy of note.

In the first place, the amount of technical competence necessary for the performance of religious duties is small. Scientific or artistic capacity is not required. Anyone can set himself up as enjoying an intimate relation with deities, and nobody can successfully dispute him. Therefore, the factor of scarcity of personnel does not operate in the technical sense.

One may assert, on the other hand, that religious ritual is often elaborate and religious lore abstruse, and that priestly ministrations require tact, if not intelligence. This is true, but the technical requirements of the profession are for the most part adventitious, not related to the end in the same way that science is related to air travel. The priest can never be free from competition, since the criteria of whether or not one has genuine contact with the supernatural are never strictly clear. It is this competition that debases the priestly position below what might be expected at first glance. That is why priestly prestige is highest in those societies where membership in the profession is rigidly controlled by the priestly guild itself. That is why, in part at least, elaborate devices are utilized to stress the identification of the person with his office—spectacular costume, abnormal conduct, special diet, segregated residence, celibacy, conspicuous leisure, and the like. In fact, the priest is always in danger of becoming somewhat discredited—as happens in a secularized society—because in a world of stubborn fact, ritual and sacred knowledge alone will not grow crops or build houses. Furthermore, unless he is protected by a professional guild, the priest's identification with the supernatural tends to preclude his acquisition of abundant wordly goods.

As between one society and another it seems that the highest general position awarded the priest occurs in the medieval type of social order. Here there is enough economic production to afford a surplus, which can be used to support a numerous and highly organized priesthood; and yet the populace is unlettered and therefore credulous to a high degree. Perhaps the most extreme example is to be found in the Buddhism of Tibet, but others are encountered in the Catholicism of feudal Europe, the Inca regime of Peru, the Brahminism of India, and the Mayan priesthood of Yucatan. On the other hand, if the society is so crude as to have no surplus and little differentiation, so that every priest must be also a cultivator or hunter, the separation of the priestly status from the others has hardly gone far enough for priestly prestige to mean much. When the priest actually has high prestige under these circumstances, it is because he also performs other important functions (usually political and medical).

In an extremely advanced society built on scientific technology, the priesthood tends to lose status, because sacred tradition and supernaturalism drop into the background. The ultimate values and common ends of the society tend to be expressed in less anthropomorphic ways, by officials who occupy fundamentally political, economic, or educational rather than religious positions. Nevertheless, it is easily possible for intellectuals to exaggerate the degree to which the priesthood in a presumable secular milieu has lost prestige. When the matter is closely examined the urban proletariat, as well as the rural citizenry, proves to be surprisingly god-fearing and priest-ridden. No society has become so completely secularized as to liquidate entirely the belief in transcendental ends and supernatural entities. Even in a secularized society some system must exist for the integration of ultimate values, for their ritualistic expression, and for the emotional adjustments required by disappointment, death, and disaster.

Government

Like religion, government plays a unique and indispensable part in society. But in contrast to religion, which provides integration in terms of sentiments, beliefs, and rituals, it organizes the society in terms of law and authority. Furthermore, it orients the society to the actual rather than the unseen world. The main functions of government are, internally, the ultimate enforcement of norms, the final arbitration of conflicting interests, and the overall planning and direction of society; and externally, the handling of war and diplomacy. To carry out these functions it acts as the agent of the entire people, enjoys a monopoly of force, and controls all individuals within its territory.

Political action, by definition, implies authority. An official can command because he has authority, and the citizen must obey because he is subject to that authority. For this reason stratification is inherent in the nature of political relationships.

So clear is the power embodied in political position that political inequality is sometimes thought to comprise all inequality. But it can be shown that there are other bases of stratification, that the following controls operate in practice to keep political power from becoming complete:

1. The fact that the actual holders of political office, and especially those determining top policy must necessarily be few in number compared to the total population.
2. The fact that the rulers represent the interest of the group rather than of themselves, and are therefore restricted in their behavior by rules and mores designed to enforce this limitation of interest.
3. The fact that the holder of political office has his authority by virtue of his office and nothing else, and therefore any special knowledge, talent, or capacity he may claim is purely incidental, so that he often has to depend upon others for technical assistance.

In view of these limiting factors, it is not strange that the rulers often have less power and prestige than a literal enumeration of their formal rights would lead one to expect.

Wealth, Property, and Labor

Every position that secures for its incumbent a livelihood is, by definition, economically rewarded. For this reason there is an economic aspect to those positions (e.g., political and religious) the main function of which is not economic. It therefore becomes convenient for the society to use unequal economic returns as a principal means of controlling the entrance of persons into positions and stimulating the performance of their duties. The amount of the economic return therefore becomes one of the main indices of social status.

It should be stressed, however, that a position does not bring power and prestige *because* it draws a high income. Rather, it draws a high income because it is functionally important and the available personnel is for one reason or another scarce. It is therefore superficial and erroneous to regard high income as the cause of a man's power and prestige, just as it is erroneous to think that a man's fever is the cause of his disease.[4]

The economic source of power and prestige is not income primarily, but the ownership of capital goods (including patents, good will, and professional reputation). Such ownership should be distinguished from the possession of consumers' goods, which is an index rather than a cause of social standing. In other words, the ownership of producers' goods is properly speaking, a source of income like other positions, the income itself remaining an index. Even in situations where social values are widely commercialized and earnings are the readiest method of judging social position, income does not confer prestige on a position so much as it induces people to compete for the position. It is true that a man who has a high income as a result of one position may find this money helpful in climbing into another position as well, but this again reflects the effect of his initial, economically advantageous status, which exercises its influence through the medium of money.

In a system of private property in productive enterprise, an income above what an individual spends can give rise to possession of capital wealth. Presumably such possession is a reward for the proper management of one's finances originally and of the productive enterprise later. But as social differentiation becomes highly advanced and yet the institution of inheritance persists, the phenomenon of pure ownership, and reward for pure ownership, emerges. In such a case it is difficult to prove that the position is functionally important or that the scarcity involved is anything other than extrinsic and accidental. It is for this reason, doubtless, that the institution of private property in productive goods becomes more subject to criticism as social development proceeds toward industrialization. It is only this pure, that is, strictly legal and functionless ownership, however, that is open to attack; for some form of active ownership, whether private or public, is indispensable.

One kind of ownership of production goods consists in rights over the labor of others. The most extremely concentrated and exclusive of such rights are found in slavery, but the essential principle remains in serfdom, peonage, encomienda, and indenture. Naturally this kind of ownership has the greatest significance for stratification, because it necessarily entails an unequal relationship.

But property in capital goods inevitably introduces a compulsive element even into the nominally free contractual relationship. Indeed, in some respects the authority of the contractual employer is greater than that of the feudal landlord, inasmuch as the latter is more limited by traditional reciprocities. Even the classical economics recognized that competitors would fare unequally, but it did not pursue this fact to its

---

[4] The symbolic rather than intrinsic role of income in social stratification has been succinctly summarized by Talcott Parsons, "An Analytical Approach to the Theory of Social Stratification," *American Journal of Sociology*, XLV (May, 1940), 841–862.

necessary conclusion that, however it might be acquired, unequal control of goods and services must give unequal advantage to the parties to a contract.

Technical Knowledge

The function of finding means to single goals, without any concern with the choice between goals, is the exclusively technical sphere. The explanation of why positions requiring great technical skill receive fairly high rewards is easy to see, for it is the simplest case of the rewards being so distributed as to draw talent and motivate training. Why they seldom if ever receive the highest rewards is also clear: the importance of technical knowledge from a societal point of view is never so great as the integration of goals, which takes place on the religious, political, and economic levels. Since the technological level is concerned solely with means, a purely technical position must ultimately be subordinate to other positions that are religious, political, or economic in character.

Nevertheless, the distinction between expert and layman in any social order is fundamental, and cannot be entirely reduced to other terms. Methods of recruitment, as well as of reward, sometimes lead to the erroneous interpretation that technical positions are economically determined. Actually, however, the acquisition of knowledge and skill cannot be accomplished by purchase, although the opportunity to learn may be. The control of the avenues of training may inhere as a sort of property right in certain families or classes, giving them power and prestige in consequence. Such a situation adds an artificial scarcity to the natural scarcity of skills and talents. On the other hand, it is possible for an opposite situation to arise. The rewards of technical position may be so great that a condition of excess supply is created, leading to at least

temporary devaluation of the rewards. Thus "unemployment in the learned professions" may result in a debasement of the prestige of those positions. Such adjustments and readjustments are constantly occurring in changing societies; and it is always well to bear in mind that the efficiency of a stratified structure may be affected by the modes of recruitment for positions. The social order itself, however, sets limits to the inflation or deflation of the prestige of experts: an over-supply tends to debase the rewards and discourage recruitment or produce revolution, whereas an under-supply tends to increase the rewards or weaken the society in competition with other societies.

Particular systems of stratification show a wide range with respect to the exact position of technically competent persons. This range is perhaps most evident in the degree of specialization. Extreme division of labor tends to create many specialists without high prestige since the training is short and the required native capacity relatively small. On the other hand it also tends to accentuate the high position of the true experts—scientists, engineers, and administrators—by increasing their authority relative to other functionally important positions. But the idea of a technocratic social order or a government or priesthood of engineers or social scientists neglects the limitations of knowledge and skills as a basic for performing social functions. To the extent that the social structure is truly specialized the prestige of the technical person must also be circumscribed.

Variation in Stratified Systems

The generalized principles of stratification here suggested form a necessary preliminary to a consideration of types of stratified systems, because it is in terms of these principles that the types must be described. This can be seen by trying to delineate types according to certain modes of variation. For instance, some of the most important modes (together with the polar types in terms of them) seem to be as follows:

(a) The Degree of Specialization

The degree of specialization affects the fineness and multiplicity of the gradations in power and prestige. It also influences the extent to which particular functions may be emphasized in the invidious system, since a given function cannot receive much emphasis in the hierarchy until it has achieved structural separation from the other functions. Finally, the amount of specialization influences the bases of selection. Polar types: *Specialized, Unspecialized.*

(b) The Nature of the Functional Emphasis

In general when emphasis is put on sacred matters, a rigidity is introduced that tends to limit specialization and hence the development of technology. In addition, a brake is placed on social mobility, and on the development of bureaucracy. When the preoccupation with the sacred is withdrawn, leaving greater scope for purely secular preoccupations, a great development, and rise in status, of economic and technological positions seemingly takes place. Curiously, a concomitant rise in political position is not likely, because it has usually been allied with the religious and stands to gain little by the decline of the latter. It is also possible for a society to emphasize family functions—as in relatively undifferentiated societies where high mortality requires high fertility and kinship forms the main basis of social organization. Main types: *Familistic, Authoritarian* (*Theocratic* or sacred, and *Totalitarian* or secular), *Capitalistic.*

(c) The Magnitude of Invidious Differences

What may be called the amount of social distance between positions, taking into account the entire scale, is something that should lend itself to quantitative measurement. Considerable differences apparently exist between different societies in this regard, and also between parts of the same society. Polar types: *Equalitarian, Inequalitarian.*

(d) The Degree of Opportunity

The familiar question of the amount of mobility is different from the question of the comparative equality or inequality of rewards posed above, because the two criteria may vary independently up to a point. For instance, the tremendous divergences in monetary income in the United States are far greater than those found in primitive societies, yet the equality of opportunity to move from one rung to the other in the social scale may also be greater in the United States than in a hereditary tribal kingdom. Polar types: *Mobile* (open), *Immobile* (closed).

(e) The Degree of Stratum Solidarity

Again, the degree of "class solidarity" (or the presence of specific organizations to promote class interests) may vary to some extent independently of the other criteria, and hence is an important principle in classifying systems of stratification. Polar types: *Class organized, Class unorganized.*

External Conditions

What state any particular system of stratification is in with reference to each of these modes of variation depends on two things: (1) its state with reference to the other ranges of variation, and (2) the conditions outside the system of stratification which nevertheless influence that system. Among the latter are the following:

(a) The Stage of Cultural Development

As the cultural heritage grows, increased specialization becomes necessary, which in turn contributes to the enhancement of mobility, a decline of stratum solidarity, and a change of functional emphasis.

(b) Situation with Respect to Other Societies

The presence or absence of open conflict with other societies, of free trade relations or cultural diffusion, all influence the class structure to some extent. A chronic state of warfare tends to place emphasis upon the military functions, especially when the opponents are more or less equal. Free trade, on the other hand, strengthens the hand of the trader at the expense of the warrior and priest. Free movement of ideas generally has an equalitarian effect. Migration and conquest create special circumstances.

(c) Size of the Society

A small society limits the degree to which functional specialization can go, the degree of segregation of different strata, and the magnitude of inequality.

Composite Types

Much of the literature on stratification has attempted to classify concrete systems into a certain number of types. This task is deceptively simple, however, and should come at the end of an analysis of elements and principles, rather than at the beginning. If the preceding discussion has any validity, it indicates that there are a number of modes of variation between different systems, and that any one system is a composite of the society's status with reference to all these modes of variation. The danger of trying to classify whole societies under such rubrics as *caste, feudal,* or *open class* is that one or two criteria are selected and others ignored, the result being an unsatisfactory solution to the problem posed. The present discussion has been offered as a possible approach to the more systematic classification of composite types.

Some Principles of Stratification: A Critical Analysis

MELVIN M. TUMIN

The fact of social inequality in human society is marked by its ubiquity and its antiquity. Every known society, past and present, distributes its scarce and demanded goods and services unequally. And there are attached to the positions which command unequal amounts of such goods and services certain highly morally-toned evaluations of their importance for the society.

The ubiquity and the antiquity of such inequality has given rise to the assumption that there must be something both inevitable and positively functional about such social arrangements.

Clearly, the truth or falsity of such an assumption is a strategic question for any general theory of social organization. It is therefore most curious that the basic premises and implications of the assumption have only been most casually explored by American sociologists.

The most systematic treatment is to be found in the well-known article by Kingsley Davis and Wilbert Moore, entitled

Reprinted from Melvin M. Tumin, "Some Principles of Stratification: A Critical Analysis," *American Sociological Review*, XVIII, No. 4 (August, 1953), 387–394, by permission of the author and the American Sociological Association. The writer has had the benefit of a most helpful criticism of the main portions of this paper by Professor W. J. Goode of Columbia University. In addition, he has had the opportunity to expose this paper to criticism by the Staff Seminar of the Sociology Section at Princeton. In deference to a possible rejoinder by Professors Moore and Davis, the writer has not revised the paper to meet the criticisms which Moore has already offered personally.

"Some Principles of Stratification."[1] More than twelve years have passed since its publication, and though it is one of the very few treatments of stratification on a high level of generalization, it is difficult to locate a single systematic analysis of its reasoning. It will be the principal concern of this paper to present the beginnings of such an analysis.

The central argument advanced by Davis and Moore can be stated in a number of sequential propositions, as follows:

1. Certain positions in any society are functionally more important than others, and require special skills for their performance.
2. Only a limited number of individuals in any society have the talents which can be trained into the skills appropriate to these positions.
3. The conversion of talents into skills involves a training period during which sacrifices of one kind or another are made by those undergoing the training.

[1] *American Sociological Review*, X (April, 1945), 242–249. An earlier article by Kingsley Davis, entitled, "A Conceptual Analysis of Stratification," *American Sociological Review*, VII (June, 1942), 309–321, is devoted primarily to setting forth a vocabulary for stratification analysis. A still earlier article by Talcott Parsons, "An Analytical Approach to the Theory of Social Stratification," *American Journal of Sociology*, XLV (November, 1940), 849–862, approaches the problem in terms of why "differential ranking is considered a really fundamental phenomenon of social systems and what are the respects in which such ranking is important." The principal line of integration asserted by Parsons is with the fact of the normative orientation of any society. Certain crucial lines of connection are left unexplained, however, in this article, and in the Davis and Moore article of 1945 only some of these lines are made explicit.

4. In order to induce the talented persons to undergo these sacrifices and acquire the training, their future positions must carry an inducement value in the form of differential, i.e., privileged and disproportionate access to the scarce and desired rewards which the society has to offer.[2]
5. These scarce and desired goods consist of the rights and perquisites attached to, or built into, the positions, and can be classified into those things which contribute to (a) sustenance and comfort, (b) humor and diversion, (c) self-respect and ego expansion.
6. This differential access to the basic rewards of the society has as a consequence the differentiation of the prestige and esteem which various strata acquire. This may be said, along with the rights and perquisites, to constitute institutionalized social inequality, i.e., stratification.
7. Therefore, social inequality among different strata in the amounts of scarce and desired goods, and the amounts of prestige and esteem which they receive, is both positively functional and inevitable in any society.

Let us take these propositions and examine them *seriatim*.[3]

(*1*) *Certain positions in any society are more*

functionally important than others and require special skills for their performance. The key term here is "functionally important." The functionalist theory of social organization is by no means clear and explicit about this term. The minimum common referent is to something known as the "survival value" of a social structure.[4] This concept immediately involves a number of perplexing questions. Among these are: (a) the issue of minimum vs. maximum survival, and the possible empirical referents which can be given to those terms; (b) whether such a proposition is a useless tautology since any *status quo* at any given moment is nothing more and nothing less than everything present in the *status quo*. In these terms, all acts and structures must be judged positively functional in that they constitute essential portions of the *status quo*; (c) what kind of calculus of functionality exists which will enable us, at this point in our development, to add and subtract long and short range consequences, with their mixed qualities, and arrive at some summative judgment regarding the rating an act or structure should receive on a scale of greater or lesser functionality? At best, we tend to make primarily intuitive judgments. Often enough, these judgments involve the use of value-laden criteria, or, at least, criteria which are chosen in preference to others not for any sociologically systematic reasons but by reason of certain implicit value preferences.

Thus, to judge that the engineers in a factory are functionally more important to the factory than the unskilled workmen involves a notion regarding the dispensability of the unskilled workmen, or their replaceability, relative to that of

[2] The "scarcity and demand" qualities of goods and services are never explicitly mentioned by Davis and Moore. But it seems to the writer that the argument makes no sense unless the goods and services are so characterized. For if rewards are to function as differential inducements they must not only be differentially distributed but they must be both scarce and demanded as well. Neither the scarcity of an item by itself nor the fact of its being in demand is sufficient to allow it to function as a differential inducement in a system of unequal rewards. Leprosy is scarce and oxygen is highly demanded.

[3] The arguments to be advanced here are condensed versions of a much longer analysis entitled, *An Essay on Social Stratification*. Perforce, all the reasoning necessary to support some of the contentions cannot be offered within the space limits of this article.

[4] Davis and Moore are explicitly aware of the difficulties involved here and suggest two "independent clues" other than survival value. See footnote 3 on [p. 370 of this volume].

the engineers. But this is not a process of choice with infinite time dimensions. For at some point along the line one must face the problem of adequate motivation for *all* workers at all levels of skill in the factory. In the long run, *some* labor force of unskilled workmen is as important and as indispensable to the factory as *some* labor force of engineers. Often enough, the labor force situation is such that this fact is brought home sharply to the entrepreneur in the short run rather than in the long run.

Moreover, the judgment as to the relative indispensability and replaceability of a particular segment of skills in the population involves a prior judgment about the bargaining-power of that segment. But this power is itself a culturally shaped *consequence* of the existing system of rating, rather than something inevitable in the nature of social organization. At least the contrary of this has never been demonstrated, but only assumed.

A generalized theory of social stratification must recognize that the prevailing system of inducements and rewards is only one of many variants in the whole range of possible systems of motivation which, at least theoretically, are capable of working in human society. It is quite conceivable, of course, that a system of norms could be institutionalized in which the idea of threatened withdrawal of services, except under the most extreme circumstances, would be considered as absolute moral anathema. In such a case, the whole notion of relative functionality, as advanced by Davis and Moore, would have to be radically revised.

(2) *Only a limited number of individuals in any society have the talents which can be trained into the skills appropriate to these positions (i.e., the more functionally important positions).* The truth of this proposition depends at least in part on the truth of proposition 1 above. It is, therefore, subject to all the limitations indicated

above. But for the moment, let us assume the validity of the first proposition and concentrate on the question of the rarity of appropriate talent.

If all that is meant is that in every society there is a *range* of talent, and that some members of any society are by nature more talented than others, no sensible contradiction can be offered, but a question must be raised here regarding the amount of sound knowledge present in any society concerning the presence of talent in the population.

For, in every society there is some demonstrable ignorance regarding the amount of talent present in the population. *And the more rigidly stratified a society is, the less chance does that society have of discovering any new facts about the talents of its members.* Smoothly working and stable systems of stratification, wherever found, tend to build-in obstacles to the further exploration of the range of available talent. This is especially true in those societies where the opportunity to discover talent in any one generation varies with the differential resources of the parent generation. Where, for instance, access to education depends upon the wealth of one's parents, and where wealth is differentially distributed, large segments of the population are likely to be deprived of the chance even to *discover* what are their talents.

Whether or not differential rewards and opportunities are functional in any one generation, it is clear that if those differentials are allowed to be socially inherited by the next generation, then, the stratification system is specifically dysfunctional for the discovery of talents in the next generation. In this fashion, systems of social stratification tend to limit the chances available to maximize the efficiency of discovery, recruitment and training of "functionally important talent."[5]

---

[5] Davis and Moore state this point briefly on [p. 375 of this vol.] but do not elaborate on it.

Additionally, the unequal distribution of rewards in one generation tends to result in the unequal distribution of motivation in the succeeding generation. Since motivation to succeed is clearly an important element in the entire process of education, the unequal distribution of motivation tends to set limits on the possible extensions of the educational system, and hence, upon the efficient recruitment and training of the widest body of skills available in the population.[6]

Lastly, in this context, it may be asserted that there is some noticeable tendency for elites to restrict further access to their privileged positions, once they have sufficient power to enforce such restrictions. This is especially true in a culture where it is possible for an elite to contrive a high demand and a proportionately higher reward for its work by restricting the numbers of the elite available to do the work. The recruitment and training of doctors in modern United States is at least partly a case in point.

Here, then, are three ways, among others which could be cited, in which stratification systems, once operative, tend to reduce the survival value of a society by limiting the search, recruitment and training of functionally important personnel far more sharply than the facts of available talent would appear to justify. It is only when there is genuinely equal access to recruitment and training for all potentially talented persons that differential rewards can conceivably be justified as functional. And

stratification systems are apparently *inherently antagonistic* to the development of such full equality of opportunity.

(3) *The conversion of talents into skills involves a training period during which sacrifices of one kind or another are made by those undergoing the training.* Davis and Moore introduce here a concept, "sacrifice" which comes closer than any of the rest of their vocabulary of analysis to being a direct reflection of the rationalizations, offered by the more fortunate members of a society, of the rightness of their occupancy of privileged positions. It is the least critically thought-out concept in the repertoire, and can also be shown to be least supported by the actual facts.

In our present society, for example, what are the sacrifices which talented persons undergo in the training period? The possibly serious losses involve the surrender of earning power and the cost of the training. The latter is generally borne by the parents of the talented youth undergoing training, and not by the trainees themselves. But this cost tends to be paid out of income which the parents were able to earn generally by virtue of *their* privileged positions in the hierarchy of stratification. That is to say, the parents' ability to pay for the training of their children is part of the differential *reward* they, the parents, received for their privileged positions in the society. And to charge this sum up against sacrifices made by the youth is falsely to perpetrate a bill or a debt already paid by the society to the parents.

So far as the sacrifice of earning power by the trainees themselves is concerned, the loss may be measured relative to what they might have earned had they gone into the labor market instead of into advanced training for the "important" skills. There are several ways to judge this. One way is to take all the average earnings of age peers who did go into the labor market for a period equal to the average length of the training period. The total income, so calculated,

[6] In the United States, for instance, we are only now becoming aware of the amount of productivity we, as a society, lose by allocating inferior opportunities and rewards, and hence, inferior motivation, to our Negro population. The actual amount of loss is difficult to specify precisely. Some rough estimate can be made, however, on the assumption that there is present in the Negro population about the same range of talent that is found in the White population.

roughly equals an amount which the elite can, on the average, earn back in the first decade of professional work, over and above the earnings of his age peers who are not trained. Ten years is probably the maximum amount needed to equalize the differential.[7] There remains, on the average, twenty years of work during each of which the skilled person then goes on to earn far more than his unskilled age peers. And, what is often forgotten, there is then still another ten or fifteen year period during which the skilled person continues to work and earn when his unskilled age peer is either totally or partially out of the labor market by virtue of the attrition of his strength and capabilities.

One might say that the first ten years of differential pay is perhaps justified, in order to regain for the trained person what he lost during his training period. But it is difficult to imagine what would justify continuing such differential rewards beyond that period.

Another and probably sounder way to measure how much is lost during the training period is to compare the per capita income available to the trainee with the per capita income of the age peer on the untrained labor market during the so-called sacrificial period. If one takes into account the earlier marriage of untrained persons, and the earlier acquisition of family dependents, it is highly dubious that the per capita income of the wage worker is significantly larger than that of the trainee. Even assuming, for the moment, that there is a difference, the amount is by no means sufficient to justify a lifetime of continuing differentials.

What tends to be completely overlooked, in addition, are the psychic and spiritual rewards which are available to the elite trainees by comparison with their age peers in the labor force. There is, first, the much higher prestige enjoyed by the college student and the professional-school student as compared with persons in shops and offices. There is, second, the extremely highly valued privilege of having greater opportunity for self-development. There is, third, all the psychic gain involved in being allowed to delay the assumption of adult responsibilities such as earning a living and supporting a family. There is, fourth, the access to leisure and freedom of a kind not likely to be experienced by the persons already at work.

If these are never taken into account as rewards of the training period it is not because they are not concretely present, but because the emphasis in American concepts of reward is almost exclusively placed on the material returns of positions. The emphases on enjoyment, entertainment, ego enhancement, prestige and esteem are introduced only when the differentials in these which accrue to the skilled positions need to be justified. If these other rewards were taken into account, it would be much more difficult to demonstrate that the training period, as presently operative, is really sacrificial. Indeed, it might turn out to be the case that even at this point in their careers, the elite trainees were being differentially rewarded relative to their age peers in the labor force.

All of the foregoing concerns the quality of the training period under our present system of motivation and rewards. Whatever may turn out to be the factual case about the present system—and the factual case is moot—the more important theoretical question concerns the assumption that the training period under *any* system must be sacrificial.

There seem to be no good theoretical grounds for insisting on this assumption. For, while under any system certain costs will be involved in training persons

---

[7] These are only very rough estimates, of course, and it is certain that there is considerable income variation within the so-called elite group, so that the proposition holds only relatively more or less.

for skilled positions, these costs could easily be assumed by the society-at-large. Under these circumstances, there would be no need to compensate anyone in terms of differential rewards once the skilled positions were staffed. In short, there would be no need or justification for stratifying social positions on *these* grounds.

(*4*) *In order to induce the talented persons to undergo these sacrifices and acquire the training, their future positions must carry an inducement value in the form of differential, i.e., privileged and disproportionate access to the scarce and desired rewards which the society has to offer.* Let us assume, for the purposes of the discussion, that the training period is sacrificial and the talent is rare in every conceivable human society. There is still the basic problem as to whether the allocation of differential rewards in scarce and desired goods and services is the only or the most efficient way of recruiting the appropriate talent to these positions.

For there are a number of alternative motivational schemes whose efficiency and adequacy ought at least to be considered in this context. What can be said, for instance, on behalf of the motivation which De Man called "joy in work," Veblen termed "instinct for workmanship" and which we latterly have come to identify as "intrinsic work satisfaction?" Or, to what extent could the motivation of "social duty" be institutionalized in such a fashion that self-interest and social interest come closely to coincide? Or, how much prospective confidence can be placed in the possibilities of institutionalizing "social service" as a widespread motivation for seeking one's appropriate position and fulfilling it conscientiously?

Are not these types of motivations, we may ask, likely to prove most appropriate for precisely the "most functionally important positions?" Especially in a mass industrial society, where the vast majority of positions become standard-ized and routinized, it is the skilled jobs which are likely to retain most of the quality of "intrinsic job satisfaction" and be most readily identifiable as socially serviceable. Is it indeed impossible then to build these motivations into the socialization pattern to which we expose our talented youth?

To deny that such motivations could be institutionalized would be to over-claim our present knowledge. In part, also, such a claim would seem to derive from an assumption that what has not been institutionalized yet in human affairs is incapable of institutionaliza-tion. Admittedly, historical experience affords us evidence we cannot afford to ignore. But such evidence cannot legiti-mately be used to deny absolutely the possibility of heretofore untried alter-natives. Social innovation is as impor-tant a feature of human societies as social stability.

On the basis of these observations, it seems that Davis and Moore have stated the case much too strongly when they insist that a "functionally impor-tant position" which requires skills that are scarce, "must command great pres-tige, high salary, ample leisure, and the like," if the appropriate talents are to be attracted to the position. Here, clearly, the authors are postulating the unavoid-ability of very specific types of rewards and, by implication, denying the pos-sibility of others.

(*5*) *These scarce and desired goods consist of rights and perquisites attached to, or built into, the positions and can be classified into those things which contribute to* (*a*) *sustenance and comfort;* (*b*) *humor and diversion;* (*c*) *self-respect and ego expansion.*

(*6*) *This differential access to the basic rewards of the society has as a consequence the differentiation of the prestige and esteem which various strata acquire. This may be said, along with the rights and perquisites, to con-stitute institutionalized social inequality, i.e., stratification.* With the classification of the rewards offered by Davis and Moore there need be little argument. Some question must be raised, however, as to whether any reward system, built into a general stratification system, must allocate equal amounts of all three types of reward in order to function effectively, or whether one type of reward may be emphasized to the virtual neglect of others. This raises the further question regarding which type of emphasis is likely to prove most effective as a differential inducer. Nothing in the known facts about human motivation impels us to favor one type of reward over the other, or to insist that all three types of reward must be built into the positions in comparable amounts if the position is to have an inducement value.

It is well known, of course, that societies differ considerably in the kinds of rewards they emphasize in their efforts to maintain a reasonable balance between responsibility and reward. There are, for instance, numerous societies in which the conspicuous display of differential economic advantage is considered extremely bad taste. In short, our present knowledge commends to us the possibility of considerable plasticity in the way in which different types of rewards can be structured into a functioning society. This is to say, it cannot yet be demonstrated that it is *unavoidable* that differential prestige and esteem shall accrue to positions which command differential rewards in power and property.

What does seem to be unavoidable is that differential prestige shall be given to those in any society who conform to the normative order as against those who deviate from that order in a way judged immoral and detrimental. On the assumption that the continuity of a society depends on the continuity and stability of its normative order, some such distinction between conformists and deviants seems inescapable.

It also seems to be unavoidable that in any society, no matter how literate its

tradition, the older, wiser and more experienced individuals who are charged with the enculturation and socialization of the young must have more power than the young, on the assumption that the task of effective socialization demands such differential power.

But this differentiation in prestige between the conformist and the deviant is by no means the same distinction as that between strata of individuals each of which operates *within* the normative order, and is composed of adults. The *latter* distinction, in the form of differentiated rewards and prestige between social strata is what Davis and Moore, and most sociologists, consider the structure of a stratification system. The *former* distinctions have nothing necessarily to do with the workings of such a system nor with the efficiency of motivation and recruitment of functionally important personnel.

Nor does the differentiation of power between young and old necessarily create differentially valued strata. For no society rates its young as less morally worthy than its older persons, no matter how much differential power the older ones may temporarily enjoy.

(7) *Therefore, social inequality among different strata in the amounts of scarce and desired goods, and the amounts of prestige and esteem which they receive, is both positively functional and inevitable in any society.* If the objections which have heretofore been raised are taken as reasonable, then it may be stated that the only items which any society *must* distribute unequally are the power and property necessary for the performance of different tasks. If such differential power and property are viewed by all as commensurate with the differential responsibilities, and if they are culturally defined as *resources* and not as rewards, then, no differentials in prestige and esteem need follow.

Historically, the evidence seems to be that every time power and property are distributed unequally, no matter what the cultural definition, prestige and esteem differentiations have tended to result as well. Historically, however, no systematic effort has ever been made, under propitious circumstances, to develop the tradition that each man is as socially worthy as all other men so long as he performs his appropriate tasks conscientiously. While such a tradition seems utterly utopian, no known facts in psychological or social science have yet demonstrated its impossibility or its dysfunctionality for the continuity of a society. The achievement of a full institutionalization of such a tradition seems far too remote to contemplate. Some successive approximations at such a tradition, however, are not out of the range of prospective social innovation.

What, then, of the "positive functionality" of social stratification? Are there other, negative, functions of institutionalized social inequality which can be identified, if only tentatively? Some such dysfunctions of stratification have already been suggested in the body of this paper. Along with others they may now be stated, in the form of provisional assertions, as follows:

1. Social stratification systems function to limit the possibility of discovery of the full range of talent available in a society. This results from the fact of unequal access to appropriate motivation, channels of recruitment and centers of training.
2. In foreshortening the range of available talent, social stratification systems function to set limits upon the possibility of expanding the productive resources of the society, at least relative to what might be the case under conditions of greater equality of opportunity.
3. Social stratification systems function to provide the elite with the political power necessary to procure acceptance and dominance of an ideology which rationalizes the *status quo*, whatever it may be, as "logical," "natural" and "morally right." In this manner, social stratification systems function as essentially conservative

influences in the societies in which they are found.
4. Social stratification systems function to distribute favorable self-images unequally throughout a population. To the extent that such favorable self-images are requisite to the development of the creative potential inherent in men, to that extent stratification systems function to limit the development of this creative potential.
5. To the extent that inequalities in social rewards cannot be made fully acceptable to the less privileged in a society, social stratification systems function to encourage hostility, suspicion and distrust among the various segments of a society and thus to limit the possibilities of extensive social integration.
6. To the extent that the sense of significant membership in a society depends on one's place on the prestige ladder of the society, social stratification systems function to distribute unequally the sense of significant membership in the population.
7. To the extent that loyalty to a society depends on a sense of significant membership in the society, social stratification systems function to distribute loyalty unequally in the population.
8. To the extent that participation and apathy depend upon the sense of significant membership in the society, social stratification systems function to distribute the motivation to participate unequally in a population.

Each of the eight foregoing propositions contains implicit hypotheses regarding the consequences of unequal distribution of rewards in society in accordance with some notion of the functional importance of various positions. These are empirical hypotheses, subject to test. They are offered here only as exemplary of the kinds of consequences of social stratification which are not often taken into account in dealing with the problem. They should also serve to reinforce the doubt that social inequality is a device which is uniformly functional for the role of guaranteeing that the most important tasks in a society will be performed conscientiously by the most competent persons.

The obviously mixed character of the functions of social inequality should come as no surprise to anyone. If sociology is sophisticated in any sense, it is certainly with regard to its awareness of the mixed nature of any social arrangement, when the observer takes into account long as well as short range consequences and latent as well as manifest dimensions.

Summary

In this paper, an effort has been made to raise questions regarding the inevitability and positive functionality of stratification, or institutionalized social inequality in rewards, allocated in accordance with some notion of the greater and lesser functional importance of various positions. The possible alternative meanings of the concept "functional importance" has been shown to be one difficulty. The question of the scarcity or abundance of available talent has been indicated as a principal source of possible variation. The extent to which

the period of training for skilled positions may reasonably be viewed as sacrificial has been called into question. The possibility has been suggested that very different types of motivational schemes might conceivably be made to function. The separability of differentials in power and property considered as resources appropriate to a task from such differentials considered as rewards for the performance of a task has also been suggested. It has also been maintained that differentials in prestige and esteem do not necessarily follow upon differentials in power and property when the latter are considered as appropriate resources rather than rewards. Finally, some negative functions, or dysfunctions, of institutionalized social inequality have been tentatively identified, revealing the mixed character of the outcome of social stratification, and casting doubt on the contention that

Social inequality is thus an unconsciously evolved device by which societies insure that the most important positions are conscientiously filled by the most qualified persons.[8]

---

[8] Davis and Moore, *op. cit.*, p. 243.

Reply

KINGSLEY DAVIS

Tumin's critique, almost as long as the article it criticizes, is unfortunately intended not to supplement or amend the Davis-Moore theory but to prove it wrong. The critique also sets a bad example from the standpoint of methodology. Nevertheless, it does afford us a

Reprinted from Kingsley Davis, "Reply," *American Sociological Review*, XVIII, No. 4 August, 1953), 394–397, by permission of the author and the American Sociological Association.

meager opportunity to clarify and extend the original discussion. The latter, limited to eight pages, was so brief a treatment of so big a subject that it had to ignore certain relevant topics and telescope others. In the process of answering Tumin, a partial emendation can now be made.

General Considerations

Our critic seems to labor under four major difficulties, two of a methodological and two of a substantive character.

First, he appears not so much interested in understanding institutionalized inequality as in getting rid of it. By insinuating that we are "justifying" such inequality, he falls into the usual error of regarding a causal explanation of something as a justification of it: He himself offers no explanation for the universality of stratified inequality. He argues throughout his critique that stratification does not have to be, instead of trying to understand why it is. Our interest, however, was only in the latter question. If Tumin had chosen to state our propositions in our own words rather than his, he could not have pictured us as concerned with the question of whether stratification is "avoidable."

Second, Tumin confuses abstract, or theoretical, reasoning on the one hand with raw empirical generalizations on the other. Much of his critique accordingly rests on the fallacy of misplaced concreteness. Our article dealt with stratified inequality as a general property of social systems. It represented a high degree of abstraction, because there are obviously other aspects of society which in actuality affect the operation of the prestige element. It is therefore impossible to move directly from the kind of propositions we were making to descriptive propositions about, say, American society.

Third, in concentrating on only one journal article, Tumin has ignored other theoretical contributions by the authors on stratification and on other relevant aspects of society. He has thus both misrepresented the theory and raised questions that were answered elsewhere.

Fourth, by ignoring additions to the theory in other places, Tumin has failed to achieve consistency in his use of the concept "stratification." The first requirement, in this connection, is to distinguish between stratified and nonstratified statuses. One of the authors under attack has shown the difference to hinge on the family. "Those positions that may be combined in the same legitimate family—viz., positions based on sex, age, and kinship—do not form part of the system of stratification. On the other hand those positions that are socially prohibited from being combined in the same legal family—viz., different caste or class positions—constitute what we call stratification."[1] This distinction is basic, but in addition it is necessary to realize that two different questions can be asked about stratified positions: (1) Why are different evaluations and rewards given to the different *positions?* (2) How do *individuals* come to be distributed in these positions? Our theory was designed to answer the first question by means of the second. But much confusion results, as illustrated by Tumin's ambiguities, if the term "stratification" is used in such a way at to overlook the distinction between the two.

The Specific Criticisms

It will be seen that these four difficulties plague Tumin throughout his remarks and lead to much obfuscation. In answering his criticisms, we shall follow his sequence in terms of the propositions attributed to us.

1. Differential Functional Importance of Positions

Tumin criticizes the idea of unequal functional importance on the grounds that the concept is unclear, unmeasurable, and evaluative, and that other systems of motivation are conceivable. The latter point is irrelevant, since the proposition in question says nothing whatever about motivation. So is the remark about "value-laden criteria," since no such criteria are advanced by us. As for the difficulty of measuring

---

[1] Kingsley Davis, *Human Society* (New York: The Macmillan Company, 1949), p. 364.

functional importance, we stated this before Tumin did, but he does not elect to discuss the two criteria suggested in our article. The difficulty of exact empirical measurement does not itself make a concept worthless; if so we should have to throw away virtually all theoretical concepts. Rough measures of functional importance are in fact applied in practice. In wartime, for example, decisions are made as to which industries and occupations will have priority in capital equipment, labor recruitment, raw materials, etc. In totalitarian countries the same is done in peacetime, as also in underdeveloped areas attempting to maximize their social and economic modernization. Individual firms must constantly decide which positions are essential and which not. There is nothing mystical about functional importance.

Tumin points out that the unskilled workmen in a factory are as important as the engineers. This is of course true, but we have maintained that the rating of positions is not a result of functional importance alone but also of the scarcity of qualified personnel. Any concrete situation is a product of both. It requires more capital to train an engineer than to train an unskilled worker, and so engineers would not be trained at all unless their work were considered important.

Actually Tumin does not deny the differential functional importance of positions. He disguises his agreement with the proposition by tendentious argumentation.

2. The Strangulation of Talent by "Stratification"

Tumin's objection to the idea of a scarcity of trained and talented personnel rests on the argument (a) that societies do not have a "sound knowledge" of talents in their populations and (b) that stratification interferes with, rather than facilitates, the selec-

toin of talented people. The first point is inconsequential, because a selective system—e.g., organized baseball—does not require a pre-existing knowledge of talent to be effective. The second point is crucial, but Tumin strangely fails to refer to a later treatment of this very problem by Davis.[2] In introducing the problem, Davis says: "One may object to the foregoing explanation of stratification [as contained in the Davis-Moore article] on the ground that it fits a competitive order but does not fit a noncompetitive one. For instance, in a caste system it seems that people do not get their positions because of talent or training but rather because of birth. This criticism raises a crucial problem and forces an addition to the theory." The addition takes the following form: The theory in question is a theory explaining the differential prestige of *positions* rather than individuals. Even though a high-caste person occupies his rank because of his parents, this fact does not explain the high evaluation of the caste's *position* in the community. The low estate of sweeper as compared with priestly castes cannot be explained by saying that the sons of sweepers become sweepers and the sons of Brahmins become Brahmins. The explanation of the differential evaluation of strata must be sought elsewhere, in the survival value of drawing qualified people into the functionally most important positions. But since this is not the only functional necessity characterizing social systems, it is in actuality limited by certain other structures and requirements. Among the latter is the family, which limits vertical mobility by the mechanism of inheritance and succession. The family's limiting role, however, is never complete, for there is some vertical mobility in any society. Thus the selective effect of the

---

[2] *Ibid.*, pp. 369–370.

prestige system exists in its pure form only abstractly, not concretely; and the same is true of the inheritance of status. Consequently, to say that in a given society there is partial inheritance of high positions is not to deny that at the same time the prestige system is operating to draw capable people into these positions.

One source of confusion in this argument is the ambiguity, mentioned above, of the term "stratification." On the one hand it is used by us to designate the institutionalized inequality of rewards as between broad strata.[3] On the other hand, it is used (as Tumin does implicitly) to mean the inheritance of class status. With the latter definition, of course, the idea that stratification contributes to upward mobility is incongruous. One cannot expect a theory designed to account for the universal existence of institutionalized inequality as between positions to be, at the same time, an explanation of the inheritance of class status. However, it is possible to extend the theory by combining with it a general analysis of the family's articulation with the differential reward system in society. This has been done by Davis, and the result is that one can understand the combined existence in the same society of (1) a differential ranking of stratified positions, (2) a certain amount of vertical mobility, and (3) a certain amount of inheritance of status. It is this extension of the theory that Tumin ignores.

3. The "No Sacrifice" Criticism

Tumin contends, in effect, that no differential rewards are necessary to induce individuals to qualify for functionally important positions, because they make no "sacrifices." In support of

his view he says (1) that the family often makes the sacrifice for the offspring, (2) that the loss of earning power during the training period is negligible, and (3) that the prestige during the training period is high.

But point (1) confirms rather than denies the theory. It makes no essential difference that the family assumes some of the burden of training; the fact is that there is a burden. The differential ability of families to make such sacrifices of course comes back to the role of the family in limiting competition for status, which has already been discussed. The claim under point (2) that the loss of earning power during training is more than made up in the years following again confirms the theory, for we have said there is a differential reward for those attaining functionally important positions. As for point (3), the fact that the trainee may enjoy a standard of living higher than that of his already working age peers comes back to the family's status, already discussed. Nor does the claim that the psychic rewards are high during training offer any objection to the theory, because these psychic rewards are mainly a reflection of the anticipated rewards of an ultimately high status to be attained through training. It is amusing that throughout his discussion of "sacrifice" Tumin, though thinking in terms of professional training, never once mentions the onerous necessity of studying. It is unfortunately true that most individuals regard hard study as burdensome, and it is something that the family cannot do for them. Many youths are unwilling to make this sacrifice and also many are incapable of doing it well enough to succeed. There are, however, many other kinds of hurdles to high position that would discourage an individual if it were not for the rewards offered. So difficult is it to get enough qualified personnel in good positions that the modern state under-

---

[3] K. Davis, "A Conceptual Analysis of Stratification," *American Sociological Review*, VII (June, 1942), 309–321.

takes to bear some of the costs, but it cannot bear them all.

4. Alternative Motivational Schemes

Our critic contends that there are "a number of alternative motivational schemes" as efficient as differential rewards in motivating people to strive for important positions. Actually he mentions three: joy in work, sense of social service, and self-interest. The third is obviously a ringer. Concerning it he asks, "To what extent could the motivation of 'social duty' be institutionalized in such a fashion that self-interest and social interest come closely to coincide?" The answer is that such coinciding is not only possible but is actually accomplished—and our theory of social inequality explains how. This leaves, then, only two alternatives that offer any possible criticism of our views. In the eight-page article under attack, it was mentioned that one consideration is the unequal pleasantness of activities required by different positions, but space did not allow us to follow out the implications of this fact. The truth is that if everybody elected to do just what he wanted to do, the whole population would wind up in only a few types of position. A society could not operate on this basis, because it requires performance of a wide range of tasks. Surviving societies therefore evolve some system of inducements over and above the joy of work which motivates people to do what they would otherwise not do. Finally, as for the sense of social service, any sociologist should know the inadequacy of unrewarded altruism as a means of eliciting socially adequate behavior. It must be remembered that the differential rewards characterizing the status scale are not all material; they also lie in the good opinion and expectations of others and in the feeling of self-satisfaction at having stood well in

others' eyes. No one will deny that joy of work and a sense of social service are actual motives, any more than one will deny the reality of the desire for esteem (in contrast to prestige) but in any society they are supplementary rather than alternative to the positional reward mechanism.

5–6. Types of Rewards

The Davis-Moore article mentioned a rough tripartite classification of types of rewards occurring in stratified positions. Tumin says these may be unequally employed, that one society may emphasize one type more than another. This is true; we said nothing to the contrary. Tumin goes on to say that societies give approval to behavior that conforms with norms. This we certainly never disputed; indeed, in connection with positions, Davis has given a name to it—*esteem*, the kind of approval that comes with the faithful fulfillment of the duties of a position.[4] The approval that comes with *having* a position, i.e., approval attached to the position and not to the degree of faithfulness in performing its duties, is called *prestige*. Whatever the words used, the distinction is important, but Tumin has confused the two. A social system, though it certainly utilizes esteem, is not entirely built on it, because there must be motivation not only to conform to the requirements of positions held but also to strive to get into positions. Esteem alone tends to produce a static society, prestige a mobile one. Tumin's statement that the position of the parent vis-à-vis the child is not part of the stratified system is true, but it agrees perfectly with Davis' distinction between stratified and non-stratified statuses, already mentioned as an essential part of the theory overlooked by Tumin.

---

[4] *Ibid.*; and Davis, *op. cit.*, pp. 93–94.

7. Inevitability and Disfunctionality

As the grand climax of his restatement of our views, Tumin has us concluding that social inequality is *inevitable* in society. Let it be repeated, we were not concerned with the indefinite or utopian future but with societies as we find them. No proof or disproof of a proposition about inevitability is possible. As "evidence" of his view of inevitability, Tumin *hopes* to see a society based on "the tradition that each man is as socially worthy as all other men so long as he performs his appropriate tasks conscientiously." But this is, once again, the idea of a society based exclusively on esteem. The question would still remain, how do people in the first place get distributed in their different positions with their "appropriate tasks?" One can hardly criticize a theory by ignoring the problem with which it deals.

Tumin goes on to point out ways in which stratification is disfunctional. In most of what he says, however, "stratification" is being used in the sense of inheritance of status. In so far as his assertion of disfunctionality is true, then, the culprit is the family, not the differential positional rewards. He also mentions unfavorable self-images, but the disfunctionality of these is not clear, because an unfavorable self-image may be a powerful stimulus to competitive and creative activity. The same comment can be made about the alleged disfunctionality of class conflict. Incidentally, in this part of his critique Tumin makes pronouncements of functionality with firm confidence, although in the early part he doubted the functionality could be determined.

The truth is that any aspect of society is functional in some ways and disfunctional in others. Our theory was designed to suggest some of the ways in which institutionalized positional inequality contributes to societies as going concerns. Otherwise it seems difficult if not impossible to explain the universal appearance of such inequality. Excrescencies and distortions certainly appear, but they do not completely negate the principle. Tumin's analysis of the disfunctions is unsophisticated because of his confusion as to what it is that *has* the disfunctions, because of his uncritical concept of function, and because of his lack of any clear notion of a social system as an equilibrium of forces of which the stratified positional scale is only one.

Comment

WILBERT E. MOORE

I generally concur with Professor Davis's reply, which is somewhat more comprehensive than the comments I had prepared independently. However, I

Reprinted from Wilbert E. Moore, "Comment," *American Sociological Review*, XVIII, No. 4 (August, 1953), 397, by permission of the author and the American Sociological Association.

should like to emphasize that there is no reason to deny to Professor Tumin the right and even the propriety of a theoretical approach to an equalitarian system, as long as relevant principles of social structure are somehow taken into account. I do not believe Professor Tumin has met the latter qualification. With regard to the relevance of his criticism of our paper, I suggest that Professor Tumin made the major mistake of not explicitly defining social stratification, which in turn led him to assume that differential rewards and inequality of opportunity are the same thing. Neither theory nor evidence will support this equation, and making it true by implicit definition can only stand in the way of theoretically significant research.

Reply to Kingsley Davis

MELVIN M. TUMIN

We advance our science by developing and expanding the existing theoretical statements formulated by our fellow scientists. It was with this aim in mind that I took the article by Davis and Moore as the best statement of a given theoretical position. I, therefore, regret that Mr. Davis has viewed my efforts in a somewhat different light. That I chose the Davis-Moore article should be ample evidence of my respect for it.

In view of Davis' objection to my suggested revisions, it now becomes possible to point up the central issues which ought to be joined.

1. Does the fact that a given institutional pattern is universal necessarily imply that it is positively functional? Are there not numerous universals which represent structurally built-in limits on human efficiency? It is important that this alternative characterization of universal patterns be offered, since Mr. Davis insists that only those patterns survive which prove to be "best for society." Clearly, he cannot use this argument in accounting for existing stratification systems without applying it equally to such other matters as institutionalized human ignorance, war, poverty and magical treatment of disease.

Reprinted from Melvin M. Tumin, "Reply to Kingsley Davis," *American Sociological Review*, XVIII, No. 6 (December, 1953), 672–673, by permission of the author and the American Sociological Association.

2. Does the universality of an institutional pattern necessarily testify to its indispensability? In the case of stratification, does Mr. Davis really mean to imply that the functions of locating and allocating talent cannot be performed by any other social arrangement? Since a theoretical mode *can* be devised in which all other clearly indispensable major social functions are performed, but in which inequality as motive and reward is absent, how then account for stratification in terms of structural and functional necessities and inevitabilities?

3. An essential characteristic of all known kinship systems is that they function as transmitters of inequalities from generation to generation. Similarly, an essential characteristic of all known stratification systems is that they employ the kinship system as their agent of transmission of inequalities. In effect, of course, this is saying the same thing in two apparently different ways. The fact is that kinship and stratification overlap in all known societies. One cannot fully describe any given kinship system without implicitly including the transmission of inequalities if one assigns the function of "status-placement" to kinship. Similarly, one cannot describe any stratification system in operation without implying the generational transmission of inequalities, if one includes the dynamics of inequality.

To the extent that this is true, then it is true by definition that the elimination from kinship systems of their function as transmitters of inequalities (and hence the alteration of the definition of kinship systems) would eliminate those inequalities which were generation-linked.

What puzzles me, therefore, is how one can assign the "villainy" of the act of transmission of inequalities to the kinship system and insist, in turn, that the stratification system is pristine in this regard.

4. Obviously, the denial to parents of their ability and right to transmit both advantages and disadvantages to their offspring would require a fundamental alteration in all existing concepts of kinship structure. At the least, there would have to be a vigilant separation maintained between the unit which reproduces and the unit which socializes, maintains and places. In theory, this separation is eminently possible. In practice, it would be revolutionary.

One of its likely consequences would be a thorough-going alteration in the motives which impel men to high effort. It was precisely to this point of alternative possible motives that I addressed much of my original argument. Dr. Davis argues against the motive of "esteem" as being inadequate on the grounds that esteem alone tends to produce a static society. This may be true by definition. Aside from that possible source of verity, there is no empirical evidence which will support Dr. Davis' contention.

Further regarding alternative motivations, Davis argues that (a) if everybody elected to do just what he wanted to do, the whole population would wind up in only a few types of position; and (b) any sociologist should know the inadequacy of unrewarded altruism as a means of eliciting socially adequate behavior. These statements are not true even by definition; and certainly we have no sound empirical studies which

will support them as Davis puts them.

It does not seem to be the best thing for a growing science to shut the door on inquiry into alternative possible social arrangements.

5. Finally, my central argument was to the effect that there are strategic functions of stratification systems which were overlooked in the Davis-Moore article. I tried to identify a number of the operations of stratification which seemed clearly to render inefficient the process of location and allocation of talent. Davis chooses in his rejoinder either to ignore these disfunctions or to attribute them to kinship rather than to stratification. But they are there clearly to be seen. Added in with the positive functions which have been identified, we get a *mixed* net result of inequality in operation.

Of course, all institutional arrangements of any complexity are bound to be mixed in their instrumentality. It is the recognition of this mixture, and the emphasized sensitivity to the undesired aspects, which impels men to engage in purposeful social reform. In turn, social scientists have been traditionally concerned with the range of possible social arrangements and their consequences for human society. One is impelled to explore that range after probing deeply into whether a given arrangement is unavoidable and discovering that it is not. One is even more impelled to such exploration when it is discovered that the *avoidable* arrangement is probably less efficient than other possible means to the stated end. It was toward such further probing that I directed my original remarks. Joining the issues here raised will, perhaps, help probe more deeply.

But Some Are More Equal Than Others

WILBERT E. MOORE

The theoretical controversy over the interpretation of social inequality is one of the most enduring disputes in contemporary sociology. Now nearing the end of a second decade since the publication of the essay by Davis and Moore[1] and more than two decades since the original version of an essay by Parsons,[2] the debate continues, with an important and extensive critical commentary by Tumin[3] as the most recent major statement on the issues. It would be naively arrogant to suppose that the present attempt to review and clarify the analysis of inequality will be taken as defini-

Reprinted from Wilbert E. Moore, "But Some Are More Equal than Others," *American Sociological Review*, XXVIII, No. 1 (February, 1963), 13–28, by permission of the author and the American Sociological Association. The title of course is borrowed from George Orwell's *Animal Farm* (New York: Harcourt, Brace & World, Inc., 1954. The present essay is partially derived from a joint work with Arnold S. Feldman, *Order and Change in Industrial Societies*, now in preparation. I also benefited from critical comments by my collaborator, but accept sole responsibility for the present formulation.

[1] Kingsley Davis and Willbert E. Moore, "Some Principles of Stratification," *American Sociological Review*, X (April, 1945), 242–249.

[2] Talcott Parsons, "An Analytical Approach to the Theory of Social Stratification," *American Journal of Sociology*, XLV (May, 1940), 841–862. See also "A Revised Analytical Approach to the Theory of Social Stratification," in Reinhard Bendix and Seymour M. Lipset, *Class, Status and Power* (New York: The Free Press, 1953), pp. 92–128.

[3] Melvin M. Tumin with Arnold S. Feldman, *Social Class and Social Change in Puerto Rico* (Princeton, N. J.: Princeton University Press, 1961), esp. Chap. 29, "Theoretical Implications." This chapter is by the senior author alone.

tive, for the issues are empirical but also semantic, theoretical but also ideological. It is even possible, though by no means certain, that the controversy prompts useful inquiry as well as providing the pleasure of polemics to participants and their partisans.

The recent statement by Tumin and earlier ones by the same author[4] and by others[5] chiefly question the *necessary* universality of social inequality, although not its empirical ubiquity, and additionally raise questions concerning the "dysfunctions" of stratification. My current view is that the Davis-Moore position was incomplete, resulting in some overstatement (as noted by Simpson[6]) and some neglect of dysfunctions. These criticisms have already been noted by Davis.[7] In addition, I should specifically reject any stable equilibrium version of "functionalism" as both incorrect and

[4] Tumin, "Some Principles of Stratification: A Critical Analysis," *American Sociological Review*, XVIII (August, 1953), 387–394; Tumin, "Obstacles to Creativity," *Review of General Semantics*, XI (Summer, 1954), 261–271; Tumin, "Rewards and Task Orientations," *American Sociological Review*, XX (August, 1955), 419–423; Tumin, "Some Disfunctions of Institutional Imbalance," *Behavioral Science*, I (July, 1956), 218–223; Tumin, "Competing Status Systems," in Arnold S. Feldman and Wilbert E. Moore, eds., *Labor Commitment and Social Change in Developing Areas* (New York: Social Science Research Council, 1960), Chap. 15.

[5] See Richard L. Simpson, "A Modification of the Functional Theory of Stratification," *Social Forces*, XXXV (December, 1956), 132–137; Richard D. Schwartz, "Functional Alternatives to Inequality," *American Sociological Review*, XXIV (December, 1959), 772–782; Leonard Reissman, *Class in American Society* (New York: The Free Press, 1959), pp. 69–94.

[6] Simpson, *loc. cit.*

[7] See Davis, "Reply to Tumin," *American Sociological Review*, XVIII (August, 1953), 394–397.

extrinsic to the position that social inequality is a necessary feature of any social system[8]. For example, constructive innovation is an intrinsic of industrial societies and of those seeking to become such—or whose leaders are seeking that goal, if one feels required to avoid anthropomorphism. This disequilibrating behavior is almost certain to be differentially rewarded, and is certainly "functional" by any of the proposed meanings or nuances of the term save only the connotation of stasis. The "functional theory of stratification" maintained only that positions of unequal importance would be unequally rewarded, and was silent, regrettably but not criminally, on the subject of systemic changes.

By use of the term "stratification" the Davis-Moore position also implied that clearcut and consistent statuses attributable to individuals could be generalized into categories for individuals of "similar" status, and the categories ranked as "strata." The utility of such summations and classifications is subject to empirical test: do the "operational" definitions of generalized status and, say, class have predictive value for social variables not included in the definition? If status inconsistency is widespread and "class" variables have weaker predictive power than the separate definitional components, such as occupation, income, and education, then this empirical situation is clearly a relevant set of specifications about the characteristics of inequality in a society. If "class" is not a very useful analytical tool as applied to contemporary complex societies, this tells us a good deal about those societies.

It does not, by any stretch of theoretical imagination or empirical confrontation, tell us that those societies are "equalitarian."

Although Davis and Moore were fairly explicit in equating "social stratification" with unequal rewards, that now appears unfortunate. I have some sympathy for Buckley's criticism[9] on this point. Thus part of the difficulty in the continuing controversy has been semantic; and part has been empirical, in the sense that the clarity of class identification and its predictive value are questions of fact.

The single issue to which the present remarks are addressed is whether social inequality is a necessary feature of social systems. It is thus not a theoretical (to say nothing of ideological) defense of "social stratification" in the limited sense of clearly identifiable social categories, mutually exclusive, hierarchically ranked, and in sum exhaustive of all members of society. The proposition that every social system must exhibit manifestations of social inequality *permits no inference whatsoever* concerning the consistency of ranking from one context of action to another, the empirical reference for "general social status," or the empirical validation of "social classes."

What we are dealing with, then, is the elementary circumstance that inequality is ubiquitous in human societies, which is not in dispute and at least partial explanation of this universal phenomenon, which is in dispute. The explanation presented here reiterates the thesis that "functional differentiation" of positions will inevitably entail unequal rewards, and adds the thesis

---

[8] A close approximation to the original Davis-Moore position, and with some resemblance to the present one, is that of Bernard Barber, *Social Stratification* (New York: Harcourt, Brace & World, Inc., 1957), esp. Chaps. 1–4. Barber, however, does appear to deal only with a stable equilibrium model.

[9] Buckley's principal criticism of the Davis-Moore position is the use of the term "social stratification," which he would limit to hereditary social strata. See Walter Buckley, "Social Stratification and the Functional Theory of Social Differentiation," *American Sociological Review*, XXIII (August, 1958), 369–375.

that differences in performance must be expected to be and will be differentially valued. The legitimacy of this kind of analysis, or its potential relation to questions of status consistency and "stratification" in the narrow sense, scarcely needs defense. To conclude, as does Buckley, that the functional theory "promotes an insuperable discontinuity in sociological research"[10] is simply tendentious.

Elementary Processes of Social Valuation

In his attempt to construct an equalitarian system, Tumin concedes the necessity of differentiating normative compliance from deviance. This concession, however, has far-reaching implications. Even in social contexts in which equality may be the norm or expectation, compliance with expectations is not automatically assured, and failure to adhere to that or any other relevant norm will be the basis for a negative valuation of *performance*.

All social relationships governed by norms (and which ones are not?) are likely to provide a scale of approximations to and departures from ideal conduct. *Qualities* also are likely to be differentially valued, perhaps as indicative of probable or expected performance. And *achievements*, a retrospective view of performances, are likely to be evaluated unless all social relationships are to be viewed as transitory and memories abolished.

This "behavioral" view of the process of social valuation involves gradations with reference to "ideals." But there is no reason to suppose that the ideal is the same for every person in every context of action. Positional gradation, too, is governed by norms, and one must have a strong urge to believe in the power of

---

[10] *Ibid.*, p. 375.

evil to view all such norms as maliciously imposed by persons of privilege.

Positional gradation may be taken as the basic feature of social inequality from a "structural" view. From that point of view the properties of individuals that prompt valuation—performance, qualities, and achievements—constitute modes of *access* to positions.[11] Valuation itself confers a status, however transitory or enduring it may be. However, once statuses are institutionalized, that is, are endowed with normatively sanctioned role requirements, they will have ranking attributed to them and to their incumbents *ex officio* somewhat independently of mode of access. For example, in the extreme case, a position may be filled by drawing lots, and yet confer prestige on its incumbent. (Perhaps "luck" may be a valued quality.)

Social differentiation is a universal and necessary fact of social existence. The Davis-Moore "functional" interpretation of inequality rested on the unequal functional importance of positions and the unequal supply of talents for filling them. That interpretation, unlike most functional analyses, was explicitly evolutionary, and like many had possible rationalistic overtones. Tumin essentially skirts the issues of importance and talents, but rejects the evolutionary explanation, for which he substitutes the view that stratification is an anachronistic survival maintained by self-perpetuating power. (That revolutionary polities establish new modes of social stratification escapes his attention.) Between those two modes of ap-

---

[11] A small conceptual point may be noted here. Parsons, in his revised essay, uses qualities, performances, and possessions as the properties of individuals subject to differential valuation. This appears less satisfactory than the distinction between access to positions and rewards to their incumbents—both of which are somewhat more extensive than Parsons' formulation would indicate.

peal to inferential evidence there is little basis of proof, and the argument must shift to other grounds.

Tumin would not abolish functional differentiation, but only differential rewards. He would declare all positions of equal value, and the sole basis of differential valuation that of "conscientiousness." Short of universal and perfect skill in instantaneous psychiatric diagnosis, I suggest that the judgment of subjective intention would promptly lead to judgments of qualities, achievements, and, especially, performance. Esteem,[12] in other words, would become the single permissible mode of evaluation or reward.

To accomplish the almost-termination of inequality, Tumin has a large and unfilled set of tasks: (1) to make all tasks equal in difficulty and in various other "intrinsic" qualities, lest elements of positional prestige creep in; (2) to achieve coordination of specialized activities without resort to graded authority; (3) and, of course, to equalize all material or financial rewards and prevent any form of differential accumulation.

The *attributes* of positions, the role requirements, may include power and influence. Thus the giving of orders, providing instruction, setting goals and procedures, creative innovation, "exemplary" conduct in the strict sense may all follow from "superior" positions in various groups and organizations. The counterparts are obedience, learning, emulation, imitation, deference, and so on. These actions bear witness to the acceptance of the normative system and the legitimacy of the role performances of the superior. It is, I suggest, impossible to imagine a social system totally lacking in these manifestations of inequality.

[12] See Davis, "A Conceptual Analysis of Stratification," *American Sociological Review*, VII (June, 1942), 309–321.

Unless intrinsic task equalization is accomplished, it would seem extremely unlikely that equality of rewards—or rather, permitting only esteem-rewards —would be institutionalized by any conceivable system of socialization. This would require a somewhat greater extension of martyrdom than any religious system has yet achieved, and religious martyrs expect future rewards. I believe that Tumin has become entrapped by an ideological position that I see no reason to accept: namely, that equality is intrinsically more equitable than inequality. The practice of equal rewards for unequal performance does not immediately recommend itself as either functionally or ethically superior to the contrary scandal of unequal rewards for equal performance. (In order to maintain the view that inequality is *ipso facto* iniquitous, Tumin consistently emphasizes unequal rewards, systematically avoids unequal demands, such as the exceptional effort required for acceptable performance in some roles or the responsibility costs of power.)

The Problem of Rewards

The possible rewards for unequal performance or performance in unequal positions are not only self-esteem, the the approval of significant others, "fame," and so on, but may include differential allocations of any scarcities such as disposable time and material goods or money. Now it is especially material or financial rewards (the two are not the same) that most upset Tumin about social inequality, and it is in fact theoretically imaginable to have a viable social order without substantial purchasing-power differentials. Income equalization might well heighten the differentials in other attributes and rewards for superior positions. Unless a market system of distribution permitting consumer choice is to be entirely abandoned, the way consuming units use their income would still probably result in invidious valuation. And it would be exceptionally difficult to prevent other sources and forms of inequality from being used instrumentally to gain a disproportionate share of scarcities.

Indeed, modes of access, attributes, and rewards of positions are all subject to possible instrumental use in the same or other contexts of action. This is one clear source for the presumed pressure for status consistency.[13] The degree to which consistency prevails, however, is not impressive in any industrial society, and especially in those with pluralistic institutional systems. Fragmentation[14] of even nominally singular statuses into incomparable analytical subsystems— for example, an administrator's involvement with occupational peers, in a structure of authority, and in the labor market—should more than offset tendencies to status coalescence. Even income, the one "universal solvent," has early limits in determining "worth" in non-economic contexts and in others it may be a necessary but not sufficient means of social placement and valued performance.

Where the contexts of social differentiations are fragmented and comparability among them minimal because of the absence of an adequate mode of mensuration, a remaining common denominator such as income may take on a special significance. But that significance arises only when a uniform standard is sought, and the occasions for doing so may be rather limited. Tumin's position here is compounded of several empirical errors: (1) a class system

"really exists"; (2) it is posited upon only one dominant "phase" of social life, the economic, which is associated with (the cause of?) prestige and power; (3) other worthwhile human endeavors are given something less than their "due" because the economy has "invaded" other institutional areas. Not only does this entail an exaggeration of status comparability in industrial societies, but it leads to a perception of status anxieties more pervasive than any evidence indicates. Tumin's convictions concerning the evils of inequality provoke him into constructing a "minor handbook of a scoundrel's guide to how to disguise inequality,"[15] which includes many of the actual characteristics of social differentiation in modern societies. The implication that obfuscation of a "general social status" represents a conspiracy is supported by no known evidence. One might just as properly view social systems characterized by complex role differentiation as conspiring against the sociologist's attempt to impose on them a simplified structure of "social stratification."

The instrumental use of elements of inequality outside their original context is only one of the intrinsic strains in stratification systems. Privilege may seek to perpetuate itself, speaking elliptically. That is, a privileged group may seek to guard its position for its "own kind," even by changing the modes of access— for example, by emphasis on irrelevant qualities such as lineage or graduation from a particular school. Being comprised of mortal members, no privileged group can literally "perpetuate itself" except by some form of recruitment. If the forms of recruitment are contrary to other values and norms—for example, relevant performance criteria or equality of opportunity—equity strains will become intensified.

---

[13] See Parsons' revised essay, previously cited.

[14] For a discussion of the process of status fragmentation in industrial societies, see Feldman, "The Interpenetration of Firm and Society," in International Social Science Council, *Social Implications of Technological Change* (Paris, 1962), pp. 179–198.

[15] "Theoretical Implications," p. 502.

To maintain that social inequality is an essential feature of social systems not only has no implications for tidy and rectilinear ranking, as noted previously, but also does not rule out value inconsistency, "dysfunctions," strain, conflict, and change. These too are empirical characteristics of social systems, perfectly integrated models being only analytical constructs of dubious utility. Certainly the proponents of the "functional theory" of inequality seem to have been less impeded in their analysis by ideological orientations than have some of the critics.[16]

The Meaning of Equalitarianism

A final critical note must be added concerning the interpretation of every manifestation of inequality as contary to the avowed value of equality, attributed to American and at least some other industrial societies.[17] Now neither inconsistency in values nor inconsistency between ideals and practice would be a surprising empirical finding, but the conclusion must be approached with some caution. Ideals as well as behavioral norms are subject to limitation by the contexts of social action. This is an elementary fact of social organization and its recognition is surely incumbent on any social analyst. An interesting and possibly significant basis of comparison through time and space would be the contexts in which, on the one hand, *common* rights and duties are the norm, and, on the other, unequal valuation of performance and position is the expectation. In other words, what are the rights of men generally and what are the rights of social units differentially?

[16] This is the position taken by Davis. See "The Abominable Heresy: A Reply to Dr. Buckley," *American Sociological Review*, XXIV (February, 1959), 82–83.
[17] See Tumin, "Theoretical Considerations," pp. 493, 497–498, 510–511.

Absolute equality may be a kind of vague and unspecified dream for the millennial future of socialist states, but certainly has been espoused by few of the ideologists of the Western democracies and cannot be taken as an established social value: equality before the law and the state, perhaps; and, later, equality of opportunity for unequal rewards, but not an absence of evaluative differentiation and consequent position. It is not even true that "all men are equal in the sight of God," unless one hastens to add, as in George Orwell's *Animal Farm*, "but some are more equal than others."

One would have to be naive indeed to suppose that income inequality has no implications for "equality before the law." It does not follow that measures to increase legal equality stem from a bad conscience about income inequality or appear solely as a diversionary tactic so that income inequality will be tolerated without revolt. Similarly, as long as the family is a primary agency of attitude-formation in children, existing differentials in social privileges may well have negative implications for equality of opportunity. But this is an empirical insight—of considerable importance—not something that is true by definition. It is even true, as Tumin maintains, that existing "systems" of social stratification tend to waste talents and real or potential skills. It does not follow that an equalitarian system would optimize their utilization. The measures to tap talents are likely to be directed toward openness rather than flatness of social positions, and diversity rather than uniformity of rewards.

Equalitarianism may indeed provide an instrumental "value" for social critics, both lay and professional, who seek to extend its application. Their efforts may bear some fruit, such as the extension of social as against private income in such fields as health and education. Yet the needs for the one or the talents for the other are not equally distributed, and it is thus opportunities and not results that are equalized.

Equity strains are evident in most contexts of social inequality, and involve questions of "proper" rewards to the "right" people. It is extremely unlikely that any system of inequality will be institutionalized and provided with a rationale in social values adequate to prevent discontent. Such strains are likely to produce changes, and in some situations a possible change may be toward equality. In most situations the more likely change is toward a restructuring of access, attributes, and rewards. Fairness is simply not a synonym for equality, and no amount of sentimentalizing about the worthiness of all men will make it so.

On Inequality

MELVIN M. TUMIN

Moore's review of some of the major points in the theory of stratification on which there has been substantial disagreement in the past provides us with a welcome opportunity to re-evaluate earlier formulations.

Part of the difficulty in past exchanges has arisen from the ambiguity of the term "social inequality." As Moore points out, we have sometimes failed to join issues because, in discussing how much inequality is unavoidable, he has referred to certain aspects of inequality, and we to others. It is crucial that we distinguish major forms of inequality, and them make our judgments regarding avoidability and functionality refer specifically to each of these forms.

The inequalities that comprise social stratification are special forms. By social stratification we refer to the presence in any society of a system by which various social units are ranked as inferior and superior to each other *on a scale of social worth, or receive unequal amounts of the de-*sired rewards available in the society. So defined, the inequalities referred to in the term "social stratification" do not by any means include all the types of social inequality one is likely to find. In short, there can be a good deal of social inequality without a corresponding or covariant amount of social stratification.

The core of our original argument, of course, concerned the question of the avoidability and functionality of those kinds of inequalities here defined as social stratificational. But one must also examine the other kinds of inequality, because they frequently form a basis of stratificational inequalities.

I want to advance, provisionally, a five-fold categorization of inequality, indicating in each case my judgment as to how unavoidable these are, and for whom and for what they may be positively functional. The order in which they are listed has no intended implication either concerning their relative importance, or ubiquity, or ranking on any other dimension. As here offered, they represent sources of possible inequality, some or all of which are found in all known societies. Whether they are unavoidable is a matter for examination.

1. The first source of inequality is that which is ordinarily termed "social differentiation," but which, for reasons that will appear later, I prefer to call "*role*

Reprinted from Melvin M. Tumin, "On Inequality," *American Sociological Review*, XXVIII, No. 1 (February, 1963), 13–28, by permission of the author and the American Sociological Association.

and attribute specification." By that term, I refer to those distinctions which take the form of neutral, that is, nonevaluative and noncomparative specifications of the responsibilities and rights attached to a given social position (e.g., father), or of the attributes and qualities assigned to a social type (e.g., woman, man, etc.).

Insofar as the status or social type is distinctively specified, and hence differentiated from others, social inequality is obviously involved. Some such distinctions exist in all societies, and at least some of these seem to be unavoidable and positively functional for social continuity, if we mean by that latter term simply the persistence of the social organization in one form or another over more than one generation. Given the helplessness of the human child, for instance, a distinction between the child and older people is unavoidable. Similarly, given the needs for replenishing the population, at least partly through reproduction, some distinctions, albeit minimal, between men and women must also be institutionalized. Finally, given the needs for certain unequal amounts of authority and power in the socialization process, some generational distinctions may have to be superimposed on the age differentiations just mentioned.

Note, however, that how much and what kind of distinctions must exist is culturally variable. Much will depend on the kind of kinship system and a good deal will also depend on the prevailing cultural definitions of the proper roles of men and women, the social goals that are desired, and the relationship forms that are preferred. There are many different ways in which the relationships of children to the older population and of men to women can be arranged. We know little at this point about the greater or lesser functionality of varying versions of these arrangements. What we do know suggests that for some goals—e.g., maximum utilization of human talent—most, if not all, of the patternings hereto-

fore practiced have served as guarantees of significant under-utilization of such talent.

Such considerations aside, however, the important thing is that the inequalities that are due to role or attribute specification do not necessarily involve any differences in evaluation and rank on a scale of social inferiority and superiority. Nor do they necessarily entail any differences in rewards. How likely they are to give rise to differential social evaluations and rewards depends very much on the prevailing ideology and has little or nothing to do with any "natural" consequence of role specification. We know this surely from the fact that in all societies the largest number of socially differentiated roles and social types do not involve differential evaluation and reward. Hence, additional cultural features are required to bring on these stratificational inequalities, and these additional features are obviously variable over time within any society, as well, of course, as between societies. If one realizes that the majority of socially differentiated roles and social types are not in any significant sense involved in the stratification system, one immediately sees the fallacy of the common argument that egalitarianism necessarily leads to monotonous uniformity: it is possible to have a society in which one would find a minimum of stratification coexistent with a profuse abundance of unranked yet differentiated and hence unequal social types and roles.

2. The second source of inequality is *rank ordering by intrinsic characteristics.* Everywhere men tend to make comparisons as to who is taller, or prettier, or quicker; and which tasks are more difficult, or more dangerous, or cleaner, or more skilled, or involve management of more subordinates. The "necessity" of making such distinctions is unclear. It may have to do with some inclinations in men to compare and contrast themselves with others, arising perhaps from

the dynamics of ego differentiation, and this in turn connected with the necessity of acquiring a clear-cut and differentiated identity. Only in the minority of cases, and only in a mediated way, does such rank ordering seem to be connected with the requirements of social continuity. When we find these connections, we always find an intervening and mediating set of values, such that patterned preferences exist for one social type as against another, or there is differential admiration for one set of skills as against another. But in and of themselves, such intrinsic characteristics can be and often are rank-ordered without any exigent or unavoidable implications for stratification.

The independence of the variability of such rank ordering from stratificational evaluating and rewarding is evident in the significant differences found from one society to another, and even within any given society, in the evaluations made of such characteristics. For example, the cleanliness and skill of only some tasks may be considered justificatory of differential evaluation and reward. Equally clean and equally skilled tasks of other kinds will not be rewarded. Consider further that in Israel a debate continues as to whether to assign higher salaries, equal salaries, or lower salaries to the more versus the less skilled jobs.

Skill has to be valued in a special way before it can become a determinant of differential social evaluation and rewards. There is nothing demonstrably "natural" about reacting to differential skills in the ways generally found in modern industrial societies. A number of additional factors, such as very particular learned motivational schemes and social goals, arranged in very particular hierarchies, are required to be present and to be understood if we are to understand in turn why we have the existing forms of occupational stratification. Clearly, numerous alternatives could be devised, invoking alternative motivational schemes and alternative systems of belief as to social obligations and rights. They may not be able to be invoked tomorrow, and in that sense to propose them as reasonable alternatives for tomorrow would be utopian. But we are not talking about what is possible tomorrow. Rather we are considering what is possible in human affairs, assuming the availability of a population with a fresh slate on which no major cultural themes have yet been written.

This distinction between the immediately probable and the theoretically possible form of social arrangements must be kept in mind if we are not to confuse practical social planning with theoretical specification of limits and possibilities.

Some have argued that the multiplication of ranked characteristics is due to the emergence of social goals and needs which, in turn, demand some rational fitting of characteristics to tasks. Even if true, this is not necessarily relevant evidence about "inevitables" in social organization. For example, in modern industrial society, one would be hard pressed to show any important connections between many lucrative secondary and tertiary industries (e.g., the movie industry) and the demands of social survival. The fact that cultural themes have arisen that generate and support such industries has little bearing upon the prerequisites of societal continuity. The differential evaluations and rewards received by participants in such industries has everything to do with what people want and what the market will bear. But no one would seriously suggest that anything and everything that the people want or that the market will bear are functionally prerequisite to anything but themselves. Most of these cultural elaborations can be functionally justified only in that meaningless sense of "functional" where all things that exist are said to be functional, or else they would not exist. I have elsewhere remarked on the nonsense that this Panglossian view generates.

3. A third source of possible inequality is generic to social organization. That is, some form of it is found in all societies and is unavoidable. It may be termed "*ranking by moral conformity.*" If a society is properly conceived of as a normative order, then concern must be expressed and standards must be developed by which actual or potential behavior is judged as morally acceptable or unacceptable. In theory, a society can be sufficiently generous and lax in its standards so that virtually every social type and role would be more or less morally acceptable. But even under these circumstances, there would necessarily be certain other types and roles that would be defined as morally unacceptable.

I do not see that a judgment of moral acceptability necessarily entails anything but the minimum amount of social stratification, if any at all. While it is true that in caste societies, for instance, moral and sacred purity are important criteria of evaluation and reward, it is equally true that in class-structured societies all classes tend to be considered within the range of moral acceptability. The differences among the classes— that is, differences of evaluation of social worth and reward—arise off a base of equal moral evaluation.

That kind of differential social evaluation which is a component of stratification is a very different matter. It has to do, as we shall see, with a judgment regarding the extent to which the statuses or social types differentially exemplify certain of the most approved and admired ideals. By contrast, the general moral conformity here referred to typically does not give rise to stratification. Quite to the contrary, it is an imperative of societies that the vast majority of patterned statuses and social types shall be considered as equal in this basic moral sense.

4. We turn now to the bases on which most current theory accounts for the existence of stratification. We may term this fourth type "*ranking by functional contribution,*" and indicate two major analytically separate subforms.

(*a*) *Ranking according to contribution to or exemplification of "ideals."* Besides the general moral conformity that every society needs to demand from the majority of its members, some hierarchical arrangement of "ideals" and "values" is also unavoidable. I am deliberately vague as to how many, how specific, and what kinds of ideals and values have to be involved, for we know very little about this. Presumably, societies can function "equally well," though with different consequences for social organization, either with a limited number of values and ideals arranged in very specific and very rigid rank order, or with a large number of such values and ideals (about which there is considerable dissensus regarding their relative importance or the specific ways in which to achieve or exemplify them).

The amount of inequality generated by ranking according to exemplification of ideals depends on the kinds of ideals that are held up for emulation. Some ideals involve scarce social resources, e.g., wealth. By contrast, some ideals are relatively abundantly accessible, e.g., the good citizen. We cannot say, a priori, that the existence of a system of ranking according to exemplification of ideals necessarily involves a great deal of actual inequality per se. Theoretically it is possible that the ideals could be structured such that all but the smallest per cent of the members of a society could fulfill the ideal expectations. This could be done even where the relevant resources are scarce, by introducing a countervailing theme that sanctions equal distribution. In short, scarcity by itself, or in combination with demand, cannot generate unequal distribution of a *patterned* sort, unless unequal distribution is otherwise provided for in cultural themes and social structures.

It cannot be gainsaid, however, that the generic sources of social deviation found in any society, no matter how egalitarian, are likely to produce recognizable differences in the degree to which the ideal behavior forms are manifested. This apparently unavoidable minimum of inequality thus arises indirectly from the need for social continuity, insofar as it can be shown that such continuity is dependent upon the existence of such ideal standards. But it is theoretically possible to arrange the standards in such a way that the unequal performances arising from unequal socialization can be kept to a bare minimum of relevance and importance.

Admittedly if statuses or social types are ranked differently on the scale of contribution to social ideals, they will tend to be judged as representing superior and inferior positions or attributes, and hence constitute a form of social stratification. It seems additionally unavoidable, moreover, that there will accrue to the statuses or types defined as superior certain informal if not formal rewards over and above those allocated to or available to inferior positions and types.

Moore has indicated this and I am now persuaded that exceptionally strict controls would be required to keep such diffusion of inequality to a minimum, and that at least some inequality in rewards as well as in evaluation seems probable.

On the other hand, it is not possible to demonstrate that the survival needs of any society require any "significant" amounts of such unequal ranking. What is required is a system of ranking, but this does not preclude the possibility or the likelihood that such differentials can be kept to a minimum without significant strain. To contend otherwise would

be to insist that there is something in human nature that demands unequal rewards for unequal achievement in the exemplification of valued ideals. We know of no such feature in human nature.

Nor is it necessary, as Moore has suggested, that all tasks should be made equal or that we must dispense with coordination through graded authority in order to keep unequal invidious ranking to a minimum. After all, in many aspects of our lives, we are motivated to exemplify the ideals which we value without particular reference to the extent to which others are doing so, or to the rewards we might receive for doing so. If, in certain selected aspects of existence, other motivational schemes more conducive to stratification seem to predominate, we are in no position to assign to either one of these actualized motivational systems a greater naturalness or fittingness for human society. Similarly, if in some spheres of endeavor, invidious evaluation of positions by some such criterion as difficulty of performance seems to be central at the moment, we cannot fail to pay attention to the simultaneous existence of spheres of existence in which quite different cultural themes predominate, so that inequalities in difficulty or in cleanliness, or some other quantity do not become a basis of invidious ranking. Again, we have no basis for asserting the greater or lesser naturalness of any of these ways of behaving, nor can we at the moment assess their long range and ramified implications for social survival. However plagued current societies may be with the demand for unequal rewards for so-called unequal work, and however relatively successful some of those societies may be compared to others, we surely cannot ignore the fact that these cultural orientations and social forms have arisen in very specific historical contexts. Moreover, we have never seriously explored the possibilities of alternative forms that might yield much more of the desired values and ideals with much less stratification than is now being practiced.

(b) *Ranking according to functional contribution to desired social goals.* Current theory attaches the greatest significance to differential functional importance as a basis of social stratification. It is argued that every society must make judgments about unequal functional importance and must allocate its scarce and desired goods at least partly in line with such judgments.

I have previously argued with these points at great length.[1] Here I will simply state the central issues.

First, at any point in the history of any society, certain goals will enjoy a higher priority in the minds of the majority, or of a ruling minority of the members of that society than other goals. In consequence, there will be more concern with rational fitting of appropriate personnel and skills to these tasks than to the others not so highly valued. Some of these high priority tasks may also require some very specialized skills that are scarce at that time in the population.

---

[1] See the following by Melvin M. Tumin: "Some Principles of Stratification: A Critical Analysis," *American Sociological Review*, XVIII (August, 1953), 387–394; "Reply to Kingsley Davis," *American Sociological Review*, XVIII (December, 1953), 672–673; "Obstacles to Creativity," *Etc., A Review of General Semantics*, XI (Summer, 1954), 261–271; "Rewards and Task Orientations," *American Sociological Review*, XX (August, 1955), 419–423; "Some Disfunctions of Institutional Imbalances," *Behavioral Science*, I (July, 1956), 218–223; "Social Conditions for Effective Community Development," *Community Development Review* (December, 1958), 1–39; "Changing Status Systems," in Symposium on *Labor Systems and Social Change*, edited by W. E. Moore and A. Feldman (New York: Social Science Research Council, 1960), pp. 277–290; (with Arnold Feldman), *Social Class and Social Change in Puerto Rico* (Princeton, N. J.: Princeton University Press, 1961). See esp. Chap. 29, "Theoretical Implications."

There will naturally be some effort to see to it that these scarce personnel are recruited for those tasks and are motivated to perform them properly.

If the personnel necessary for the functionally important tasks are scarce, and *if* unequal rewards of various kinds, or the promise of them, are required to induce the scarce personnel to take up these tasks and to perform them conscientiously, then unequal rewards will probably be allocated—*if* the society is rational.

Much of current theory fails to take account of the importance of the "if's" in the propositions stated above, and to realize that these propositions must be prefaced with "ifs," since the conditions specified are culturally variable. The biggest and most important "if" has to do with the methods by which scarce and valued personnel can be motivated to take up the necessary tasks. In a culture that trains its people to be motivated by differential rewards and places high value on such differential rewards, and that requires considerable sacrifice to train one's self to achieve scarce and valued skills, stratification is likely to be at a maximum. On the other hand, under other cultural circumstances the important cultural tasks can be and will be filled by appropriate personnel without significant differential evaluation and material reward, or, at least, with much less enduring forms of such invidious distinction. To contend otherwise would be to insist that no other motivational schemes and no other cultural themes regarding work and performance are possible, except at great strain to "human nature," and this is untrue. Tasks may be highly unequal in many regards without invoking judgments of unequal social worth and unequal entitlement to rewards, if people are socialized to view matters in this way.

Admittedly, positional deference is found in any hierarchical arrangement.

Admittedly, too, there must be differentials and hence inequalities in the amount of task-specific power or authority required for the coordination of specialized activities. Nothing in present theory or research, however, suggests any significant amount of unavoidable diffusion of task-specific differences to differences on ladders of *general* social worth or to claims to unequal material rewards.

Moreover, one can now see some mechanisms by which the possible diffusion of task-specific inequalities beyond the boundaries of the task itself can be kept to a minimum or eliminated. Important are such countervailing influences as well-socialized norms that encourage men to feel obliged or pleased to do that for which they are most suited. If properly institutionalized, such norms and their accompanying sanctions could effectively impede the diffusion of unequal authority and rewards beyond their task-specific limits.

Moore has argued that this would require an extension of martyrdom beyond any heretofore achieved limits and adds that he suspects I arrive at this position by being trapped by an ideological commitment to the effect that equality is intrinsically more equitable than inequality. I think, rather, it is he who has been beguiled by the unanalyzed implications of the term "unequal work." We have shown before how nominally unequal work need not at all be defined as deserving of unequal evaluation regarding the social worth nor as deserving of unequal rewards. The vast majority of the inequalties we have heretofore listed do not get taken up into the stratification system. Only under the conditions that the prevalent ideology defines such unequal evaluation and rewards as justified will the unequal tasks be incorporated in the stratification system.

Martyrdom—and the implied strain and hence unrealism—seems to me to be irrelevant here, unless, again, one assumes, without any empirical justification, that any and all different things will naturally generate any and all other kinds of differences. Even where tasks are unequal with regard to the demands placed upon the task performance, no martyrdom, but only ordinary human motivation, quite within the range of demonstrated possibilities, is required to institutionalize the persuasion that men should do what they are capable of doing. Nowhere in the world are difficulty, dirt, or danger of task uniformly evaluated and rewarded. Within our society, jobs of equal difficulty receive very unequal evaluations and rewards. Obviously, only *some* kinds of difficulties, attached to only *some* kinds of tasks, result in the kind of unequal evaluation and reward that Moore sees as unavoidable for all tasks so defined. And that they do so is due to very special cultural themes that are obviously limited in time and in durability.

The enduring mistake in much current stratification theory is to impute to total social systems a kind of rationality with regard to society-wide prestige and reward that may pertain in only very limited ways to very selected aspects of the occupational structure.

5. *Diffusions of differentials in property, power, and prestige.* Thus far we have considered how inequalities in ranking on a scale of moral values and on a scale of functional contributions to desired goals may result in further inequalities in ranking on a general scale of social worth and in the rewards allocated to the unequal statuses or types.

Now we must also reckon with an additional source of inequality in any society, namely, the tendency for any inequality to increase over time and to diffuse to other situations, unless otherwise restrained. I choose to identify this as a separate source of inequality since the mechanisms that sanction it or inhibit it are different from those that sanction or inhibit the original inequality. That is, the mechanisms by which wealthy people become wealthier, and perhaps acquire prestige and power because of their wealth, may be different from the mechanisms by which they became wealthy in the first place, especially if their initial wealth arose as a result of unequal rewards for unequal task performance. I also feel it important to identify this diffusion as an additional source of inequality, and frequently of stratification because it is at least debatable whether more of the total inequality found in any society is due to the presumed rational allocation based upon task or type, or is due to the diffusion of inequality, once initiated.

It is in my judgment no longer reasonable to dismiss the diffusion of inequality either on the ground that it is an aberration or that it is primarily attributable to other systems, such as the kinship system. The kinship system may be the vessel through which the diffusion of inequality operates. But the themes which make possible or which justify such diffusion are *general* social themes and are not by any means necessarily specific to the kinship system per se.

It is with regard to this diffuse stratification that one can feel most justified in noting the absence of any functional necessity whatsoever so far as societal continuity is concerned. To be sure, particular cultural themes may arise, such that the right to augment and transmit one's unequal position over generations may become an important part of the motivational scheme of some of those personnel whose conscientious performance of functionally important tasks is required for survival. But in such cases societies would have much less difficulty in denying the right to diffusion of inequality, without impairment of motivation, however much difficulty

they might have in denying the right to unequal rewards for one's self, without impairing motivation.

Finale

We have seen that some role specification is required, though minimal; further, some rank ordering according to intrinsic characteristics may be required, but this is uncertain; a definite standard of moral conformity is required; some rank ordering by contribution to ideals and to functionally important tasks is probably required. But none of these need result in anything but the minimum of stratification, where the requirements are measured in terms of social survival over two generations.

It must be clear by now that the criterion of social survival is useful only as a beginning touchstone for social analysis. Little is learned about human society by asking what is required for minimum social survival. Once we list obvious categories of social tasks that must be performed, nothing else of much significance is derivable from the need for continuity. Everything else that then comes into our analysis has to assume or postulate certain levels and kinds of cultural organization, for which one or another form of social arrangement may be more or less functional.

Following another line of analysis, we must ask, "Under what conditions do we get more and less of various forms of inequality, and why, and with what consequences for whom?" If we put our questions that way, we shall not be beguiled into seeking rational accounts for the existence and continuity of various cultural forms, most of which seem to be accidental products of human social history which arise very much by chance, and persist often simply by virtue of impersonal social drift, or inertia, or by the contrivances of various elites who find the social situation to their liking and wish to preserve it.[2]

If this is the case, we will gain nothing and lose much by trying to "account" for such stratification within a framework of concepts relevant to "rational" behavior of societies, based on normative consensus, system integration, and social productivity. Most existing stratification, we insist, enjoys little or no consensus, has little to do with social integration, and is probably seriously dysfunctional for social productivity.

Moral Postscript

Moore has raised some serious questions regarding equity and equality. He argues that equity does not necessarily demand equality of reward, however much Western traditions have emphasized the equity of moral opportunity. These are matters of moral preference, but it is appropriate and important to consider them. To me there is one position that cannot be overcome, unless one invokes a feudal notion, derivative from the concept of the divine right of kings or the lesser *droit de seigneur*. That position states simply that no society can expect or demand from an individual any more than that of which he is capable. Differences in social development and capabilities are due to two sources: (1) the inherited capa-

cities, and (2) the trained and patterned utilization of these capacities. Among people of equal native capacity, differences in their socially relevant talents are functions of training and learning over which the average society has dominant control. Thus to reward them differently, assuming equal conscientiousness, is to reward differences in opportunity which were socially generated in the first place.

Among persons of unequal native ability, differences in socially relevant capacities are due both to biological and environmental factors. Assuming equal conscientiousness, and assuming the unjustifiability of differentially rewarding unequal opportunity, one is left only with the possible justifiability of rewarding unequal biological inheritance, a principle which, presumably, democratic Western societies have specifically denied as legitimate. However, under the pressures of national competition and under the pressures of those with privileged position, there has been considerable movement to substitute an aristocracy of talent for an aristocracy of birth. In effect, the aristocracy of talent is no different than the aristocracy of birth, except insofar as it specifies what it is about native inheritance that seems deserving of special reward.

If one cannot reasonably ask of a man more than that of which he is capable, and if that of which he is capable is set and determined by factors over which he has little or no control, then what can the possible basis be, from a moral point of view, of allocating unequal rewards for unequal performance? Societies may exigently need some stratificational schemes for very specific and very limited cultural purposes, once the underlying and supporting cultural themes are already present. But this seems to me to have little or nothing to do with equity and justice, and almost as little to do with social continuity.

---

[2] Moore has himself hinted at some such state of affairs when, in writing about the conduct of the modern corporation, he says, "The 'justification' of executive salaries in corporations rests upon the presumed scarcity of talent and the highly competitive market for the limited supply. Yet the peculiar talents of the highest-paid executives as compared with those at much lower salaries, even within the business world, are rather difficult to specify, and they invite the suspicion that they do not exist." Wilbert E. Moore, *The Conduct of the Corporation* (New York: Random House, Inc., 1962), p. 14.

Rejoinder

WILBERT E. MOORE

The opportunity for this further exchange has served both to reduce radically the previous area of disagreement and—because Tumin has addressed himself to the general issues of inequality creatively and not just defensively—to open up some new issues worthy of theoretical and empirical attention. Let me note some of the major points of agreement. (These represent a substantial modification of "original" positions on both sides of the controversy.)

It is agreed that performances will be differentially evaluated in terms of approximations to social values and normatively defined standards of conduct.

It is agreed that some social differentiation entails "intrinsic" inequality of position.

It is agreed that the relationship between such ubiquitous "inequalities" on the one hand and "stratification" as generalized and ranked social categories on the other is subject to investigation but by no means definitionally the same. Thus, one may theoretically imagine and, here and there, empirically encounter social differentiation with unequal rewards without this becoming a component of a "generalized" social status. Put the other way around, what Tumin calls the "diffusion" of inequality and its self-reinforcement have no intrinsic and necessary relationship to differential valuation of performance or differential valuation of functional positions.

Reprinted from Wilbert E. Moore, "Rejoinder," *American Sociological Review*, XXVIII, No. 1 (February, 1963), 13–28, by permission of the author and the American Sociological Association.

It seems also to be agreed that the "utilization of human potential" is suboptimal in all known social systems, and that in all known social systems the institutionalization of existing differentials is incomplete and subject to dynamic tensions. The implications of these dysfunctions and dynamic properties of these dysfunctions and dynamic properties of unequal valuations seem still in dispute. I see no reason to suppose that the predictive inference to be drawn from them is a tendency to greater equality of position and reward.

Now what remains in useful contention? The first debatable issue, I suggest, revolves around Tumin's "minimal" estimate of the relevance of inequality. Let me start with his assertion of "the fact that in all societies the largest number of socially differentiated roles and social types do not involve differential evaluation and reward." Now if this allegation refers to evaluation of *performance* it is not only contradictory to the clearly stated concession on this point, but, more to the scientific point, it is overwhelmingly contravened by the evidence. If *positional* differentiation is the basis of the allegation, the matter is in principle subject to mensuration but none is in fact at hand. In the present state of knowledge, I suggest that the formulation is a non-fact. And although I shall note below that I dislike Tumin's extreme relativism concerning societies and cultures, I suggest here that any measurement of positions differentially evaluated or not would be highly relative to the degree of coalescence and consistency in status categories in one or another system of social "stratification." Thus the allegation appears patently false in a traditional "caste" system and probably in a totalitarian system of bureaucratic positions, as, say, in the Soviet Union.

I have spent some precious space on this point because Tumin reiterates twice more the assertion that most differentiation does not involve invidious valuation, but in the modified context of "stratification," narrowly speaking. I think it *is* agreed that functionally specific inequalities *may* not be generalized into a singular status or aggregates of such statuses into a stratum, but it is not at all established that functional differentiation and unequal valuation are independently variable.

The general position Tumin has espoused in his latest statement is debatable in several respects that warrant specification. He has adopted an extremely relativistic view of cultural values and social institutions that seem to me empirically unwarranted and theoretically doubtful. Without using the Sumnerian phrase, "the mores can make anything right," that is the position he has taken. As I read the evidence, the evaluation of functionally differentiated positions is by no means as randomly variable as his discussion asserts or implies. I suggest that behavior relevant to the maintenance of order, the provision of economic support, the protection of the society, and the exemplifications of religious and esthetic values *always* involves differential positional as well as merely personal valuation. Tumin's cultural relativism and his notion that anything is possible through socialization represent a kind of denial of orderly and reliable generalizations about human societies. I do not think this denial is immoral; it is just wrong.

Although Tumin asserts that scarce personnel can be motivated to take up functionally critical tasks without differential rewards, "or at least with much less and much less enduring forms of such invidious distinctions," there is surely no evidence for the bald assertion, without

the modification, which he reiterates in subsequent paragraphs. I spoke of improbable "martyrdom" in the performance of exceptional tasks without unequal recognition, and I still have no reason to retreat from my critical position.

Tumin links an extreme cultural relativism and extensive randomness of cultural components with an extreme bio-social determinism within a *given* system. His final moral argument in behalf of rather extensive equality is to the effect that there is little social justice in rewarding differential talent (and performance?) which derives either from hereditary accident or the character of socialization that is imposed by the very system that allocates rewards. But here he uses a tell-tale, saving phrase, "assuming equal conscientiousness." Surely by now our understanding of the complex interplay between the individual and the social order does not permit so deterministic a view of human motivation or so easy a dismissal of the importance of purpose in human behavior. Though it is extremely unlikely that any social system will be able to overlook the consequences of the accident of birth in either the biological or sociological sense, since differential placement will likely take such consequences into account, there surely remains some interstitial area of human effort, or purpose, or conscientiousness that cannot be readily reduced to the influence of human heredity or the social environment. Though it is clearly the business of the sociologist to seek out the social sources and correlates of patterned human behavior, I do not think the evidence warrants the comfortable and individual guilt-absolving or excellence-degrading view that society is all and the complexities of individual motivation a purely dependent variable. Perhaps this difference of view only confirms the notion that assumptions regarding human nature underlie most if not all structural propositions of substantial generality.

Tumin and I have both been guilty, in these short statements, of anthropomorphizing "society." Such ellipsis is normally harmless, but I do want to dissent on one point. When Tumin stipulates as a condition for the "functional theory" of social inequality that the society be "rational," I suggest two modifications. The first is the evolutionary, "survival" test which Tumin has earlier doubted but not destroyed. The second point is that the denial of rationalism in a social decision-making is untenable, since it conspicuously exists as a norm in all contemporary societies, and, now and then, as a practice.

The protagonists in the current renewal of an enduring controversy are scarcely the designated spokesmen for recognizable clienteles. And lest it be thought that the issues relevant to stratification are all resolved or clarified, it should be noted that the whole concept of "class" as an explanatory variable has been barely touched in this exchange. Tumin in his suggested desiderata for the next steps in analysis of social inequality happily does not use the term "class"—which unfortunately our neighboring social scientists think is one of our most useful analytic tools—and his way of putting the questions does not presuppose that conceptual category. Can we get anyone to join the joyful march to sensible investigation?

The Functionalist Theory of Stratification: Two Decades of Controversy

GEORGE A. HUACO

Long after Functionalism is discarded as a pseudo-explanation, Kingsley Davis and Wilbert E. Moore's attempts to explain stratification will be remembered as a brilliant effort. What is known as the Davis and Moore theory of stratification was first put forth in April, 1945. The authors argued that there is a "universal necessity which calls forth stratification in any social system." On the one hand, different positions have different degrees of functional importance for societal preservation or survival. On the other hand, the amount of talent and training available in the population is scarce. So the system attaches greater rewards to the functionally more im-

portant positions in order to insure that the individuals with greatest talent and training occupy these positions. Although the authors warned that due to space limitations they were emphasizing the universal aspects of stratification (and conversely, not giving much attention to variable features found in different systems), some peculiar consequences seemed to follow from this analysis. In the first place, Davis and Moore seemed to be describing all stratification systems as if they were pure achievement systems. In the second place, our authors seemed to suggest that the rich, powerful, and prestigeous were not only the more talented and better trained but also the incumbents of roles which made a greater contribution to societal preservation and survival. These rather philistine implications aroused much opposition, and as we shall see, this opposition appears as the general background of the controversy that followed.

In his 1945 textbook, *Human Society*,

Reprinted from George A. Huaco, "The Functionalist Theory of Stratification: Two Decades of Controversy," *Inquiry*, IX (1966), 215–240, by permission of the author and the publisher, Universitetsforlaget, Oslo.

Kingsley Davis added a major modification to the original theory:

One may object to the foregoing explanation of stratification on the ground that it fits a competitive order but does not fit a non-competitive one. For instance, in a a caste system it seems that people do not get their positions because of talent or training but rather because of birth. This criticism raises a crucial problem and forces an addition to the theory. . . . The necessity of having a social organization—the family—for the reproduction and socialization of children requires that stratification be somehow accommodated to this organization. Such accommodation takes the form of status ascription.[1]

In the new 1948 version, Davis conceptualized stratification in terms of a polarity:

At one theoretical pole is the type which we might call absolutely closed, at the other pole the type which we might call absolutely open. The first would be one in which inheritance of the parental status (and hence the influence of the family) is complete; the second would be one in which there is no inheritance of the parental status and hence no family influence. Obviously, neither pole has ever been realized in practice. It is impossible to eliminate all competition for status, just as it is impossible to eliminate all ascription of status. In other words the role of the family in this matter is never absolute, nor is it ever nil. Thus the stratified systems we actually find in human society are mixed types.[2]

The addition of the ascriptive dimension results in a sizeable modification. We can now examine briefly the logical structure of the theory as a whole.

The 1945 Version

a. Different positions have different degrees of functional importance (i.e. make different contributions to societal preservation or survival).

b. Adequate performance of different positions requires different amounts of talent and training.

c. Personnel with adequate amounts of talent and training is scarce.

d. Societies exhibit "stratification"; here defined as "unequal rewards attached to different positions." *Causal account:* (a) on the one hand, and (b) and (c) on the other, determine (d) in the following manner: greater rewards are attached to those positions which have greater functional importance and greater requirements of talent and training. In turn, (d) determines or "insures" (e):

e. The mobility of the more talented and trained individuals into the more highly rewarded positions.

Basic assumption: The achievement of condition (e) makes for societal preservation or survival (with the implication that the cause of (e), namely "stratification," also contributes to societal preservation or survival).

The 1948 Modification

A. Condition (e) describes an analytically pure achievement order.

B. In all societies the achievement of condition (e) is prevented partially or almost fully by status ascription.

C. The cause of status ascription is the family.

Before going on to the controversy a few initial comments are in order:

    I. Items (b), (c), and (d) are fairly straightforward empirical generalizations.

    II. The status of item (a) is unclear. It must be either a directly verifiable empirical generalization or an indirectly testable explanatory postulate, but it seems to be neither. It is not an empirical generalization, because degrees of differential functional importance are not part of the observable social universe. It is not a valid explana-

[1] Kingsley Davis, *Human Society* (New York: The Macmillan Company, 1948), pp. 369–70.
[2] *Ibid.*, pp. 388–89.

tory postulate, because it lacks the logical derivations or deductions which alone would make it indirectly testable.

III. The causal account contains two minor assumptions: (1) that those positions with greatest functional importance tend to require the greatest amounts of talent and training; and (2) that those positions with greatest functional importance tend to receive the highest rewards. The validity of these two assumptions is as questionable as the validity of item (a). Furthermore, their very existence rules out the use of talent, training, or rewards as either indicators or measures of differential functional importance.

IV. In terms of historical evidence the basic assumption is probably false: societies which approach the achievement of condition (e) might be more rational and more just, but there is as yet no evidence that they are either stronger or survive longer than the more ascriptive traditional societies.

V. Since the functionalist aspects of the theory consist precisely of item (a) together with the basic assumption, it follows that it is precisely the functionalist character of this theory which is most in question.

The critical controversy proper began in August, 1953, with Melvin M., Tumin's "Some Principles of Stratification: A Critical Analysis."[3] Tumin questioned the logical status of the notion of differential functional importance as being unmeasurable and intuitive. Further, he suggested that the derivation of differential functional importance from so-called societal functions is a useless tautology since "any *status quo* to any given moment is nothing more and nothing less than everything present in the *status quo*." Next, Tumin questioned differential scarcity of personnel as an adequate determinant of stratification.

He argued that in practice most stratification systems artificially restrict the development of whatever potential talent and skill may exist in the population; "and the more rigidly stratified a society is, the less chance does that society have of discovering any new facts about the talents of its members." Next Tumin raised the issue of the possible existence of "functional equivalents" or alternatives to unequal rewards. He suggested two possible alternatives: intrinsic job satisfaction, and social service, as adequate motivations "for seeking one's appropriate position and fulfilling it conscientiously." At the linguistic level Tumin questioned the appropriateness of using the term "sacrifice" to describe the situation of those individuals who postpone joining the labor force by undergoing a lengthy period of specialized training. His second linguistic objection suggested that it would be more appropriate to speak of unequal "resources" rather than of unequal "rewards." Finally, he suggested that different positions have attached to them "certain highly morally-toned evaluations of their importance for the society," and implied that these evaluations stem from scarce and unequally distributed goods and services (and not from differential functional importance). Tumin also said that some of the vocabulary of analysis used by Davis and Moore came close to being "a direct reflection of the rationalizations, offered by the more fortunate members of a society, of the rightness of their occupancy of privileged positions."[4]

Kingsley Davis replied that Tumin had examined the original 1945 version but ignored the modified 1948 version of the theory. He agreed that "differential functional importance" is difficult to measure, but protested that Tumin had not bothered to examine the "two in-

[3] Melvin M. Tumin, "Some Principles of Stratification: A Critical Analysis," *American Sociological Review*, XVIII (August, 1953), 387–94.

[4] *Ibid.*, p. 389.

dependent clues" mentioned in the 1945 version. He added that:

Rough measures of functional importance are in fact applied in practice. In wartime, for example, decisions are made as to which industries and occupations will have priority in capital equipment, labor recruitment, raw materials, etc. In totalitarian countries the same is done in peacetime, as also in underdeveloped areas attempting to maximize their social and economic modernization. Individual firms must constantly decide which positions are essential and which are not.[5]

Next, Davis agreed that in practice stratification systems often artificially restrict the manifestation of talent and training in the population, but argued that the 1948 version of the theory had already met this objection by explaining ascription in terms of the role of the family. Also, and quite correctly, he pointed out that Tumin had used the term "stratification" in a manner different from that of Davis and Moore (1945) and Davis (1948): Tumin's use of the term included "inheritance of class status"; while Davis and Moore's use of the term was limited to "unequal rewards attached to different positions". On the issue of possible "functional equivalents" to unequal rewards, Davis argued that intrinsic job satisfaction and social service "are supplementary rather than alternative to the positional reward mechanism." Davis rejected the notion that the theory was either evaluative or justificatory, and suggested that Tumin was being Utopian and "not so much interested in understanding institutionalized inequality as in getting rid of it"; and stated that the Davis and Moore theory explains how the individual pursuit of self-interest actually coincides with social interest.[6]

In his brief "Reply to Kingsley Davis,"[7] Tumin took issue with still another aspect of the Davis-Moore theory: he challenged the suggestion that the universality of stratification is any evidence for its alleged "necessity." On the issue of possible "functional equivalents" to unequal rewards, he quite correctly pointed out that their feasibility cannot be ruled out on *a priori* grounds; and that if Davis and Moore want to argue that alternatives are impossible, they have to present some evidence to that effect. In summary, in this first exchange between critic and defenders, the critic succeeded in challenging two major aspects of the Davis and Moore theory: first, Tumin succeeded in questioning the scientific validity of the notion of "differential functional importance" by suggesting that it might be nothing more than a set of hidden tautologies. Second, Tumin succeeded in questioning the necessity of "unequal rewards" by suggesting the feasibility of "functional equivalents." The real weight of this second challenge lies in the fact that the admission of equivalents or alternatives effectively destroys the theory's predictive power.

In August 1955, Richard Schwartz' "Functional Alternatives to Inequality,"[8] challenged the explanatory and predictive aspects of the Davis and Moore theory on the basis of a year's study of stratification phenomena in two Israeli settlements: a bureaucratic and collectivistic kibbutz called Orah, and an individualistic Moshav co-op called Tamin. Schwartz described how the collectivistic and bureaucratic kibbutz developed what might be described as a compensatory informal pattern of posi-

[5] Kingsley Davis, "Reply," *American Sociological Review*, XVIII (August, 1953), 395.

[6] *Ibid.*, p. 396.

[7] Melvin M. Tumin, "Reply to Kingsley Davis," *American Sociological Review*, XVIII (December, 1953), 672.

[8] Richard D. Schwartz, "Functional Alternatives to Inequality," *American Sociological Review*, XX (August, 1955), 424–30.

tions and positional changes. This informal pattern, which included such things as relatively greater mechanization of routine tasks, job rotation, and individualistic outside jobs, contributed to job satisfaction by offsetting the dominant pattern of the group. Likewise, in the individualistic small-landowner's co-op, the development of a collectivistic informal pattern, which included such things as sharing scientific agricultural information and a process of collective decision-making, tended to increase job satisfaction by offsetting the dominant group pattern. Schwartz described how the populations of these two settlements had been self-selected in the sense that those individuals with a more collectivistic orientation chose to join the kibbutz and those with a more individualistic orientation joined the co-op. Further, he showed that this process of a population changing to fit the positional pattern received a powerful impetus from child socialization: the kibbutz children were socialized in a collectivistic direction, the co-op children were trained toward individual decision-making. Both settlements had a pattern of unequal rewards attached to different positions.

On the basis of this study Schwartz argued that "inequality as analyzed by Davis and Moore has functional alternatives";[9] or more specifically, that changes in the positional structure as well as changes in the characteristics of the population could be considered as feasible functional equivalents or alternatives to unequal rewards. The trouble here is that while Davis and Moore argued that unequal rewards insure that qualified individuals occupy positions with different requirements of talent and training, Schwartz argued that changes in positional structure and changes in population characteristics were adequate ways of promoting job

satisfaction and role performance by position incumbents. But mobility into positions is not the same as job satisfaction or adequacy of role performance within positions; and thus Schwartz failed to prove what he was trying to prove. Nevertheless, and at a purely logical level, the Schwartz critique re-emphasized the previous criticism of Tumin to the effect that Davis and Moore had failed to deal adequately with the possibility of functional alternatives to inequality of rewards.

In December, 1956, Richard L. Simpson's "A Modification of the Functional Theory of Social Stratification," made a new attack on several aspects of the Davis and Moore 1945 version:

The adequacy of this theory and its assumptions can be questioned on several grounds: (1) the importance of a position is difficult if not impossible to evaluate. (2) Some positions exist and are rewarded which do not seem to contribute to society at large; for example, the valet or the kept woman. (3) Some positions are given greater rewards than appears warranted by either their importance to society or the difficulty of training for them; for example, motion picture stars. (4) The theory implies an assumption that any scheme of stratification is somehow the best that could be had, that the prevailing distribution of rewards comes into being somehow because it is "functionally necessary".[10]

Objections (2) and (3) are irrelevant, because the identification of highly rewarded yet parasitical roles in no way challenges the Davis and Moore theory: economic contribution and degree of functional importance are not identical notions. Objection (4) is technically incorrect (despite Davis's remark to the effect that stratification systems are so arranged that the pursuit of individual self-interest coincides with social inter-

[9] Ibid., p. 424.

[10] Richard L. Simpson, "A Modification of the Functional Theory of Stratification," Social Forces, XXXV (December, 1956), 132.

est). Objection (1) alone is relevant, and here Simpson has tried to examine the two "clues" given by Davis and Moore, namely, "uniqueness" and "degree to which other positions are dependent on the one in question."

Now, it may be admitted that a position which is uniquely capable of performing an essential function is important, but this statement still begs the question of how essential a given function is. Is public entertainment an essential function? If so, is only a movie star capable of performing it, or could a juggler or a bowling alley proprietor meet this social need equally well? The important criterion in imputing uniqueness of this sort would seem to be whether the public *thinks* that a given position or its incumbent is unique or important, not whether a sociologist considers that society could manage without the position or a given incumbent of it.[11]

Now this is very confused. The notion of "differential functional importance" presumably refers to an objective state of affairs; namely, the extent to which a given position contributes to the preservation or survival of the society. This is not the same as the opinion of a given sociologist or the opinion of the public. Furthermore, Davis has expressly rejected using "the position's prestige" as an indicator of functional importance, because this "constitutes circular reasoning." Simpson goes on:

Let us consider the positions of janitor and garbage collector. These positions are presumably about equal in functional uniqueness and in the extent to which other positions depend on them. Yet we might feel that the garbage collector is more important, since uncollected refuse presents a more serious problem to society than unswept floors. Granting this, it is probable that the garbagemen's prestige is lower than that of the janitor, as is the intrinsic pleasantness of his work, while their pay may be about equal. Thus

the rewards of the positions are inversely related to their importance, and their importance cannot be explained by Davis' and Moore's clues.[12]

The trouble with this exercise in uncontrolled speculation is that it goes too far, and in so doing, fails to establish contact with the Davis and Moore claim. Our theorists have argued that positions will *tend* to be rewarded in some manner commensurate with their degree of functional importance, *not* that there is a one-to-one correspondence between degree of functional importance and unequal rewards. Furthermore, differential functional importance is only one of the alleged determinants of unequal rewards attached to different positions, the other determinant being differential scarcity of personnel. Given this rather flexible apparatus, it would be very simple for Davis and Moore to say in answer to Simpson something to the effect that the apparent non-correspondence between functional importance and rewards (in the above example) is due to differential scarcity of personnel.

Simpson completes his critique by examining the attempt to derive differential functional importance from so-called "functional prerequisites."

Some might claim that the importance of a position can be judged by seeing whether it contributes to the fulfillment of a "functional prerequisite" or "universal need" of the society. . . . Any investigator is free to invent his own list, and no one can gainsay him, for no one has found a way to test the validity of such a list. . . . Furthermore, the reasoning with regard to these universal social needs is often circular. Positions are said to be important because they meet one of the needs, but one suspects that some of the needs have been invented to account for the existence of the positions.[13]

Here Simpson repeats the earlier charge

---

[11] *Ibid.*

[12] *Ibid.*, p. 133.
[13] *Ibid.*

by Tumin to the effect that the claim that positions have different degrees of functional importance rests on nothing more than a set of hidden tautologies.

Two years later, in August, 1958, Walter Buckley's 'Social Stratification and the Functional Theory of Social Differentiation' attacked Davis and Moore on both ideological and linguistic grounds. After reviewing the objections of Tumin, Schwartz, and Simpson, Buckley argued that the Davis-Moore theory

accepts outmoded concepts and assumptions of classical economics, such as "inherent scarcity" of social ends and the inviolability of competition, all of which results in a picture of theoretical necessity and reproduces with remarkable faithfulness a culturally circumscribed ideology. . . . The manner in which the functionalists present the stratification system as actually operating is rather the way in which many persons desire and believe that it would work in contemporary society if only the class structure did not exist to hinder it.[14]

This critique of the ideological implications of the Davis-Moore theory focuses on the understandable feelings of outrage aroused in some critics by a theory whose original version, in effect, tells us that those members of our society who have the greater amounts of wealth, power, and prestige, are also the ones who make (thanks to their positions) the greatest contributions to the preservation or survival of the society. It is also obvious that however applicable this critique might be to the Davis-Moore 1945 version (which did not attempt to explain status ascription), it is not applicable to the Davis 1948 version (which attempted to explain ascription in terms of the family). The Davis 1948 version, in effect, suggests that if the family did

not exist, and if society were organized as a pure achievement order, then the positions with greater rewards would also be the ones that make the greater contribution to the preservation and survival of the society, but that since the family does exist, and since all societies exhibit different mixtures of achievement and ascription, this correspondence between high rewards and high functional importance is no longer the case.

Buckley's second criticism concerns the Davis and Moore use of the term "stratification."

The Davis-Moore theory specifies the central defining criterion of the concept of stratification as follows: "If the rights and prerequisites of different positions in a society must be unequal, then the society must be stratified, because that is precisely what stratification means." We shall argue, however, that this is not precisely what stratification has meant to most students. It is (or was) rather firmly imbedded in usage that stratification involved the existence of *strata*, generally agreed to refer to specifiable collectivities or subgroups that *continue through several generations* to occupy the same relative positions and to receive the same relative amounts of material ends, prestige, and power. The statement quoted above, on the other hand, refers only to the fact of the differentiation of social positions as seen at any one point in time, and implies nothing about the existence of strata, which, to extend our above definition, implies groupings of individuals with biological and social continuity whose movements into the differentiated positions can be predicted to some degree (if only statistically).[15]

Buckley's criticism is twofold: (a) that the Davis-Moore use of 'stratification' is much too *abstract* (in that it refers to unequal rewards attached to positions and not to specific *strata*); and (b), that it fails to include the notion of *ascription* (in that it does not refer to "groupings

[14] Walter Buckley, "Social Stratification and the Functional Theory of Social Differentiation," *American Sociological Review*, XXIII (August, 1958), 369–73.

[15] *Ibid.*, p. 370.

of individuals with biological and social continuity"). And both of these criticisms seem to be in error. It is a commonplace that scientific theories require a fairly high level of abstraction; and if this abstraction makes possible an increase in analytical precision, then the desirability of abstraction is beyond question. As to the second criticism, it is applicable to the Davis and Moore 1945 version, but inapplicable to the Davis 1948 version.

Kingsley Davis's "The Abominable Heresy: Reply to Dr. Buckley" was an emotional and sarcastic counterattack. Davis affirmed his right to define 'stratification' in a manner different from Buckley, and added that:

the most significant thing about Dr. Buckley's paper is that he himself proposes no alternative theory of positional inequality or, for that matter, of what he calls stratification. If he had any specific curiosity about the subject one would expect him not only to refute an existing theory but to supply another in its place. Instead he falls back on a tenet of Marxian faith. "For an explanation of its ubiquity,' he writes, "we must turn . . . to the sociocultural dynamics of particular times and places. . . ." The real heresy in the Davis-Moore article . . . is rather the sin of believing that *any* scientific explanation of social inequality can be found.

The Davis-Moore theory of social inequality can certainly be improved upon. Along with others I have tried to do so in writings that my critic conveniently ignores. Improvement in the theory will come, however, by modification and extension rather than by all-out attack without replacement. The fact remains, of course, that the more the theory is improved as a scientific explanation, the more intransigent will be the attacks on it as a heresy.[16]

The scientific import of this reply is questionable, and it seems a bit absurd to castigate a critic for limiting his role to making a negative contribution.

In December, 1959, Dennis H. Wrong's "The Functional Theory of Stratification: Some Neglected Considerations" attempted to mediate between theory and its critics:

The functional theory of stratification advanced by Davis and Moore attempts to explain the universality and necessity of inequality in societies with a complex division of labor, a task that is independent of efforts to explain the division of labor itself or the intergenerational perpetuation of inequalities along family lines. The theory is so general, however, that it excludes none of the Utopian models of "classless societies" proposed by Western thinkers and, its critics to the contrary notwithstanding, says nothing whatsoever about the range of inequality and the determinants of that range in concrete societies. The theory appears to understate the degree to which positions are inherited by failing to view societies in long range historical perspective. In common with the arguments of its critics, it also ignores the possible disruptive consequences of mobility and equality of opportunity, a theme notably neglected by American sociologists.[17]

Here the opening formulation is incorrect. Davis and Moore do not attempt "to explain the universality and necessity of inequality." but attempt to explain the universality of inequality by its alleged necessity. This aspect of the Davis-Moore theory, in effect, exemplifies the typical functionalist maneuver of explaining a cultural universal by claiming that it is necessary for the preservation or survival of a system. The observation that the Davis and Moore theory neglects "the power element in stratification," and is "lacking a truly historical perspective,"[18] is quite accurate.

---

[16] Kingsley Davis, "The Abominable Heresy: A Reply to Dr. Buckley," *American Sociological Review*, XXIV (February, 1959), 83.

[17] Dennis H. Wrong, "The Functionalist Theory of Stratification: Some Neglected Considerations," *American Sociological Review*, XXIV (December, 1959), 772.

[18] *Ibid.*, pp. 774–78.

In 1960, Tumin's "Competing Status Systems," a contribution to Arnold S. Feldman and Wilbert E. Moore's *Labor Commitment and Social Change in Developing Areas*, repeated Tumin's earlier contention that "there is nothing inevitable at all about the need for unequal rewards for unequal work."[19] The following year, in his book *Social Class and Social Change in Puerto Rico*, Tumin argued that:

We must conclude that the actual shape of any reward system or any system of inducement and recruitment into tasks will be a function of the relevant powers of the sectors who hold differing judgments about the respective importance of tasks. Stratification, then, to the extent to which, as some have suggested, it can be defined by the system of unequal allocation of scarce, valued goods and services, is something very different from an unconsciously evolved device by which societies insure that the most competent persons will be induced to take on the tasks considered most functionally important to the society. It is rather an outcome, specified partly by social reward distributions, which is a function of the competition among variable definitions of what is important to the respective powers available to the competing sectors to implement their decision [the passage is italicized in the original].[20]

Since "the actual shape of any reward system" refers to the range of inequality, Tumin is here suggesting that the actual configuration of power is a crucial determinant of the range of unequal rewards attached to different positions. He is also suggesting that the effective power of relevant sectors implements their evaluation of which positions are more important than others by the allocation of greater rewards to these positions.

It seems quite possible, however, to account for the universal presence of ranking and evaluation systems, and for the presence of inequalities in scarce, valued goods and services in nearly all societies, without relying upon some very restricted notion of the conditions under which actors will be induced to take up certain roles and perform them conscientiously. It would be equally reasonable to imagine an earlier historical condition where differences in age and strength made it possible for some members of groups to seize what they wanted when they wanted them, and to proceed to institutionalize their power over others by allocating the goods and services as they saw fit. Once in control of the socialization of the young, it is not much of a trick to teach certain patterns of deference which no longer require differences in physical strength to maintain.[21]

This formulation seems to involve some confusion. Tumin is unquestionably correct in taking power as a major determinant of role *ascription;* and a power explanation goes a long way in accounting for why the present incumbents of high-reward positions are who they are. But can a power explanation be equally effective in accounting for the inequality of rewards attached to positions? The difference can perhaps be made clear by appealing to a well-known historical example. The Aryan invasion is said to have been the historical origin of the Hindu caste system. This power event explains why the high-reward positions of priest and warrior were occupied exclusively by members of the conqueror group. It does *not* explain why both the conquerors and the conquered alike (together with many other similar traditional societies) should have regarded the roles of priest and warrior as high-reward positions.

In February, 1963, Wilbert E. Moore's "But Some Are More Equal

[19] Melvin M. Tumin, "Competing Status Systems," in Arnold S. Feldman and Wilbert E. Moore, eds., *Labor Commitment and Social Change in Developing Areas* (New York: Social Science Research Council, 1960), p. 279.

[20] Melvin M. Tumin with Arnold S. Feldman, *Social Class and Social Change in Puerto Rico* (Princeton, N. J.: Princeton University Press, 1961), p. 491.

[21] *Ibid.*, p. 508

than Others" answered Tumin and made a re-appraisal of the original Davis-Moore 1945 version.

My current view is that the Davis-Moore position was incomplete, resulting in some overstatement (as noted by Simpson) and some neglect of dysfunctions. These criticisms have already been noted by Davis. In addition, I should specifically reject any stable equilibrium version of "functionalism" as both incorrect and extrinsic to the position that social inequality is a necessary feature of any social system. . . . The "functional theory of stratification" maintained only that positions of unequal importance would be unequally rewarded, and was silent, regrettably but not criminally, on the subject of systemic changes. . . . Although Davis and Moore were fairly explicit in equating "social stratification" with unequal rewards, that now appears unfortunate. I have some sympathy for Buckley's criticism on this point.[22]

After these modifications Moore turned to re-affirm the original thesis of the 1945 version:

The single issue to which the present remarks are addressed is whether social inequality is a necessary feature of social systems. . . . The explanation presented here reiterates the thesis that "functional differentiation" of positions will inevitably entail unequal rewards—and adds the thesis that differences in performance must be expected to be and will be differentially valued.[23]

Here Moore reviews the many ways in which "inequality" can arise from the social valuation of "performances, qualities, and achievements," but this misses the point, because neither Tumin nor anyone has argued for the viability of a completely egalitarian order: the issue concerns only the possibility and feasibility of "equivalents" or "alternatives" to "unequal rewards"; namely, whether or not something other than unequal rewards can motivate individuals to occupy the different positions. Moore does not think so.

Unless intrinsic task equalization is accomplished, it would seem extremely unlikely that equality of rewards—or rather, permitting only esteem rewards—would be institutionalized by any conceivable system of socialization. This would require a somewhat greater extension of martyrdom than any religious system has yet achieved—and religious martyrs expect future rewards. I believe that Tumin has become entrapped by an ideological position that I see no reason to accept: namely that equality is intrinsically more equitable than inequality.[24]

On the causes of "stratification" (unequal rewards attached to different positions), Moore repeated the 1945 formulation and rejected Tumin's modification:

The Davis-Moore "functional" interpretation of inequality rested on the unequal functional importance of positions and the unequal supply of talents for filling them. That interpretation, unlike most functional analyses, was explicitly evolutionary, and like many had possible rationalistic overtones. Tumin essentially skirts the issues of importance and talents but rejects the evolutionary explanation, for which he substitutes the view that stratification is an anachronistic survival maintained by self-perpetuating power. (That revolutionary polities establish new modes of social stratification escapes his attention.)[25]

This account of Tumin's views is not quite accurate. Although Tumin did not discuss revolutionary polities, their existence does not constitute a counterexample to his argument. Tumin suggested that the values of relevant power sectors constitute a decisive determinant of "the actual shape of any reward sys-

[22] Wilbert E. Moore, "But Some Are More Equal than Others," *American Sociological Review*, XXVIII (February, 1963), 14–15.

[23] *Ibid.*, p. 15.

[24] *Ibid.*, p. 16.
[25] Moore, *loc. cit.*

tem." And as we saw when we analyzed his argument with the aid of a concrete historical example, power is most certainly a decisive determinant of positional ascription, but it is questionable whether power can explain why within a given socio-historical setting some positions are given high rewards and not others.

Moore argued that the class system of industrial societies exhibits "fragmentation of even nominally singular statuses into incomparable analytical subsystems," and that:

Tumin's position here is compounded of serveral empirical errors: (1) a class system "really exists"; (2) it is posited upon only one dominant "phase" of social life, the economic, which is associated with (the cause of?) prestige and power; (3) other worthwhile human endeavors are given something less than their "due" because the economy had "invaded" other institutional areas. Not only does this entail an exaggeration of status comparability in industrial societies, but it leads to a perception of status anxieties more pervasive than any evidence indicates.[26]

Moore's formulation, in turn, would seem to rest on an exaggeration. If no class system "really exists" in industrial society because the "analytical subsystems" are really "incomparable," then it would seem to follow that most theories of stratification, including the Davis and Moore theory, are either irrelevant or inapplicable.

In "On Inequality," his reply to Moore, Melvin Tumin argued that the range of social inequality is much greater than that which is institutionalized in unequal rewards.

Any of the diverse inequalities found in society can become subject to stratification. These inequalities arise from: (1) role specification; (2) ranking according to characteristics intrinsic to the role; (3) ranking according to moral conformity; (4) ranking according to contribution to (a) value and moral ideals and (b) functionally important tasks; (5) diffusion and transfer. Types (1), (2), and (4), have higher likelihood of being taken up into the stratification system, but none need so result. Considerable inequality can therefore coexist with little or no stratification.[27]

Here Tumin's main point represents a harmonious addition to the Davis and Moore theory. Tumin's secondary claim that some types of inequality "seem unavoidable as system features for survival of a society over two generations" is more complex and seems to involve disparate elements. First, Tumin is referring to parent-child, man-woman role differentiations (which Davis has explicitly ruled out as possible bases for stratification). Second, Tumin is referring to the universality of invidious valuations: "Everywhere men tend to make comparisons as to who is taller, or prettier, or quicker" (but need he follow the arbitrary functionalist maneuver of translating a cultural universal into an alleged functional necessity?). Third, Tumin is referring to "ranking by functional contribution," which he divides into two major analytical sub-types: (a) "Ranking according to contribution to or exemplification of ideals"; and (b) "Ranking according to functional contribution to desired social goals." In connection with the latter he says:

Current theory attaches the greatest significance to differential functional importance as a basis of social stratification. It is argued that every society must make judgments about unequal functional importance and must allocate its scarce and desired goods at least partly in line with such judgments.[28]

As an account of what Davis and Moore

[26] Ibid., p. 17.

[27] Melvin M. Tumin, "On Inequality," American Sociological Review, XXVIII (February, 1963), 18.

[28] Ibid., p. 23.

claim this is surely in error. Once again, it must be emphatically pointed out that differential functional importance is not the same as the judgments or valuations of a given society. Differential functional importance is, presumably, the degree of contribution which each position makes to the preservation or survival of the society.

In his "Rejoinder" to Tumin, Wilbert E. Moore agreed that social inequality and unequal rewards are definitionally different, but he argued that they are empirically closer than Tumin allows. He questioned Tumin's "extremely relativistic view of cultural values and social institutions," and suggested that there is an underlying pattern of necessary functions:

As I read the evidence, the evaluation of functionally differentiated positions is by no means as randomly variable as his discussion asserts or implies. I suggest that behavior relevant to the maintenance of order, the provision of economic support, the protection of the society, and the exemplifications of religious and aesthetic values *always* involves differential positional as well as merely personal valuation.[29]

To say that positions in these general areas involve differential valuation is not very enlightening, since presumably all positions in a given society have some degree of positive or negative valuation. Furthermore, and as is the case with all lists of so-called functional prerequisites, the general areas listed by Moore add up to a fairly standard definition of society. It follows from this that the claim that these positions "always" involve valuation is little more than a tautology.

In October, 1963, Arthur L. Stinchcombe's "Some Empirical Consequences of the Davis-Moore Theory of Stratifi-

cation" attempted to demonstrate that differential functional importance really exists and can be tested. With explicit reference to the Davis-Moore 1945 version, Stinchcombe argued that:

Davis and Moore's basic argument is that unequal rewards tend to accrue to positions of great importance to society, provided that the talents needed for such positions are scarce. "Society" (i.e., people strongly identified with the collective fate) insures that these functions are properly performed by rewarding the talented people for undertaking these tasks. This implies that the greater the importance of positions, the less likely they are to be filled by ascriptive recruitment. (Footnote: The theory holds that the most important positions, if they require unusual talents, will recruit people who otherwise would not take them, by offering high rewards to talent. This result would take place if one assumed a perfectly achievement-based stratification system. Some have asserted that Davis and Moore's argument "assumes" such a perfectly open system, and hence is obviously inadequate to the facts. Since the relevant results will be obtained if a system recruits more talented people to its "important" positions but ascribes all others, and since this postulate is not obviously false as is the free market assumption, we will assume the weaker postulate here. It seems unlikely that Davis and Moore ever assumed the stronger, obviously false, postulate.)[30]

This seems to be very confused. First, Davis and Moore (1945) argued that high rewards (not "unequal rewards") "tend to accrue" to positions of high functional importance and high but scarce requirements of talent and training. Second, nothing in this proposition, or in the entire 1945 version, permits anyone to draw any inferences about "ascriptive recruitment." The reason

[29] Wilbert E. Moore, "Rejoinder," *American Sociological Review*, XXVIII (February, 1963), 27.

[30] Arthur L. Stinchcombe, "Some Empirical Consequences of the Davis-Moore Theory," *American Sociological Review*, XXVIII (October, 1963), 805.

for this is obvious: the 1945 version did not discuss ascription and the 1948 version attempted to remedy this lack by introducing the role of the family as the explanation of ascription. Furthermore, the 1948 version accounted for concrete stratification systems as approximations to two theoretical extremes: a complete achievement order versus a completely ascriptive one. Nothing in this formulation allows Stinchcombe to infer an inverse relationship between functional importance and ascription. Finally the assertion that "a system recruits more talented people to its "important" positions but ascribes all others," implies a dichotomy between important and non-important positions; and this is clearly at variance with the usage of Davis and Moore, for whom, presumably, *every* position within the system has a *different degree* of functional importance.

Next, Stinchcombe gives us his first concrete example of what he regards as differential functional importance.

It is quite difficult to rank tasks or roles according to their relative importance. But certain tasks are unquestionably more important at one time than at another, or more important in one group than another. For instance, generals are more important in wartime than in peacetime.[31]

But this is simply a misunderstanding. Here the position "general" is compared to itself in two different time periods (wartime versus peacetime), but the notion of differential functional importance in Davis and Moore refers to a comparison of different positions in the same time period. But then can we not say that in wartime the position 'general' makes a greater contribution to societal survival than, say the position "housewife"? In one obvious sense this is true, but this is not the sense involved in Davis and Moore's differential func-

tional importance. A nation at war involves the co-ordination of social resources for the pursuit of a system-goal. This co-ordination involves the temporary and dichotomous classification of all system-positions into two categories: (a) those positions which are necessary or essential for the pursuit of the war (e.g., general, arms manufacturer, nuclear scientist, etc.), and (b) those positions which are not necessary or essential for the pursuit of the war (e.g., housewife, luxury-goods manufacturer, artist, etc.). Our improved version of Stinchcombe's example will not do for at least three good reasons: (1) differential functional importance involves, presumably, different *degrees* of contribution to societal survival attached to the various positions (and a dichotomy is useless for this purpose); (2) the example is set in wartime, and this involves a system whose positions are coordinated as means for the pursuit of a system-goal, and this is not the usual condition of social systems throughout history (in other words, even if this example of differential functional importance were a valid one, which it is not, the possibility of generalizing to peacetime would still be in question); (3) the assertion that generals, foot soldiers, arms manufacturers (or any war specialists) are "necessary" for the pursuit of war is not an empirical statement but a tautology.

Stinchcombe's second example of differential functional importance involves changes in the position "king."

The kingship in West European democratic monarchies has consistently declined in political importance as the powers of parliament have increased. . . . Their rewards have also changed, emphasizing more ceremonial deference and expressions of sentiment, less wealth and power. . . . Changes in the nature of the role-requirements and of the rewards indicate a shift of functions. At the least these changes indicate that some ceremonial functions of the king-

---

[31] *Ibid.*

ship have declined much less in importance than the political functions. But to have a nonpolitical function in a political structure is probably to be less important in the eyes of the people.[32]

In the first place, this example is open to the same criticisms made of the last example: the position "king" is compared to itself over two or more time periods, but differential functional importance involves the comparison of different positions among themselves within one time period. In the second place, what does "to be less important in the eyes of the people" have to do with differential functional importance? What degree of contribution to societal survival was made by the position "king" before the rise of parliament? After the rise of parliament?

Stinchcombe's third example is a bit confused in that it is unclear whether it is intended as an example of differential functional importance, differential talent of personnel, or both.

In some industries individual talent is clearly a *complementary* factor of production, in the sense that it makes other factors much more productive; in others, it is more nearly *additive*. To take an extreme case of complementarity, when Alec Guinness is "mixed" with a stupid plot, routine supporting actors, ordinary production costs, plus perhaps a thousand dollars for extra makeup, the result is a commercially very successful movie; perhaps Guinness increases the value of the movie to twice as much by being three times as good as the alternative actor. But if an equally talented housepainter (three times as good as the alternative) is "mixed" with a crew of 100 average men, the value of the total production goes to approximately 103 per cent. Relatively speaking then, individual role performance is much more "imporant" in the first kind of enterprise.[33]

"Much more important" here means

"makes a greater contribution to the economic or commercial value of the product." All speculation apart, the film example is unfortunate because in the case of Guinness his commercial value resides in his role as a film star and not in his role as a dramatic actor, and the two are not the same (in fact, in Hollywood they come close to being inversely related). Therefore it is very questionable whether it is the dramatic talent of Guinness which is the complementary input into the "commercially very successful movie." But beyond all this, what sense does it make to compare special creative talent and ordinary skill? And if the sense of the comparison is to tell us that creative talent generally receives greater rewards than ordinary skill, don't we know this already? Stinchcombe goes on to make up two lists of "enterprises" in which talent is said to be primarily complementary and primarily additive.

Talent Complementary Factor
Research
    Universities
Entertainment
Management
Teams in athletics and other "winner take all" structures
Violin Concertos

Talent Nearly Additive
Teaching
    Undergraduate colleges
    High Schools
Manufacturing
Manual Work
Groups involved in ordinary competition in which the rewards are divided among the meritorious
Symphonies.[34]

Now a simple inspection of the activities grouped under these two lists reveals that the first contains an appreciably greater proportion of high reward activities, and also of activities which involve

[32] *Ibid.*, p. 806.
[33] *Ibid.*
[34] *Ibid.*

special creative talents. Stinchcombe "predicts" that this will be the case. He again "predicts" that activities in the second list will involve a greater amount of ascription by age, time-in-grade, and seniority. It is difficult to see what is proved by these two lists beyond the well known fact that in the United States (the lists are culture-specific) role incumbents with special creative talents will generally receive greater rewards than those with ordinary skills (and that the latter will be more prone to seek the compensatory security of devices such as seniority).

In October, 1963, Walter Buckley's "On Equitable Inequality" replied to some of the points raised by Wilbert E. Moore's February, 1963, article. Buckley argued that the Davis-Moore theory involves a "competitive fallacy" because it interprets stratification in all societies in terms of an atypical case: "the competitive-achievement syndrome of contemporary industrial societies." He repeated Tumin's point (granted by Moore) that stratification limits or restricts the development of potential talent. He accused Moore of confusing "inequality" with "inequity" (or with using "inequality" in such a way that the meaning of the term shifts from "objective differences" to "inequity"). He argues that the real task of stratification studies should be to determine the minimum range of unequal rewards compatible with an industrial order. Finally, Buckley pointed out that Moore's claim that a class system does not really exist is an artifact created by an artificially restricted definition of "stratum"; and that to adopt Moore's usage would force us to say that "no known society is or has ever been stratified."[35]

In October, 1963, George A. Huaco's "A Logical Analysis of the Davis-Moore Theory of Stratification" attempted a detailed analysis of the notion of differential functional importance.

The postulate of unequal functional importance means that for any given society, the performance of some roles contributes more to the preservation of survival of that society than the performance of other roles. For this statement we need an independent definition of survival. We also need criteria to measure how much a given role contributes to survival vis-à-vis any other role. Davis mentions the following examples of such criteria.

"Rough measures of functional importance are in fact applied in practice. In wartime, for example, decisions are made as to which industries and occupations will have priority in capital equipment, labor recruitment, raw materials, etc. In totalitarian countries the same is done in peacetime, as also in underdeveloped areas attempting to maximize their social and economic modernization. Individual firms must constantly decide which positions are essential and which are not."[36]

The difficulties with these examples are twofold:

a. Each of them provides a dichotomous (essential/nonessential) criterion which seems to be tautologically derived from an over-all system goal. But what we need is criteria that permit us to measure the *degree* of contribution to societal survival of any role vis-à-vis any other role; in short, we need ranking criteria.

b. Each of these examples is drawn from a partially or totally planned economic system, and as such, useless for drawing inferences applicable to unplanned systems (and most societies throughout history have been unplanned).[37]

Huaco examined the two "clues" mentioned in the Davis and Moore 1945 version (role uniqueness, and degree to which other positions are dependent on

---

[35] Walter Buckley, "On Equitable Inequality," *American Sociological Review*, XXVIII (October, 1963), 800.

[36] Davis, "Reply," *op. cit.*, p. 395.
[37] George A. Huaco, "A Logical Analysis of the Davis-Moore Theory of Stratification," *American Sociological Review*, XXVIII (October, 1963), 803.

the functionalist theory of stratification **425**

the one in question). He pointed out that there is absolutely no empirical basis for admitting uniqueness and dependency as indicators of anything beyond themselves. Next he examined a claim made by Davis in both the 1945 and 1948 versions. Davis wrote:

Owing to the universal necessity of certain functions in society, which require social organization for their performance, there is an underlying similarity in the kind of positions put at the top, the kind put at the middle, and the kind put at the bottom of the scale. . . . For this purpose we shall select religion, government, economic activity, and technology.[38]

Huaco remarked that this selection of four "necessary" societal "functions" is not only familiar, but it is also in the right order. And that:

As described by Davis, the selected "functions" roughly correspond to the four analytical levels of a well-known model of society:

Davis	Marx
Religion	Upper layer of superstructure
Government	Lower layer of superstructure
Economic Activity	Relations of production
Technology	Forces of production

The sole purpose of this comparison is to suggest that Davis and Moore's "universal" and "necessary" societal "functions" are really the various analytical parts of their implicit model of society, or are derived by a series of hidden tautologies from such an implicit model. The "necessity" involved is clearly analytical or logical necessity. It follows from this that Davis' claim that what he has selected are four "universal" and "necessary" societal "functions" is simply a tautology.[39]

Huaco concluded that differential functional importance is "a complete un-

known," and that "it cannot serve as a legitimate explanation for unequal rewards."

In Retrospect

Now let us return to our initial analysis of the logical structure of the Davis and Moore theory to try and sort out those portions which have been destroyed by the critics from the more solid and promising fragments. In the first place, it is fairly obvious that the basic concept of the theory, the postulate of differential functional importance, is a fallacy. There is not a shred of evidence that different positions make different degrees of contribution to societal preservation or survival. In the second place, it is also obvious that the assumption to the effect that societies whose stratification systems approach a pure achievement order have greater survival or endurance than more ascriptive societies is not only unwarranted, but probably false. Nevertheless, the remaining fragments of the theory seem to hold considerable promise.

I. *Unequal rewards attached to different positions are a cause of the mobility of individuals into positions.* Despite the technical issue of possible "alternatives," it now seems fairly certain that this is one of the most solid portions of the theory. Evidence for this is indirect, but impressive, and it comes from the area of experimental psychology known as learning theory. Very briefly, Davis and Moore's comprehensive definition of "rewards" corresponds to the psychological notion of "reinforcement." The notion of "high rewards" corresponds to "positive reinforcement" and "low rewards" to negative reinforcement." Learning theorists have considerable experimental evidence that both animals and humans learn and act in response to the manipulation of positive and negative reinforcements.

---

[38] Davis, *Human Society, op. cit.*, p. 371.
[39] Huaco, *op. cit.*, p. 804.

II. *The existence and operation of the institution of the family is cause of status ascription.* That the particularistic character of kinship bonds tends to generate status ascription is probably self-evident. It is also evident that the existence of the family is an insufficient or incomplete explanation of ascription. We can set up a conceptual model in which the ascriptive propensities of the family are held in abeyance and in which a sizeable amount of status ascription is nevertheless generated. The Norman conquest of England will do as a point of departure: we know that the Norman conquerors reserved for themselves most high reward positions, and limited the conquered Saxons to low reward positions. We know that both societies had extensive family ascription; but the point is that similar ascriptive results would have followed a similar conquest even if both societies had been completely achievement oriented. The explanation of why the conquering Normans reserved for themselves most high reward positions cannot be found in the Norman family, but must be traced to the conquest itself, that is to say to the phenomenon of power.

III. *Differential scarcity of qualified personnel is a cause of "stratification" (unequal rewards attached to different positions).* Let us modify the statement to read: differential scarcity of qualified personnel is a cause of *the range* of unequal rewards attached to different positions. This interesting notion deserves to be developed beyond its brief formulation by Davis and Moore. It seems that we can posit variation along two different dimensions: on the one hand the positional structure of a given society may have high or low requirements for talent and training, on the other hand the population of the same society may have high or low amounts of effective talent and training. A state of relative differential scarcity of personnel can be said to exist whenever there is a sizeable gap between the amount of effective talent and training available in the population and the amount of talent and training required by the positional structure of the society. We can now set up a fourfold table and examine the various possibilities:

		Amount of Talent and Training Required by the Positional Structure of the Society	
		High	Low
Amount of Talent and Training Available in the Population	High	Mature Industrial Society	Pre-Revolutionary Society
	Low	Industrializing Society	Traditional Society

1. *Traditional Society:* Here the amount of talent and training required by the positional structure of the society is low and the amount of effective talent and training available in the population is also low. Here it makes little or no sense to speak of a differential scarcity of personnel; and whatever may be the range of unequal rewards, the scope of this range must be explained in terms of other (as yet unidentified) factors.

2. *Industrializing Society:* Here the amount of talent and training required by the positional structure of the society is high but the amount of effective talent and training available in the population remains low. Here there is a differential scarcity of personnel, and the hypothesis would predict that the range of unequal rewards would tend to increase. Historically speaking, this would seem very much to be the case. The period of early West European industrialization, the nineteenth-century American expe-

rience, and the period of Soviet industrialization all seem to exhibit an increased range of unequal rewards.

3. *Mature Industrial Society:* Here the amount of talent and training required by positional structure of the society is high, and the amount of effective talent and training available in the population also tends to become high. With a gradual diminution of differential scarcity of personnel, we can predict that mature industrial societies will exhibit a trend toward a gradual shortening of the range of unequal rewards. Again, the historical evidence seems to support this prediction.

4. *Pre-Revolutionary Society:* Here the amount of talent and training required by the positional structure of the society is relatively low but the amount of effective talent and training available in the population becomes relatively high.

Instead of a differential scarcity of personnel we have a differential surplus of personnel. This was the situation of Russia in 1917 with its highly educated and underemployed intelligentsia; and it is also the situation of many colonial societies where the colonial administration fosters the simultaneous education and underemployment of a native intelligentsia.

What remains of the Davis and Moore functionalist theory of stratification? Two decades of controversy seem to have effectively sorted out the metaphysical postulate and questionable assumptions from the more valuable ingredients. These ingredients contain considerable insight, but by themselves they do not add up to a fully adequate theory of social inequality, mobility, and ascription, much less of stratification.

Dissonance and Dissensus in Evaluation

MELVIN M. TUMIN   **ARNOLD FELDMAN**

The dissonance between objective and subjective ranking is a feature of every social system on which we have any evidence. Nor is the strain necessarily more often toward modifying the subjective ranking system to bring it into greater consonance with the objective inequalities. In the case of modernized societies, at least, one notes a bi-vectored strain.

Some efforts seem to be made to reduce this dissonance by elite attempts at persuasion, through the available media, of the rightness of the distribution of

Reprinted from Melvin M. Tumin with Arnold S. Feldman, *Social Class and Social Change in Puerto Rico* (Princeton, N. J.: Princeton University Press, 1961), pp. 486–493, by permission of the authors and the publisher.

rewards in property and power and of the idea that the possession of these rewards marks the worth of an actor.

But contrary strains also seem to be at work in both modern and other societies. On the one hand, there are techniques of strata insulation and isolation which dim the publicly symbolized differences in the appearances and advantages between strata. Often enough, these insulations and isolations are self-imposed. But often simultaneous with this isolation and insulation, the relatively lower groups (at least those in the modern societies) exert considerable effort to secure a greater share of the society's rewards. Their effort is ignited precisely because they do not agree that their work is less important to the society and less deserving of its rewards. Curiously, an important reason why they press for a larger share is that they have partially accepted the idea that possession of these rewards is a proper criterion by which to measure an actor's work. But the presence of this idea always seems to be accompanied, and usually preceded, by a public denial that possession of scarce valued properties has any proper bearing on ranking; at least, there is denial that such possession has the significance attributed by the official ideology and by the elite rankers who articulate this ideology.

We can now make a provisional summary of factors determining the relationship between possessions of valued properties and ranking on a hierarchy of social and moral worth:

1. In every social system, some values and properties will be commonly affirmed as desirable by nearly all actors of all strata. The degree of consensus will usually depend on how vaguely stated these values and properties are, and how operationally difficult it is to make any precise measurements and comparisons. The vaguer and more operationally difficult, the greater the likelihood of consensus (for example, the desirability of success, the value of truth, loyalty, and so forth).

2. Significant distinctions will always be found between properties which are valued and abundant and those which are valued and scarce. All social systems must, by virtue of being normative systems, have both sets of properties and must, in their institutional operations, give credit and social recognition to both. Scarce valued properties will generally be confined to material goods and services and a small number of talents; abundant valued properties will generally refer to moral qualities, capacities for social intercourse, and so forth.

3. Differences will always be found among the actor's own enunciations of the rank orders of social worth of various types of positions and actors. The differences are largely a function of the different combinations of scarce valued and abundant valued properties which the actors themselves possess. Actors with a relatively large share of the scarce properties will naturally tend to give them greater weight in their ranking systems, without, however, denying the significance of the abundant valued properties. By contrast, actors with relatively small shares of the scarce properties will tend to give proportionately less weight, if any at all, to the significance of these properties for ranking; they will emphasize, instead, the overriding significance of the valued abundant properties to which they can lay claim.

5. The dissensus about rank ordering which flows from these differential ratios of properties will increase, depending on how much the official ideology of the society stresses the "ultimate equality" and "equal worth" of all men. But since, in any social system, some official stress *must* be laid upon the importance of abundant valued properties—for example, moral conduct—actors at lower socio-economic positions will always have a legitimized basis on which to justify their claims to a higher rank that their social superiors accord them. When the official ideology proclaims the ultimate inequality of all types of actors and when this ideology is institutionally enforced, transmitted effectively over time through the agencies of socialization, and reinforced by strict controls over deviations, the dissensus about ranking will tend to a minimum.

With these observations, we can now formulate a provisional answer to the problem regarding the conditions under which consensus and dissensus will vary. The consensus here refers primarily to agreement by actors at all levels of rank on the correctness of the ranks assigned to them by others; it also refers to actors' agreement on the ranks which ought to be assigned to everyone else. Dissensus can exist on either or both counts, that is, on actors' own ranks, or on the ranks assigned to others.

Therefore, dissensus with regard to rank will tend to approach a maximum when there are simultaneously present:

1. An official ideology of the equal moral and social worth of all actors or strata of actors, predicated on the great social importance of otherwise unrewarded normative conduct;
2. An affirmation, on the ideal level, of the equal importance to the system of all of of its major phases and the activities appropriate thereto:
3. A highly unequal distribution of the scarce, valued goods and services, publicly justified and rationalized as inducements and rewards for talents and performances appropriate to only one phase of the system.

Not only will there tend to be dissensus about one's own rank and about those enjoyed by others, but serious dissensus is also likely on the right distribution of the scarce valued goods and services—who is getting the disproportionate amounts of rewards, and the amount of their shares.

By contrast, consensus will tend to approach a maximum in a social system when there are:

1. An official ideology of the ultimate moral and social inequality of worth of all actors or strata of actors, predicated on presumably inherited properties or qualities, not subject to any empirical confirmation or denial;
2. An affirmation, on the ideal level, of the relatively small importance to the system of certain of its phases, and of the predominant importance of one of its phases;
3. A distribution of the scarce, valued goods and services in highly unequal shares, the dominant portions going to the hereditary elite, justified in terms of their hereditary qualities as such and their natural fitness for the tasks (phase activities) considered most important to the system.

Here, too, consensus will be found not only with regard to the subjective rank enjoyed by oneself and ascribed to others, but also with regard to the distribution of the scarce valued goods and services.

Now, we may ask, under what conditions are most or all strata likely to accept the propriety of unequal distribution of scarce valued goods and services and yet disagree on the ranking on a hierarchy of moral and social worth? From the variables posited above, we can see one of the occasions where this kind of dissensus will occur: where it is generally agreed that one set of phase activities is functionally more important than others, and that talented performers in this phase require and/or deserve disproportionate shares of the scarce valued goods, but where there is, nevertheless, an official ideology which proclaims that all the social actors are ultimately of equal worth. This official evaluation is predicated on some theological or similar nonempirical ground and/or on the avowal that all other phase activities are vital even though their role performances occasion no institutional expectations of or provisions for hierarchical rewards.

We can specify important outcomes of the interplay of the variables described above, and this reinforces the importance of our distinctions. Those distinctions are, in summary: (1) between the unequal distributions of scarce valued goods and services and the assignments of unequal rank on a hierarchy of social and moral worth; (2) between valued properties which are scarce and those which are abundant; (3) between consensus on the order of importance of the phases and appropriate reward structures in any social system, and the consensus on the rank order of worth of actors.

The first two sets of distinctions need not be elaborated further now, though we shall refer back to them subsequently.

But it is important to look more carefully at the implications of the third distinction. The focus of attention is primarily upon ranking, in relative importance, the different phases of the system or, variously, assigning different functional importance to various roles and tasks.

The first important implication of this distinction is that we may not safely assume the existence of consensus on the rank ordering of phases of the system, or on the ranking of roles. Nor may we safely assume in any given case that we can account for the ranking of roles by their ranking of phases, until we know—and this always remains to be discovered empirically and highly subject to variation—whether there is consensus on the ranking of the phases and also the appropriateness of assigning rank in accordance with roles played in the high-ranked phases.

There is some good theoretical ground on which to insist that some dissensus will always be found—except in the limiting case specified before—on both the ranking of the phases and the appropriateness of ranking roles by their phase contributions. This latter dissensus must always be expected, at least to some degree, precisely because one must always expect some degree of disagreement about phase ranking.

It seems certain that in a normal condition of any social system (short of extreme crises), three sets of rank orders of phases are always simultaneously present:

1. The first rank ordering assigns, for the moment in the society's history, what almost everyone generally concedes or what some insist upon and enforce as the highest priority importance to a particular aspect or a major phase of a system. Some of these temporary assignments of priority prove so enduring that they resemble in all but words a permanent priority. But the crucial fact is that they are publicly defined as temporary.

2. The second rank order always present in a social system is the assignment, usually with general agreement of every sector, of equal importance to all phases in view of the long-range requirements of the system.

3. The third rank ordering is partly derivative from the second, yet analytically separable. It refers to the process by which role players in every phase of the system are officially persuaded to believe and act as if their roles are as important as those played in any other phase of the system; derivatively, these role players ascribe the highest order of system importance, insofar as they personally are concerned, to their roles (for example, wife-mothers being socialized and encouraged to believe and act as if their roles are indispensable to the system, as important as any other in general, and more important than any other, as far as they themselves are concerned).

There are two reasons for this process. First, the notion of the equal importance of all roles derives from the second rank ordering described above. Second, the notion of the *greater* importance of the roles derives from the fact that it would otherwise be impossible to recruit players for these roles and to motivate them to conscientiously perform their roles, especially since these roles are otherwise publicly unrewarded, and often psychologically ungratifying. That a role can be both equal and greater in importance presents no difficulty if we realize that it is *equal* from the *overall* point of view, and *more important* from the point of view of the player himself. Not only is there official *permission* for him to conceive his role as more important, but there is official *pressure* and institutional *support* for him to do so. In short, every social system appears to encourage a series of differing judgments on role importance; competition and conflict among these differences are reduced by the technique of making the greater importance specific to the role player and not commensurably greater on any comparative basis. Thus the wife-mother may properly claim that her role is more important than any other, where her contribution to her social groups and to the social system is concerned, without necessarily courting disagreement or conflict with the husband-father-breadwinner's point of view that his roles are most important, in terms of his possible contribution to the same groups and to the system.

A fundamentally important consequence of the third type of rank ordering has to do with the psychic deficits which an actor incurs from playing low-ranked and low-rewarded roles in the phase of dominant emphasis. The deficit in self-estimate is made up for by discounting the significance of the low-ranked role in the dominant phase and emphasizing the significance of the unranked roles he plays in the less dominant phases. Thus the low-ranked breadwinner, incurring a psychic deficit because of his low rank in the occupational sphere, restores his self-image and, in his judgment, justifies a rank of equality with everyone else by appealing in his own internal conversations and public protestations to the equal, if not greater, importance of his other roles in the maintenance of the system. Thus he says: "I am a decent man; I obey the laws; I raise my children to respect authority and to show decent manners; I am friendly to my neighbors; I pay my taxes; I vote; I work hard at my job and I help make things which everyone wants to have; I go to church regularly; I teach my children reverence for God; I help them learn to desire to get ahead and make a way for themselves in life; I see to it that they get as much school as I can afford; I give my family everything my income makes possible; and so on." If this same kind of actor must admit, on confrontation, that his

task within the division of labor is not as materially well rewarded as others and/or does not involve as much "responsibility," this is almost the only basis on which he must admit lesser contribution to the maintenance of system process—assuming that he agrees with these criteria of functional importance of tasks; and he has a long list of his other equal contributions which more than adequately compensate for and equalize the single invidious distinction.

Given these three coexisting rank ordering of phases in every social system, it becomes apparent that the attempt to account for the rank ordering of roles on the basis of their "functional importance" or "contribution to system process" raises as many, if not more, problems than it solves. For, three sets of definitions of system process and functional importance are always present and institutionally sanctioned and legitimized; and, for reasons stated earlier, there is bound to be some disagreement among these definitions, even if differential power quotients enable some role players to implement their decisions more than others. Moreover, as we have previously noted, it seems certain that the amount of disagreement about rank ordering of the *worth* of role players will vary directly with the amount of inequality in the distribution of the scarce, valued goods if, at the same time, there exists either an official ideology of the equal worth of all actors regardless of role and/or any significant emphasis on the social importance of the unrewarded roles.

Can it therefore be said that the allocation of scarce, desired rewards is made on the basis of the proportionate contribution to the maintenance of system process, or on the judgment of the "functional importance" of the task? Only as far as those sectors of actors who assert the relative greater importance of one set of tasks over another have the power with which to implement this judgment in the reward structure and, previously, in the inducement and recruitment structure.

We must conclude that the actual shape of any reward system, or any system of inducement and recruitment into tasks, will be a function of the relevant powers of the sectors who hold differing judgments about the respective importance of tasks. Stratification, then, to the extent to which, as some have suggested, it can be defined by the system of unequal allocation of scarce, valued goods and services, is something very different from an unconsciously evolved device by which societies insure that the most competent persons will be induced to take on the tasks considered most functionally important to the society. It is, rather, an outcome, specified partly by social reward distributions, which is a function of the competition among variable definitions of what is important to the society, and among the respective powers available to the competing sectors to implement their decisions.

The fundamental dimensions of any stratification system are more complex than even these formulations suggest. Some disparity is always expected between the system of distribution of valued goods and services and the actor's subjective rank ordering of social worth. We have previously indicated the numerous bases on which dissensus in ranking can occur. It only disguises the complexity of these issues to formulate the matter of prestige allocation by some statement which begins, "Prestige is accorded, etc.," unless that statement contains reference to who is doing the according and to the meaning of prestige being accorded. We recall, in this regard, that a distinction must be drawn between two possible meanings of prestige; that which, when assigned to tasks, implies a judgment that the task is more important than others, or the skill is harder to come by, the income is more

desirable, and so on; and that which involves the ascription of moral and social worth to the role players who possess the valuable skills, desired income, and so on.

The studies of empirical rankings indicate quite clearly that there can be a relatively wide degree of consensus about how skilled a task is, how good it is to have more rather than less money, and so on; at the same time, there can be substantial dissensus on what these variable possessions imply for ranking on some hierarchy of moral and social worth. For these reasons, it is crucial that the dimensions of prestige be distinguished in any proposition regarding the distribution or allocation of prestige. It is equally crucial that those who are making the judgments be specified.

Facing the question of how to account for the distribution of prestige in the society, we must first see the distribution as multiple—always referring to variable and incommensurable components (skill vs. morality)—and, secondly, as always possibly differing by strata; this difference is in accordance, at the minimum, with their respective amounts of the goods worthy of prestige.

Thus the shape of the society's prestige system is a function of:

1. Competing definitions of system process
2. Competing powers to implement these decisions
3. Competing criteria of prestige
4. The power to shape one's own self-appraisal and to verify the correctness of one's appraisal

There are probably no unavoidable or fixed limits upon the power of actors to shape their own self-appraisal and to secure verification for the correctness of these appraisals. There are always strains working against highly idiosyncratic and unshared self-appraisals. But every society has some mechanisms by which actors can more or less successfully collect and sustain a reasonably favorable self-image. At the extreme, there can be recourse to the private worlds of delusion.

But we must also reckon with the fact that behavior which is often highly dysfunctional for system process is exhibited by those whose self-definitions seriously swerve from definitions of themselves which they perceive their effective others to hold. This behavior can take the form of withdrawal of interest, of identification, loyalty, and energy—some form of demoralization followed by retreat. Or it can manifest itself in aggressive creations of subcultures which compete with the dominant cultural emphases. The various versions of withdrawal or campaigns against the culture have earlier been specified in detail by Merton,[1] and more recently and fully by Dubin,[2] Cloward,[3] and Merton.[4] The important point here is that no system can, except at danger to itself, permit the distributions of material rewards and worth-ranks to generate significant numbers of such deviant actors. In short, every system can be said to have a vested interest in allowing the maximum number of the member actors to receive verification of their own self-estimates, at least from *some others;* there is a further

vested interest, proportionate to the level of actors' effective participation that the system seeks, in making it possible for the maximum of member actors to secure *publicly and officially symbolized* verifications of the favorable self-images they seek.

If the system develops to the point where almost all of its public symbols of approbation are exclusively confined to the dominant phase and to the unequal rewards distributed according to role situation in that dominant phase, a maximum number of actors are forced to eke out relatively small-scale, private, and unreassuring confirmation of their worth by others.

Again, the American case is an empirical example. Members of this society seem to be deriving decreasing comfort and reassurance of their worth out of their satisfactory performances in roles other than occupational; and they find smaller and smaller comfort from the less-than-enthusiastic ritual pronouncements that the good, law-abiding, citizen-breadwinner, however humble in socio-economic status, is as worthy and important as anyone else in the system. Instead, occupational role situation and the income and consumption correlatives have become nearly the sole bases on which worth is ascribed officially and on which the various actors calculate their own worth. The appeals of the lower socio-economic strata to their moralty and respectability as marks of their worth seem to be diminishing in their frequency, vigor, and tone of conviction.[5]

These observations suggest, in turn,

[1] Robert K. Merton, "Social Structure and Anomie," Chap. 4 in his rev. ed. of *Social Theory and Social Structure* (New York: The Free Press, 1957).

[2] Robert Dubin, "Deviant Behavior and Social Structure: Continuities in Social Theory," *American Sociological Review*, XXIV, No. 2 (April, 1959), 147–64.

[3] Richard A. Cloward, "Illegitimate Means, Anomie and Deviant Behavior," *American Sociological Review*, XXIV, No. 2 (April, 1959), 164–76.

[4] Robert K. Merton, "Social Conformity, Deviation and Opportunity Structures: A Comment on the Contributions of Dubin and Cloward," *American Sociological Review*, XXIV, No. 2 (April, 1959), 177–89.

[5] See the excellent recent reevaluation of the sources of anomie, as these relate to access to goal-achievement, in Dorothy Meier and Wendell Bell, "Anomia and Differential Access to the Achievement of Life Goals," *American Sociological Review*, XXIV, No. 2 (April, 1959), 189–202.

that any system can "get away with" having both an *official ideology* of the ultimate equality of all and an actual commitment to highly unequal rewards in scarce, valued goods for role performance in one dominant phase. Yet it can keep deviation and apathy to a minimum only by preventing the unequal scarce possessions from assuming too much significance in the worth-ranking system. Or, variously, if it cannot prevent what seems to be a natural growth in this direction, it must deliberately cultivate other mechanisms by which the relatively low-rewarded actors can secure reassurance of their worth.

A Theory of Social Mobility

SEYMOUR MARTIN LIPSET   HANS L. ZETTERBERG

The lion's share of the studies of social mobility to date are descriptive. Most researchers have been preoccupied primarily with the construction of measures and with the establishing of rates of mobility,[1] or, they have been concerned with the background of members in certain élite groups.[2] It is our contention that enough descriptive material has now been collected to suggest a shift in the emphasis of future research. While we still have to answer many further questions of the type *"how much* mobility?"* we might now also begin to ask such questions as *"what causes* account for this rate of mobility?"* and *"what consequences* follow from this rate of mobility?"* more consciously and systematically than has been done in the past.

To contribute to this shift from descriptive to verificational studies we would like to offer a simple theory of social mobility. We shall present (1) a few definitions delineating different kinds of mobility, and (2) a few hypotheses about factors affecting (*a*) the extent of mobility, and (*b*) the political or ideological consequences of various kinds of

Reprinted from Seymour Martin Lipset and Hans L. Zetterberg, "A Theory of Social Mobility," *Transactions of the Third World Congress of Sociology*, III (1956), 155–177, by permission of the authors and the publisher. The preparation of this paper was facilitated by funds made available by the Bureau of Applied Social Research, Columbia University, from a grant by the Ford Foundation for an inventory of political research, and a grant from the Ida K. Loeb Fund. We are also indebted to the Center for Advanced Study in the Behavioral Sciences for assistance. We would like to acknowledge the advice of Professor Leo Lowenthal, Dr. Natalie Rogoff, Mr. Juan Linz, and Mr. Yorke Lucci. None of these institutions or individuals have any responsibility for the statements made in this article.

---

[1] Among the best studies analyzing mobility in large populations are Theodore Geiger, *Soziale Umschichtungen in einer dänischen Mittelstadt* (Aahrus Universitet, 1951), Natalie Rogoff, *Recent Trends in Occupational Mobility* (New York: The Free Press, 1953), and David V. Glass, ed., *Social Mobility in Britain* (London: Routledge & Kegan Paul, Ltd., 1954).

---

[2] References to various élite studies will be found in Donald R. Matthews, *The Social Background of Political Decision Makers* (Garden City, N. Y.: Doubleday & Company, Inc., 1954), S. M. Lipset and Reinhard Bendix, "Ideological Equalitarianism and Social Mobility in the United States," in *Transactions of the Second World Congress of Sociology*, II (London: International Sociological Association, 1954), pp. 53–54.

mobility. These hypotheses will be illuminated with some data already available, but for the main part, they require a great deal of additional empirical support.

I. Some Dimensions of Mobility

Max Weber has indicated how useful it is to conceive of stratification along many dimensions.[3] More recently Parsons has suggested that one way of viewing stratification is to conceive of it as "the ranking of units in a social system in accordance with the standards of the common value system."[4] This approach also affords a multitude of cross-cutting stratifications. Of this multitude we would like to single out a few for discussion. They deal with the ranking of occupational and economic statuses, and with the ranking of certain properties of role relationships such as intimacy and power.

1. Occupational Rankings

From Plato to the present, occupation has been the most common indicator of stratification. Observers of social life— from novelists to pollsters—have found that occupational class is one of the major factors which differentiate people's beliefs, values, norms, customs and occasionally some of their emotional expressions.

We now have good measures of the prestige ranks of various occupations that can be used as bases for computation of occupational mobility. Occupations are differentially esteemed and studies

show a remarkable agreement as to how they rank in esteem. In a well-known survey ninety occupations ranging from "Supreme Court Justice" and "Physician" to "Street Sweeper" and "Shoe Shiner" were ranked by a national sample of the United States.[5] On the whole, there is substantial agreement among the rates from different areas of the country, different sizes of home towns, different age groups, different economic levels, and different sexes. Lenski reports that occupations not mentioned in the survey can be fitted into the original rank order with high reliability.[6] Thus it appears that we have available a technique which makes the notion of occupational rank quite feasible for the researcher. Occupations receiving approximately the same rank will be called an *occupational class*. There appears to be a great deal of international consensus about occupational prestige classes. A recent analysis by Inkeles and Rossi compares the relative position of occupational categories as judged by samples of Americans, Australians, Britons, Japanese, Germans, and Russian defectors.[7] They report a very high degree of agreement among the people of these six countries. The fact, however, that these studies were for the most part conducted separately, and that the analysis could only deal with published results, did not make possible any basic study of the variations in occupational prestige, or in the relative desirability of different occupations as occupational goals in different countries. Popular as well as academic con-

[3] Max Weber, *The Theory of Social and Economic Organization* (New York: Oxford University Press, Inc., 1947), p. 425, see also pp. 424–429, and Max Weber, *Essays in Sociology* (New York: Oxford University Press, Inc., 1946), pp. 180–195.
[4] Talcott Parsons, *Essays in Sociological Theory* (New York: The Free Press, 1954), p. 388.

[5] National Opinion Research Center, "Jobs and Occupations: A Popular Evaluation," *Opinion News* (September 1, 1947), 3–13.
[6] G. H. Lenski, "Status Crystallization: A Non-vertical Dimension of Social Status," *American Sociological Review*, XIX (1954), 405–413.
[7] Alex Inkeles and Peter Rossi, "Cross National Comparisons of Occupational Ratings," *American Journal of Sociology*, LXI (January, 1956), 329–339.

sensus (which, of course, cannot be trusted as a substitute for actual measurement) suggests that civil service occupations have higher prestige in much of Europe than they do in America. Similarly, most American intellectuals believe that intellectual positions have lower prestige in the United States than they do in Europe. (The aforementioned study of the prestige of occupations in the United States, incidentally, throws doubt upon the common belief of American intellectuals that businessmen are overly appreciated as compared with themselves; a college professor ranks higher than an owner of a factory that employs one hundred people.) New cross-national research might want to focus on such presumed difference in the prestige of occupations.

The above approach to occupational classes in the form of ranking of different occupational titles is theoretically neat and operationally easy. However, one must be aware that it sometimes obscures significant shifts such as those involved in movements from a skilled manual occupation to a low-level white-collar position, or from either of these to a modest self-employment. All these occupations might at times fall in the same prestige class. The difficulties inherent in relying solely on this method of classification can be observed most vividly in the fact that many changes in social position which are a consequence of industrialization would *not* be considered as social mobility since they most frequently involve shifts from a low rural to a low urban position. This points to the need of recording not only occupational class but also *occupational setting*, that is, the kind of social system in which the occupation is found. Changes between occupational settings may also be important: white-collar workers behave differently in specified ways from small businessmen or skilled workers although the prestige of their occupational titles

may not differ greatly. For example, most researchers in the United States place small business ownership higher than white-collar employment, and the latter, in turn, higher than the blue-collar enclave of the same corporation. When estimating their own social status level, white-collar workers and small businessmen are much more likely to report themselves as members of the "middle class" than are manual workers who may earn more than they do.[8] Studies of occupational aspirations indicate that many manual workers would like to become small businessmen.[9] Political studies suggest that at the same income level, manual workers are more inclined to support leftist parties which appeal to the interests of the lower classes, than are white-collar workers or self-employed individuals.[10]

2. Consumption Rankings

It is theoretically and empirically useful to separate occupational and economic status. For example, economists have for good reasons differentiated between their subjects in their status as "producers" in the occupational structure, and in their status as "consumers." Both statuses might be ranked but it is not necessarily true that those who receive a higher rating in their producing capacity would also receive a high consumption rating.

The ranking of consumer status is difficult. Yet it is plain that styles of life differ and that some are considered more "stylish" than others. Those whose style

[8] Richard Centers, *The Psychology of Social Class* (Princeton, N. J.: Princeton University Press, 1949), p. 86.

[9] Nancy C. Morse and Robert S. Weiss, "The Function and Meaning of Work and the Job," *American Sociological Review*, XX (1955), 191–198.

[10] S. M. Lipset, *et al.*, "The Psychology of Voting: An Analysis of Political Behaviour," in G. Lindzey, ed., *Handbook of Social Psychology* (Reading, Mass.: Addison-Wesley Publishing Company, Inc., 1954), p. 1139.

of life carries approximately the same prestige might be said to constitute a *consumption class*. Changes in consumption class may or may not be concomitant with changes along other stratification dimensions.

At the same occupational income level, men will vary in the extent to which they are oriented toward acting out the behaviour pattern common to different social classes. For example, highly-paid workers may choose to live either in working-class districts or in middle-class suburbs. This decision both reflects and determines the extent to which workers adopt middle-class behaviour patterns in other areas of life. A study of San Francisco longshoremen has indicated that longshoremen who moved away from the docks area after the income of the occupation improved tended to be much more conservative politically than those who remained in the docks area.[11] A British Labour Party canvasser has suggested that one can differentiate between Labour Party and Conservative voters within the working class by their consumption patterns. The Tory workers are much more likely to imitate middle-class styles.

The changes which have occurred in many Western countries in recent years in the income of different occupational groups point up the necessity to consider consumption class as a distinct stratification category. In countries such as the United States, Sweden, and Great Britain, the lower classes have sharply improved their economic position, while the proportion of the national income going to the upper fifth of the population has declined.[12] An interesting result in many countries having a long-term full employment economy combined with a reduced working-class birth rate is that a large number of families headed by men in low prestige occupations receive higher incomes than many middle-class families in which the wife does not work, and the children receive a prolonged education. A vivid illustration of this may be seen in the fact that over 100,000 families in the United States, whose principal bread winner is a "laborer," have an income of over $10,000 a year.[13] (This income is, of course, in most cases a consequence of having more than one wage-earner in the family.)

It is plain that as an index to consumption class, total income is inadequate, although it obviously sets the ultimate limit for a person's consumption class. It is the way income is spent rather than the total amount, that determines a man's consumption class. The best operational index to consumption class is, therefore, not total income, but amount of income spent on prestigious or cultural pursuits. The fact, however, that lower prestige occupations now often have incomes at the level of white-collar occupations is likely to affect both the style of life and the political outlook of manual workers in a high income bracket and of salaried members of the white-collar class in a relatively lower income position. A comparison of these two groups in terms of their consumption patterns or styles of life is thought to be of particular importance in forecasting future political behaviour, as well as crucial for an understanding of the factors related to other types of mobility in different societies.

It is, of course, difficult to measure the extent of the shift up or down in consumption class. In part, this might be

---

[11] Unpublished study of Joseph Aymes, former graduate student in the Department of Psychology, University of California at Berkeley.

[12] Selma Goldsmith, *et al.*, "Size Distribution of Income Since the Mid-thirties," *The Review of Economics and Statistics*, XXXVI (1954), 26.

[13] Fortune Magazine, *The Changing American Market* (Garden City, N. Y.: Hanover House, 1955).

done by comparing the consumption pattern of families at the same income level whose occupational class or income has changed over some particular period of time. Perhaps the best, although most expensive way of dealing with the problem, is to employ a "generational" panel. That is, to interview the parents of a portion of the original random sample, and to compare income in father's and son's family, and their scores on a consumption scale.

3. Social Class

Much of the research in stratification in America has been concerned with *social class*. This term, as used by American sociologists, refers to roles of intimate association with others. Essentially, other classes in this sense denote strata of society composed of individuals who accept each other as equals and qualified for intimate association. For example, the Social Register Association of American Cities only considers candidates for membership after three or more individuals already belonging to the Social Register certify that they accept the candidate as a person with whom they associate regularly and intimately. Men may change their occupational class by changing their job, but they may improve their social class position only if they are admitted to intimate relationships by those who already possess the criteria for higher rank.

One method of studying social class mobility would be a comparison of the occupational or economic class position of husbands and wives before marriage, or of the respective in-laws.[14] Another index of social class might be obtained

___

[14] See S. M. Lipset and Natalie Rogoff, "Class and Opportunity in Europe and America," *Commentary*, XIX (1954), 562–568; and David V. Glass, ed., *op. cit.*, pp. 321–338, 344–349.

by asking respondents in a survey to name the occupational status of their best friends. These latter methods would give us some measure of the extent to which upward or downward mobility in the occupational structure is paralleled by upward or downward movement in the social class structure. Such research would be best done in the context of a study which used a "generational" panel.

4. Power Rankings

Certain role-relationships are also authority or power relationships, that is, they involve subordination on one part and superordination on the other. The extent to which a person's role-relationship affords the means to impose his version of order upon the social system might be ranked as his power, and persons having approximately the same power might be said to constitute a *power class*. It is plain that power classes may be, in part at least, independent of other classes. A labour leader may have a low occupational status and yet wield considerable political influence. A civil servant or parliamentarian whose office is vested with a great deal of political power may enjoy a high occupational and social class, but not be able to meet the consumption standards of these classes. Power as a vehicle for other kinds of social mobility has so far been a neglected area of research.

The most feasible way of using information about improvements in power status is to analyse its effects on economic and occupational position and political orientation. The findings of a recent British study are suggestive in this regard. On the basis of a study of participation in community affairs in Wales we learn that "the adult sons of [low-level unpaid] local union leaders . . . achieved middle-class occupational status much more frequently than others of their generation."[15] In a study of members of the Typographical Union in New York City it was found that men holding the equivalent of shop steward's positions in the union were much more likely to say that they would try to get a nonmanual occupation if beginning their work career over again, than were men who did not hold these offices.[16] When one considers that at least 10 per cent of the members of the trade union movement hold some unpaid union office, and that many more have held one in the past, it is probable that this avenue to power mobility plays an important role in the dynamics of social mobility. Of course, politics, itself, may be even more important (than trade unions) in providing opportunity for power-mobility. Various students of American politics have pointed out the way in which different ethnic groups, in particular the Irish, have been able to improve their position through the medium of politics. In Europe, the Labour and Socialist parties undoubtedly give many lower-class individuals an opportunity to secure power and status far above their economic position. Robert Michels, among others, has suggested that the children of socialist leaders of working-class origin, often secure higher education and leave the working-class.[17]

An operational index to power class is difficult to construct. The public debate in Western societies seems rather shy when it comes to matters of power. While there is a fairly freely admitted consensus about the desirability of high occupational consumption and social status, there is less consensus about the loci of power, and less admittance that power might be desirable. Perhaps the best one can do at present is to ask a panel of informed social scientists to list the various types of power positions available to individuals at different class levels. Among workers in the United States, for example, these might include positions in political parties, trade unions, veterans' organizations, and ethnic groups. After collecting the data on all positions held by members of a sample, it should be possible to rank the relative importance of different posts.

The complexity of this problem is of such a magnitude that one cannot anticipate more than fragmental findings on *individual* changes of power class position. The relative power position of various *groups*, however, may change over time, as witnessed, for example, by the return to power of the industrialists in Germany, the decline of the gentry in England, and throughout the Western world the manifest increase in the power of organized labour. It is plain that individuals change in their power class to the extent that they belong to these groups. Such membership (easy to ascertain by survey methods) may reflect itself in different feelings of political involvement and influence; for example, a study of two cities in Sweden by Segerstedt and Lundquist indicates that workers have these feelings to a greater extent than the white-collar class.[18] Likewise, the British worker may experience himself and his class as politically less impotent than, say, the American worker.

This concludes the discussion of the dimensions of social stratification which seem to us theoretically most rewarding and which are accessible by available re-

[15] T. Brennan, "Class Behaviour in Local Politics and Social Affairs," in *Transactions of the Second World Congress of Sociology*, II, *op. cit.*, pp. 291–292.

[16] S. M. Lipset, Martin Trow and J. S. Coleman, *Union Democracy* (New York: The Free Press, 1956).

[17] Robert Michels, *Political Parties* (New York: The Free Press, 1949), pp. 280–281.

[18] Torgny Segerstedt and Agne Lundquist, *Människan i industrisamhället II: Fritidsliv samhällsliv* (Stockholm: Studieförbundet Näringsliv och Samhälle, 1955), pp. 287–290.

search techniques. Previous studies of class mobility have, for the most part, ignored the possibility that a society may have a higher rate of mobility on one of these dimensions and a lower one on others. Similarly, an individual may rank high along one dimension while occupying a lower rank along another. We would like to draw attention to the possibility that such a multi-dimensional approach makes it possible to draw more qualified and accurate conclusions about comparative mobility and stratification systems, and above all, might enable us to deal with many interesting problems of intra-society dynamics, particularly in the realm of politics.

A Methodological Note

A basic difficulty inherent in most discussions of social mobility has been the absence of a comparative frame of reference. That is, when faced with a table showing that a given per cent of males in certain occupations are of lower class origins, one does not know whether this proportion is relatively high or low. The conception of high or low mobility, after all, assumes a comparison with something else which is higher or lower. Basically, there are three types of comparison which can be made. The first is a comparison with the past, i.e., is there more or less social mobility today than in the past. The second comparison is with other areas or countries; is the U.S. a more mobile society than Germany or Great Britain. Efforts at such comparisons lead into the third type, comparison with a model expressing equal opportunity. How nearly does a given country approach the utopian concern for complete equality? Thinking of mobility in terms of equality rather than absolute rates leads us to recognise that there may more mobility in country A than in country B, and yet less equality of opportunity. For example, if a country is 90 per cent peasant, even with completely equal opportunity, most children of peasants must remain peasants. Even if every non-peasant position is filled by a peasant's son, only about 11 per cent of them could change their occupation. On the other hand, if a country under-

goes rapid economic transformation and the proportion of nonmanual positions increases to, say, one half of all positions, then 50 per cent of the children of manual workers would have to secure nonmanual work in order to meet the criterion of equality.[19]

A word should be said about the conventional operational method of ascertaining mobility in comparing a father's position with that of his son. If one asks in a survey "what is your occupation?" and "what is your father's occupation?" most of the time we obtain the father's position at the peak of his career while the information for the son refers to a period prior to his peak occupation. It is, therefore, wise to record also the occupation of the father at an earlier time, for example, by asking "what was your father's occupation when he was at your age?" Also, one should not overlook the possibility of measuring intragenerational mobility, that is advancement from the first position held to the present. It might well be that the length of the leap along the rank ladder might be substantially greater in one country than in another although the same proportion of the population can obtain a better position than their parents in both countries.

2. Some Causes of Social Mobility

Much of the discussion about the degree of openness of a given society is confused by the failure to distinguish between two different processes, both of which are described and experienced as social mobility. These are:

1. The Supply of Vacant Statuses

The number of statuses in a given

<hr />

[19] For statistical techniques developed to handle this problem, see Donald Marvin, "Occupational Propinquity as a Factor in Marriage Selection," *Publications of the American Statistical Association*, XVI (1918), 131–150; Natalie Rogoff, *op. cit.*, pp. 29–33; David V. Glass, ed., *op. cit.*, pp. 218–259: see also Federico Chessa, *La Trasmissione Ereditaria delle Professioni* (Torino: Fratelli Bocca, 1912), for early presentation of the logic of this approach.

stratum is not always or even usually constant. For example, the expansion in the proportion of professional, official, managerial, and white-collar positions, and the decline in the number of un-skilled labour positions require a surge of upward mobility, providing that these positions retain their relative social standing and income. Demographic factors also operate to facilitate mobility, when the higher classes do not reproduce themselves and hence create a "demographic vacuum."[20]

2. The Interchange of Ranks

Any mobility which occurs in a given social system, which is not a consequence of a change in the supply of statuses and actors must necessarily result from an interchange. Consequently, if we think of a simple model, for every move up there must be a move down. Interchange mobility will be determined in large part by the extent to which a given society gives members of the lower strata the means with which to compete with those who enter the social structure on a higher level. Thus the less emphasis which a culture places on family background as a criterion for marriage, the more class mobility that can occur, both up and down, through marriage. The more occupational success is related to educational achievements, which are open to all, the greater the occupational mobility.

The description of these processes does not, of course, account for *motivational* factors in mobility. If mobility is to occur, individuals need to be motivated to aspire to secure higher positions. The obvious common sense starting point for a discussion of mobility motivation is the

observation that people do not like to be downwardly mobile: they prefer to keep their rank or to improve it.

An insightful motivation theory which accounts for men's desire to improve themselves, as well as to avoid falling in social position may be found in Veblen's analysis of the factors underlying consumption mobility.

Those members of the community who fall short of [a] somewhat indefinite, normal degree of prowess or of property suffer in the esteem of their fellowmen; and consequently they suffer also in their own esteem, since the usual basis for self-respect is the respect accorded by one's neighbours. Only individuals with an aberrant temperament can in the long run retain their self-esteem in the face of the dis-esteem of their fellows.

So as soon as the possession of property becomes the basis of popular esteem, therefore, it becomes also a requisite to that complacency which we call self-respect. In any community where goods are held in severality, it is necessary, in order to ensure his own peace of mind, that an individual should possess as large a portion of goods as others with whom he is accustomed to class himself; and it is extremely gratifying to possess something more than others. But as fast as a person makes new acquisitions, and becomes accustomed to the resulting new standard of wealth, the new standard forthwith ceases to afford appreciably greater satisfaction than the earlier standard did. The tendency in any case is constantly to make the present pecuniary standard the point of departure for a fresh increase of wealth; and this in turn gives rise to a new standard of sufficiency and a new pecuniary classification of one's self as compared with one's neighbours. So far as concerns the present question, the end sought by accumulation is to rank high in comparison with the rest of the community in point of pecuniary strength. So long as the comparison is distinctly unfavourable to himself, the normal, average individual will live in chronic dissatisfaction with his present lot; and when he has reached what may be called the normal pecuniary standard of the community, or of his class in the community, this chronic dissatisfaction will give place to

[20] See P. Sorokin, *Social Mobility* (New York: Harper & Row, Publishers, 1927), pp. 346–377; and Eldridge Sibley, "Some Demographic Clues to Stratification," *American Sociological Review*, VII (1942), 322–330.

a restless straining to place a wider and ever-widening pecuniary interval between himself and this average standard. The invidious comparison can never become so favourable to the individual making it that he would not gladly rate himself still higher relatively to his competitors in the struggle for pecuniary reputability.[21]

Implicit in this passage seem to be the following hypotheses:

1. The evaluation (rank, class) a person receives from his society determines in large measure his self-evaluation.
2. A person's actions are guided, in part at least, by an insatiable desire to maximize a favourable self-evaluation.

Hence, if the society evaluates a high consumption standard favourably, the individual will try to maximize his consumption level, since he thereby maximizes his self-evaluation. This theory can easily be generalized to any other dimension of class. Since any ranking is an evaluation by the society, it will be reflected in a person's self-evaluation; since any person tries to maximize his self-evaluation, he tries to maximize his rank. This would go for all the rankings we discussed earlier, that is, occupational consumption, social and perhaps also power classes. The basic idea is that persons like to protect their class positions in order to protect their egos and improve their class positions in order to enhance their egos. For example, societies with a more visible occupational stratification—such as Western Europe —are likely to produce stronger ego-needs favouring occupational mobility. Societies which place less emphasis on visible signs of occupational class and stress themes of equality—for example, the United States—are likely to produce less strong ego-needs favouring mobility. We cannot discuss here all the qualifi-

cations that modern research must impose on the Veblen theory of motivation for mobility. However the theory is interesting from the point of view that it does not assume that mobility occurs only as a result of specific social norms, pressuring people to be mobile; instead the motivations for mobility are placed in the realm of more or less universal ego-needs operating within stratified societies. This is not to say that the presence of norms to the effect that people should be mobile, are without enough authority to be a general law of social psychology that those who follow them out are rewarded by more favourable sentiments from their environment.[22] Motivation arising from norms pressuring for mobility might supplement the motivations to rise derived from ego-needs. It is perhaps precisely in societies where these ego-needs are weakest due to cultural themes of equality that mobility norms are most necessary. Thus, the intriguing paradox arises that the United States because of the emphasis on equality must emphasize also mobility norms in order to furnish the motivation necessary to fill higher positions.

This theory, stressing supply of actors and statuses, interchange of rank, and universal ego-needs, goes a long way to explain one of the most intriguing findings that seems to emerge from comparative mobility research. Popular and academic consensus have long held that occupational mobility in the United States is higher than in Western Europe. Examination of available evidence suggests that this is perhaps not the case.[23] It is now possible to expand the empirical basis for this conclusion. It has been possible to locate data from ten countries which have been collected by survey methods on national samples. The

[21] Thorstein Veblen, *The Theory of the Leisure Class* (New York: The Modern Library, 1934), pp. 30–32.

[22] H. W. Riecken and G. C. Homans, "Psychological Aspects of Social Structure," in G. Lindzey, ed., *op. cit.*, pp. 787–789.

[23] See Lipset and Rogoff, *op. cit.*

TABLE 1   Social Mobility in Ten Populations

Father's occupation

Respondent's occupation	France[a] Nonman.	Man.	Farm	Germany[b] Nonman.	Man.	Farm	Russian emigrés[d] Nonman.	Man.	Farm
Nonmanual	73%	35%	16%	58%	27%	19%	90%	28%	20%
Manual	18	55	13	38	68	28	10	68	36
Farm	9	10	71	4	5	54	—	3	44
N	(1109)	(625)	(1289)	(579)	(406)	(321)	(265)	(376)	(541)

Respondent's occupation	Switzerland[e] Nonman.	Man.	Farm	U.S.[f] Nonman.	Man.	Farm	U.S.[h] Nonman.	Man.	Farm
Nonmanual	84%	44%	27%	71%	35%	23%	81%	30%	—
Manual	13	54	19	25	61	39	19	70	—
Farm	3	3	54	4	4	38	—	—	—
N	(582)	(239)	(303)	(319)	(430)	(404)	(259)	(399)	(—)

Respondent's occupation	Germany[c] Nonman.	Man. and farm lab.	Farm	U.S.[g] Nonman. and farm owners	Man.	Farm
Nonmanual	80%	30%	12%	64%	31%	24%
Manual	20	60	19	34	67	46
Farm	—	10	70	1	2	30
N	(236)	(210)	(139)	(180)	(291)	(323)

Finland[i]

Respondent's occupation	"White-collar class"	"Working class"	"Farmer"
Nonmanual	64%	11%	9%
Manual	24	56	21
Farm	12	33	70
N	(590)	(1868)	(2302)

Great Britain[j]

	High levels of nonman. and farm owners	Routine nonman. and farm workers
Higher levels of nonman. and farm owners	51%	20%
Routine nonman., man., and farm workers	49	80
N	(1144)	(2358)

Denmark[k]

	High levels of nonman. and farm owners	Routine nonman. and farm workers
High levels of nonman. and farm owners	56%	22%
Routine nonman. and farm workers	44	78
N	(796)	(1174)

Sweden[m]

Sons, aged 22–28	Nonmanual	Man.	Farm
Nonmanual	67%	59%	44%
Manual	32	39	44
Farm	1	2	12
N	(57)	(101)	(73)

Italy[l]

	Nonman. and well-to-do peasants	Manual, farm labor and poor peasants
Nonman. and well-to-do peasants	66%	8%
Manual, farm labor and poor peasants	34	92
N	(224)	(472)

Sweden[n]

Father's occupation	Respondent's occupation Better situated	Middle class	Worker
Better situated	54%	5%	—
Middle class	39	72	35
Worker	7	23	65

(N's are not given)

While these studies, viewed comparatively, constitute a significant addition to our knowledge of international variations in stratification and mobility, they present many difficulties to anyone who is interested in making any systematic generalizations. Only a few of the sets of data were collected for stratification or social mobility studies. For example, six of the national surveys which collected mobility data did so in the context of research focusing on other problems. The German and one set of American data have never been published, since they were unrelated to the major problem of the research. These were obtained through private correspondence. But more important than this is the fact that most of the data were gathered without any reference to the need for international or even national comparisons. For example, the three American studies are not comparable with one another. One reports only the relationship between the occupation of fathers and sons who are urban dwellers. The other two report mobility patterns for the entire population, but one secured the information about father's principal occupation while the other asked for the occupation while "you were growing up." The Italian study used a third method, by asking for the father's occupation when he was the respondent's age, while the Danish study contrasts occupations of father and son at age 20. It is possible to argue that each form of the question is worthwhile, but clearly, using different versions makes comparison difficult if not impossible.

An even more serious problem is inherent in the system of classification of respondents and their fathers. Most of the studies employed noncomparable systems of classification. Thus, the Danish, British, Italian, and second Swedish studies differ from the others in classifying rural occupations in the same categories as urban occupations of presumed comparable status. Farm owners are grouped with high level nonmanual occupations, while farm labourers are placed in the same category as semi- and unskilled urban workers. All other studies differentiate between urban and rural occupational strata. The British and Danish study, in addition, does not differentiate between manual and nonmanual occupations. Lower levels of nonmanual employment are classified with skilled workers, while all other studies keep manual and clerical occupations separate. Some of the European studies classify "artisans," i.e., self-employed workers such as carpenters, together with manual workers, while other studies group them with independent businessmen. We have reclassified for consistency and placed artisans in the same category as other nonmanual jobs. Some studies differentiate between salaried and free professionals, the first group being classified as "officials," while others use the category "professional" for both groups. The Finnish study differed from all the others in using a different system of classification for fathers and sons. All the studies except the second Swedish one are given in terms of the relationship between fathers' and sons' occupations. The latter does not allow us to present it in comparable terms since the number of cases in each cell is not given. It should also be noted that all the tables, except the Finnish and Swedish, deal with fathers' and sons' occupations. The latter ones include women among the respondents.

a M. Bresard, "Mobilité sociale et dimension de la famille," Population, V, No. 3 (1950), 533-67.

b This table was computed from the data kindly supplied by the U.N.E.S.C.O. Institute at Cologne, Germany, which were secured in their study of German attitudes in 1953.

c This table was computed from data kindly supplied by the Institut für Demoskopie, at Allensbach, Germany, from one of their national surveys of West German opinion.

d Robert A. Feldmesser, "Observations on Trends in Social Mobility in the Soviet Union and Their Implications," in A. Kassof et al., "Stratification and Mobility in the Soviet Union: A Study of Social Class Cleavages in the U.S.S.R." (Cambridge: Harvard Russia Research Center, 1954), mimeo, p. 8.

e Recalculated from data kindly supplied by Professor Roger Girod from his paper in this volume.

f This table was derived by Natalie Rogoff from data published by the National Opinion Research Centre. See N.O.R.C., "Jobs and Occupations," Opinion News (September 1, 1947), 3–13.

g This table was computed from data kindly supplied by the Survey Research Centre, which were secured in their study of the 1952 presidential election.

h Richard Centers, The Psychology of Social Classes (Princeton, N. J.: Princeton University Press, 1949), p. 181.

i Tauno Hellevuo, "Poimintatutkimus Säätykerrosta" (A Sampling Study of Social Mobility), Suomalainen Suomi, No. 2 (1952), 93–96.

j This table was adapted from material in David V. Glass, ed., Social Mobility in Britain (London: Routledge & Kegan Paul, Ltd., 1954.)

k We are indebted to Professor K. Svalastoga, University of Copenhagen, Denmark, for these data based on a probability sample.

l L. Livi, "Sur la mesure de la mobilité sociale," Population (January-March, 1950), 65-76.

m This table was computed from data kindly supplied by Svenska Institutet för Opinionsundersökningar, Stockholm, Sweden, from a probability sample of youth.

n Elis Håstad, "Gallup" Och Den Svenska Väljarkåren (Uppsala: Hugo Gebers Förlag, 1950), p. 271.

studies comprise Denmark, Finland, Germany (two studies), Great Britain, Italy, Soviet Russia (post-war emigrés), Sweden (two studies), and the United States (three studies). The studies afford only very crude international comparisons, largely using the three categories of manual, nonmanual, and farm occupations. In presenting these materials in Table 1 we make the assumption that a move from manual to nonmanual employment constitutes upward mobility among *males*. This assumption may be defended primarily on the grounds that most male nonmanual occupations receive higher prestige than most manual occupations, even skilled ones. It is true, of course, that many white-collar positions are lower in income and prestige than the higher levels of skilled manual work. Most of the less rewarded white-collar positions, however, are held by women. The men who hold them are often able to secure higher level supervisory posts. Consequently, we believe that using the division between manual and nonmanual occupation as indicators of low and high occupational status is justified as an approximate dichotomous break of urban male occupations. It is important to recognize, however, that like all single item indicators of complex phenomena, this one will necessarily result in some errors.

When examining the results of these studies, especially the ones for the United States, France, Switzerland, and Germany (which are most comparable), there can be little doubt that the advanced European societies for which we have data have "high" rates of social mobility, if by a high rate we mean one which is similar to that of the United States. In each country, a large minority is able to rise above the occupational position of their fathers, while a smaller but still substantial minority falls in occupational status. A British research group, under the direction of David Glass, attempted a quantitative comparison of their data with the findings from the French, Italian and the third American study. Glass and his associates concluded that Britain, the U.S. and France had similar rates of mobility.[24] The Italian and Finnish findings, however, indicate a lower rate of social mobility than in the other countries. It is difficult to make any clear judgment concerning the Finnish data, since the father's occupation in the Finnish study is based on the reply to "what class do you consider your father belongs(ed): white-collar, working-class, or farmer?" while the sons are grouped according to their objective occupation.[25] The British, Danish, Italian and second Swedish

---

[24] David V. Glass, ed., *op. cit.*, pp. 260–265.

[25] The findings indicating considerable fluidity in the occupational class structure outside of America are buttressed by the results of studies of mobility in individual cities in different countries. A study based on a random sample of the Tokyo population indicates that about one-third of the sons of fathers employed in manual occupations were in nonmanual jobs when interviewed, while about 30 per cent of the sons of men in nonmanual occupations had become manual workers. (A. G. Ibi, "Occupational Stratification and Mobility in the Large Urban Community: A Report of Research on Social Stratification and Mobility in Tokyo, II," *Japanese Sociological Review*, IV (1954), 135–149. We describe the results of this study in general terms since close to twenty per cent of the men were in occupational categories which we could not fit into the conventional manual-nonmanual farm groups without more knowledge about Japanese occupational titles.) A study of mobility among a group of young residents of Stockholm indicates that over half of the sons of manual workers who grew up in Stockholm were in nonmanual occupations at the age of twenty-four (Gunnar Boalt, "Social Mobility in Stockholm: A Pilot Investigation," in *Transactions of the Second World Congress of Sociology*, II, *op. cit.*, pp. 67–73). Two excellent studies of social mobility in a Danish (Geiger, *op. cit.*) and an American (Rogoff, *op. cit.*) provincial city permit an even more detailed comparison of mobility between Europe and America, which is presented in Lipset and Rogoff, *op. cit.* It is clear that there is no substantial difference in the patterns of social mobility in Aarhus and Indianapolis.

studies combine urban and rural occupations in the same classes. This has the consequence of increasing downward mobility since many sons of farmers who are middle class become urban workers. It also reduces upward mobility since children of farm laborers are less likely to move up than the offspring of manual workers.

The data from these studies tend to challenge the popular conception that America is a land of wide-open occupational mobility as compared to Europe, where family background is alleged to play a much more important role in determining the position of sons. It is important to note, however, that the available data should not be treated as if they were a set of quantitatively comparable censuses of mobility in different countries. All that we can say from the existing survey studies is that they do not validate the traditional assumptions. Considerable mobility occurs in every country for which we have data. Furthermore, available historical material tends to indicate that much of Europe had occupational mobility rates from 1900 to 1940 which are similar to the present, and which did not lag behind the American one.[26] Whether there are significant differences among these countries can only be decided after the completion of an integrated comparative research project, which employs the same methods of collecting, classifying, and processing the data. Thus far, no such study exists.

According to our theory, the explanation of these findings has to be sought in structural and motivational factors which are similar on both continents. Both Europe and America have experienced differential fertility, that is, the tendency of those in upper classes to have fewer children, a condition that leaves room for the lower classes to rise. Both have seen an expansion in the number of white-collar positions at the expense of manual workers, thus creating a surge of upward occupational mobility to the extent that new industrial labour is drawn from farm areas. Bendix has compared the ratio of administrative (white-collar) and production (manual) workers over the last half-century in the United States, the United Kingdom and in Sweden, and finds the parallel in trends very great. Thus, in the United States in 1899 there were 8 administrative employees per 100 production workers while in 1947 there were 22 administrative employees per 100 production workers. The corresponding rise in Britain between 1907 and 1948 is from 9 to 20 administrative employees per 100 production workers, and in Sweden the figures jump from 7 in 1915 to 21 administrative employees per 100 production workers in 1950.[27]

---

[26] For example, a study which secured questionaire data from over 90,000 German workers in the late 1920's reported that almost one-quarter of the males in this group came from manual working-class families (Gewerkschaftsbund der Angestellten, *Die wirtschaftliche und soziale Lage der Angestellten* (Berlin, 1931), p. 43; see also Hans Speier, *The Salaried Employee in German Society*, Vol. I (New York: Department of Social Science, Columbia University, 1939), pp. 86–98. An early British survey of the social origins of the owners, directors and managers in the cotton industry found that over two-thirds of this group had begun their occupational careers either as manual workers or in low-status clerical positions [S. J. Chapman and F. J.

Marquis, "The Recruiting of the Employing Classes from the Ranks of Wage Earners in the Cotton Industry," *Journal of the Royal Statistical Society* (February, 1912), pp. 293–306]. Pitirim Sorokin (*op. cit.*) who made an extensive analysis of social mobility research around the world before 1927 also concluded that the assumption that the United States was a more open society in terms of occupational mobility than the industrial sections of Europe was not valid. For early data on mobility in the city of Rome, see Chessa, *op. cit.*

[27] Reinhard Bendix, *Work and Authority in Industry* (New York: John Wiley & Sons, Inc., 1956).

Likewise, the United States and Western Europe have experienced a parallel process in interchange of ranks. On both continents the majority of non-manual and high-status positions are no longer in the category of self-employment. A bureaucrat father unlike a businessman cannot give his job to his son. Many non-self-employed middle-class parents have little to give their children except a better opportunity to secure a good education and the motivation to attempt to obtain a high-class position. If for any reason, such as the early death of the father or family instability, a middle-class child does not complete a higher education, he is in a worse position in terms of prospective employment than the son of a manual worker who completes college, lycee, or gymnasium. Clearly, some proportion of the children of the middle class are so handicapped, and many of them fall in socioeconomic status. In addition, some simply do not have the abilities to complete higher education or to get along in a bureaucratic hierarchy, and fall by the wayside. Thus, whatever the reason that some persons of middle-class origin move downward, they leave room for others of lower-class background to rise.

Given these structural prerequisites for mobility, it seems to make little difference that Americans are exposed to stronger norms and more vivid models encouraging mobility. The more visible occupational class distinctions in Europe actually may make for stronger ego-needs pressuring for upward mobility. Thus the resulting motivation to move upward appears approximately equal on both continents. There is, unfortunately, little available data on the aspiration level of men in the same class in different countries.

The more pronounced presence of mobility norms in the American "open class" value system might, however, make for more "planned" mobility in the United States, while mobility in Europe would be more "unplanned." That is, the emphasis placed on mobility in the value system of the United States should lead more Americans than Europeans to make conscious plans to secure the skills necessary to be upwardly mobile. On the other hand, the age of marriage and the age of parents at the arrival of the first child in Northern and Western Europe is somewhat higher than in the United States. Consequently, a European will have a longer period without family responsibilities to take risks or advance his skills. In this sense, "unplanned" mobility may be facilitated in Europe and restricted in America.

The norms dictating class behaviour in a social class oriented society may actually serve to open the occupational ladder for lower strata individuals since they sometimes operate to inhibit the sons of higher strata families from securing the type of education which will enable them to obtain a high position in the economic structure. The fact that in some European countries engineering and other high level industrial positions appear to have less prestige in the eyes of the upper classes than high posts in the civil service, or the military, has the effect of eliminating from competition for industrial posts some men who could secure them if they so desired. This means that room is left for individuals of lower social origins to secure these high positions.

3. Some Political Consequences of Mobility

Earlier, we called attention to the fact that most studies of social mobility have been descriptive in character and have not attempted to relate findings concerning mobility to other aspects of the society. In this concluding section, we shall discuss the relevance of mobility theory and research to political analysis. Our guiding general assumption is that many of the major political problems facing contemporary society are, in part, a consequence of the conflict and tensions resulting from the contradictions inherent in the need for both aristocracy and equality.[28]

Much of the writing in the general area of social stratification has been concerned with the problem of equality. Writers from the time of the Greek civilization on have pointed to the need for tenure in high status positions and the inheritance of social position as requirements for the stability of complex societies. These theorists have suggested that the division of labour requires differential rewards in prestige and privilege as the means of motivating individuals to carry out the more difficult leadership or other positions requiring a great deal of intelligence and training. Also, given a system of differential rewards, the particularistic values which are a necessary part of family organization require high-statused individuals to attempt to pass their gratifications to their children. The simplest way to assure these rewards for their children is to pass their privileged positions on to them. Thus, a strain towards aristocracy, or the inheritance of rank, is, as Plato indicated, a necessary concomitant of a stratified society.

The legitimation of inherited rank immediately gives rise to another problem, that is the problem of reconciling the legitimation of inherited privilege with the social need to encourage some men born into lower status positions to aspire to and attain higher positions. Thus all economically expanding societies such as the United States, most of Western Europe, India, the Soviet Union, South Africa, and many others, must encourage individuals to aspire to higher or at least different occupational positions from those held by their parents. The dilemma confronting a society in doing this may best be seen in the problems faced by the Soviet Union. Soviet writers have complained that most Russian school-children only desire important bureaucratic and military positions. They have castigated the school system for failing in its obligation of making the children of workers and peasants proud of their fathers' occupations.[29] Yet, while the new ruling class of the Soviet Union attempts on the one hand to reduce the ambitions of lower-class youth, its goal of an expanding industrial society forces it to recruit constantly from the ranks of the lower classes.

However, social mobility is not only an issue for the politicians, it is also a force generating political and ideological pressures. There can be little doubt that a system of differential rewards and inherited privilege entails internal strains which make for instability. Such a system requires a large proportion of the population to accept a lower conception of its own worth as compared with others (this follows from the first hypothesis we derived from Veblen). This barrier to the possibility of enhancement of the self may in some cases lead to a rejection of self, described as "self-hatred" in the analyses of the personalities of lower-status minority group members. Such a rejection, however, is necessarily difficult to maintain, and in all stratified societies, some men have tended to reject the dominant valuation

---

[28] See Talcott Parsons, "A Revised Analytical Approach to the Theory of Stratification," in R. Bendix and S. M. Lipset, eds., *Class, Status and Power*, 1st ed. (New York: The Free Press, 1953), p. 117; and K. Davis and W. E. Moore, "Some Principles of Stratification," *American Sociological Review*, X (1945), 242–249. For a critique of this position and an answer to it, see M. M. Tumin, "Some Principles of Stratification: a Critical Analysis," *American Sociological Review*, XVIII (1953), 387–394; K. Davis, "Reply to Tumin," *ibid.*, pp. 394–397.

---

[29] Alex Inkeles, "Social Stratification and Mobility in the Soviet Union: 1940–1950," in R. Bendix and S. M. Lipset, eds., *op. cit.*, pp. 611–621.

placed on the upper classes. Sometimes this rejection takes the form of lower-class religious values which deny the moral worth of wealth or power; at other times it may take the form of rebellious "Robin Hood" bands, or formal revolutionary or social reform movements; often it may lead to individual efforts to improve one's status through legitimate or illegitimate means.

It is entirely conceivable that the political consequences of class deprivation might be different depending on what dimension of class is challenged. Some recent analysts of the development of rightist extremism in the United States have suggested that this movement is, in part, a response to insecurity about social class position.[30] Essentially, these analyses assume that when the occupational and consumption aspects of stratification are salient, the ideological debate and the political measures will be concerned with the issues of job security, redistribution of property, and income. Political movements with this motivation are most common in times of depression when many see their economic position decline. On the other hand, when the social class dimension is challenged or confused, the ideological debate will contain endless discussions of traditional values of ascription, often with elements of irrationality and scapegoating. Political movements with this motivation are likely to occur in times of high occupational and consumption mobility when the old upper class feels itself threatened by *nouveaux arrivées*, and when the latter feel frustrated in not being accepted socially by those who already hold high social position.

The political themes related to threats to social class position, or to frustrations in achieving higher position in the social class structure are likely to be more irrational than those related to the desire for economic security or achievement. Franz Neumann has suggested that the adoption of a conspiracy theory of politics, placing the blame for social evils on a secret group of evil-doers is related to social class insecurity.[31] Groups in this position account for the actual or potential decline which they desire to avert by blaming a conspiracy rather than themselves or their basic social institutions. In doing so, they can continue to believe in the ongoing social structure which accords them their status, while at the same time feel that they are taking action to eliminate the threat to their social status.

It might be interjected at this point that the above is not untestable speculation. We already know how to measure the kinds of mobility which are the independent variables of the hypotheses. The dependent variables—the political themes—can also be measured by the conventional kind of public opinion poll questions. In fact, many already existing questions presumed to measure along a conservatism-liberalism continuum would tap some of the themes, and for the others equally simple items can be constructed. It is also easy to ascertain by survey methods memberships in groups or associations known to embrace any of the above political themes.

Short of having survey data, it is possible to present some impressionistic evidence for the hypothesis that strains introduced by mobility aspirations or anxieties will predispose individuals towards accepting more extreme political views. Political literature knows several suggestions that class discrepancies, e.g., high social class and lower economic position, has this effect. Such hypotheses

---

[30] See the various essays reprinted in Daniel Bell, ed., *The New American Right* (New York: Criterion Books, 1955); and Richard Hofstadter, *The Age of Reform* (New York: Alfred A. Knopf, Inc., 1955), esp. pp. 131–172.

[31] Franz Neumann, "Anxiety in Politics," *Dissent* (Spring, 1955), 135–141.

about rank discrepancies are not strictly hypotheses about social mobility. However, it is plain that whenever social mobility occurs, rank discrepancies are likely to occur, since it is extremely rare that a person would rise or decline at the same rate along all dimensions of class. For example, this hypothesis has been suggested in explaining political behaviour in contemporary Canada. In the province of Saskatchewan, governed since 1944 by a socialist party, it was found that the leaders of the socialist party who were either businessmen or professionals, were largely of non-Anglo-Saxon origin, that is, of low social class. On the other hand, the big majority, over 90 per cent, of the middle-class leaders of the Liberal and Conservative Parties, were Anglo-Saxons.

Socially, the businessmen of the ethnic minority are part of the lower class group of the Saskatchewan population. They are not exploited economically, but they are deprived socially of many of the privileges that usually go with business status. The cleavage between them and the Anglo-Saxon "upper class" is often as great as the split between the farmers and the business community. Subject to the cross pressures of contradictory statuses, many members of minority groups have seen fit to identify themselves with the political party which is opposed by the "upper class" and which promises to strike at the community power of these dominant groups.[32]

Robert Michels, in his analysis of European socialism before World War I made a similar hypothesis explicit:

The origin of this predominant position [of the Jews in the European socialist movement] is to be found, as far at least as concerns Germany and the countries of eastern Europe, in the peculiar position which the Jews have occupied and in many respects still occupy. The legal emancipation of the Jews has not been followed by their social and moral emancipation. . . . Even when they are rich, the Jews constitute, at least in eastern Europe, a category of persons who are excluded from the social advantages which the prevailing political, economic, and intellectual system ensures for the corresponding portion of the Gentile population: Society in the narrower sense of the term is distrustful of them, and public opinion is unfavourable to them.[33]

Evidence derived from analysis of electoral behaviour, or the composition of the membership or leadership of political parties in different countries, indicates that Jews still react in the same way in more recent times. In the United States the bulk of the Jewish middle class supports the more liberal or left-wing parties, even though their occupational and economic position would seem to suggest a more conservative outlook.[34] It would be interesting to see how well this would hold in countries with relatively little anti-Semitism, for example, Scandinavia. In such countries where presumably Jews are achieving a higher social class position we would not expect them to have the same extent of leftist political orientation.

So far, we have reported hypotheses which have predicted a political orientation to the left when a group's social class position is lower than its occupational or economic position, in spite of the fact that the latter normally would predispose a conservative outlook. It has also been suggested, however, that a rightist orientation also occurs among people in such positions. It has been argued, for example, that *nouveaux riches* are sometimes even more conservative than the old rich, because some of them seek to move up in the social class struc-

[32] S. M. Lipset, *Agrarian Socialism* (Berkeley, Calif.: University of California Press, 1950), p. 191.

[33] Robert Michels, *op. cit.*, pp. 260–261.
[34] Lawrence A. Fuchs, "American Jews and the Presidential Vote," *American Political Science Review*, XLIX (1955), 385–401.

ture by adapting to the value and behaviour patterns which they believe are common in the class above them, or more simply, perhaps because they have not developed patterns of *noblesse oblige*, characteristic of established upper classes. Riesman and Glazer have argued that the economically successful upwardly mobile Irish in America have become more conservative as a concomitant of their search for higher status.[35]

The political orientation of a group whose social class position is higher than their occupational-economic class should be also affected by this discrepancy in class positions. We have already reported hypotheses which indicate that this may result in rightist political behaviour. On the other hand, however, are suggestions that a discrepancy in status may lead an old but declining upper class to be more liberal in its political orientation. For example, most observers of British politics have suggested that the emergence of Tory Socialism, the willingness to enact reforms which benefited the working class, was a consequence of the hostility of the old English landed aristocracy toward the rising business class, which was threatening its status and power. W. L. Warner reports a situation in which members of old families in an American city characterized by a high degree of emphasis on ascriptive social class supported the efforts of a radical trade union to organize the plants, which were owned by newly wealthy Jews.[36]

Unfortunately, there is no empirical research and little speculation on the conditions which are related to such varying reactions. Much of the specula-

tion and evidence presented above suggests alternative reactions to seemingly similar social pressures. That is, both rightist and leftist political behaviour has been explained as a reaction to discrepancies in status. Three studies of electoral choice offer a similar dilemma. These studies were made by the Survey Research Center of the University of Michigan in 1952, by the UNESCO Institute of Social Science in Cologne, Germany, in 1953, and by the Finnish Gallup Poll in 1949. The Finnish and German studies suggest that middle-class individuals of working-class origin are more likely to vote for the more liberal or left-wing party, than are those who are in the same class position as their fathers. The American data, on the other hand, indicate that successfully upward mobile sons of workers are even more conservative in their party choice than those middle-class individuals whose fathers held occupations comparable to their own[37] (Table 2).

---

[35] David Riesman and Nathan Glazer, "The Intellectuals and the Discontented Class," in D. Bell, ed., *op. cit.*, pp. 66–67.

[36] W. L. Warner and J. O. Low, *The Social System of the Modern Factory* (New Haven: Yale University Press, 1947); see also S. M. Lipset and R. Bendix, *op. cit.*, pp. 230–233.

[37] Two other American studies suggest similar conclusions. Maccoby found that upward mobile youth in Cambridge were more Republican than nonmobiles in the class to which the upward mobile moved. Eleanor E. Maccoby, "Youth and Political Choice," *Public Opinion Quarterly* (Spring, 1954), 35. The M.I.T. Center for International Studies interviewed a random sample of 1,000 American business executives in 1955. These data show that only 5 per cent of the children of manual workers are Democrats as compared with 10 per cent Democratic among the executive sons of middle- or upper-class fathers. Hans Speier in his study of white-collar workers in pre-Hitler Germany estimated that 50 per cent of the members of the Socialist white-collar union were the sons of workers, while less than 25 per cent of the members of the two conservative white-collar unions were sons of workers. This finding is similar to the pattern in contemporary Germany, see Speier, *op. cit.*, pp. 92–93.

Hence three American studies agree that the upward-mobile are more conservative than the stationary middle-class, while two German and one Finnish study find that the upward-mobile in these countries are more radical than the stationary nonmanual workers.

TABLE 2   Left Vote of Finnish, German and American Middle-Class Men Related to Their Social Origins[a]

Father's occupation	Per cent both Left parties	Finland, 1949 Per cent Social-Democratic	Per cent Communist	Germany, 1953 Per cent Social-Democratic	Per cent Democratic U.S., 1952	U.S., 1948
Manual	23	20	3 (157)	32 (200)	22 (67)	35 (72)
Nonmanual	6	5	1 (356)	20 (142)	30 (79)	39 (83)
Farm	10	10	— (183)	22 (58)	34 (59)	49 (61)

[a] The data from which these tables were constructed were funished by the Finnish Gallup Poll, the UNESCO Institute of Social Science and the Survey Research Center. We would like to express our thanks to them. Non-voters and persons not expressing a party choice are eliminated from this table.

TABLE 3   Left Vote of Finnish, German and American Workers Related to Their Social Origins

Father's occupation	Per cent both Left parties	Finland, 1949 Per cent Social-Democratic	Per cent Communist	Germany, 1953 Per cent Social-Democratic	Per cent Democratic U.S., 1952	U.S., 1948
Manual	81	53	28 (1017)	64 (357)	62 (119)	82 (101)
Nonmanual	42	34	8 (50)	52 (58)	54 (37)	64 (36)
Farm	67	56	11 (378)	38 (75)	58 (87)	89 (64)

It would be easy to construct some *ex post facto* interpretations for the variations in the consequences of upward social mobility in Finland, Germany and the United States. Rather than do so at this point, we prefer to simply present these results as another illustration of both the complexities and potential rewards inherent in cross-national comparisons.

While the political consequences of upward mobility vary among Germany, Finland and the United States, downward mobility seems to have the same result in the three countries. The working-class sons of middle-class fathers are less likely to back the left parties than are the sons of workers (Table 3).

It is clear from these data that the more consistent the class position of a worker and his father, the more likely he is to accept the dominant political pattern of his class.[38] Also, there can be little

---

[38] Similar patterns are suggested in other American studies. Richard Centers reported

that workers who have middle class fathers are more likely to give conservative responses on questions designed to measure liberalism-conservatism, while the successfully upward mobile sons of manual workers do not differ from these in nonmanual occupations whose fathers held similar posts. Centers, *op. cit.*, p. 180. A study of the United Automobile Workers Union found that 78 per cent of the sons of workers were Democrats in 1952 as compared to 60 per cent of the offspring of middle-class fathers. Arthur Kornhauser, *When Labor Votes—A Study of Auto Workers* (New Hyde Park, N.Y.: University Books, 1956). Two studies of trade union membership indicate that mobile individuals are less likely to belong to, or be active in, trade unions. S. M. Lipset and Joan Gordon, "Mobility and Trade Union Membership," in R. Bendix and S. M. Lipset, eds., *op. cit.*, pp. 491–500 and Arnold Tannenbaum, *Participation in Local Unions* (Ann Arbor: University of Michigan Survey Research Center, 1954), mimeo, p. 292. It is interesting to note that one study based on survey materials, which attempted to relate social mobility to ethnic prejudice in an American city found that both upward and downward mobile persons were more prejudiced than individuals who were in the same social position as their fathers. This result suggests that the socially mobile, whether upward or downward, are more insecure in their dealings with others

doubt that the facts of downward social mobility go at least a part of the way in accounting for conservatives among the working class.

These two studies, like the qualitative and more speculative political analyses reported earlier, only begin to open up the area of the impact of stratification dynamics on political behaviour. The consequences of social mobility, and the determinants of political behaviour are, of course, much more complex than has been hinted above. There is obviously a need for further exploratory research in order to suggest hypotheses that are better than random guesses. From this point of view, it would be gratifying if public opinion surveys concerning political matters see fit to include, in the future, mobility information as a standard category.

---

than those who are stationary in the class structure. It is congruent with our findings that the socially mobile in America are more conservative than the nonmobile at the same level. See Joseph Greenblum and Leonard I. Pearlin, "Vertical Mobility and Prejudice: A Socio-Psychological Analysis," in R. Bendix and S. M. Lipset, eds., *op. cit.*, pp. 480–491.